THE CLASSICS OF WESTERN SPIRITUALITY
A Library of the Great Spiritual Masters

iii

HILDEGARD of BINGEN
SCIVIAS

TRANSLATED BY
MOTHER COLUMBA HART AND JANE BISHOP

INTRODUCED BY
BARBARA J. NEWMAN

PREFACE BY
CAROLINE WALKER BYNUM

PAULIST PRESS
NEW YORK ● MAHWAH

Cover art: MOTHER PLACID DEMPSEY, a Benedictine nun of the Abbey of Regina Laudis in Bethlehem, Connecticut, is also a sculptor, painter, graphics designer and book illustrator. Regarding the cover and inside illustrations she says: "Doing art work for this volume became a unique personal experience in which I was struck by three things. First, I realized there has existed for centuries a body of illustrations of the Visions that are traditionally ascribed to St. Hildegard's 'direct supervision.' Despite their obvious differences in style, which suggest not merely different artists but entirely different historical periods, they have enjoyed a long history of commentaries by various spiritual writers and important scholars, including, in our time, Dr. Carl Jung. Recognizing their unique value in terms of tradition and their own intrinsic aesthetic beauty, I chose to represent them here in all their clarity and forthrightness. In so doing, I came to appreciate that, in a very real sense, they do proceed from her 'direct supervision.' Secondly, I came to understand directness and supervision as the marks of St. Hildegard, who looked upon the mystery of nature and mankind with the radical and comprehensive 'eye' of Faith, that is, through supernatural 'seeing' or, as one may say, through 'Super-Vision,' and this is what I have tried to express on the cover. Thirdly, I realized that her 'Super-Vision' includes the hidden bringing together of many persons to share and creatively carry out that Vision. In this regard I wish to express my debt to her and, through her, to the Abbess and members of my own community, to Sr. Mary Charles, R.S.M., Dr. John Farina, children's book illustrator Mercer Mayer, and to Jeanne Parr."

Copyright © 1990 by the Abbey of Regina Laudis: Benedictine Congregation Regina Laudis of the Strict Observance, Inc.

Library of Congress Cataloging-in-Publication Data

Hildegard, Saint, 1098–1179.
    [Scivias. English]
    Scivias/Hildegard of Bingen: translated by Columba Hart and
Jane Bishop; introduction by Barbara Newman; preface by Caroline
Walker Bynum.
       p.   cm.—(The Classics of western spirituality)
    Translation of: Scivias.
    Includes bibliographical references.
    ISBN 0-8091-0431-8 ISBN 0-8091-3130-7 (pbk.)
    1. Mysticism—Early works to 1800. I. Hart, Columba, 1903– .
II. Bishop, Jane, 1950– . III. Title. IV. Series.
BV5080.H5413 1990
248.2′2—dc20

                                                         89-29315
                                                           CIP

Published by Paulist Press
997 Macarthur Boulevard
Mahwah, New Jersey 07430

Printed and bound in the United States of America

Contents

BOOK THREE: THE HISTORY OF SALVATION
SYMBOLIZED BY A BUILDING

Translators of this Volume

MOTHER COLUMBA HART, O.S.B. was graduated from Smith College in 1924 *summa cum laude,* having studied under Eleanor S. Duckett and Howard R. Patch. She remained for the M.A. degree in English and continued graduate work at Radcliffe and Harvard in romance philology, Middle English, and Latin paleography under John L. Lowes, John S. Tatlock, and Charles H. Haskins. She earned a second M.A. at Radcliffe in 1926. After European travel she studied French while living in Paris for two years, and later translated *Ouvrons la Bible* by Roger Poelman (*How to Read the Bible,* New York: Kenedy, 1953, and London: Longmans, 1955). Her first original book, *Mary of the Magnificat,* had come out in 1942 (Sheed & Ward). The work of translating from the Latin *The Exercises of Saint Gertrude* (Newman, 1956) brought to her attention the dearth of information about Gertrude's life and suggested research on thirteenth-century women, especially the Flemish mystics. Thus she discovered Hadewijch, some of whose letters she presented in *The American Benedictine Review* (1962). Her translation from the Latin of William of Saint Thierry's *Exposition on the Song of Songs* was begun at this time and appeared in Cistercian Fathers Series (1970). In 1972 Mother Columba contributed to *The American Benedictine Review* another article on medieval women "*Consecratio Virginum:* Thirteenth-Century Witnesses." In 1980 she brought out a volume in The Classics of Western Spirituality Series, which may well be considered her masterpiece, the translation of *The Complete Works* of Hadewijch.

At 86, Mother Columba has retired from active research for publication and remains a beloved elder and resource person in her Benedictine community of the Abbey of Regina Laudis in Bethlehem, Connecticut, where she has been a member for forty years.

JANE BISHOP received her B.A. from Vassar College and her M. Phil. and Ph.D. from Columbia University. After a precarious few years as an adjunct professor at Barnard College, Pace University, Iona College, the New School for Social Research and Manhattan College, she is now Assistant Professor of Ancient and Medieval History at The Citadel, Charleston, South Carolina. Dr. Bishop has written articles for *Trends in History* and the *Dictionary of the Middle Ages,* and "Bishops as Marital Advisors in the Ninth Century" for *Women of the Medieval World,* ed. Julius Kirshner and Suzanne Wemple (Basil Blackwell, Oxford, 1985). She was a founding member of the Institute for Research in History, which unfortunately became defunct in 1989. Dr. Bishop's specialties are Byzantine and papal political and social history, which makes Hildegard's mysticism a holiday from her main preoccupations. She is now seeking a publisher for her book *Pope Nicholas I and the First Age of Papal Independence.*

Author of the Introduction

BARBARA J. NEWMAN is Associate Professor of English at the Northwestern University College of Arts and Sciences. She received her B.A. from Oberlin College, her M.A. Div. from the University of Chicago Divinity School and her Ph.D. from Yale University, Department of Medieval Studies. Dr. Newman's publications include: *Sister of Wisdom: St. Hildegard's Theology of the Feminine* (University of California Press, 1987) and *Hildegard of Bingen: Symphonia,* critical edition with translations and commentary (Cornell University Press, 1988).

Author of the Preface

CAROLINE WALKER BYNUM is Professor of History at Columbia University and a MacArthur Fellow. She is the author of a number of scholarly works on medieval spirituality including *Jesus as Mother: Studies in the Spirituality of the High Middle Ages* (University of California Press, 1982) and *Holy Feast and Holy Fast: The Religious Significance of Food to Medieval Women* (University of California Press, 1987).

Preface

U ntil recently the visionary women of the Western European Middle Ages were neglected by scholars. German historians tended to see the two great twelfth-century Rhineland prophets, Hildegard of Bingen and Elizabeth of Schönau, and the mystical group at the convent of Helfta in the thirteenth century as important only insofar as they foreshadowed Protestantism. The intense affective female piety of the early fourteenth century described in the collections of visions and pious biographies known as *Nonnenbücher* made scholars so nervous that they neglected these works altogether except as philological evidence of the development of the German language. English students of mysticism denigrated the female mystics of their own and the continental tradition as "experiential," and judged their works, along with those of such male devotional writers as Richard Rolle, inferior to speculative, neo-Platonic mystical writing. Historians of science and psychology, as well as phenomenologists of religion, repeatedly explained women's visionary experiences as neurosis or disease (migraine, hysteria, anorexia nervosa, and so on). Further, as Peter Dronke has pointed out, there is no major female writer from the Middle Ages whose works modern scholars have not attributed (often with very little evidence) to a man.[1] If I had written this preface in 1950, I might well have argued that the only thing the diverse female writers of the Middle Ages had in common was their neglect by modern scholarship.

All that has changed. Not only has the field of women's history emerged as a branch of research with considerable methodological sophistication, but women's theological writing and piety have received particular emphasis. Two anthologies of medieval women writers in translation have recently appeared, and religious texts predominate. At least two current series are devoted exclusively to women's texts.[2] The plays of Hrotsvitha of Gandersheim and Hildegard of Bingen are now performed by college drama departments and church groups; several recordings of Hildegard's liturgical songs are on the market; extravagant claims about the effectiveness of women's medicine and midwifery circulate; radical feminists today appropriate from medieval texts insights they characterize as female or feminist and use them to challenge or reform or profoundly reinterpret the modern church. In the 1980s female authorship is often attributed to anonymous texts, sometimes on the shakiest of bases. A German postage stamp in 1979 honored the eighth-hundredth anniversary of the death of Hildegard of Bingen; the postwar, apocalyptic German artist, Anselm Kiefer, includes the thirteenth-century beguine and visionary Mechtild of Magdeburg as the only woman in his monumental painting "Germany's Spiritual Heroes."

The recent enthusiasm for visionary women in general and for the immensely talented polymath Hildegard of Bingen in particular raises disturbing interpretative questions. For Hildegard is in no way typical, either as a nun or as a visionary or as a female writer. As Professor Newman notes in her introduction, Hildegard was profoundly different from such later figures as Catherine of Siena and Teresa of Avila, the only women taken seriously as theologians or as mystics by the Catholic church until recently. Nor is Hildegard, who is in any case an extremely difficult writer, made easier to understand by isolating her from her twelfth-century German, monastic context and relocating her in a tradition of female spirituality running from Perpetua (d. 203) to Therese of Lisieux (d. 1897). A Benedictine abbess, Hildegard advocated a monastic life of obedience and communal prayer—not the extravagant and individualistic asceticism of some later medieval women. A proponent of Gregorian reform, Hildegard proselytized for clerical purity and power, and argued that women should not hold priestly office, although she (virtually alone among medieval women) undertook preaching missions with ecclesiastical approval. Authorized to write by God's command (as were many other medieval women), Hildegard dominated her confessors, scribes and illustrators in a way not common with female saints, some of whom (such as Elizabeth of Hungary or Angela of Foligno) were so controlled by their confessor-scribes that it is indeed hard to know whether their piety and even their words represent truly the divine message they heard in the inner recesses of their hearts.[3] Moreover, Hildegard was a prophetic seer whose visions had political content and were based in a physical experience of light and pain. She wrote in Old Testament images of precious stones and noble buildings, of agriculture and organic growth, of courts and war and beautiful garments—images radically different from the more tender, domestic, even sentimental meditations on the Holy Family and the human experience of Jesus common in Rhineland convents of the fourteenth century. A visionary who took her revelations as a text for exegesis, not an experience for re-living, Hildegard was not, technically speaking, a mystic at all. She wrote not about union but about doctrine, although her attention to bodily phenomena such as sexual desire or menstrual cramps sets her apart from other visionary theologians of the twelfth century (such as Hugh or Richard of St. Victor).

Readers who come to the complex and difficult text presented here equipped with a background in feminist theology or in women's history may be surprised by many things—among them Hildegard's sense of inferiority as a female and her confident self-assertion in castigating the clergy. Readers who approach the *Scivias* with knowledge of later medieval apocalyptic or mystical writing may be puzzled by the virtual absence of nuptial imagery—usually thought, quite incorrectly, to be characteristic of women writers—and by the lack of a spirituality of *imitatio Christi* and self-punishing asceticism. In presenting Hildegard's obscure yet brilliant visions to such readers, it is therefore tempting merely to underline their idiosyncrasy and leave it at that. This would, however, be unwise. The flood of questions raised by recent work on women's piety needs to be addressed, if only by spelling out clearly two issues at stake. First, is there a female spirituality in the period between 1100 and 1517? Second, did medieval women speak with their own voices and out of their own experience, or is their work merely the inscription of the misogynist and patriarchal values of the dominant religious tradition? Although related, these are not the same question.

To ask the first question is really to ask whether there are consistent and identifiable ways in which women's religious concerns, considered across decades, classes and national or linguistic lines, differ from those of men. The question does not, as some have argued, make essentialist assumptions about the "eternal feminine." To be sure, there were biological constraints affecting women's roles in the medieval period—constraints of which Hildegard, with her keen medical curiosity, was well-aware. But no modern theorist would explain women's religious options or opinions as biologically determined. There were, however, institutional and educational constraints not rooted in biology that were constant throughout the later Middle Ages. Women were prohibited from holding priestly office and increasingly from exercizing roles as preachers and spiritual counselors. They were cut off from the new scholastic education of the twelfth and thirteenth centuries, yet found encouragement and opportunities to write when vernacular languages and genres emerged in that much-studied shift from oral to written culture.[4] The question of women's piety is therefore in part a question of whether social, educational and institutional limitations were so powerful an influence as to differentiate fundamentally women's insights from men's.

Recent studies of medieval saints have suggested that certain themes such as the religious significance of illness and the need for charismatic authorization do characterize women's religious experience. Analyses of the structure of women's prose and women's visions also suggest that particular fears shaped women's intellectual efforts, and indeed that the act of writing itself was often for a woman both service to others and audacious self-integration. Some recent scholarship has even argued that gender-related imagery is used differently by males and females, although the best of such work eschews any assumption that women are generally drawn to feminine or men to masculine images. Research on medieval medical texts has established that learned and folkloric traditions shared an emphasis on the threatening physicality of females; some historians would argue that such traditions underlie the extravagant physiological imagery in women's writing as well as the extraordinary bodily miracles such as stigmata, miraculous lactation, and so forth performed by women from the thirteenth century on.[5]

It is clear that this recent research cannot be ignored in a study of Hildegard. Different as she may be from later, more affective female mystics, her *Scivias* nonetheless scintillates with a concern for embodiment—as both glorious and deplorable—that puts her in the company of Mary of Oignies, Angela of Foligno and Catherine of Genoa. Atypical as we may find her moderate Benedictinism, her assumption of quasi-clerical roles and her exegetical rather than experiential stance toward her visions, the act of writing that wrenched her from depression into leadership reminds us of the stunning personal integration and religious creativity achieved by Beatrice of Nazareth, Catherine of Siena and Teresa of Avila in similar acts.

The second question asked in recent decades about women's writing is also complex. Both radical feminists and conservative students of mysticism have queried whether what we have in women's texts from the twelfth to the fifteenth century are women's voices at all. In a culture where official theology was defined by scholastic debate and papal pronouncement, where reception of the eucharist required the recipient to submit to previous scrutiny by a male confessor, where increasingly elaborate rules were devised for "testing" charismatic gifts, which could be adjudged "feigned sanctity," how can we be sure we hear women speaking freely? Can phrases such as Hildegard's repeated assertion of female inferiority really be accepted as women's own, even when penned or dictated by the woman herself?[6]

Some scholars have wished to decide this issue a priori, declaring women's writings either a vague echo of more theoretically powerful works by orthodox males or a species of "false consciousness" that reflects merely patriarchal repression. This position assumes not only that women's courage, serenity, self-sacrifice and loyalty were self-delusion but also that the power to repress is the only effective power in human history. To this a priori assumption scholarly scrutiny of texts can, of course, provide no rebuttal. But recent scholarship not committed to this ideological position has found in Hildegard, as in Catherine of Siena or Julian of Norwich or even—for all their orientation toward male advisers—Elizabeth of Schönau or Dorothy of Montau, the wellings up of profound female experience. The low-keyed irony with which Hildegard reminded corrupt clerics that God had been forced to choose an inferior mouthpiece because *they* had fallen so low, like the cheeky casuistry with which the fourteenth-century English woman Margery Kempe met the admonition not to preach, have hardly seemed to all recent interpreters an internalizing of misogyny.[7] Nor have all scholars read as repression Hildegard's glorious sense of the power and independence conferred on women by virginity.

It would, however, be misleading to close with general methodological issues raised by the current discussion of female spirituality. Attentive readers will find that Hildegard directs her audience not to a consideration of woman but to a consideration of humankind. She meditates not on the experience of *anima* as *sponsa*, languishing with desire for Christ her bridegroom, but on the place of the human person (*homo*) in a divine plan that marches from creation through Christ's incarnation to last judgment and final redemption. For a lyrical evocation of soul seeking the sensual delights of ecstatic union, one must turn, in the twelfth century, to Cistercian or Carthusian monks. The *homo* of whom Hildegard writes is a lump of mire, although surrounded with jewels (pt III, vision 1). The body this *homo* wears as a garment is crucial to its self and will rise at the last day gendered and intact, but body is useful to *homo* not as a locus of earthly or celestial sensations but as an instrument of self-discipline.

Hildegard's Latin is less beautiful than that of her more affective and evocative Cistercian contemporaries; her concern is more ecclesiological; her vision of the divine economy more historical; her piety is tougher and less individualistic. Readers who expect to be moved or inspired as Bernard of Clairvaux moves and inspires may be initially disappointed. But if one pauses for a moment while reading and looks beyond the elaborate and often confusing details of Hildegard's revelations, one realizes one has been shown the structure of salvation. With Hildegard one does not feel; one sees. Before the eyes of the mind pass such vivid images as the first human being, formed of clay, refusing to pluck the flower of obedience (pt II, vision 1); the great maternal figure *Ecclesia*, with souls going in and out of her womb (pt II, vision 3); the pillar of Christ's humanity, up and down which the virtues climb as on a ladder (pt III, vision 8); the bones of the dead leaping together at the end of time into figures whose very appearance reveals their status as saved or damned (pt III, vision 12); the crystalline beauty of the heavens in eternity, filled with light and song (pt III, vision 13). Hildegard's visions are in fact one vision: a primer and a *summa* of Christian doctrine.

Hildegard spoke to recall the lukewarm and their faithless leaders to God. Her speaking required courage. It also required troubled times and divine inspiration. Indeed she believed God had called upon a weak woman to rage against evil only because humankind had turned away from heaven and bent its will toward the dust from which it had been created. But rage she did, with confidence and power. It is hard not to see in her parable of the apostles (pt III, vision 7) a description of her own prophetic role:

And so . . . the Holy Spirit came openly in tongues of fire. . . . And, because the apostles had been taught by the Son, the Holy Spirit bathed them in Its fire, so that with their souls and bodies they spoke in many tongues; and, because their souls ruled their bodies, they cried out so that the whole world was shaken by their voices.

And the Holy Spirit took their human fear from them, so that no dread was in them, and they would never fear human savagery when they spoke the word of God; all such timidity was taken from them, so ardently and so quickly that they became firm and not soft. . . . And then they remembered with perfect understanding all the things they had heard and received from Christ. . . .

And so, going forth, they made their way among the faithless peoples who did not have roots. . . . And to these they announced the words of salvation and of true faith in Christ.

NOTES

1. Peter Dronke, *Women Writers of the Middle Ages: A Critical Study of Texts from Perpetua (+ 203) to Marguerite Porete (+ 1310)* (Cambridge: Cambridge University Press, 1984), ix.

2. *Medieval Women Writers*, ed. Katharina M. Wilson (Athens, GA: The University of Georgia Press, 1984); *Medieval Women's Visionary Literature*, ed. Elizabeth A. Petroff (Oxford: Oxford University Press, 1986). See also the *Matrologia Latina* series, edited by Margot King and published by Peregrina Publishing Co.; and the projected series *Femina*, to be edited by Jane Chance and published by Focus Publishing.

3. See *Sankt Elisabeth: Fürstin, Dienerin, Heilige: Aufsätze, Dokumentation, Katalog*, ed. Philipps-Universität Marburg (Sigmaringen: Thorbecke, 1981); Paul Lachance, *The Spiritual Journey of the Blessed Angela of Foligno According to the Memorial of Frater A.*, Studia Antoniana 29 (Rome: Pontificum Athenaeum Antonianum, 1984).

4. Herbert Grundmann, "Die Frauen und die Literatur im Mittelalter: Ein Beitrag zur Frage nach der Entstehung des Schrifttums in der Volkssprache," *Archiv für Kulturgeschichte* 26 (1936), 129–61. On the shift from orality to scribality, see M. T. Clanchy, *From Memory to Written Record: England, 1066–1307* (Cambridge, MA: Harvard University Press, 1979); Per Nykrog, "The Rise of Literary Fiction," in *Renaissance and Renewal in the Twelfth Century*, ed. Giles Constable and Robert Benson

(Cambridge, MA: Harvard University Press, 1982), 593–612; Brian Stock, *The Implications of Literacy: Written Language and Models of Interpretation in the Eleventh and Twelfth Centuries* (Princeton: Princeton University Press, 1983).

5. See Donald Weinstein and Rudolph Bell, *Saints and Society: The Two Worlds of Western Christendom, 1000–1700* (Chicago: University of Chicago Press, 1982), 234–35; Richard Kieckhefer, *Unquiet Souls: Fourteenth-Century Saints and Their Religious Milieu* (Chicago: University of Chicago Press, 1984), 57–58; Petroff, 28–32 and 37–44; Marie-Christine Pouchelle, *Corps et chirurgie à l'apogée du Moyen Age* (Paris: Flammarion, 1983); Caroline Walker Bynum, " '... And Woman His Humanity': Female Imagery in the Religious Writing of the Later Middle Ages," in *Gender and Religion: On the Complexity of Symbols*, ed. Bynum, Harrell and Richman (Boston: Beacon, 1986), 257–88; idem, "The Female Body and Religious Practice in the Later Middle Ages," *Zone* 3–5 (1989), to appear.

6. See *Frauenmystik im Mittelalter*, ed. Peter Dinzelbacher and D. Bauer, Wissenschaftliche Studientagung der Akademie der Diozese Rottenburg-Stuttgart 22.–25. February 1984 in Weingarten (Ostfildern: Schwabenverlag, 1985); Caroline Walker Bynum, *Holy Feast and Holy Fast: The Religious Significance of Food to Medieval Women* (Berkeley: University of California Press, 1987), 13–30 and 277–96; P. Dinzelbacher, "Zur Interpretation erlebnismystischer Texte des Mittelalters," *Zeitschrift für deutsches Altertum und deutsche Literatur* 117 (1988), 1–23; Ursula Peters, "Frauenliteratur im Mittelalter? Überlegungen zur Trobairitzpoesie, zur Frauenmystik und zur feministischen Literaturbetrachtung," *Germanisch-Romanische Monatschrift*, N.F. 38 (1988), 35–56.

7. Dronke, 149 and 201; Clarissa W. Atkinson, *Mystic and Pilgrim: The Book and the World of Margery Kempe* (Ithaca, NY: Cornell University Press, 1983), 108–9.

Introduction

S t. Hildegard (1098–1179), founder and first abbess of the Benedictine community at Bingen, is one of the most fascinating spiritual figures of the twelfth century. The bearer of a unique and elusive visionary charism, she was also a prophet in the Old Testament tradition—the first in a long line of prophetically and politically active women—yet at the same time a representative of the German Benedictine aristocracy in its heyday. Proudly aware of belonging to a social and spiritual elite, she was profoundly humble before God, awed by the audacity of her own mission, and by turns diffident and strident about her gifts.

Measured in purely external terms her achievements are staggering. Although she did not begin to write until her forty-third year, Hildegard was the author of a massive trilogy that combines Christian doctrine and ethics with cosmology; a compendious encyclopedia of medicine and natural science; a correspondence comprising several hundred letters to people in every stratum of society; two saints' lives; several occasional writings; and, not least, a body of exquisite music that includes seventy liturgical songs and the first known morality play. Although other women had written before her, their works had fallen back into silence; the names of Perpetua, Egeria, Baudonivia, Dhuoda and Hrotsvitha were unknown to her. Nor was she aware of her great French contemporary, Heloise. We must not underestimate the courage she needed as the first woman, to the best of her knowledge, to take up wax tablets and stylus in the name of God. Even greater, perhaps, was the daring required to embark on her career as a public preacher of monastic and clerical reform. This mission led her to undertake four prolonged preaching tours, beginning at the age of sixty; she spoke mainly to monastic communities, but on occasion addressed clergy and laity together in the public squares. In the meantime she continued to guide and administer the two nunneries she had founded, the first despite strong opposition from her abbot. Its daughter house, located in the Rhineland village of Eibingen, is still thriving today.

To her contemporaries Hildegard was "the Sibyl of the Rhine," an oracle they sought out for advice on everything from marital problems and health troubles to the ultimate fate of their souls. Often she gave her advice unsought—most notably to her patron, the emperor Frederick Barbarossa, whom she rebuked fiercely for his role in the German papal schism. Her books enjoyed a modest circulation and a widespread notoriety. By later medieval generations she was remembered primarily as an apocalyptic prophet. Her fiery but enigmatic writings about the Antichrist and the last stages of world history were collected by a Cistercian monk in 1220 and continued to circulate until the Reformation, when she was perversely hailed as a proto-Protestant because she had prophesied the confiscation of ecclesiastical wealth by princes and the dissolution of monasteries.

In our own day the voice that Hildegard had called "a small sound of the trumpet from the living Light" is resounding once more. In Germany she still enjoys a wide popular cult, and the abbey at Eibingen has become a center of scholarship and pilgrimage. Herbalists have rediscovered some of her prescriptions and begun to experiment with their use in modern homeopathic practice. Musicians have performed her liturgical songs and her drama, the *Ordo virtutum*, to great acclaim. To students of spirituality Hildegard remains of compelling interest, not only as a rare feminine voice soaring above the patriarchal choirs, but also as a perfect embodiment of the integrated, holistic approach to God and humanity for which our fragmented era longs. While the movement for creation-centered spirituality has exaggerated certain elements of her teaching and denied its more ascetic and dualistic aspects, it remains true that Hildegard unites vision with doctrine, religion with science, charismatic jubilation with prophetic indignation, and the longing for social order with the quest for social justice in ways that continue to challenge and inspire.

Hildegard's Life and Works

Hildegard's life, which is well-known from her own writings as well as a variety of contemporary documents, presents a mixed image of oppression and privilege.[1] Born into a noble family of Bermersheim near Alzey, she enjoyed the inestimable advantages of wealth, high birth, membership in a large and well-connected family and easy access to the holders of political and ecclesiastical power.[2] At the time of her birth the Cistercian order was in its infancy and the first stirrings of the apostolic poverty movement had barely begun. Benedictine monasticism, especially in Germany, remained an option for the elite, and many communities had close connections with the houses of their noble founders or patrons. On the other hand, the ethic of world-renouncing asceticism held a strong appeal for these powerful families, so it was not unusual when the daughter of the Count of Sponheim, a woman named Jutta, decided in 1106 to adopt the solitary life of a recluse.

Jutta's family was closely connected with Hildegard's, and her conversion provided an ideal opportunity for Hildegard's parents, Hildebert and Mechthild, to perform a pious deed. They offered their eight-year-old daughter, the last of ten children, to God as a tithe by placing her in Jutta's hermitage.[3] As a handmaid and companion to the recluse, Hildegard was also her pupil: She learned to read the Latin Bible, particularly the Psalms, and to chant the monastic Office. In time, other women joined Jutta and Hildegard, and the hermitage became a nunnery professing the Benedictine Rule. As a teenager Hildegard made her formal profession of virginity. We hear nothing more of her until 1136 when Jutta died and Hildegard was elected abbess in her stead. Five years later she received the prophetic call that eventually led her to compose the *Scivias* and embark on her public mission.

Although the outward circumstances of Hildegard's life were in no way remarkable until that date, her inner life had always been mysterious. In the personal memoirs that form part of her official biography she reports not early mystical longings or a precocious sense of vocation, but rather a peculiar temperament, which doomed her to chronic ill health and, at the same time, gave her a propensity for visions from earliest childhood. She could see things that were invisible to those around her; she foretold the future; and her visual field was filled at all times with a strange luminosity that she later came to call "the reflection of the living Light." In this light she perceived a variety of figures, ranging from human forms to elaborate architectural models, which she was able to interpret with the aid of a "voice from heaven." Finally, on rare occasions she came into contact with a greater brightness, which she called "the living Light" itself; her description of this experience (written at the age of 77) suggests a direct encounter with the divine presence.[4] Initially, however, her visions were merely baffling. Hildegard confided them only to Jutta and to the monk Volmar, her teacher and later her secretary and close friend.

The early genesis of these visions, their connection with the "aerial fires" and other illnesses that plagued Hildegard, and above all, the fact that she experienced visions for forty years before receiving her prophetic call and learning to interpret them as a gift from God, strongly suggest a physiological basis. Charles Singer and, more recently, Oliver Sacks have concluded that the abbess suffered from "scintillating scotoma," a form of migraine.[5] But illness did not prevent her from living an extraordinarily active life and surviving to the ripe age of eighty-one. Moreover, she always stressed that she received her visions while "fully awake in mind and body" and without any impairment of her normal sense functioning—a description that would exclude any seizures, ecstasies or trance states. It is even clearer that she did not in any way seek to induce the visions. As a Benedictine she practiced and counselled only moderate fasting and avoided mortifications; nor is it reported that she spent long hours in private prayer. Her visionary experience, then, was one of the givens of her physical and psychological make-up. It took decades of painfully acquired self-knowledge—and the authority of an abbatial position—before she was able to understand the visions as a vehicle for divine revelation. Her spirituality thus stands in contrast with that of later mystics who deliberately cultivated visions and other paranormal experiences. Nevertheless, her visions set a seal on the prophetic authority she claimed: without them she would have had neither a message nor an audience. Illness, on the other hand, kept her constantly aware of her human frailty and furnished one of the abiding themes of her spirituality, that of divine power made perfect in weakness.[6]

Hildegard's prophetic call came to her in 1141 in the form of a fiery light that permeated her whole heart and brain and gave her an infused knowledge of all the books of Scripture. In the *Scivias* preface, where she describes this illumination, she is careful to give her exact age at the time as well as the names of all her superiors (the reigning emperor, the archbishop of Mainz and the abbot of St. Disibod). This scrupulous dating follows a literary convention established by the Hebrew prophets and continued by the seer John of Patmos; like them, Hildegard was keenly aware of history and her own historical moment. The illumination, with the subsequent command to "cry out and write," had come to her not because she was any more devout or deserving than others, but because the times were desperate. Unlike modern historians Hildegard did not perceive the mid-twelfth century as a time of spiritual fervor and renewal, but as an "effeminate age" in which the Scriptures were neglected, the clergy "lukewarm and sluggish" and the Christian people ill-informed. Her mission, then, was to do with her prophetic charism what professional clerics had failed to do with their priestly charism: teach, preach, interpret the Scriptures and proclaim the justice of God.

After she overcame her initial hesitation about writing, it took Hildegard ten years to complete the *Scivias* with the editorial help of Volmar and the assistance and moral support of her favorite nun, Richardis von Stade.[7] This decade was marked by numerous crises in her life. Through the agency of Volmar and of her bishop, Henry of Mainz, Hildegard's fame eventually reached the ears of Pope Eugenius III, who happened to be presiding over a synod of bishops at Trier in the winter of 1147–48. Eugenius, a Cistercian, had been a disciple of St. Bernard before his elevation. Not long before the synod of Trier, Hildegard had written to the abbot of Clairvaux to seek confirmation of her gifts, and Bernard intervened on her behalf with the pope. The upshot was that Eugenius took advantage of his proximity to Hildegard's convent to procure a copy of her unfinished *Scivias*, which he read in public before the assembled bishops and then officially endorsed, sending the seer a letter of apostolic greeting and benediction to continue her work.[8] The importance of this papal seal of approval cannot be overestimated. Not only did it increase Hildegard's confidence and security in the face of continuing self-doubt, but it also authenticated her publicly and protected her from the censure she was bound to attract for violating the deutero-Pauline strictures on female silence and submission.

At about the time of the synod Hildegard received a vision in which she was instructed to leave St. Disibod, the male community to which she and her nuns were attached, and found a new convent on the site of a ruined Carolingian monastery near Bingen. This plan met with vehement objections from her abbot along with many of the nuns, who were loath to leave their comfortable surroundings for a desolate wilderness. Hildegard's desire for independence from the monks—juridical and financial as well as spiritual—embroiled her in prolonged conflict with the abbot of St. Disibod.[9] In addition, some of her daughters refused to move; her beloved Richardis left to become abbess of another monastery, much to Hildegard's chagrin; and her migration exposed her to ridicule from the local nobility, whose goodwill was essential if the new community was to prosper. Nevertheless she persevered, using her family connections to secure the land and a miraculous "charismatic illness" to persuade the abbot that her departure was the will of God. Her new monastic church of St. Rupert was formally consecrated in 1152.

During the 1150s Hildegard devoted herself to securing the welfare of her monastery, the Rupertsberg, with every means at her disposal.[10] She worked to establish monastic discipline by teaching and preaching; supervised construction of the new buildings; obtained gifts and bequests to make her community financially secure; fought for a charter of independence from St. Disibod; and fostered the cult of her new patron, St. Rupert, by writing his *vita*. To instruct her nuns she wrote a commentary on the Athanasian creed, and she enriched their liturgical life with the repertoire of songs that she eventually gathered into her *Symphonia*.[11] To this period also, in all likelihood, belong the final version of her music drama, the *Ordo virtutum* (*Play of Virtues*), and the mysterious *Lingua ignota*, which she seems to have created as a kind of secret language to instil a sense of mystical solidarity among her nuns.[12]

This intense burst of activity directed toward her daughters was complemented by an ever-widening correspondence with the outside world. Hildegard's growing fame brought a constant stream of pilgrims and miracle-seekers, as well as prospective nuns, to the Rupertsberg gates. Most of her correspondents were fellow abbesses, abbots and priests, although there is an impressive sprinkling of secular rulers and prelates and a less prestigious, though perhaps more revealing, selection of letters to ordinary laymen and women. It is difficult to evaluate Hildegard's correspondence in its present state, however, since her secretaries edited freely in order to upgrade the status of her associates and enhance her image as an inspired oracle of God—possibly with a view to imminent canonization. A forthcoming critical edition of her letters will make it possible, for the first time, to assess the actual scope and influence of her correspondence.[13]

According to an autobiographical preface, it was in the same decade of almost unbelievable energy that Hildegard composed her two scientific works. The *Book of Simple Medicine*, also called *Nine Books on the Subtleties of Different Kinds of Creatures*, summarizes the natural science of her age in a logical encyclopedic format. Four books on animals, two on herbs and trees, and three on gems, metals and "elements" combine a wealth of empirical observation with medical notes on the wholesome and poisonous properties of creatures, moral symbolism belonging to the genre of bestiary lore, and magical charms to be used in healing. A companion volume, the *Book of Composite Medicine* or *Causes and Cures*, was apparently never redacted in final form. Along with more or less systematic material on diseases and their treatment, it contains a fascinating miscellany of traditions about Adam and Eve, observations on sexuality and even astrological lore.[14]

It is significant that these works, unlike the *Scivias* and Hildegard's later visionary writings, make no claim to divine inspiration. Neither she nor her secretaries ever made any attempt to disseminate them, nor are they included in the huge manuscript of her collected works, prepared at the Rupertsberg shortly after her death. This omission suggests that Hildegard made a sharp distinction between God's work and her own, yet her creativity and curiosity knew no bounds. The medical works, especially *Causes and Cures*, were probably compiled for her personal use. A tradition of miraculous healings ascribed to her suggests that she practiced medicine informally, like many monastics; on the evidence of these writings, she used both natural and supernatural means.[15] Only in her last written work did she attempt to combine her scientific interests with her prophetic and theological mission.

Around 1158, Hildegard was ready to turn her restless mind in new directions. The Rupertsberg, strengthened and stabilized by two charters from the new archbishop of Mainz, was now well enough established that she could risk prolonged absence for the sake of preaching. Over the next five years she undertook three major tours, despite the burden of illness. Travelling along Germany's great rivers, the Rhine and the Main, she preached at numerous monasteries and gave fiery apocalyptic sermons in the cathedral towns of Cologne and Trier. Many of these communities subsequently requested transcripts of her sermons, which can be found among her correspondence.[16] This period also saw the composition of a new visionary work, the *Liber vitae meritorum* (*Book of Life's Merits*), which became the second volume of her trilogy. Based on her own experience as a spiritual director, it deals with moral psychology and penance in the context of an overarching christological vision. This little-known work represents a novel synthesis of at least three medieval genres: the *psychomachia* or virtue-vice debate, the penitential and the otherworld vision. It is an important early witness to the developing doctrine of purgatory and represents an interesting compromise between the older medieval concept of virtues and vices as static entities and the newer psychological dynamism favored by the Victorines and Cistercians.[17]

By the time she had completed the *Book of Life's Merits* Hildegard was sixty-five and in constant ill health, but her old age witnessed both the most remarkable literary work and the bitterest conflicts of her long career. Although the abbess could inspire deep loyalty and devotion in her friends, she also had a talent for making enemies. Her sheer force of will, combined with a dazzling array of spiritual and intellectual gifts, a courage hardened by decades of struggle, and a prophetic persona, which she displayed in season and out, made her a formidable opponent; and she did not take defeat easily. When Richardis left her to become abbess of Bassum, Hildegard contested the election and appealed the case all the way to the pope, who ruled against her; she relented only when her young disciple took sick and died at the height of the conflict.[18] The monks of St. Disibod, too, had tasted her wrath when they objected to her plans for independence. But the conflicts of her last years show Hildegard in a more disinterested light, taking considerable risks for the sake of her principles.

The most celebrated of these quarrels set the prophet against the emperor, Frederick Barbarossa.[19] The two had earlier been on excellent terms. Sometime in the mid-1150s Frederick had summoned Hildegard to his palace at Ingelheim to give a prophetic oracle, the contents of which neither party ever disclosed in writing. In 1163 he gave her an imperial charter of protection for the Rupertsberg, guaranteeing valuable liberties. But from an ecclesiastical point of view, Frederick was already schismatic at this time, for in 1159 he had supported an antipope, Victor IV, in opposition to Alexander III. Most of the German bishops had been willing to support Victor, but when he died in 1164 and Frederick appointed a successor instead of seeking reconciliation with the legitimate pope, the prelates were outraged and Hildegard added her prophetic voice to the chorus, calling her imperial patron a madman. She continued to oppose the emperor when he named a third antipope in 1168, thus refusing to let her loyalties be dictated by political self-interest.[20] Her staunchly orthodox stance is also demonstrated by a polemic she wrote against the Cathars in 1163 at the request of the canons of Mainz.[21]

In the meantime Hildegard had begun work on her final visionary opus, the *Liber divinorum operum* or *Book of Divine Works* (also called *De operatione Dei* or *On the Activity of God*).[22] This work, inspired by an overpowering vision of Caritas or Divine Love, sets forth Hildegard's cosmology and her most mature views of history and eschatology. Like the *Scivias*, it ends with an apocalyptic scenario, which was eagerly scrutinized for centuries to come. The heart of the book, however, lies in a pair of carefully balanced commentaries on the Johannine prologue and the first chapter of Genesis. This construction holds the key to Hildegard's whole theological vision, which revolves around the identity of the Creator with the incarnate Word. Reverent meditation on the cosmos and its proportions, which all have their analogues in the microcosm of the human body, leads to the same eternal center as meditation on history in its divinely ordained stages. Just as the human form is inscribed in the center of the universe in a celebrated illustration of this text, so Christ or incarnate Love is inscribed in the center of time.[23] The consequences of this vision are worked out in detail by means of the ingenious allegories and intricate numerological correlations so dear to Hildegard's age.

Before completing the *Book of Divine Works* the abbess lost her secretary, Volmar, who died in 1173. He was replaced first by Gottfried of St. Disibod, who began to compose her *vita*, and then by the extraordinary Guibert of Gembloux, a Belgian monk.[24] Through hearsay Guibert had become fascinated by Hildegard's visions, and it is to his insatiable curiosity that we owe most of what she recorded about her inner experience. In return for this spiritual favor he rendered her invaluable aid by coming to serve as secretary and provost of the Rupertsberg during her final years. Despite the impatience of his own community, Guibert did not leave Hildegard even in 1178, when her feisty and unyielding temper led to the unexpected consequence of an interdict.[25] The occasion was the burial of a nobleman, at one time excommunicated, in her monastic churchyard. Learning of the incident, the prelates of Mainz demanded that the corpse be exhumed, but Hildegard maintained that the deceased had died in a state of grace and refused to obey even at the price of being excommunicated herself. For six months she and her nuns endured deprivation of Mass, sacraments and their unique liturgical chant. The abbess continued to fight until the interdict was lifted only a few months before her death. At this date the underlying cause of the prelates' antagonism is no longer clear, but Hildegard's resistance stands as a final testament to her courage and the loyalty of her disciples. The controversy also occasioned one of her most profound and poignant letters, an apologia for music and its role in the spiritual life.[26]

Hildegard's Spirituality

Although Hildegard is frequently classified as a mystic, she may be more precisely identified as a visionary and prophet. Classical definitions of mysticism stress the union of the soul with God and the whole system of ascetic and contemplative disciplines that aim to facilitate that union. But Hildegard, while she certainly had a powerful sense of the divine presence, did not follow the unitive way. "Prayer" to her meant primarily petition and liturgical praise, while "the love of God" meant reverence, loyalty and obedience to his commands. In the rare texts where she portrays herself as a partner in dialogue with God, she is not the enamored bride longing for divine union, as in St. Bernard's *Sermons on the Song of Songs,* but the fragile and woefully inadequate mortal—"ashes of ashes, and filth of filth"—trembling before the great commission she has received. Like Moses "stuttering and slow of speech," and like Isaiah "of unclean lips," she offers the prophet's classic response to a calling she has not chosen, yet cannot do other than obey.

The essentially prophetic character of Hildegard's spirituality explains the startling lack of interest in her own subjectivity. In spite of her unusual inner experiences, she recorded only as much as she had to reveal in order to authenticate her works. Thus only at the beginning and end of each book does she describe its genesis in visions; elsewhere the emphasis rests firmly on the content, and still more on the meaning, of the things seen. Moreover, her autobiographical prefaces and endings tend to focus as much on the seer's disabilities (her femaleness, poor health and lack of education) as they do on her revelations. These disclaimers, far from representing a simple "modesty topos," also serve the aim of authentication; they are meant to persuade readers that, because the author is not "wise according to worldly standards," her weakness and foolishness have been empowered by God alone.[27]

Hildegard's prophetic self-awareness pervades all her writings except for her scientific works, and accounts for many of their stylistic features as well as their characteristically objective or outer-directed teaching. Because she saw herself as the voice of another, not as a speaker in her own right, she often seems disturbingly unaware of the human element in her writings. Not only does she lapse easily from speaking about God in the third person, as preacher, to speaking *for* him in the first person, as prophet; she also claims direct verbal inspiration for her entire opus and threatens terrible divine vengeance on anyone who dares to add, delete or alter a word. This instrumental view of her activity also required her to deny any education beyond "simple reading," although she was already well-acquainted with the Church Fathers and standard biblical commentaries when she wrote the *Scivias*, and by the end of her life was a woman of remarkably wide culture. Her posture as a simple, unlearned person was not intended to deceive; aside from reinforcing her prophetic persona, it constitutes an implicit critique of the learned clerics whose negligence, she believed, had necessitated her mission.

Hildegard never went beyond her limited and stylized self-disclosures to reveal more of her inner life until she was in her seventies, and even then she did so only at the request of hagiographically inclined admirers. For her first biographer, Gottfried, she wrote or dictated a valuable autobiographical memoir; and for the adoring Guibert she supplied this celebrated and oft-quoted account of her "mode of seeing":

> In this vision my soul, as God would have it, rises up high into the vault of heaven and into the changing sky and spreads itself out among different peoples, although they are far away from me in distant lands and places. And because I see them this way in my soul, I observe them in accord with the shifting of clouds and other created things. I do not hear them with my outward ears, nor do I perceive them by the thoughts of my own heart or by any combination of my five senses, but in my soul alone, while my outward eyes are open. So I have never fallen prey to ecstasy in the visions, but I see them wide awake, day and night. . . . The light that I see thus is not spatial, but it is far, far brighter than a cloud that carries the sun. I can measure neither height, nor length, nor breadth in it; and I call it "the reflection of the living Light." And as the sun, the moon, and the stars appear in water, so writings, sermons, virtues, and certain human actions take form for me and gleam within it.
>
> Now whatever I have seen or learned in this vision remains in my memory for a long time, so that, when I have seen and heard it, I remember; and I see, hear, and know all at once, and as if in an instant I learn what I know. But what I do not see, I do not know, for I am not educated. . . . And the words in this vision are not like words uttered by a human mouth, but like a shimmering flame, or a cloud floating in a clear sky.
>
> Moreover, I can no more recognize the form of this light than I can gaze directly on the sphere of the sun. Sometimes—but not often—I see within this light another light, which I call "the living

Light." And I cannot describe when and how I see it, but while I see it all sorrow and anguish leave me, so that then I feel like a simple girl instead of an old woman.[28]

This is not the kind of experience that could be taught or learned. Readers might be reminded of Augustine's theory of illumination, which was probably familiar to Hildegard, or of the variant form of Neoplatonic light-mysticism that reached medieval Europe through Pseudo-Dionysius. A still closer parallel can be found in the experiences of Simeon the New Theologian and the Byzantine hesychasts, who sought by means of spiritual exercises to attain purity of heart and thus behold the uncreated light of Mount Tabor. Hildegard could not possibly have known this latter tradition, however; and as we have seen, she made no effort to cultivate or promulgate her special mode of seeing. Nor did she theologize about her visionary experience *per se*.

Aside from the dynamics of prophetic inspiration, Hildegard's spirituality is best understood through the ecclesiastical roles she played: Benedictine abbess, Gregorian reformer and apocalyptic preacher. As mistress of the Rupertsberg, she was indeed a Benedictine to the core. The *Scivias* opens with a vision of two thoroughly monastic virtues, Fear of the Lord and Poverty of Spirit; one has eyes on every side, and the other is inundated with the glory of God, indicating that only the humble possess true vision. Throughout Hildegard's works, but especially in the *Scivias*, the foundational virtues are humility, obedience and discretion, which, like Benedict, she called "the mother of virtues." In governing her community and advising her fellow superiors, she advocated a middle way between laxity and self-indulgence on the one hand and excessive abstinence on the other. She placed a premium on unity, and her teaching is pervaded with classical monastic themes: spiritual warfare, knowledge of good and evil, the conflict between soul and body, the acquisition of virtues, the special merit of chastity. Monks and virgins, in her view, were "new planets" which first appeared in the heavens at Christ's nativity;[29] she never doubted that they formed an elite corps among Christians and, if they persevered in their vows, would receive a special reward.

Although she herself was raised by a recluse, Hildegard was not particularly sympathetic to the eremitic life. A number of abbots and abbesses sought her counsel because they longed to lay down the burden of governing and work out their salvation in a hermit's cell; she always replied that this was a temptation to be resisted.[30] In fact, Hildegard's originality in so many fields should not obscure the fact that she represented a rather old-fashioned type of monasticism. Her reaction to the newer currents is neatly epitomized in her quarrel with the abbess Tengswich of Andernach, sister of the canonical reformer Richard of Springiersbach.[31] Richard and Tengswich were pioneers in the movement for apostolic poverty, and Tengswich had criticized Hildegard sharply (under the veil of ironic praise) because the abbess of Bingen accepted only noble girls in her convent. What is more, she allowed them to wear jewelry when they received communion. In a spirited reply Hildegard defended the principle of class discrimination: One would not put beasts of different species in the same stall, and even angels had their hierarchy. As for wearing jewels, it was perfectly acceptable for the brides of Christ to dress like noble ladies because, as virgins, they were exempt from the rule of female subordination that required matrons to wear veils and lay aside their elegant attire. This blend of renunciation with privilege continues the long tradition of high-born abbesses, who gave up the titles and secular powers of nobility while retaining its influence, prestige and corporate wealth.

As a reformer Hildegard belongs squarely within the Gregorian camp. In fact, as Jeffrey Russell wrote of Gregory VII himself, her life "is proof that a burning spirit can dwell within a breast committed to order."[32] *Ordo* is indeed a key word in the *Scivias*. Hildegard did not call for radical change of social or ecclesiastical structures; it was the abuse of authority, not the nature of it, that she opposed. Her ideal was a Christendom wherein the secular power would be firmly subordinate to the spiritual, princes and prelates would rule with vigilance and justice, and subjects and layfolk would offer prompt obedience. Yet because her message was largely directed to those in power, and particularly to the ecclesiastical hierarchy, she concerned herself far more with the negligence of clerics and the arrogance of rulers than with the sins of subjects. Three issues that particularly concerned her were clerical celibacy, simony and the subservience of prelates to the secular power—a burning question in Barbarossa's Germany where the bishops were virtually ministers of state. All of these issues, of course, continued the eleventh-century struggle of the reformed papacy against what it perceived as lay encroachments on the dignity of the church.

In addition, Hildegard was zealous for orthodoxy and thus deeply troubled by the hierarchy's failure to offer any effective resistance to the Cathars, who were making numerous converts even as she composed the *Scivias* and had infiltrated the Rhineland by the 1160s. Their alarming success may account for the space she devoted to the sacraments of marriage and the eucharist, which were particularly reviled by these dualistic sectarians. In her most vehement and memorable preaching the abbess highlighted purity of doctrine along with sexual purity, both of which could be symbolized by the powerful image of the virgin Ecclesia. Hildegard not only personified Mother Church in this ancient symbol; in a sense, she impersonated her, making herself a mouthpiece for the pure but continuously imperilled bride of Christ.[33] In short, she placed her zeal for reform at the service of an essentially clerical vision of the church and a hierarchical vision of society. For her there could be no conflict between the spirit of prophecy and the spirit of order.

Hildegard's apocalyptic preaching must be understood in its proper context.[34] As she was not a radical reformer, neither was she a millenarian; she did not envisage an imminent Second Coming or look forward to a golden age of the Spirit. Rather, her apocalyptic message is closely akin to that of the Old Testament prophets. She shared their perception that divine judgment inevitably follows on human sin, and especially on the sins of rulers. If the princes of the church did not renounce their greed, fornication, oppression and negligence, they would be punished by the loss not only of their wealth and power, but even of the dignity they had signally abused. The perpetrators of this vengeance would be princes and people, not because Hildegard believed that kings were superior to prelates or that laypeople had a right to choose their own priests, but because she saw that the secular power could serve as God's scourge to punish his faithless people, just as the Assyrians of old had been allowed to punish Israel. Apocalyptic imagery coupled with the preaching of reform carries the same message that Jonah brought to the Ninevites: If the preaching is obeyed, it is just possible that the prophesied disasters will be averted.

But there is another dimension to Hildegard's apocalyptic. Like all prophets she was deeply concerned with history, and in both the *Scivias* and the *Liber divinorum operum* she surveyed the course of salvation history from beginning to end, from the creation to the final judgment.[35] In order to understand the present it was necessary to consider the past—the successive dispensations of grace before the birth of Christ—as well as the future, in which his work of salvation would at last be fulfilled. Hildegard's vision of the end, as set forth in *Scivias* III.11–12, entails a grim succession of evils that must come to pass before the judgment. As elaborated in the *Liber divinorum operum*, however, her scenario for the last times represents neither a gradual improvement nor a progressive deterioration in the state of the world. On the contrary, history is now seen as "one thing after another": ages of justice and injustice, each with its own deformations or reforms, would alternate until the coming of Antichrist. Hildegard did not presume to say when he would arrive, but she did frequently speak of her own era as an "effeminate age," which had succeeded the virginal epoch of paradise and the masculine epoch of the apostles and would in turn cede to still worse times. In one passage she even suggested that this effeminate age, signalled by the advent of feminine prophets, began around the time of her own birth.[36] But as a rule, the succession of periods is not dated even in the flexible and teasing manner that is typical of apocalyptic. Later generations could and did interpret the prophecies as they pleased, inserting themselves into the sequence wherever they chose.[37]

The *Scivias*

The title *Scivias* is short for *Scito vias Domini,* or *Know the Ways of the Lord.* The firstfruits of Hildegard's prophetic labor, this book was ten years in the making (1141–51), and during her lifetime it remained the best-known of all her works. Pope Eugenius III's approval granted it an instant celebrity, which it has retained among modern cognoscenti in large part because of the splendid illuminations that adorn an early manuscript. The *Scivias* resulted directly from Hildegard's prophetic call and was addressed to a largely clerical and monastic audience, more specifically to indolent male theologians: "Unlock for them the enclosure of mysteries which they, timid as they are, conceal in a hidden and fruitless field. Burst forth into a fountain of abundance, and overflow with mystical knowledge, until they who now think you contemptible because of Eve's transgression are stirred up by the flood of your irrigation."[38] The visionary's gender is defiantly flaunted as a challenge to idle and "effeminate" clerics.

For modern readers the initial challenge of the *Scivias* lies in its distinctive style and structure. The text is divided into three books of unequal length, dealing respectively with the orders of creation, redemption and sanctification. The third book contains as many visions as the first two combined. Within each vision, or major structural unit, the organization is complex but uniform. Hildegard always begins with a simple and usually brief description of what she has seen; her visionary experience itself is taken for granted. Occasionally she is addressed by a divine voice or a figure within the vision. At the end of each vision proper, its interpretation is introduced by a formula: "And I heard a voice from heaven, saying . . ." From this point onward the initial vision becomes a "text" to be interpreted phrase by phrase, just as a traditional monastic commentator would gloss a text from Scripture. First the visual phenomena are interpreted allegorically; then more or less elaborate teaching follows, clarifying points of doctrine and morality that have been suggested by the vision.[39] Within each of these doctrinal units, scriptural passages are introduced as proof texts, and these in turn receive allegorical readings. The didactic and exegetical nature of the whole is signalled by the recurrent pedagogical questions, *Quid est hoc?* and *Quomodo?*—"What does this mean?" Finally each unit closes with an admonitory formula that remains constant for all the visions in a particular book, thus lending further structural unity.

The order of visions is carefully arranged to afford multiple perspectives on the system of Christian doctrine. In the division into three books focusing on creation, redemption and sanctification, there is an allusion to the works of the Trinity. The first book explores connections between macrocosm and microcosm, things above and things below, the created world and the fallen world. In the second book, which is dominated by the figure of Ecclesia or Mother Church, Hildegard presents her teaching on the sacraments of redemption: baptism, confirmation, priesthood, penance and the eucharist. She apparently regarded monastic vows as a sacrament too, for they are treated at length. (Marriage, as a sacrament of the original creation, is discussed in Book I.)[40] Book III has a double structure, at once historical and moral. Most of the visions in this part develop the image of a complex allegorical building, the "edifice of salvation," which is upheld by divinity and inhabited by the Virtues. Hildegard's depiction of its walls, pillars and towers traces the successive ages of salvation history from creation through the last judgment, while her visions of the personified Virtues allow her to present a theology of the moral life. The two themes coalesce in the last vision, a symphony of praise for the inhabitants of heaven. Both history and moral struggle are here transcended and consummated.

Read as a visionary text the *Scivias* is unique; read as a compendium of Christian doctrine, it takes its place alongside many similar works of the period. The closest parallel is provided by Hugh of St. Victor's summa, *On the Sacraments of the Christian Faith*, written only a decade before (c. 1134; Hugh died in the year Hildegard began to write).[41] As an early scholastic who was also a noted teacher of contemplation, Hugh bridged the gap between the older monastic theology represented by Hildegard and the newer, more systematic mentality of the schools. In his summa the Victorine theologian used the method of scholastic argument rather than inspired visions, and he claimed only human authority. But a comparison of his table of contents with Hildegard's will show the essential similarity of matter (see below), if not of manner, between the two contemporary works. The twenty-six *Scivias* visions treat subjects closely akin to Hugh's thirty sections. Of the topics covered by Hugh, Hildegard omits only philosophical subjects like causality, predestination and natural law, along with certain "priestly" matters like vestments, masses for the dead and ceremonials for the dedication of a church. On the other hand, she includes an extensive treatment of the virtues, which Hugh omits. If Hildegard had been a male theologian, her *Scivias* would undoubtedly have been considered one of the most important early medieval summas.

The fact of visionary inspiration, of course, gives her work a tone and style quite unlike Hugh's. Where he argues, she asserts; where he speaks in his own person, she speaks *in persona Dei*. Her untutored Latin is often difficult and idiosyncratic, despite the fact that she had Volmar as a copy

INTRODUCTION

On the Sacraments of the Christian Faith by Hugh of St. Victor

Book I   [On the Creator and the Dispensation of the Law]
1. On the six days of creation
2. On the primordial causes
3. On the Trinity
4. On the will of God and its signs
5. On the creation of the angels, and on free will
6. On the creation of man
7. On the fall of the first man
8. On the restoration of man
9. On the institution of the sacraments
10. On faith
11. On the natural law
12. On the written law (the Ten Commandments)

Book II   [On the Redeemer and the Dispensation of Grace]
1. On the incarnation of the Word
2. On the church and its orders, and on the secular power
3. On the spiritual power, or the ranks of clergy
4. On sacred garments
5. On the dedication of a church
6. On the sacrament of baptism
7. On confirmation
8. On the sacrament of the body and blood of Christ
9. On sacramentals
10. On simony
11. On the sacrament of marriage
12. On vows
13. On vices and evil works
14. On confession
15. On the anointing of the sick
16. On death, hell, and prayers for the dead
17. On the end of the world
18. On the renewing of the world

editor to correct her mistakes in grammar. Occasionally she uses picturesque technical terms of her own devising; for instance, one of her standard phrases for *monk* is *vivens odor vovens iter secretae regenerationis* ("a living fragrance vowing the way of secret regeneration"). A *priest* is a *pigmentarius*, or "perfumer," perhaps with reference to the aromatic chrism of his anointing, and *viriditas* (literally, "the color green") means not only verdure or foliage, but all natural and spiritual life as quickened by the Holy Spirit.

The *Scivias*, then, can be approached from many angles: It is a prophetic proclamation, a book of allegorical visions, an exegetical study, a theological summa. Finally, it may be considered as a multimedia work in which the arts of illumination, music and drama contribute their several beauties to enhance the text and heighten the visionary message.[42] The earliest manuscript to survive until modern times was prepared around 1165 in the Rupertsberg scriptorium and illuminated with thirty-five remarkable miniatures. These paintings were produced at great expense, using costly gold and silver leaf as well as colors, and they are iconographically unique.[43] In style, too, they diverge from contemporary manuscript illumination as strikingly as Hildegard's Latin differs from that of a rhetorically trained twelfth-century humanist. Recent literature has presented the abbess herself as painter, but there is no medieval evidence to support this hypothesis, and if it were true both Hildegard and her biographers would surely have mentioned such a notable achievement. Given the peculiarities of the work, however, it seems likely that the artist (or artists) lacked formal training and worked under the visionary's personal supervision. The painter may have been a gifted Rupertsberg nun, or perhaps a monk from St. Disibod or another monastery closely associated with Hildegard.

Whoever the artist, he or she stayed close to the text of the visions and apparently eschewed the use of models, recombining iconographic motifs in new forms as creatively as Hildegard re-envisioned the familiar themes of Christian doctrine. The paintings are thus far more than illustrations; insofar as possible, they draw the viewer into the numinous world of the visionary's own experience. In this respect they resemble the didactic and meditative diagrams sprinkled through the works of Hugh of St. Victor.[44] The originality of these miniatures becomes even clearer when they are compared with illustrated Hildegard manuscripts prepared outside the Rupertsberg, such as the Heidelberg *Scivias* and the Lucca manuscript of the *Liber divinorum operum*.[45]

Unfortunately the famed Rupertsberg *Scivias* vanished in the bombing of Dresden and has not been seen since 1945. But a photocopy had been providentially made in 1927, and the twentieth-century nuns of Eibingen devoted seven years to the preparation of a hand-copied and hand-painted facsimile on parchment. This manuscript (1927–33), with miniatures painted by Dame Josepha Knips, is today our only surviving source for the original colors. Although the black-and-white copies reproduced in this volume do not convey the beauty of the originals, they may serve the reader as points of orientation when details of the text are difficult to visualize. Readers must be wary, however; although the correspondence between text and miniature is close, it is not exact, and discrepancies should be noted.

In the last *Scivias* vision Hildegard introduced music to end her work in a triumphant chorus of praise. We know from epistolary evidence that she was already celebrated for her lyrics as early as 1148 and as far away as Paris.[46] The fourteen pieces included in *Scivias* III.13, which were later incorporated in her *Symphonia*, comprise seven antiphons and seven responsories in honor of the Virgin Mary, the angels and the hierarchy of heaven. Although the *Scivias* manuscripts do not supply musical notation, Hildegard's melodies have come down to us in the two extant *Symphonia* manuscripts, and several of these pieces are now available on record.[47] In Hildegard's lifetime they were undoubtedly sung by the Rupertsberg nuns as part of the Divine Office.

Following the songs is a short play, which brings the reader from heaven back to earth, from the Church Triumphant to the Church Militant. It presents the struggle of a soul tempted by the enemy but rescued and strengthened by a choir of Virtues, until it finally attains salvation and sees the devil bound. In this short form the play admirably summarizes the themes of Book III. It was probably not long afterward that Hildegard expanded it into the longer version known as the *Ordo virtutum* and composed its melodies, if indeed she had not already done so.[48] This liturgical drama (also available on record) antedates other known morality plays by about a century and a half.[49] Unlike other moralities, it is set entirely to music, with the exception of the devil's speeches; as the spirit opposed to all harmony, he is incapable of song. While later morality plays, composed in the vernacular, aimed at wide popular appeal and often included humor, Hildegard's Latin drama is thoroughly monastic and aristocratic in character.[50] Its performance at the Rupertsberg may have coincided with the dedication of the nuns' new church in 1152, a year after the *Scivias* was completed.

Synopsis of the Visions

Because of the length of this volume it has unfortunately been impossible to provide detailed annotation. Hence the reader may find it helpful to use these capsule summaries as a *vade mecum* alongside the translation. The synopsis provided below highlights the salient features of symbolism, iconography and doctrine presented by each vision and its accompanying miniatures. It may be read either as an overview of the *Scivias* or as an introduction to the individual sections.

Book One: The Creator and Creation

1. *The mountain of God.*   Hildegard sees the Lord of the universe enthroned as "angel of great counsel" on an iron-colored mountain, which represents the eternity of his kingdom. The commentary highlights divine majesty vis-à-vis mortal humility, for the two Virtues irradiated by the glory of God are Fear of the Lord and Poverty of Spirit—both images of the seer's own state of mind as she confronts this awesome vision. One Virtue represents the beginning of wisdom, and the other, the first beatitude. Like Isaiah in his vision of the Temple (Is 6:1–8), Hildegard is called and sent by the Lord to proclaim his justice. She is then granted insight into the mystery of human intentions as God sees and judges them.

2. *Creation and the fall.*   In highly compressed and allegorical form this vision depicts the fall of Lucifer and his angels (represented as "living lamps" or stars) and the subsequent fall of Adam and Eve. The iconography is unusual and full of arcane significance. Eve, for instance, appears as a shining cloud full of stars because she is the "mother of all living," and her unborn children are meant to replace the fallen angels. Hildegard's commentary on the Genesis narrative largely exonerates Eve and lays the greatest burden of blame on Satan, breaking with the usual tendency to interpret this text in a misogynist vein.[51]

Representation of the first human couple serves as a vehicle for teachings on sexuality and marriage. Hildegard's message here is in complete conformity with mainstream Catholic doctrine. She teaches that marriage is good, but virginity is better; divorce, adultery and fornication are wrong; consanguinity is a bar to marriage; procreation is a natural process designed by God but tainted by original sin; and sexual relations are permissible only when both partners are fertile. In the relations between man and woman she affirms male supremacy yet stresses mutuality, even to the point of misquoting 1 Corinthians 11:9. Where Paul said "Man was not created for woman, but woman for man," Hildegard states that "woman was created for the sake of man, and man for the sake of woman." She adds that there is no reason why a menstruating woman should not attend church, although a bride who has just lost her virginity and a man who has been wounded in battle should abstain.

The vision ends on a note of reassurance. Although Adam and Eve were cast out of paradise, the sinless Redeemer delivered them by means of chastity, humility, charity and other virtues. Likewise, human disobedience caused the whole creation to rebel, destroying its original harmony, yet God preserved paradise inviolate as a sign of great mercy to come.

3. *The cosmos.* This vision of the cosmic egg, depicted in loving detail by the miniaturist, represents the universe as a symbolic, layered structure in which God sustains powerfully contesting forces in a delicate balance. Moving from the outermost layer inward, Hildegard sees zones of luminous and shadowy fire, representing divine purification and judgment; pure ether, which signifies faith; a watery layer for baptism; and finally the globe made up of four elements. Each of the heavenly bodies also has its allegorical meaning: the solar disk is Christ, sun of justice; the moon is the church, which reflects his light; stars are the works of piety; and so forth. Surprisingly, Hildegard does not develop the creation and birth mythology that the egg shape may suggest to readers; rather, she represents this form—"small at the top, large in the middle and narrowed at the bottom"—as symbolizing the stages of human history. The rest of the allegory also focuses on the mysteries of the incarnation and the church, in keeping with the overall theme of the *Scivias*.

In the *Liber divinorum operum* I.2 Hildegard presents an alternative vision of the universe in the form of a sphere. Her interpretation there correlates its proportions with those of the human body, since a major theme of that book is the correspondence of macrocosm and microcosm. To explain the discrepancies between her two visions she remarks that the egg shape better demonstrates the distinction between the various elements, while the sphere more accurately represents the measurements of the cosmos.[52]

The vision concludes with a long polemic against astrology, magic and divination. The seer argues that heavenly bodies are the servants of God and have no power in themselves for good or evil; people who scrutinize the stars to learn their fate are guilty of pride and fall prey to the devil's seductions. It is difficult to reconcile this polemic with the deterministic lunar astrology set forth in *Causes and Cures.*[53]

4. *Soul and body.* In this three-part vision Hildegard begins with a powerful myth, continues with teaching on human nature and psychology, and closes with a series of moral exhortations. The vision must have been a favorite with the artist, who illustrated it with three separate paintings.

The structure is unusual in that a lengthy myth precedes interpretation of the vision proper. Hildegard introduces a lonely pilgrim soul wandering in the "tabernacle" of her body and lamenting because she has lost her mother, the heavenly Zion. The soul's poignant lament recalls the lamentations of Israel in the wilderness, seeking the promised land and the new tabernacle in which God dwelt. Attentive readers will hear echoes of Job, Jeremiah and other biblical sufferers. There is also a strong Platonic coloring, for the soul grieves that it is oppressed by the sinful and burdensome flesh; the mother-daughter dynamics may even suggest Demeter and Kore, with the devil cast in the role of Pluto. The myth is illustrated in the right-hand column of the first miniature, reading from bottom to top; here the artist has depicted the soul led captive by demons, tortured on the rack, assaulted by savage beasts, hiding in a cave, scaling a mountain and, at last, given wings to soar up to its heavenly tabernacle, where the devil continues to attack it in vain. This vividly realized *psychomachia* is akin to the *Ordo virtutum*.

The heavenly voice next explains the vision itself, which represents the infusion of the soul into the embryo in its mother's womb. Conception and pregnancy are described by means of the ancient folk analogy of milk curdling into cheese; the quality of the milk or semen determines the strong, weak or bitter character of the product. This vision is illustrated in the left side of the miniature, which shows men and women—the ancestors of the unborn child—carrying bowls of cheese, into which a devil insinuates corruption. There follows a discussion of the natural powers of soul and body: the intellect or moral judgment, the will, the reason and the senses. Soul and body are meant to cooperate harmoniously; the body is not inherently evil, but through the devil's temptations it is a continual source of tribulation to the soul.[54] The second miniature portrays a Christian kneeling in prayer to receive strength against demonic attack.

In a third painting angels and demons struggle for possession of the soul as it passes from the dying person's mouth. This image of the four last things (death and judgment, heaven and hell) corresponds to Hildegard's classic teaching on the Two Ways. Every soul must choose between the sacred East, where the sun of justice rises, and the bitter North, where Satan rules his realm of darkness and cold (Is 14:12–15).

5. *The synagogue.* This brief vision personifies the people of the covenant in the form of a woman, Synagoga, who is the "mother of the incarnation" and thus the mother-in-law of the church. Hildegard is adapting a traditional iconography, which depicted the two women as rivals—Synagoga rejected and blinded because of her unbelief and supplanted in God's favor by Ecclesia, or the Gentile church.[55] The stereotype of the Jews as a literal, carnal people is present in force. But the "true believers" in Israel—Abraham, Moses and the prophets—enjoy a privileged status and are allowed to admire the new bride's beauty from afar. Like many of the figures in Hildegard's visions, Synagoga can be "read" vertically from head to feet as an allegory of successive historical periods. In the end, the seer teaches, the Jews will be converted and "run back with great haste to the way of salva-

tion." This commonplace view, derived from Romans 11, was shared by Bernard of Clairvaux, Honorius and many other contemporaries.

6. *The choirs of angels.* The nine choirs of angels were conventionally ranked, in ascending order, as angels, archangels, virtues, powers, principalities, dominations, thrones, cherubim and seraphim, and arrayed in three clusters of three. Hildegard's text supplies an alternative division into two, five and two so that her nine choirs can provide analogues for human nature. Angels and archangels signify body and soul, the cherubim and seraphim, as always, symbolize the knowledge and love of God, and the five middle orders represent the five senses. Further allegorical details pertain to the incarnation and the life of virtue. From Pseudo-Dionysius Hildegard takes the notion that the celestial hierarchy above mirrors the ecclesiastical hierarchy below. Her vision of the choirs as "armies arrayed like a crown" inspires the artist's brilliant mandala-like image of nine concentric circles ranged about a void to signify the ineffable Presence.[56]

The reason for placing the synagogue and the angels in this section of the *Scivias* is not immediately apparent. But Hildegard may have meant to show that while the synagogue prefigures the work of salvation and the angels assist in it, true redemption could not be accomplished until the advent of Christ and the church—the subject of Book II.

Book Two: The Redeemer and Redemption

1. *The Redeemer.* This initial vision recapitulates important themes of Book I—Hildegard's prophetic call, the creation and the fall of man—but the emphasis has now shifted to the Second Person of the Trinity. Vision I.2 focused on Satan and Eve; this vision concentrates on Christ and Adam. Hildegard first sees an unquenchable fire that is "wholly living and wholly Life," with a sky-blue flame to represent the eternity of the Word. After creating the first human being, the triune God offers him "the sweet precept of obedience" in the shape of a fragrant flower, but Adam fails to pluck it and thereby falls into thick darkness. The forbidden fruit of Genesis is here transmogrified into a blossom that the man is *supposed* to pluck, so that his sin becomes one of omission; thus obedience is seen as a positive good and evil as a privation. This revisionist view expresses Hildegard's idea that the "knowledge of good and evil" is God's gift to humanity rather than the devil's temptation.

Redemption proceeds in gradual stages. First the night of sin is illumined by the shining stars of the patriarchs, then by the prophets, culminating in John the Baptist; finally Christ appears as the radiance of dawn. By his passion and resurrection he delivers Adam, whose fate is contrasted with that of the unrepentant Satan. In the miniature Adam is represented three times: as the creature fashioned from mud (*adamah* = "red earth"); as the young man who withholds his hand from the flower; and as the old man who has fallen into darkness and "returned to his earth." The artist's vision diverges significantly from the text. He or she has added a central medallion to represent the six days of creation, and the unity of Creator and Redeemer is brilliantly figured in symmetrical spheres of light at the top and bottom of the miniature. A "finger of God" stretches downward from the light to awaken the newly created Adam, while the radiance of the risen Christ flames upward to redeem the fallen Adam.[57]

2. *The Trinity.* Somewhat illogically, this vision of the triune God follows that of the Redeemer, perhaps because the Trinity was first revealed to humankind through the incarnation. Father, Son and Holy Spirit are signified by a radiant light, a sapphire-hued figure and a glowing fire; the exposition stresses the unity and inseparability of the Persons. Hildegard then introduces three similitudes from created things: a stone with its dampness, solidity and kindling power; a flame with its light, heat and color; and a word with its sound, breath and meaning. The analogies of the flame and the word are ancient, but they are developed here in original fashion. It is noteworthy that none of these analogues is gender-specific, and the naming of Father and Son is balanced by a reference to "the embrace of God's maternal love," which is charity.

From the rather abstract language of Hildegard's text the artist has conceived another mandala-image. "Light" and "fire" become concentric circles glimmering with gold and silver leaf, and quivering lines suggest the vitality and energy of the living God.[58]

3. *The church, bride of Christ and mother of the faithful.* This is the first of four visions that center around the figure of Ecclesia and the sacraments. Baptism, the sacrament of her maternity, is represented in striking imagery faithfully reproduced by the artist. Reading the miniature from top to bottom and from right to left, the four panels illustrate successive moments of Hildegard's vision. (a) Ecclesia, the bride of Christ, lovingly embraces his altar. (b) She prepares to give birth to God's children; festive angels prepare their places in heaven. (c) Baptism. Two ancient images, the womb of Mother Church and the net of Peter, are conflated here. Converts or catechumens, represented as "black children," race to enter their mother's womb to be reborn; she gives birth "through her mouth," that is, through the words of blessing and the breath of the Spirit. The luminous disk, familiar from the previous visions, represents invocation of the Trinity. As the newly baptized Christians emerge, they shed their dark skins and are clothed in the "pure

white garments" of initiation. (d) Christ instructs the newly baptized in the Two Ways of sin and justice.

The teaching in this vision emphasizes the majestic and mysterious powers granted to the church as well as the grace of baptism. The church will never be conquered by hell; her secrets transcend comprehension; her crown is the teaching of the apostles, and her heart, the virginity of Mary. Following patristic doctrine Hildegard uses the symbol of Ecclesia's virginity to accentuate her pure faith, inviolate in the face of heresy and schism. But in her capacity as mother, Ecclesia grieves over the sins and rebellions of her children.

Baptism, Hildegard teaches, is analogous to circumcision under the old covenant, but is accessible to people of both sexes and all ages. It opens the kingdom of heaven to believers and remits the sin of Adam. Several brands of Donatism are rejected in passing; for example, baptism does not depend on the holiness of the priest, but on the invocation of the Trinity; infant baptism is acceptable to God; a layman may baptize in case of emergency. The symbolism of rebirth inspires an interesting digression on literal birth, which includes a surprising analogy between a man's motives in procreation and God's motives in creation. But the superior excellence of virginity is reiterated.

4. *Confirmation.* After the faithful are cleansed in baptism, they must receive the Holy Spirit through the sacrament of anointing with holy oil, which is reserved to the bishop. The vision depicts the power of the Spirit as a lofty tower that upholds and strengthens the woman Ecclesia. Her children appear in varying guises to indicate their spiritual and ecclesiastical status; thus, contemplatives are distinguished from lay Christians by the more glorious light on which they fix their gaze. But in each category some are more zealous in devotion, others more vigorous in justice. Hildegard teaches that while the sacraments are necessary for salvation, they are not sufficient; they must be accompanied by repentance and good works.

5. *Three orders in the church.* Ecclesia appears in her glory, clothed in radiant light of many colors: crystal clarity to signify the priesthood, the rosy glow of dawn for virginity, purple for monastic imitation of Christ's passion, and cloudy brightness for the secular life. This vision strongly affirms the principle of hierarchy in the church: spiritual people are to secular as day is to night, and monks rank as high above clergy as archangels do above angels. It is permissible to move from a lower order into a higher, but not to descend from a higher to a lower.

Hildegard treats the priesthood briefly, stressing clerical celibacy and commending the life of regular canons. Her vision of virginity is more lyrical, characterized by imagery of music, flowers and feminine beauty. Virgins, she says, imitate the example of Christ and John the Baptist; they alone are entitled to sing the new song in paradise [Rv 14:3–4]; they go beyond the letter of the Law to fulfill the counsels of perfection. On the subject of monasticism Hildegard addresses several points of contemporary controversy. Although monks rank higher than priests, they may be ordained and preach if the church has need of them. Since God considers the intention rather than the outward habit of the monk, children should not be offered as oblates without their consent. Renegade monks, on the other hand, must be brought back to the monasteries they have fled. Married couples cannot separate to take monastic vows unless both partners consent.

Although Hildegard's position on oblates and her emphasis on intention are in keeping with the spirit of twelfth-century monastic reform, she expresses a highly critical view of new orders. Praising St. Benedict as a "second Moses," she inveighs against diversity, novelty and singularity and proclaims that God will judge innovators. The faithful monk ought to be "humble and content with what his predecessors instituted for him." This kind of humility is equivalent to conservatism; in her view innovation can spring only from pride.

The last part of the vision elaborates on the unforgivable sin of "blasphemy against the Holy Spirit," which Hildegard defines as despair of God's mercy in the form of either final impenitence or suicide.

6. *Christ's sacrifice and the church.* This vision, by far the longest in the *Scivias*, deals with subjects of burning interest to twelfth-century theologians: the nature of the eucharist and of the priesthood. In the vision proper Hildegard draws on a patristic typology that enjoyed wide diffusion in medieval art. The crucifixion is represented as the wedding of Christ and the church: As Christ hangs on the cross his predestined bride, Ecclesia, descends from heaven and is united with him, receiving his body and blood as her dowry. Whenever Mass is celebrated, Ecclesia, as heavenly archetype of the celebrant, devoutly offers this dowry to the Father and renews her marriage union with the Son.

The numerous doctrinal points in this section can be grouped under six headings: eucharistic theology, liturgical practice, communion, requirements for the priesthood, sexual ethics and penance. Under the first heading Hildegard offers a commentary on the Mass, focusing particularly on the consecration of the gifts. Although she does not use the word *transubstantiation* and its related Aristotelian vocabulary, her teaching is in essence identical with the doctrine later defined by Fourth Lateran and elaborated by Thomas Aquinas. A surprising emphasis falls on the role of the Virgin Birth. The Virgin Annunciate becomes a model for priests, who bring Christ's body into the world by uttering the words of consecration just as Mary did by uttering her *fiat;* and the wheat of the eucharistic bread is made to symbolize the purity of Christ's virginal flesh. Since original sin is transmitted through the taint of lust, the Redeemer's body and blood must be free from every hint of sexuality in order to cleanse the sinful flesh of mortals.

After treating various points of ritual—fasting before communion, reception in both kinds, the use of traditional words and vestments—Hildegard presents a typology of communicants. The second miniature for this vision illustrates the five types: faithful believers, doubters, the unchaste and lustful, the malicious and envious, the warlike and oppressive. According to the quality of their faith and repentance, Christians may communicate either unto salvation or unto judgment.

In the section on priesthood Hildegard condemns simony (the purchase and sale of ecclesiastical office) and pluralism (the holding of multiple benefices by a single cleric). She also reiterates traditional criteria for the priesthood: a candidate must be adult, male and sound in body. (Women, she says, are "an infirm and weak habitation appointed to bear children," but as virgins they can possess the priesthood vicariously through their bridegroom, Christ.) The bulk of this section is devoted to clerical celibacy. Priests must have no wife except for the church and the justice of God; a married priest is an adulterer and serves the devil. Hildegard answers the objection that priests were married in apostolic times by arguing that God formerly permitted this aberration "because there were so few priests," just as he permitted the patriarchs to marry their female kin because there were so few people. "But now the church is adult and strong, and her ministers are many," so a higher standard of celibacy can be enforced.

The polemic against clerical marriage leads into a long catalogue of sexual sins: cross-dressing, fornication, homosexuality, "unnatural" intercourse, masturbation, bestiality and "nocturnal pollution." This list of prohibitions in turn raises the subject of confession and penance, which is treated more briefly. Confession resurrects sinners from death; it may be heard by a layman in case of emergency; and it is strengthened by almsgiving—especially if the recipients are among the "deserving poor." Hildegard urges priests to use their power of binding and loosing effectively and condemns those who abuse this authority through anger or negligence.

7. *The devil.* Hildegard's placement of this vision is pivotal. The threat of satanic temptation ends this book as the promise of angelic assistance ended Book I, but the vision of the devil bound anticipates the dramatic victory that closes Book III.

The hideous multicolored "worm" or dragon symbolizes the many kinds of vice and temptation with which the Evil One assaults people. As in Hildegard's previous visions of the church, Christians are divided into categories according to their degrees of faith and justice. Satan assails the "spiritual people" (priests and monastics) in one manner, the secular people in another, while heretics are represented as wholly in his power. Some features of the heresy Hildegard attacks suggest the Cathars; for example, they revile the sacraments and the clergy, feign Catholicism out of fear and lay claim to a pretended sanctity. Other accusations, for instance of devil-worship and obscene sacrifices of human seed, are ancient slanders earlier hurled at Christians and gnostics of the subapostolic age. Satan's power appears to be formidable, even though he is bound firmly by a chain and in the end the saints trample on him.

An interesting feature of the vision is the image of Vanity Fair, possibly inspired by Revelation 13:17 and 18:11–17. This scene is illustrated in the lower panel of the second miniature, where the artist has depicted the sinister merchants in the hats worn by medieval Jews.

Book Three: The Virtues and the History of Salvation

1. *God, Lucifer and humanity.*   This vision at first recapitulates I.1: Hildegard sees a figure of God enthroned in majesty and her calling is reaffirmed. The poignant novelty here is an image of newly created humanity: God "held to his breast what looked like black and filthy mire, as big as a human heart, surrounded with precious stones and pearls." The operative theological idea is an old, half-mythical opinion that humanity was created to replace a "tenth choir" of angels who fell with Lucifer. An eloquent miniature represents Hildegard's vision of these angels as shooting stars that are gradually extinguished as they fall, until only cinders remain. But their departing light is not quenched; it returns to the bosom of God, and since Satan fell "without an heir," God treasures his inheritance of light for a new creation. Unlike the angels, human beings are then fashioned with a "vile earthly nature" to preserve them from pride and consequent ruin.

The vision thus supplies one possible answer to a question that must arise among all theists who denigrate the body, namely, why a good God should have created such a "miserable form" in the first place. Despite the wretchedness of human nature, however, the Son of God has assumed it in the incarnation, so that no angel dares to despise it. Moreover, the filthy mire is held firmly to God's heart and adorned with the gems and pearls of sanctity. The vision is meant to inspire humility and gratitude as well as fear of God's justice; the commentary stresses that unlike the fallen angels, human beings can and therefore must repent of their misdeeds.

2. *The edifice of salvation.* This vision sets forth a blueprint of the symbolic building that will be expounded in detail through the remainder of the book. The miniature provides an indispensable diagram, although it depicts a square building where Hildegard describes a rectangular one. Built on the mountain of God, grounded in faith and fear of the Lord, the city or edifice of salvation has a double symbolism representing, on the one hand, the course of salvation history, and on the other, the doctrines and virtues every Christian must believe and acquire to be saved.

The most important wall links the East (represented on top, as is usual in medieval maps) with the North (shown to the left). In the East lies the figurative realm of Christ, in the North that of Satan, and the luminous wall between the two therefore signifies *speculativa scientia,* or the knowledge of good and evil. This is not "speculative knowledge" in the sense of abstract thought, but "reflective knowledge" in the sense of moral judgment (the adjective is from *speculum,* a mirror); this faculty is the cognitive aspect of free will.[59] The remaining three walls are of masonry, which has several meanings: the joined stones denote human flesh and its labors, the Law and the works of justice. Thus moral knowledge must be conjoined with right action for the upbuilding of salvation.

Hildegard gives two interpretations for the points of the compass. In one reading, East and West signify the dawn of salvation and the sunset of the Law, while North and South represent the fall and restoration of Adam. Alternatively, the diagram may be read counterclockwise beginning at the right. The four cornerstones are successive covenants between God and humanity: At the South stands Adam, at the East Noah (the dawn of justice), at the North Abraham and Moses as representatives of the Law (the beginning of war against Satan), and at the West Christ (the revelation of the Trinity).[60] The proportions of the building also receive numerological meanings.

This vision assigns further theological value to the despised body. Again human beings are contrasted with angels: The latter are purer and more luminous, but humans are more valiant and meritorious soldiers of God because they have to do battle against their own nature. In ascetic struggle "they conquer themselves, chastising their bodies, and so know themselves to be in [God's] army."

3. *The tower of anticipation of God's will.* From now on the exploration of the building proceeds counterclockwise, beginning with the northeast wall. Hildegard first examines the "tower of anticipation" of God's perfect will, which was manifested in the incarnation and first prefigured in the Abrahamic covenant of circumcision.[61] Aside from foreshadowing baptism, this covenant is taken primarily as a sign of sexual discipline: The initial

"cutting off" of unchastity leads by stages to the perfect virginity of Christ and Mary.

Within each portion of the building Hildegard sees a group of feminine Virtues appropriate to that particular moment of salvation history. The Virtues occupy an important place in her theology; they are not exclusively human qualities but "brilliant stars given by God, which shine forth in human deeds." The Latin *virtus* means "energy" or "power" as well as "virtue," and Hildegard plays on both senses. In effect, a virtue is a divine quality that becomes an operative force in willing souls and fully incarnates itself in right action; it is a synthesis of grace and moral effort. As Hildegard puts it, the Virtues do not work of their own accord, but with the cooperation of the person who has received them from God. They appear in feminine form in keeping with a long tradition of virtue-vice allegory that goes back to Prudentius, but also because in Hildegard's symbolic theology the feminine represents the sphere of synergy in which divinity and humanity work together for salvation.

The first three Virtues in this tower represent the initial manifestations of the ascetic life: Celestial Love, Discipline and Modesty. There follow two christological Virtues: Mercy (associated with the Virgin Mary and Christ's birth) and Victory (connected with his conquest of Satan). Standing somewhat to the side are Patience, who imitates Christ's passion, and Longing, who clings to a crucifix. Hildegard's allegorical technique further characterizes the Virtues by assigning intricate symbolism to their iconography—colors, garments and attributes.[62] In addition, each Virtue utters a self-defining motto; similar formulas recur in the *Ordo virtutum* where they are set to music.

4. *The pillar of the Word of God.*   Near the northern corner stands the pillar of the Word, signifying both the incarnate Word and the written word of Scripture. The latter has not two parts as one would expect, but three: Old Testament, New Testament and commentary, or "the profound and rich wisdom of the principal doctors." Such is the authority that Hildegard, in accord with monastic tradition, assigned to patristic exegesis. The first two sides of this triangular pillar display the saints of the old and new covenants: first, patriarchs and prophets, seen as precursors of Christ, and then apostles, martyrs and other Christian heroes. The third side, representing the exegetes, shows by its shape that wisdom arose from a small beginning, increased in the course of time, but will dwindle again in the last days. At the top of the pillar perches the dove of the Holy Spirit.

The Virtue in this vision is the Knowledge of God, more a divine than a human figure. More awesome in appearance than the other Virtues, she embodies the mystery of God's mercy and judgment in bringing sinners to grace through the scourge of calamity. Illness and other chastisements may redeem sinners by making them physically incapable of their former vices, which otherwise they would never voluntarily leave. These reluctant Christians are the wedding guests whom Christ has "compelled to come in" (Lk 14:23).

5. The jealousy of God. "The Lord is a jealous God and avenging, the Lord is avenging and wrathful; . . . The Lord is slow to anger and of great might, and will by no means clear the guilty" (Na 1:2–3). This grim vision presents the vengeance of God against evil, symbolized by a wrathful crimson face and three silently beating wings. Naturally the head faces north, directing its vigilance against Satan and his kingdom.

In the face of God's jealousy no sin goes unpunished. If it is not avenged by voluntary penance it will exact its price either in earthly suffering or in the torments of purgatory or hell. Though vengeance may appear to strike without warning, God is always just, for human beings have been granted judgment to discern good from evil; ignorance of the Law is no excuse. Hildegard's ethical stance is one of uncompromising self-denial; the choice of good is associated with struggle and anxiety, and that of evil with self-will, desire and pleasure. Certain sins, such as desecration or robbery of a church, simony and withholding of tithes, are singled out as special objects of God's vengeance because they defile the honor of his house.

6. The stone wall of the old Law. The northwest wall of the building signifies the Old Testament Law, the period of history between Abraham and Christ, and the political order. Most of the commentary in this vision asserts and defends the principles on which Christian feudal society was based.

The human race, Hildegard maintains, is divided into two unequal orders, the spiritual and the secular, and each of these classes has its proper hierarchy. Among the secular people there are the higher and lower nobility, free men and women and serfs; among the spiritual there are "the excellent and the superior, the obeyers and the enforcers." Hildegard has no doubt that these distinctions were ordained by providence; they "were and are and always will be." Two ideological justifications for hierarchy are set forth: (a) it prevents anarchy, because without rulers people would "kill each other off and perish"; and (b) it teaches by the example of earthly authority how divine authority should be loved and feared. Though the spiritual power is more exalted than the secular, princes as well as prelates represent God's justice and mercy. The "greater" deserve to rule the "lesser" because God has chosen them for their superior abilities—intelligence, integrity, eloquence —just as he chose Jacob to rule over Esau. But usurpation of power, whether through bribery or simony, violence or black magic, is harshly condemned —despite the same Jacob's example! Subjects ought of course to be obedient; if they suffer persecution from rulers, they can imitate Christ's passion.

Eight Virtues inhabit this section of the building. The first group consists of Abstinence, Liberality and Piety: self-denial is the prerequisite for generosity toward God and neighbor. In the second group Truth, Peace and Beatitude appear, representing three stages in the victory over evil. Slightly apart stand two Virtues embodying God's temporal and eternal gifts: Discretion, associated with secular justice, and Salvation of Souls. The latter manifests herself in two phases: In her "Jewish" period she has a swarthy complexion, dark curls and a multicolored tunic, but after Christ's birth she takes on a luminous white aspect, stripping off all "diversity."

7. *The pillar of the Trinity.* In *Scivias* II.2 Hildegard presented the Trinity as an eternal living reality. Her focus in this vision is on the Trinity as a saving doctrine revealed by Christ at a particular moment of history. Hence the pillar appears at the west corner of the building, symbolizing the prophetic "end of the ages." It is triangular, like the pillar of the Word (III.4), and its three edges are sharp swords cutting off all infidels: heretics, Jews and pagans, symbolized respectively by chaff, broken wings and rotten wood. Hildegard adds a lengthy parable, which she then interprets as an allegory of the apostles' preaching, and supplies some rather cloudy similitudes for the Trinity. As if to defend their obscurity, she stresses that this divine mystery must be humbly accepted and not presumptuously scrutinized.

8. *The pillar of the Savior's humanity.* This important vision depicts the incarnation as the primary locus of the Virtues, that is, the context in which humanity is enabled to collaborate with God. The pillar closely resembles Jacob's ladder, but in place of the angels seen by the patriarch, Hildegard perceives "all the virtues of God ascending and descending." Her imagery is indebted to that of an earlier visionary, Hermas (third century), who in *The Shepherd* had described a host of celestial maidens in the guise of stonemasons working to build up the church.[63] Hildegard's maidens also carry stones, representing "the winged and shining deeds people do . . . to win salvation." These Virtues descend to human beings through the humanity of Christ and return to heaven through his divinity.

The miniature shows the influence of a traditional pictorial motif, the ladder of salvation, whereby Christians climb up from earth to heaven on the rungs of virtue. Based on classic texts like the Benedictine Rule and John Climacus's *Ladder of Perfection*, the image was particularly favored by monks and nuns. Many representations of it show demons on either side of the ladder, picking off unwary souls with their arrows;[64] Hildegard's image is more positive and depicts supportive Virtues in their place. At the top of the ladder stands the Grace of God, clothed as a bishop to admonish and exhort the faithful.

The seven principal Virtues (proceeding from top to bottom) are Humility, Charity, Fear of God and Obedience on the right, and Faith, Hope and Chastity on the left. Humility is the queen of Virtues, as in the *Ordo virtutum*, but Charity is the most important and has the longest speech. She wears the sapphire blue associated with the Word of God and is assimilated to him as Chastity is to the Virgin Mary. The latter is overshadowed by the dove of the Holy Spirit and appears pregnant with a child named Innocence. In several places the text echoes earlier visions: for example, Fear of the Lord first appeared in I.1, and Hope with her crucifix is very similar to Longing in III.3.

A more perplexing cross-reference points back to I.4, for Hildegard observes that the pillar of the Savior's humanity stands "in the same place" as the radiant diamond-shaped figure she had earlier seen. But that figure was independent of the allegorical building, so Hildegard must be implying that a consistent "inner geometry" persists through all her visions. In both contexts the figure in question signifies the incarnation, but in I.4 Hildegard was discussing the means by which every soul enters its body when it is formed in the womb, while here she stresses the uniqueness of Christ's birth from the Virgin.

The central teaching of the vision concerns synergy, or cooperation with God. Hildegard teaches that God's grace will not forsake even the most hardened sinner, but it is not irresistible; the human will always retains the freedom to choose or reject salvation. To the sinner grace brings first self-knowledge, then repentance, finally hope and amendment of life. The discourse of this Virtue should be compared with earlier teaching on the Knowledge and the Jealousy of God. In a lengthy digression Hildegard draws an analogy between the seven Virtues and the seven gifts of the Holy Spirit resting on Christ [Is 11:2], thus reinforcing the centrality of the God-man.

9. *The tower of the church.* This tower stands at the southern corner of the building and represents the whole history of the church; it is therefore unfinished. But somewhat inconsistently, the seven turrets at its summit, standing for the gifts of the Holy Spirit, are already built. This detail clearly indicates how allegorical significance prevails over the logical coherence of the image. The motifs of the heavenly ladder and the cooperation of Virtues are continued from the previous vision.

Wisdom, God's feminine co-worker in creation, stands atop the "house of seven pillars" described in Proverbs 9:1. As the first of the cardinal virtues, she precedes Justice, Fortitude and temperance. The last of the four, however, is given not her classical name but the more impressive title of Sanctity—an index of the importance Hildegard ascribed to sobriety and self-denial. Unique among the Virtues, Sanctity has three heads. Two are sexless, but the left one, labelled Self-Sacrifice, is significantly female.

Hildegard's doctrine of the church stresses the role of the apostles and doctors. The faithful, as always, are divided into various categories: some cherish and preserve their baptismal garment, others feel constrained by it but keep on struggling, while still others throw off the garment and return from the church into the world. Worst of all are the simoniacs with their filthy lucre. Continuing her polemic, Hildegard claims that they purchase offices "by means of [their] spiritual father, money—for in that transaction money becomes [their] bishop." But the attack on unjust authority is balanced once again by a call for obedience to the powers that be; they will perish horribly in God's judgment, but the time is not yet.

10. *The Son of Man.* This vision completes the circuit of the building, returning to the eastern corner where the Son of Man is seated on a throne beneath that of the Shining One (God the Father). He exhorts the people of God on self-knowledge, obedience and sexual discipline, reminding the married that coupling is only permissible out of desire for children, and the celibate that mere outer virginity does not suffice for their salvation. True continence is the gift of God and should not be promised hastily or presumptuously. A consecrated virgin should rely on divine strength alone and prepare for a lifetime of ascetic struggle.

Five more Virtues fill up the complement of the city. They are Constancy, Celestial Desire (symbolized by the thirsty hart of Psalm 41), Compunction, Contempt of the World (safely ensconced within the wheel of God's mercy) and Concord (winged like an angel because she prefigures the life of heaven). Christ appears in his human aspect in a rather understated form. Like Ecclesia, he is visible only from the navel upward because his lower parts represent ages of history yet to unfold. Some of these mysteries will be disclosed in the apocalyptic visions that follow.

11. *The last days and the fall of Antichrist.* This is the vision that won Hildegard her greatest celebrity as a prophet. Although she draws on earlier apocalyptic scenarios, notably that of the tenth-century monk Adso,[65] the seer adds powerful imagery of her own. Her three principal themes are (a) the "five ferocious epochs" to come; (b) the career of Antichrist; and (c) the rape and recovery of the church.

The upper left panel of the miniature depicts five beasts that symbolize future epochs of world history: a fiery dog, a yellow lion, a pale horse, a black pig and a gray wolf. Each of these animals suggests the temperament of villainous rulers to come. In the *Liber divinorum operum,* vision III.10, the description of these eras is considerably expanded, and ages of justice and reformation are posited in between the ages of misrule. All the beasts appear in the North, since they belong to Satan's kingdom; but no term is set to their rule. Hildegard says only that the world is now in its seventh age, "approaching the end of time." This is a conventional view, however, which has nothing to do with her symbolism of the beasts. In the sixth age of the world Christ was incarnate, just as on the sixth day Adam was created. The seventh age is a "sabbath," which may be indefinitely prolonged. One apocalyptic sign, however, is the fact that Hildegard herself prophesies. God has called her because his duly appointed authorities now languish in idleness, and the world order is showing signs of decrepitude.

The approaching Antichrist is represented as a parodic inversion of Christ.[66] Born of a harlot who feigns that she is a virgin, he will be wholly possessed by the devil from his mother's womb and trained by her in the magical arts. Through preaching and false miracles, even the feigned resurrection of the dead, he will make many converts; finally he himself will simulate death and resurrection and promulgate his own scriptures. As Hildegard emphasizes Christ's virginity throughout the *Scivias,* she also stresses the Antichrist's lawless sexuality. Not only is he a child of fornication, but he himself will reject continence and all other forms of self-denial. For a time he will be opposed by the "two witnesses," Enoch and Elijah, whom God is reserving in heaven for the last times, but eventually they will suffer martyrdom for the faith.

The most daring part of the vision concerns the Antichrist's rape and bloody violation of the church, depicted in the lower panel of the miniature. Her private parts now become visible, with the monstrous head of the Antichrist appearing in place of her genitals, for he is both her son and her seducer. As Satan corrupted Eve, so will the son of perdition attempt to corrupt the virgin Ecclesia. But Christ's bride will emerge triumphant, though bruised, bloodied and in large part deceived by his wiles. After enduring persecution and martyrdom, she will be vindicated by her heavenly Bridegroom (upper right panel) and united to him in marriage. Scatology and eschatology merge as the Antichrist, self-exalted on a mountain of excrement, is struck down by a thunderbolt from on high.

12. *The last judgment, the new heaven and the new earth.* At an unspecified time after the fall of Antichrist, the last judgment with its terrors will come to pass and history will have ended. In Hildegard's vision there are no surprises in the judgment: Good and evil are plainly manifest in the forms of

the newly awakened dead. Sentence is passed on the reprobate without appeal, and unbelievers are not even allowed to stand trial, for they are damned in advance. The saints, on the other hand, receive bliss and glory from Christ, who comes in majesty on the clouds of heaven, yet with his wounds still open from the cross.

As the Son of Man sits in judgment, all creation is "shaken by dire convulsions" in which the elements are purged of mortality. Hildegard sees a "black skin" peeled away from them, recalling her image of the newly baptized in II.3. There follows a chillingly Platonic vision of permanence: In the new heaven sun, moon and stars will stand motionless, and on the new earth shall be fire without heat, air without density, a sea without waves. The vision ends on a note of everlasting stasis: "And so there was no night, but day. And it was finished."

13. *Symphony of praise.* This magnificent coda is not really a vision but a concert. The songs Hildegard records in this section do indeed, as she claims, marvelously summarize all the meanings she has presented before. In the first fourteen pieces she offers praise to the Virgin Mary, the choirs of angels and five categories of saints: prophets, apostles, martyrs, confessors and virgins. Each rank of the celestial hierarchy is honored with an antiphon and a responsory, although the liturgical genres of these pieces are not specified here as they are in the *Symphonia* manuscripts.

Heaven is not populated only with saints, but also with repentant sinners. The second part of this section is a lament and prayer of intercession for the fallen. In the final portion a penitent soul's pilgrimage to heaven (earlier presented mythically in I.4) is set forth in dramatic form. The soul slips from well-meaning innocence to impatience when she asks the Virtues for a "kiss of the heart," and they warn instead that she must do battle by their side. At this point the devil intervenes and easily leads her into sin. In contrast to later morality plays, Hildegard is not interested in dramatizing the soul's adventures in evil; instead she presents a verbal contest between the devil and the Virtues to fill the time until the soul's repentance. In the end the Virtues receive the weeping penitent, and led by their queen Humility and celestial Victory, they conquer and bind the devil.[67]

The play is followed by a brief commentary and a tribute to the power of music, anticipating the apologia Hildegard was to write at the end of her life. In liturgical song "words symbolize the body" and the humanity of Christ, she writes, "and the jubilant music indicates the spirit" and the Godhead. An allegorical reading of Psalm 150, in which the different instruments are made to symbolize the varieties of saints, leads into a final affirmation of the prophet's mission and brings the *Scivias* to a close.

INTRODUCTION

Hildegard's Place in the Tradition

Although Hildegard occupies a central place at the crossroads of twelfth-century culture, the question of "sources and influences" has always posed difficulties for students of her work. One reason for the problem has already been addressed: Hildegard's prophetic persona demanded that she present herself as a "simple and unlearned little woman," and her claim to direct visionary inspiration barred appeal to merely human authorities. Thus, although she was undoubtedly well-versed in theological and spiritual writers, she virtually never cited her sources in even the most conventional or formulaic way. In addition, her distinctive literary style makes it difficult to recognize quotations, except for the scriptural texts that she chose to gloss. Since the exegetical tradition in which she worked was both conservative and cumulative, any one of a dozen writers might be cited with equal plausibility as the source for a given doctrine or interpretation. Only in rare cases, such as the seer's debt to the *Shepherd* of Hermas in *Scivias* III.8, or to Adso's treatise *On the Antichrist* in III.11, can we point with confidence to an individual writer.

In general, the most pervasive influences in the *Scivias* are the Bible and its commentaries, the liturgy, the Benedictine Rule and the works of such widely read Church Fathers as Augustine, Jerome, Gregory the Great and Bede.[68] In all of these Hildegard's monastic heritage is evident. She was steeped in the Divine Office with its spirit of formal, communal praise; her idea of heaven (*Scivias* III.13) is a thoroughly Benedictine one, which emphasizes not the vision of God or the mystical union, but the unending liturgy of the saints. She was familiar with the moral as well as the exegetical works of the Fathers, particularly with their teachings on virginity. And if her knowledge of early Christian writings included a moderately obscure author like Hermas, it probably embraced a fair amount of apocryphal literature as well. Attempts to trace her reading in classical authors, including scientific writers, have remained highly conjectural.[69] Unfortunately we have no library catalogue for either the Rupertsberg or the monastery of St. Disibod; even if we had, a list of manuscripts would not take account of the rich oral tradition, so important even in the literate world of the monastery. Some of Hildegard's arcane lore about Adam and Eve, for instance, seems to come from Jewish tradition and may have been acquired firsthand,[70] and much of her medical knowledge was surely gained through oral transmission and experience.

Hildegard probably acquired her knowledge of the Church Fathers from florilegia and earlier medieval adaptations as well as original texts. Among late antique and Carolingian authors she would surely have known Isidore of Seville, Rabanus Maurus, Paschasius Radbertus and the hymnodist

Notker of St. Gall. The Neoplatonic tradition, which strongly colored her cosmology—accounting for affinities with more "avant-garde" authors like Bernard Silvestris and Alan of Lille—may have reached her through John Scotus Eriugena.[71] On the other hand, she might have known this author only indirectly through his twelfth-century popularizer, Honorius Augustodunensis. Among her contemporaries Hildegard stands closest to Honorius himself, a prolific author who apparently spent the latter part of his life in Regensburg,[72] and to Rupert of Deutz, a Benedictine who wrote numerous works of theology and exegesis.[73] We have already noted similarities between the *Scivias* and the work of Hugh of St. Victor. Other reformers, such as Gerhoch of Reichersberg and Godfrey of Admont, furnish useful points of comparison and contrast for Hildegard's ecclesiastical program.[74] And she was undoubtedly familiar with certain writings of Bernard of Clairvaux, the recipient of her first letter, although Cistercian spirituality had only a limited influence on her outlook. While she admired Bernard's personal holiness and shared the order's preoccupation with Caritas, or divine love, the physical and aesthetic austerities of the white monks were foreign to her. Her version of "bridal spirituality" is more indebted to traditional literature on virginity, such as the *Speculum virginum*,[75] than to Cistercian currents.

In sum, Hildegard's opus presents us with a synthesis of classical Benedictine theology, exegetics and spirituality as they stood in the mid-twelfth century, touched but not yet deeply permeated by the new modes of piety that were already changing the face of the church.[76] Yet conservative as she was, nothing she ever wrote can be mistaken for the work of another author. All is charged with the urgency of her prophetic mission, shaped by her powerfully original visionary and poetic gifts, and not least, colored subtly but pervasively by her feminine self-awareness. Hildegard's place in the tradition of women's spirituality is a complex question.[77] While that tradition may be theoretically helpful in understanding her life and work, we must remember that it was a hidden tradition that Hildegard herself did not know; any similarities between her spirituality and that of earlier female writers must result from common solutions to common problems, not conscious or even unconscious influence. With regard to later female writers the case is very different; there we must reckon with Hildegard herself as a significant role model.

Her community at Bingen, unlike the famous convent at Helfta a century later, never became a vital center of feminine spiritual culture. It may be that Hildegard's own presence was too overbearing, or her visionary gift too intimately bound up with her unique psychology and temperament, to inspire imitation. In any case, there was never a "school of Hildegard" as there was, so to speak, a "school of St. Bernard," of St.-Victor, or of Eckhart. Nevertheless the seer did have one unsought "disciple," her younger contemporary

Elisabeth of Schönau.[78] Excited by Hildegard's growing fame, this young Benedictine began to have visions a year after the *Scivias* was published. She visited Hildegard, corresponded with her, honored her as a spiritual mother, named one of her books after the *Scivias* and even adopted the older nun's conception of an "effeminate age" to justify feminine prophecy. Like Hildegard, too, Elisabeth felt herself called to preach reform, write epistles of spiritual counsel and utter apocalyptic warnings. One contemporary chronicler saw the two visionary nuns as partners in a single divine visitation.[79]

Yet a comparison between Hildegard and Elisabeth reveals precisely which elements of the older woman's spirituality belonged to the future and which to the past. As Elisha to Hildegard's Elijah, Elisabeth "inherited" her prophetic spirit along with her gift of visions, her fiery reformist zeal, her role as moral adviser to all who sought (or were subjected willy-nilly to) her advice, and her willingness to intervene in politics—though the two women were not always on the same side.[80] Like Hildegard, Elisabeth was spiritually sensitive and physically frail, prone to continual illness which often accompanied her visions. These shared traits continued to dominate the profile of women's spirituality in the later Middle Ages; we meet them again in Catherine of Siena, Birgitta of Sweden and a host of lesser-known women.

Yet there was much in Hildegard that Elisabeth found less congenial, or at any rate less imitable. The abbess of Bingen's systematic review of Christian doctrine, her Platonism, her scientific and cosmological interests, her deep learning, her idiosyncratic style and brilliant, esoteric symbology, her artistic gifts (expressed not only in her musical and dramatic creations but also in the careful, architectonic structure of her books)—all these remained foreign to the seer of Schönau. In short, it is the complexity, variety and sheer intellectual difficulty of Hildegard's opus that marks her and not Elisabeth as a woman of the twelfth-century Renaissance. Although the two nuns were contemporaries, one senses that Elisabeth would have been equally at home in a community of consecrated women a century later, while Hildegard would have been an anachronism.

What Elisabeth may have found lacking in her spiritual mother, and what she in turn supplied and passed on to later religious women, was precisely her mysticism. In her one finds ecstasies, deliberate cultivation of mystical experience, a highly developed subjectivity and deeply personal (as opposed to communal) relationships with the saints; one also finds a characteristically intimate and mutually dependent relationship with her confessor, so different from Hildegard's clearly dominant position vis-à-vis her secretary Volmar.[81] Even in their approach to their common Benedictine heritage the two nuns differed remarkably. Hildegard translated her private visions into the public medium of liturgical praise, which her whole community could share; Elisabeth translated her public experience of the liturgy into private mystical conversations with the angels and saints.

My point here is not to make invidious comparisons between the two visionaries, so close and yet so fundamentally different, but rather to show how Hildegard's life and work were received by subsequent generations. In fact, the late medieval public recreated the spiritual mother in the image of her daughter, whose works were copied and read far more widely.[82] Thus Hildegard was long remembered and celebrated as the visionary, prophet and apocalyptic preacher that she was; she was quickly forgotten as the learned writer, monastic theologian and gifted composer that she also was. The Cistercian prior Gebeno of Eberbach kept her prophetic reputation alive by publishing an extremely popular anthology of her apocalyptic prophecies, which he entitled *Speculum futurorum temporum* or *Pentachronon* (1220); this collection proved much more appealing to later medieval tastes than Hildegard's original writings.[83] On Gebeno's authority she was known to the Flemish mystic Hadewijch as "Hildegaert die alle die Visione sach," and cited at length by Lodewijk van Velthem as an anti-fraternal prophet.[84] Somewhat later, as the generic image of a late medieval "holy woman" came to be superimposed on her dimly remembered figure, she was taken for a mystic and ecstatic.

The Christian humanists of the Renaissance took a new kind of interest in Hildegard. Trithemius, abbot of Sponheim (1462–1516), published enthusiastic if dubiously accurate reports of her career,[85] and Jacques Lefèvre d'Etaples printed the first edition of the *Scivias* (1513). But the Reformation contributed two further distortions. Andreas Osiander claimed Hildegard as a Protestant in 1527, because of her prophecies against negligent clergy,[86] and in due time a more "virile age," which she had also prophesied, vented its misogyny by denying her the dignity of authorship altogether, ascribing her works to Volmar or some other pseudonymous male.[87]

The rediscovery and authentication of Hildegard's oeuvre is the work of twentieth-century scholarship, which has gradually chipped away at the falsified, stereotypical image of the female mystic and the a priori notion that a medieval woman could not, and therefore did not, write.[88] But as Hildegard and her work become known to the public through popular as well as scholarly presentations, through concerts and recordings as well as articles and books, new stereotypes arise to replace the old. Just as the later Middle Ages and the Reformation found in Hildegard the role model they needed, so our own era has created the image of Hildegard the feminist, the liberationist, the "creation-centered mystic," the holistic health practitioner, the prophet of ecological justice.[89] This model of sanctity has proven useful and inspiring to many women and men, and it contains a grain (but only a grain) of historical truth. The image of a saint, however, is always a work of synergy. Hildegard teaches that a virtuous life is the joint creation of God and humanity. By extension, a saintly life is the joint creation of the era that produces the saint and the era that venerates him or her. Those who admire Hildegard's contemporary icon will find it lovingly painted elsewhere. For those who wish to become acquainted with Hildegard the author, this faithful and unabridged translation of the *Scivias* lets her speak for herself.

NOTES

1. The primary source for Hildegard's life is a *vita* by the monks Gottfried of St. Disibod and Dieter of Echternach, begun a few years before her death and completed shortly afterward; it includes autobiographical memoirs supplied by the abbess. *Vita S. Hildegardis*, ed. J.-P. Migne, *Patrologia latina* [PL] 197 (Paris, 1855): 91–130; trans. Anna Silvas, "Saint Hildegard of Bingen and the *Vita S. Hildegardis*," *Tjurunga: An Australasian Benedictine Review*, 29 (1985): 4–25; 30 (1986): 63–73; 31 (1986): 32–41; 32 (1987): 46–59. There are two modern biographies in German: Adelgundis Führkötter, *Hildegard von Bingen* (Salzburg, 1972); and Eduard Gronau, *Hildegard von Bingen, 1098–1179* (Stein-am-Rhein, 1985).

2. On Hildegard's family see Marianna Schrader, *Die Herkunft der hl. Hildegard,* rev. ed. (Mainz, 1981).

3. Guibert of Gembloux, *Hildegardis vita* (fragment), ed. J.-B. Pitra, *Analecta S. Hildegardis*, vol. 8 of *Analecta sacra* (Monte Cassino, 1882): 408.

4. Letter to Guibert of Gembloux "de modo visionis suae," Ep. 2, ed. Pitra: 331–34.

5. Charles Singer, "The Scientific Views and Visions of Saint Hildegard," *Studies in the History and Method of Science* 1 (Oxford, 1917) pp. 1–55; Oliver Sacks, *Migraine: Understanding a Common Disorder* (Berkeley, 1985) pp. 106–8.

6. Barbara Newman, "Divine Power Made Perfect in Weakness: St. Hildegard on the Frail Sex," in *Peaceweavers*, vol. 2 of *Medieval Religious Women*, ed. Lillian T. Shank and John Nichols (Kalamazoo, 1987) pp. 103–22. On this theme in women's spirituality generally see Elizabeth Petroff, ed., *Medieval Women's Visionary Literature* (Oxford, 1986) pp. 32–44.

7. Ildefons Herwegen, "Les collaborateurs de Ste. Hildegarde," *Revue bénédictine* 21 (1904): 192–203, 302–15, 381–403. Recent research has indicated that Volmar's role was limited to copy editor and scribe; he did no significant stylistic revision.

8. Ep. 1, PL 197: 143ab. Cf. Marianna Schrader and Adelgundis Führkötter, *Die Echtheit des Schrifttums der hl. Hildegard von Bingen* (Cologne, 1956) pp. 111–19.

9. See the letter from Hildegard to her daughters, PL 197: 1065b–67a.

10. Maria Brede, "Die Klöster der hl. Hildegard Rupertsberg und Eibingen," in *Hildegard von Bingen, 1179–1979*, ed. Anton Brück (Mainz, 1979) pp. 77–94.

11. Barbara Newman, ed. and trans., *Symphonia armonie celestium revelationum* (Ithaca, 1988).

12. This work is still unedited, but see fragments in Pitra, 496–502, and Wilhelm Grimm, "Wiesbader Glossen," *Zeitschrift für deutsches Alterthum* 6 (1848) pp. 334–40.

13. Lieven Van Acker, "Der Briefwechsel der hl. Hildegard von Bingen: Vorbemerkungen zu einer kritischen Edition," *Revue bénédictine* 98 (1988): 141–68; 99 (1989): 118–54.

14. Irmgard Müller, *Die pflanzlichen Heilmittel bei Hildegard von Bingen* (Salzburg, 1981); Karl-Heinz Reger, *Hildegard-Medizin;* Joan Cadden, "It Takes All Kinds: Sexuality and Gender Differences in Hildegard of Bingen's 'Book of Compound Medicine,' " *Traditio* 40 (1984): 149–74.

15. *Vita*, Bk. III; *Acta inquisitionis de virtutibus et miraculis sanctae Hildegardis,* PL 197: 131–40.

16. See, for example, Ep. 48, PL 197: 244–53 (Cologne) and Ep. 49, PL 197: 254–58 (Trier).

17. Angela Rozumek, *Die sittliche Weltanschauung der hl. Hildegard von Bingen: Eine Darstellung der Ethik des Liber vitae meritorum* (Eichstätt, 1934).

18. Schrader and Führkötter, *Echtheit,* 131–41; Peter Dronke, *Women Writers of the Middle Ages* (Cambridge, 1984): 154–59.

19. Heinrich Büttner, "Die Beziehungen der hl. Hildegard zur Kurie, Erzbischof und Kaiser," in *Universitas: Festschrift für Bischof Stohr* 2 (Mainz, 1960).

20. On the schism see M. G. Cheney, "The Recognition of Pope Alexander III: Some Neglected Evidence," *English Historical Review* 84 (1969): 474–97; Robert Somerville, *Pope Alexander III and the Council of Tours (1163): A Study of Ecclesiastical Politics and Institutions in the Twelfth Century* (Berkeley, 1977).

21. "De Catharis," Pitra, 348–51; Raoul Manselli, "Amicizia spirituale ed azione pastorale nella Germania del sec. XII: Ildegarde di Bingen, Elisabetta ed Ecberto di Schönau contro l'eresia catara," *Studi e materiali di storia delle religioni* 38 (1967): fasc. 1–2, 302–13; Gerhard Müller, "Die hl. Hildegard im Kampf mit Häresien ihrer Zeit: Zur Auseinandersetzung mit den Katharern," in Brück, *Hildegard von Bingen,* 171–88.

22. The title *De operatione Dei,* used by Heinrich Schipperges for his German translation, appears in the oldest and best MS. (Ghent, Universiteitsbibliotheek, Cod. 241), but it appears to be a later scribal addition. Contemporary lists of Hildegard's works give the title *Liber divinorum operum.*

23. On this MS. see Anna Masetti and Gigetta dalli Regoli, *Sanctae Hildegardis revelationes, MS. 1942* (Lucca, 1973); Rita Otto, "Zu denen gotischen Miniaturen einer Hildegardhandschrift in Lucca," *Mainzer Zeitschrift* 71–72 (1976/77) pp. 110–26.

24. Albert Derolez, ed., *Guiberti Gemblacensis Epistolae* I, CCCM66 (Turnhout, 1988): 216–57.

25. Epistles 8 and 9, PL 197: 159–61; Dronke, 196–99.

26. Ep. 47, PL 197: 218–21.

27. Barbara Newman, "Hildegard of Bingen: Visions and Validation," *Church History* 54 (1985), pp. 163–75; Christel Meier, "Prophetentum als literarische Existenz: Hildegard von Bingen," in *Deutsche Literatur von Frauen* I, ed. Gisela Brinker-Gabler (Munich, 1988) pp. 76–87.

28. Epistle to Guibert of Gembloux, Pitra, 332–33.

29. Letter to the monks of St. Disibod, Pitra, 354.

30. See Epistles 32, 33, 37, 42, 44, 66, 70, 74, 77, 78, 86, 100, 101, 108, and 112 in PL 197; Sabina Flanagan, "Hildegard of Bingen as Prophet: The Evidence of her Contemporaries," *Tjurunga* 32 (1987): 16–45.

31. Alfred Haverkamp, "Tenxwind von Andernach und Hildegard von Bingen: Zwei 'Weltanschauungen' in der Mitte des 12. Jahrhunderts," in *Institutionen, Kultur und Gesellschaft im Mittelalter: Festschrift für Josef Fleckenstein,* ed. Lutz Fenske, Werner Rösener and Thomas Zotz (Sigmaringen, 1984): 515–48.

32. Jeffrey Russell, *A History of Medieval Christianity: Prophecy and Order* (Arlington Heights, 1968), p. 123.

33. Barbara Newman, *Sister of Wisdom: St. Hildegard's Theology of the Feminine* (Berkeley, 1987), chap. 6.

34. See Charles Czarski, *The Prophecies of St. Hildegard of Bingen*, diss., University of Kentucky, 1983; Kathryn Kerby-Fulton, *The Voice of Honest Indignation: Reformist Apocalypticism and Piers Plowman* (Cambridge, 1989), chap. 1.

35. Elisabeth Gössmann, "Zyklisches und Lineares Geschichtsbewusstsein im Mittelalter: Hildegard von Bingen, Johannes von Salisbury und Andere," in *L'Homme et son univers au moyen âge*, 2 ed. Christian Wénin (Louvain, 1986), pp. 882–92.

36. *Vita* 2.16, PL 197: 102cd. Cf. PL 197: 167b, 185c, 254cd, 1005ab.

37. Cf. Robert Lerner, "Medieval Prophecy and Religious Dissent," *Past & Present* 72 (1976): 3–24.

38. *Scivias* I.1.

39. Christel Meier, "Zwei Modelle von Allegorie im 12. Jahrhundert: Das allegorische Verfahren Hildegards von Bingen und Alans von Lille," in *Formen und Funktionen der Allegorie*, ed. Walter Haug (Stuttgart, 1979), pp. 70–89.

40. The sacramental system was still quite fluid in Hildegard's day, and the notion of seven sacraments not yet universally accepted.

41. Hugh of St. Victor, *On the Sacraments of the Christian Faith* [*De Sacramentis*], trans. Roy Deferrari (Cambridge, MA, 1951).

42. Cf. Heinrich Schipperges, "Das Schöne in der Welt Hildegards von Bingen," *Jahrbuch für Ästhetik und allgemeine Kunstwissenschaft* 4 (1958/59): 83–139.

43. The full-color illustrations are reproduced in the Latin edition of the *Scivias* (CCCM, vols. 43–43a) and in the German translation by Maura Böckeler, *Wisse die Wege* (Salzburg, 8th ed., 1987).

44. Grover Zinn, "Mandala Symbolism and Use in the Mysticism of Hugh of St. Victor," *History of Religions* 12 (1972/73): 317–41.

45. On the miniatures see Josef Schomer, *Die Illustrationen zu dem Visionen der hl. Hildegard als künstlerische Neuschöpfung* (Bonn, 1937); Rita Otto, "Zu einigen Miniaturen einer *Scivias*handschrift des 12. Jahrhunderts," *Mainzer Zeitschrift* 67–68 (1972/73): 128–37; Christel Meier, *Text und Bild im überlieferten Werk Hildegards von Bingen* (Wiesbaden, 1978).

46. Letter of Odo of Soissons, Ep. 127, PL 197: 352a.

47. *A feather on the breath of God:* Sequences and hymns by Abbess Hildegard of Bingen, Gothic Voices (Hyperion A66039); *Geistliche Musik des Mittelalters und der Renaissance*, Instrumentalkreise Helga Weber (TELDEC 66.22387); *Gesänge der hl. Hildegard von Bingen*, Schola der Benediktinerinnenabtei St. Hildegard (Psallite 242/040 479 PET); *Hildegard von Bingen: Symphoniae*, Sequentia (Harmonia Mundi 1C 067-19 9976 1).

48. Peter Dronke, "The Composition of Hildegard of Bingen's *Symphonia*," *Sacris Erudiri* 19 (1969/70): 381–93; "Problemata Hildegardiana," *Mittellateinisches Jahrbuch* 16 (1981): 97–131.

49. Performance edition by Audrey Davidson, *The "Ordo virtutum" of Hildegard of Bingen* (Kalamazoo, 1985); recording by Sequentia, *Hildegard von Bingen: Ordo virtutum* (Harmonia Mundi 20395/96); liner notes include an English translation by Peter Dronke.

50. Robert Potter, "The *Ordo Virtutum*: Ancestor of the English Moralities?" *Comparative Drama* 20 (1986): 201–10.

51. Newman, *Sister of Wisdom*, chap. 3.

52. Kent Kraft, *The Eye Sees More Than the Heart Knows: The Visionary Cosmology of Hildegard of Bingen*, Ph.D. diss. University of Wisconsin, 1977.

53. On the basis of this inconsistency earlier scholars rejected the authenticity of all or part of *Causae et curae:* Hans Liebeschütz, *Das allegorische Weltbild der hl. Hildegard von Bingen* (Leipzig, 1930); Bertha Widmer, *Heilsordnung und Zeitgeschehen in der Mystik Hildegards von Bingen* (Basel, 1955); Heinrich Schipperges, *Heilkunde* (Salzburg, 1957). For more recent views see Dronke, *Women Writers,* 173–79; Newman, *Sister of Wisdom,* chap. 4.

54. Magna Ungrund, *Die metaphysische Anthropologie der hl. Hildegard von Bingen* (Münster, 1938).

55. Charles Singer, "Allegorical Representation of the Synagogue in a Twelfth Century Illuminated Manuscript of Hildegard of Bingen," *Jewish Quarterly Review,* n.s. 5 (1915): 267–88.

56. Heinrich Schipperges, *Die Welt der Engel bei Hildegard von Bingen,* 2d ed. (Salzburg, 1979).

57. On the iconography see Christel Meier, "Zum Verhältnis von Text und Illustration im überlieferten Werk Hildegards von Bingen," in Brück, *Hildegard von Bingen,* 159–69.

58. Heinrich Ostlender, "Dante und Hildegard von Bingen," *Deutsches Dante-Jahrbuch* 27 (1948): 159–70; Ernst Benz, "Die Farbe im Erlebnisbereich der christlichen Vision," *Eranos Jahrbuch* 41 (1972): 273–82; Peter Dronke, "Tradition and Innovation in Medieval Western Colour-Imagery," *Eranos Jahrbuch* 41 (1972): 98–106.

59. Margot Schmidt, "Hildegard von Bingen als Lehrerin des Glaubens: *Speculum* als Symbol des Transzendenten," in Brück, *Hildegard von Bingen,* 95–157.

60. Barbara Maurmann-Bronder, *Die Himmelsrichtungen im Weltbild des Mittelalters: Hildegard von Bingen, Honorius Augustodunensis und andere Autoren* (Munich, 1976).

61. Peter Dronke, "Arbor Caritatis," in *Medieval Studies for J.A.W. Bennett,* ed. P.L. Heyworth (Oxford, 1981), pp. 228–33.

62. Christel Meier, "Die Bedeutung der Farben im Werk Hildegards von Bingen," *Frühmittelalterliche Studien* 6 (1972): 245–355.

63. Hermas, *Pastor, Sources chrétiennes* 53 (Paris, 1958); J.B. Lightfoot, trans., *Excluded Books of the New Testament* (London, 1927), pp. 249–403. See especially Vision III and Similitude IX.

64. Cf. Herrad of Hohenbourg, *Hortus Deliciarum,* reconstructed by Rosalie Green, Michael Evans, et al. (London, 1979): II, 352, Plate 124.

65. Adso of Moutier-en-Der, *De ortu et tempore Antichristi,* ed. D. Verhelst, CCCM 45, trans. John Wright in *The Play of Antichrist* (Toronto, 1967).

66. Cf. Wilhelm Kamlah, *Apokalypse und Geschichtstheologie: Die mittelalterliche Auslegung der Apokalypse vor Joachim von Fiore* (Berlin, 1935); H.D. Rauh, *Das Bild des Antichrist im Mittelalter* (Munich, 1973); Richard Emmerson, *Antichrist in the Middle Ages: A Study of Medieval Apocalypticism, Art, and Literature* (Seattle, 1981).

67. Peter Dronke, "Hildegard of Bingen as Poetess and Dramatist," in *Poetic Individuality in the Middle Ages* (Oxford, 1970), pp. 169–79.

68. The edition of Führkötter and Carlevaris (CCCM, 43–43a) provides meticulous annotation and comprehensive indices of scriptural and liturgical texts, patristic and medieval authors and key words in the *Scivias.*

69. The most ambitious source studies are those of Hans Liebeschütz, *Das allegorische Weltbild der hl. Hildegard von Bingen* (Leipzig, 1930); and Bertha Widmer, *Heilsordnung und Zeitgeschehen in der Mystik Hildegards von Bingen* (Basel, 1955).

INTRODUCTION

Recent writers, with the notable exception of Peter Dronke, have been more skeptical about the extent of Hildegard's classical learning.

70. According to her *Vita* (II.1), Hildegard disputed with Jews and tried to convert them: PL 197: 105b.

71. Heinrich Schipperges notes the affinities but does not believe that either Hildegard or the Chartrian poets were acquainted with the new Arabic learning: "Einflüsse arabischer Medizin auf die Mikrokosmosliteratur des 12. Jahrhunderts," in *Antike und Orient im Mittelalter*, ed. Paul Wilpert (Berlin, 1962), pp. 129–53.

72. Valerie Flint, "The Place and Purpose of the Works of Honorius Augustodunensis," *Revue bénédictine* 87 (1977): 97–127.

73. John Van Engen, *Rupert of Deutz* (Berkeley, 1983).

74. Cf. Wolfgang Beinert, *Die Kirche—Gottes Heil in der Welt: Die Lehre von der Kirche nach den Schriften des Rupert von Deutz, Honorius Augustodunensis und Gerhoch von Reichersberg* (Münster, 1973).

75. On this influential work, which Hildegard certainly knew, see Matthäus Bernards, *Speculum virginum: Geistigkeit und Seelenleben der Frau im Hochmittelalter* (Cologne, 1955); an edition by Jutta Seyfarth is forthcoming in the CCCM series.

76. Friedhelm Jürgensmeier, "St. Hildegard 'Prophetissa Teutonica,' " in Brück, *Hildegard von Bingen*, pp. 273–93.

77. There is much recent work on this subject. For overviews of the tradition see Dronke, *Women Writers*; Petroff, *Medieval Women's Visionary Literature*; Katharina Wilson, ed., *Medieval Women Writers* (Athens, GA, 1984). On Hildegard and the theme of gender see Elisabeth Gössmann, "*Ipsa enim quasi domus sapientiae*: Zur frauenbezogenen Spiritualität Hildegards von Bingen," in *Eine Höhe, über die nichts geht*, ed. Margot Schmidt and Dieter Bauer (Stuttgart, 1986); Caroline Bynum, " '. . . And Woman His Humanity': Female Imagery in the Religious Writing of the Later Middle Ages," in *Gender and Religion: On the Complexity of Symbols*, ed. Caroline Bynum, Paula Richman, and Stevan Harrell (Boston, 1986): 257–88; Newman, *Sister of Wisdom*, chap. 7.

78. Josef Loos, "Hildegard von Bingen und Elisabeth von Schönau," in Brück, *Hildegard von Bingen*, pp. 263–72; Kathryn Kerby-Fulton and Dyan Elliott, "Self-Image and the Visionary Role in Two Letters from the Correspondence of Elizabeth of Schönau and Hildegard of Bingen," *Vox Benedictina* 2 (1985): 204–23; Elisabeth Gössmann, "Das Menschenbild der Hildegard von Bingen und Elisabeth von Schönau . . . ," in *Frauenmystik im Mittelalter*, ed. Peter Dinzelbacher and Dieter Bauer (Ostfildern, 1985), pp. 24–47.

79. *Annales Palidenses* ad 1158, MGH.SS. 16, p. 90.

80. For instance, Elisabeth supported Barbarossa's candidate, Victor IV, in the German papal schism.

81. While Volmar was initially Hildegard's teacher and served as provost of her convent, in the second half of her life she exercised an unmistakable intellectual and spiritual dominance. Elisabeth, on the other hand, subordinated herself humbly to her brother and abbot, Ekbert, whose guidance shaped the course of her visions.

82. About 150 manuscripts of Elisabeth's works survive, as opposed to about three dozen of Hildegard's.

83. The work is unedited except for fragments in Pitra, 483–88.

84. Lodewijk van Velthem, *Voortzetting van den Spiegel Historiael*, Book VII (1316), vol. 3, ed. Herman vander Linden and Willem de Vreese (Brussels, 1938); Ernest McDonnell, *The Beguines and Beghards in Medieval Culture* (New Brunswick, 1954), pp. 292–94. Henry of Langenstein may have been the first to call Hildegard the

INTRODUCTION

"German Sibyl": G. Sommerfeldt, "Die Prophetien der hl. Hildegard von Bingen in einem Schreiben des Magisters Heinrich von Langenstein (1383)," *Historisches Jahrbuch* 30 (1909): 43–61.

85. *Chronicon Hirsaugiense* ad 1149, 1150, 1160, 1180; *Chronicon Sponheimense* ad 1136, 1148–1150, 1179, 1498; *Catalogus illustrium virorum* [sic] *Germaniae*, p. 138; *De scriptoribus ecclesiasticis*, p. 281; all in *Opera historica*, ed. Marquand Freher (Frankfurt, 1601; rpt. 1966).

86. Widmer, *Heilsordnung und Zeitgeschehen*, 260. In 1680 Jerome Baptista, Lord Bishop of Albarazin, published a pamphlet entitled "The Nunns Prophesie, or, The True, Wonderful, & Remarkable Prophesie of St. Hildegard, First Nunn, and then Abess: concerning the Rise & Downfall of those Fire Brands of Europe, the whole Order of Jesuits."

87. Johann Wilhelm Preger, *Geschichte der deutschen Mystik im Mittelalter* I (Leipzig, 1874). J.P. Schmelzeis, in *Das Leben und Wirken der hl. Hildegardis* (Freiburg im Breisgau, 1879), maintained that Hildegard transcribed her Latin writings directly from heaven without understanding a word of them.

88. The epoch-making work was the historical and paleographic study of Marianna Schrader and Adelgundis Führkötter, *Die Echtheit des Schrifttums der hl. Hildegard von Bingen* (Cologne, 1956), together with the studies by Liebeschütz, Widmer, Schipperges and Dronke already cited.

89. This is the image promulgated in the publications of Bear & Company: Gabriele Uhlein, *Meditations With Hildegard of Bingen* (Santa Fe, 1982); Matthew Fox, *Illuminations of Hildegard of Bingen* (Santa Fe, 1985); and translations of the *Scivias* by Bruce Hozeski (Santa Fe, 1986), and of the *Liber divinorum operum* by Robert Cunningham (Santa Fe, 1987).

Translator's Note

Scivias, St. Hildegard's great work of religious genius, is composed of a relatively brief Prologue (Declaration) and three Books, each Book being made up of several Visions. That Hildegard saw each Book as a unit is clear both from the climactic movement of each of her three main parts and from the fact that she employs three closing sentences of a poetic character. By the first of these she concludes all six of the Visions of Book One; by the second, all seven of the Visions of Book Two; and by the third, all thirteen of the Visions of Book Three.

Every Vision contains a varying number of subdivisions, unequal in length, indicated by numbered subtitles. Certain illustrations in the twelfth-century manuscript (reproduced in colors and gold both in Böckeler's German translation and in the Brepols 1978 critical Latin text, and in black and white in this translation) show that Hildegard herself wanted the subdivisions and corresponding subtitles. My translation therefore retains both subdivisions and corresponding subtitles; to save space, I have abridged the more lengthy subtitles.

For each separate Vision Hildegard uses the following literary procedure: First she gives the reader a poetic and obscure account of what she "saw," then she goes on to repeat and develop each sentence or phrase of the preliminary account, disclosing gradually the Vision's deep significance. And yet she never says, "I have outlined all the points, and now I will repeat and develop them." Therefore, for the assistance of the reader, italics are used in each vision both for her initial account and for her repetitions of each sentence or phrase thereof in her subsequent explanation.

Because of the extreme length of *Scivias,* I have reduced explanations, inserted between square brackets, to a minimum. Hildegard's three poetic expressions—"chrism makers" (*pigmentarii*) for "bishops and priests," "living fragrance" (*vivens odor*) for "monk," and "vowing the way of secret regeneration" (*vovens iter secretae regenerationis*) for "making monastic profession"—I translated literally only in the preliminary occurrences, reverting thereafter to the commonplace terms.

Mother Columba Hart, O.S.B.

55

TRANSLATOR'S NOTE

Co-Translator's Note

My contribution to this translation has been in two main areas. First, while remaining faithful to the meaning of the Latin, I have rendered it somewhat less literal to make it read better in English. In Book Three, Vision Thirteen, where Hildegard breaks into poetry to express the songs sung in heaven, I have carried out Mother Columba's decision to do them in poetic rather than prose form in English: I have put them into a very loose pentameter, not because that corresponds to any discernible meter in the original but to reflect Hildegard's poetic intentions.

Second, I have tried to correct a practice in the English of the last few hundred years that is not justified by the Latin. English has tended to translate the Latin *homo*, "human being," by the word *man*, which increasingly in our time is understood to refer exclusively to males. Latin has the word *homo* for "person," and *vir* and *mulier* for "man" and "woman"; because its pronouns agree in gender with the nouns they modify rather than with the beings they express, it is possible to write for long stretches in Latin without any suggestion of an exclusionary "his" or "her," which is unavoidable in English. Hildegard is writing for and about both men and women most of the time in this work and writes of them as "humans"; when she represents God speaking to her, He calls her not "O mulier" but "O homo," "O human being." Consequently, with some slight loss in resonance in the English because we are used to grand rhetoric about "men" and "mankind," I have translated the various forms of *homo* by "person," "humans," "people" or "humanity" wherever possible. It has sometimes been necessary to use a singular, personal collective noun for Humanity, in which case I have used the capitalized "Man"; otherwise, wherever the words "man" and "woman" appear here, they reflect Hildegard's talk of the different situations of *viri* and *mulieres* in the original.

Jane Bishop

HILDEGARD of BINGEN
SCIVIAS

THE SEERESS

Declaration

These Are True Visions Flowing from God

And behold! In the forty-third year of my earthly course, as I was gazing with great fear and trembling attention at a heavenly vision, I saw a great splendor in which resounded a voice from Heaven, saying to me,

"O fragile human, ashes of ashes, and filth of filth! Say and write what you see and hear. But since you are timid in speaking, and simple in expounding, and untaught in writing, speak and write these things not by a human mouth, and not by the understanding of human invention, and not by the requirements of human composition, but as you see and hear them on high in the heavenly places in the wonders of God. Explain these things in such a way that the hearer, receiving the words of his instructor, may expound them in those words, according to that will, vision and instruction. Thus therefore, O human, speak these things that you see and hear. And write them not by yourself or any other human being, but by the will of Him Who knows, sees and disposes all things in the secrets of His mysteries."

And again I heard the voice from Heaven saying to me, "Speak therefore of these wonders, and, being so taught, write them and speak."

It happened that, in the eleven hundred and forty-first year of the Incarnation of the Son of God, Jesus Christ, when I was forty-two years and seven months old, Heaven was opened and a fiery light of exceeding brilliance came and permeated my whole brain, and inflamed my whole heart and my whole breast, not like a burning but like a warming flame, as the sun warms anything its rays touch. And immediately I knew the meaning of the exposition of the Scriptures, namely the Psalter, the Gospel and the other catholic volumes of both the Old and the New Testaments, though I did not have the interpretation of the words of their texts or the division of the syllables or the knowledge of cases or tenses. But I had sensed in myself

59

wonderfully the power and mystery of secret and admirable visions from my childhood—that is, from the age of five—up to that time, as I do now. This, however, I showed to no one except a few religious persons who were living in the same manner as I; but meanwhile, until the time when God by His grace wished it to be manifested, I concealed it in quiet silence. But the visions I saw I did not perceive in dreams, or sleep, or delirium, or by the eyes of the body, or by the ears of the outer self, or in hidden places; but I received them while awake and seeing with a pure mind and the eyes and ears of the inner self, in open places, as God willed it. How this might be is hard for mortal flesh to understand.

But when I had passed out of childhood and had reached the age of full maturity mentioned above, I heard a voice from Heaven saying, "I am the Living Light, Who illuminates the darkness. The person [Hildegard] whom I have chosen and whom I have miraculously stricken as I willed, I have placed among great wonders, beyond the measure of the ancient people who saw in Me many secrets; but I have laid her low on the earth, that she might not set herself up in arrogance of mind. The world has had in her no joy or lewdness or use in worldly things, for I have withdrawn her from impudent boldness, and she feels fear and is timid in her works. For she suffers in her inmost being and in the veins of her flesh; she is distressed in mind and sense and endures great pain of body, because no security has dwelt in her, but in all her undertakings she has judged herself guilty. For I have closed up the cracks in her heart that her mind may not exalt itself in pride or vainglory, but may feel fear and grief rather than joy and wantonness. Hence in My love she searched in her mind as to where she could find someone who would run in the path of salvation. And she found such a one and loved him [the monk Volmar of Disibodenberg], knowing that he was a faithful man, working like herself on another part of the work that leads to Me. And, holding fast to him, she worked with him in great zeal so that My hidden miracles might be revealed. And she did not seek to exalt herself above herself but with many sighs bowed to him whom she found in the ascent of humility and the intention of good will.

"O human, who receives these things meant to manifest what is hidden not in the disquiet of deception but in the purity of simplicity, write, therefore, the things you see and hear."

But I, though I saw and heard these things, refused to write for a long time through doubt and bad opinion and the diversity of human words, not with stubbornness but in the exercise of humility, until, laid low by the scourge of God, I fell upon a bed of sickness; then, compelled at last by many illnesses, and by the witness of a certain noble maiden of good conduct [the nun Richardis of Stade] and of that man whom I had secretly sought and found, as mentioned above, I set my hand to the writing. While I was doing it, I sensed, as I mentioned before, the deep profundity of scriptural exposition; and, raising myself from illness by the strength I received, I brought this work to a close—though just barely—in ten years.

These visions took place and these words were written in the days of Henry, Archbishop of Mainz, and of Conrad, King of the Romans, and of Cuno, Abbot of Disibodenberg, under Pope Eugenius.

And I spoke and wrote these things not by the invention of my heart or that of any other person, but as by the secret mysteries of God I heard and received them in the heavenly places.

And again I heard a voice from Heaven saying to me, "Cry out therefore, and write thus!"

Book One

THE CREATOR AND CREATION

THE ONE ENTHRONED

VISION ONE
God Enthroned Shows Himself to Hildegard

I saw a great mountain the color of iron, and enthroned on it One of such great glory that it blinded my sight. On each side of him there extended a soft shadow, like a wing of wondrous breadth and length. Before him, at the foot of the mountain, stood an image full of eyes on all sides, in which, because of those eyes, I could discern no human form. In front of this image stood another, a child wearing a tunic of subdued color but white shoes, upon whose head such glory descended from the One enthroned upon that mountain that I could not look at its face. But from the One who sat enthroned upon that mountain many living sparks sprang forth, which flew very sweetly around the images. Also, I perceived in this mountain many little windows, in which appeared human heads, some of subdued colors and some white.

And behold, He Who was enthroned upon that mountain cried out in a strong, loud voice saying, "O human, who are fragile dust of the earth and ashes of ashes! Cry out and speak of the origin of pure salvation until those people are instructed, who, though they see the inmost contents of the Scriptures, do not wish to tell them or preach them, because they are lukewarm and sluggish in serving God's justice. Unlock for them the enclosure of mysteries that they, timid as they are, conceal in a hidden and fruitless field. Burst forth into a fountain of abundance and overflow with mystical knowledge, until they who now think you contemptible because of Eve's transgression are stirred up by the flood of your irrigation. For you have received your profound insight not from humans, but from the lofty and tremendous Judge on high, where this calmness will shine strongly with glorious light among the shining ones.

"Arise therefore, cry out and tell what is shown to you by the strong power of God's help, for He Who rules every creature in might and kindness floods those who fear Him and serve Him in sweet love and humility with the glory of heavenly enlightenment and leads those who persevere in the way of justice to the joys of the Eternal Vision."

1 The strength and stability of God's eternal Kingdom

As you see, therefore, *the great mountain the color of iron* symbolizes the strength and stability of the eternal Kingdom of God, which no fluctuation of mutability can destroy; and *the One enthroned upon it of such great glory that it blinds your sight* is the One in the kingdom of beatitude Who rules the whole world with celestial divinity in the brilliance of unfading serenity, but is incomprehensible to human minds. But that *on each side of him there extends a soft shadow like a wing of wonderful breadth and length* shows that both in admonition and in punishment ineffable justice displays sweet and gentle protection and perseveres in true equity.

2 Concerning fear of the Lord

And before him at the foot of the mountain stands an image full of eyes on all sides. For the Fear of the Lord stands in God's presence with humility and gazes on the Kingdom of God, surrounded by the clarity of a good and just intention, exercising her zeal and stability among humans. And thus *you can discern no human form in her on account of those eyes.* For by the acute sight of her contemplation she counters all forgetfulness of God's justice, which people often feel in their mental tedium, so no inquiry by weak mortals eludes her vigilance.

3 Concerning those who are poor in spirit

And so *before this image appears another image, that of a child, wearing a tunic of subdued color but white shoes.* For when the Fear of the Lord leads, they who are poor in spirit follow; for the Fear of the Lord holds fast in humble devotion to the blessedness of poverty of spirit, which does not seek boasting or elation of heart, but loves simplicity and sobriety of mind, attributing its just works not to itself but to God in pale subjection, wearing, as it were, a tunic of subdued color and faithfully following the serene footsteps of the Son of God. *Upon her head descends such glory from the One enthroned upon that mountain that you cannot look at her face;* because He Who rules every created being imparts the power and strength of this blessedness by the great clarity of His visitation, and weak, mortal thought cannot grasp His purpose, since He Who possesses celestial riches submitted himself humbly to poverty.

4 They who fear God and love poverty of spirit are the guardians of virtues

But *from the One Who is enthroned upon that mountain many living sparks go forth, which fly about those images with great sweetness.* This means that many exceedingly strong virtues come forth from Almighty God, darting fire in divine glory; these ardently embrace and captivate those who truly fear God and who faithfully love poverty of spirit, surrounding them with their help and protection.

5 The aims of human acts cannot be hidden from God's knowledge

Wherefore *in this mountain you see many little windows, in which appear human heads, some of subdued color and some white.* For in the most high and profound and perspicuous knowledge of God the aims of human acts cannot be concealed or hidden. Most often they display both lukewarmness and purity, since people now slumber in guilt, weary in their hearts and in their deeds, and now awaken and keep watch in honor. Solomon bears witness to this for Me, saying:

6 Solomon on this subject

"The slothful hand has brought about poverty, but the hand of the industrious man prepares riches" [Proverbs 10:4]; which means, a person makes himself weak and poor when he will not work justice, or avoid wickedness, or pay a debt, remaining idle in the face of the wonders of the works of beatitude. But one who does strong works of salvation, running in the way of truth, obtains the upwelling fountain of glory, by which he prepares himself most precious riches on earth and in Heaven.

Therefore, whoever has knowledge in the Holy Spirit and wings of faith, let this one not ignore My admonition but taste it, embrace it and receive it in his soul.

MAN'S FALL

VISION TWO
Creation and the Fall

*T*hen I saw as it were a great multitude of very bright living lamps, which
received fiery brilliance and acquired an unclouded splendor. And behold!
A pit of great breadth and depth appeared, with a mouth like the mouth of
a well, emitting fiery smoke with great stench, from which a loathsome cloud
spread out and touched a deceitful, vein-shaped form. And, in a region of brightness, it blew upon a white cloud that had come forth from a beautiful human
form and contained within itself many and many stars, and so doing, cast out
both the white cloud and the human form from that region. When this was done,
a luminous splendor surrounded that region, and all the elements of the world,
which before had existed in great calm, were turned to the greatest agitation and
displayed horrible terrors. And again I heard Him Who had spoken to me
before, saying:

1 No unjust impulse takes the blessed angels from the love and
praise of God

No impulse of injustice makes those withdraw in terror who follow
God with faithful devotion and burn with worthy love through affection for
Him, from the glory of heavenly beatitude; while they who serve God merely
in pretence not only fail to advance to greater things but, by just judgment,
are cast out from the things they erroneously suppose they possess. This is
shown by the *great multitude of very bright living lamps;* they are the vast
army of heavenly spirits, shining in the blessed life and living in great beauty
and adornment, because when they were created by God they did not grasp
at proud exaltation but strongly persisted in divine love. For, *receiving fiery
brilliance, they acquired an unclouded splendor,* because when Lucifer and his
followers attempted to rebel against the supreme Creator, they, with zeal for
God in his and his followers' downfall, clothed themselves in the vigilance of
divine love, while the others, not wishing to know God, embraced the torpor
of ignorance. In what way? At the fall of the Devil great praise burst forth
from these angelic spirits who persevered in rectitude with God, because
with keenest sight they knew that God continues immovable, without any
change of any mutability in His power, so that no warrior can ever conquer

Him. And thus, burning in His love and persevering in righteousness, they despised all the dust of injustice.

2 Lucifer, for pride in his beauty and power, was cast forth from Heaven

But Lucifer, who because of his pride was cast forth from celestial glory, was so great at the moment of his creation that he felt no defect either in his beauty or in his strength. Hence when he contemplated his beauty, and when he considered in himself the power of his strength, he discovered pride, which promised him that he might begin what he wished, because he could achieve what he had begun. And, seeing a place where he thought he could live, wanting to display his beauty and power there, he spoke thus within himself about God: "I wish to shine there as He does here!" And all his army assented, saying, "What you wish we also wish." And when, elated with pride, he tried to achieve what he had conceived, the jealousy of the Lord, reaching out in fiery blackness, cast him down with all his retinue, so that they were made burning instead of shining and black instead of fair. Why did this happen?

3 God would have been unjust if He had not cast them down

If God had not cast down their presumption, He would have been unjust, since He would have cherished those who wished to divide the wholeness of divinity. But He cast them down and reduced their impiety to nothing, as He removes from the sight of His glory all who try to oppose themselves to Him, as My servant Job shows when he says:

4 Words of Job on this subject

"The lamp of the wicked shall be put out and a deluge shall come upon them; and He shall distribute the sorrows of His wrath. They shall be chaff before the face of the wind, and sparks scattered by the whirlwind" [Job 21:17–18]. This means the flagrant filth of wanton wickedness that emerges from false prosperity, like a distinguishing mark on the carnal will of those who do not fear God but spurn Him in perverse rage, disdaining to know that anyone can conquer them, while in the fire of their ferocity they want to consume whatever they oppose. In the hour of God's vengeance this filth will be trodden underfoot like dirt; and by the supreme judgment these impious ones will be cast down in wrath by all who are under heaven, because they are harmful both to God and to humans. Therefore, since God does not allow them to have what they want, they are scattered everywhere among people, tormented by pain in the rage of their madness, because they burn to possess what God does not allow them to devour. And since they withdraw in this way from God, they become entirely useless, able to do nothing good for either God or humanity, cut off from the seed of life by the foreseeing eye of God's contemplation. For which reason they are given over to misery, wasting themselves in the flat taste of evil fame, since they do not receive the downpouring rain of the Holy Spirit.

5   On Hell, which in its voracity keeps souls swallowed up

But *the pit of great breadth and depth* that appeared to you is Hell, having within it, as you see, the breadth of vices and the depth of losses. It has a mouth indeed like the mouth of a well, emitting a fiery smoke with great stench, because in its voracity to swallow up souls, it shows them sweetness and gentleness, and with perverse deception leads them to the torments of perdition, where rises a burning fire with black smoke pouring out and a boiling, deadly stench; these dire torments were prepared for the Devil and his followers, who turned away from the Supreme Good, not wishing to know or understand it. Therefore they are outcast from all good, not because they did not know it, but because in their great pride they despised it. What does this mean?

6   In the casting down of the Devil Hell was created

In the casting down of the Devil this exterior darkness, full of all kinds of pains, was created; for these evil spirits, in contrast to the glory that had been prepared for them, were subject to the misery of many punishments, and in contrast to the brightness they had had, endured the thickest darkness. How? When the proud angel raised himself on high like a snake, he received the prison of Hell, because it could not be that anyone should prevail over God. For how could two hearts possibly exist in one breast? Likewise, there could not be two gods in Heaven. But since the Devil and his followers chose proud presumption, therefore he found the pit of Hell prepared for him. So also the people who imitate them in their actions become sharers of their pains, according to their deserts.

7   Gehenna is for the impenitent, other torments for those who can be saved

Some souls, having reached the point of damnation, are rejected from the knowledge of God, and therefore they shall have the pains of Hell without the consolation of deliverance. But some, whom God has not consigned to oblivion, experience a higher process and undergo purgation of the sins into which they have fallen, and at last feel the loosing of their bonds and are delivered into rest. How is this? Gehenna is ready for those who have impenitently forgotten God in their hearts, but other torments for those who, though they perform bad works, do not persevere in them to the end, but at last, groaning, look back to God. For this reason let the faithful flee from the Devil and love God, casting away evil works and adorning good works with the beauty of penitence; as My servant Ezekiel, inspired by Me, urges, saying:

8   Words of Ezekiel on this subject

"Be converted, and do penance for all your iniquities; and iniquity shall not be your ruin" [Ezekiel 18:30]. That is to say: O you people! who till now have wallowed in sin, remember your name of Christians, be converted to the way of salvation, and perform all your works in a gush of penitence, who previously had innumerable vices and committed many crimes. Thus as you rise from your evil habits, that iniquity by which you had been soiled will not sink you deep in the ruin of death, since you cast it off in the day of your salvation. Therefore the angels will rejoice over you, because you have abandoned the Devil and run to God, knowing Him better in your good actions than you did when you endured the mockery of the ancient seducer.

9   The Devil's fraud, which deceived Adam through the serpent

That *a loathsome cloud spread out from the pit and touched a deceitful, vein-shaped form* means that from the bottom of perdition the Devil's fraud came forth and invaded the serpent, who already bore within itself the crime of fraudulent intention, in order to deceive humanity. In what way? Because, when the Devil saw Man in paradise, he cried out with great aversion, saying, "Oh! who touches me in the mansion of true beatitude?" And so he knew that he had not yet perfected in any creature the malice he had within himself, but seeing Adam and Eve walk with childlike innocence in the garden of delight, with great wonder he rose up to deceive them through the serpent. Why? Because he understood that the serpent more than any other animal resembled him and was eager to accomplish by its deceitfulness what he could not do openly in his own form. So when he saw Adam and Eve turn away in soul and body from the forbidden tree, he understood that they were obeying a divine precept, and that in the first work they began he could very easily throw them down.

10   Only from Eve's reply did the Devil know the tree was forbidden

For he would not have known that this tree was forbidden them unless he had proved it by guileful questioning and by their answers. Wherefore *in that bright region he blew upon a white cloud, which had come forth from a beautiful human form and contained within itself many and many stars* because, in that place of delight, Eve—whose soul was innocent, for she had been raised out of innocent Adam, bearing in her body the whole multitude of the human race, shining with God's preordination—was invaded by the Devil through the seduction of the serpent for her own downfall. Why was this? Because he knew that the susceptibility of the woman would be more easily conquered than the strength of the man; and he saw that Adam burned so vehemently in his holy love for Eve that if he, the Devil, conquered Eve, Adam would do whatever she said to him. Hence the Devil *cast out both the cloud and the human form from that region* because that ancient seducer cast out Eve and Adam by his deception from the seat of blessedness and thrust them into the darkness of destruction. How? By first misleading Eve, so that she might flatter and caress Adam and thus win his assent, since she more than any other creature could lead Adam to disobedience, having been made from his rib. Thus woman very quickly overthrows man, if he does not hate her and easily accepts her words.

11   What things are to be observed and avoided in marriage

Because a mature woman was given not to a little boy but to a mature man, namely Adam, so now a mature woman must be married to a man when he has reached the full age of fertility, just as due cultivation is given to a tree when it begins to put forth flowers. For Eve was formed from a rib by Adam's ingrafted heat and vigor, and therefore now it is by the strength and heat of a man that a woman receives the semen to bring a child into the world. For the man is the sower, but the woman is the recipient of the seed. Wherefore a wife is under the power of her husband because the strength of the man is to the susceptibility of the woman as the hardness of stone is to the softness of earth.

But the first woman's being formed from man means the joining of wife to husband. And thus it is to be understood: This union must not be vain or done in forgetfulness of God, because He Who brought forth the woman from the man instituted this union honorably and virtuously, forming flesh from flesh. Wherefore, as Adam and Eve were one flesh, so now also a man and woman become one flesh in a union of holy love for the multiplication of the human race. And therefore there should be perfect love in these two as there was in those first two. For Adam could have blamed his wife because by her advice she brought him death, but nonetheless he did not dismiss her as long as he lived in this world, because he knew she had been given to him by divine power. Therefore, because of perfect love, let a man not leave his wife except for the reason the faithful Church allows. And let them never separate, unless both with one mind want to contemplate My Son, and say with burning love for Him: "We want to renounce the world and follow Him Who suffered for our sake!" But if these two disagree as to whether they should renounce the world for one devotion, then let them by no means separate from each other, since, just as the blood cannot be separated from the flesh as long as the spirit remains in the flesh, so the husband and wife cannot be divided from each other but must walk together in one will.

But if either husband or wife breaks the law by fornication, and it is made public either by themselves or by their priests, they shall undergo the just censure of the spiritual magisterium. For the husband shall complain of the wife, or the wife of the husband, about the sin against their union before the Church and its prelates, according to the justice of God; but not so that the husband or wife can seek another marriage; either they shall stay together in righteous union, or they shall both abstain from such unions, as the discipline of church practice shows. And they shall not tear each other to pieces by viperous rending, but they shall love with pure love, since both man and woman could not exist without having been conceived in such a bond, as My friend Paul witnesses when he says:

12   Words of the apostle on this subject

"As the woman is of the man, so is the man for the woman; but all are from God" [1 Corinthians 11:12]. Which is to say: Woman was created for the sake of man, and man for the sake of woman. As she is from the man, the man is also from her, lest they dissent from each other in the unity of making their children; for they should work as one in one work, as the air and the wind intermingle in their labor. In what way? The air is moved by the wind, and the wind is mingled with the air, so that in their movement all verdant things are subject to their influence. What does this mean? The wife must cooperate with the husband and the husband with the wife in making children. Therefore the greatest crime and wickedest act is to make by fornication a division in the days of creating children, since the husband and wife cut off their own blood from its rightful place, sending it to an alien place. They will certainly incur the deceit of the Devil and the wrath of God, because they have transgressed that bond God ordained for them. Woe to them, therefore, if their sins are not forgiven! But although, as has been shown, the husband

and wife work together in their children, nevertheless the husband and the wife and all other creatures come from the divine disposition and ordination, since God made them according to His will.

13   Why before the Incarnation some men had several wives

Before the Incarnation of My Son, however, certain men among the ancient people had several wives at once, as they wished; they had not yet heard the open prohibition of My Son, Who when He came into the world showed that the right fruit of this union of husband and wife as long as they live is the fruit manifest in the union of Adam and Eve, a union to be exercised not by the will of Man but by the fear of God. For it is better to have this right union, by the arrangement of the prudence of the Church, than to crave fornication; but you humans ignore this, and pursue your lusts not only like humans but like beasts.

But let there be right faith and pure love of the knowledge of God between husband and wife lest their seed be polluted by the Devil's art and divine vengeance strike them because they are biting and tearing each other to pieces and sowing their seed inhumanly with the wantonness of beasts. In such a case jealousy will torture them like a viper, and without the fear of God and without human discipline a defiled excess of seed will be stored up in them, and often, by the just judgment of God, this perversity of theirs will be chastised by having those born of them deprived of limbs and of health in their lives; unless I receive their penitence and show Myself propitious to them. For if any shall call upon Me in penitence for their sins, I will accept their penitence for the love of My Son; for if anyone lifts a finger to Me in penitence, that is, reaches out to Me in penitence and groaning in his heart, saying, "I have sinned, Lord, before You!" My Son, Who is the Priest of priests, will show Me that penitence; for penitence which is offered to priests for the love of My Son obtains the purgation of the sinners. Therefore, people who worthily do penance escape from the jaws of the Devil, who, trying to swallow the hook of divine power, has grievously wounded his jaw; and now, therefore, faithful souls pass out of perdition and arrive at salvation. How?

Because the priests at the altar, invoking My name, will receive the confession of the peoples and show them the remedy of salvation. So, in order to find God propitious, let them not contaminate their seed by various vices, since those who emit their semen in fornication or adultery render their children, born of them thus, unsound. How? Can he who mixes mud or ordure with pure clay make a lasting vessel? Likewise, will he who contaminates his semen in fornication or adultery ever beget strong sons? But many work in different ways in their inmost being, and many of these become prudent toward the world and toward God. And with these the heavenly Jerusalem is filled; deserting vice and loving virtue, they imitate My Son in chastity and in great works, carrying in their bodies, as much as they are able, His martyrdom.

But when I do not wish a person to have children, I take away the virile power of the semen, that it may not coagulate in the mother's womb; so also I deny the earth the power to bear fruit when by My just judgment I will to do so. But do you wonder, O human, why I let children be born in adultery and similar crimes? My judgment is just. For, since the fall of Adam, I have not found in human seed the justice that should have been in it, for the Devil drove out this justice by the taste of the fruit. Therefore I sent My Son into the world born of a virgin, so that by His blood, in which there was no carnal pollution, He might take away from the Devil those spoils that he had carried off from humanity.

14   No human or angel but only the Son of God could deliver Man

For neither a human being, conceived in sin, nor an angel, who has no covering of flesh, could save Man, wallowing in sins and laboring under the heaviness of the flesh, from the power of the Devil; but only He Who, coming without sin, with a pure and sinless body, delivered him by His Passion. Therefore, though human beings are born in sin, I nevertheless gather them into My heavenly kingdom when they faithfully seek it. For no wickedness can take My elect from me, as Wisdom testifies, saying:

15   Words of Wisdom on this subject

"The souls of the just are in the hand of God; and the torment of death shall not touch them" [Wisdom 3:1]. Which is to say: The souls of those who embrace the path of rectitude with devout affection are aided by the celestial Helper; so that, because of the good works by which in the height of justice they strive for Heaven, the torment of perdition does not break them, for the true Light strengthens them in the fear and love of God. But after Adam and Eve were driven out of the place of delight, they knew in themselves the work of conceiving and bearing children. And falling thus from disobedience into death, when they knew they could sin, they discovered sin's sweetness. And in this way, turning My rightful institution into sinful lust, although they should have known that the commotion in their veins was not for the sweetness of sin but for the love of children, by the Devil's suggestion they changed it to lechery; and, losing the innocence of the act of begetting, they yielded it to sin. This was not accomplished without the Devil's persuasion; for that purpose he sent forth his darts, and it did not come to pass without his suggestion; as he said, "My strength is in human conception, and therefore humanity is mine!" And, seeing that if Man consented to him he would become a sharer in his punishment, he said again within himself: "All iniquities are against Most Powerful God, since He is certainly not unjust." And that deceiver put this as a great seal on his heart, that Man, who had consented to him of his own accord, could not be taken away from him.

Therefore I took secret counsel within Myself, to send My Son for the redemption of humanity, that Man might be restored to the heavenly Jerusalem. And no iniquity could withstand this counsel, for My Son, coming into the world, gathered unto himself all who, forsaking sin, chose to hear and imitate Him. I am just and righteous, not willing the iniquity that you, O human, embrace when you know you can do evil. For Lucifer and Man each tried at the beginning of their creation to rebel against Me and could not stand firm, but fell away from good and chose evil. But Lucifer laid hold of total evil and rejected all good, and did not taste the good at all, but fell into death. Adam, however, tasted the good when he accepted obedience, but he longed for evil, and in his desire accomplished it by his disobedience to God. Why this happened is not for you, O human, to investigate; mortal cannot know what there was before the creation of the world or what may happen after the last day, but God alone knows this, except insofar as He permits His elect to know it.

But that fornication, which is commonly done by people, is abominable in My sight, for I created male and female from the beginning in integrity and not in wickedness. Therefore those hypocrites who say it is lawful for them to commit fornication, with animal appetites, with whomever they wish, are unworthy of My eyes, because, despising the honor and loftiness of their rationality, they look to the beasts and make themselves like them. Woe to those who live so and persevere in this wickedness!

16   Blood relatives may not be united in marriage

I also do not wish the blood of relatives to be mingled in marriage, where the ardor of family love is not yet weakened, lest there arise shameless love in the relation of consanguinity; but let the blood of different families flow together, which feels no blood relationship burning within it, so that human custom may work there.

17   Example of milk

Milk that is cooked once or twice has not yet lost its flavor, but by the time it is coagulated and cooked the seventh or eighth time, it loses its qualities and does not have a pleasant taste except in case of necessity. And as one must not have sexual relations with a relative who is one's own spouse, so also one must abhor a sexual relationship with a relative related not to one but to one's spouse; let no human being join in such a coupling, which the Church by its Doctors, who established it in great responsibility and honor, has forbidden.

18 Blood relatives could marry in the Old, but not in the New Testament

Under the Old Testament people married their blood relatives by the precept of the Law, but that was allowed because of their hardheartedness, so that they might be at peace among themselves and charity be strengthened in them; so that these tribes would not break My Covenant by dividing and mixing with the pagans in marriage, until the time came when My Son brought the fullness of charity, changing the joining of relatives in carnal bonds into marriages with different people in bashful modesty. Thus, since the Bride of My Son [the Church] now possesses in holy baptism a bond of My fear and righteous justice, let such joinings of relatives be far from her; for the embraces of a man and woman related by blood would be wickedly enkindled into shameless fornication and ceaseless lust much more than those of unrelated people. I am explaining this by this person [Hildegard], to whom this human operation is unknown; she is receiving this explanation not from human knowledge, but from God. What next?

19 A man should be adult to marry and take only a wife of marriageable age

When a male is at the age of strength, so that his veins are full of blood, then he is fertile in his semen; then let him take in lawfully instituted marriage a woman who is also at the age of heat, that she may modestly receive his seed and bear him children in the path of rectitude.

20 On the avoidance of illicit and lustful pollution

But let not a man emit his semen in excessive lust before the years of his strength; for if he tries to sow his seed in the eagerness of lust before that seed has enough heat to coagulate properly, it is proof that he is sinning at the Devil's suggestion. And when a man is already strong in his desire, let him not exercise his strength in that work as much as he can; because if he thus pays attention to the Devil, he is doing a devilish work, making his body contemptible, which is entirely unlawful. But let the man do as human nature teaches him, and seek the right way with his wife in the strength of his heat and the vigor of his seed; and let him do this with human knowledge, out of desire for children.

But I do not want this work done during the wife's menses, when she is already suffering the flow of her blood, the opening of the hidden parts of her womb, lest the flow of her blood carry with it the mature seed after its reception, and the seed, thus carried forth, perish; at this time the woman is in pain and in prison, suffering a small portion of the pain of childbirth. I do not remit this time of pain for women, because I gave it to Eve when she conceived sin in the taste of the fruit; but therefore the woman should be cherished in this time with a great and healing tenderness. Let her contain herself in hidden knowledge; she should not, however, restrain herself from going into My temple, but faith allows her to enter in the service of humility for her salvation. But because the Bride of My Son is always whole, a man who has open wounds because the wholeness of his members has been divided by the impact of a blow shall not enter My Temple, except under the fear of great necessity, lest it be violated, as the intact members of Abel, who was a temple of God, were cruelly broken by his brother Cain.

21 A woman shall not enter the temple after birth or defloration by a man

So a woman, too, when she bears offspring, may not enter My Temple except in accordance with the law I give her, because her hidden members have been broken, that the holy sacraments of My Temple may be unviolated by any masculine or feminine pain or pollution; because the most pure Virgin bore My Son, and she was whole without any wound of sin. For the place that is consecrated in honor of my Only-Begotten should be untouched by any corruption of bruise or wound, because My Only-Begotten knew in himself the integrity of the Virgin Birth. Therefore, let a woman who breaks the wholeness of her virginity with a man also refrain from entering My Temple while injured by the bruise of her corruption, until the injury of that wound is healed, in accordance with the sure instruction of church teaching. For when His Bride was wedded to My Son on the wood of the cross, she kept herself hidden until My Son commanded His disciples to teach the truth of the Gospel throughout the whole world; but afterward she arose openly and publicly preached the glory of her Bridegroom in the regeneration of the Spirit and water. So let a virgin who is joined to a husband do the same, namely remain hidden with modest shame until the time which church opinion appoints for her; and when she has given herself over to the love of her husband in her concealment, let her come forth openly.

22   Those who have intercourse with the pregnant are murderers

I do not want that work of man and woman to take place from the time when the root of a little child has already been placed in the woman, lest the development of that little child be polluted by excessive and wasted semen, until her purification after childbirth. After that it may be done again, in rectitude and not in wantonness, for the love of children. Thus the human race may procreate by honest human custom, and not as foolish people babble when they claim it is lawful to satisfy their lust at will, saying, "How can we contain ourselves so cruelly?" O humans, if you pay attention to the Devil, he will incite you to evil and destroy you with his deadly poison; but if you raise your eyes to God, He will help you and make you chaste. Do you not desire chastity in your works rather than lust? The woman is subject to the man in that he sows his seed in her, as he works the earth to make it bear fruit. Does a man work the earth that it may bring forth thorns and thistles? Never, but that it may give worthy fruit. So also this endeavor should be for the love of children and not for the wantonness of lust.

Therefore, O humans, weep and howl to your God, Whom you so often despise in your sinning, when you sow your seed in the worst fornication and thereby become not only fornicators but murderers; for you cast aside the mirror of God and sate your lust at will. Therefore the Devil always incites you to this work, knowing that you desire your lustfulness more than the joy of children. Hear, then, you who are among the towers of the Church! In your fornication do not accuse Me, but consider yourselves; for when you despise Me and run to the Devil you do unlawful things, and therefore you do not wish to be chaste; as My servant Hosea says, speaking of the corrupted people:

23   Hosea on this subject

"They will not set their thoughts to return to their God; for the spirit of fornication is in the midst of them, and they have not known God" [Hosea 5:4]. Which is to say: Evil people who do not know God hide the countenance of their heart, and do not do the various things that would bring it back to true brightness; that is, they do not see with clear eyes the things that are of God, but nurture evil in themselves; for, by the Devil's persuasion, the breath of wanton impurity weakens the virile strength they should have, and they cannot put good faith in God because the Devil turns them away from the life of felicity.

24 Commendation of chastity

But now I will turn to My most loving sheep who are securely placed in My heart, the seed of chastity. Virginity was made by Me, for My Son was born of a virgin. And therefore virginity is the most beautiful fruit of all the fruits of the valleys, and the greatest of all the persons in the palace of the unfailing King; for it was not subject to the precept of the law, since it brought My Only-Begotten into the world. Therefore, listen, all those who wish to follow My Son, in the innocence of free chastity or in the solitude of mourning widowhood: Virginity unspotted from the beginning is nobler than widowhood oppressed under the yoke of a husband, even though widowhood, after the grief of the loss of a husband, would imitate virginity.

For My Son bore many pains in His body and underwent the death of the cross; therefore you also, in His love, will suffer much anguish when you conquer in yourselves what was sown in the lust of sin by the taste of the fruit. But though you will endure in your seed flowing rivulets from the conflagration of lust, since you cannot be so chaste as to prevent human weakness from appearing in you secretly, you should in that labor imitate the Passion of My Son and resist yourselves; that is, extinguish within yourselves the burning flame of lust and other things of this world, casting out anger, pride, wantonness and other vices of that sort and attaining this victory by a great struggle. These battles are to Me full of great beauty and much fruit, brighter than the sun and sweeter than the love of spices; for when you trample under foot the burning lust within you, you imitate My Only-Begotten in His pains. And when you persevere in this, you will attain much glory for it in the celestial kingdom.

O sweetest flowers! My angels marvel at your struggle, for you escape from death, so as not to be polluted by the poisonous mud of the world; you have a carnal body, but you tread it under foot, and so you will be glorious in their company since you will appear unpolluted in their likeness. Therefore rejoice that you thus persevere, for I am with you when you receive Me faithfully and with joy in your hearts receive My voice; as I show in a secret vision of My beloved John, saying:

25 John on this subject

"Behold, I stand at the door and knock; if any shall hear My voice and open the door, I will come in to him and will sup with him, and he with Me" [Apocalypse 3:20]. That is to say: O you who faithfully love Me, your Savior, look and see how, wishing to aid you, I wait at the tabernacle of your heart, seeing what you have in the self-knowledge of your conscience, and with the breath of your memory I knock at your spirit, that its goodwill may open and grant admission. And if then the faithful heart, which fears Me, hears My knock, I join Myself to him, embracing him and taking with him the unfailing food, since he offers Me that sweet taste, himself, in his good works; therefore he too shall have that food of life in Me, because he loves what brings life to those who desire justice.

26   After Adam was expelled, God closed Paradise in

But, as you see, after Adam and Eve were expelled from Paradise, *a luminous splendor surrounded that region,* since when they went forth from the place of delight because of their transgression, the Power of the Divine Majesty took away every stain of contagion from the place and fortified it with His Glory, so that from then on it would be touched by no encroachment; which also showed that the transgression which had taken place there would one day be abolished by His clemency and mercy.

27   Creation opposed Man because he rebelled against God

And so *all the elements of the world, which before had existed in great calm, were turned to the greatest agitation and displayed horrible terrors,* because when Man chose disobedience, rebelling against God and forsaking tranquillity for disquiet, that Creation, which had been created for the service of humanity, turned against humans in great and various ways so that Man, having lowered himself, might be held in check by it. What does this mean? That Man showed himself a rebel against God in the place of delights, and therefore that Creation, which had been subjected to him in service, now opposed itself to him.

28   On the delightfulness of Paradise

But Paradise is the place of delight, which blooms with the freshness of flowers and grass and the charms of spices, full of fine odors and dowered with the joy of blessed souls, giving invigorating moisture to the dry ground; it supplies strong force to the earth, as the soul gives strength to the body, for Paradise is not darkened by shadow or the perdition of sinners.

29   Why God made Man such that he could sin

Therefore listen and understand me, you who say in your hearts, "What are these things and why?" Oh, why are you so foolish in your hearts, you who have been made in the image and likeness of God? How can such great glory and honor, which is given to you, exist without testing, as if it were an empty case of nothing? Gold must be tested in the fire, and precious stones, to smooth them, must be polished, and all things of this kind must be diligently scrutinized. Hence, O foolish humans, how can that which was made in the image and likeness of God exist without testing? For Man must be examined more than any other creature, and therefore he must be tested through every other creature. How?

Spirit is to be tested by spirit, flesh by flesh, earth by water, fire by cold, fight by resistance, good by evil, beauty by deformity, poverty by riches, sweetness by bitterness, health by sickness, long by short, hard by soft, height by depth, light by darkness, life by death, Paradise by punishments, the Heavenly Kingdom by Gehenna, earthly things by earthly things and heavenly things by heavenly things. Hence Man is tested by every creature, in Paradise, on earth and in Hell; and then he is placed in Heaven. You see clearly only a few things among many that are hidden from your eyes. So why do you deride what is right, plain and just, and good among all good things in the sight of God? Why do you think these things unjust? God is just, but the human race is unjust in transgressing God's precepts when it claims to be wiser than God.

30   Man should not examine the highest things since he cannot the lowest ones

Now tell me, O human: What do you think you were when you were not yet in soul and body? Truly you do not know how you were created. But now, O human, you wish to investigate Heaven and earth, and to judge of their justice in God's disposition, and to know the highest things though you are not able to examine the lowest; for you do not know how you live in the body, or how you may be divested of the body. He Who created you in the first human foresaw all these things; but that same most gentle Father sent His Only-Begotten to die for the people, to deliver humanity from the power of the Devil.

31   Man now shines brighter in Heaven than before

And thus Man, having been delivered, shines in God, and God in Man; Man, having community in God, has in Heaven more radiant brightness than he had before. This would not have been so if the Son of God had not put on flesh, for if Man had remained in Paradise, the Son of God would not have suffered on the cross. But when Man was deceived by the wily serpent, God was touched by true mercy and ordained that His Only-Begotten would become incarnate in the most pure Virgin. And thus after Man's ruin many

87

shining virtues were lifted up in Heaven, like humility, the queen of virtues, which flowered in the virgin birth, and other virtues, which lead God's elect to the heavenly places. For when a field with great labor is cultivated, it brings forth much fruit, and the same is shown in the human race, for after humanity's ruin many virtues arose to raise it up again. But you, O humans, oppressed by the heaviness of the flesh, do not see that great glory God's full justice has prepared for you, without stain or unworthiness, so that no one can throw it down. For before the structure of the world was made, God in true justice had foreseen all these things. Therefore, O human, consider this comparison:

32 Man's condition symbolized by a garden, a sheep and a pearl

The master who seeks to set out a garden without being wearied first chooses a suitable site, and then, deciding on a place for each planting, reflects on the fruit of good trees and the utility, taste, fragrance and high esteem of various spices. And so this master, if he is a great philosopher and expert contriver, lays out each of the plantings where he sees that it will be most useful; and then he thinks of enclosing it with great walls, so that none of his enemies can destroy his planting. Then he appoints his experts, who know how to water the garden and who collect its fruit and make from it many fragrant things. Therefore consider well, O human: If that master foresaw that his garden, bringing forth no fruit or any kind of use, was to be destroyed, why would so great a philosopher and contriver have made, planted, watered and fortified it so eagerly and with so much labor?

Hear, therefore, and understand! God, Who is the Sun of Justice, made His splendor rise over the filth that is Man's wickedness; and that splendor shone with great brightness, as that filth stank exceedingly. The sun gleamed forth in its brightness, and the filth putrefied in its foulness; and therefore the sun was embraced by those beholding it with much greater love than if the filth had not been there opposite it. But as foul as the filth is compared to the sun, so evil is Man's wickedness compared to God's justice. Hence justice, being beautiful, must be loved, and iniquity, being foul, must be rejected.

Into this foulness fell a sheep belonging to the master who had planted this garden. But this sheep was separated from its master by its own consent, not by his negligence; afterward the master sought it again with great zeal and justice. Therefore the choir of angels shone with great honor, for the angels saw a human in Heaven. What does this mean?

When the innocent Lamb was suspended on the cross, the elements trembled, because the most noble Son of the Virgin was slain in the body by the hands of murderers; by His death the lost sheep was brought back to the pastures of life. For the ancient persecutor saw that because of the blood of the innocent Lamb, which the Lamb had poured out in remission of the sins of humanity, he must lose that sheep, and only then first recognized who that Lamb was; previously he had not been able to understand how the Celestial Bread, without a man's semen and without any desire for sin, had become incarnate of the Virgin by the overshadowing of the Holy Spirit.

For that persecutor, when first he was created, raised himself up in the haughtiness of pride, throwing himself into death and expelling Man from the glory of Paradise; but God did not will to resist him by His power, but conquered him by humility through His Son. And because Lucifer derided God's justice, by God's just judgment he was unable to know the incarnation of God's Only-Begotten. For by this hidden decision the lost sheep was brought back to life. Therefore, O rebellious humans, why are you so hard-hearted? God did not will to forsake humanity, but sent His Son for its salvation; thus God crushed the head of pride in the ancient serpent. For when Man was snatched from death, Hell opened its gates, and Satan cried, "Alas, alas, who will help me?" And the Devil's whole band was torn with great agitation, marvelling that there was a power so great they and their prince could not resist it, since they saw the souls of the faithful being taken away from them. Thus Man was lifted up above the heavens because through the Son of God God appeared in Man and Man in God. Likewise, that master who lost the sheep but brought it so gloriously back to life had, like that sheep, a precious pearl that slipped from him and fell into the mud. But he, not allowing it to lie in the dirt, mercifully drew it forth and purified it of the filth in which it had lain, as gold is purified in the furnace, and restored it to its former honor with even greater glory. For God created Man, but the latter at the Devil's instigation fell into death, from which the Son of God saved him by His blood and brought him gloriously to the glory of Heaven. And how? By humility and charity.

33 Commendation of humility and charity above all other virtues

For humility caused the Son of God to be born of the Virgin, in whom was found humility, not eager embraces or beauty of flesh or earthly riches or gold ornaments or earthly honors. But the Son of God lay in a manger, because His Mother was a poor maiden. Humility always groans, weeps and destroys all offenses, for this is its work. So let anyone who wishes to conquer the Devil arm himself with humility, since Lucifer fervently flees it and hides in its presence like a snake in a hole; for wherever it finds him, it quickly snaps him like a fragile thread.

And charity took the Only-Begotten of God, who was in the bosom of the Father in Heaven, and placed Him in the womb of a mother on earth, for it does not spurn sinners or publicans but seeks to save all. Therefore it often brings forth a fountain of tears from the eyes of the faithful, thus softening hardness of heart. In this, humility and charity are brighter than the other virtues, since humility and charity are like a soul and body that possess stronger powers than the other powers of soul and bodily members. How? Humility is like the soul and charity like the body, and they cannot be separated from each other but work together, just as soul and body cannot be disjoined but work together as long as a person lives in the body. And as the various members of the body are subject, according to their powers, to the soul and to the body, so also the other virtues cooperate, according to their justice, with humility and charity. And therefore, O humans, for the glory of God and for your salvation, pursue humility and charity; armed with them, you shall not fear the Devil's snares but shall have everlasting life.

Therefore whoever has knowledge in the Holy Spirit and wings of faith, let this one not ignore My admonition, but taste it, embrace it and receive it in his soul.

THE UNIVERSE

91

VISION THREE
The Universe and Its Symbolism

After this I saw a vast instrument, round and shadowed, in the shape of an egg, small at the top, large in the middle and narrowed at the bottom; outside it, surrounding its circumference, there was bright fire with, as it were, a shadowy zone under it. And in that fire there was a globe of sparkling flame so great that the whole instrument was illuminated by it, over which three little torches were arranged in such a way that by their fire they held up the globe lest it fall. And that globe at times raised itself up, so that much fire flew to it and thereby its flames lasted longer; and sometimes sank downward and great cold came to it, so that its flames were more quickly subdued. But from the fire that surrounded the instrument issued a blast with whirlwinds, and from the zone beneath it rushed forth another blast with its own whirlwinds, which diffused themselves hither and thither throughout the instrument. In that zone, too, there was a dark fire of such great horror that I could not look at it, whose force shook the whole zone, full of thunder, tempest and exceedingly sharp stones both large and small. And while it made its thunders heard, the bright fire and the winds and the air were in commotion, so that lightning preceded those thunders; for the fire felt within itself the turbulence of the thunder.

But beneath that zone was purest ether, with no zone beneath it, and in it I saw a globe of white fire and great magnitude over which two little torches were placed, holding that globe so that it would not exceed the measure of its course. And in that ether were scattered many bright spheres, into which the white globe from time to time poured itself out and emitted its brightness, and then moved back under the globe of red fire and renewed its flames from it, and then again sent them out into those spheres. And from that ether too a blast came forth with its whirlwinds, which spread itself everywhere throughout the instrument.

And beneath that ether I saw watery air with a white zone beneath it, which diffused itself here and there and imparted moisture to the whole instrument. And when it suddenly contracted it sent forth sudden rain with great noise, and when it gently spread out it gave a pleasant and softly falling rain. But from it too came a blast with its whirlwinds, which spread itself throughout the afore-mentioned instrument.

And in the midst of these elements was a sandy globe of great magnitude, which these elements had so surrounded that it could not waver in any direction.

But as these elements and these blasts contended with each other, by their strength they made it move a little.

And I saw between the North and the East a great mountain, which to the North had great darkness and to the East had great light, but in such a way that the light could not reach the darkness, nor the darkness the light.

And again I heard the voice from Heaven, saying to me:

1 The visible and temporal is a manifestation of the invisible and eternal

God, Who made all things by His will, created them so that His Name would be known and glorified, showing in them not just the things that are visible and temporal, but also the things that are invisible and eternal. Which is demonstrated by this vision you are perceiving.

2 The firmament in the likeness of an egg and what it signifies

For this *vast instrument, round and shadowy, in the shape of an egg, small at the top, large in the middle and narrowed at the bottom,* faithfully shows Omnipotent God, incomprehensible in His majesty and inestimable in His mysteries and the hope of all the faithful; for humanity at first was rude and rough and simple in its actions, but later was enlarged through the Old and New Testaments, and finally at the end of the world is destined to be beset with many tribulations.

3 On the bright fire and the shadowy zone

Outside it, surrounding its circumference, there is bright fire with, as it were, a shadowy zone under it. This shows that God consumes by the fire of His vengeance all those who are outside the true faith, and those who remain within the Catholic faith He purifies by the fire of His consolation; thus He throws down the darkness of devilish perversity, as He did also when the Devil wanted to oppose himself to God though God had created him, and so fell defeated into perdition.

4 On the placement of the sun and the three stars

And in that fire there is a globe of sparkling flame, so great that the whole instrument is illuminated by it, which in the splendour of its brightness shows that within God the Father is His ineffable Only-Begotten, the sun of justice with the brilliance of burning charity, of such great glory that every creature is illumined by the brightness of His light; *over which three little torches are*

94

arranged in such a way that by their fire they hold up the globe lest it fall; that is, [the Trinity] shows how by its arrangement the Son of God, leaving the angels in the heavenly places, descended to earth and showed humans, who exist in soul and body, heavenly things, so that, glorifying Him by serving Him, they reject all harmful error, and magnify Him as the true Son of God incarnate through the true Virgin, when the angel foretold Him and when humans, living in soul and body, with faithful joy received Him.

5   On the ascent of the sun and what it signifies

Therefore *the globe sometimes raises itself up, so that much fire flies to it and therefore its flames last longer.* This means that when the time came that the Only-Begotten of God was to become incarnate for the redemption and uplifting of the human race by the will of the Father, the Holy Spirit by the power of the Father brought celestial mysteries wonderfully to pass in the Blessed Virgin; so that when the Son of God too in virginal chastity showed marvellous splendor and made virginity fruitful, virginity became glorious; for the longed-for Incarnation was brought to pass in the noble Virgin.

6   On the descent of the sun and what it signifies

So, indeed, *sometimes it sinks downwards and great cold comes to it, so that its flames are more quickly subdued.* This shows that the Only-Begotten of God, born of a virgin and hence inclined to be merciful to human poverty, incurred many miseries and sustained great physical anguish; but after He had shown Himself to the world in a bodily shape, He passed from the world and returned to the Father, while His disciples stood by, as it is written:

7   Words from the Acts of the Apostles

"While they looked on He was lifted up, and a cloud received Him" [Acts 1:19]. Which is to say: When the children of the Church had received the Son of God in the interior knowledge of their hearts, the sanctity of His body was lifted up into the power of His Divinity, and in a mystical miracle the cloud of secret mystery received Him, hiding Him from mortal eyes, and the blasts of the winds showed themselves His servants.

8   On the first wind and its whirlwinds

But, as you see, *from the fire that surrounds the instrument issues a blast with whirlwinds,* which shows that from Almighty God, Who fills the whole world with His power, truth rushes forth and spreads with words of justice, which truly demonstrate to humanity the same living and true God.

9 On the second wind and its whirlwinds

But from the zone beneath it rushes forth another blast with its own whirlwinds because the rage of the Devil, knowing God and fearing Him, sends out the worst dishonor and the most evil utterances, *which diffuse themselves hither and thither throughout the instrument,* since in the world useful and useless rumors spread themselves abroad in many ways among the peoples.

10 On the dark fire and the thunder and the sharp stones

In this zone also there is a dark fire of such horror that you cannot look at it. This means that the ancient betrayer's most evil and most vile snares vomit forth blackest murder with such great passion that the human intellect cannot fathom its insanity; *whose force shakes the whole zone,* because murder includes in its horror all diabolical malignities. In the first man born hatred boiled up out of anger and led to fratricide, *full of thunder, tempest and exceedingly sharp stones large and small,* for murder is full of avarice, and drunkenness and extreme hardness of heart, which run riot relentlessly both in great murders and in minor vices. *While it makes its thunders heard, the bright fire and the winds and the air are all in commotion,* because when murder cries out in its eagerness to shed blood, it arouses the justice of Heaven and an outburst of flying rumors and an increased disposition to vengeance on the part of right judgment; *so that lightning precedes those thunders, for the fire feels in itself the turbulence of the thunder,* for the manifestation of divine scrutiny exceeds and suppresses evil, since the Divine Majesty, before the sound of that insanity manifests itself in public, foresees it with that watchful eye to which all things are naked.

11 The purest ether and the placement of the moon and two stars

But beneath that zone is purest ether, with no zone beneath it; for beneath the snares of the ancient betrayer shines most serene faith, with no uncertainty or infidelity hiding in it, since it is not founded by itself but dependent on Christ; *and in it you see a globe of white fire and great magnitude,* which is a true symbol of the unconquered Church, which, as you can see, asserts in faith innocent brightness and great honor; *over which two little torches are placed, holding that globe so that it does not exceed the measure of its course,* which signifies that the two Testaments given from Heaven, the Old and the

New, connect it to the divine rules of the celestial mysteries, holding the Church back from rushing into a variety of different practices, for both the Old and the New Testaments show it the blessedness of the supernal heritage.

12   The placement of the other stars and what it signifies

And therefore *in that ether are scattered many bright spheres, into which the white globe from time to time pours itself out and emits its brightness;* for in the purity of faith many splendid works of piety are done by which the Church, though it may suffer words of disdain, passes on the beauty of its miracles. Though plunged in sorrow, it still marvels at the brightness of the works done by the perfected through others; and therefore, *it moves back under the globe of red fire and renews its flames from it, and then again sends them out into those spheres;* for, moving in contrition back under the protection of the Only-Begotten of God, and receiving from Him the pardon of divine consolation, it again shows the love of heavenly things in blessed works.

13   The third wind and its whirlwinds and what they signify

Therefore also *from the ether a blast comes forth with its whirlwinds, which spreads itself everywhere throughout the instrument;* for from the unity of faith there comes forth to help humanity a strong tradition of true and perfect statements, which swiftly penetrate to the ends of the earth.

14   The watery air and the white zone and what they signify

And beneath that ether you see watery air with a white zone beneath it, which diffuses itself here and there and imparts moisture to the whole instrument; for thus, under the faith possessed by the ancient and the modern fathers, baptism in the Church for the salvation of believers is truly shown to you, which, founded on blessed innocence and stability, propagates itself everywhere by divine inspiration and brings to the whole world the overflowing waters of salvation for believers. *When this zone suddenly contracts, it sends forth sudden rain with great noise, and when it gently spreads out it gives a pleasant and softly falling rain;* for sometimes baptism is presented by the apostles of truth with all their enthusiasm of preaching and depth of mind, and so manifests itself to the astonishment of humans with a rapid abundance of words and a flood of preaching; and sometimes that same baptism is presented by those preachers with sweet moderation, so that it reaches the people for whom it is meant discreetly by a gentle watering.

BOOK ONE

15 On the fourth wind and its whirlwinds

Therefore *from that air too comes a blast with its whirlwinds that spreads itself throughout the aforementioned instrument;* for when the flood of baptism brings salvation to believers, a true report of the words of forcible sermons goes forth and pervades the whole world with its manifest blessedness, so that the people, forsaking infidelity and seeking after the Catholic faith, openly declare it.

16 On the sandy globe of the earth and what it signifies

And in the midst of these elements is a sandy globe of great magnitude, which these elements have so surrounded that it cannot waver in any direction. This openly shows that, of all the strengths of God's creation, Man's is most profound, made in a wondrous way with great glory from the dust of the earth and so entangled with the strengths of the rest of creation that he can never be separated from them; for the elements of the world, created for Man's service, wait on him, and Man, enthroned as it were in their midst, by divine disposition presides over them, as David says, inspired by Me:

17 Words of David on this subject

"Thou hast crowned him with glory and worship, and given him dominion over all the works of Thy hands" [Psalms 8:6–7]. Which is to say: You, O God, Who have marvellously made all things, have crowned Man with the gold and purple crown of intellect and with the sublime garment of visible beauty, thus placing him like a prince above the height of Your perfect works, which You have distributed justly and rightly among Your creatures. Before all Your other creatures You have conferred on Man great and wonderful dignities.

18 On the movement of the earth and what it signifies

But, as you see, *as these elements and these blasts contend with each other, by their strength they make the globe move a little;* for at certain times the report of the Creator's miracles comes to all of God's creation, so that miracle is piled on miracle in a great thunder of words; and then Man, struck by the greatness of these miracles, feels the impact on his mind and body, and in these wondrous deeds considers with astonishment his own weakness and frailty.

19   The great mountain between the North and the East

And you see between the North and the East a great mountain, which to the North has great darkness and to the East has great light. This shows Man's great choice between devilish impiety and divine goodness, evil deception giving the many miseries of damnation to the reprobate, and salvation giving the great happiness of redemption to the elect; *but in such a way that the light cannot reach the darkness, nor the darkness the light;* for the works of light do not come down among the works of darkness, and the works of darkness do not ascend to the works of light; though the Devil often tries to obscure the latter through evil people, like pagans, heretics and false prophets, and those whom they try to attract to themselves by fallacious deception. How? Because they want to know what it is not for them to know, imitating the one who panted to be like the Most High. And because they follow him, by their own will he shows them a lie as the truth. Hence they are not with Me, and I am not with them; for they do not walk in My ways, but love strange paths, seeking out the false things a foolish creature shows them about future events. And in their perverse seeking this is what they wish to have, despising Me and rejecting My saints, who love Me with a sincere heart.

20   Those who perversely examine the future by means of creatures

But these people who obstinately tempt Me by perverse art, examining creatures that were made for their service and asking them to show them things their wilfulness wishes to know—can they, by practicing this art, lengthen or shorten the time their Creator has given them to live? They cannot, by a day or by an hour. Or can they postpone what God has predetermined? In no way. O wretches! Do I not sometimes permit creatures to show you what will happen? They can show you these signs because they fear Me, God, as a servant can sometimes display the power of his master, and as the ox, the ass and other animals show the will of their masters when they faithfully do their bidding. O fools! When you consign Me to forgetfulness, neither looking to Me nor adoring Me, but looking to a creature subject to you for what it portends and shows, then you are obstinately casting Me aside, worshipping the frail creature instead of your Creator. Therefore I say to you: O human, why do you worship that creature, which cannot console you or help you and which cannot make you prosper in happiness, though it is affirmed that they can by astrologers, teachers of death and followers of pagan unbelief, who say the stars give life to you humans and determine all your actions? O wretches, Who made the stars?

But at times, with My permission, the stars by certain signs do manifest themselves to humanity, as My Son shows in His Gospel, where He says:

21 Words of the Gospel

"There shall be signs in the sun and the moon and the stars" [Luke 21:35]. Which is to say: By the light of these lights service is rendered to humanity, and in their revolutions the times of times are displayed. So in the latest times, by My permission lamentable and dangerous epochs will be foretold in them, so that the radiance of the sun and the splendor of the moon and the brightness of the stars will be dimmed, that human hearts may be stirred up to action. Thus also by My will the Incarnation of My Son was shown by a star. But no human being has a star of his own, which determines his life, as a foolish and erring people tries to assert; all stars are at the service of all people. That star only shone more brightly than all other stars because My Only-Begotten, unlike all other humans, was born without sin from a virgin birth. But that star gave My Son no aid, except in faithfully announcing His Incarnation to the people; for all stars and other creatures, fearing Me, fulfil My command, but do not have any knowledge of anything about any creature. For creatures fulfil My commands when it pleases Me, in the same way as when a minter, making a coin, strikes it with the requisite form; then that coin displays the form stamped on it, but has no power to know when the minter may decide to impress another form on it, for neither in the long nor in the short run does it understand the form it has. What does this mean?

O human, if a stone lay before you on which, if you looked carefully, you could read what was going to happen to you, then in your mistaken thoughts, saddened by your misfortune or elated by your prosperity, you would say, "Alas, [ach] I shall die!" or "O joy, [wach] I shall live!" or "Alas, what misfortune," or "O joy, what prosperity is mine!" Now what would that stone have conferred on you? Would it have taken away or given you anything? It could not be either against you or for you.

And likewise neither stars nor fire nor birds nor any other creatures of this kind can either harm you or help you by your examining them. But if, rejecting Me, you trust in a creature made for your service, I also in My just judgment will cast you out of My sight, taking from you the felicity of My kingdom. For I do not want you to scrutinize stars or fire or birds or other creatures for signs of future events; and if you persist in scrutinizing them, your eyes are obnoxious to Me, and I will cast you out like the lost angel, who deserted the truth and threw himself into damnation.

O human! When the stars and the other creatures were made, where were you? Did you give God advice about their arrangement? But the presumption of such scrutiny arose in the first of all dissensions, when Man forgot God to such an extent that he arrogantly inspected one kind of creature after another and sought in them signs of future events. And thus, indeed, the error arose about Baal, because people who were deceived worshipped the creature of God instead of God, to which the Devil's mockery incited them, because they were mindful of the creature rather than the Creator and desired to know what they were not meant to know.

22 How the Devil mocks humanity by the art of magic

Therefore, worse things than this appeared, for humans through the Devil began to be crazy for magic arts, so that now they see and hear the Devil, and he speaks to them deceitfully and shows them one sort of creature in their scrutiny as if it were another. It is not My will to say how the first seducers were taught by the Devil, so that now those who seek him see and hear him; but they are very guilty in this wickedness of theirs, for they deny Me, their God, and imitate the ancient seducer. O human! I have sought you by the blood of My Son, not in malicious iniquity but in great justice; but you forsake Me, the true God, and imitate him who is a liar. I am justice and truth; and therefore I admonish you by faith and exhort you by love and recapture you by penitence, so that, though you are bloody in the pollutions of sinners, you may yet rise from your fall into ruin. But if you despise Me, understand the comparison in this parable; which says:

23 Parable on this subject

A certain lord who had many servants under him gave each of them a full set of warlike arms, saying, "Be upright and useful, and renounce tardiness and indolence." But while they were marching with him, these servants saw beside the road a certain impostor, inventor of evil arts; and some of them, being deceived, said, "We wish to learn this man's arts!" And, casting away their arms, they ran to him. The others said to them, "What are you doing, imitating this impostor and provoking our lord to anger?" And they answered, "How does this harm our lord?" But their lord said to them, "O wicked servants! Why have you thrown away the arms I gave you? And why is it dearer to you to love this vanity than to serve me, your lord, whose servants you are? Go, then, follow this impostor as you desire, for you do not wish to serve me, and see how his folly will profit you." And he cast them out. Which is to say:

This lord is Almighty God, ruling all peoples with His power, Who has armed every person with intellect, commanding him to be active and vigilant in the exercise of virtue, and rid himself of perverseness and negligence. But as people are going along the way of truth, disposed to walk in the divine commands, they are met by many temptations; for the Devil, the seducer of the whole world and the wicked contriver of many vices, waits for them not in the way of truth but in deceptive ambushes. Therefore, certain of them, who love injustice more than right, are seduced by the Devil and are more eager to imitate the vices of the ancient seducer than to embrace the virtues of God. And that intellect, which they ought to have used for the divine commandments, they twist to the vices of earthly iniquity and submit themselves to the Devil. The Doctors, as their companions, cite to them often the sacred Scriptures, reproaching them for their deeds and loudly asking why they follow the Devil's illusions and bring down divine vengeance on themselves. But they almost always deride these admonitions, claiming that they sin in few things and do not offend God by pride at all. Therefore, when they persevere in that obduracy, they receive the divine sentence; for these servants of iniquity are asked why they suffocated their God-given intellect and why they preferred the deceptions of the ancient seducer to loving their Creator, Whom they should actively have served. Thus they too are despised for devilish illusions according to their works, since they refused to serve God, and they are forced to consider what their wicked seduction has profited them since, thus cast out, they incur damnation, because they have disregarded the divine precepts and tried to follow the Devil rather than God.

For I do not will that humans should despise Me, when they ought to know Me in faith; for if they reject Me to examine a creature subject to them, thus imitating the ancient seducer, then I permit them to achieve the desires of their hearts both as to the creature and as to the Devil; and thus they learn by experience how much the creature they have adored will profit them, and what the Devil whom they have followed will give them.

24   Humans go out of the world whenever their salvation and use is complete

And, O foolish humans, why do you scrutinize a creature about the length of your life? For none of you can either know or avoid or get through the period of his life except as I decide he will live; for, O human, when your salvation is complete in both worldly and spiritual matters, you will leave the present world and pass on to that which has no end. For when a person has such fortitude that he burns for Me more ardently than other people, and, aware of the earthly dregs of stinking sin, is active in avoiding the snares of the ancient serpent, I do not take his spirit from his body before his fruits have fully ripened with sweetest fragrance. But if I find one who is of such frailty that in pain of his body and terror of the evil lurker he is too delicate to bear My yoke, I take him away from this world before his soul, wasting away in weakness, begins to dry up. For I know all things. But I want to caution the human race with all possible justice, so that no person can excuse himself: When I strike them with a sentence of death as if they were about to die, when in fact they are to live for a long time yet, I warn and exhort people to do justice. For no one can have or make for himself any time unless I see usefulness in him and by My will allow him to live; as indeed Job testifies, when he says:

25 Words of Job on this subject

"You have appointed his bounds, which cannot be passed" [Job 14:5]. Which is to say: You Who are above all and foresee all before it comes to pass have indeed established in the secret of Your majesty the bounds of human life, so that they cannot be exceeded by humans either by knowledge, by prudence or by understanding, for any reason, in infancy, youth or old age, except according to Your secret providence, which willed to make Man for the glory of Your Name.

26 Words of God on this subject

I, O human, knew you before the foundation of the world. Nevertheless, I will to consider your days in your works and judge of their usefulness, and diligently and sharply examine your deeds. But if I suddenly withdraw anyone from this life, the usefulness of his life is complete; and if his life were extended longer, it would not keep on in freshness bearing good fruits but, tainted by the faith of the flesh, would only give off smoke like the empty sound of words and not attain to Me in the inmost depth of its heart. Therefore I do not grant him a prolongation of this life, but withdraw him from this world before he falls into the apathy of this infertility. But to you, O human, I say: Why do you despise Me? Did I not send My prophets to you, and give My Son on the wood of the cross for your salvation, and choose My apostles to show you the way of truth through the Gospel? So, having all good things through Me, you cannot excuse yourself. And why then do you put Me off?

27 God will no longer tolerate auguries from creatures

But I will no longer tolerate this perverse error, your seeking signs for your actions in the stars or fire or birds or any other creatures; all those who by the Devil's persuasion first fell into this error despised God and threw down His precepts, for which they themselves are despised. But I shine above every creature in the glory of My Divinity, and My miracles are manifested to you in My saints; so I wish you not to practice this error of augury any more, but to look toward Me.

28 Concerning human foolishness and stubbornness

O fool! Who am I? None other than the Supreme Good. Therefore I grant you all good things when you diligently seek Me. And whom do you believe Me to be? I am God, above all things and in all things, but you want to treat Me as a serf who fears his lord. How? You want Me to do your will, while you despise My precepts. God is not thus. What does this mean? He does not remember a beginning nor fear an end. The heavens contemplate Me and resound with My praises and obey Me in that justice by which I established them. The sun, moon and stars appear among the clouds of heaven on their proper course, and the blasts of the wind and the rain move through the air as is appointed for them, and all do the bidding of their Creator. But you, O human, do not fulfil My precepts, but follow your own will, as if for you the law's justice were neither established nor manifested. And although you are but ashes, you are in such a state of contumacy that the justice of My law does not suffice for you, though it is plowed and cultivated in the body and blood of My Son and well trodden out by My saints of the Old and New Testaments alike.

29 Analogy of the goat, the hart and the wolf

But in your great foolishness you wish to lay hold of Me, threatening Me and saying, "If God wants me to be just and good, why does He not make me righteous?" Wishing to catch Me like this is as if a wanton goat wished to catch a hart; it would be thrown back and pierced by the hart's strong horns. So, when you try to behave wantonly and play with Me, I too will crush you in My just judgment by the precepts of the law as if by My horns. These trumpets resound in your ears, but you do not follow them; you run off after the wolf, which you think you have so mastered that it cannot hurt you. But the wolf will devour you, saying, "This sheep strayed from the road and did not want to follow its shepherd but ran after me; therefore I will to have it, for it chose me and forsook its shepherd." O human, God is just; so everything He does in heaven and earth is justly ordained.

30 Analogy of the physician

I am the great Physician of all diseases and act like a doctor who sees a sick man who longs to be cured. What does this mean? If the illness is slight, he cures it easily, but if it is serious, he says to the sick person, "I require silver and gold from you. If you will give them to me, I will help you." I too, O human, do this. Lesser sins I wipe away in people's groans and tears and good resolutions, but for graver faults I say, O human, apply yourself to penitence and amendment, and I will show you My mercy, and give you eternal life. You shall not scrutinize the stars and other creatures about future events, or adore the Devil, or invoke him or ask him anything. For if you seek to know more than you ought to know, you will be deceived by the ancient seducer. The first man sought more than he should have sought, and was deceived by him and went to perdition. But the Devil did not foresee the redemption of Man, when the Son of Man slew death and broke Hell asunder. The Devil at first conquered Man through the woman; but God at last crushed the Devil through the woman who bore the Son of God, who wondrously brought the works of the Devil to naught; as My beloved John testifies, saying:

31 Words of John

"For this reason the Son of God appeared, that He might destroy the works of the Devil" [1 John 3:8]. What does this mean? The great brightness, the Son of God, appeared for the health and salvation of humanity, taking on the poverty of a human body, but shining like a burning star amid shadowy clouds. He was placed on the wine-press, where wine was to be pressed out without the dregs of fermentation, because He the cornerstone fell upon the press and made such wine that it gave forth the greatest odor of sweetness. He, shining as a glorious human being amid the human race, without any admixture of polluted blood, trod with His warlike foot upon the head of the ancient serpent; He destroyed all the darts of his iniquity, full of rage and lust as they were, and made him utterly contemptible.

Therefore, whoever has knowledge in the Holy Spirit and wings of faith, let this one not ignore My admonition, but taste it, embrace it and receive it in his soul.

BODY AND SOUL

THE SOUL AND HER TABERNACLE

VISION FOUR
Soul and Body

*T*hen I saw a most great and serene splendor, flaming, as it were, with
many eyes, with four corners pointing toward the four parts of the world,
which was manifest to me in the greatest mystery to show me the secret of
the Supernal Creator; and in it appeared another splendor like the dawn, con-
taining in itself a brightness of purple lightning. And behold! I saw on the earth
people carrying milk in earthen vessels and making cheeses from it; and one part
was thick, and from it strong cheeses were made; and one part was thin, and from
it weak cheeses were curdled; and one part was mixed with corruption, and from
it bitter cheeses were formed. And I saw the image of a woman who had a perfect
human form in her womb. And behold! By the secret design of the Supernal
Creator that form moved with vital motion, so that a fiery globe that had no
human lineaments possessed the heart of that form and touched its brain and
spread itself through all its members.

But then this human form, in this way vivified, came forth from the
woman's womb and changed its color according to the movement the globe made
in that form.

And I saw that many whirlwinds assailed one of these globes in a body and
bowed it down to the ground; but, gaining back its strength and bravely raising
itself up, it resisted them boldly and said with a groan:

1   Lament of the soul returning by God's grace from the path of
    error to Zion

"A pilgrim, where am I? In the shadow of death. And in what path am I
journeying? In the path of error. And what consolation do I have? That
which pilgrims have. For I should have had a tabernacle adorned with five
square gems more brilliant than the sun and stars, for the sun and stars that
set would not have shone in it, but the glory of angels; the topaz would have
been its foundation and all the gems its structure, its staircases made of
crystal and its courtyards paved with gold. For I should have been a companion of the angels, for I am a living breath, which God placed in dry mud;
thus I should have known and felt God. But alas! When my tabernacle saw
that it could turn its eyes into all the ways, it turned its attention toward the

North; ach, ach! and there I was captured and robbed of my sight and the joy of knowledge, and my garment all torn. And so, driven from my inheritance, I was led into a strange place without beauty or honor, and there subjected to the worst slavery. Those who had taken me struck me and made me eat with swine and, sending me into a desert place, gave me bitter herbs dipped in honey to eat. Then, placing me on the rack, they afflicted me with many tortures. And stripping me of my garments and dealing me many wounds, they sent me out to be hunted, and got the worst poisonous creatures, scorpions and asps and other vermin, to hunt and capture me; and these spewed out their poison all over me so that I was made helpless. Therefore they mocked me, saying, 'Where is your honor now?' Ach, and I trembled all over and with a great groan of woe said silently to myself, 'Oh, where am I? Ach, from whence did I come here? And what comforter shall I seek in this captivity? How shall I break these chains? Oh, what eye can look on my wounds? and what nose can bear their noisome stench? and what hands will anoint them with oil? Ach, who will have mercy on my affliction?

" 'May Heaven graciously hear my cry, and earth tremble at my grief, and every living thing incline with pity toward my captivity. For the bitterest sorrow oppresses me, who am a pilgrim without comfort and without help. Oh, who will console me, since even my mother has abandoned me when I strayed from the path of salvation? Who will help me but God? But when I remember you, O mother Zion, in whom I should have dwelt, I see the bitter slavery to which I am subjected. And when I have called to memory the music of all sorts that dwells in you, I feel my wounds. And when I remember the joy and gladness of your glory, I am horrified by the poisons that pollute them. Oh, where shall I turn? and where shall I flee? My sorrows are without number; for if I continue in these evils, I shall become the companion of those whom I knew to my shame in the land of Babylon. And where are you, O mother Zion? Woe is me that I so unluckily drew back from you; if I had not known you, I would sorrow more lightly! But now I will flee from these evil comrades, for wicked Babylon has put me in a leaden dish and crushed me with heavy bludgeons so that I hardly breathe. And when I pour out my tears and groans to you, O my mother, wicked Babylon sends forth such a noise and roar of sounding waters that you cannot hear my voice. So with great care I will seek the narrow ways by which to escape my evil comrades and my unhappy captivity.'

"And when I had said these things, I went away by a narrow path and hid myself from sight of the North in a small cave, bitterly weeping for the loss of my mother, and also for all my sorrows and all my wounds. And so many tears did I shed, weeping and weeping, that my tears soaked all the pain and all the bruises of my wounds.

"And behold! A most sweet fragrance touched my nostrils, like a gentle breath exhaled by my mother. Oh, what groans and tears I poured forth then, when I felt the presence of that small consolation! And in my joy I uttered such cries and shed such tears that the very mountain in whose cave I had hidden myself was shaken by it. And I said, 'O mother, O mother Zion, what will become of me? And where is your noble daughter now? Oh, how long, how long have I been deprived of your maternal sweetness, in which with many delights you gently brought me up!' And I delighted in these tears as if I saw my mother.

"But my enemies, hearing these cries of mine, said, 'Where is she, whom up to now we kept with us as we liked, so that she completely carried out our will? Look how she is calling upon the dwellers in Heaven. Let us therefore use all our arts and guard her with such great zeal and care that she cannot escape us, for before she was completely subject to us. If we do this, she will follow us again.'

"But I came secretly out of the cave in which I had hidden and tried to go up to such a height that my enemies would be unable to find me. They, however, set in my way a sea of such raging heat that I could not pass over it. There was, indeed, a bridge, but so small and narrow a one that I could not cross by it. And on the shore of that sea appeared a mountain range so high that I could not make my way across it. And I said, 'Oh, wretched woman that I am, what shall I do now? For a little while just now I felt the sweetness of my mother's presence, and I thought she was trying to call me to her; but ach! is she now leaving me again? Ach! where shall I turn? For if I return to my former captivity, my enemies will deride me more than before, because I tearfully cried out to my mother and for a little while felt her gentle sweetness, but now I am forsaken by her again.'

"But because of that sweetness which my mother had lately sent me, I was for the first time filled with such strength that I turned to the East and resumed my way along the narrow path. But the paths were so hedged in by thorns and thistles and such obstacles that I could scarcely take a step. However, with great labor and sweat I struggled through them at last, so worn out by my travail that I could scarcely breathe.

"Thus, at last, I attained with the utmost fatigue to the summit of the mountain in which I had hidden before and turned downward to the valley into which I had to descend; and behold! there in my way were asps, scorpions, serpents and other like crawling things, all hissing at me. Terrified I uttered the loudest of shrieks, crying, 'O mother, where are you? I would suffer less if I had not lately felt the sweetness of your presence; for I am falling again into the captivity in which I lay just now. Where now is your help?' And then I heard my mother's voice, saying to me:

III

2   On the wings of the soul

" 'O daughter, run! For the Most Powerful Giver whom no one can resist has given you wings to fly with. Therefore fly swiftly over all these obstacles!' And I, comforted with great consolation, took wing and passed swiftly over all those poisonous and deadly things.

3   On the tabernacle it entered

"And I came to a tabernacle, whose interior was all of the strongest steel. And, going in, I did works of brightness where I had previously done works of darkness. And in that tabernacle I placed at the north a column of unpolished steel, on which I hung fans made of diverse feathers, which moved to and fro. And, finding manna, I ate it. At the east I built a bulwark of square stones and, lighting a fire within it, drank wine mixed with myrrh and unfermented grape juice. At the south I built a tower of square stones, in which I hung up red shields and placed trumpets of ivory in its windows. And in the middle of this tower I poured out honey and mixed it with other spices to make a precious unguent, from which a great fragrance poured forth to fill the whole tabernacle. But at the west I built nothing, for that side was turned toward the world.

"And while I was absorbed in this work, my enemies seized their quivers and attacked my tabernacle with their arrows, but I was so absorbed in the work I was doing that I did not notice their madness until the gates of the tabernacle were full of arrows. But none of the arrows could penetrate the door or the steel lining of the tabernacle, so that I also could not be injured by them. When they saw this, they sent a tremendous flood of water to wash away both me and my tabernacle, but their malice accomplished nothing. Wherefore I boldly mocked them, saying, 'The architect who built this tabernacle was wiser and stronger than you. Collect your arrows and put them down, for from now on they cannot make your will triumph over me. See, what wounds have they given me? With great pain and labor I have waged many wars against you, and you tried to put me to death, but you could not; for I was protected by the strongest armor and brandished sharp swords against you and thus vigorously defended myself from you. Retreat, therefore, retreat, for you will have me no longer.' "

4   Lament of the soul while resisting the Devil's whirlwinds with God's help

But I, fragile and untaught, saw that many whirlwinds rushed upon another of these globes and tried to throw it down, but could not; for it resisted strongly and gave them no room to rage. It nonetheless spoke with lamentation, saying: "I am a poor little thing, but I have a great duty. Oh, what am I? and what is the theme of my outcry? I am the living breath in a human being, placed in a tabernacle of marrow, veins, bones and flesh, giving it vitality and supporting its every movement. But alas! Its sensibility gives rise to filth, licentiousness and wantonness of conduct and every kind of vice. Ach! Oh, how great is the groaning of my complaint! For when the works of my tabernacle prosper, the Devil's persuasion meets me and ensnares me, and uplifts me in haughty pride, so that I say, 'I want to act according to the joys of earthly fertility.' For inside my tabernacle I understand all works, but I am so impeded by its ardent desires that before I can discern my proper work I see dire wounds in me. Oh, what a cry I let out! and I say, 'O God, did You not create me? Look how vile earth oppresses me!' And I start to run away. How is this? When my tabernacle knows carnal desire, then, because I take pleasure in its carnal acts, I myself fulfill those acts. But reason, which along with knowledge lives in me, shows me that I was created by God. And by reason I remember that Adam, when he had transgressed God's command, was afraid and hid himself. So I too am afraid and hide myself from the face of God when I sense that my works in my tabernacle are contrary to God. But when I think above all of the leaden scale of sin, I condemn all those works that burn with carnal desire.

5   On the whirlwinds engendered by the Devil's persuasion

"Alas for me, a pilgrim! How can I survive among these dangers? And what happens when the Devil's persuasion invades me, saying, 'Is a thing good which you do not know and cannot see and cannot do?' and again, 'Why forsake what you do know and do understand and can do?' What shall I do then? Full of sorrow, I will answer, 'Ach miserable me! for harmful poisons were instilled into me through Adam, when he disobeyed God and was cast out into the world and joined his tabernacle to carnal things. For in the taste of the fruit he knew by disobedience, a harmful sweetness poured itself into his blood and flesh, producing the corruption of vice. And therefore I feel the sin of the flesh in me, and intoxicated by this sin, I neglect the Most Pure God. But I must not follow the taste my tabernacle has in it. For since Adam was pure and honest when God created him and he first appeared, I fear God, knowing that I too was created pure and honest. But now, through the evil habits of vice, I dwell in disquietude. Oh, in all these ways I am a pilgrim!

"Therefore the whirlwinds tell me lies in many voices, which rise up within me, saying, 'Who are you? and what are you doing? and what are these battles you are fighting? You are indeed unhappy, for you do not know whether your work is good or bad. Where will you go? and who will save you? and what are these errors that are driving you to madness? Are you doing what delights you? Are you escaping what distresses you? Oh, what will you do when you know this and are ignorant of that? For what delights you is not lawful for you, and what distresses you God's precept compels you to do. And how do you know whether these things are so? It would be better for you if you did not exist!' And after these whirlwinds have risen up thus within me, I begin to tread another path that is hard for my flesh to bear, for I begin to practice righteousness. But then I doubt as to whether or not the Holy Spirit has given this to me, and I say, 'This is useless.' And I wish to fly above the clouds. How? I wish to fly above my faculties and start things I cannot finish. But when I try to do these things, I only stir up great sadness in myself, so that I do no works, either on the heights of sanctity or on the plains of good will; but I bear within me the disquietude of doubt, desperation, sadness and oppression in all things. And when the Devil's persuasion disturbs me then, oh, how great a calamity overtakes me! For I am overcome in my unhappiness by all the evils that are or can be in blame, malediction, mortification of body and soul and shameful words against the purity, healing and loftiness that are in God. And then wickedness suggests to me that all the felicity and all the good which is in Man as well as God will be to me harmful and oppressive, offering me death rather than life. Ach! How unhappy is this struggle, which forces me from labor to labor, from sorrow to sorrow, from discord to discord, depriving me of all happiness.

6   From what cause these errors come into being

"But from whence does the evil of these errors come into being? From this: that the ancient serpent has within himself astuteness and deceptive cunning and the deadly poison of iniquity. For by his astuteness he infuses me with stubbornness in sinning and withdraws my intellect from the fear of God, so that I am not afraid to sin, and say, 'Who is God? I do not know who God is.' And by his deceptive cunning he instils obduracy into me, so that I am hardened in evil. And by the deadly poison of iniquity he takes spiritual joy away from me, so that I can rejoice neither in Man nor in God, and thus incites me to despairing doubt, so that I do not know whether or not I can be saved. Oh, what are these tabernacles that they should suffer so much danger from the deception of the Devil?

"But when, by God's gift, I remember that God created me, then in the midst of these oppressions I give this answer to the Devil's tempting: 'I will not yield to the frail clay, but furiously wage war!' How? When my tabernacle tries to do works of unrighteousness, I will tread upon marrow, blood and flesh in the wisdom of patience, the way the strong lion defends itself and the serpent fleeing a mortal blow hides itself in its hole. For I must not let myself be struck by the Devil's arrows or practice the pleasures of the flesh. How?

7 How anger, hatred and pride are restrained

"When anger tries to burn up my tabernacle, I will look to the goodness of God, Whom anger never touched; and thus I will be sweeter than the air, which in its gentleness moistens the earth, and have spiritual joy because virtues are beginning to show themselves in me. And thus I will feel God's goodness.

"And when hatred tries to darken me, I will look to the mercy and the martyrdom of the Son of God, and so restrain my flesh, and in faithful memory receive the sweet fragrance of the roses that spring from thorns. And so I will acknowledge my Redeemer.

"And when pride tries to build in me a tower of vanity without foundation on the rock, and to erect in me the loftiness that wants no one to be like itself but always to be taller than the rest—oh, who will help me then, when the ancient serpent who fell into death by wishing to be above everyone is trying to cast me down? Then I say with grief, 'Where is my King and my God? What good can I do without God? None.' But then I look to God Who gave me life, and I run to the Most Blessed Virgin who trod underfoot the pride of the ancient abyss, and thus I am made a strong stone of God's edifice; and that rapacious wolf, who choked on the divine hook, from now on cannot conquer me. And thus in God's sublimity I know the sweetest good, which is humility, and feel the sweetness of the unfailing balsam and rejoice in the delightfulness of God as if I were amid the fragrance of all perfumes. And thus I ward off the other vices by the impregnable shield of humility."

8 Lament of a soul that with fear goes forth from its tabernacle

But then I, poor creature, saw that another of the globes freed itself from the lineaments of the form it was in and untied all its bonds, and with a groan drew itself out of them, and broke away lamenting from its abode. And it said, "I will go forth from my tabernacle. But, miserable and full of grief as I am, where shall I go? I shall go through dreadful and fearsome paths to the judgment where I shall be judged! There I will show the works that I have performed in my tabernacle, and there I will be requited according to my merits. Oh, what great fear, and oh, how much anguish will be there for me!" *And when it had thus freed itself, there came certain spirits, some of light and some of darkness, who had been its life's companions according to its behavior in its abode, and who waited for its release so that they could lead it away with them. And I* heard a living voice saying to them, "Let her be led from place to place according to her works."

And again I heard a voice from Heaven saying to me, "The Blessed and Ineffable Trinity showed itself to the world when the Father sent into the world his Only-Begotten, conceived by the Holy Spirit and born of the Virgin, so that humans, born so diversely and bound by so many sins, should be brought back by Him to the way of truth; and thus those who, when released from their ties to the heavy body, carry good and holy works with them might gain the joys of the celestial inheritance."

9   God's knowledge is clouded by no obscurity

That you, O human, may grasp this more profoundly and show it more clearly, *you see a most great and serene splendor, flaming, as it were, with many eyes, with four corners pointing toward the four parts of the world.* This signifies the knowledge of God, great in its mysteries and pure in its manifestations, radiant with the most profound clarity, which extends its all-piercing gaze in fourfold firmness to the four corners of the earth. There this knowledge most clearly foresees those who will be rejected as well as those who will be gathered in; this shows the mystery of the Celestial Majesty, which, as you see, is presented to you in this image of great loftiness and profundity. *In it appears another splendor like the dawn, containing in itself a brightness of purple lightning;* for the knowledge of God also indicates that the Only-Begotten of the Father, taking flesh from the Virgin, hastened to shed His blood in the purity of faith for the salvation of humanity, while in the same knowledge of God the good and the evil are made known, for it is clouded by no obscurity of any kind. But you, O human, are saying, "What is Man to do, when God knows in advance everything Man is going to do?" And I, O human, say this to you:

10   In the beauty of God's justice no injustice can be found

O fool! In the wickedness of your heart you are imitating the one who first refused the way of truth and opposed it with a lie, because he wished to make himself like the Supreme Goodness. Who can obscure the Beginning and the End, Who is, was and will remain? And what are you, who are a spark among ashes? And what did you know when you were nothing? But you, with your lamentable beginning and miserable end, speak against the thing you do not know and should not know, the indescribable beauty of God's justice, in which no suspicion of injustice is found, or has been found, or will be found. O fool, for whom do you take the father of wickedness whom you imitate? What does this mean? When pride swells up within you,

you want to be raised above the stars and the other creatures and the angels, who fulfil God's precepts in all things. But you shall fall, as the one fell who opposed a lie to the truth. For he loved the lie, and therefore, entangled in death, he fell into the abyss. Therefore, O human, pay attention. If you do not contemplate the charity with which God freed you, and if you pay no heed to the number of good things God constantly gives you, and if you do not consider how, when you fall into many sins and love death rather than life, He calls you back from death; nonetheless, when you finally remember the Scriptures and the doctrines the faithful fathers of antiquity set before you, telling you to avoid evil and do good, then if you say from your inmost heart, "I have sinned gravely, wherefore I must return with due penitence to my Father who created me," your Father will receive you lovingly and place you in His bosom and clasp you in sweet embraces. But now you disdain to know that blessedness, which God sets before you, and you refuse to hear or to do God's justice. If it were possible to do, would you not reprimand God's justice as unjust rather than true? For that reason, if you had not been redeemed by the blood of the Son of God, you would be lying lost in perdition. But God's judgment is true and just. Wherefore, O human, what advantage will it give you if in My judgment you destroy yourself? In the choir of the angels and in My chosen vineyard resounds the praise of those who laud Me and say, "Glory to You, Lord!"; and, because they are just, they do not contradict My judgment. But what did it profit the Devil to oppose Me? He, seeing that his brightness was great, tried to exalt himself above all, so that a countless band of proud spirits joined with him; all of whom the Divine Power cast down with him in the zeal of Its rectitude. And so also are cast down all who persevere in evil and seek to avert God's justice, laboring to pervert the Supreme Good into perverse wickedness. So God never established anything unjust, but in the equity of His goodness He ordained all that is right.

11 On idols, and that they must be forsaken

But when the race of people to whom Adam and Eve had narrated how they were made by God and how they had been expelled from Paradise passed away, those people arose in the wantonness of vanity who in their unfaithfulness abandoned God, making themselves idols into which the Devil entered and mocked them. Others who followed them in perversity worshipped God's creature rather than the Creator Himself, and thought things that were not alive could determine their lives. So let all who are still foul with this infidelity forsake their stupidity and be converted in faith to Him Who broke the Devil's snares, laying aside old ignorance and embracing new life, as My servant Ezekiel exhorts, saying,

12 The prophet Ezekiel on this subject

"Cast away from you all your transgressions in which you have transgressed, and make for yourselves a new heart and a new spirit" [Ezekiel 18:31]. Which is to say: O you who want to persevere in rectitude under the Sun in Whose paths go the blessed sheep, cast out of your heart's knowledge inquiry into those secret things that in the highest wisdom are useless. By them you sought to fly to a vain height but were plunged into a deep pit, in which dwells no honor but only that horrible desire that does not know God. And when you do this, for your salvation go in the way of truth, where you will find in your heart the newness of the sparkling heavens, and where you will have in your spirit the newness of living breath.

13 On the inequality of human seed and the diversity of people made from it

You see also on the earth people carrying milk in earthen vessels and making cheese from it; these are the people in the world, both men and women, who have in their bodies human seed, from which the various races of people are procreated. *One part is thick, and from it strong cheeses are made;* for that strong semen, which is usefully and well matured and tempered, produces energetic people, to whom brilliant spiritual and bodily gifts are given by their great and noble ancestors, making them flourish in prudence, discretion and usefulness in their works before God and Man, and the Devil finds no place in them. *And one part is thin, and from it weak cheeses are curdled;* for this semen, imperfectly matured and tempered in a weak season, produces weak people, who are for the most part foolish, languid and useless in their works in the sight of God and the world, not actively seeking God. But also *one part is mixed with corruption, and from it bitter cheeses are formed;* for that semen is basely emitted in weakness and confusion and mixed uselessly, and it produces misshapen people, who often have bitterness, adversity and oppression of heart and are thus unable to raise their minds to higher things. Many of them nonetheless become useful; though they suffer many tempests and troubles in their hearts and in their actions, they come out victors. For if they were left in peace and quiet, they would become languid and useless, and therefore God forces them and leads them to the path of salvation, as it is written:

14 Words of Moses on this subject

"I will kill, and I will make live; I will strike, and I will heal; and there is none who can deliver out of My hand" [Deuteronomy 32:39]. Which is to say: I Who Am, having neither beginning nor end, slay in their deeds wicked people who, steeped in vice by the Devil's filth, are deceived by the diabolic pits into sowing unhappy births. Oh, how crafty is the bite of the viper, which so poisons them that death tries to enter into them! Therefore I deprive them of prosperity in this world, where they are slain by many calamities that they cannot overcome but which by just judgment are always with them. But I, Who am thrown down by no darkness, also cause these people to live wonderfully elsewhere, when I draw the spirit that lives in them upward from the earth, so that it may not perish within them. I also afflict with wounds of weakness in their life's labor those who try in their pride of mind to rise to an absurd height, thinking that no one can cast them down; but I Who am present everywhere also sometimes raise them to true health, so that they will not be destroyed by vanity amid deceitful dangers. And in all these things there is no human or other creature who can subvert these works of Mine by any cunning or fierceness of his, for there is no one who can resist My will and justice.

15 Why stunted and deformed infants are born

And often, as you see, when male and female unite in forgetfulness of Me and in the mockery of the Devil, those who are born are found to be stunted so that their parents, who transgressed My precepts, may feel anguish at having these children and so return to Me in penitence. Often also I let these strange births take place among people for My glory and that of My saints, so that when those who are thus deformed are restored to health by the help of My elect, My name may be more ardently glorified among people. But those who bind themselves by an agreement to seek the glory of virginity ascend like the dawn to the secret places of Heaven, since for the sake of My Son's love they deprive themselves of the delights of the body.

16 An infant is vivified in the womb and confirmed by a soul on leaving it

And you see the image of a woman who has a perfect human form in her womb. This means that after a woman has conceived by human semen, an infant with all its members whole is formed in the secret chamber of her womb. And behold! *By the secret design of the Supernal Creator that form moves with vital motion;* for, by God's secret and hidden command and will, fitly and rightly at the divinely appointed time the infant in the maternal womb receives a spirit, and shows by the movements of its body that it lives, just as the earth opens and brings forth the flowers of its use when the dew falls on it. *So that a fiery globe which has no human lineaments possesses the heart of that form;* that is, the soul, burning with a fire of profound knowledge, which discerns whatever is within the circle of its understanding, and, without the form of human members, since it is not corporeal or transitory like a human body, gives strength to the heart and rules the whole body as its foundation, as the firmament of Heaven contains the lower regions and touches the higher. *And it also touches the person's brain;* for in its powers it knows not only earthly but also heavenly things, since it wisely knows God; *and it spreads itself through all the person's members;* for it gives vitality to the marrow and veins and members of the whole body, as the tree from its root gives sap and greenness to all the branches. *But then this human form, in this way vivified, comes forth from the woman's womb, and changes its color according to the movement the globe makes in that form;* which is to say that after the person has received the vital spirit in the maternal womb and is born and begins his actions, his merits will be according to the works his soul does with the body, for he will put on brightness from the good ones and darkness from the evil ones.

17 How the soul shows its powers according to the powers of the body

The soul now shows its powers according to the powers of the body, so that in a person's infancy it produces simplicity, in his youth strength, and in adulthood, when all the person's veins are full, it shows its strongest powers in wisdom; as the tree in its first shoots is tender and then shows that it can bear fruit, and finally, in its full utility, bears it. But then in human old age, when the marrow and veins start to incline to weakness, the soul's powers are gentler, as if from a weariness at human knowledge; as when winter approaches the sap of the tree diminishes in the branches and the leaves, and the tree in its old age begins to bend.

18 A person has three paths within himself

But a person has within himself three paths. What are they? The soul, the body and the senses; and all human life is led in these. How? The soul vivifies the body and conveys the breath of life to the senses; the body draws the soul to itself and opens the senses; and the senses touch the soul and draw the body. For the soul gives life to the body as fire gives light to darkness, with two principal powers like two arms, intellect and will; the soul has arms not so as to move itself, but so as to show itself in these powers as the sun shows itself by its brilliance. Therefore, O human, who are not just a bundle of marrow, pay attention to scriptural knowledge!

19   On the intellect

The intellect is joined to the soul like an arm to the body. For as the arm, joined to the hand with its fingers, branches out from the body, so the intellect, working with the other powers of the soul, by which it understands human actions, most certainly proceeds from the soul. For before all the other powers of the soul it understands whatever is in human works, whether good or evil, so that through it, as through a teacher, everything is understood; for it sifts things as wheat is purified of any foreign matter, inquiring whether they are useful or useless, lovable or hateful, pertinent to life or death. Thus, as food without salt is tasteless, the other powers of the soul without intellect are insipid and undiscerning. But the intellect is also to the soul as the shoulder is to the body, the very core of the other powers of the soul; as the bodily shoulder is strong, so it understands the divinity and the humanity in God, which is the joint of the arm, and it has true faith in its work, which is the joint of the hand, with which it chooses among the various works wisely as if with fingers. But it does not work in the same way as the other powers of the soul. What does this mean?

20   On the will

The will activates the work, and the mind receives it, and the reason produces it. But the intellect understands the work, knowing good and evil, just as the angels, who have intellect, love good and despise evil. And where the heart is in the body, there the intellect is in the soul, exercising its power in that part of the soul as the will does in another part. How? Because the will has great power in the soul. How? The soul stands in a corner of the house, that is, by the prop of the heart, like a man who stands in a corner of his house, so that looking through the whole house he may command all its contents, lifting his right arm to point out what is useful in the house and turning to the East. Thus the soul should do, looking along the streets of the body toward the rising sun. Thus it puts its will, like a right arm, as the support of the veins and marrow and the movement of the whole body; for the will does every work, whether it be good or bad.

21   Analogy of fire and bread

For the will is like a fire, baking each deed as if in a furnace. Bread is baked so that people may be nourished by it and be able to live. So too the will is the strength of the whole work, for it starts by kneading it and when it is firm adds the yeast and pounds it severely; and, thus preparing the work in contemplation as if it were bread, it bakes it in perfection by the full action of its ardor, and so makes a greater food for humans in the work they do than in the bread they eat. A person stops eating from time to time, but the work of his will goes on in him till his soul leaves his body. And in whatever differing circumstances the work is performed, whether in infancy, youth, adulthood or bent old age, it always progresses in the will and in the will comes to perfection.

22 How in the will's tabernacle all powers are activated and come together

But the will has in the human breast a tabernacle, the mind, upon which the intellect and that same will and a sort of force of the soul all breathe in strength. And all these are activated and come together in the same tabernacle. How? If anger arises, gall is produced and brings the anger to its height by filling the tabernacle with smoke. If wicked delight rises up, the flame of lust touches its structure, and so the wantonness that pertains to that sin is elevated and in that tabernacle united with it. But there is another, lovely kind of joy, which is kindled in that tabernacle by the Holy Spirit, and the rejoicing soul receives it faithfully and perfects good works in the desire of Heaven. And there is a kind of sadness that engenders in the tabernacle, out of those humors that surround the gall, the sloth which produces disdain, obduracy and stubbornness in people and depresses the soul, unless the grace of God comes quickly to rescue it.

But since in that tabernacle there occur contrary conditions, it is often disturbed by hatred and other deadly emotions, which kill the soul and try to lay it waste in perdition. But when the will wills, it can move the implements in the tabernacle and in its burning ardor dispose of them, whether they are good or evil. But if these implements please the will, it bakes its food there and offers it to people to enjoy. So in that tabernacle a great throng of good and evil things arises, like an army gathered in some place of assembly; when the commander of an army arrives, if the army pleases him he accepts it, but if it displeases him he orders it to disband. The will does the same. How? If good or evil arises in the breast, the will either carries it out or ignores it.

23 On the reason

But both in the intellect and in the will reason stands forth as the loud sound of the soul, which makes known every work of God or Man. For sound carries words on high, as the wind lifts the eagle so that it can fly. Thus the soul utters the sound of reason in the hearing and the understanding of humanity, that its powers may be understood and its every work brought to perfection. But the body is the tabernacle and support of all the powers of the soul, since the soul resides in the body and works with the body, and the body with it, whether for good or for evil.

24 On the senses

It is the senses on which the interior powers of the soul depend, so that these powers are known through them by the fruits of each work. The senses are subject to these powers, since they guide them to the work, but the senses do not impose work on the powers, for they are their shadow and do what pleases them. The exterior human being awakens with senses in the womb of his mother before he is born, but the other powers of the soul still remain in hiding. What is this? The dawn announces the daylight; just so the human senses manifest the reason and all the powers of the soul. And as on the two commandments of God hang all the Law and the prophets, so also on the soul and its powers depend the human senses. What does this mean?

The Law is ordained for human salvation, and the prophets show forth the hidden things of God; so also human senses protect a person from harmful things and lay bare the soul's interior. For the soul emanates the senses. How? It vivifies a person's face and glorifies him with sight, hearing, taste, smell and touch, so that by this touch he becomes watchful in all things. For the senses are the sign of all the powers of the soul, as the body is the vessel of the soul. What does this mean? A person is recognized by his face, sees with his eyes, hears with his ears, opens his mouth to speak, feels with his hands, walks with his feet; and so the senses are to a person as precious stones and as a rich treasure sealed in a vase. But as the treasure within is known when the vase is seen, so also the powers of the soul are inferred by the senses.

25 That the soul is the mistress and the flesh the handmaid

The soul is the mistress, the flesh the handmaid. How? The soul rules the body by vivifying it, and the body is ruled by this vivification, for if the soul did not vivify the body it would fall apart and decay. But when a person does an evil deed and the soul knows it, it is as bitter for the soul as poison is for the body when it knowingly takes it. But the soul rejoices in a sweet deed as the body delights in sweet food. And the soul flows through the body like sap through a tree. What does this mean? By the sap, the tree grows green and produces flowers and then fruit. And how is this fruit matured? By the air's tempering. How? The sun warms it, the rain waters it, and thus by the tempering of the air it is perfected. What does this mean? The mercy of God's grace, like the sun, will illumine the person, the breath of the Holy

Spirit, like the rain, will water him, and so discernment, like the tempering of the air, will lead him to the perfection of good fruits.

26 Analogy of a tree to the soul

The soul in the body is like sap in a tree, and the soul's powers are like the form of the tree. How? The intellect in the soul is like the greenery of the tree's branches and leaves, the will like its flowers, the mind like its bursting firstfruits, the reason like the perfected mature fruit, and the senses like its size and shape. And so a person's body is strengthened and sustained by the soul. Hence, O human, understand what you are in your soul, you who lay aside your good intellect and try to liken yourself to the brutes.

27 The soul inclined to sin leaves it when stung with remorse

But you, O human who are seeing these things, consider also that *many whirlwinds assail one of these globes in a body and bow it down to the ground.* This means that as long as a person lives in soul and body, his soul is disturbed by many invisible temptations, which incline it to sins of earthly desire through the pleasure of the flesh. *But that globe, gaining back its strength and bravely raising itself up, resists them boldly;* because when the faithful and careful person sins, by God's gift he is often stung with remorse and forsakes his sin; placing his hope in God, he rejects the Devil's lies and faithfully seeks his Creator, as the faithful soul truly showed when it lamented its miseries as above.

28 The soul tempted by the Devil evades his darts by celestial inspiration

And you see that *many whirlwinds rush upon another of these globes and try to throw it down, but cannot.* This means that the Devil assails this soul with many snares, trying to draw it into many sins and crimes, but cannot by his illusions prevail over it; *for it resists strongly and gives them no room to rage;* that is, fortifying itself with celestial inspiration, it drives away the darts of lying deception and hastens back to its Savior, as it declared in the words of its complaint quoted above.

29 The soul that forsakes its body awaits its sentence with great fear

And, as you see, *another of the globes frees itself from the lineaments of the form it is in and unties all its bonds.* This means that the soul, forsaking the members of its bodily dwelling, breaks its relationship with them when the time comes for the body's dissolution. *And with a groan it draws itself out of them and breaks away lamenting from its abode;* for, taking itself out of the body with anguish, it tremblingly allows its habitation to fall, dreading the imminent tribunal of the Celestial Judge, at which it will perceive by God's just judgment the merits of its works, as it too shows in its complaint already quoted. That is why, *when it has thus freed itself, there come certain spirits, some of light and some of darkness, who have been its life's companions according to its behavior in its abode;* because in that dissolution, when a person's soul forsakes its habitation, by God's just and true ordinance both good and evil angelic spirits are present who have observed its deeds done in the body by means of the body. *They wait for its release so that they can lead it away with them;* for they await the sentence of the Just Judge on that soul when it is separated from the body, so when it leaves the body they lead it where the Celestial Judge will judge it on the merits of its deeds, as has been faithfully demonstrated, O human, to you.

30 Words of God to humanity, that they should obey the divine precepts

Therefore, O My dearest children, open your eyes and ears and obey My precepts! Why do you despise your Father, Who has delivered you from death? The choirs of angels sing, "You are just, O Lord!" [Psalm 118:137], because God's justice has no flaw in it; for God delivered Man not by power but by mercy, when He sent His Son into the world to redeem him. No smear of dung soils the sun; and likewise no wickedness of injustice can touch God. But you, O human, with reflective knowledge consider good and evil. What are you when you soil yourself with many desires of the flesh? and what are you when the brightest gems of the virtues shine in you? The first angel despised good and desired evil; therefore he received it, dying into eternal perdition and being entombed in death for rejecting the good. But the good angels condemned evil and loved good, seeing the fall of the Devil, who wanted to overthrow the truth and set up a lie. Thus they burned with love of God and firmly based themselves on all that is good, so that they wanted nothing but what pleased God, never ceasing to praise Him. The first man also knew God and loved Him in simplicity and, receiving His precepts, set himself to obey; but then he inclined toward evil and committed disobedience. For when the Devil suggested evil to him, he forsook good and perpetrated evil, and hence he was cast out of Paradise. Therefore, evil must be thrown down into the perdition of death, and good embraced in love of life.

But you, O human, when you consider good and evil, are standing, as it were, where two roads branch off. If you despise the darkness of evil and want to see Him Whose creature you are, and Whom you acknowledged in holy baptism where the old sin of Adam was nullified in you; and if you say, "I want to fly from the Devil and his works and follow the true God and His precepts"; then think how you have been taught to turn away from evil and do good, and how the Heavenly Father did not spare His Only-Begotten but sent Him for your deliverance; and pray to God to help you. And He, hearing you, will say, "These eyes are pleasing to me!" And if you then cast off weariness and run courageously in God's commands, He will always hear the cry of your prayers. Therefore you should subdue your flesh and subjugate it to the rule of the soul. But you say, "I have in my flesh so many great burdens that I cannot conquer myself; but since God is good, He will make me good. How can I subdue my flesh, being human? God is good; He will perfect all good things in me. For when it pleases Him, He can make me good."

But I say to you: If God is good, why do you put such little value on knowing His goodness, which gave His Son over to deliver you by many sorrows and labors from death? When you say that you cannot do good works, you speak in unjust wickedness. For you have eyes to see with, ears to hear with, a heart to think with, hands to work with and feet to walk with, so that with your body you can stand up and lie down, sleep and wake, eat and fast. Thus God created you. Therefore, resist the desires of your flesh, and God will help you. For when you set yourself against the Devil like a strong warrior against his enemy, God delights in your struggle, wanting you to invoke Him in every hour, in all your troubles, constantly. But when you do not try to subdue your flesh, you make it feast with vice and sin, for you free it from the bridle of the fear of the Lord, with which you should be curbing it lest it go to perdition.

At such a time you are looking to the Devil, as he himself looked to wickedness when he fell into death. And, rejoicing in your perdition, he says, "Here is a person who is like us!" And then he falls on you and instils into you at his will his death-shadowed ways. But God knows what good you are capable of. For the Law is laid down for you according to what you can perform. God wishes from the beginning to the end of the world to take pleasure in His elect, that they may be faithfully crowned, adorned with the brightness of virtue. How shall this be? Let Man resist the pleasure of the flesh, lest he be caught up in the delights of the world; and let him not live securely, as if he could remain in the house he inhabits; for he is a pilgrim, whose Father awaits him if he chooses to return to Him in the place where he knows He is. Therefore, O human, if you turn your eyes to the two roads, good and evil, then you will learn, for you will understand both great things and small. How? Through faith you know the One God, in His divinity and humanity; and in evil you see the Devil's works. And when you know the just and the unjust roads, I will question you: "Which road do you wish to travel on?" If you wish to travel in good paths, and if you faithfully hear My words, pray to God assiduously and sincerely to help you and not abandon you, since your flesh is fragile; and bow your head in humility, and shake off and quickly cast away from you such of your works as are evil.

God requires this of you. For what if someone were to offer you gold and lead, and say "Stretch out your hand for whichever you want"? You would eagerly seize the gold and leave the lead, for you love gold better than lead. So too you should prefer the country of Heaven to the downward slope of sin. But if you have fallen into sin, quickly rise by confession and pure penitence, before death lays claim to you. For your Father wants you to cry out, weep and ask for help so as not to remain in the squalor of sin. For if you have been wounded, you seek a physician lest you die. Does not God often send people troubles, so that they will more intently invoke Him? But you, O human, say "I cannot do good works!" I say you can. And you say "How?" And I say, "By thought and action." And you answer, "I lack decision." And I answer, "Learn to fight against yourself!" And you say, "I cannot fight against myself unless God helps me." Hear then how you can fight against yourself. When evil rises up in you and you do not know how to get rid of it, then, touched by My grace, which reaches you in the paths of your inner vision, at once cry out, pray, confess and weep so that God will help you, and remove evil from you, and grant you strength in good. For this good is yours by the knowledge that lets you understand God by the inspiration of the Holy Spirit. If you were someone's workman, oh, how often you would have to do what your body found difficult! Would you not bear many trials for the sake of your earthly wages? Then why do you not serve God, Who gave you both soul and body, for the sake of heavenly wages? For if you wanted to possess a temporal object, oh, how you would labor that you might have it quickly!

But now it wearies you to seek what has no end. As the ox is roused by the goad, so you should exert yourself in body for fear of the Lord; if you do, God will not cast you out. If some tyrant were to capture you, you would at once turn to anyone who could help you, and beg him, pray him and promise him your property if he would come to your aid. Do this also, O human, when iniquity captures you; turn to God, beg, pray and promise Him your reformation, and He will help you. But you, O human, are blind when you need to see, deaf when you need to hear and senseless when you need to defend yourself, since the intellect and the five bodily senses God gave you are no more to you than filth and emptiness. Do you not have intellect and knowledge? The Kingdom of God can be bought, but not acquired in jest. Hear therefore, O humanity, and do not despise entry into the heavenly Jerusalem, or touch death, or deny God and acknowledge the Devil, or increase in sins and diminish in good deeds. You do not wish to hear God, when you refuse to walk in His precepts, and you run to the Devil, when you seek to gratify the pleasure of your flesh. Recover therefore and be strengthened, for it is necessary for you.

So let the faithful person recognize his pain and seek a physician before he falls dead. If he considers his pain and seeks a physician, the latter when found will show him the bitter medicine that can save him; that is, the bitter words by which he must be tested to see whether his penitence comes from the root of his heart or only from his unstable breath. And when he has tested this, he will give him the wine of penitence, with which to wash away the pus from his wounds, and the oil of mercy, with which to anoint the wounds to heal them. Then he will enjoin him to be careful of his health, saying, "See that you keep taking this medicine carefully and regularly, and do not tire of it, for your wounds are serious." There are many who accept penance for their sins only with difficulty; but, though with much effort, they nonetheless carry it out for fear of death. But I give them My hand, and change their bitterness into sweetness, so that they may fulfil tranquilly that penance they began with such difficulty. But he who neglects repentance for his sins, saying it is hard for him to chastise his body, will be wretched, for he does not want to look at himself, or seek a physician, or have his wounds healed, but hides the dreadful wound in himself and covers over death with false appearances to conceal it. Thus he is averse to tasting penance, unwilling to look to the oil of mercy or seek the consolation of redemption; and so he will go into death, since he has loved death and not sought the Kingdom of God.

Therefore, O ye faithful, run in God's precepts lest the damnation of death seize upon you. Imitate the new Adam and cast off the old. For to him who runs, the Kingdom of God is open, but to him who lies on the ground it is closed. But miserable are they who worship the Devil, not knowing God. How? Because they do not adore one God in Trinity and do not seek to know the Trinity in Unity. So let the one who wishes to be saved be unwavering in the true Catholic faith. What is this?

31 On the Catholic faith

He who denies the Son does not worship the Father, and he who does not know the Father does not love the Son, and he who rejects the Holy Spirit has neither the Father nor the Son, and he who does not adore the Father and the Son does not receive the Holy Spirit. Therefore the Unity must be understood in the Trinity, and the Trinity in the Unity. O human, can you be alive without a heart and without blood? Even so it must not be believed that the Father is without the Son or the Holy Spirit, or the Son without the Father and the Holy Spirit, or the Holy Spirit without Them. For the redemption of humanity the Father sent the Son into the world and then took Him back to Himself, the way a person sends out the thoughts of his heart and then recalls them to himself. Wherefore Isaiah speaks of the salvific mission of God's Only-Begotten by the will of the Celestial Majesty, saying:

32 Words of Isaiah

"The Lord sent a word unto Jacob, and it has lighted upon Israel" [Isaiah 9:8]. Which is to say: The Lord, that is the Supernal Father, sent the Word by Whom all things were made, that is God's Only-Begotten, Who was in divinity in the Father's heart forever without any beginning, into Jacob through the mouths of the prophets; and they faithfully foretold that the same Son of God would come into the world for human salvation, so that people forewarned and strengthened by them could overthrow the Devil and wisely reject his crafty deceptions. And the same Word lighted upon Israel when the Only-Begotten of God came into the high fecundity of the Virgin, into which no man had penetrated but which had inviolably kept its flower, so that He, born of the Virgin, might lead back those who were erroneously blind to the light of truth into the true way.

Therefore whoever has knowledge in the Holy Spirit and wings of faith, let this one not ignore My admonition, but taste it, embrace it and receive it in his soul.

EVADING THE DEVIL'S DARTS

THE SYNAGOGUE

VISION FIVE
The Synagogue

A fter this, I saw the image of a woman, pale from her head to her navel and black from her navel to her feet; her feet were red, and around her feet was a cloud of purest whiteness. She had no eyes, and had put her hands in her armpits; she stood next to the altar that is before the eyes of God, but she did not touch it. And in her heart stood Abraham, and in her breast Moses, and in her womb the rest of the prophets, each displaying his symbols and admiring the beauty of the Church. She was of great size, like the tower of a city, and had on her head a circlet like the dawn. And again I heard the voice from Heaven saying to me: "On the people of the Old Testament God placed the austerity of the Law in enjoining circumcision on Abraham; which He then turned into sweet Grace when He gave His Son to those who believed in the truth of the Gospel, and anointed with the oil of mercy those who had been wounded by the yoke of the Law."*

1   The Synagogue is the mother of the Incarnation of the Son of God

Therefore *you see the image of a woman, pale from her head to her navel;* she is the Synagogue, which is the mother of the Incarnation of the Son of God. From the time her children began to be born until their full strength she foresaw in the shadows the secrets of God, but did not fully reveal them. For she was not the glowing dawn who speaks openly, but gazed on the latter from afar with great admiration and alluded to her thus in the Song of Songs:

2   Words of Solomon

"Who is this who comes up from the desert, flowing with delights and leaning upon her beloved?" [Song of Solomon 3:6, 8:5]. Which is to say: "Who is this new Bride, who with many good works comes up through the deserts of the pagans, who reject God's lawful precepts and adore idols, and ascends to heavenly desires, abounding in the delights of the gifts of the Holy Spirit, panting with great zeal and leaning on her spouse, the Son of God?" For it is she who blooms with the resplendent virtues given her by the Son of

God and flows with brooks of Scripture. And the same Synagogue, lost in admiration of the children of this new Bride, speaks thus by My servant the prophet Isaiah:

3 Words of Isaiah the prophet

"Who are these who fly like clouds, and like doves to their windows?" [Isaiah 60:8] That is to say: Who are these who, withdrawing themselves in mind from earthly and fleshly desires, fly full of desire and devotion to heavenly things, and with the simplicity of doves and without the bitterness of gall fortify their senses and with the great ardor of virtue seek the protection of that firm rock that is the Only-Begotten of God? For these are they who in supernal love tread underfoot earthly kingdoms and seek heavenly ones. The Synagogue therefore was marvelling at the Church, for she knew herself not to be adorned with those virtues she foresaw in her; for the Church is surrounded by angelic guardians to keep the Devil from harming her and casting her down, while the Synagogue, deserted by God, lies in vice.

4 On the varying color of the Synagogue

That is why *you see her black from her navel to her feet,* for from the time of her fullest strength to the end of her time she was soiled by deviation from the Law and by transgression of the heritage of her fathers, for she disregarded the divine precepts in many ways and followed the pleasures of the flesh. *Her feet are red, and around her feet is a cloud of purest whiteness;* for at the end of her time she killed the Prophet of Prophets and therefore slipped and fell down herself, while at the same time a most clear and acute faith arose in the minds of believers; for as the Synagogue ended, the Church arose, when after the death of the Son of God the apostolic doctrine spread throughout the world.

5 Her blindness, and why the prophets stand within her

That image *has no eyes, and has put her hands in her armpits;* for the Synagogue did not look on the true light, since she held the Only-Begotten of God in despite, and she conceals the works of justice under the apathy of her laziness, remaining in her torpor and negligently hiding them as if they did not exist. *She stands next to the altar that is before the eyes of God, but she does not touch it;* for she did in fact know superficially the Law of God, which she received by divine precept and divine visitation, but she did not plumb its depths, for she shrank from it rather than loved it, neglecting the sacrifice and the incense of devout prayers to God.

And in her heart stands Abraham; for he was the beginning of circumcision in the Synagogue; *and in her breast Moses;* for he brought the divine Law
into human hearts; *and in her womb the rest of the prophets;* that is, they stand
in that tradition that was given them by God as observers of the divine
precepts; *each displaying his symbols and admiring the beauty of the Church;* for
they displayed the miracles of their prophecies by marvelous symbols and
with great wonder waited for the noble beauty of the new Bride.

6   That she is as great as a tower and has a circlet like the dawn

The Synagogue *is of great size like the tower of a city,* because she
received the greatness of the divine laws and so foreshadowed the bulwarks
and defenses of the noble and chosen City. *And she has on her head a circlet
like the dawn,* because she prefigured in her rising the miracle of God's
Only-Begotten and foreshadowed the bright virtues and mysteries that followed. For she was crowned, as it were, early in the morning, when she
received the divine precepts, following Adam, who at first accepted God's
commands, but afterward by his transgressions fell into death. So also did the
Jews, who originally submitted to the divine Law, but then in their unbelief
rejected the Son of God. But as humanity in the last days will be snatched
from the perdition of death by the death of God's Only-Begotten, so too the
Synagogue, stirred up by divine clemency, will before the last day abandon
her unbelief and truly attain to the knowledge of God. How is this? Does not
the dawn rise before the sun? But the dawn recedes, and the sun's brightness
remains. How is this? The Old Testament receded, and the truth of the
Gospel remains; for what the early people observed in the flesh in legal rites,
the new people of the New Testament practice in the spirit, and what the
former showed in the flesh, the latter perfect in the spirit. For circumcision
has not passed away, because it has been transformed into baptism; as the
older race was marked in one member, the newer race is marked in all its
members. Hence the old precepts have not passed away but are transformed
into better ones; and in the last times the Synagogue will also transform itself
faithfully into the Church. For, O Synagogue, when you were wandering in
many iniquities, polluting yourself with Baal and the others, shamefully
breaking the custom of the Law and lying naked in your sins, I did what My
servant Ezekiel tells of, when he says:

7   Words of Ezekiel

"I spread my garment over you and covered your shame; and I swore to
you, and I entered into a covenant with you" [Ezekiel 16:8]. Which is to say:
I, the Son of the Most High, in the will of My Father have spread My

Incarnation over you, O Synagogue, to save you, taking away your sins, which you have committed in many times of forgetfulness; I have promised you the remedy of salvation, showing you the ways of My covenant for it when I made known to you by apostolic doctrine the true faith, so that you might obey my precepts as a wife ought to submit to the power of her husband. For I have taken from you the harshness of the exterior Law and given you the sweetness of spiritual doctrine and in it shown you all My mysteries in Myself; but you have deserted Me, Who am just, and allied with the Devil.

8   Analogy of Samson, Saul and David

But, O human, understand that Samson's wife left him, and so he was deprived of his eyesight, and the Synagogue likewise forsook the Son of God, spurning Him stubbornly and rejecting His doctrine. But later, when his hair grew again, as the Church of God was strengthened the Son of God in His might overthrew the Synagogue and deprived her children, who were crushed by God's jealousy by means of pagans who did not know God. For she had undergone many errors of confusion and discord, and polluted herself by wicked transgressions. But as David at last called back the wife he had first married, but who had polluted herself with another man, so also the Son of God at the end of time will call back the Synagogue, which had first been joined to Him in His Incarnation but had rejected the grace of baptism and followed the Devil, and she will forsake the errors of unbelief and return to the light of truth. For the Devil drew the Synagogue away in her blindness, and gave her over to error and unbelief; and he will not cease to do this until the coming of the son of perdition. But the latter will fall in the exaltation of his pride as Saul fell, slain on Mount Gilboa, after driving David out of his land; as the son of iniquity will try to drive out My Son in His elect. But My Son, when the Antichrist has been cast out, will call back the Synagogue to the true faith, as David took back his first wife after the death of Saul; for at the end of time the people will see the one who deceived them conquered and run back with great haste to the way of salvation. For it was not fitting for the truth of the Gospel to precede the shadow of the Law, as it is fitting that fleshly things should precede and spiritual things should follow; the servant announces his master's coming, and the master does not go before the servant to serve him. So too the Synagogue went before as a foreshadowing sign, and the Church came after in the light of truth.

Therefore whoever has knowledge in the Holy Spirit and wings of faith, let this one not ignore My admonition, but taste it, embrace it and receive it in his soul.

THE CHOIRS OF ANGELS

137

VISION SIX
The Choirs of Angels

*T*hen I saw in the secret places in the heights of Heaven two armies of *heavenly spirits who shone with great brightness. Those in one of the armies had on their breasts wings, with forms like human forms in front of them, on which human features showed as if in clear water. Those in the second army also had wings on their breasts, which displayed forms like human forms, in which the image of the Son of Man shone as if in a mirror. And I could see no other form either in these or in the others. These armies were arrayed in the shape of a crown around five other armies. Those in the first of these five armies seemed as if they had human forms that shone with great splendor from the shoulders down. Those in the second shone with such great brightness that I could not look at them. Those in the third had the appearance of white marble and heads like human heads, over which torches were burning, and from the shoulders down they were surrounded by an iron-gray cloud. Those in the fourth had forms like human forms and feet like human feet, and wore helmets on their heads, and marble tunics. And those in the fifth had nothing human in their appearance, and shone red like the dawn. And I saw no other form in them.*

But these armies were also arrayed like a crown around two others. Those in the first of these other armies seemed to be full of eyes and wings, and in each eye appeared a mirror and in each mirror a human form, and they raised their wings to a celestial height. And those in the second burned like fire, and had many wings, in which they showed as if in a mirror all the Church ranks arrayed in order. And I saw no other shape either in these or in the others. And all these armies were singing with marvellous voices all kinds of music about the wonders that God works in blessed souls, and by this God was magnificently glorified.

And I heard the voice from Heaven, saying to me:

1   God wonderfully formed and ordered His creation

Almighty and Ineffable God, Who was before all ages and had no beginning and will not cease to be when all ages are ended, marvellously by His will created every creature and marvellously by His will set it in its place. How? He destined some creatures to stay on the earth, but others to inhabit the celestial regions. He also set in place the blessed angels, both for human salvation and for the honor of His name. How? By assigning some to help humans in their need, and others to manifest to people the judgements of His secrets.

Therefore *you see in the secret places in the heights of Heaven two armies of heavenly spirits who shine with great brightness;* thus, as is shown to you in the height of secret places that the bodily eye cannot penetrate but the inner sight can see, these two armies indicate that the human body and soul should serve God, since they are going to have the brightness of eternal blessedness with the citizens of Heaven.

2   On the appearance of the angels and its meaning

And those in one of the armies have on their breasts wings, with forms like human forms in front of them, on which human features show as if in clear water. These are the angels, who spread the desires in the depths of their minds like wings; not that they have wings like birds, but that in their desires they are quick to accomplish God's will, the way a person's thoughts speed swiftly; and by their forms they display in themselves the beauty of reason, by which God closely examines human deeds; for as a servant who hears his master's words carries them out according to his will, so the angels pay attention to God's will for humans and show Him human actions in themselves.

3   On the appearance of the archangels and its meaning

And so those in the second army also have wings on their breasts, which display forms like human forms, in which the image of the Son of Man shines as if in a mirror. These are the archangels, who contemplate God's will in the desires of their intellect and display in themselves the beauty of reason; they magnify the Incarnate Word of God in the purest way, because, knowing God's secret decrees, they have often prefigured the mysteries of the Incarnation of the Son of God. *And you can see no other form either in these or in the others;* for in both the angels and the archangels there are many secret mysteries that the human intellect, weighed down by the mortal body, cannot understand. *But these armies are arrayed in the shape of a crown around five other armies.* This shows that the human body and soul must, by virtue of their strength, contain the five human senses, purify them by the five wounds of My Son, and lead them to the righteousness of governance from within.

4   On the appearance of the Virtues and its meaning

And so *those in the first of these five armies seem as if they have human forms that shine with great splendor from the shoulders down.* These are the

Virtues, which spring up in the hearts of believers and in ardent charity build in them a lofty tower, which is their works; so that in their reason they show the deeds of the elect, and in their strength bring them to a good end with a great glory of blessedness. How? The elect, whose inner understanding is clear, cast away all their wickedness of evil, being enlightened by these Virtues in the enlightenment of My will, and fight vigorously against the snares of the Devil; and these Virtues unceasingly show to Me their Creator these struggles against the Devil's throng. For people have within themselves struggles of confession and of denial. How? Because this one confesses Me, and that one denies Me. And in this struggle the question is: Is there a God or not? And the answer comes from the Holy Spirit Who dwells in the person: God is, and created you, and also redeemed you.

But as long as this question and answer are in a person, the power of God will not be absent from him, for this question and answer carries with it penitence. But when this question is not in a person, neither is the answer of the Holy Spirit, for such a person drives out God's gift from himself and, without the question that leads to penitence, throws himself upon death. And the Virtues display to God the battles of these wars, for they are the seal that shows God the intention that worships or denies Him.

5   On the appearance of the Powers and its meaning

Those in the second army shine with such great brightness that you cannot look at them. These are the Powers, and this means that no weak, mortal sinner can understand the serenity and beauty of the power of God or attain a likeness to it, for God's power is unfailing.

6   On the appearance of the Principalities and its meaning

Those in the third have the appearance of white marble and heads like human heads, over which torches are burning, and from the shoulders down they are surrounded by an iron-gray cloud. These are the Principalities, and they show that those who by God's gift are rulers of people in this world must assume the true strength of justice, lest they fall into the weakness of instability. They should contemplate their Head, Who is Christ the Son of God, and direct their government according to His will for human needs, and seek the grace of the Holy Spirit in the ardor of truth, that until their end they may continue firm and unshaken in the strength of equity.

7   On the appearance of the Dominations and its meaning

Those in the fourth have forms like human forms and feet like human feet, and wear helmets on their heads, and marble tunics. These are the Dominations; they show that He Who is the Lord of all has raised human reason, which had lain polluted in the dust of humanity, from earth to Heaven, when He sent to earth His Son and His Son in His righteousness trod underfoot the ancient seducer; and thus the faithful should faithfully imitate Him, Who is their Head, placing their hope in Heaven and fortifying themselves with the strong desire of good works.

8   On the appearance of the Thrones and its meaning

And those in the fifth have nothing human in their appearance and shine red like the dawn. These are the Thrones, showing that when for human salvation the Only-Begotten of God, He Who was uninfected by human sin, put on a human body, Divinity bent down to humanity; for He, being conceived by the Holy Spirit in the dawn, which is to say in the Blessed Virgin, received flesh with no spot of uncleanness whatsoever. *And you see no other form in them,* for there are many mysteries of the celestial secrets that human frailty cannot understand. *But these armies are also arrayed like a crown around two others.* This means that the faithful who direct their body's five senses to celestial things, knowing that they have been redeemed through the five wounds of the Son of God, attain with every turn and working of their mind, because they ignore the heart's pleasure and put their hope in inward things, to love of God and their neighbor.

9   On the appearance of the Cherubim and its meaning

Therefore, *those in the first of these other armies seem to be full of eyes and wings, and in each eye appears a mirror and in each mirror a human form, and they raise their wings to a celestial height.* These are the Cherubim, who signify knowledge of God, by which they see the mysteries of the celestial secrets and fulfil their desires according to God's will. Thus, possessing in the depth of their knowledge the purest clarity, they miraculously foresee all those who know the true God and direct their hearts' desires, like wings on which nobly and justly to arise, to Him Who is above all; and, instead of lusting after the transitory, love the eternal, as they show by the high-mindedness of their desires.

10   On the appearance of the Seraphim and its meaning

And those in the second army burn like fire, and have many wings, in which they show as if in a mirror all the Church ranks arrayed in order. These are the Seraphim, and this means that just as they burn for love of God and have the greatest desire to contemplate Him, they also by their desires display with shining purity the ranks, both secular and spiritual, which flourish in the mysteries of the Church, for the secrets of God show wondrously in them. Therefore all who, loving sincerity with a pure heart, seek eternal life, should ardently love God and embrace Him with all their will, that they may attain to the joys of those they faithfully imitate.

But you see no other shape either in these or in the others. This is to say that there are many secrets of the blessed spirits that are not to be shown to humans, for as long as they are mortal they cannot discern perfectly the things that are eternal.

11 All these armies sing of the miracles God does in blessed souls

But all these armies, as you hear, are singing with marvellous voices all kinds of music about the wonders that God works in blessed souls, by which God is magnificently glorified. For spirits blessed in the power of God make known in the heavenly places by indescribable sounds their great joy in the works of wonder that God perfects in His saints; by which the latter gloriously magnify God, seeking Him in the depth of sanctity and rejoicing in the joy of salvation; as My servant David, the observer of celestial secrets, testifies when he says:

12 The Psalmist on this subject

"The voice of rejoicing and of salvation in the tabernacles of the just" [Psalm 117:15]. Which is to say: The song of the gladness and joy of those who tread the flesh underfoot and lift up the spirit is known, with unfailing salvation, in the dwellings of those who reject injustice and do the works of justice; they might do evil at the Devil's temptation, but by divine inspiration they do good. What does this mean? Man often has inappropriate exultation at committing an improperly desired sin; but in that state he does not have salvation, for he has gone against the divine command. He, however, who strongly does the good he ardently desires shall dance in the true exultation of the joy of salvation, for while in the body he yet loves the mansion of those who run in the way of truth and turn aside from lying error.

Therefore, whoever has knowledge in the Holy Spirit and wings of faith, let this one not ignore My admonition, but taste it, embrace it and receive it in his soul.

Book Two

THE REDEEMER AND REDEMPTION

THE REDEEMER

147

VISION ONE
The Redeemer

*A*nd I, a person not glowing with the strength of strong lions or taught by their inspiration, but a tender and fragile rib imbued with a mystical breath, saw a blazing fire, incomprehensible, inextinguishable, wholly living and wholly Life, with a flame in it the color of the sky, which burned ardently with a gentle breath, and which was as inseparably within the blazing fire as the viscera are within a human being. And I saw that the flame sparked and blazed up. And behold! The atmosphere suddenly rose up in a dark sphere of great magnitude, and that flame hovered over it and gave it one blow after another, which struck sparks from it, until that atmosphere was perfected and so Heaven and earth stood fully formed and resplendent. Then the same flame was in that fire, and that burning extended itself to a little clod of mud which lay at the bottom of the atmosphere, and warmed it so that it was made flesh and blood, and blew upon it until it rose up a living human. When this was done, the blazing fire, by means of that flame which burned ardently with a gentle breath, offered to the human a white flower, which hung in that flame as dew hangs on the grass. Its scent came to the human's nostrils, but he did not taste it with his mouth or touch it with his hands, and thus he turned away and fell into the thickest darkness, out of which he could not pull himself. And that darkness grew and expanded more and more in the atmosphere. But then three great stars, crowding together in their brilliance, appeared in the darkness, and then many others, both small and large, shining with great splendor, and then a gigantic star, radiant with wonderful brightness, which shot its rays toward the flame. And in the earth too appeared a radiance like the dawn, into which the flame was miraculously absorbed without being separated from the blazing fire. And thus in the radiance of that dawn the Supreme Will was enkindled.

And as I was trying to ponder this enkindling of the Will more carefully, I was stopped by a secret seal on this vision, and I heard the voice from on high saying to me, "You may not see anything further regarding this mystery unless it is granted you by a miracle of faith."

And I saw a serene Man coming forth from this radiant dawn, Who poured out His brightness into the darkness; and it drove Him back with great force, so that He poured out the redness of blood and the whiteness of pallor into it, and struck the darkness such a strong blow that the person who was lying in it was touched by Him, took on a shining appearance and walked out of it upright. And so the serene Man Who had come out of that dawn shone more brightly than human tongue can tell, and made His way into the greatest height of inestimable glory, where He radiated in the plenitude of wonderful fruitfulness and fragrance. And I heard the voice saying to me from the aforementioned living fire: "O you who are wretched earth and, as a woman, untaught in all learning of earthly teachers and unable to read literature with philosophical understanding, you are nonetheless touched by My light, which kindles in you an inner fire like a burning sun; cry out and relate and write these My mysteries that you see and hear in mystical visions. So do not be timid, but say those things you understand in the Spirit as I speak them through you; so that those who should have shown My people righteousness, but who in their perversity refuse to speak openly of the justice they know, unwilling to abstain from the evil desires that cling to them like their masters and make them fly from the face of the Lord and blush to speak the truth, may be ashamed. Therefore, O diffident mind, who are taught inwardly by mystical inspiration, though because of Eve's transgression you are trodden on by the masculine sex, speak of that fiery work this sure vision has shown you."

The Living God, then, Who created all things through His Word, by the Word's Incarnation brought back the miserable human who had sunk himself in darkness to certain salvation. What does this mean?

1   On God's omnipotence

This blazing fire that you see symbolizes the Omnipotent and Living God, Who in His most glorious serenity was never darkened by any iniquity; *incomprehensible*, because He cannot be divided by any division or known as He is by any part of any of His creatures' knowledge; *inextinguishable*, because He is that Fullness that no limit ever touched; *wholly living*, for there is nothing that is hidden from Him or that He does not know; *and wholly Life*, for everything that lives takes its life from Him, as Job shows, inspired by Me, when he says:

2   Words of Job on this subject

"Who is ignorant that the hand of the Lord has made all these things? In His hand is the soul of every living thing and the spirit of all human flesh" [Job 12:9–10]. What does this mean? No creature is so dull of nature as not to know what changes in the things that make it fruitful cause it to attain its full growth. The sky holds light, light air, and air the birds; the earth nourishes plants, plants fruit and fruit animals; which all testify that they were put there by a strong hand, the supreme power of the Ruler of All, Who in His strength has provided so for them all that nothing is lacking to them for their use. And in the omnipotence of the same Maker is the motion of all living things that seek the earth for earthly things like the animals and are not inspired by God with reason, as well as the awakening of those who dwell in human flesh and have reason, discernment and wisdom. How?

The soul goes about in earthly affairs, laboring through many changes as fleshly behavior demands. But the spirit raises itself in two ways: sighing, groaning and desiring God; and choosing among options in various matters as if by some rule, for the soul has discernment in reason. Hence Man contains in himself the likeness of heaven and earth. In what way? He has a circle, which contains his clarity, breath and reason, as the sky has its lights, air and birds; and he has a receptacle containing humidity, germination and birth, as the earth contains fertility, fruition and animals. What is this? O human, you are wholly in every creature, and you forget your Creator; you are subject to Him as was ordained, and you go against His commands?

3 That the Word was and is indivisibly and eternally in the Father

You see that *that fire has a flame in it the color of the sky, which burns ardently with a gentle breath, and which is as inseparably within the blazing fire as the viscera are within a human being;* which is to say that before any creatures were made the Infinite Word was indivisibly in the Father; Which in course of time was to become incarnate in the ardor of charity, miraculously and without the stain or weight of sin, by the Holy Spirit's sweet freshness in the dawn of blessed virginity. But after He assumed flesh, the Word also remained inseparably in the Father; for as a person does not exist without the vital movements within his viscera, so the only Word of the Father could in no way be separated from Him.

4 Why the Son of God is called the Word

And why is He called the Word? Because, just as a word of command uttered by an instructor among local and transitory human dust is understood by people who know and foresee the reason he gave it, so also the power of the Father is known among the creatures of the world, who perceive and understand in Him the source of their creation, through the Word Who is independent of place and imperishable in His inextinguishable eternal life; and as the power and honor of a human being are known by his official words, so the holiness and goodness of the Father shines through the Supreme Word.

BOOK TWO

5 By the power of the Word of God every creature was raised up

And you see that *the flame sparks and blazes up*. This is to say that when every creature was raised through Him, the Word of God showed His power like a flash of flame; and when He became incarnate in the dawn and purity of virginity, it was as if He blazed up, so that from Him trickled every virtue of the knowledge of God, and Man lived again in the salvation of his soul.

6 God's incomprehensible power made the world and the different species

And the atmosphere suddenly rises up in a dark sphere of great magnitude. This is the material of Creation while still formless and imperfect, not yet full of creatures; it is a sphere, for it is under the incomprehensible power of God, which is never absent from it, and by the Supernal Will it rises up in God's great power in the twinkling of an eye. *And that flame hovers over it like a workman and gives it one blow after another, which strike sparks from it, until that atmosphere is perfected and so Heaven and earth stand fully formed and resplendent.* For the Supernal Word, Who excels every creature, showed that they all are subject to Him and draw their strength from His power, when He brought forth from the universe the different kinds of creatures, shining in their miraculous awakening, as a smith makes forms out of bronze; until each creature was radiant with the loveliness of perfection, beautiful in the fullness of their arrangement in higher and lower ranks, the higher made radiant by the lower and the lower by the higher.

7 After the other creatures Man was created from earthly mud

But then the same flame that is in that fire and that burning extends itself to a little clod of mud, which lies at the bottom of the atmosphere; this is to say that after the other creatures were created, the Word of God, in the strong will of the Father and supernal love, considered the poor fragile matter from which the weak frailty of the human race, both bad and good, was to be produced, now lying in heavy unconsciousness and not yet roused by the breath of life; *and warms it so that it is made flesh and blood,* that is, poured fresh warmth into it, for the earth is the fleshly material of humans, and nourished it with moisture, as a mother gives milk to her children; *and blows upon it until it rises up a living human,* for He aroused it by supernal power and miraculously raised up a human being with intelligence of body and mind.

8 Adam accepted obedience, but by the Devil's counsel did not obey

When this is done, the blazing fire, by means of that flame which burns ardently with a gentle breath, offers to the human a white flower, which hangs in that flame as dew hangs on the grass. For, after Adam was created, the Father in His lucid serenity gave to Adam through His Word in the Holy Spirit the sweet precept of obedience, which in fresh fruitfulness hung upon the Word; for the sweet odor of sanctity trickled from the Father in the Holy Spirit through the Word and brought forth fruit in greatest abundance, as the dew falling on the grass makes it grow. *Its scent comes to the human's nostrils, but he does not taste it with his mouth or touch it with his hands;* for he tried to know the wisdom of the Law with his intelligence, as if with his nose, but did not perfectly digest it by putting it in his mouth, or fulfil it in full blessedness by the work of his hands. *And thus he turns away and falls into the thickest darkness, out of which he cannot pull himself.* For, by the Devil's counsel, he turned his back on the divine command and sank into the gaping mouth of death, so that he did not seek God either by faith or by works; and therefore, weighed down by sin, he could not rise to true knowledge of God, until He came Who obeyed His Father sinlessly and fully.

And that darkness grows and expands more and more in the atmosphere; for the power of death in the world was constantly increased by the spread of wickedness, and human knowledge entangled itself in many vices in the horror of bursting and stinking sin.

9 Abraham and Isaac and Jacob and the other prophets drove back the darkness

But then three great stars, crowding together in their brilliance, appear in the darkness, and then many others, both small and large, shining with great splendor. These are the three great luminaries Abraham, Isaac and Jacob, symbolizing the Heavenly Trinity, embracing one another both by their works of faith and by their relationship in the flesh, and by their signs driving back the darkness in the world; and, following them, the many other prophets both minor and major, radiant with many wonders.

10 The prophet John, glittering with miracles, foretold the Son of God

And then a gigantic star appears, radiant with wonderful brightness, which shoots its rays toward the flame. This is the greatest prophet, John the Baptist, who glittered with miracles in his faithful and serene deeds, and pointed out by their means the true Word, the true Son of God; for he did not yield to wickedness, but vigorously and forcefully cast it out by works of justice.

11   At the Incarnation of the Word of God the great counsel was seen

And in the earth too appears a radiance like the dawn, into which the flame is miraculously absorbed, without being separated from the blazing fire. This is to say that God set a great splendor of light in the place where He would bring forth His Word and, fully willing it, sent Him there, yet not so as to be divided from Him; but He gave that profitable fruit and brought Him forth as a great fountain, so that every faithful throat could drink and never more be dry. *And thus in the radiance of that dawn the Supreme Will is enkindled;* for in the bright and roseate serenity was seen the fruitfulness of the great and venerable counsel, so that all the forerunners marvelled at it with bright joy.

12   Humans must not scrutinize God's secrets beyond what He wishes to show

But you, O human, who seek in the way of humans to know more fully the loftiness of this counsel, are opposed by a concealing barrier; for you must not search into the secrets of God beyond those things the Divine Majesty wills to be revealed for love of those who trust in Him.

13   Christ by His death brought back His elect to their inheritance

And you see a serene Man coming forth from this radiant dawn, Who pours out His brightness into the darkness; and it drives Him back with great force, so that He pours out the redness of blood and the whiteness of pallor into it, and strikes the darkness such a strong blow that the person who is lying in it is touched by Him, takes on a shining appearance and walks out of it upright. This is the Word of God, imperishably incarnate in the purity of unstained virginity and born without pain, and yet not separated from the Father. How? While the Son of God was being born in the world from a mother, He was still in Heaven in the Father; and at this the angels suddenly trembled and sang the sweetest praises of rejoicing. And, living in the world without stain of sin, He sent out into the darkness of unbelief His clear and blessed teachings and salvation; but, rejected by the unbelieving people and led to His Passion, He poured out His beautiful blood and knew in His body the darkness of death. And thus conquering the Devil, he delivered from Hell his elect, who were held prostrate there, and by His redeeming touch brought them back to the inheritance they had lost in Adam. As they were returning to their inheritance timbrels and harps and all kinds of music burst forth, because Man, who had lain in perdition but now stood upright in blessedness, had been freed by heavenly power and escaped from death, as through My servant Hosea I have stated thus:

14 Words of Hosea on this subject

"The iniquity of Ephraim is bound up; his sin is hidden. The sorrows of a woman in labor shall come upon him; he is an unwise son; for now he shall not stand in the contrition of the sons. I will deliver them out of the hand of death, from death I will redeem them. I will be your death, O Death; I will be your destruction, O Hell!" [Hosea 13:12–14]. What does this mean? The Devil's perverse iniquity is bound by heavy fetters, since he does not deserve that God's zeal should release him; for he has never rightfully acknowledged Him as do those who faithfully fear Him. For the Devil always raises himself against God, saying, "I am God!"; and he always goes astray over the Blessed One of the Lord, opposing the name of Christians because of Him. Thus his malice is so ingrained that his sin, cruelly committed in filthy pride, can never deserve by any reparation to be covered by salvation. Therefore he will be in perpetual pain, as a woman in labor is afflicted by despair when she doubts she can survive the opening of her womb. For this misery will remain with him, that he is forsaken by beatitude because the wisdom of the sons flees from him, and he does not come to himself, as that man came to himself who returned to his father from his wickedness.

Thus he will never stand trusting in that action by which the children of salvation in the Heavenly Son crush death in its hardened iniquity, which the cunning serpent brought forth when he suggested deceit to the guileless first man. But since those children despise the poison of that unclean advice and look to their salvation, I will deliver them from slavery to idols; for idols are by their deceptiveness in the power of perdition, and for them the unfaithful forsake the honor of their Creator, entangling themselves in the Devil's snare and doing his works at his will.

And so I will redeem the souls of those who love and worship Me, the Holy and the Just, from the pain of Hell; for no one can be released from the Devil's fetters, which bind him with bitterest death by his transgression of God's precepts, except by the redemption of Him Who will redeem His elect with His own blood. This is how I will slay you, O Death, with utter destruction, for I will take from you the thing you think to live by, and you will be called a useless corpse; at the height of your strength you will lie prostrate, as a corpse without the soul lies prostrate awaiting decay. For when the happy souls are mercifully raised up to celestial bliss through the new Man, Who will not be a party to poisonous deception, the fountain of living water will drown you. Thus also to your confusion I will be your destruction, O Hell!, when My strong power will take from you your ill-gotten spoils, so that you too, justly despoiled, will never again appear whole and laden with riches, but will lie prostrate and confounded forever, bearing wounds and decay.

15 The Son of God rising from the dead showed Man the way from death to life

And, as you see, *the serene Man Who has come out of that dawn shines more brightly than human tongue can tell,* which shows that the noble body of the Son of God, born of the sweet Virgin and three days in the tomb (to confirm that there are three Persons in one Divinity), was touched by the glory of the Father, received the Spirit and rose again to serene immortality, which no one can explain by thought or word. And the Father showed Him with His open wounds to the celestial choirs, saying, "This is My beloved Son, Whom I sent to die for the people." And so joy unmeasurable by the human mind arose in them, for criminal forgetfulness of God was brought low, and human reason, which had lain prostrate under the Devil's persuasion, was uplifted to the knowledge of God; for the way to truth was shown to Man by the Supreme Beatitude, and in it he was led from death to life.

16 The risen Christ appeared frequently to His disciples

But just as the children of Israel, after being liberated from Egypt, wandered in the desert for forty years before coming into the land flowing with milk and honey, so too the Son of God, rising from the dead, showed Himself for forty days to His disciples and the blessed women who wept and had a great desire to see Him. This He did to encourage them, lest they should waver in faith and say, "We did not see Him, so we cannot believe that He is our salvation!" He showed Himself to them frequently, to strengthen them that they might not fall.

17 When Christ ascended to the Father His Bride was given many ornaments

And He makes His way into the greatest height of inestimable glory, where he radiates in the plenitude of wonderful fruitfulness and fragrance. This is to say that the Son of God ascended to the Father, Who with the Son and the Holy Spirit is the height of lofty and excelling joy and gladness unspeakable;

where that same Son gloriously appears to His faithful in the abundance of sanctity and blessedness, so that they believe with pure and simple hearts that He is true God and Man. And then indeed the new Bride of the Lamb was set up with many ornaments, for she had to be ornamented with every kind of virtue for the mighty struggle of all the faithful people, who are to fight against the crafty serpent.

But let the one who sees with watchful eyes and hears with attentive ears welcome with a kiss My mystical words, which proceed from Me Who am life.

THE TRINITY IN THE UNITY

159

VISION TWO
The Trinity

hen I saw a bright light, and in this light the figure of a man the color of a sapphire, which was all blazing with a gentle glowing fire. And that bright light bathed the whole of the glowing fire, and the glowing fire bathed the bright light; and the bright light and the glowing fire poured over the whole human figure, so that the three were one light in one power of potential. And again I heard the living Light, saying to me:

1 On the perception of God's mysteries

This is the perception of God's mysteries, whereby it can be distinctly perceived and understood what is that Fullness, Whose origin was never seen, and in Which that lofty strength never fails that founded all the sources of strength. For if the Lord were empty of His own vitality, what then would have been His deeds? And therefore in the whole work it is perceived Who the Maker is.

2 On the Three Persons

Therefore you see *a bright light,* which without any flaw of illusion, deficiency or deception designates the Father; *and in this light the figure of a man the color of a sapphire,* which without any flaw of obstinacy, envy or iniquity designates the Son, Who was begotten of the Father in Divinity before time began, and then within time was incarnate in the world in Humanity; *which is all blazing with a gentle glowing fire,* which fire without any flaw of aridity, mortality or darkness designates the Holy Spirit, by Whom the Only-Begotten of God was conceived in the flesh and born of the Virgin within time and poured the true light into the world. *And that bright light bathes the whole of the glowing fire, and the glowing fire bathes the bright light; and the bright light and the glowing fire pour over the whole human figure, so that the three are one light in one power of potential.* And this means that the Father, Who is Justice, is not without the Son or the Holy Spirit; and the Holy Spirit, Who kindles the hearts of the faithful, is not without the Father or the Son; and the Son, Who is the plenitude of fruition, is not without the Father or the Holy Spirit. They are inseparable in Divine Majesty, for the

Father is not without the Son, nor the Son without the Father, nor the Father and the Son without the Holy Spirit, nor the Holy Spirit without Them. Thus these three Persons are one God in the one and perfect divinity of majesty, and the unity of Their divinity is unbreakable; the Divinity cannot be rent asunder, for it remains inviolable without change. But the Father is declared through the Son, the Son through Creation, and the Holy Spirit through the Son incarnate. How? It is the Father Who begot the Son before the ages; the Son through Whom all things were made by the Father when creatures were created; and the Holy Spirit Who, in the likeness of a dove, appeared at the baptism of the Son of God before the end of time.

3   People must not forget to invoke the One God in Three Persons

Hence let no person ever forget to invoke Me, the sole God, in these Three Persons, because for this reason I have made Them known to Man, that he may burn more ardently in My love; since it was for love of him that I sent My Son into the world, as My beloved John testifies, saying:

4   John on the charity of God

"By this the charity of God has appeared toward us: that God has sent His Only-Begotten Son into the world, that we may live by Him. In this is charity, not that we have loved God, but that He has loved us, and sent His Son to be a propitiation for our sins" [1 John 4:9–10]. What does this mean? That because God loved us, another salvation arose than that we had had in the beginning, when we were heirs of innocence and holiness; for the Supernal Father showed His charity in our dangers, though we deserved punishment, in sending by supernal power His Holy Word alone into the darkness of the world for the people's sake. There the Word perfected all good things, and by His gentleness brought back to life those who had been cast out because of their unclean sins and could not return to their lost holiness. What does this mean?

That through this fountain of life came the embrace of God's maternal love, which has nourished us unto life and is our help in perils, and is the deepest and sweetest charity and prepares us for penitence. How?

God has mercifully remembered His great work and His precious pearl, Man, whom He formed from the mud of the earth and into whom He breathed the breath of life. How? By devising the life of penitence, which will never fail in efficacy. For through his proud suasion the cunning serpent deceived Man, but God cast him into penitence, which calls for the humility the Devil did not know and could not practise; for he knew not how to rise up to the right way.

Hence this salvation of charity did not spring from us, and we were ignorant and incapable of loving God for our salvation; but He Himself, the Creator and Lord of all, so loved His people that for their salvation He sent His Son, the Prince and Savior of the faithful, Who washed and dried our wounds. And He exuded the sweetest balm, from which flow all good things for salvation. Therefore, O human, you must understand that no misfortune or change can touch God. For the Father is the Father, the Son is the Son, and the Holy Spirit is the Holy Spirit, and these Three Persons are indivisible in the Unity of the Divinity. How?

5   On the three qualities of a stone

There are three qualities in a stone and three in a flame and three in a word. How? In the stone is cool dampness and solidity to the touch and sparkling fire. It has cool dampness that it may not be dissolved or broken; solidity to the touch that it may make up habitations and defenses; and sparkling fire that it may be heated and consolidated into hardness. Now this cool dampness signifies the Father, Who never withers and Whose power never ends; and this solidity of touch designates the Son, Who was born of the Virgin and could be touched and known; and the sparkling fire signifies the Holy Spirit, Who enkindles and enlightens the hearts of the faithful. What does this mean?

As a person who in the body often touches the cool dampness of stone falls sick and grows weak, so one who in his unsteady thoughts rashly tries to contemplate the Father loses his faith. And as people build their dwellings and defend themselves against their enemies by handling the solidity of stone, so too the Son of God, Who is the true cornerstone, is the dwelling of the faithful people and their protector from evil spirits. And as sparkling fire gives light to dark places by burning what it touches, so also the Holy Spirit drives out unbelief and consumes the blight of iniquity.

And as these three qualities are in one stone, so the true Trinity is in the true Unity.

6   On the three qualities in a flame

Again, as the flame of a fire has three qualities, so there is one God in three Persons. How? A flame is made up of brilliant light and red power and fiery heat. It has brilliant light that it may shine, and red power that it may endure, and fiery heat that it may burn. Therefore, by the brilliant light understand the Father, Who with paternal love opens His brightness to His faithful; and by the red power, which is in the flame that it may be strong, understand the Son, Who took on a body born from a Virgin, in which His divine wonders were shown; and by the fiery heat understand the Holy Spirit, Who burns ardently in the minds of the faithful. But there is no flame seen where there is neither brilliant light nor red power nor fiery heat; and thus also where neither the Father nor the Son nor the Holy Spirit is known God is not properly worshipped.

Therefore as these three qualities are found in one flame, so Three Persons must be understood in the Unity of the Divinity.

7 On the three causes of human words

And as three causes for the production of words are seen, so the Trinity in the Unity of the Divinity is to be inferred. How? In a word there is sound, force and breath. It has sound that it may be heard, meaning that it may be understood, and breath that it may be pronounced. In the sound, then, observe the Father, Who manifests all things with ineffable power; in the meaning, the Son, Who was miraculously begotten of the Father; and in the breath, the Holy Spirit, Who sweetly burns in Them. But where no sound is heard, no meaning is used and no breath is lifted, there no word will be understood; so also the Father, Son and Holy Spirit are not divided from one another, but do Their works together.

So as there are these three causes for one word, the celestial Trinity is likewise in the celestial Unity. So as in a stone there exists and there operates no cool dampness without solidity to the touch and sparkling fire, or solidity to the touch without cool dampness and sparkling fire, or sparkling fire without cool dampness and solidity to the touch; and as in a flame there exists and there operates no brilliant light without red power and fiery heat, or red power without brilliant light and fiery heat, or fiery heat without brilliant light and red power; and as in a word there exists and there operates no sound without meaning and breath, or meaning without sound and breath, or breath without sound and meaning, but all keep indivisibly together to operate; so also these Three Persons of the true Trinity live inseparably in the majesty of the Divinity and are not divided from each other.

Thus, O human, understand the One God in Three Persons. In the foolishness of your mind you think that God is so powerless that He cannot truly live in three Persons, but only exist weakly in one. What does this mean? God is, in three Persons, the true God, the First and the Last.

8 On the unity of essence

But the Father is not without the Son, or the Son without the Father, or the Father and the Son without the Holy Spirit, or the Holy Spirit without Them; for these three Persons are inseparable in the Unity of the Divinity.

How? A word sounds from a person's mouth, but the mouth does not sound without a word, nor does the word sound without life. Where does the word stay? In the person. And from whence does it go forth? From the person. And how? Because the person is living. Thus the Son is in the Father, Whom the Father sent into the dark world for human salvation, conceived in the Virgin by the Holy Spirit. As the Son is the Only-Begotten in the Divinity, He is the only-begotten in virginity; as he is the Only One of the Father, He is the only-born of the Mother; as the Father begot Him before time began, the Virgin Mother bore the same Only One within time, and after childbirth remained a virgin.

Therefore, O human, in these Three Persons recognize your God, Who created you in the power of His Divinity and redeemed you from damnation. And do not forget your Creator, as Solomon urges you when he writes:

9 Words of Solomon

"Remember your Creator in the days of your youth, before the time of affliction comes, and the years draw nigh of which you shall say: They please me not." [Ecclesiastes 12:1] What does this mean? With your mental powers remember Him Who created you when, in the days of your false confidence, you think it is possible for you to walk according to your own desires, and raise yourself on high to throw yourself into the abyss, and stand in prosperity to fall into calamity. For the force of life in you always strives to perfect itself, until the time when it is complete. How? From birth a child grows up to full stature and remains an adult, leaving the mental license that is in foolish behavior and thinking carefully about how to manage his affairs, as he did not do in the foolishness of childhood. So let the person of faith do too. Let him leave childish behavior and grow up to fullness of virtue and persevere in its strength, leaving the pride of his desire, which pants after foolish vice; but let him with anxious care meditate what may be useful for him, though before he stooped childishly to childish ways.

Therefore, O human, embrace your God in the daylight of your strength, before the hour comes for the purgation of your works, when all things will be manifest and nothing will be overlooked, when the times come that will be complete and will never end; about which times your humanity murmurs a little, saying, "These changes do not please me, for I do not understand whether they will give me good fortune or calamity." For the human mind always wavers on this subject, since when it does good works it is anxious about whether or not they will please God, and when it does bad ones it is afraid to lose forgiveness and salvation.

But let the one who sees with watchful eyes and hears with attentive ears welcome with a kiss My mystical words, which proceed from Me Who am life.

MOTHER CHURCH

167

VISION THREE
The Church, Bride of Christ
and Mother of the Faithful

A *fter this I saw the image of a woman as large as a great city, with a wonderful crown on her head and arms from which a splendor hung like sleeves, shining from Heaven to earth. Her womb was pierced like a net with many openings, with a huge multitude of people running in and out. She had no legs or feet, but stood balanced on her womb in front of the altar that stands before the eyes of God, embracing it with her outstretched hands and gazing sharply with her eyes throughout all of Heaven. I could not make out her attire, except that she was arrayed in great splendor and gleamed with lucid serenity, and on her breast shone a red glow like the dawn; and I heard a sound of all kinds of music singing about her, "Like the dawn, greatly sparkling."*

And that image spreads out its splendor like a garment, saying, "I must conceive and give birth!" And at once, like lightning, there hastened to her a multitude of angels, making steps and seats within her for people, by whom the image was to be perfected.

Then I saw black children moving in the air near the ground like fishes in water, and they entered the womb of the image through the openings that pierced it. But she groaned, drawing them upward to her head, and they went out by her mouth, while she remained untouched. And behold, that serene light with the figure of a man in it, blazing with a glowing fire, which I had seen in my previous vision, again appeared to me, and stripped the black skin off each of them and threw it away; and it clothed each of them in a pure white garment and opened to them the serene light, saying to them one by one:

"Cast off the old injustice, and put on the new sanctity. For the gate of your inheritance is unlocked for you. Consider, therefore, how you have been taught, that you may know your Father Whom you have confessed. I have received you, and you have confessed Me. Now, therefore, behold the two paths, one to the East and the other to the North. If you will diligently contemplate Me with your inner vision, as in faith you have been taught, I will receive you into My kingdom. And if you love Me rightly, I will do whatever you shall wish. But if you despise Me and turn away from Me, looking backward and not seeking to know or understand Me, Who am recalling you by pure penitence though you are filthy with sin, and if you run back to the Devil as to your father, then perdition will take you; for you will be judged according to your works, since when I gave you the good you did not choose to know Me."

But the children who had passed through the womb of the image walked in the splendor that surrounded her. And she, benignly gazing on them, said in a sad voice, "These children of mine will return again to dust. I conceive and bear many who oppress me, their mother, by heretical, schismatic and useless battles, by robberies and murders, by adultery and fornication, and by many such errors. Many of these rise again in true penitence to eternal life, but many fall in false obduracy to eternal death."

And again I heard the voice from Heaven saying to me: "The great edifice of living souls, which is constructed in Heaven from living stones, is adorned with the immense beauty of its children's virtues, encircling them as a great city encircles its immense throngs of people, or as a wide net does a multitude of fishes; and however much the work of the faithful thrives in the Christian name, by so much does it blossom with celestial virtues."

1   The building of the Church, who redeems her children by Spirit and water

Wherefore now *you see the image of a woman as large as a great city;* this designates the Bride of My Son, who always bears her children by regeneration in the Spirit and in water, for the strong Warrior founded her on a wide base of virtue, that she might hold and perfect the great crowd of His elect; and no enemy can conquer or storm her. She expels unbelief and expands belief, by which it should be understood that in the mortal world each of the faithful is an example to his neighbor, and so they do great works of virtue in Heaven. And when the just, one by one, shall come to join the children of light, the good they have worked will appear in them, which cannot be seen here among mortal ashes, concealed as it is by the shadow of trouble.

2   The Church in her origin was adorned by apostles and martyrs

She has a wonderful crown on her head; for at her origin, when she was raised up by the blood of the Lamb, she was fittingly adorned with apostles and martyrs, and thus betrothed with true betrothal to My Son, since in His blood she faithfully formed herself into a firm edifice of holy souls.

3   The Church is adorned by the priesthood and almsgiving

And from her arms a splendor hangs like sleeves, shining from Heaven to earth. This is the work of power done by priests, who with purity of heart and hands and in the strength of good works offer the holiest of sacrifices upon the holy altar in the sacrament of the body and blood of their Savior. And the most glorious of their works is to show mercy, always offering generous help for every grief and distributing alms to the poor with a gentle heart while saying with their whole soul, "This is not my property, but that of Him Who created me." And this work, inspired by God, is before His eyes in Heaven, when by the teaching of the Church it is done among the faithful on earth.

4　On the maternal kindness of the Church

Her womb is pierced like a net with many openings, with a huge multitude of people running in and out; that is, she displays her maternal kindness, which is so clever at capturing faithful souls by diverse goads of virtue, and in which the trusting peoples devoutly lead their lives by the faith of their true belief. But He Who casts the net to capture the fishes is My Son, the Bridegroom of His beloved Church, whom He betrothed to Himself in His blood to repair the fall of lost humanity.

5　The Church, not yet perfected, will be brought to perfection near the end

She does not yet have legs or feet, for she has not yet been brought to the full strength of her constancy or the full purity of her fulfillment; for when the son of perdition comes to delude the world she will suffer fiery and bloody anguish in all her members from his cruel wickedness. By this calamity, with bleeding wounds, she will be brought to perfection; then let her run swiftly into the heavenly Jerusalem, where she will sweetly rise anew as a bride in the blood of My Son, entering into life with ardor in the joy of her offspring.

6　How the Church devoutly offers up her children in purity

But she stands balanced on her womb in front of the altar that stands before the eyes of God, embracing it with her outstretched hands; for she is always pregnant and procreating children of hers by the true ablution, and offering them devoutly to God by the purest prayers of the saints and the sweet fragrance of chosen virtues both hidden and manifest; which are plain to the clear understanding of the mind's eye when all stain of falsity and all noises of human praise are removed, as incense is purged of a noxious stench that corrupts its smell. This good work is in God's sight the sweetest sacrifice, at which the Church constantly labors, striving with her whole desire for heavenly things in bringing virtues to fruition, and by increase of such fruit thirtyfold, sixtyfold and a hundredfold building the high tower of the celestial walls.

7 No wickedness of devilish art can obscure the Church

And she gazes sharply with her eyes throughout all of Heaven; for her purpose, which she devoutly keeps to in the heavenly places, can be obscured by no wickedness: no persuasion of devilish art, nor error of a wavering people, nor storms over the various countries in which madmen tear themselves to pieces in the fury of their unbelief.

8 The human mind cannot fully understand the secrets of the Church

You cannot make out her attire, which is to say that the human intellect, weighed down by fragile weakness, cannot fully understand her secrets; *except that she is arrayed in great splendor and gleams with lucid serenity,* for the True Sun shines everywhere around her by the bright inspiration of the Holy Spirit and her most becoming adornments of virtue.

9 On the virginity of Mary

And on her breast shines a red glow like the dawn; for the virginity of the Most Blessed Virgin when she brought forth the Son of God glows with the most ardent devotion in the hearts of the faithful. *And you hear a sound of all kinds of music singing about her, "Like the dawn, greatly sparkling";* for, as you are now given to understand, all believers should join with their whole wills in celebrating the virginity of that spotless Virgin in the Church.

10 On the expansion of the sacrament of the true Trinity

And that image spreads out its splendor like a garment, saying that she has to conceive and give birth, which means that in the Church the sacrament of the true Trinity will more widely expand, for it is her garment in which to shelter the faithful peoples, through whom she grows by the building up of the living stones, who are washed white in the pure font; thus she herself affirms that it is necessary to salvation that she conceive children in blessing and bring them forth in cleansing, by regeneration in the Spirit and water.

11 The ministry of angels is at hand for each of the faithful

And at once, like lightning, there hasten to her a multitude of angels, making steps and seats within her for people, by whom the image is to be perfected;

because for each of the faithful there is at hand a fearsome and desirable ministry of blessed spirits; they are building stairs of faith and seats of sovereign quiet for those faithful souls, in whom that happy mother, the Church, will attain to her full beauty.

12   Those regenerated by the Church their mother in the faith of the Trinity

Then you see black children moving in the air near the ground like fishes in water, and they enter the womb of the image through the openings that pierce it. This signifies the blackness of those foolish people who are not yet washed in the bath of salvation, but love earthly things and run about doing them, building their dwelling on their unsteadiness; they come at last to the mother of holiness, contemplate the dignity of her secrets and receive her blessing, by which they are snatched from the Devil and restored to God. Thus they enter the confines of the churchly order in which the faithful person is blessed by salvation, when he says within himself, "I believe in God," and the rest of the articles of faith.

But she groans, drawing them upward to her head, and they go out by her mouth, while she remains untouched. For this blessed mother sighs inwardly when baptism is celebrated by the sacred anointing of the Holy Spirit, because the person is renewed by the true circumcision of the Spirit and water, and thus offered to the Supreme Beatitude Who is the Head of all, and made a member of Christ, regenerated unto salvation by invocation of the Holy Trinity. But in this that mother suffers no hurt, for she will remain forever in the wholeness of virginity, which is the Catholic faith; for she arose in the blood of the true Lamb, her intimate Bridegroom, Who was born of the untouched Virgin without any corruption of integrity. So too that Bride will remain untouched, so that no schism can corrupt her.

She will often, however, be bothered by the wicked, but with the help of her Bridegroom she will always most strongly defend herself, like a virgin who is often assailed by the cravings of desire through the Devil's art and the arguments of men, but pours out her prayers to God and is forcibly liberated from their temptations and her virginity preserved. So also the Church resists her wicked corrupters, the heretical errors of Christians, Jews and pagans, who infest her and try to corrupt her virginity, which is the Catholic faith. She resists them strongly, lest she be corrupted, for she was and is and will remain a virgin; the true faith which is her virginity keeps its wholeness against all error, so that her honor as a chaste virgin remains uncorrupted by any touch of lust in the modesty of her body.

And thus the Church is the virginal mother of all Christians, since by the mystery of the Holy Spirit she conceives and bears them, offering them to God so that they are called the children of God. And as the Holy Spirit overshadowed the Blessed Mother, so that she miraculously conceived and painlessly bore the Son of God and yet remained a virgin, so does the Holy Spirit illumine the Church, happy mother of believers, so that without any corruption she conceives and bears children naturally, yet remains a virgin. How is this?

13 Analogy of the balsam, onyx and diamond

As balsam oozes from a tree, and powerful medicines pour from an onyx vessel in which they are stored, and bright light streams without impediment from a diamond, so the Son of God, unopposed by corruption, was born of the Virgin; and so too the Church, His Bride, brings forth her children without being opposed by error, yet remains a virgin in the integrity of her faith.

14 The Trinity in baptism takes away black sins and confers a white garment

And you see how *that serene light with the figure of a man in it, blazing with a glowing fire, which you saw in your previous vision, again appears to you.* This means that the true Trinity in the true Unity is again shown to you to confirm your faith, as you saw it in that previous exceedingly true vision, with the serene Father and His sweet Son who was in divinity before all time in the Father, conceived within time in the flesh by the Holy Spirit and born of the Virgin. For in holy baptism Heaven opens and that Blessed Trinity appears to the baptized, so that the faithful person may receive the knowledge of how to worship the One God in the true Trinity, Which truly appeared in the first sacrament of baptism.

And it strips the black skin off each of them and throws it away; and it clothes each of them in a pure white garment and opens to them the serene light, speaking to them one by one words of blessed admonition. For the Divine Power, looking into human hearts, mercifully takes from them the crimes of their unbelief by the washing of baptism, and throws those crimes out of the Way, Which is Christ; for in Christ there is no death, but life through pure confession and the washing away of sins. Through Him each of them is clothed in the purity of salvation, and through Him the brightness of the blessed inheritance, from which the first human being was expelled, is opened to them. And each of the faithful is admonished by words of truth that he should lay aside the old ways of iniquity and accept the new gift of grace for salvation.

And the children who have passed through the womb of the image walk in the splendor that surrounds her; which means that they, who through the font of sacred baptism have the Church as their happy mother, should remain in and keep to the divine law by which that mother is illuminated and adorned, for if they renounce it by infidelity they will again be stained by the sins from which they had been cleansed.

15 On the Church's lament over the error of her children

So she, benignly gazing on them, says in a sad voice that these children of hers will return again to dust. For this blessed mother, loving them with deepest love and feeling their pain in the depths of her viscera, laments that they whom she brought forth in the washing of regeneration and who were made pure in the heavenly places have longed again for earthly things and become filthy with sin. How? Because many who outwardly receive the faith inwardly oppose it by various vices and tread the way of error instead of the way of truth. Many of them recover from this falsity, but many persist in wickedness; their mother shows this by her words quoted above.

16 Two signs are given to people with which to defend themselves

Two signs of the law for those who were signed were handed down and are known to humanity: circumcision among the ancient fathers, and baptism among the new doctors. By these people are guided like an ox by its yoke; for, though the ox is corrected by the goad, it would still make a crooked furrow if it were not bound to the yoke. Likewise, people would not go forward in My ways if they were not bound to the yoke of their signs.

17 Analogy of the young man

This would be as if a young man were to start off on a journey and his father were to say to him, "Go the right way," but not give him a sword or any weapons of war with which to defend himself. What would happen then? He would flee naked, neither daring nor able to defend himself from the danger that stands in his way and hinders his journey; and he would hide himself, not being signed with the fearsome armor that would have defended him. So would My people be naked if they were not baptized; but now they are fearsome to their enemies who see them signed with the anointing of baptism, by which they resist all who try to destroy them, whether it be a human throng or a devilish army.

18 Why the twofold law was not given to Adam

But the twofold law was not given to Adam. Why? I gave him a law about the tree when he regarded Me in the innocence of his heart. But he spurned Me and agreed with the cunning serpent, and that was so dangerous that no mortal eye will be able to see Me as long as it remains in this transitory world. And because Adam transgressed My precept, he and his race were without a law until the time that prefigured the nobility of My Son.

19 The ancient serpent was fought by Noah and Abraham and bound by the Church

But the warning of the Holy Spirit appeared in Noah as the human race was on the verge of perishing, when I raised the ark above the Flood. For before the ages I foresaw that this evil race, which had completely polluted itself with black wickedness, would have to be replaced by a new stock. For after the death of Adam, his progeny went astray, not knowing that I am God, saying, "Who is God? Who is God?" And then every evil arose in their midst, so that the ancient serpent slithered among them with unhampered power, persuading them to do all his will. He was then free from bondage in fetters, for before the Flood the warning of the Holy Spirit did not strike him; but I threatened him in Noah, from whom the new stock arose, for I so instructed My people that they could never forget the teaching.

Thus the warning of the Holy Spirit first threatened him in Noah, but then circumcision in Abraham struck him in the jaw; and at last the Church bound him in the last days, until the world passes away on the final day. I permitted the Devil to exercise his power in the world before the Flood because of the ancient contest in which he conquered Adam, until he had filled his belly with the carcass of all iniquity; and I allowed this because My judgment is just. Therefore I raised up the towering mass of the Flood and slew the sinners, but in My mystery preserved Noah, whom Satan could not despoil, because by My will he stayed above the Flood. And in the Flood I symbolized the righteous offspring, My Son, announcing to the new age that He Who would silently come into the world and make known the Holy Trinity was truly to be worshipped. How?

20 On the three wings and what they signify

He displayed three wings, which symbolize the Holy Trinity; for which you, O Synagogue, shall deny Me and an alien people shall receive Me, and for which you, O Abraham, shall be magnified. O Abraham, you are encircled with circumcision, you are walled round by the ancient covenant, and you are adorned with the dawn of the Church's sun. I gave circumcision to you and your race until the coming of My Son, who openly forgave the sins of humanity; but with Him the physical circumcision of the flesh of the foreskin came to an end, and in the sanctification of the washing of My Son, the true font of baptism poured forth.

21   Men who were uncircumcised in the time of circumcision were transgressors

But those of your race who in the time of circumcision were not circumcised when they were told to be, whether they were of lesser or greater age, transgressed the terms of My covenant; except women, on whom circumcision is not enjoined. For a woman is not to be circumcised, since the maternal tabernacle is hidden within her body and cannot be touched except as flesh embraces flesh; and also she is under the power of a husband like a servant under his master.

22   Adam's creation had three causes and so does a man who begets children

For a man has three causes for his act: desire, potency and zeal. His desire enkindles his potency, and thus in both the man and his work there is zeal to complete the work and burning will. In the same way there were three causes at work in the creation of Adam: God's will formed Man by means of His power and perfected Him in great loving-kindness in His own image and likeness. So in God's will note a parallel with a man's desire, and in God's power, a man's potency, and in the loving-kindness of God's will and power the zeal of the man's desire and potency.

In this way the human race is begotten by men on women, as God made humanity from the mud of the earth; and as the earth in its freshness is constituted to bring forth from seeds the fruits of the field, so women are to bring forth children in the waters of birth. What does this mean?

A woman from time to time becomes aware of moisture in her, which diffuses itself through her in the fluid of fertility with heat. Otherwise she would not willingly receive her husband, but refuse him and not consent to his will or procreate children. For if she did not have the fluid of fertility with heat, she would remain fruitless like dry ground, which does not yield itself to any fruitful use. But this fluid of fertility is not always inflamed into the ardor of desire in a woman, unless she has previously been touched by a man and so knows the passion of the ardor of desire; for desire in her is not as strong and burning as in a man, who is as strong as a lion in his desire for the deed of begetting. He, therefore, has the strength of the desire and the deed, and a woman's business is only to submit to the command of his will; she is then occupied with the procreation of her offspring until she brings them into the world.

23 A woman who is a virgin for the love of God is by God greatly ornamented

But she who desires My Son and wants to keep her virginity for His love is greatly ornamented in His nuptial chamber, for she sets at naught the burning she endures for the sake of His love, but perseveres in chastity, choosing not to be consumed by the fire of ardent lust; and in her spiritual marriage she despises [the idea of] a fleshly husband, and renounces the thought of one to strive with her whole desire after My Son. O dearest seeds, O flowers sweeter and more exquisite than any perfumes, whose soft fragility rises like the dawn to betrothal with My Son, loving Him dearly with chaste love; she is His bride and He is her Bridegroom, for this race of virgins loves Him dearly and is to be adorned in the Heavenly Kingdom with glorious ornaments! But what else?

24 A man who refuses marriage for love of God is a consort of the Son of God

And when the strength of a man refuses to lead a consort in marriage, so that the man for love of My Son controls himself in the vigor of his nature, whose fulfillment is the begetting of children, but he restrains his body so as not to fulfil the desires of the flesh; that this man conquers himself in this manner is extremely pleasing to Me. Therefore I make him too a consort of My Son and place Him like a calm mirror before his face, because he resists the Devil, who drew the human race to himself by filthy and wicked infidelity. To save humanity from this snare I sent My Son into the world, born of the sweet Virgin without any stain of sin; and that innocent Lamb brought and consecrated the font of salvation, abolishing in it the foreskin of the ancient sin. What is this?

This bitter foreskin is the crime of Adam's transgression, and My Son took it away, entering the font of salvation Himself and nobly setting apart the Christian multitude, that the ancient serpent who deceived humanity might in that same washing be drowned. How? The Son fulfilled the Father's terms, and took His inheritance. What does this mean? The race of Adam was driven for his transgression out of the place of delight, but in the baptism of salvation was recalled to life by My Son. How? He Himself spoke the words of blessing over the unbelievers who resisted My precepts, so that, terrified, they would seek pardon in a spirit of contrition, which My servant Isaiah testifies as I told him to, saying:

25 Words of Isaiah the prophet

"And the children of those who afflicted you shall come and bow down to you, and all who slandered you shall worship your footsteps" [Isaiah 60:14]. What does this mean? O You Who are celestial Peace and the purest Sun! By You shall burst forth the living root, which is regeneration by the Spirit and water, and those who had lain prostrate under the heaviest curse in the filth of horrible impurity shall come eagerly to acknowledge You; and thus bowed down, they will rise at last to truth and justice. How?

They will suck the maternal sweetness of the true faith, not knowing it by sight but grasping it by faithful belief. And who are they? Those who sprang in sin from a race that never saw You in Your burning charity but persistently afflicted and oppressed You as if You were not their destined ruler; but who came to their senses and most sweetly loved You.

And so when they come to follow the true faith they will accept You as King, and adore You as Lord and run swiftly in the holy paths You have shown them; they will gaze on You always with uplifted hands and keep constant vigil before You by good works, never growing weary of seeing You by faith; and all this will be done by those who formerly tore You without shame or reverence, and divided You in hatred and envy; but now they will embrace You ardently in the mirror of faith. What does this mean?

26 Heaven was closed to Man by Adam's fault until the Son of God came

The fall of Adam closed Heaven through My wrath; for Man spurned Me and listened to the cunning serpent, and therefore all the glory of Paradise was closed to him. This closure lasted until the coming of My noble Son, Who by My will entered the flowing Jordan, where My voice resounded mercifully when I said that He was My beloved Son in Whom I was well pleased. I willed this so that at the end of time I might redeem humanity through My Son, Who cleaves to Me in brightest warmth of love as the comb to the honey; therefore I sent Him into the font, which symbolizes Me the Fountain of living water, so that He Himself Who is the fountain of salvation might raise up those souls whom the Holy Spirit by water would redeem from sin and from eternal death. Wherefore the Holy Spirit appeared there too, for through Him remission of sins is given to the faithful; that is, in the mystical secret when My Only-Begotten was pointed out by the Holy Spirit in the form of a dove, which bird is of simple and honest behavior, and likewise the Holy Spirit is simple unfailing justice and goodness above all good. And this was fitting, for My Son was born of the Virgin without any stain of sin, and in baptism a person who is born with sin from a man and a woman is splendidly and gloriously born again without sin, as My Son says to Nicodemus in the Gospel:

27   Words of the Gospel

"Truly, truly I say to you, unless a man is born again of water and the Spirit, he cannot enter the Kingdom of Heaven" [John 3:5]. What does this mean? With firmest certainty and not with wavering doubt, I say to you who are born of filth that Man, risen out of burning heat and wrapped in a poisonous form, will be confounded by his apathy unless in the true joy of a new child he is born again from the water of sanctification and the spirit of illumination. How? Because Man, who overflows like water with the spirit of his enlivening, will not be able to enter into salvation as an heir to the Kingdom of his Creator unless he is purified by the true regeneration, as water cleans the dirty and spirit gives life to the inanimate; for he is guilty of the sin of the first parent, who was fraudulently deceived by the Devil. How?

As the thief who wishes to steal the King's most noble and precious possession sneaks in furtively, so the deceptive idea crept in by the maw of the Devil, by which he wickedly stole the beloved jewel of holy innocence and chastity in which dwelt the Holy Spirit; so it must now be cleansed by the holy ablution. For the death-bearing heat, which comes out of transgression of Almighty God's commands and is kindled by lust in the curdling of desire, must now be drowned in Him, Who never grudgingly hides His wonders, but generously shows them forth in infinite mercy.

28   Words of God in exhortation

Hear My Son, therefore, in this plan of regeneration, which is the revelation of My Kingdom; and learn from Him, that you may fulfil My precepts. Do this and so please Me, and beware lest the ancient serpent seduce you; and if you keep to your baptism, which was commanded for you in the name of the Blessed Trinity, you shall not die. And as often as you fall, rise again with greater penitence, in accordance with My mercy on your sins.

O you My dearest children, know the goodness of your Father Who by Himself has delivered you from the jaws of the Devil through pure confession and true pardon and given you all the good things with which to labor to possess the celestial Jerusalem, which you lost by crafty deception; for no one can seek out his lost inheritance except by the sweat of his labor. But you can easily receive supernal blessedness, your just inheritance, by a simple rule. For the Holy Spirit, as was said before, expels Satan's power from Man in baptism, sanctifying him as a new person in regeneration, so that he can receive his lost joys. Therefore, let anyone who desires to be saved not refuse to be regenerated for the purgation of his sins.

29 In circumcision one member was circumcised, but all members are in baptism

For to the men of the race of Abraham I gave circumcision in one member, but in My Son I commanded all men and women of all people to be circumcised in all their members. How? The circumcision of baptism sprang from the baptism of My Son, and so it shall remain till the last day, and then its sanctity will abide for eternity and know no end. And those who are thus circumcised in the washing of baptism will truly be saved, if they faithfully keep this washing by just works; for I will receive any person, whether of lesser or of greater age, who will keep My covenant, which he has made with Me, believing in Me and confessing the true Trinity either by himself or by those who speak for him, as an infant or a person unable to speak asks by another's mouth. And I will not destroy him in eternity, like one who refuses to receive this font and the works of faith, as is written in the Gospel in the teaching of My Son:

30 Words of the Gospel

"He who believes and is baptized shall be saved; but he who does not believe shall be condemned" [Mark 16:16]. What does this mean? A person who sees by his knowledge, which is his inner eye, what is hidden from his outer sight and does not doubt it, most certainly believes; and this is faith. For what a person perceives outwardly, he knows outwardly, and what he sees inwardly, he understands inwardly. Therefore, when human knowledge ardently perceives in the mirror of life the incomprehensible Divinity the outer eye cannot see, the lusts of the flesh are thrown to the ground and trampled on.

Thus the spirit of that person sighs for true loftiness and feels the regeneration brought by the Son of Man, He Who was conceived by the Holy Spirit, whose mother did not receive him from the flesh of a man, but from the mystery of the Father of all. And when He sweetly came He showed in water the pure and living mirror that makes Man live in regeneration. For as Man was born in the flesh when divine power created him in the form of Adam, so the Holy Spirit revives the life of the soul by the pouring out of water; It receives into Itself the spirit of the person, restoring him to life, as he is first brought into life on a wave of blood when he comes out of the vessel of the body. And just as a human form is then lovingly formed and called human, so now the soul of the person is vivified in water before the eyes of God, so that God knows that he is an inheritor of life.

Wherefore he who receives the font of salvation and the covenant of justice finds life in salvation, because he has faithfully believed. But he who does not will to believe is dead, for he does not have the breath of the Spirit with which to fly in the heights of Heaven, but gropes his way by touch with blinded eyes, and in the darkened knowledge of the flesh is not truly alive; for he lacks the vital teaching God has breathed into one who against the will of his flesh ascends on high. That person, then, will be condemned to the death of unbelief, because he did not have the washing of salvation. For I have not excluded any age or race from this salvation, but through My Son I have mercifully instituted this calling for all people.

31 God receives in baptism both sexes at all ages

For in whatever hour and of whatever sex or age a person may be, male or female, infant or decrepit, when he comes to baptism with loving devotion I will receive him with My merciful help. And I do not refuse the washing of baptism to an infant, as certain false deceivers declare who lyingly say I reject such an offering; as in the Old Testament I did not spurn the circumcision of an infant, though he did not request it with his own voice or receive it of his own will, but his parents supplied it for him.

So now in the new grace I do not reject the baptism of an infant, although he does not ask it by speech or by consent; his parents do this for him.

32 In honor of the Trinity there must be three present at the font

But if he wants to attain salvation, he should then in all justice fulfil the faithful promise that those who stood with him at the sacred font made for him. In honor of the Holy Trinity these ought to be three people, the priest who pours the water on him and the two who give the words of faith for him. But those who are thus joined to the baptized in the washing of baptism cannot enter into marriage relations with him, for they are joined to him by spiritual relationship. In the baptism of My Son, I the Father thundered, which the priest re-enacts when he gives the benediction for the washing; and the Holy Spirit was seen in the form of a gentle animal, whose place is held by the man who speaks to and teaches the person to be baptized in simplicity of heart; and My Son was present to be baptized in the flesh, which is symbolized by the woman who stands by in the sweetness of a nurturer in the place of the sweet Incarnation of My Only-Begotten. And what then?

33 Analogy of a baby

And as a baby is nourished in its body by milk and the food another grinds up for it, so also a baptized person must observe from his inmost heart the doctrine and the faith given to him in his baptism. But if the baby does not suck at its mother's breast or take the food ground up for it, it will die at once; and so also if a baptized person does not receive the nurturing of his most loving mother, the Church, or retain the words his faithful teachers proposed to him at baptism, he will not escape a cruel death for his soul, for he has refused his soul's salvation and the sweetness of eternal life. And as, when the baby cannot chew its bodily food with its teeth, someone else grinds it up for it to swallow lest it should die, so too in baptism, since it lacks words to confess Me, of necessity there are spiritual helpers there for it, who provide it with the food of life, namely the Catholic faith, lest it fall into the snare of perpetual death. How?

A master gives his orders to his servant in a commanding voice, and the latter carries them out in anxiety and fear; likewise a mother teaches her daughter charity, and the latter fulfils her words in obedience; and in the same way, let those who have vowed the faith offer the words of salvation at the proper time to the baptized person, that he may carry them out with faithful devotion for the love of Heaven.

34 In baptism all sins are remitted

No matter how grave are the sins with which a person is burdened, if he enters into holy baptism in the name of the sacred Trinity I truly efface all the crimes of his wickedness; as in an infant, when he is washed in the bath of regeneration, I truly take away the old sin of Adam. But do not marvel, O human, that in the font of baptism a person is justified of all his sins and mercifully relieved of their weight. For the innocent Lamb, who entered the font of baptism without any stain of sin, mercifully removes the evil of human sins in baptism by the great mystery of His Incarnation. But I perceive and scrutinize all things most keenly both in this world and in eternity, where there is no bodily death and all things are manifest. What does this mean?

Gehenna is tested by the works of death and eternal life by the works that pertain to life. How? Death is tested by death, for when a man dies by God's just judgment in his sins, without penitence and without mercy because he did not ask for it, his death is received into the deathliness of Hell. And Life is tested by life, so that good works shine in Heaven, for they are ruled by eternal life.

So also they who are baptized in the font of blessing are tested by the holiness of the second regeneration. And I am invoked by the benediction of the priest, so that My ears are attentive to the words of faith, even if he who invokes me is in the grasp of sin.

35 Even if a priest is a sinner, God accepts a baptism from him

For even if a priest is a sinner, I nonetheless accept the office of baptism from him, if he performs it faithfully by the invocation of My Name. His iniquity will condemn him if he perseveres in it without penitence. But I do not refuse to receive from him the celebration of baptism when he invokes Me with the words of faith. Why is this?

36 Analogy of the rich man

If a rich man has a steward who dispenses his goods justly to his dependents and so faithfully fulfils his duties, yet that steward is guilty in another deed, his master will not disdain to accept his duties from him; but he will say to him nonetheless, "Servant wicked in your deeds!" He will be indignant at him in his mind, but he will not disdain to accept from him the duties he performs with justice. So I too, Who have many stewards, do not refuse to receive My sacrament from a priest who is duly anointed and remains faithful to his duties, though he must be blamed for his other deeds; I judge him My enemy from his other unjust acts, but I do not disdain to receive from him what is Mine.

37 In a case of necessity, any person of faith may baptize

But if some person who is scheduled to be baptized thinks his separation from the body is near and asks for baptism, and a priest cannot be found to baptize him, if anyone pours the water on him with the invocation of the Triune Majesty, he is baptized; and he will receive the remission of his sins and the grace of heavenly blessedness through this pouring, for he has been washed in the Catholic faith, and this baptism cannot be changed.

But in this invocation no Person of the Three ineffable Persons can be omitted; for if due to unbelief one of Them is not invoked, the truth is not conferred by salvation but falsehood has caused deception. The invocation of the ineffable Trinity must not be lacking, for the Trinity was not lacking at the pure baptism of My Son, but there declared Its marvels wonderfully through Itself. Therefore, let those who want to be saved receive the regeneration of life unto salvation, and not neglect to receive it lest they perish; for, as an aborted fetus is rejected and perishes without the heat of life, and does not remain in its mother's womb either to be formed or to be quickened, so they who have nothing to do with the sacraments of the Church, the mother of all sanctity, either in mind or in deeds are in danger of death without the consolation of the Holy Spirit.

This let all peoples hear and understand who wish to enter the Kingdom of God in the regeneration of the Spirit and water, according to what is given to them in the holy Scriptures through the gift of the Holy Spirit.

But let the one who sees with watchful eyes and hears with attentive ears welcome with a kiss My mystical words, which proceed from Me Who am life.

CONFIRMATION

VISION FOUR
Confirmation

*A*nd then I saw the image of an immense round tower, all made of a single *white stone, with three windows in its summit from which shone so much brilliance that even the roof of the tower, which was constructed like a cone, showed very clearly in its light. These windows were adorned all round with beautiful emeralds. And the tower stood directly in back of the image of the woman described in the previous vision, just as a tower is placed in the wall of a city, so that because of its strength the image could not fall.*

And I saw those children who, as mentioned before, had passed through the womb of that image, shining with great brightness; some of them were adorned with gold color from their foreheads to their feet, but others lacked that color and had only the brightness. And some of these children were looking at a pure and brilliant splendor, but the rest at a turbulent red flash located in the East. Of those who were meditating on the pure and brilliant splendor, some had clear eyes and strong feet and were marching forward vigorously in the womb of the image; but others had weak eyes and crippled feet and were blown here and there by the wind. These, however, had a staff in their hands, and they flew in front of the image and touched it at times, though languidly. Still others had calm eyes but weak feet, and they moved back and forth in the air before the image; and others had weak eyes and strong feet, but they walked before the image languidly. But of the ones who were contemplating the turbulent red flash, some were well-ornamented and advanced into the image with vigor; but others tore themselves away from her and attacked her and broke her established rules. Among these, some by the fruit of penitence humbly returned to her, but others by obstinacy and neglect remained in the elation of the way of death. And again I heard the voice from Heaven saying to me:

1   Each baptized person should be anointed and confirmed by a bishop

After the illumination of baptism, which rose with the Sun of Justice Who sanctified the world by His own washing, the new Bride of the Lamb was adorned and confirmed in the fire of the ardor of the Holy Spirit for the perfection of her beauty. So also each of the faithful who is regenerated by the Spirit and water should be decorated and confirmed by a bishop's anointing, so that he will be strengthened in all his members toward achieving beatitude and find himself most perfectly adorned with the full fruits of highest justice.

Therefore, *this tower that you see* represents the flaming forth of the gifts of the Holy Spirit, which the Father sent into the world for love of His Son, to enkindle the hearts of His disciples with fiery tongues and make them stronger in the name of the Holy and True Trinity. Before the coming upon them of the Holy Spirit in fire, they were sitting shut up in their house, protecting their bodies, for they were timid about speaking of God's justice and feeble in facing their enemies' persecutions. Because they had seen My Son in the flesh, their inner vision was unopened and they loved Him in the flesh, and thus did not yet see the bright teaching that afterward, when they were made strong in the Holy Spirit, they spread abroad in the world. But by Its coming they were so confirmed that they did not shrink from any penalty, but bravely endured it. And this is the strength of that tower, which strengthened the Church so much that the insane fury of the Devil can never overcome it.

2 Confirmation confers the immense sweetness of the Holy Spirit

You see the tower as immense and round, all made of a single white stone. This means that the sweetness of the Holy Spirit is boundless and swift to encompass all creatures in grace, and no corruption can take away the fullness of its just integrity. Its path is a torrent, and streams of sanctity flow from it in its bright power, with never a stain of dirt in them; for the Holy Spirit Itself is a burning and shining serenity, which cannot be nullified, and which enkindles ardent virtue so as to put all darkness to flight.

3 In confirmation the Trinity manifests itself by verdant virtues

It has three windows in its summit from which shine so much brilliance that even the roof of the tower, which is constructed like a cone, shows very clearly in its light; for the ineffable Trinity is manifested in the outpouring of the gifts of the power of the Holy Spirit. And from the blessed Trinity so much clarity of justice emanates through the teaching of the apostles that in it the great power of Divinity, which in the height of its omnipotent majesty is incomprehensible, is shown more clearly to mortal creatures, that is, humans. But it can be grasped only as much as possible for the faith of a believing and faithful person.

Hence these windows are adorned all round with beautiful emeralds; for the

Trinity is declared openly throughout the world by the verdant virtues and tribulations of the apostles, which are never greeted with arid apathy. How? Because it is known how ravening wolves sought to tear apart the apostles for their faith in the truth, and these various calamities strengthened them for the struggle, so that by fighting they constructed the Church and strengthened her with strong virtues to build up the faith and adorned her with many brilliancies. And because the Church, through the inspiration of the Holy Spirit, has been so strengthened by them, she desires and asks that her children also be adorned in this anointing by the Holy Spirit, Which penetrated the hearts of the faithful in that high and mystical mercy when by the will of God the Father It came into the world in fiery tongues. Therefore, the person who was baptized with the baptism of salvation must also be confirmed by the anointing of that excellent Teacher, as the Church is confirmed on the firm rock.

4 How the Church, fortified by the Holy Spirit, can never fall into error

Hence the tower stands directly in back of the image of the woman described in the previous vision, just as a tower is placed in the wall of a city, so that because of its strength the image cannot fall. For the Holy Spirit has worked marvels in the exceeding strength of Him Who is the true Bridegroom of the Church, and It shows the Church to be so strong in her defenses that, because of the fortitude she derives from Its fiery gift, she can never be thrown down by any error of wickedness. Under heavenly protection she will always rejoice, without spot or wrinkle, in the love of her Bridegroom, because My Only-Begotten was conceived nobly by the Holy Spirit and born without stain of the Virgin, as I said to Moses:

5 Words of Moses on this subject

"Behold, He said, there is a place with Me, and you shall stand upon the rock. And when My glory shall pass by, I will set you in a hole of the rock and protect you with My right hand, until I pass. And I will take away My hand, and you shall see My back parts" [Exodus 33:21–23]. What does this mean? The miracle is at hand that will be fulfilled in My will. But first you will fight with harsh legal precepts whose force is in their outward significance and where you will not find the sweetness and gentleness that will be revealed in My Son. And this harshness of the Law, which by My command you will write down, will stand in hard and stony hearts until you and your followers have shown all the glory that is to be rendered to Me until the coming of My Son. And when this is fulfilled in the Law you are writing, I will be glorified, and I will place you inside the pierced rock. How? I will place you in the hardness of the Law, appointing you to be over it as master of the old times, which will be pierced by My Son, when I send Him into the world at the right time and He expounds it farther than you have in His mystical words. So His strength will protect you, for He will bring words more acute than yours; and He will open the Law's commands that are now closed until He returns to Me. What does this mean?

He, taking on a body from the Virgin, will in that body give words of salvation to the world until in it He passes through death. Then I will take away My hand, when I lift Him up to Me above the stars and lay bare all His mysteries through the Holy Spirit; and thus you will see His Incarnation as a person is seen from the back and not the front, seeing Him when incarnate but not grasping His Divinity. For your children will see him when he returns to Me, more than they understood Him when He lived visibly among them.

6 The baptized are adorned when they are anointed by the bishop

And you see those children who, as mentioned before, had passed through the womb of that image, shining with great brightness. These are they who in the innocence of a clean and pure heart have gained a mother, the Church, in the font of regeneration, as was shown to you before, and are children of light, for their sins are washed away. *Some of them are adorned with gold color from their foreheads to their feet;* for from their beginning in good works to their end in sanctity, they are adorned with the shining gifts of the Holy Spirit by their anointing with chrism in the true faith at the hand of the bishop. How? Just as gold is adorned by having precious stones set into it, so baptism is adorned with the chrism given to those baptized in faith by the hand of the bishop, as it is written:

7 Words of the Book of Kings on this subject

"The King went over the brook of Cedron, and all the people marched toward the way of the olive trees, which led to the desert" [2 Kings 15:23]. What does this mean? The Son of the Virgin, who rules the whole world like an earthly king, left the people behind and went into the flowing waters of the blessed washing, which by the teaching of the Holy Spirit shows the way of salvation to one of strong desire. What does this mean? Christ left death and crossed over to life, revealing supreme beatitude in the regeneration by the Spirit and water, which are the great ornaments of the celestial Jerusalem, which never ends. Therefore all the people who believed in Him, by the inspiration of the Holy Spirit, went by the anointing with oil to the way that had been hidden; and they looked out over the desert of Adam's sin, which bore no trace of the beauty of God's just inheritance, and considered whether or not that way led back to salvation. For the wound of the first man's sin required that he be anointed by the office of the priest; this was not required for the Son of the Virgin, since He was wholly conceived in sanctity and His mother's womb was not wounded or corrupted but remained whole.

But whatever is weakened and confounded by the wounds of the Devil's advice must be strengthened and adorned by the anointing of oil, that the gaping bloody wound of fleshly desire may be wiped clean.

8   Those baptized but not confirmed have light but not adornment

But others, as you see, lack that color and have only the brightness. For, having been cleansed only by the ablution of baptism, they lack the anointing with chrism by the bishop, which is the sign of the ardent Holy Spirit. What does this mean? The anointing with the gifts of the Holy Spirit by confirmation is the special ability of the episcopal office, which is to be done among the faithful after the regeneration of the Spirit and water, to found the believer upon a firm rock. How? My Son received baptism in His body and thus sanctified it by His flesh, which was not divided, for He alone is the Son of the Virgin, and therefore is called the Son of Man, but the Virgin did not conceive him by a man but gave birth to him with unbroken virginity. After the affliction of His Passion and the glory of His Resurrection, in that same flesh He entered Heaven and returned to Me; and then the Holy Spirit illuminated the world in fiery ardor, confirming all justice in the hearts of His disciples and revealing to them what had before been hidden. How?

The Holy Spirit enkindled their hearts as the sun, beginning to appear from around a cloud, shows its burning heat by its shining light. What does this mean? Love of My Son was secretly burning in their minds, and thus the fire of the Holy Spirit passed through them and showed the bright sunlight of their teaching. For this is the testimony the Holy Spirit gave to the Church, that death cannot resist the justice of God.

9   Confirmation should be conferred by bishops alone

Therefore, O children of Truth, hear and understand the confirmation of the Holy Spirit, which He offers you in the sweet unction of His teaching, being Himself the master of all anointing. This anointing, therefore, in honor of the Holy Spirit should be conferred only by the bishop. For every ecclesiastical order is instituted in the Holy Spirit, and therefore this anointing is of the Holy Spirit.

Therefore, a person who has received the mystery of regeneration unto life has not taken possession of the fullness of churchly ornaments unless he is anointed in this way, as the Church is adorned by the glorious Holy Spirit. And as the Church is perfected by the gifts of the Holy Spirit, a believer ought to be confirmed by the anointing of the bishop, who is the reverend master in the honor of the Holy Spirit; for the Holy Spirit by Its fire brings forth and kindles sure doctrine in the Christian people.

10 The one confirmed may not marry those who held his hands

Hence those who stood by the one anointed in this unction by the Holy Spirit may not enter into earthly conjugal relations with that person, to whom they are joined in the Holy Spirit. What does this mean? Faith brings a person to this anointing, and the one who then holds his hands symbolizes faith, which does not seek the things of the flesh but always goes toward the things of the spirit. For My eye sees a person as he will be when he comes to Me in his deeds.

11 One who returns to the Devil after baptism is condemned unless he repents

But if, O human, you forsake Me after baptism and return to the Devil, by My just judgment you shall be condemned for it, since I gave you the great gift of intellect and showed you My mercy in the font of baptism. For all who ask for My mercy in baptism will find it freely, for the sake of My Son Who came into the world and endured many labors in the body; therefore, O human, you should patiently endure the conflicts of your soul and body, and for My Son's sake I will receive you.

And no one must be turned away from the washing of baptism if he faithfully seeks it in My name, for I receive a person ardently at whatever time he seeks Me. But if his works thereafter are wicked, they condemn him to death. Therefore, O human, be cleansed in the regeneration of salvation and be anointed in the unction of holiness, and flee death and seek life. For the Church, mother of the faithful, prays constantly that her children may escape death and find life. How? God gave her a voice to supplicate for her children until the full number of them enter the tabernacle of the celestial city. And she has such a voice to tell Me Who am before all ages always to see and think of My Only-Begotten's Incarnation, so that for love of Him I may spare her children, whom she received in the regeneration of the Spirit and water. For unless they are saved they cannot enter the heavenly kingdom.

12 Three ways in which the Church resounds like a trumpet

Therefore she cries out, "Fear the Father, love the Son, burn in the Holy Spirit!" How? This cry is given to her by Me the Father in the Son through the Holy Spirit; it is the voice resounding in her like a trumpet in a city. And she speaks in her children no other way than this. Therefore, Omnipotent God is reminded by His Son to spare human sins, which by their penitence can be forgiven without their damnation, because the Son of God took on humanity without sin. Because God is just and the splendor of Heaven is not touched by any unclean stain, He was not clothed with polluted flesh conceived by the seed of sin; and how should Man, stained with immense foulness, enter the Kingdom of Heaven unless through My Son, incarnate without uncleanness? He receives sinners who are purified by penitence; and who could do this except God? Hence the Church too turns back to her children and cherishes them with maternal love.

13 On the many differences among the baptized

And you see that *some of these children are looking at a pure and brilliant splendor, but the rest at a turbulent red flash located in the East.* This means that among the children of the Church, whom she procreates by the power of God in the innocence of her incorruption, some direct their attention to spiritual purity and shine with serene virtue, treading earthly things underfoot for love of the true Sun; but others have bodily senses that different vices throw into disorder, yet they too burn for the true faith and aspire to eternity for the supernal reward. *Of those who are meditating on the pure and brilliant splendor, some have clear eyes and strong feet and are marching forward vigorously in the womb of the image;* for when they pursue celestial things they fix their just thoughts on God's commandments and direct their footsteps toward the good end, and thus walk in the close embrace of their mother's love, lessening their devotion neither in temporary nor in eternal things.

But others have weak eyes and crippled feet, for they do not hold to a clear purpose nor a strong performance in the work of perfection. Therefore *they are blown here and there by the wind,* for they are thrown into unstable conduct by various prideful temptations.

But these have a staff in their hands, and they fly in front of the image and touch it at times, though languidly; for they place obstinate confidence in their works, show themselves to the Church of God with empty pomp, and fatuously attend to her from time to time for reasons of worldly prudence. But when by this false pretense they appear wise in the sight of humans, before God they appear as vainglorious fools.

Still others have calm eyes but weak feet, and they move back and forth in the air before the image; the divine commands are known to them through their insight in contemplation, but they are lame in the feet of fulfillment, and thus they appear before the Bride of Christ in restless instability. Seeking wisdom in the dark, and thinking they have it before it has really taken hold on their minds, they derive no power from it.

Others have weak eyes and strong feet, but they walk before the image languidly; for they hold onto a mild inclination toward good works, when they should be advancing more vigorously in deeds of justice, but they do not go in the ways of the Church, for they fix their minds on earthly things more than heavenly. Therefore they are foolish before God, for they wish to grasp by worldly prudence what they cannot attain.

But of the ones who contemplate the turbulent red flash, some are well-ornamented and advance into the image with vigor; for these, though they possess earthly things, carry their beautiful works nonetheless into the very heart of the Church; they do not disdain to set the foot of righteousness in the divine law, but obey God's commandments, and receive strangers, clothe the naked and feed the hungry. Oh, how happy they are, since thus they receive God, and He Himself dwells with them!

But others tear themselves away from her and attack her and break her established rules. They abandon the maternal womb and the sweet nourishment of the Church and trouble her with many errors, and with different oppressions tear to pieces her laws, which God established. *Among these, some by the fruit of penitence humbly return to her;* for their grave offenses they inflict grave punishments on themselves by doing worthy penance for the restoration of life. *But others by obstinacy and neglect remain in the elation of the way of death;* for they reject life and receive the judgment of death for their hard hearts and contumacious folly. As Ezekiel says in his mystical vision:

14   Words of Ezekiel

"The King shall mourn, and the prince shall be clothed with sorrow, and the hands of the people of the land shall be troubled. I will do to them according to their way, and I will judge them according to their judgments, and they shall know that I am the Lord" [Ezekiel 7:27]. What does this mean? The soul in which Reason is king, feeling the pleasure of sin at hand, assents to it mournfully because it knows the evil of it. How? Because its reason, wisdom and knowledge are inspired by God; and thus, though the body consents, it finds the evil shameful, knowing that it is not good.

Therefore, when it is polluted with many crimes by the acts of the flesh, it heaves deep sighs and yearns for God. And when in the breath of pride the sinful deed is done, the body is clothed with confusion like an unworthy prince, having exercised its sovereignty in uncleanness; for as a person grieves when clothed in vile garments, so also he is sad when a shameful reputation originates, to his confusion, in himself. Therefore the bad deeds of those prostrate in their evils on the ground will be confounded by heavenly commands, for such do not have the garments of salvation, which is beatitude with God; and evil confusion will possess those who lack this happiness. And so I will deal with them in the road of iniquity in which they stand, honoring the path of sin and putting no justice into their hearts though warned by the Holy Spirit; I will grant them no mercy, because they do not know the good or fear Me, but disdain Me, the Creator of all, with raging wickedness, and do whatever they like.

Therefore I will judge them according to their own judgments, which are the works they desire and do; I will give them no rewards of happiness, but set the punishment of damnation in their way, since they show Me no honor; and they shall know that no one can free them from it except Me, the Lord of all.

But let the one who sees with watchful eyes and hears with attentive ears welcome with a kiss My mystical words, which proceed from Me Who am life.

THE MYSTICAL BODY

199

VISION FIVE
The Three Orders in the Church

*A*fter this I saw that a splendor white as snow and translucent as crystal had shone around the image of that woman from the top of her head to her throat. And from her throat to her navel another splendor, red in color, had encircled her, glowing like the dawn from her throat to her breasts and shining from her breasts to her navel mixed with purple and blue. And where it glowed like the dawn, its brightness shone forth as high as the secret places of Heaven; and in this brightness appeared a most beautiful image of a maiden, with bare head and black hair, wearing a red tunic, which flowed down about her feet.

And I heard the voice from Heaven saying, "This is the blossom of the celestial Zion, the mother and flower of roses and lilies of the valley. O blossom, when in your time you are strengthened, you shall bring forth a most renowned posterity."

And around that maiden I saw standing a great crowd of people, brighter than the sun, all wonderfully adorned with gold and gems. Some of these had their heads veiled in white, adorned with a gold circlet; and above them, as if sculpted on the veils, was the likeness of the glorious and ineffable Trinity as it was represented to me earlier, and on their foreheads the Lamb of God, and on their necks a human figure, and on the right ear cherubim, and on the left ear the other kinds of angels; and from the likeness of the glorious and supernal Trinity golden rays extended to these other images. And among these people there were some who had miters on their heads and pallia of the episcopal office around their shoulders.

And again I heard the voice from on high, saying, "These are the daughters of Zion, and with them the harps of the harpers and all sorts of musical instruments, and the voice of all gladness, and the joy of joys."

But beneath that splendor, which glowed like the dawn, I saw between Heaven and earth a thick darkness appear, the horror of which exceeded what human tongue can utter.

And again I heard the voice from Heaven saying, "If the Son of God had not suffered on the cross, this darkness would mean that no person could attain celestial glory."

And where the splendor shone, which was mixed with purple and blue, it encircled the woman's image with strong ardor. But another splendor, like a white cloud, decently enveloped that image from the navel down, to the point at which it had not yet grown further. And these three splendors around that image shone afar, showing that within her many steps and ladders were well and properly placed.

And when I saw these things, I was seized with extreme trembling; my strength failed me, and I fell to the ground, unable to speak. And behold! A great splendor touched me like a hand, and I recovered my strength and voice. And from that splendor again I heard a voice, saying;

"These are great mysteries. For consider the sun and the moon and the stars. I formed the sun to give light by day, and the moon and stars to give light by night. The sun symbolizes My Son, Who went forth from My heart and illuminated the world when in the latest times He was born of the Virgin, as the sun goes forth and lights the world when it rises at the end of the night. And the moon symbolizes the Church, betrothed to My Son in true and celestial betrothal. And as the moon is so made that it always increases and decreases, but does not burn of itself unless it is kindled by the light of the sun, so too the Church has a cycle of movement: her children sometimes rise in increase of virtues and sometimes decline by inconstant behavior or harm by outside forces. For she is often assailed in her mysteries by ravening wolves, that is to say malicious people, whether bad Christians or Jews or pagans; and she is not fired to endurance by herself, but lit up by Me through My Son to persevere in good. But the stars, which differ from each other in the brightness of their glory, symbolize the people in the differing religious orders of the Church."

1 Apostles and their followers, the priests, surround the Church with teaching

Thus you see that *a splendor white as snow and translucent as crystal shines around the image of that woman from the top of her head to her throat.* For the Church, who is the incorrupt Bride, is surrounded by apostolic teaching, which reveals the pure Incarnation of Him Who descended from Heaven into the Virgin's womb and Who is the strong and clear mirror of all the faithful. And this teaching, which shines so brightly around the Church, constantly surrounded her from the start, from the time she first began to be built until she attained the strength to swallow the food of life. How?

The apostolic teaching shone around the head of the Church when the apostles first began to build her up by their preaching; moving through different places, they collected workers who would strengthen her in the Catholic faith and make themselves into priests and bishops and all the ecclesiastical orders, to establish faithfully the rights of men and women who married and all other such institutions. Therefore, the chrism-makers [bishops and priests] conform to that teaching; they are like the priests of the

Testament of the Law, who were appointed to nourish the multitudes with inner food under the law of circumcision. Hence also the apostles chose those orders with which, by heavenly inspiration, they adorned the Church. What does this mean?

That their followers, who took their places, faithfully traverse streets and farms and cities and other places, regions and lands, carrying the health-giving chrisms and announcing the divine law to the people. For they are fathers and stewards, carefully chosen to make church rules known to the people by their teaching and to distribute to them the food of life; and therefore they must show themselves such in their lives that My sheep will not be offended by their works, but walk uprightly after them. For they have this office that they may openly serve the bread of life to the people, and for each one individually set in order the duties of faith; therefore they must so restrain themselves as not to desire carnal union, since they must give the spiritual food to believers and offer to God the spotless sacrifice prefigured in innocent Abel. For of him it is written:

2 Example of Abel

"Abel also offered of the firstlings of his flock, and of their fat." [Genesis 4:4] What does this mean? That at the beginning of time there shone forth in him, who was innocent in his life, a blessed and kingly manifestation, which by God's gift touched not earth but Heaven. How? Because Abel in his integrity offered to God the purpose and the full service of his will, resolving in his heart to offer Him the first increase of his substance and successfully doing so, thus honoring the Supreme Father and showing Him proper reverence.

So, as Abel was in charge of his flock, pasturing and guarding it and with simple devotion offering its increase and its fatty nourishment to God, let the aforementioned chrism-makers, who are set over the children of the Church, who are the sheep of Christ, pasture them according to His plan, faithfully nourish them by their words, teaching them the church rules, and protect them forcefully from the snares of the ancient waylayer, and offer gifts from some of them, with sincere reflection, to the Observer of all. How?

If they cannot make them perfect in all respects, let them nonetheless offer to God some fruit that comes from them: first, like the increase of the firstborn of the flock, their good intentions, and then, like the sweet fruit of its fatlings, the perfect work of activity in their will. But why did Abel worship God so devoutly? The fact is that the wholeness of his chastity impelled him to such great devotion.

3 The ministers of the Church must keep their chastity

Therefore let those who are appointed by consecration to offer to God the sacred sacrifice approach His altar in the sweetness of chastity. For if they themselves are authors of corruption, how can they offer to others wounded by corruption the hand of salutary healing? And so, that they may be able to give others health-giving remedies with confidence, I will them to imitate My Son most forcefully in love of chastity. But if they should fall, let them hasten to rise immediately by penitence and flee as if naked from the shamefulness of sin; let them seek the wholesome remedy and faithfully follow Abel, whose sacrifice was acceptable to God.

4 Those who live in obedience when unsupervised gain an eternal reward

But those churchmen who enclose themselves in a cloister of obedience and behave according to the ordinances of their superiors, which the latter made by My inspiration, even though they do not have bishops carefully watching over them and do not bear the burden of their anxiety, gain for themselves with those bishops the celestial reward in the city of the chosen, because they subject themselves to their superiors for the sake of eternal reward alone.

5 On the noble and joyous state of perfect virginity

But you see that from her throat to her navel another splendor, red in color, encircles her. This means that after the teaching of the apostles had so invigorated the Church that she could truly discern the saving food and make it the source of her interior strength, there arose the noblest perfection of churchly religion, which tasted heavenly sweetness with burning ardor and stringently restrained itself in order to gird itself with secret power; rejecting the union of human coupling, it avoided the division caused by the bitterness of the flesh. How? *That splendor glows like the dawn from her throat to her breasts;* for this perfection arose from the taste of the excitement of miracles and extended in virginal gladness to the sweet nourishment of churchly religion. *And it shines from her breasts to her navel mixed with purple and blue;* for she fortified herself for the stringency of inner chastity by the noblest training, namely by imitating the Passion of My Son to gain the celestial love He guarded in His heart. Therefore, *where it glows like the dawn, its brightness shines forth as high as the secret places of Heaven;* for the perfection that flowers in the state of virginity directs its strength not downward toward earthly things, but miraculously upward to what is in Heaven.

6   On the image of the maiden

In this brightness appears a most beautiful image of a maiden, with bare head and black hair. This is serene Virginity, innocent of all foulness of human lust. Her mind is unbound by any shackle of corruption, but is not yet perfectly able to bar troubled and dark thoughts from the minds of her children, as long as they are in the world; but she forcefully resists and opposes such thoughts.

Therefore *she wears a red tunic, which flows down about her feet;* for she perseveres toward the goal of widest and most blessed perfection by the sweat of her labor in virtuous works, surrounded with the variety of virtues and imitating Him Who is the plenitude of sanctity. She is also, as is shown you in this hidden and supernal light, the noble daughter of the celestial Jerusalem, the glory and honor of those who have shed their blood for love of virginity or in radiant humility preserved their virginity for the sake of Christ and died sweetly in peace. For she was betrothed to the Son of Almighty God, the King of all, and bore Him a noble brood, the elect choir of virgins, when she was strengthened in the peace of the Church.

7   The throng that stands around that maiden

And around that maiden you see standing a great crowd of people, brighter than the sun, all wonderfully adorned with gold and gems. This is to say that noble Virginity is surrounded and ardently embraced by a wonderful crowd of virgins. They all shine before God more brightly than the sun does on the earth; for they have conquered themselves and bravely trodden death underfoot in the glorious works they have humbly performed for Christ, and so are adorned beautifully with the highest wisdom. *Some of them have their heads veiled in white, adorned with a gold circlet;* for, shining in the glory of virginity, they indicate that those who seek its rank should veil their minds from harmful heat all around, and grasp the purity of innocence which is adorned with the beautiful splendor of chastity.

Above them, as if sculpted on the veils, is the likeness of the glorious and ineffable Trinity as it was represented to you earlier; which shows that these people's minds firmly and strongly uphold the honor of the celestial and glorious Trinity, Which was truly shown you before in a mystery, by their knowledge of love and steadfast chastity.

On their foreheads is the Lamb of God, and on their necks a human figure, and on the right ear cherubim, and on the left ear the other kinds of angels; which declares that in their reverent chastity they will imitate the mildness of the Son of God, laying aside stiffnecked wantonness and knowing themselves to be frail humans. In prosperity they will listen to and embrace true and unfailing knowledge; at the approach of adversity they will listen for angelic aid. So *from the likeness of the glorious and supernal Trinity golden rays extend to these other images,* for the ineffable Trinity unceasingly works the miracles of Its profound wisdom among the faithful who seek virtue and flee the seductions of the Devil.

And among these people there are some who have miters on their heads and pallia of the episcopal office around their shoulders. For among those who flourish in the honor of virginity there are some in the celestial city who ably held the rank of the ancient fathers and the glory of higher offices in the world, yet did not lose the ornament of virginity. Hence, as you hear, all those who in their desire kept their integrity for the sake of celestial love are called "daughters of Zion" in the celestial habitations; for in their love of virginity they imitated My Son, Who is the flower of virginity. Therefore the sounding echoes of the blessed spirits and the outpouring of voices and the winged decorations of happy minds and the golden vision of shining stones and jewels are all with them. How? Because the Son of God grants them this, that a sound goes forth from the Throne in which the whole choir of virgins joins in singing with great desire and harmonizing in the new song, as John, the beloved virgin, testifies, saying:

8 Words of John

"And they sang, as it were, a new song before the throne, and before the four living creatures and the ancients" [Revelation 14:3]. What does this mean? In those faithful ones who embrace chastity for a good purpose and preserve their virginity unstained for love of God, good will bursts forth wonderfully in praise of their Creator. How? In the dawn-light of virginity, which always surrounds the Son of God, steadfast praise is hidden; no worldly office and no tie of the law can resist it, and it sings in the voice of exultation a celestial song to the glory of God. How?

That song, which was not heard before the Only-Begotten of God, the true flower of virginity, returned in the body from earth to Heaven and sat again on the right hand of the Father, has a swift course and makes itself heard wonderfully in new liberty. And, since new customs, which have not been seen before, are regarded with amazement when they are seen, this new and unheard-of mystery resounded in Heaven in honor of virginity, before the majesty of God (for God could do this) and before the four wheels that rolled into the four corners of the earth bearing the truth of justice and the humanity of the Savior like the living creatures in the new Law, and before those ancients who were imbued with the Holy Spirit and showed the path of righteousness to the people under the old Law. Why is this? Because God by the new grace softened the rigor of the old institution.

9 Virginity offered to God must be carefully preserved

But since virginity is so glorious before God, those who have offered it to God of their own will must carefully preserve it; for this holy purpose, undertaken with great devotion to virginity, must be faithfully kept. So let those who have undertaken this mystery take care not to fall back. For when they offer themselves to God, not joined by any bond of marriage or burdened by any secular business but spurning carnal coupling and desiring to cleave to the glorious innocence of the innocent Lamb, they are beloved imitators of My Son.

So a man who decides in his mind not to join himself to any rib, but wants to persevere in the modesty of virginity for love of My Son, will become his companion, if he perseveres in the works of chastity; for he has offered these holy gifts to My Son for the glory of a heavenly reward by the vow of a most sacred pact of churchly religion.

But if he then breaks this pact because of an evil stinging of his flesh and commits adultery, he reduces his liberty to servitude, for by his shameful pleasure he has wickedly brought low his head when he ought to have chastely imitated My Son; and he has uttered a lie, vowing to live chastely and not fulfilling it. Therefore, if he perseveres in his rash fault he will undergo the strict judgment of the Just Judge, for no shame or lie can appear in celestial glory.

But if before his death the man does penance for his guilt with bitter tears, My Son's flowing blood will receive him, since he abhors his sin; but this does not place him back among his companions who shine with the glory of integrity, for he has deserted their society, casting away the liberty of his pact and reducing it to the slavery of sin.

10 She who breaks the vow of virginity will be not a lady but a handmaid

And a maiden who of her own will is betrothed in holiness to My Son is becomingly received by Him, for He wishes to have her united with Him in companionship. How? That she may embrace Him with chaste love, and He may love her in secret; for to Him she is always lovable, since she seeks Him rather than an earthly bridegroom. But if she then transgresses this pact, she is polluted in the sight of those who are in celestial joy; and if she perseveres in this rashness, by just judgment she will be deprived of heavenly glory. But if she repents, she will be received as a handmaid and not as a lady, since she has deserted her royal betrothal and loved another more than Him she should have loved. And let him who seduced and violated her, if he wants to atone for his guilt, repent as if he had broken open Heaven; only thus will he escape the condemnation of death, for he rashly violated a heavenly betrothal. What does this mean?

11 Illustration of this issue

If some great ruler had a bride exceedingly dear to him, who was adulterously corrupted by a servant of his servants, what would that lord do? He would certainly send his army to destroy him in greatest wrath, since this man had struck him to the very viscera. But if this servant, fearing the army, should beg his master to intercede for him, and fall at his feet with tears to ask him to spare him, then that king would suffer him to live because of his own goodness and the other's petition, and restore him to the society of his fellow-servants. But he would not reward him like his close and familiar friends, even though he did show him the favor he deserved among his fellow-servants of the same rank. So it will be for one who seduces and violates a bride of the eternal King. For that King, issuing His judgments in righteous zeal, will send him to perdition, because in this deed he disregarded Him and held Him in scorn.

But if the wretch, looking forward in fear to that day of wrath, humbly begs God's elect to ask pardon for him from the Lord and tearfully contemplates the Humanity of his Savior until he is absolved from sin by His grace, then the King, mindful of the blood that was shed for the redemption of the human race, and for love of the citizens of Heaven, will save him from his guilt and from the power of the Devil and accord him the salvation of the blessed so that he will not go to perdition. But He will not adorn him in the dance of the royal wedding, at which the other friends of God will rejoice with those sacred virgins who in celestial betrothal are dedicated to My Son; just as He will not crown with the rank of virginity one who has lost the modesty of virginity, even though He grants him with His other elect joy in the celestial city and an inestimable reward.

12 The great difference between celestial desire and earthly lust

But beneath that splendor, which glows like the dawn, you see between Heaven and earth a thick darkness appear, the horror of which exceeds what human tongue can utter. This is to say that under the glory of virginity, the fall of our first parent openly stands between the spiritual and the carnal intellect; and that fall was the darkest shadow of unfaithfulness, so that no person could expound its terror. Why?

Because in the Incarnation of the Son of God, born of the Virgin, celestial desire was supreme and earthly lust was lacking; so Adam's transgression was miraculously remade into salvation by the blood of the Son of God; not earlier, since no other but the Only-Begotten of God, sent into the world by the Father, could cancel that transgression and permit entry into Heaven. Therefore, as you hear in this vision, unless the Son of God had shed His blood for human salvation, that transgression would have weighed Man down so much that he could not have attained to the joy of the citizens of Heaven.

13   On monks who enter into monastic profession

And where the splendor shines, which is mixed with purple and blue, it encircles the woman's image with strong ardor. This symbolizes the perfection of those who imitate the Passion of My Son in the ardor of their love and strongly adorn the Church with their self-restraint. How? Because they are the high building of the growing treasury of the divine counsel. For when the Church was invigorated and grew stronger, to increase her beauty there came forth a living fragrance [monks], vowing the way of secret regeneration [making monastic profession]. What does this mean? That there then arose the wonderful order, which attained to My Son in the beauty of His example; for as My Son came into the world separated from the common people, so this army lives in the world separated from the rest of the people. This people first arose in the desert and in hiding, as balsam sweetly oozes from the tree, and then grew into a great multitude, as the tree extends its branches. And I blessed and sanctified this people, for they are to Me the lovely flowers, roses and lilies, which grow in the fields without human labor; for no law constrains these people to desire such a narrow way, but they undertake it of their own will without any legal command, as I inspire them, and do more than they are told to. Therefore, they gain a very great reward from Me, as is written in the Gospel, where the Samaritan brought that wounded man to an inn:

14   Words of the Gospel

"And the next day he took out two pence and gave them to the innkeeper, and said, 'Take care of him, and whatever you spend over and above this, I will repay you when I return' " [Luke 10:35]. What does this mean? On the first day of salvation, that is, when the miraculously incarnate Son of God was abiding in the world in His body and until His resurrection, He performed in His Humanity many marvellous works, by which He wholesomely brought the wounded man to true remedies. But the next day, that is, after His resurrection, when all the mysteries of truth had been openly given to the Church, He figuratively offered the New and Old Testaments as a sure proof of eternal life and a sweet food for the believing people.

And He gave these writings by His grace to the pastors of the Church, who keep His flock; and He said to them with sweet admonition, "Use churchly rules to look after the company of Christians redeemed in My blood, which I have entrusted to you, taking care that they do not err or lack in what pertains to life. But whatever you may add in your goodwill to what I have ordered you to keep, doing more than is commanded of you, I your Leader and Savior, who now leave the world and ascend to the Father but will return to judge the world and establish it forever, with no wearing away through the passage of time, will then repay you for your labor and your goodwill, with added fruits. And I will say to you 'O faithful and righteous servant, who has ministered faithfully!' Whoever willingly adds more than the Law commanded him will receive a twofold reward; for I hold him glorious in My name, since he has loved Me greatly." And I say:

15 The orders of virgins and monks are not found in the precepts of the Law

Neither the race of virgins nor this singularly devoted order, nor those who imitate them, such as desert hermits, are commanded by the Law; as the prophets too were not appointed by people under the laws of the flesh, for they arose imbued only by My inspiration. But they do more than was commanded them, which priests and those pertaining to their order do not, for these things were commanded by Abraham and Moses in the Old Testament, and the apostles took them from the Law, set them up in My will by the Holy Spirit and handed them on to be kept by the Church. And the same apostolic teaching was set forth in the Gospel by My Son, when His disciples were sent out to spread abroad the words of truth to the whole world.

What then? As the apostles announced the way of salvation to the people, the bright dawn of the daughters of Zion arose in the love of My Son, that is, the dawn of those who strongly repressed their flesh and harshly mortified their evil desires. And as this chaste virginity followed My Son in ardent love, that singularly devoted order greatly pleasing to Me also imitated His Incarnation. These are My true temples, where I am worshipped as if by choirs of angels; they bear in their bodies the Passion and death and burial of my Only-Begotten, not in that they die by the sword or other human terrors, but in that they imitate My Son by renouncing the will of their own flesh, separating themselves from all worldly things and ornaments in which the world rejoices. Which is written in the Gospel about John, the lamp of the world:

16 Example of John the Baptist

"And the same John had a garment of camel's hair and a leathern girdle about his loins" [Matthew 3:4]. What does this mean? Divine grace had woken miraculous abstinence in him, and by that grace he had a defense of his virtue, for in his mind he had despised honor and earthly riches, and in his body he had tamed the wanton urges through the restraints that, to mortify vice, he had put on the pleasures of the flesh. For, advancing through hard and rough ways and trampling down earthly lust, he built greater towers of virtue than his predecessors. How?

Because, vigorously performing many works of virtue, he ardently loved chastity and showed the way of healing to those who devotedly sought it. Therefore, all monks who make profession should follow John in his way of life, who shone by his lofty works of blessed virtue amid the great darkness of the world; they should flee from the meaningless expanse of worldly things, restrain their wandering minds and so force their bodies to renounce evil desire. Thus they will outshine by more excellent means those who before their time walked simply in the way of the Lord and made their simple habitations; they will take the steep and narrow path by firmly treading underfoot those things that are the pleasures of the world. How? Because, despising themselves and subjecting their bodies to the service of Christ in the work of the virtues, they will shun wantonness by austere behavior and so shine brightly for others by their good examples. For they faithfully imitate the angelic choir. How? By renouncing worldly things; for, as the angels do not seek or long for the things of earth, these people follow them miraculously in despising all fleeting things.

17 Monks for the needs of the Church may take Church offices

So as My Son brings the message of the healthful sacraments, and is the Priest of priests and the Prophet of prophets and the builder of blessed towers, if a necessity arises a monk who is firmly rooted and competent for it may be a messenger and priest, prophet and counselor of the Church. He is not to be kept away from these offices, as long as his sight is clear and he does not slumber at his churchly duty but attends to his teaching; he must only reject being occupied by secular business and its contagion. For neither angels nor priests nor prophets will hide God's justice, but will make it known in truth from His precepts; as in the Gospel it is written again of John, whose austerity they follow, that he was not a reed shaken in the wind.

18 Words of the Gospel concerning John

"And all the country of Judea went out to him, and all the inhabitants of Jerusalem; and they were baptized by him in the river Jordan, confessing their sins" [Mark 1:5]. What does this mean? They, whose hearts had been struck by fear of death and love of life, went out with sighs and groans from the pleasures of vice to him who had the divine grace to do everything for them, by means of simple confession from their devoted wills and visions of peace. How? Because John, the forerunner of the Truth, conveyed to them both bitterness and sweetness. Therefore they entreated from his rectitude an outpouring of penance, so that, by avoiding evil deeds and doing good ones and confessing their crimes, they might deserve to reach Him Who would confer on them true salvation in the light of the New Testament instead of the remedy in the shadow of the Old. And just as John taught those who came to him and baptized them in the river after receiving their words of repentance in honor of the Savior to come, so now, in the name of the Savior Who has come and brought salvation to the faithful, let those who add shining works to the testimony of sanctification not neglect to do so. Inspired by the Holy Spirit, let them reach new heights of austerity in renouncing worldly things, following the model they adopted when they listened to that testimony and put on the new man through the regeneration of the Spirit and water, rejecting the service of the Devil. And, when necessity impels, let them offer the hand of assistance to those who ask, admonishing, uplifting and healing; and if they have worthily attained an office by churchly promotion, let them faithfully imitate their Forerunner, so as truly to complete in the new light what he showed in the shadow.

For the monks are the girdle of the Church and strongly encircle her, since they are concerned with My Son's Incarnation and also exercise the function of the angels; that is, they do not cease at any hour to sing melodiously or pray in compunction, with the freshness of remorse and not with the useless dry dust of noisy cries, and they do not seek to handle worldly things but examine themselves thoroughly with charity and humility.

Oh, these are My strong and loving people, for in them I contemplate the sufferings that My Son underwent in the flesh; and they die His death, when they forsake their own will and submit to obedience for the sake of eternal life, walking in the commands of their superiors.

19 The monks' unique garment symbolizes Christ's Incarnation and burial

Therefore their garment is unlike that of other people, for it symbolizes the incorrupt Incarnation of My Son, which is completely different from the procreation of other people. For the command of the Law concerning men and women did not touch the Incarnation, in the same way that no written law obliges these people to their strictness of life; though one who undertakes it with a vow by his own will for the love of God should persevere in it, lest he recoil and fall, like Lucifer who forsook light and went into darkness.

And this garment flies with wings of subtlety like the glitter of supernal spirits, and points to the Incarnation and burial of My Son; for one who gives himself up to strictest obedience has on his garment the sign of My Son's Incarnation, and one who renounces secular business for the works of justice has on his garment the sign of My Son's burial. Hence one who by purity of will is clothed in this garment is uplifted by a heathful remedy.

And therefore, let one who receives it with blessings and the invocation of the Holy Spirit not renounce it; for he who despises it in persistent and evil rejection will be with the one who spurned the order of angels and was entombed in death. What does this mean? These people are not spurred on by any precept of the Law to their strictness of life, but have undertaken to observe My pact of their own will and thus make My Church illustrious by the holiness of their ways. How? This order rose after the apostles' preaching as the sun rises after the first light of day. What does this mean?

20   Benedict, who is a second Moses, made this order a separate way

The first light of day designates the faithful words of the apostolic teaching; the dawn, the beginning of this way of life, which following that teaching first came about in solitude and in caves; but the sun symbolizes the separate and well-disposed way I then brought about through My servant Benedict, whom I passed by in burning fire, teaching him to honor the Incarnation of My Son in the garment of his way of life, and imitate His Passion in the abnegation of his will. For Benedict is like a second Moses, lying in the cleft of the rock and tormenting and repressing his body with great harshness for the love of life, as the first Moses wrote on the stone tablets at My command and gave the Jews a Law that was harsh and hard. But as My Son penetrated that same Law with the sweetness of the Gospel, so also My servant Benedict by the sweetness of the Holy Spirit's inspiration made the plan of this order a separate and level path, which before him was an exceedingly hard way of life. And he gathered together by it large numbers for his order, as My Son, through the sweetness of His fragrance, gathered to Himself the Christian people.

And so then the Holy Spirit spoke in the hearts of His elect who sighed for life, telling them that as in the washing of baptism the crimes of the peoples are washed away, so they themselves should renounce the pomps of the world as a sign of the Passion of My Son. How? Because in holy baptism a person is converted from the power of the Devil and rejects his old stains of sin, and thus these too should reject earthly business by the sign of their garment, which is also an angelic sign. How? Because by My will they are appointed protectors of the people.

21 For Church necessities a proven monk may receive priesthood

For this reason, those of them who are found proven in their holy way of life may be established as pastors of My Church, as the angels, who are touched by no stain from earthly affairs, are the guardians of My people. For, as the angels hold before God a twofold rank, so the people of this religious order live in a twofold life. How? The angels in the heavenly places serve God without interruption, and on earth continually protect people from the snares of the Devil. So these people imitate the angelic order when they despise earthly things and serve God daily, and also defend all other people from evil spirits day and night by their prayers. Therefore, if My Church does not have a fitting pastor, let the people of this religious order come to her aid, crying out and weeping; and let the one among them who is found proven defend her with vigorous zeal, receiving priesthood too if necessary.

22 No one should undertake this order without being very closely examined

But no one should undertake the religious life of this order suddenly and as if just waking from a dream, but let him first be tested with close examination as to the self-control of his mind, and whether he can persevere in this purpose; for if he were to undertake it by his own will in the pact of blessing and later in perverse error renounce it and impenitently mock Me, he would perish miserably in the condemnation of death. Therefore, O my dearest children, who are so scattered by opposition, rise up quickly in humility and charity, and manfully and unanimously consent to your holy purpose.

23 Secular people who keep God's laws greatly adorn the Church

But, as you see, another splendor, like a white cloud, decently envelops that image from the navel down, to the point at which it has not yet grown further. This is the secular life, which with pure and calm purpose surrounds the Church with reverence and renders her just assistance, from the fullness of her growing strength until the point past which she has not yet developed in her children. How? Because what lies closest to the navel is the womb, from which the whole human race is procreated. Therefore this refers to the secular people in the Church, through whom she must be brought to the full number of her orders, for here are gathered kings and dukes, princes and rulers, and their subjects, rich and poor, and the destitute living among the others. And by all these the Church is exceedingly adorned, for when lay-people faithfully observe the Law of God, which is laid down for them, they beautify the Church greatly; when they obey their superiors with sincere humility and devotion, and chastise their bodies for God's love by alms and vigils and continence and widowhood and other good works that are of God, they embrace God with many embraces. Therefore they who keep the law appointed for them by My will are most lovable to Me.

24   Married people cannot become monastics unless both agree to do it

If any layperson desires to renounce worldly things to bear the yoke of My liberty, let him come to Me quickly, unless he is in the bonds of a fleshly union. This tie he may not rashly loose unless his consort wills it. How? Husband may not leave wife and wife may not leave husband for this purpose unless it is the will of both, and they both decide either to remain in the world or to separate from the world; for it cannot be that a whole person can remain well if one foot remains with his body and the other is cut off from it. So it is not fitting for a husband to worship the world while his wife deserts the world, or for a wife to reside in the world while her husband flees the world, if they wish to have glory in celestial life; for if this is done indiscreetly and foolishly, it will be called a robbery rather than an offering. So let those who are legally joined in a fleshly union live together with one mind, and not foolishly separate from each other without a dispensation or declaration from Church authority, as is written again in the Gospel:

25   Words of the Gospel

"What therefore God has joined together, let not Man put asunder" [Matthew 19:6]. What does this mean? God, creating the human race, took flesh out of flesh and joined them in a union, and thus established that this connection must not be hastily broken. How? Because in the union of man and woman flesh will be united to flesh and blood to blood by a legal ceremony, so that they cannot be divided from each other in foolish haste, unless both dissolve the bond for a just cause or a rightful devotion; for God in His secret wisdom graciously formed this union of male and female for the propagation of people. And because He so rightly constituted this union, foolish human desire should not cause a breach between the two parts, and neither part should take the dowry of its blood to an alien place; for, as God commanded that people should not slay each other, He also commanded that they should not divert their blood from its rightful place by cruel fornication.

Therefore, let people repress the ardor of their longing and not transmit their flame to an alien fire. For if an ardent will takes hold of the will of another and stirs it up to fervent lust for a stronger or weaker reason, the two will coalesce into one by the first person's mental desire and the other's consent to be embraced by it. For the sight of the outer eye makes the inner heat burst into flame. And even if the one body does not sin with the other, the living will still makes them burn, so that all their viscera are shaken by their feelings. Therefore, let the outer person be guarded with such caution that the inner person may never be wounded by carelessness.

26   These orders consolidate the Church in their ranks and degrees

And you see that *these three splendors around that image shine afar;* which is to say that these three institutions surround and consolidate the blessed Church in a wondrous way in honor of the heavenly Trinity, causing her to burst forth with buds and spread out with blessed verdure. Therefore *they show that within her many steps and ladders are well and properly placed.* These are the various orders of laypeople and religious, in which the Church by good habits and the practice of virtue guides her children, educated in sweet reverence, to Heaven. How? When they spurn earthly things and love celestial ones. What does this mean? When they faithfully fulfil in divine love the precepts instituted for them.

27   Each order must avoid diversity, singularity and novelty in way of life

But as in three Persons there is one God, so in these three orders there is one Church, founded by Him Who has planted all good things. For whatever He has not planted will not be able to stand. And thus those institutions He has not instituted will fall into great errors. How? Those institutions that in haughty pride seek to ascend and do not wish to be subject to those higher than they were not planted by God. And this happens when a lesser order strives to raise itself above a greater one, which was constituted by My will on the ancient counsel of the first Fathers; and when it tries in its madness to appear more important by distinctive signs in its vestments; as if the order of angels tried to raise itself above the order of archangels. What would this mean? That they were nil and useless, since with vain ideas they tried to divide the orders duly constituted by God. But this should not be.

So it is not fitting that I should be invoked by those who, with a mania for diversity, always wish for a new purpose, and who, not knowing their own minds, leave the well-trodden path and the well-plowed ground of the early Fathers, who were inspired by the Holy Spirit. Many of these, in the greatness of their pride, forsake the established ordinances that the Church has from the early Fathers, and make schisms in their various institutions. And they wish in their wanderings to be called fruitful trees, but they cannot even be called empty reeds, as is shown by the beloved John, who writes about those who wither in apathy and are cut off:

28 Words of John

"I know your works, that you are neither cold nor hot. I would you were cold or hot! But because you are lukewarm and neither cold nor hot, I will spew you out of my mouth" [Revelation 3:15–16]. What does this mean? O fools, who are shamefully withering up inside, I Who am the Knower of Secrets see with the eye of knowledge the works of your desires; you have not fled utterly from the works of the fire of the fiery Enlightener, and yet you have not renounced the works that produce the ice of frigid stiffness. How? You are not entirely given over to works of cold evil, and you are not entirely burning for good deeds, but you waver toward each in the instability of your mind, like a lukewarm wind; and you do not think either about the deserved punishments of evil or about the worthy rewards of good. How? Because you look into such a deep abyss that you cannot find its bottom, but you also give your attention to such a high mountain that you cannot scale its summit.

Oh, how much better it would be for you to know yourself as an unprofitable servant and a sinner, rather than remaining in lukewarmness and hardly glancing at what is right. For if you were separated from good actions you would know yourself to be a sinner, and if you withdrew yourself from evil works you would have some hope of life. But now you are like a lukewarm wind, which gives neither moisture nor heat to the fruits. For you are one who begins, but not one who finishes; you touch the beginning of good, but you never feed on its perfection, like the wind that blows around a person's mouth and not the food that reaches his stomach. Which is more precious, an empty noise or a finished work? Of course a finished work is more acceptable than an empty noise.

Work, then, in the silence of humility, and do not puff yourself up with pride; for anyone who forsakes the holy society of My docile and loving servants, and undertakes with eager boasting a work he disdains to complete with sweet mildness, will be counted as nothing.

But if you begin in rectitude to try to penetrate the meaning of My words, which offer food to the faithful, but are then sluggish in them and show no sweetness of justice to those you encounter, and so fall to worse things, I will begin to cast you out by that same meaning of My words for your lukewarm negligence. For you show no savor of sweetness in doing your works and do not pant after the blessed reception of inner gifts. And, being so cast out, you will be trodden underfoot, like food that is so insipid in taste that a person spits it out of his mouth before it can reach his stomach. But what now?

The wind blows, and its noise resounds, but it puts forth no flower from its roots nor reproduces itself. For they, who should be under My yoke, are willful and undisciplined. What does this mean? They neglect the right path and make themselves useless tabernacles. For such people, who are sluggish inside and have no fervor for justice, neither burn for the laws set up for them nor follow the way of life of their fathers before them; but each of them nurtures some singularity in himself and lays down laws for himself according to his own will, and so in wavering thoughts and inflated pride raises himself up to fly. And, since they do not keep to the righteous pact of their fathers, they are always new and unskilled, and they wander here and there in great instability, following their own will.

29 Analogy of a craftsman

Therefore I compare them to stupid craftsmen who are building a large building, yet do not follow the wisdom of previous craftsmen who are well-trained in the use of their tools and knowledgeable about how to plan and raise a building; but they carelessly and foolishly trust in themselves, wanting to excel others in wisdom, and build their buildings such that they will be shaken by storms and thrown down by the winds. For they will not be built on rock, but on sand.

And thus do those who trust to themselves in their pride and seek to seem wiser than the early Fathers; they do not want to walk according to their covenant, but lay down shaky laws for themselves at their own will, and thus, leaning not on Christ but on their own unstable conduct, they are often stirred up to sin by the temptations of the Devil.

30 The institution of his predecessors suffices for one who is humble

Therefore, lest the breath of the Holy Spirit, which suffused the early Fathers, be expelled by these people's swelling pride, I desire the faithful person to be humble and content with what his predecessors instituted for him. For if he should vainly will more than he ought humbly to seek, he might later grow lukewarm and draw back from it and be shamefully confounded, as it is written in the Gospel:

31 Words of the Gospel on this subject

"When you are invited to a wedding, do not take the first place, lest one more honorable than you should be invited, and he that invited you both should come and say to you, 'Give this man place'; and you with shame must go and take the last place" [Luke 14:8–9]. What does this mean? When you are told by divine inspiration that because of your faithful labors you are summoned to that holy tabernacle that flourishes in a bridal way of life, unceasingly rejoicing with purity and honor and holiness in the virginal branch and in the blessed Mother the Church, with no sadness of corruption or confusion or degradation of the bud or the flower, then curb your mind in humility and do not uplift it in pride. How?

When for love of God you free your body from earthly affairs, you will grow as a beautiful flower, blossoming and never withering in the heavenly Jerusalem with the Son of God, in Whom are all ornaments for souls; for the old person produces all human abominations, but the new builds all the holiness of virtue. So when you have come to such holiness, blush to imitate the ancient serpent, who cast himself out of the place of beatitude because he was hungry for vainglory. What does this mean? If you see anyone better adorned than you, do not in eagerness of mind ascend above him, saying, "I want to be above him or like him!" If you exalt yourself so, are you a faithful servant, since you are provoking the Lord to anger by opposing yourself to Him? But if you see that someone has stronger resources than you, and out of envy disparage him, you are not walking in the plain road but going by trackless ways.

So be eager to serve God in humility and do not give yourself up madly to pride; and do not exalt yourself in vain pretense over one who, if assessed justly, shines with a greater desire of eternal life than you burn with yourself, and who for his heavenly ardor is invited to the height of blessedness by Him Who loves all lovers of truth. For if you do, He Who by His inspiration summoned you to the service of humility and the other to the gift of charity may come with the eye of knowledge and judge you with His righteous judgment, saying, "You lifted yourself up in eager pride to a place for which you are not fit; leave your vainglory and submit in duty, and give this beloved one of mine the place of honor you so rashly seized!" And what will become of you then?

If you are overthrown in this way, in anguish of grief and sadness you will begin to feel extreme dejection and abhor yourself as contemptible; for the Protector of souls will take from you the honor you usurped when you opposed yourself to Him and tried to seize what was not yours to have. So what you wanted will be taken from you, and what you did not want will be given to you. And so also when a lesser order exalts itself over a greater one it will be suppressed, overthrown by My just judgment, for I do not wish that pride to be anything but thrown down and confounded. For if a handmaid exalts herself above her mistress, she will be despised the more by all who see her, for she tried to become what she should not have desired.

32 The Gospel on those who make laws after their own hearts

Therefore, those who make laws for themselves according to their own hearts, not seeking My will, fail rather than go forward, as My Son testifies in the Gospel, saying, "Every plant which My Heavenly Father has not planted will be rooted up" [Matthew 15:13]. What does this mean? That every offshoot of the knowledge of heart, mind or conduct will be destroyed if, arising out of the fecundity of human nature, it is so sown in a person that he burns to unite himself with a willful desire; and if it is then changed into mental pride or carnal wantonness or overflowing pollution or self-excuse for sin or changeful actions that rush up and down without examining whether they are useful or useless. It will be destroyed by just judgment, for truly My Father in Heaven, who dwells in justice, has not planted this plant; it will be uprooted and wither, because it thrives not on the dew of Heaven but on the moisture of the flesh. How? Because the person has done the deed in foolish knowledge, wishing not to contemplate the justice and will of his Creator but to look to the one who tirelessly spins the wheel of his body.

For what seems good to people who have not fixed their eye sharply on God will prove ruinous unless it is warmed by the breath of the Holy Spirit, for it will have changed into vainglory. For when vain people are afflicted by boredom, they will often revert to vainglory, sometimes uplifting themselves to pride, pretense and jealousy of spirit, and sometimes tearing themselves to pieces in annoyance, disdain and opposition to institutions that came from Me; and also discouraging each other from doing good things, which spring not from apathetic boredom but from the ardor of desire to make daily progress.

For what flows from Me is a sweet and delightful taste to the soul; it goes forward in perseverance and does not look back in indecision. Therefore, blessed is the one who, confiding in Me, puts his hope and the beginning and end of his works not in himself but in Me. He who does these things shall not fall; but he who tries to stand without Me will go to ruin. And who does the latter? Those who vaingloriously embrace novelty and, bored with My precepts, trust in themselves. But though an old garment is vexatious to human minds, I in My gifts must not be spurned, for in their simplicity they are always new, and the older they are the more precious they are.

Hence those things people devise themselves without My inspiration in the vanity of their habits will melt away amid their vain exertions. And though these things in human eyes may sometimes seem to last, I reject them from My sight and hold them as nothing, as it is written in the Gospel:

33 Further words of the Gospel

"Let them alone, for they are blind leaders of the blind. And if the blind lead the blind, both shall fall into the ditch" [Matthew 15:14]. What does this mean? Allow perverse livers to dissipate themselves in perversity, for they refuse to correct themselves by righteousness of works. And because in their own estimation they call themselves just, when in their actions they are vain, they become blind from their very qualities, disdaining to walk in the way of justice and proposing to those who follow them in bad deeds the way of iniquity instead of truth. So they who have not the right vision of justice think they are just when they are unjust, and when they show the path of false justice to people ignorant of the road of true doctrine, they fall into the ditch of despair, because neither they nor their followers know where they are going.

34 God casts down some innovators and leaves others whom He will judge later

And in these cases I sometimes in My wrath cast down innovations in the sight of humanity; but in My foreseeing vision I silently tolerate others in human sight for a while, which I will nonetheless do justice on in future by the weighing of My just judgment. Therefore, let one who is faithful yearn to ascend to the height of virtue, not to descend to the depths of worldliness. How?

35 One may go from a lower to a higher degree but not from higher to lower

One who is in a lower degree can ascend to a higher, but one who is in a higher degree should not descend to a lower. What does this mean? Counts can rise to be dukes, and dukes can rise to be kings, but it is not fitting that kings should descend to be dukes or dukes stoop to be counts. For if kings subjected themselves to dukes and dukes submitted to counts, all the people would shout, "Wach!" and hold them in derision.

Thus laypeople can enter the order of priests and bishops, and these clerics can join those who have taken vows as monks; but it is not fitting that vowed monks should go over to the order of clerics, or that clerics should rush back to the laity. And if monks go to be clerics, or clerics return to the laity, the souls of the just will say of them, "Alas, alas, alas!" and they will be rejected in My sight unless they turn to fitting penance; for if a higher rank falls upon a lower one, both will be destroyed.

So will it be for those who leave the right path and go backward. For if one has put on My Son, what other son His equal could he put on? None, and truly none. But rejoice in your Father; for often I find the greater people in the lower ranks and the lesser in the higher, since pride falls and humility ascends.

36 Example of souls and angels

Therefore have peace and charity and humility among you, as the souls of the just have with the angels and the angels with the archangels. For the souls of the just do not envy the office of the angels, and the angels are not angry at the glory of the archangels. Why is this? Archangels point out the greatest things in the greatest times of necessity, and the angels announce lesser things in the normal course of events, while the faithful people humbly obey. Therefore, let each fulfil his office faithfully. How?

Let those who are vowed monks, like the archangels, renew their powerful assistance whenever there is a great occasion of necessity in the Church; and let those who have the office of clerics, like the angels, do their business in the daily life of their institution; and let people who want to attain to supreme beatitude faithfully receive their words. How?

37 Monks symbolize grain, clerics fruit and laypeople meat

Because they who are vowed monks are like grain, which is the strong, dry food of humans; so this people of Mine is bitter and harsh to the taste of the world. And the clerics are like fruits, sweet to the taste, and show themselves sweet to people by the usefulness of their office. And the common laypeople are like meat, but meat comes partly from chaste birds; thus those who live in the world according to the flesh have children, but among them are found followers of chastity, such as widows and the continent, who fly to heavenly desires by their appetite for virtue.

38 These three churchly institutions take two separate paths

But these churchly ranks live in two ways. How? Of spiritual and secular people. How? Like day and night. What does this mean? Spiritual people are like the day, and secular people are like the night, since they live in temporal human life. What does this mean? Day holds the sun's brightness and the serenity of the shining sky; this symbolizes the fact that the spiritual kind includes both the order of vowed monks and the order of clerics. Night holds the light of moon and stars and the blackness of the dark; this means that secular people include among themselves both just people, who shine in their works, and sinners weighed down by the darkness of their sins. But let one who forsakes the night of the seculars and is converted for love of life to the day of the spirituals be constant in this action; for if he goes backward, he will be compared to old Adam who transgressed the command of life and was driven out into the calamities of the world.

Therefore, let no one hasten to leave the world and boldly enter into My covenant of his own will until he is thoroughly examined and tested; for I do not want one who has seized the robe of My Son to let it go. For is it fitting that one who has clothed himself with His Incarnation and received His cross into his hands should renounce his Lord? By no means. Therefore listen to this.

39 To renounce the sign of religious life will mean harsh judgment

A person who has willingly confessed in his heart and vowed in his soul's devotion to bear My yoke and renounce worldly things, and then with ardent heart and desirous soul and just purpose received the sign of the religious life, must remain in it, for if he renounces it and scorns the resulting evil he will be strictly judged. Why is this? Because he has spurned Him Whose sign he has received and then trampled on, just as the Jews spurned Him when in the madness of unbelief they afflicted Him on the cross. And, as the Jews did not fear that wicked deed, so this one does not fear to reject that same Passion in rejecting his vow. For what a person promises he must fulfil, as David testifies, saying:

40 Words of David on this subject

"I will go into Your house with burnt offerings; I will pay You my vows, which my lips have uttered" [Psalm 65:13-14]. What does this mean? By resolving to do good and just deeds, I will go, O my God, into the order that You in Your holiness have given, leaving the couch of pleasure in ardent desire, for nothing is sweeter to me than to pursue You, the Creator of all. And therefore I will pay you my vows, which my mouth uttered together with my soul. For I wish to perfect what I promised You, the Just Judge, in my ardent desire: to direct my actions toward You, against Whom I have foolishly transgressed. And I desire to hasten back to You, to avoid evil deeds and do good ones; for the reason and the intellect that burn in me seek to aspire in true penitence toward You, the Living God, rather than to imitate the Devil by deceitful contrariety.

Therefore, O human, when you thus offer Me your heart, think on how you may wisely accomplish this. For My eye sees most sharply what human will tells me; and whatever is Mine, I will most strictly require.

Why then, O foolish and more than foolish, do you take on yourselves such great burdens, as if you thought it easy to set aside the will of the flesh? According to the law My commands have given you, you are not obliged to leave the world unless you first train yourselves by so many labors that you are able to bridle the carnal desires in you.

41   Those who take the sign of religion for the wrong reason are like Balaam

But you are like a lukewarm wind, for vainglory blows upon your minds; and so after some adversity you say, "I want not to work any more in the world, but speedily to flee it. Why should I wear myself out in vain labor like this?" And when you say these things to yourself, you think it will turn out as you expect. But many seek Me with a vacillating mind, so that they are marked only outwardly with the sign of religious life, not seeking Me with pure eyes or looking simply about them with true doctrine to see how to escape the Devil who seeks to devour them; as the dove, seeing reflected in pure water the bird that seeks to seize her, takes to flight. But these people do not flee from the Devil when they see him coming in doctrinal writings; but in sudden stupefaction, born of the blindness of their minds, they blow toward Me like a lukewarm wind.

For some undertake the religious life renouncing not their own will but only their secular clothes, because they have experienced misery and poverty instead of riches in the world; they leave the world because they cannot have it as they wish. Others are foolish and simple about the world and, being unable to guide themselves, are contemptible to people; so they flee from the world because they are mocked by it. Others labor greatly under the calamities of sickness and bodily weakness, and so leave the world not for My sake but to remedy these afflictions more easily. Yet others suffer such great anguish and oppression from the temporal lords to whom they are subject that they withdraw from the world for fear of them, not so as to obey My precepts but only so that those lords can no longer have power over them.

So all these come to the religious life not for the sake of celestial love but for the sake of the earthly troubles they have, not knowing whether I am salted with wisdom or insipid, sweet or bitter, a dweller in Heaven or on earth. What does this mean? They do not look for the spice or the sweetness of the Scriptures, or consider how I dwell in the hearts of those who seek celestial things. And since, neglecting to fear Me and advancing according to their own wills, they will not examine these things, they are alien to Me and fugitives.

Therefore I do not count them as having left the world and come to Me; but they are guilty of fearing the servant and despising the master; for they follow earthly business and do not fear Me, and thus they are counted afraid of the least important and reckless of the most important things. Therefore, they become like Balaam, who, seeing the Israelite people beautiful in their tents, longed with a false longing to join with them, saying:

42   Example of Balaam

"Let my soul die the death of the just, and my last hour be like theirs" [Numbers 23:10]. What does this mean? When a person is stirred up in his soul to begin deeds of justice, then with mounting desire he sighs and longs for them, saying, "I, a wretch entangled in many sins and bonds, yearn to have my soul reject carnal desires and leave behind all malice of wickedness, and, by that contrition which makes the just despise themselves, abide in the dwelling place of good works. How? That in my good deeds my end may be like that of the ones who do God's justice, so that the result of My good works may equal the beginning of their just purpose." But if the person who says these things is then, when his sighing is over, tempted by evil spirits and conquered by carnal desire so that he returns to iniquity, he does what Balaam did when he was deceived by the wickedness of his greed. How? Because at first he wanted to curse My people, and I opposed him both by My angel and by his ass; and by My zeal I led him to bless My people with the blessing of the words I placed in his mouth and to desire to be made like to My people Israel in his death. But afterward, touched by the spirit of dissension, he returned to his first separation and scattered that people for a deathly reward by the fornication of his counsel, as he promised when he said:

"But yet, going to my people, I will give counsel what your people shall do to this people in the latter days" [Numbers 24:14]. What does this mean? Just this: When I turn back to the path of desires related to the pleasures of the flesh, I will begin again those lusts I had previously known. How? Because I know what I am in my flesh and serve it fittingly; and I know well the motives that always act upon it. "So, O human, to you who burn for these delights I, the Devil, show in my secret mind incentives for your desires; and by my delightful suggestions I so enkindle your ardor that through knowledge of the ancient joys of earth, which flower in your heart, you will extinguish that burning desire which previously impelled you toward holy works, first stopping them and at last leaving them as if you had never known them."

Therefore, O human, just as Balaam stooped to wrong desires after first looking upward with righteous longing, so do those who seek Me feignedly. For when they see those who have truly renounced the world go forward sincerely and persevere laudably and truthfully in strict and blessed ways of life, they call them beautiful and sweet, and on sudden impulse undertake their life and want to be like them. But after they have joined themselves to them, as Balaam looked to the Israelite people, they are often recalled to carnal desires, by which they were dominated before, by the various villainies they had in their hearts while still in the world. And when they are thus entangled, they contaminate My chosen flock with poison and hostility, shaking them with storms and scattering them with their wicked counsel. For when they deceitfully withdrew from the world, they did not call upon Me in their prayers to help them or ask Me to test their bodies to see if they could persevere in their purpose. So I leave them to find out how much their own will can help them when they trust in themselves.

Oh, how foolish and fruitless are their lives, for they are not provided with the written Law of God or the fruitfulness of His word; and so they did not consider what to do when they entered on the strict way, as good earth considers when it brings forth useful fruit. So let them listen: O human, only today you were a fiery furnace, burning fiercely in your flesh with carnal desires; and who gave you such a great respite that you could escape the great fire of your passion?

43   One who takes the sign of religion foolishly and ends badly is ruined

Truly one who wishes to undertake these things should examine with his inner eyes how to begin them through Me and by My help perfect them; for if he begins them foolishly and fails to fulfil them he may go to ruin, like the ancient enemy, who, confiding in himself, was cast out by the wrath of My zeal. So shall they also be cast out who, considering neither Me nor themselves, clothe themselves with the Passion of My Son in unthinking and hasty pride, and afterward find it too much for them and renounce it in disgust. Therefore, let those who submit themselves to the Passion take heed how they love it, as Jeremiah the prophet, inspired by the Holy Spirit, urges, saying:

44 Words of Jeremiah

"O all you that pass by the way, attend and see if there is any sorrow like to my sorrow! For He has made a vintage of me, as the Lord spoke in the day of His fierce anger" [Lamentations 1:12]. What does this mean? O all you who have deserted vices, rejecting the worldly and imitating the spiritual, and so are passing by the Way that is Life and Truth, which is I, the Son of God: Attend when you begin good works, lest when you start to imitate My Passion you forget My sorrow; and take care, for the sake of perfect justice, that the sorrow you impose on yourselves for My sake is like My sorrow. How?

By persevering unfailingly to a good end in these miseries you bear for My sake, as I also persevered in My sorrow in My purpose of dying for you; for I was oppressed and trampled in the Passion of the cross, as a grape of the vine is crushed in the winepress, that you might eat My Body and drink My Blood. The Ruler of Heaven and earth foresaw this with His all-seeing eye in the beginning, when Adam forsook life and accepted death; My Heavenly Father foresaw that in the latter days He would conquer the ancient seducer and deliver the human race with celestial aid, through Me his Son, incarnate of the Virgin to oppose the Devil with the great strength of justice. Therefore let the person, of whatever age or sex he is, who clothes himself with the Passion of Christ take care to retain it firmly, lest if he renounce it by an error of neglect he may later be unable to find it when he wants to have it.

45 Children may enter the holy way of life only with their informed consent

Therefore also, let people who want to subject their children to that Passion in humility of life not do it with imprudent and inconsiderate haste, but examine the matter with wise discretion and not force them to do without their consent what the people themselves could not bear. How?

If you offer your child to Me when discerning intellect is not in him, but all his understanding lies undeveloped, and that offering is against his will because you have not sought his consent to it, you have not acted rightly; you have offered a ram. How? If someone offers a ram at My altar without binding its horns strongly with ropes, the ram will certainly run away. So also if a father or mother offer their child, who is the ram, to My service, but do not honor his will, which is his horns, by assiduous care or supplication or entreaty or diligent exhortation, which are the ropes that bind him, since by all these the child should be brought to consent in good will; not having been proved by these tests, he will certainly run away, physically or mentally, unless God guards him by miracle.

And if you, O human, confine that child with such great strictness of bodily discipline that he cannot free himself from the pressure of his will's repugnance, he will come before Me arid and fruitless in body and soul because of the captivity unjustly inflicted on him without his consent. Then I will say to you, O human who has bound him:

46 Example of the field

I had a green field in My power. Did I give it to you, O human, that you might make it put forth whatever fruit you wished? And if you sow sand in it, can you make it grow into fruit? No. For you do not give the dew, or send forth the rain, or confer fresh moisture, or draw warmth out of the burning sun, all of which are necessary to produce good fruit. So too, you can sow a word in human ears, but into his heart, which is My field, you cannot pour the dew of compunction, or the rain of tears, or the moisture of devotion, or the warmth of the Holy Spirit, through all of which the fruit of holiness must grow.

And how did you dare so rashly to touch one dedicated and sanctified to Me in baptism, that without his will you handed him over to bear My yoke in strict captivity; so that he became neither dry nor green, not dying to the world or living to the world? Why have you so oppressed him that he can do neither? If I comfort him by miracle so that he may remain in the spiritual life, that is not for humans to look into; for I want his parents not to sin in his oblation, offering him to Me without his will.

But if anyone, father or mother, wishes to offer their child to My service, let them say before presenting him, "I promise God that I will keep my child with skillful care until he reaches the age of reason, entreating, beseeching and exhorting him to go permanently into God's service. And if he says yes, I will speedily offer him to the service of God; but if he does not consent, may I be guiltless in the sight of God's Majesty."

And if the parents of the child have brought him up in this way until the age of reason, and if then the child turns away and will not give his consent, then they have shown their devotion in him as far as they could and must not offer him against his will or force him to enter that servitude which they themselves do not want to bear or perform.

47 Those who maliciously turn others from following God commit sacrilege

But one who wishes with a devoted mind to be subject to Me should be strongly exhorted to do it and is not to be drawn back from his good intention by the envy of any spiteful soul. For if anyone deflects from his purpose one who desired to follow Me, he commits sacrilege, since he breaks My covenant in the other's mind. And therefore he will render account in the just judgment if he remains firm in this evil, since he turned away one who wished to serve Me, which he should not have done, as it is written:

48   Words of Moses

"Anything that is devoted to the Lord, whether it be man, or beast, or field, shall not be sold, neither may it be redeemed" [Leviticus 27:28]. What does this mean? When a person's longing soul, in its full knowledge, touches his good sense with the conviction that he should do a certain thing, his will accepts it and says, "This is fitting for the honor of God." And so the person promises the thing to God with good devotion and just reverence, and offers himself to Him by a kiss of the heart, that is by the will of his desire. Therefore, the thing has been offered to God as the dowry of holiness. How? Because God, seeing the person's will working in him, accepts this will by a ring of sanctification, as a husband undertakes by a betrothal ring to keep his bride in a pact of alliance that means that from now on he will never forsake her.

Hence when God has accepted this will from the manly strength of a person who forces himself to leave what he has and give what he possesses more to God than to himself, that bond of consecration must remain, and he must not forsake his devotion. Why? Because his wisdom has known it and his good sense has understood it and his will has built it up in God's honor; so whether it is a person who has offered himself to God, or an animal, owned by a person, which is offered to God, or a field bringing forth fruit, which was consecrated to God, it must not be given for a high price or held for a low profit lest God's honor be counted a trifling matter.

49   One who begins God's service and then rejects it must be recalled to it

But even as no one must be forced against his will to turn from the secular way to the spiritual path, so too one who undertook My service with devoted will and then despised and rejected it must be recalled by just judgment to resume it. How? If he has upright guides and spiritual masters full of My zeal, they should call him back to My service. In doing this, let them first soothe him by supplication, exhortation and caressing speech, and then proceed to correct him by blows, cold, hunger and similar punishments, so that these miseries will warn him by recalling to his mind the pains of

Hell; and, fearing them, he may cast from him the filthiness of his soul and be recalled to the path he had deserted. As is written of these things in the Gospel:

50 Words of the Gospel

"Go out into the highways and byways, and compel them to come in, that my house may be filled" [Luke 14:23]. What does this mean? You who are a spiritual shepherd and a just guide and an upright master, leave your original habits, which you got from your first parents, and enter the strait and narrow way of unyielding precepts, written by men sure of themselves in the design of the Holy Spirit. And consider most sharply in My zeal those who, living under these precepts and your rule, undertook or vowed, by their own will and not by the undue urging of another, to observe the holy purpose of My covenant, but then esteemed it lightly and yearned to go back to their old vices. And, by sweet and bitter reproofs, compel them to enter into church discipline, that the house I have dowered may be filled, both with those who have been strongly reproved and with those who have been sweetly admonished. For some must be called to life by various punishments, and others by various blandishments. How?

As the righteous shepherd anxiously seeks his lost sheep, so must spiritual masters seek with great diligence their underlings who go astray through vice, and force them by their cleverness to return to the house of justice from which they went out or wished to go out, that the Church may be filled with sheep, some bitterly reproved and some gently exhorted, to be brought to the heavenly pastures.

51 The undisciplined who refuse correction must be expelled to save the rest

But if any are so stubborn as to refuse to correct themselves, either by bodily punishment inflicted on them in My zeal by their superiors, or for fear of Me Who am the God Who does not wish iniquity, or for love of the blood poured out by My Son Who suffered for them; and if these labor to pollute with their filth My faithful friends who are moving quickly in My ways, then these friends of Mine must expel them like wolves, lest they contaminate the flock, which My friend Paul urges, saying:

52 Words of the Apostle

"Put away the evil one from among you" [1 Corinthians 5:13]. What does this mean? You who are at the height of governing yet remain in humble subjection, expel this evil one from among you; for he despises fear of Me and opposes Me, the Creator of Heaven and earth. Expel him from among you with such force that he may never fix a root in your consciousness or set his foot in your company, lest the sweet unguents of your good works become worthless. But if any of these shall wish to return in penitence and shall seek Me his Creator with a pure heart, I will receive him even if he comes at the end of his course, for I judge all things justly.

53 Feigned converts are deceived, sincere converts received by God

But if someone hides and reserves the treasure of his heart, saying, "Until I feel myself about to die I will not turn away from secular affairs," and so defers his conversion until his last gasp; and then, when he can no longer breathe and despairs of longer life, tries to renounce the world; he deceives his soul, for his conversion is deceptive, made in jest and taken as a jest. But if one is close to death and renounces the world with his whole heart, for his sins and for love of Me, and desires to serve Me ardently as long as he lives, I will truly accept his devotion with all the choirs of angels and grant him the glory of life. For though a person may be involved in great crimes, when he faces up to his sins and weeps bitterly over his offenses, and does this simply because he has provoked Me to wrath, I will raise him up from death to salvation and not deny him the celestial inheritance, as the psalmist David testifies in My Spirit, saying:

54 Words of David

"In what day soever I shall call upon you, behold! I know You are my God" [Psalm 35:10]. What does this mean? In whatever day of my life divine grace shall illumine my mind with celestial brightness as I lie in the dark, so that in bitter remorse for my sins and with a heavy and wounded heart I call upon You, Who grant to all who call on You with a pure heart the remedy of Your loving kindness, by this visitation I know that You Who mercifully bring all these things to pass are my God. What does this mean? When by Your grace You Who can do it shall lead me to know You as my God in works of justice, and humble myself for my deeds of wickedness; then You will receive me, for I sincerely seek you and tearfully cry out after you and know You in renewal of soul, and I exhaust my body in true penitence and know it to be of no worth.

When a person performs his penance thus, he will find the remedy for his sins. How? Because he knows Me to be his God. How? Because he has forsaken his sins, and therefore he will see with the eye of penitence that those things he did before in his evil desire were vain.

55 Blasphemers against the Holy Spirit and suicides are rejected by God

Let no one therefore neglect to seek the remedy of penitence. If one neglects penitence when he is sound of body, let him nonetheless be eager to seek it in his last moments, and I will receive him into salvation; for however great the stain of sin is, by pure penitence it is washed away for the sake of My Son. But this is not true of anyone who has impenitently uttered blasphemy against the Holy Spirit, and anyone who has obdurately flung his own body into death; these two things are like one. And in the glory of eternal life I will not acknowledge these people, as it is written in the Gospel:

56 Words of the Gospel

"Every sin and blasphemy shall be forgiven to people; but the spirit of blasphemy shall not be forgiven" [Matthew 12:31, misquoted]. What does this mean? Every sin committed as an excess of the flesh, or in lust or bitterness or such vices, or blasphemy, which is the worship of idols, where the true God is not known and a false image is adored, or the invocation of demons, where the true God is known but in human perversity the Devil is called upon; all these things are forgiven people who are truly repentant and, stung by tears from their inmost hearts, faithfully seek the true God Who grants His mercy to all who call upon Him. For though people who do these things go gravely astray in sin, if they do not utterly renounce God, Who reigns in the heavens in sovereignty and power, they will seek and find His helping hand.

But if they persevere in their infidelity, so that they never recover from their wickedness but deny God with firm heart and consenting soul; if they say to themselves, "What is this that is called God? For there is no God in any mercy or truth Who could want or have power to help me," and therefore remain impenitent because they do not believe that they can be cleansed of sin or saved; then they are blasphemers of God. And if they persist in this, they cannot receive pardon for the blasphemy because of the wickedness of their obduracy, for they so stifle the understanding of their hearts that they cannot aspire upward. For they regard as nonexistent the One by Whose mercy they must be saved, as the psalmist David asserts, saying:

57 Words of David

"The fool has said in his heart, 'There is no God' " [Psalm 13:1]. What does this mean? In his foolish utterance he who lacks wisdom and understanding has denied God in his heart, unable to know Him. How? Because he did not want to know or understand the true God, saying to himself, "What is God? God does not exist. And what then am I? I do not know what I am!" He who says these things is a fool, for he has not the true wisdom by which God is known. But anyone who has really known God, reigning in power, is wise even if a sinner. Hence anyone who has despair of God's mercy fixed in his heart, saying, "God is nothing; I know Him not because He has not known me, and I deny Him because He has denied me;" such a one will not rise again to life or inherit joy, for since he regards the Creator as nothing, all creatures will desert him.

And one who despairs because of his sins and believes that their great weight makes it impossible for him to be saved is faithless; he shall not attain to life, for he contradicts the One Who gives life to all. But if any of these is led by penitence and truly seeks Me, he shall find Me, for I reject no one who comes to me with a sincere heart.

58 Anyone who resists blasphemous despair is quickly helped by God

And if the blackest tempests of blasphemy and despair fall on anyone, and he does not consent to them in his heart or his will or any perverted taste but struggles against them in great torment; then if he perseveres in the fight and strongly resists, I will quickly help him. And let him not doubt because he must struggle, for I say he is a strong warrior against the greatest of storms, and I will help him most speedily and hold him as a friend; for, patiently enduring, he has nobly conquered great misfortunes for love of Me.

59 One who separates his body and soul, which God has joined, is damned

But just as one who does not choose to know Me, the true God, in faith or hope, does not rise again to life, as has been said; so one who throws himself into bodily death, not waiting for the separation I appoint for everyone but dividing himself without hope of mercy, will fall into perdition, for he has killed the thing with which he should have done penance. For one who separates from a person what I have placed in the person incurs great guilt, as My Son shows in the Gospel, saying:

60 Words of the Gospel

"You have heard that it was said of old, 'You shall not kill. And whoever shall kill will be in danger of the judgment' " [Matthew 5:21]. What does this mean? You who want to stand upon the rock, note that the voice that comes from the Root of all reason tells you that Scripture, interpreted for you by the finger of God, forbade your ancient predecessors to divide in a person what divine arrangement united in him. What does this mean? That He Who forbade Adam the tree of the knowledge of good and evil, saying, "In whatever day you eat of it, you shall die the death" [Genesis 2:17], also said to Adam's race through Moses, "You shall not kill" [Exodus 20:13]; so you shall not destroy what is made in the image of God. And, just as Adam in transgressing God's command deprived himself and his progeny of the life of salvation, so also the person who destroys God's creation in human form cuts off from his soul and body faithful generations of works of salvation; and, thus incurring the judicial sentence, goes into the exile of misery.

Therefore one who has made such a cruel separation in a person casts himself into calamity. He has separated what is Mine, for I placed body and soul together in humans, and who is he to dare to separate them? And if one who kills another is weighed down with immense sin, what will he be who gives himself to death and lays in the dust the thing with which he should have wiped out his crimes?

For one who kills himself imitates that lost angel who found wickedness in the beginning and gave himself to damnation by killing himself. How? By envying God, Who has no beginning and no end and Who rules all things that are in Heaven and on earth. And as the Devil in his pride chose not to look at Me when he cast himself into perdition, so the person who violently cuts himself asunder does not deign to know Me, and so falls into death, like the other who brought perdition on himself. For before he fell he tried to uplift his iniquity on the wings of the wind and to fly in the heavenly places like a bird flying in the air; and in this presumption he cast himself down from beatitude to misfortune.

But I formed Man from earth to ascend from lower to higher things, and to begin and perfect good works and thus build the splendid virtues needed for hard tasks. Therefore let Man, who has both a body and a soul, not kill himself when he can do good works and repent, lest he reach that place where he can have neither work nor penitence, like the Devil who killed himself and was cast into Hell.

But let the one who sees with watchful eyes and hears with attentive ears welcome with a kiss My mystical words, which proceed from Me Who am life.

CHRIST'S SACRIFICE AND THE CHURCH

235

THE FOOD OF LIFE

VISION SIX
Christ's Sacrifice and the Church

*A*nd after these things I saw the Son of God hanging on the cross, and the aforementioned image of a woman coming forth like a bright radiance from the ancient counsel. By divine power she was led to Him, and raised herself upward so that she was sprinkled by the blood from His side; and thus, by the will of the Heavenly Father, she was joined with Him in happy betrothal and nobly dowered with His body and blood.

And I heard the voice from Heaven saying to Him: "May she, O Son, be your Bride for the restoration of My people; may she be a mother to them, regenerating souls through the salvation of the Spirit and water."

And as that image grew in strength, I saw an altar, which she frequently approached, and there each time looked devotedly at her dowry and modestly showed it to the Heavenly Father and His angels. Hence when a priest clad in sacred vestments approached that altar to celebrate the divine mysteries, I saw that a great calm light was brought to it from Heaven by angels and shone around the altar until the sacred rite was ended and the priest had withdrawn from it. And when the Gospel of peace had been recited and the offering to be consecrated had been placed upon the altar, and the priest sang the praise of Almighty God, "Holy, Holy, Holy, Lord God of Hosts," which began the mystery of the sacred rites, Heaven was suddenly opened and a fiery and inestimable brilliance descended over that offering and irradiated it completely with light, as the sun illumines anything its rays shine through. And, thus illuminating it, the brilliance bore it on high into the secret places of Heaven and then replaced it on the altar, as a person draws in a breath and lets it out again; and thus the offering was made true flesh and true blood, although in human sight it looked like bread and wine.

And while I looked at these things, suddenly there appeared before my eyes as if in a mirror the symbols of the Nativity, Passion and burial, Resurrection and Ascension of our Savior, God's Only-Begotten, as they had happened to the Son of God while He was on earth. But when the priest sang the song of the innocent Lamb, "O Lamb of God, Who takest away the sins of the world," and prepared to take the Holy Communion himself, the fiery brilliance withdrew into Heaven; and as it closed I heard the voice from thence saying, "Eat and drink the body and blood of My Son to wipe out Eve's transgression, so that you may be restored to the noble inheritance." And as other people approached the priest to receive the sacrament, I noticed five modes of being in them. For some were bright of body and fiery of soul, and others seemed pale of body and shadowed of soul; some were hairy of body and seemed dirty in soul, because it was pervaded with unclean human pollution; others were surrounded in body by sharp thorns and leprous of soul; and others appeared bloody of body and foul as a decayed corpse in soul. And all these received the same sacraments; and as they did, some were bathed in fiery brilliance, but the others were overshadowed by a dark cloud.

And when these mysteries were finished, as the priest withdrew from the altar the calm light from Heaven, which, as said, had shone round the whole altar, was drawn up again into the secret places of Heaven. And again I heard the voice from the supernal heavens, saying to me:

1 The Church was joined to Christ in His Passion and dowered with His blood

When Jesus Christ, the true Son of God, hung on the tree of His Passion, the Church, joined to Him in the secret mysteries of Heaven, was dowered with His crimson blood; as she herself shows when she often approaches the altar and reclaims her wedding gift, carefully noting with what degree of devotion her children receive it when they come to the divine mysteries. Therefore *you see the Son of God hanging on the cross, and the aforementioned image of a woman coming forth like a bright radiance from the ancient counsel; and by divine power she is led to Him.* For when the innocent Lamb was lifted up on the altar of the cross for human salvation, the Church suddenly appeared in Heaven by a profound mystery, in purity of faith and all the other virtues; and by the Supreme Majesty she was joined to the Only-Begotten of God. What does this mean? That when blood flowed from the wounded side of My Son, at once salvation of souls came into being; for the glory from which the Devil and his followers were driven out was given to humanity when My Only-Begotten suffered temporal death on the cross, despoiled Hell and led the faithful souls to Heaven. Therefore, in His disciples and their sincere followers faith began to increase and strengthen, so that they became heirs of the celestial Kingdom. Hence that image *raises herself upward so that she is sprinkled by the blood from His side; and thus, by the will of the Heavenly Father, she is joined with Him in happy betrothal.* For when the strength of the Passion of the Son of God flows burningly forth and rises to the height of the celestial mysteries, as the perfume of spices diffuses itself upward, the Church, fortified by that strength in the pure heirs of the eternal Kingdom, is faithfully joined by the high Father's decision to the Only-Begotten of God. How? As a bride, subjected to her bridegroom in her offering of subordination and obedience, receives from him a gift of fertility and a pact of love for procreating children, and educates them as to their inheritance. So too the Church, joined to the Son of God in the exercise of humility and charity, receives from Him the regeneration of the Spirit and water to save souls and restore life, and sends those souls to Heaven.

Therefore *she is nobly dowered with His body and blood;* for the Only-Begotten of God conferred His body and blood in surpassing glory on His faithful, who are the Church and her children, that through Him they may have life in the celestial city. How?

2   God conquered the ancient serpent by His Son's humility, not His power

By giving His body and blood to sanctify those who believe; and so the Heavenly Father delivered Him up to the Passion for the redemption of the peoples and conquered the ancient serpent through Him in humility and justice. He did not want His Son to conquer by His power and strength, for God is just and does not will iniquity, as the Psalmist declares, saying:

3   Words of the Psalmist

"Blessed is the man who has not walked in the counsel of the ungodly, or stood in the way of sinners, or sat in the seat of the pernicious" [Psalm 1:1]. What does this mean?

God is the Father of all the bliss and happiness of His creatures and shows many and various signs in them; and the Incarnation of His Son dripped with the sweet taste of delight, for in Him the heavenly virtues built many mansions through which humanity can return to the supernal Kingdom, which is darkened by no shadow of death. And thus the strongest powers of virtue were shown to be in the Heavenly Father, for it was He through His Only-Begotten who slew death and broke Hell; and on the last day He will make the world anew and better.

Therefore, He has not, through any wavering of His heart, wandered away into the paths of the evil spirits, who forsook the truth and seized on the lie. How? They wanted to use the lie to divide the truth. How? By trying to overthrow the Ancient of Days, Who was before days and hours began; and by yearning to make a partner for Him of the ancient serpent, who before time began was not. But that could not and should not be, for there is one God. And therefore the Devil is a liar, for he withdrew from God and forsook life to find death. And so, indeed, God did not stand in the path that sinners walk; He condemned Adam's choice and did not love his sin, but when he was seduced by the Devil He drove him from Paradise. And He did not reign in any seat of wicked power, as does the whole human race, which is bound up with death and sits in its shadow because it arrogantly deserted the truth. What does this mean? That God did not oppose either devilish presumption or human disrespect by His power or cast them out by His strength. Why? If there were two fighters, one stronger than the other, surely the stronger would show the weaker how much more he was capable of, conquering and confounding him and not yielding to him in any way. But God did not act thus; He resisted the work of iniquity by supreme goodness, sending into the world His Son, Who in His body brought back His lost sheep to Heaven with great humility. How? The blood that came forth from His body appeared in Heaven as soon as it flowed from His open wounds, pleading that the salvation of souls should be granted. How? Every creature who lives in the Son of God shows that through His Passion and death lost humanity was restored to life. How? Because the Only-Begotten of God, Who is life, offered Himself for His Passion on the altar of the cross for the redemption of the human race; and, as you have truly heard proclaimed by the voice from Heaven, in that place He chose the Church as His Bride, to be a mother to the believing peoples to restore salvation and by spiritual regeneration send them without stain to the celestial realms.

4   The growing Church offers her dowry to God and shows Him the sacraments

But as that image grows in strength, you see an altar, which she frequently approaches, and there each time looks devotedly at her dowry and modestly shows it to the Heavenly Father and His angels. For when the Church, as mentioned, suddenly increased in strong and blessed virtues, by the inspiration of the Holy Spirit the mystical altars were sanctified by the deep longings of the faithful, as is clearly shown to you. And the Church, with steady purpose, turns her footsteps there by example and devotedly offers her dowry, which is the body and blood of the Son of God, to the Creator of all in humble obedience, in the presence of those living and burning lights who are the citizens of Heaven. Why is this? Because as the flesh of My Only-Begotten came into being in the pure womb of the Virgin Mary, and then was delivered up for human salvation, so now His flesh, augmented by the incorrupt purity of the Church, is often given to sanctify the faithful.

5   Analogy of gold

For, as the goldsmith first unites his gold by melting it in the fire, and then divides it when it is united, so I, the Father, first glorify the body and blood of My Son by the sanctification of the Holy Spirit when it is offered, and then, when it is glorified, distribute it to the faithful for their salvation.

6 When the priest approaches the altar, the angels bring a brightness there

Hence *when a priest clad in sacred vestments approaches that altar to celebrate the divine mysteries, you see that a great calm light is brought to it from Heaven by angels.* For when he who has the charge of souls is girded with the sacred cincture and approaches the life-giving table to immolate the innocent Lamb, at once the great light of the heavenly inheritance drives away the darkness, shining with the help of celestial spirits from the secret places of Heaven. And it completely illumines the plan of sanctification, for here is the food of the soul by which believers are saved. How? Because the Church in the voice of the priest seeks her dowry, which is the body and the poured-out blood of My Son, in order to be fit for blessed childbearing in saving souls; for when that precious blood was poured out she was increased by a great multitude of peoples. And so then I, Who am the unfailing Light, illumine the place of that consecration with My holiness, to the honor of the body and blood of My Only-Begotten.

7 In the sacrament of the altar God remembers His Son's Passion

For when the priest begins to invoke me on the sanctified altar, and I consider that My Son offered Me bread and wine at the supper of death just before leaving the world; then I see that My Son did this in the hour of His death, as he was about to perish on the wood of the cross, so that when the blessed offering of the holy sacrifice is offered to Me by a priest I might always have His Passion in My sight, never blotting it from My sharp vision. For He too offered Me bread and wine in the outpouring of His blood, when He cast down death and raised up humanity.

8 Why in the sacrament bread, wine and water are offered

But because He Who went into and came out of the cloister of virginal purity was not of human nature but of divine power, the flesh of My Only-Begotten can be produced by consecration from wheaten bread and His blood from grape wine mixed with water, as I have shown through My faithful servant the prophet Joel, saying:

9 Words of Joel

"And the floors shall be filled with wheat, and the presses shall overflow with wine and oil. And I will restore to you the years that the locust and the canker-worm and the rust and the caterpillar have eaten, My great host which I sent upon you; and you shall eat in plenty and shall be filled, and praise the name of your God, Who has dealt wondrously with you; and My people shall not be confounded forever" [Joel 2:24–26]. What does this mean? Through the miraculous arrangement of God the floors of the faith of the believing Church will be filled with all good things. For I will make the grain of the wheat into the body of My Son, though for their true salvation, to call My faithful back to their rightful land, I will also make adversities abound, through which for My name's sake they will crush the desires of their flesh. And likewise I will transform the juice of the grape for them into the blood of My Only-Begotten and give them the oil of mercy. How?

I will restore to you in another form, changed into salvation for you, that time consumed by the locust of forgetfulness in ignorant unbelief in a round of vanities, when villianies first arose among the children of Adam; they forgot the fruitfulness of My justice, as a person forgets his necessary food after he has put it in his stomach, and in their impiety they tore apart My justice as the locust gnaws the fruit. How? When the locust of negligence with slothful mind destroys the utility of good fruit, the canker-worm of foulness also wraps itself around it in filth; for people like this wrap themselves in the filth of idolatry and other schisms, and probings into diabolism, and magical arts, and the search for auguries in the Creator's creatures as to future happenings in human life, and vile deeds of murder and fornication, and feed on them as the canker-worm feeds on mud. How? Wherever the canker-worm of shame cherishes the stench of filth, the rust of bitterness will consume the metal of shining faith; and these people, opposing God's justice, labor to obscure it, as rust is wont to take away the beauty of metals. How?

Where the rust of biting speech stains the brilliance of good deeds, there also the caterpillar of harmful actions will rob the flourishing green crops of their usefulness; for these people cast away in wicked malice such noble virtues as simplicity, chastity and virtuous constancy, illumined by the Holy Spirit in fresh beatitude, and try to destroy them as the caterpillar destroys the crops. But in all these things My exceeding strength is declared, which in its great power conquered the opposition of the Devil when I sent it among you for your salvation. How?

I the Father sent My Son into the world, physically born of the Virgin, that through Him I might redeem you from the perdition of death; so that I might dwell in you and you in Me, since My own Son underwent the Passion and gave you His flesh to eat and His blood to drink. Hence you shall eat this sacrament devotedly for your salvation and feed blessedly upon it; and thus, through the oil of My mercy, the hunger of your souls' perdition shall be satisfied. For My Son brought you penitence as a medicine for your wounds, and My Son's Bride was adorned with all justice and truth. And therefore you shall faithfully praise My name; for I am one God in true Trinity, and I govern you and display My wonders in you, miraculously snatching you from the power of the Devil. And therefore, My people, whom I have brought forth so wonderfully from the jaws of Hell, shall not be confounded by death in the eternity that is to come.

10 God does not leave the priest until he has completed the mystery

And you see that *the calm light shines around the altar until the sacred rite is ended and the priest has withdrawn from it.* For that light is an eternal sight, and shows itself by miracle with great brightness until the mysteries of this hallowed office are finished and the dispenser of the sacred rites, having completed them, withdraws from the holy spot. Why is this? Because it is fitting that the Divine Majesty manifest Its power most fully in these blessed rites, and because as long as a person remains within these things that belong to God, God's help will never leave him.

11 When the mystery of the sacrament begins, an unknown light shines on it

And when the Gospel of peace has been recited and the offering to be consecrated has been placed upon the altar, and the priest sings the praise of Almighty God, "Holy, Holy, Holy, Lord God of Hosts," which begins the mystery of the sacred rites, Heaven is suddenly opened and a fiery and inestimable brilliance descends over that offering. For when the fresh and living breath of the royal kiss has been given, and the fruit of noble life, which is to be sanctified and purified, has been put as a stone into God's wall, and the messenger of truth utters the sweet sound of the threefold invocation of the Lord of Hosts in praise of the Creator of all and thus begins the mystery of the shining dawn, the Incarnation of the Son of God in the Virgin; then suddenly the glorious tabernacle opens on the mystery of the sacrament, and an inconceivably calm and lofty brilliance shines down. *And it irradiates [the offering] completely with light, as the sun illumines anything its rays shine through;* in the power of the Father the holy heat so strikes the sparkling circle of that oblation that the radiant splendor wholly enters into the thing it falls upon. What does this mean?

The Bride of My Son offers the gift of bread and wine on My altar with a most devoted purpose. How? To remind Me in faithful memory by the hand of the priest that in this same oblation I delivered up the body and blood of My Son. How? Because the sufferings of My Only-Begotten are seen perpetually in the secret places of Heaven; and thus that oblation is united to

My Son in My ardent heat in a profoundly miraculous way and becomes most truly His body and blood. And thence the Church is quickened with blessed strength.

12   The divine light bears the oblation on high and makes it flesh and blood

For, thus illuminating it, as was said, the brilliance invisibly bears it on high into the secret places of Heaven; for that fiery brilliance, which streams through and illumines the sacrament, bears it upward with invisible power to those places mortal eye cannot see. *And then it replaces it on the altar,* for with gracious condescension it sweetly puts it back upon the table of sanctification; as a person draws in a breath and lets it out again, when by the wonderful arrangement of God he draws into himself the breath that makes him quicken and live, and then, also that he may live, expels it. *And thus the offering is made true flesh and true blood, although in human sight it looks like bread and wine;* for God is truthful and without illusion, and His sacrament also is firmly fixed on high where no one can throw it down, and is true flesh and blood without deception. For, just as a soul truly exists within flesh and blood while a person is alive in body, so too this mystery exists within bread and wine when it is worshipped in the true celebration and appears before people. And as the blind human eye cannot fully see God, so too a person cannot physically perceive these mysteries; as a person sees another's body but not his soul, so also a person can see the bread and wine but not the sacraments. Why is this?

The calm light that shone over the body of the Son of God when He was buried in the tomb, and raised Him to life again from the sleep of death, also shines on the altar over the sacrament of the body and blood of God's Only-Begotten, covering it from human sight so that people cannot see its holiness except as bread and wine, the form in which the oblation is placed on the altar. In just this way the Divinity that was in the Son of God was so concealed from people by His Humanity that they could see him only as a human being, living with them as a human being even though He was without sin. What does this mean?

I, Who created all things, benignly accept the oblation when it is offered to Me by the Church at the hand of the priest; for as Divinity displayed its wonders in the womb of the Virgin, it shows its secrets also in this oblation. How? Because here are manifested the body and blood of the Son of God. How?

VISION SIX

13   Analogy of ointment and sapphire

That oblation, by the power of God, is invisibly borne on high and brought back again in an instant, and so warmed by the heat of the Divine Majesty that it becomes the body and blood of God's Only-Begotten. People do not perceive this mystery with their bodily senses; it is as if someone encased a precious unguent in simple bread and dropped a sapphire into wine, and I then changed them into a sweet taste, so that in your mouth, O human, you could not taste the unguent in the bread or the sapphire in the wine, but only the sweetness—as My Son is sweet and mild. What does this mean? The unguent symbolizes My Son, born of the Virgin, Who was anointed with precious ointment. How? He was clothed with holy humanity, which is a precious unguent, pouring so sweetly over the deadly wounds of humans that when they turn back to Him they will no longer putrefy or stink with Adam's perdition. And the sapphire symbolizes the Divinity in My Son, Who is the Cornerstone; He is meek and humble, for he did not grow from the root of human flesh begotten by a man and a woman, but was miraculously incarnate by My fire in the sweet Virgin, and therefore his body and blood are sweet and delightful for believers to take in.

14   Why humans cannot take this spiritual gift in visible form

But you, O human, cannot take this spiritual gift visibly, as if eating visible flesh and drinking visible blood; for you are filth of filth. But, as the living spirit in you is invisible, so also the living sacrament in that oblation is invisible and must be received invisibly by you. For, as the body of My Son came about in the womb of the Virgin, so now the body of My Only-Begotten arises from the sanctification of the altar. What does this mean? The human soul, which is invisible, invisibly receives the sacrament, which exists invisibly in that oblation, while the human body, which is visible, visibly receives the oblation that visibly embodies that sacrament. But the two are one, just as Christ is God and Man, and the rational soul and the mortal flesh make up one human being; and so a person who contemplates Me in right faith receives the sacrament faithfully to make him holy. What does this mean?

My Son was miraculously born from the most pure Virgin, whose body was untouched and never burned in the sweetness of lust, for the virginal vessel in which I willed My Only-Begotten to be incarnate was the purest possible. Thus I did not permit this sweet Virgin's vessel to melt in fiery ardor, since in it My Son miraculously took on a human body.

15 Offered by a faithful priest the oblation becomes Christ's body and blood

But the Blessed Virgin heard true words of consolation from the angel in secret, and believed; she uplifted the sighs of her soul and said, "Behold the handmaid of the Lord; be it unto me according to your word" [Luke 1:38]. Thus she conceived the Only-Begotten of God. This indicates that the priest who is performing this office must invoke with his words Almighty God, faithfully believing in Him, offering Him in devotion of heart a pure oblation and speaking the words of salvation in the service of humility; then the Supernal Majesty will receive this oblation and transmute it with miraculous power into the body and blood of the Holy Redeemer. How? As My Son miraculously received humanity in the Virgin, so now this oblation miraculously becomes His body and blood on the altar. Therefore this sacrament is wholly perfect, being invisible and visible, as My Only-Begotten is wholly perfect, Who is invisible as to His Divinity and visible on earth as to His Humanity.

16 Analogy of a chick and a butterfly

For as a chick emerges from an egg, or a butterfly springs from a cocoon, and the living creature flies away while the thing it came from remains, so also in this oblation the truth that My Son's body and blood are there must be held by faith, though the oblation appears to human sight as bread and wine.

17 In the sacrament of the altar Christ's mysteries appear as in a mirror

And therefore, *while you are looking at these things, suddenly there appear before your eyes as if in a mirror the symbols of the Nativity, Passion and burial, Resurrection and Ascension of our Savior, God's Only-Begotten, as they happened to the Son of God while He was on earth.* For, as you see in a true vision, the mysteries of Him Who came to earth to save humanity—His birth from the Virgin, suffering on the cross, burial in the tomb, rising again from the dead and ascension into Heaven—shine brightly in the sacrament of the altar, since when God's Only-Begotten lived for a time among people in the world, these things happened to Him in His body by the will of the Father for the redemption of the human race. What does this mean? Before My eyes it is manifest that My Son suffered in the world for the love of humanity, for the Nativity, Passion, burial, Resurrection and Ascension of My Son slew the death of the human race. Hence these mysteries shine before Me in the heavenly places; for I have not forgotten them, but they will appear before Me in great brightness like the dawn until the end of the world. What does this mean?

18 When the Lord's Prayer is said Christ's Passion will move God to mercy

Until the world ends I will see in that Passion all who will believe in it or reject it. For it will always shine before me, as long as people are obliged to recite what My Son taught His disciples to say in praying to God: "And forgive us our debts as we forgive our debtors" [Matthew 6:12]. What does this mean? You Who have all things in Your power, look upon the outpouring of the blood that was shed for the human race, and forgive us, who are children of transgression, the debts we should have paid you but have not because of the baseness of our hearts. What does this mean?

We have not fulfilled what we promised in baptism, for we have transgressed Your precepts and thrown away our innocence, just as Adam in paradise disobeyed you and spoiled the garment of innocence. But because You are kind, do not punish us according to our wickedness, but forgive us our transgression according to Your loving-kindness; as we also who are transgressors, although we have much malice in us, for fear and love of our Savior forgive those who wrong us for the injuries they have done us. How? There are those who should love us because we are human, but instead trouble us, failing to love You and ignoring Your precepts. But we do not persecute them, as they deserve for their malice toward us; we contemplate Your just judgment and do not swiftly avenge ourselves on them, so that You too, O God, Who are just and good, may be gracious to us.

Hear, then, O human! As long as you need help, and as long as you can succor others, My Son's Passion will appear before Me in mercy, and His body and blood will be consecrated on the altar to be received by believers for their salvation and the purgation of their crimes. For when My Only-Begotten was in the world in the body, His body was physically sustained by wheat and wine; and therefore His body and blood is now consecrated on the altar in the oblation of wheat and wine, that the faithful may be refreshed in soul and body. For My Son miraculously redeemed humanity from Adam's perdition and now mercifully absolves people from the daily evil into which they often lapse. For whatever My Son suffered physically in His body for the redemption of humanity appears when the oblation is consecrated; and My will is not to hide this, for I draw His elect on high to the heavenly places, that through them His body may be perfected in its predestined members.

19 The oblation never appears as flesh except by miracle in great
necessity

Thus I miraculously show all these mysteries in that oblation, since
when it is placed upon the altar the oblation becomes the body and blood of
My Son; but it appears in human eyes to be bread and wine, for human frailty
is so delicate that people would shudder at receiving bleeding flesh and
trickling blood. For, as long as a person is mortal, he cannot contemplate
Divinity. And therefore the mystery that is the whole of Divinity is for
humans covered with obscurity, and they perceive it invisibly; namely, that
My Only-Begotten, being immortal, dies no more. And so, O human, I give
you His body and blood in the oblation of bread and wine, so that by true
faith you may perceive by that which is visible that which is invisible. And by
divine power you receive this sacrament with true certainty, yet so that it is
not visible to you, except in cases of great necessity; it has sometimes been
shown to My elect at times when they were in great affliction. And I do all
these things to be loving and helpful to humanity. But, though every creature
is subject to My precepts, you, O human, are always rebellious against Me; so
you are blind and deaf. Yet you cannot rebel against Me. Do I not do what I
will without your seeing it? You do not see with your physical eyes or hear
with your physical ears how I send a human soul into the body and how I take
it out of the body; but your soul will understand Me when it has left its
mortal body. And so also I give the body of My Son to be eaten and His blood
to be drunk, and I do this by My power, O human, without your seeing it.

20 As the song of the Lamb is sung the faithful communicate for
their good

Therefore, as you see, *when the priest sings the song of the innocent Lamb,
"O Lamb of God, Who takest away the sins of the world," and prepares to take the
Holy Communion himself, the fiery brilliance withdraws into Heaven;* for as
that minister announces the praise of Him Who in His mild innocence bore
the wickedness of humanity, and opens his inmost heart and his outward
devotion to these mysteries, the unconquered serenity that is here showing
its power withdraws itself into the supernal secret. *And as Heaven closes, you
hear the voice from thence saying* that believing and faithful people should eat
and drink with true devotion the body and blood of their Savior, Who for
them suffered temporal death, to wash away the contamination our first
parents brought into the world when they transgressed God's precept; so
that those people, cleansed from this transgression, may be faithfully restored to the rightful inheritance that by obstinacy they had lost.

For, as the Only-Begotten of God gave His body and blood to His disciples at the Supper, so now on the altar He gives His flesh and His blood to His faithful ones, donating it for human use, as a person does when he has finished the work he wanted to do. For the Son of God, fulfilling the precepts of His Father, offered Himself for people's salvation and gave His body and blood to be eaten and drunk for their sanctification, as the Bridegroom declares to his friends in the Song of Songs, saying:

21 Words of Solomon in the Song of Songs

"Eat, my friends; drink, and be inebriated, my dearly beloved!" [Song of Songs 5:1]. What does this mean? Eat in faith, you who through holy baptism have come to My friendship; for the spilled blood of My Son has purged you from Adam's fall, and as you chew the true medicine in the body of My Only-Begotten, the repeated deeds of crime and injustice you have done will be mercifully wiped out for you. And also drink in hope from this Vine, which has brought you out of eternal punishment; receive the cup of salvation, that you may firmly and strongly believe in that grace by which you have been redeemed, for you are bathed in the blood that was shed for you. And be inebriated with love, you who are so dear to Me, and flow with brooks of Scripture so that you will know best how to break away from carnal desires; and then I will awake in you splendid virtues pleasing to Me and give you the blood of My Only-Begotten. He Himself gave this sacrament to His disciples, as is written in the Gospel:

22 The meaning of the Lord's words to His disciples about this mystery

"And while they were at supper, Jesus took bread, and when He had blessed it, He broke it and gave it to His disciples, saying, 'Take and eat: This is My body.' And He took the chalice, and when He had given thanks He gave it to His disciples, saying, 'Drink of this, all of you. This is My blood of the New Testament, which will be shed for many for the forgiveness of sins. And I say to you: I will not drink henceforth of this fruit of the vine, until that day when I shall drink it with you new in the Kingdom of My Father'" [Matthew 26:26–29]. What does this mean?

When the Son of God celebrated with His disciples that consummation by which He was to pass out of the world, no longer, as before, living among the events of the world but enduring the Passion of the cross in accordance with His Father's will, with supreme devotion He took the bread in remembrance of His body for human salvation. With all His longing He reminded His Father how He came forth from Him and wanted to return to Him, and prayed Him to consider whether it was possible, because of the weakness of

His flesh, for the chalice He was to drink to pass from Him; but this was not to happen. And therefore He blessed that bread in remembrance of the sweat of His body; for in the anguish of His Passion, as He submitted to His Father's command and was willing to die on the cross, He gave His body and blood to His disciples, so that they would not forget His example.

And he broke it for them; for that Passion was hard for His body to bear. But nonetheless He obeyed His Father and conquered cruel death by the death of His body; and so He showed that His body and blood were also to be given to believers in Him in the mystery of the oblation.

And He gave it to His disciples for true salvation, that they too might do such things in His name as He was doing for love of them; thus He was saying in a gentle voice, "You who humbly wish to follow Me, take with ardent love this example I leave you, My Passion and My works I have done at My Father's command, when He sent Me to teach and to manifest His Kingdom; and eat faithfully what I give you, for it is My body." What does this mean? "Eat My body, for you must imitate My works in your spirits and your flesh, whenever the Holy Spirit inspires them in your hearts, as a person swallows the food he is sending to his stomach; as you and all who wish to keep My precepts should follow Me in My works, so too you should eat My body."

And then the Son of God, taking for salvation the saving cup, gave thanks to His Father; for when the blood poured out from His side, grace was given to believers that was so strong that it conquered the ancient serpent, delivered lost humanity and strengthened the whole Church in faith. How? The Savior in the sweetness of His love gave His precious example to all His faithful, summoning them with gentle inspiration by saying, "Drink with confidence from this saving cup, all you who desire to follow Me faithfully, that for love of Me you may chastise your bodies by privation and restrain your blood by toil, and deny yourselves to strengthen the Church; even as I submitted Myself to the Passion, and shed My blood for your redemption, not thinking of the tenderness of My flesh but thirsting for your salvation. For this blood, which is shed for you, is not that blood of the Old Testament, which was shed in shadow, but My blood of the New Testament, which was given for the salvation of the peoples. How? I Who am the Only-born of My mother, the Son of the most pure Virgin, shed My blood on the cross to redeem people who contemplate Me by faith. And as I then gave it for the deliverance of the human race, so now I give it on the altar for humanity, to cleanse those who faithfully receive it.

"For in the Supper of My Passion I gave you My body and My blood to be eaten and drunk; and so now you may do the same on the altar in memory of Me. Therefore I unfold the truth and say to you, my faithful followers: I will not again drink this cup of anguish in this oppression I now suffer from the Jews until that day when I rise from the dead and Death is overthrown, and I bring in the day of salvation. Then I will drink with you the cup of your redemption and show you who are Mine your new reason for rejoicing: that the perdition of the ancient crime is taken away, and the Kingdom is opened to you that My Father has prepared for those who love Him. What does this mean? That by My death, which I suffered on the cross, you will know the salvation of souls; and when I ascend after My Resurrection, you will receive the Spirit, the Comforter, and you will newly understand true doctrine. And then for My name's sake you will endure many tribulations, and I will endure them with you; not because I will suffer any miseries in the body after this, as I did when I was in the world in the body, but because you will endure them in My name. Therefore I will endure them with you, since you are in Me and I am in you."

And thus, as was said, you who faithfully believe in Me shall receive the body and blood of My Son to wipe out your sins, so that, gladdened by this sacrament, you may attain supernal strength, as My servant David exclaims by My burning will, saying:

23   Words of David

"The earth shall be filled with the fruit of your works, bringing forth grass for cattle and green crops for the service of people, that you may bring forth bread out of the earth, and wine may rejoice the human heart; that faces may be gladdened with oil, and bread strengthen the human heart" [Psalm 103:13–15]. What does this mean?

O God, Whose magnificence is above everyone, by the faith that is the fruit of virtue in Your wisdom, and by which You are truly known, Man shall be filled; one who adheres to faith shall end the hunger of unbelief by taking the way of justice, though he had not known the truth before and had fainted from a dearth of rectitude. Now he will fulfil his mind's contrition by doing good works and offer to the simple, knowing their weakness, an example of humility. He will grow and flourish in virtue and show in abundant security a fertility of true righteousness, by which he will serve those who now long for earthly things. For he will labor to be useful to them, and by his services of support and defense lead faithful souls to heavenly joys, as do all who in their strength and protectiveness firmly defend those whom they are set to guard. And these works prevail in people by Your will, O God, so that when they are adorned with these virtues You may miraculously give them, out of the fruit of the pure fertility of the earth, the body of Your Son; as Your Only-Begotten, coming in the body out of the womb of virginal chastity, mercifully gave the bread of life to those who believe in Him.

And You perform a further miracle: that the blood of Your Only-Begotten, which was shed for the salvation of souls, gladdens the internal strength of people, their souls, by remitting their sins. How? Because, as once the body of Your Son was offered on the cross for the redemption of the human race, so now his flesh and blood are consecrated on the altar for the salvation of those who believe. And when this is miraculously accomplished in Your will, then this sacrament will gladden the face, which is to say the Church, sprinkling it with the oil of mercy. For those who believe and embrace mercy with joyous faith appear beautiful in the eyes of the Lord; and when the Salvation of the world hung on the cross and mercifully delivered humanity from the snare of the Devil, He also generously freed people from the bonds of sin, that they might faithfully believe in God with joyful and sincere hearts and never cease with devoted ardor to help the wretched.

And the faithful should burn in this love, so that the bread that offers life to its tasters may strengthen the minds of those who are wavering in inconstancy; and thus the purpose of their hearts may not decline to evil, but ascend in strength to that which is life.

24 This cleansing sacrament is to be worshipped by all up to the last

This bread is the flesh of My Son, which is obscured by no shadow of sin and clouded by no stain of iniquity, so that they who receive it are bathed with heavenly light in soul and body and cleansed by faith from their inner uncleanness. And therefore let there be no doubt about this most sacred flesh; for He Who formed the first man neither from flesh nor from bone is certainly able to produce the sacrament in this way. Therefore, O virginal Origin, You arise, grow, spread out and produce a great branch with many shoots from which to build the heavenly Jerusalem, beginning not in a man's semen but in a mystical breath. You are bound by no stain of sin at Your beginning, but developed in miraculous virtue, for You arose in an unplowed field, a flower so excellent that it will never wither from any accident of mortality, but in full freshness will last forever. Wherefore this sacrament of Your body and blood must be worshipped in the Church in a true service, until the last person to be saved by the mystery appears at the end of the world. For it comes from the secret mind of God to bring salvation to believers, as David testifies, saying:

25 Further words of David

"And He commanded the clouds from above, and opened the doors of Heaven, and rained down manna upon them to eat, and gave them the bread of Heaven. Man ate the bread of angels; He sent them provisions in abundance" [Psalm 77:23–25]. What does this mean?

From the heights of Heaven the Celestial Father showed this to the patriarchs and prophets in the power of His glory and in the secrets of His mysteries to prepare human minds; for in the Holy Spirit they truly foretold His Son, and in the precepts of the Law, the blood of goats and other demonstrations they miraculously foreshadowed Him to the people. And thus, opening the sweetness and affection of His heart in mildness and burning charity, He sent them His Son, that through Him they might be refreshed from the hunger of unbelief and fed on heavenly things that would satisfy their faith and give them the fullness of happiness and beatitude. And so, when the Supreme Father sent those blessed refreshments in abundance of spiritual joy, through the humanity of the Son of God Man received that bread with whose sweetness the angels of Heaven who contemplate God can never be sated. And therefore let the faithful faithfully listen:

O you faithful people, who are the fruits of the Church! Listen and understand your souls' remedy, by which you are not children of the Devil but heirs of the celestial Kingdom; and consider how I, the mild and benign Father, have surrounded you with the manifold happiness of your salvation. Pay heed therefore to the goodness of your Father, by Whom the thing that will save you has been arranged, for though you are vile ashes the Humanity of My Son still implores for your salvation. How? My Son was born of the incorrupt Virgin, who knew nothing of any pain, but remained in the fresh purity of her integrity, like grass that flourishes in verdant glory when the dew falls on it from Heaven.

26　Why bread is offered in the sacrament of the altar

And because it was from the pure Virgin that My Son took on flesh without sin, it is fitting that His flesh should now be made from that fruit which is without the sap of bitterness. How? The grain of wheat is the strongest and best of all the fruits there are; it has in its stalk no sap or pith like other trees, but its stem rises to a spike that leads to the fruit, and it never produces bitter juice either in heat or in cold, but yields dry flour. So too the flesh of My Son was dry, with no filth of the human pollution that produces the human race through the lustful embraces of a man and a woman. Not so was My Only-Begotten born, for He came forth in verdant integrity as the stalk brings forth the clustered grains of wheat. For as a stalk of wheat, flourishing without pith, produces dry grain at the end of its pure spike, so too the Blessed Virgin, conceiving without male power, brought forth her most holy Son in simple innocence. He drew from His mother no sap of sin, because she conceived Him without the pith of a man; as the stalk gives no sap to the grain, because it flourishes not by the pith of a tree but by the sun and rain and gentle breeze. So the pure Virgin brought forth her Only-Begotten in sweet chastity, not because of a man but because she was overshadowed by the power of the Most High and imbued by the outpouring of the Holy Spirit.

Therefore, though the Virgin herself originated in the will of a man and a woman, she did not thus bring forth her Son, but without the will of a man bore in her wholeness Him Who came from Heaven, true God and purest Man. As she bore Him in her virginity to be pure and stainless, now the bread that is truly consecrated as His flesh and is pure in its integrity should be received by the faithful in purity of heart and without any element of contradiction. This I predicted to the children of Israel, as by My will it is written:

27   Words of Moses

"Remember this day in which you came forth out of Egypt, and out of the house of bondage; with a strong hand has the Lord brought you forth out of this place, so look that you eat no leavened bread" [Exodus 13:3]. What does this mean?

You who wish to be imitators of My Son, turn your eyes from death to life and keep in mind the salvation of that Day which is My Son, Who trampled death and gave life, so that you went forth from the wretched exile of perdition; you threw off the thick darkness of infidelity and tore yourselves away from the house of the Devil, to whom Adam's transgression had given you. Turn your eyes from earthly to heavenly actions, for by divine power I the Lord have led you out of evil; I Who rule over all with such strength that no obstacle can stand against My might, but I sharply penetrate all things. So through My Son I have snatched you from the place where you shamefully lay in your wickedness, serving death by your infidelity instead of doing good works.

And now that you are freed in My Only-Begotten from that oppression, go from strength to strength and take care not to admit into your consciences the infidelity, which does not strengthen but bitterly weighs down your heart. What does this mean? Do not follow the arts of the Devil or the other fictions people devise for themselves, corrupted by philosophers, pagans and heretics; but imitate My Son as a mirror of faith, Who delivered you from the prison of Hell when He gave Himself for you to the suffering of the cross. And, that you may more carefully follow in His steps, strengthen your hearts with the celestial bread, and so with faithful devotion receive His body. For he came from Heaven and was born of the sweet and pure Virgin, and, by suffering for you on the cross, gave you His very self; so that now you may receive the sweet and pure bread, which is His body, consecrated on the altar by divine invocation, without any bitterness but with sincere affection, and thus escape from humanity's inner hunger and attain to the banquet of eternal beatitude.

28 Why wine is offered in the sacrifice of the altar

And in the wine that comes from the vine I also will show wonders, making it by the same invocation the sacrament of His blood. What does this mean?

The blood of My Son flowed from His side as the grape drips from the vine. And as the grape is trodden by feet and is crushed in the winepress, and sweet strong wine flows out to strengthen human blood, so too when My Only-Begotten in the sweat of His agony was bruised by blows and scourges, and pressed to the wood of the cross, noble and precious blood issued from His wounds and sprinkled the believing peoples with life-giving freedom. And the grape is unlike other fruits, which can be eaten out of hard shells, while people usually suck grapes rather than eat them; so too My Son was different from all other people in the matter of sin. For they are weighed down by wickedness and subjected to passions, while My Only-Begotten, miraculously born of the chaste Virgin, lacked all contamination of sin. Therefore, and because the grape is so delicate in texture, I will that wine should be consecrated as the blood of My Son.

For as wine flows out of the vine, so My Son went forth from My heart; and My Only-Begotten too was the true Vine, and many branches went forth from Him, for in Him the faithful have been planted who through His Incarnation are fruitful in good works. And as that liquor comes out of the sweetest and strongest fruit of the vine, all merciful and true justice appears out of the Incarnation of My Son, and all who faithfully seek Him find these virtues in Him. How? Those who faithfully cleave to Him are made by Him green and fruitful, so that they bring forth noble fruits of virtue; as He too, being sweet and mild, brought forth precious offshoots in holiness and justice and cleansed those who believed in Him from every stain of infidelity, as is written of Him in the Song of Songs:

29 Words of the Song of Songs

"A cluster of grapes of Cyprus is my beloved to me in the vineyards of Engedi" [Song of Songs 1:13]. What does this mean?

BOOK TWO

The Son of God, Who saved me the exile by His Passion, also mercifully gave me in His Resurrection the cup of life. How? As a cluster of grapes of Cyprus has in itself a strong fullness of drink, so too the excellence that is in God's Only-Begotten has in itself an unfailing magnitude, so that the Son of God will never be exhausted, but will always give the drink of life to those who thirst. For He is the Savior of Life. And we, who formerly fell short, now are strengthened by the manifestation and the knowledge of the true holiness of good works; and through Him we eat the food of life and go on through knowledge of God to life. In the Old Testament we endured great hunger and were unable to rise to salvation, for it was shadowed and did not show the full explanation but displayed many different meanings. But now we are satisfied, for we drink in Him the saving cup, tasting Who God is in true faith; Whom we cannot see with the outer and carnal vision, but Whom we have within by spiritual understanding, as strong wine shows its power in people's veins, though the people do not feel it but only know that it is within them.

And so the Bridegroom of souls is the cluster of grapes of Cyprus, Whose fruit will not fail. How? A blind man who has come in through the door asks for his sight. How? The person who did not have the vision of faith attains to faith and enters by the squeezing of the winepress into the dew of the blood of Christ. How? Just as we have life in our souls through His commands, so too we receive cleansing in our bodies through His gift; for we were born in Adam's transgression and are unclean, but in Christ's blood we are sanctified. Hence the betrothed soul says of Him in the Holy Spirit, "My Beloved, Who is sweet and lovable to my heart, is to me like strong wine in the full sanctification of His blood. For though I am unclean in that I am planted in flesh, as a vineyard lies in thorns when it is as yet uncultivated, He, the Fountain of Salvation, mercifully washes sinners clean of their stains and gloriously sanctifies them in His secret mysteries. As He came sweetly forth from the heart of His Father, He now sweetly displays His blood as wine; and as He was miraculously born of the Virgin, so His body is miraculously manifested in bread, for He is the cluster of grapes that will never suffer defect or loss."

And by the will of the Father He is trodden on the altar as if in the winepress, so that Man, who cannot subsist by himself, may not fall in his frailty and weakness. For as human blood is replenished by drinking, humanity is sanctified by the blood of the Son of God. And as people must refresh themselves by drinking lest their blood without watering dry up, so wine must not be lacking for consecration as the blood of the Son of God, but in the sacrament of that mystery will always be upon the altar.

VISION SIX

30 Why water must be present with the wine in the sacrament

But note clearly also, O human, that in this consecration water must be mixed with the wine, because blood and water issued from My Son's side; His Divinity is understood by the wine, and His Humanity is seen in the water. And thus, since there is both Divinity and Humanity in Him, there must be water and wine in that consecration; for as the wine symbolizes His Divinity, the water indicates His Humanity, which is pure and clean without the admixture of the blood of a man. For My Only-Begotten, the fountain of living water, when He came into the world for human salvation cleansed people by the regeneration of the Spirit and water from the ancient sin of Adam and transported them to Heaven, as it is written:

31 Words of Wisdom

"I, like a river channel and like an aqueduct, came forth from Paradise" [Ecclesiastes 24:41]. What does this mean? God strengthened Man with the faculty of reason and gave him many mystical gifts; breathing the breath of life into him, by reason he exalted him. But then he was seduced and was falling into death; so I, the Son of God, came to free him, flowing forth in the beauty of the stream of abiding charity and issuing in an outpouring of true and unfailing purity. I came forth from the secret place of celestial delight so that humanity, which was perishing because of its guilt, might be mercifully snatched from perdition. How? By pouring out for its sake in the agony of the Passion the unoffending blood of supreme innocence. How? When Adam transgressed and was expelled from Paradise, because he was guilty his blood was driven to overflow with anguish, and in that anguish was diluted and mixed with watery sweat. And thus water is present in human blood through sweating.

Therefore, O human, as the Only-Begotten of God began to be distressed in His body, when He willed to suffer for the human race, His blood came forth in drops of sweat; and later, when He hung on the cross, water flowed with blood from the wound in His side. And therefore, in the sacrament where the mystery of His Passion is celebrated, water must be present with the wine, because water and blood flowed from the wound in the Son of God's side. But in that sacrifice the wine must be more abundant than the water; for blood surpasses the liquid that dilutes it, just as milk exceeds the watery substance that moistens it. So let those who celebrate this mystery do so in the way that was shown them, as the people exhort who speak by My inspiration in the words of Wisdom, as it is written:

32 More from the Book of Wisdom

"Come, eat My bread, and drink the wine that I have mixed for you" [Proverbs 9:5]. What does this mean? You who wish to lay aside folly, come out of that ignorance which makes you disdain God, and that defilement which sent you into exile, and return into the pure place that is yours, shown to you in the mirror of faith in the fountain of living water; and with gentle devotion eat My bread, not sown in the field by a man or given growth by the earth, but issuing from God and remaining in Him. For as bread is eaten but earth is trampled, so the Son of God Who is the Living Bread excels the children of humanity; for the Son of God is steadfast in the power of His Divinity, while the children of humanity are unbalanced due to the weakness of their flesh. The Son of God, while physically in the world, did not have in His flesh any weak tendency to sin; for as a fire which bakes bread dries it and leaves no soft moisture in it, so the Only-Begotten of God, conceived by the mighty fire of the Holy Spirit and born of the chaste Virgin, had no contamination of sin in His body. And as bread nourishes people, the Son of God nourishes believers in faith, for He is the strong fruit that shall never fail.

Therefore, O ye faithful who eat this bread, drink also with pure purpose this wine, which is devoid of every uncleanness and which never enters that state of futility in which corruption devours noble innocence and turns it to poison.

33 Adam began with pure blood but his sin turned it to impure filth

When he was created, the first man was pure in this respect: He was not divided within himself but was pure in flesh and blood. But after he committed his transgression, he was ruined, and always after that poured out his blood in stinking and unclean adultery. For he had cast away his innocent honor, and therefore his blood lost its red color and was perverted in the act of conception into the liquid of pollution. In that liquid there is no form, until blood is engendered again; that blood takes on a new form, and after its beginning lies dormant, until it comes to its full strength and is secretly quickened to sensation. And then clean flesh and blood appear again, purified from poison, until it is struck by harmful heat, which produces the scum of uncleanness. But the Son of God was pure in respect to all these things: He had clean flesh and blood and was never touched by harmful heat, so that He remained in a holy and honorable state of verdant chastity, never profaned by contamination. But when He was in the agony of the Passion, He poured out water with the blood from His side; for blood is not poured out without water, but their proportions are such that the blood thickens the water rather than the water diluting the blood.

34 Those who take Christ's body and blood are most sweetly vivified

Therefore, you who wish devoutly to worship God because you love salvation, receive this cup of sanctification; I have so tempered it for you with mild forgiveness that you will never feel harsh punishment. For in the supernal Son there is both Divinity and Humanity, and through His Passion you are delivered from death and quickened by His body and blood, so as to have a part in the eternal habitation. But I, Who am the Beginning and the End, again say to you, O human, that My noble Son is the flower of roses and lilies of the valley, born of the chaste Virgin who brought Him forth in wholeness, and that birth was such as to appease Me for the wickedness of the first parents of the human race, who by their transgression provoked Me to wrath.

Therefore, when I see My Son's body and blood daily consecrated on the altar in My name, and you, O human, being sanctified by that sacrament, eating His flesh and drinking His blood, I always contemplate that birth. For when the priest does his office as is appointed him, invoking Me in sacred words, I am there in power, just as I was there when My Only-Begotten, without discord or stain, became incarnate. Thus His body was pure and sweet and all-holy; and they who now faithfully receive His flesh and blood will be so sweetly enlivened that they will never be despised or rejected. As it is written in the Song of Songs:

35 Words of Solomon

"Who shall give you to me for my brother, sucking the breasts of my mother, that I may find you out of doors and kiss you, and no one will despise me?" [Song of Songs 8:1] What does this mean? With groans and devotion and with sure faith the people of the Church say, "Who will be merciful and give me, a miserable human in tribulation, You, the Bridegroom of the Church?—You, Whom I name my brother because of Your Incarnation, and Who sucks the mercy and truth that nourish humanity from the Divinity, which is my mother in my creation, giving me life and growth?" What does this mean? "The nourishments of the Church too are full of Your grace, for You Who are the Living Bread and the fountain of living water make her fully abound in the sacrament of Your body and blood. And this You do that I may surely find You out of doors, knowing that You are the Son of God in Heaven but seeing You as a man on earth, for my mortal eyes cannot perceive You in Divinity; and that I may find You in the bread and wine of the divine mystery, the sacrament without deception or artifice. And thus I may kiss You, for You were incarnate for my salvation, and You now make me a sharer in Your body and blood; no creature that is subject to You and follows Your precepts can despise me now for being a rebel against Your commands and opposing You, for You came into the world for my sake and have given me Yourself."

36 At the priest's invocation at the altar the sacrament is perfected

Now therefore, O human, as you see, when the sacrifice has been offered at the altar and the priest begins to invoke Me in those words appointed for him by the Holy Spirit, verily I say to you that I am there in My burning heat, and with full will I perfect that sacrament. How? To effect this mystery I extend over this offering My ardent charity at the moment when the priest invokes Me and remembers that My Son blessed bread and wine in the agony of His Passion as the sacrament of His body and blood, giving them to His disciples that they might do the same for the salvation of the people. Truly I say to you that there will never be an invocation over such an offering in remembrance of My Only-Begotten without the mystery of His body and blood being perfected in it; though the carnal eye cannot see it, as long as it is mortal dust, except by the perception of humble and devoted faith. How? As a bird sees that an egg has been laid in its nest; it eagerly flies to cover it and nurtures it with its warmth until the chick emerges; and then the shell remains, and the chick flies away. What does this mean?

When the offering of bread and wine has been laid on the altar and dedicated to My name in memory of My Son, I the Almighty miraculously illumine it with My power and glory and transform it into the body and blood of My Only-Begotten. How? By the same miracle through which My Son took on a body from the Virgin, the consecrated oblation becomes His flesh and blood. How? As when My Son lived in the world with people, He was also with Me in Heaven; and so now, living with Me in Heaven, He also remains with people in earth. But this is a spiritual and not a physical phenomenon.

37 God exercises the power of His will in every creature as He wishes

I the Father am present to every creature and withdraw Myself from none; but you, O human, do withdraw yourself from creatures. For instance, when you look into water, your face appears in it, but your reflection can exercise none of your powers, and when you turn away you no longer appear in the water. But I do not appear to creatures thus changeably; I am present to them in a true manifestation, never withdrawing My power from them but doing in them by the strength of My will whatever I please. And so too I truly display My majesty in the sacrament of the body and blood of My Son, and wondrously perform My miracles there from the beginning of the priest's secret words until the time when that mystery is received by the people.

38 The Mass may be said from the first to the ninth hour as necessary

And this priestly office may be done for the faithful from the first to the ninth hour of the day, according to the time made necessary by the habits of the people; for Adam arose in the morning and was seduced in the ninth hour, and the Passion of My Son began at daybreak and was completed in the ninth hour, when He expired on the cross and overcame Death by His death. And the Church stood by My Only-Begotten in that place and received her wedding gifts; and these must now be celebrated by the children of the Church.

39 All must communicate fasting except in danger of death

But this office of sacrifice is to be celebrated by the priests with empty stomachs and not in repletion, lest the digestion of the food destroy spiritual desire; spiritual feasting should precede physical refection, thus honoring the spirit and reviving the body. For this sacrament is to be received with spiritual desire, not with carnal greed, and therefore it should be taken fasting and not after a meal except in an emergency, if a person is thought to be about to leave the world. My Son gave His body and blood to His disciples around the end of the day and brought them the morning of true life; and at the end of the world, death will pass away from temporal humanity, and the elect will shine like the sun in My Kingdom.

40 God raised fallen Man and not the Devil because Man was tempted

Thus My Only-Begotten in His Resurrection drew the souls of the just out of Hell and restored the human race to eternal life, which the reprobate angels lost when without temptation by another they chose death; for they were seduced by no other tempter but themselves, since they had in themselves no taste of sin as a human has in his weak body. Therefore, Man, who was physically weak and seduced by a tempter, was restored to life by the Uplifter; but the Devil, who had not been hampered by a body, was left in his perversity. And Man was given true and salutary refreshment in receiving the body and blood of My Son; invisibly revived in soul by this sacrament, he can arise and manfully resist his invisible adversary.

41   In this sacrament not quantity but holiness must be considered

But let those who receive this sacrament in greater or lesser quantity understand that the receivers of more and of less have received the same amount of power, for the sacrament consists not in quantity but in holiness. It saves those who receive according to their faith, as is written of the manna:

42   Analogy of the manna

"And the children of Israel did so and gathered, some more and some less. And they measured by the measure of an omer, and the one who gathered more had nothing over, and the one who gathered less did not lack; but each had gathered according to what he could eat" [Exodus 16:17–18]. What does this mean? The children of election, who ardently desire to see God, long for the supernal sacrament as has been commanded them, and as their teachers instruct them they gather it in their hearts. And in their souls they scrutinize it as they have learned to do; but in their secret hearts one person has more devotion and another a lesser resolve, and in their thoughts they measure by the measure of what they feel in their souls. They determine how much faith in God they have, which is not divided but remains whole, and think about the degree and kind of devotion with which they receive the body and blood of their Redeemer. So this sacrament will not be holier for the one who receives more of it, or of lesser effect for one who receives less of it; but it will illumine the recipient according to his faith. Therefore, O human, it need not be taken in great quantity, for our mighty God is present as much in a small offering of this mystery as in a great one; so let those who receive it take care only that they have God, the Three and One, in their hearts with firm and perfect faith. And let each of the faithful collect the powers of his soul with sincere and righteous heart, as his capacity for faith permits, and beware of searching into Divinity more exaltedly or profoundly than his senses or thought can grasp, but do it soberly as the Holy Spirit teaches; let him be subject to the fear of the Lord, since Man is only poor ashes.

43   What is on the altar is the true body and blood of Christ

But do not doubt, O foolish people, that this sacrament which is thus manifested to you is the body and blood of My Son. Remember from what I created the flesh and blood of Adam—from earthly mud. How, then, does it seem to you: Is it easier for Me to make the flesh and blood of My Son from this oblation, or to make Man from the mud of the ground? A man pours forth semen from his blood, and a woman receives it; what else do they add?

Nothing at all toward the formation or the body of the little baby; and who then forms the person in its flesh and bones and marrow and its beautiful face but I, the Father of all? But the father and mother have no power to make or create the little baby, except to send forth their blood in burning lust; after that they have no role in forming it. Can you see how it is done, when you cannot perceive the methods?

But you say, O human, "I do not see that this oblation is flesh and blood the way I see that a person is body and blood." To which I answer: You saw My Son in His body and blood when He was mortal on earth, as He is now immortal in Heaven; so you cannot see Him now with bodily eyes. Nor can you see how His flesh and blood are consecrated on the altar in a sacrament that exists for the glory not of a priest but of My Only-Begotten, Who did the office in the Supper with His disciples. As long as you are mortals, you cannot see Me in My glory; and so also with your physical eyes you cannot physically see the flesh and blood of My Son, because you cannot perceive that which is invisible, but with your mortal gaze can take in only that which is visible.

44 In the sacrament three things must be offered in honor of the Trinity

This sacrament must be offered to Me in three forms. What? Bread, wine and water, for the honor of the Trinity. If any of these three is lacking, the Trinity is not truly worshipped, for the Father is understood by the wine, the Son by the bread, and the Holy Spirit by the water. Thus one who offers wine without bread or water worships the Father but denies the Son and Holy Spirit; one who gives bread without wine or water holds the Son but casts away the Father and Holy Spirit; and one who uses water without wine or bread heeds the Holy Spirit but refuses the Father and the Son. One who gives wine and bread without water holds the Father and the Son but casts away the Holy Spirit; one who offers wine and water without bread worships the Father and the Holy Spirit but denies the Son; and one who uses bread and water without wine heeds the Son and the Holy Spirit but denies the Father. Therefore, let no division take place in this sacrament, as I, remaining undivided in Three Persons, am One Indivisible God; in the same way that thought, will and deed are in one human being, and without them that person is not.

45 A priest who neglects, refuses or forgets to offer these must be punished

But if there is a defect in the sacrifice, so that either bread or wine or water is left out of it, truly the one by whose neglect it happened will be liable to grave punishment. If it is done knowingly in negligent apathy, or faithlessly because of doubting unbelief, I will cast the guilty one out of My sight unless he comes to himself and punishes himself with severe penitence. And if it happens unknowingly through forgetful neglect, the guilty one will be answerable to Me for his fault and subject to penance, because he was not acute enough in ensuring that everything pertaining to My sacrifice was there. For when My Son hung upon the cross, nothing that pertained to salvation was lacking there, since He brought salvation to humanity by the outpouring of His blood; and so nothing must be absent in the celebration of His mystery. For this sacrament is the all-holiest sanctification, and so this flesh and this blood must be received with all faith and devotion.

46 How the body and blood of Christ should be distributed to the people

But let not anyone who receives this sacred flesh refuse to take the blood of the mystery too; for My Son is pure above all things and a mirror of virtue, and so His noble blood must be received. An exception is made if the recipient is weak in mind, and the priest fears the danger of spilling; in that case the recipient is given the treatment accorded to the simplicity of children, to whom bread is given and wine is denied. So let the sacrosanct flesh be granted to such a person, but the flowing blood be withheld, lest a greater danger arise from giving it; for the holy flesh is united with the blood and the blood with the flesh in one sanctity. But if the person has enough discernment to keep the mystery safe, when the sacred flesh is given him to eat let him also be given the blood of that flesh to drink.

47 The priest must use the vestments and words instituted by the Fathers

Let the priest who celebrates this sacrament take care to be clothed in those vestments that the early Fathers, instructed by the Holy Spirit, appointed to be worn at this office; and let him take great care to speak those words which the Holy Spirit gave those Fathers for the celebration of the mystery, and not omit anything from them, or go beyond the example of My Son when He took bread and the chalice and gave them to His disciples to eat and drink. One who unknowingly does something wrong in forgetful neglect as to vestments or words pertaining to this office must be corrected by a severe and salutary penance; but if he seeks My mercy he shall find it, for he did not perpetrate the transgression voluntarily in malice of heart. But if one transgresses knowingly in these sacramental rites, either from mental apathy or from wickedness of heart, I will be offended, and say to him:

48   Words of the Lord to the negligent priest

"You wicked servant, why were you not rightly clothed in the priestly vestment, when your great early teachers instituted it for you in the Holy Spirit, and your spiritual office has the same meaning as the ministry of My angels to Me? And why have you ignored the form of words your fathers bequeathed to you in the Holy Spirit for the consecration of the body and blood of My Son and the salvation and glory of the human race?" And thus he who is guilty of such a charge must answer for it to Me, unless he punishes himself by inflicting on himself a severe penance.

49   The priest who offers the sacrament must take it himself

And let not a priest who offers this feast at My altar withdraw from it fasting himself, but let him receive his soul's refreshment in the body and blood of My Son. If he knows himself to be weighed down by grave burdens and unworthy of the feast, let him not presume to approach My table or touch My Son unwashed from the filth of his sins; as those people contaminated the table and the glory of the king's birthday who cruelly cut off the head of the shining light [John the Baptist]. Let the contaminated man therefore show the nature of his sickness to the High Priest, My Son, and accuse himself before another priest who is mortal; the latter will give him the remedy of comfort and penance, and so, purified at last, he may return to his office.

50   The priest at the altar must use the words instituted

But I, the Father of all, will that the secret order of sacred words by which the priest invokes Me at the altar must not be inflated and long, but as the ancient teachers rightly ordained it who taught how to address Me by the Holy Spirit. It should not be multiplied by foolish wisdom, but kept in simplicity of heart, for I delight not in long speech but in the purity of heart of those who seek Me devoutly and embrace Me willingly in burning charity. Everywhere else I give My grace to My elect by the exchange of the gifts of the Holy Spirit, but here in this sacrament I show Myself wholly: My Son in Me, and I in Him, and the Holy Spirit in Us, and We in Him, One in Divinity, as the body and soul and powers of anyone make up one living person. Therefore, let anyone who approaches this sacrament take care not to come in such a state as to offend the glory of Divinity.

51 On the five states of those who communicate

But you, O human, as other people approach the priest to receive the sacrament, notice five modes of being in them. For those who wish to receive the divine mystery from their priest should cleanse the five senses of their body from the dregs of their sins and worthily and laudably keep themselves from furtive uncleanness, that they may healthfully receive the sacrament.

52 Those who are bright of body and fiery of soul

Therefore, of those you see approaching this sacrament, *some are bright of body and fiery of soul.* For these are clear in faith about the sacrament and do not doubt that it is the true body and the true blood of My Son. And so, perceiving this by faith, they are strengthened and made holy in body, and because they are sanctified by this mystery they will appear in this same body in Heaven after the resurrection of the dead; and their souls are transformed and enkindled by the fiery gift of the Holy Spirit, so that, flooded with enlightenment, they reject earthly things and long for heavenly ones. How? As a fire is stirred to a blaze by the wind, they are inspired by this sacrament to burn with celestial love.

53 Those who are pale of body and shadowed in soul

But others seem pale of body and shadowed of soul. For these are weak in faith and do not firmly believe in this sacrament, but find it as hard to understand wisdom as a child whose deeds are done in foolishness. They hear outwardly with the hearing of the ear and perceive with sluggish hearts what is said to them about the sacrament, and would gladly embrace it in perfect faith; but because of the doubt that is in them they cannot understand the great holiness it has. Therefore too their inner being is plunged in darkness, for they cannot lift their minds to that perfection; conceived in sin, they are too borne down by the weight of bodily weakness to be perfect in belief, though their spirit may consent to it, and they would gladly have understanding of faith if their apathy of heart would let them.

And indeed those who are not yet weighed down in their deeds by grave burdens of sin should consent to the Spirit, even as it were unwillingly; for the soul is not yet destroyed by sin in such a case, and still has power to subject the body to its will. For the body and the soul fight with each other; the soul seeks to dominate the body, since the desire for sin in the flesh goes against its wishes, and the body disdains the righteousness that is the desire of the life-loving soul. What does this mean? What is dead longs for what is dead, and what is living desires what is living. How? The flesh loves sin, and the soul loves justice, and so they oppose each other and rarely agree. But as a child is fed and satisfied without working or understanding, so these people are revived by the sacrament almost in ignorance; for they do not madly or wickedly scorn it, but only embrace it with simple minds.

54   Those who seem hairy in body and dirty in soul

Some are hairy of body and seem dirty in soul, because they are pervaded with unclean human pollution; for they are evil and unchaste in flesh, shame-lessly polluting themselves with the ordure of vice, and contaminating their souls with the stains of filthy human sin as a swine rolls its body in the mud. And because they do not fear to approach the sacrament of the body and blood of My Son unwashed after staining themselves with these vices, they must be cleansed from their presumption by a severe scrutiny. But when they are thus purged, I do not deny them My mercy, because I see worthy penitence arising in their minds.

55   Those surrounded in body by sharp thorns and leprous of soul

But others are surrounded in body by sharp thorns and leprous of soul. For these are surrounded in their hearts by anger, hate and envy, and by these thorns of iniquity they drive out of themselves gentleness, sweetness and charity; and, desiring evil and abandoning good, and troubling other people with mockery and invective, they make their souls as impure as if covered with terrible sores. And those who approach the divine mystery in such a state gravely injure themselves; but nevertheless, if they then bitterly punish themselves and seek My grace by repentance, I turn My eyes toward them.

56   Those bloody in body and foul as a decayed corpse in soul

And others appear bloody of body and foul as a decayed corpse in soul. For they make divisions among people with bloody hand and render their souls foul with the putrefying corruption of cruel wickedness; they have no thought of fearing Me, but in their cruelty reject the part I placed in Man. And if they do not fear to receive the body and blood of My Son while defiled by this contamination, they destroy themselves with severe wounds, for they presume to touch the sacrament in their uncleanness. But the foun-tain of salvation will still flow for them if they take care to wash themselves from this wickedness of theirs by worthy penitence.

57 Those who take the sacrament with pure faith and with wavering mind

And all these receive the same sacraments; and as they do, some are bathed in fiery brilliance, but the others are overshadowed by a dark cloud. For as believers approach to take the mystery of My Son's body and blood, those who are radiant with good deeds and receive it with devout mind and pure faith are illumined by the gift of the Holy Spirit for the salvation of body and soul; while those who eat it wallowing in bad deeds with contrary hearts and wavering minds bring on themselves the darkness of misfortune to their outer and inner detriment, because they have rashly presumed to unite themselves to sanctity while impure. For one who is so rebellious and stubborn that he does not fear to pollute himself, either by fornicating with himself by touching and pleasuring his own body, or by doubly fornicating in producing seed with a man or a woman, or by tearing himself with anger, hatred or envy of other people, or by staining himself with the blood of others in acts of murder, and who then presumes to approach the body and blood of My Son unpurified and uncorrected, without being purged by confession or rectified by penance, that one by his misdeed knowingly and consciously enters the fire of judgment. How? He will be tried as to his presumption and his sin like gold in a furnace, and no dust of that presumption will be left in him by which he approached the communion of the innocent Lamb polluted and uncorrected. For, as was said, whoever shall approach the holiness of My Son's body and blood unwashed and thus receive the sacrament will receive it to his own condemnation. How? As My most loving Paul says:

58 Words of the Apostle

"Therefore whoever shall eat this bread or drink this chalice of the Lord unworthily shall be guilty of the body and blood of the Lord. Let a person test himself, and then let him eat of that bread and drink of that chalice. For he who eats and drinks unworthily eats and drinks judgment on himself, not discerning the body of the Lord. Therefore are there many infirm and weak among you, and many sleep" [1 Corinthians 11:27-30]. What does this mean?

Truly I say to you, anyone who, being unworthy and foul with sin, eats the bread of life or receives the cup of salvation, which is the sacrament of Him Who is the Lord of Heaven and earth, shall feel himself at fault for it. How? Because he receives the body and blood of the Lord, the Savior of the world, snarling and dying; inclined to evil and polluted with uncleanness, he forgets the fear of the Lord and approaches the palace of healing redemption in a state of contamination. And so he commits murder there. How? By treating the sacrament presumptuously, concealing his crimes without cleansing or washing them by penance; and so with many wounds he tears himself to pieces.

Therefore I say to him: "O most miserable and most bitter one! How did you dare to cast your Lord, Whom the citizens of Heaven always long to see, into such a lake of misery? You will be tried in body and soul by bitter penance; and if you do not correct your guilt, you will still be found wanting after the resurrection of the dead." And so let anyone who wants to purge himself examine himself faithfully, and in that devout self-knowledge partake of the bread of sanctity and taste of the cup of sweetness, and so escape from the hunger of his soul's weakness and attain to the unfailing nourishment. For one who mistreats this sacrament and receives it unworthily, without purging himself from the filth of iniquity, passes on himself a sentence of vengeance for eating and drinking it unpurged; he cannot injure or obscure the mystery by his presumption, but he condemns himself. And when you presume to approach the sacrament when foul with vice, there are many infirm in your company, those who choose not to seek medicine for their souls in that holiness but impose on themselves bitter infirmity, receiving those sacraments to judgment; as well as other weak people, who are so infirm in God's law that they refuse to know Who He is Whom they are so unworthily receiving. What does this mean? They do not want to think how they should fear and worship their Lord, or how they should punish with bitter penance their flesh, which they have nourished on vice. And since they are so negligent, many of them fall asleep in forgetful neglect, not knowing or wishing to know how they should be lamenting their sins, as a sleeping person does not know or understand the state of his body.

Therefore, O human, if you receive the body and blood of My Son unwashed, not self-purified by confession or penance, in the terrible day of inquiry you will be tried for your presumption about your filthy sins, as new wine when it ferments throws off and is purged of the impurities in it.

59   The sacrament must be treated carefully by priest and people

This sacrament must be treated and guarded with great care and solicitude both by the priest and by the people, so that it does not fall to the ground by accident. For if due to apathetic neglect it falls to the ground, I in My wrath will avenge that arrogance either on the ground or on the person, unless that person punishes himself by penance and bitter blows; for flesh and blood must make restitution to flesh and blood. How? Human flesh and blood shall groan in that person because the flesh and blood of My Son have been carelessly treated by that person, as the earth quaked and people were shaken by fear when My Son gave up His spirit on the cross.

60 The mystical secrets of the Lord's body and blood must not be looked into

But if you, O human, say to yourself in your vacillating heart, "How did the oblation on the altar become the body and blood of God's Son?" I will answer you: Why, O human, do you ask this, and for what purpose do you inquire about it? Do I require you to know it? Why do you peer into My secrets about the body and blood of My Son? You should not seek out these things, but only keep them diligently and accept them in fear and veneration. Do not pause at this mystery any longer, for you must not tempt Me so rashly. What are these things to you? Only seek after Me by sure faith. For when I look into all your faith, I do not ask you to know what is the nature of the body and blood of My Son, or how this mystery is consecrated on the altar. And who asks you, O human, to stand in fire and not feel its burning? No one. So do not rashly peer into My secrets, lest you be wounded thereby. But if in your devout mind you wish to seek them, do so in diligent prayer and weeping and fasting, as your early Fathers certainly sought and often found them. And when you have thus sought and found, you will give what is left to the Holy Spirit.

But let those who approach those sacraments come not by devious paths but by the right way, lest they be cast out from them and suffer ruin in soul. How?

61 Churchmen who go in by wrong ways imitate the Devil, Baal and crucifiers

The evil deceiver who wrongly usurps the chair of the episcopal office without being elected or properly anointed, and the wicked robber who expels his pastor by the whispers of his henchmen and violently invades his throne, will either undergo grave expiation by their own will or incur serious condemnation by My wrath. For they are in the worst possible state of bitterness, imitating the one who wanted the highest honor for himself and was cast out of glorious happiness into death, and following Baal, who so deluded himself that he wrongly named himself a god and was given over to destruction. And if in their lying and presumptuous wickedness they pretend to confer My holy orders, those who receive from them ordure rather than orders are accounted in My sight no more than those who are jestingly appointed by children in their games to be laughed at by people. As this kind of thing is nonsense among people, so what these intruders pretend to do in their deceit is mockery to Me.

Thus their edifice is wicked and cannot stand, for it is a void. And if they appeared to set up anything in My temple in holy orders, it must be abolished, for it has no righteousness and is thus worthless. Let them, therefore, turn back from their temerity, lest they share the punishment of him who sought more than he should have and was thrown from the summit into the abyss. And the butcher who insanely approaches My altar without the anointing of the priestly office, as if I were as great an impostor as he is a jester, and rashly touches the table consecrated to My name to offer the sacred oblation without having the qualifications, does not fear to wound My Son with dire torment. How? As the unbeliever assails God with his incredulity, and the madman in his insanity runs into burning fire, so this one, not knowing that I am God or feeling My burning fire, casts off his fear of Me and does not love My mercy; but, with unanointed lips, he dismembers those words My Only-Begotten gave His bride when He dowered her with His body and blood, and thus wounds My Son. And it will be said to this rash attacker: "Who touches My Son, so arrogant and unanointed?"

But he who thus approaches My altar and presumes to invoke My Son with the secret words tries to wound Him not because he can put him to any pain, but because he fearlessly and presumptuously touches Him. If he persists without penitence in this contempt, he will stand in the place of punishment among those who causelessly wounded My Son. Lest he feel these torments, then, let him adopt as his own the lamentation of affliction and never again presume to approach the ministry of My altar. And let those who hold some church office that involves serving under a priest never presume to usurp his ministry unjustly, for if they wrongfully claim that righteousness for themselves, they may justly be judged unformed and rough and rejected for the construction of the edifice of the Church. For I will that My ministers shall be pure in My sight, without deceit and without stain. How? They should be duly chosen to approach My altar, and once there they should serve Me without impurity. How?

62 Priests should observe chastity like the apostles

Let them not look to an earthly marriage, for they have chosen a spiritual one. How? By entering upon My service. And if any of them suffers from the burning lust of the flesh, let him subdue his body with abstinence and fasting and chastise himself with cold and scourging. And if after all he defiles himself with a woman, let him fly from that contamination as from a burning fire or a deadly poison and cleanse his wounds with bitter penance; for I wish to be served in chastity. How? Because My Son was the height of chastity, and He represented in Himself all ecclesiastical ranks. How? Those that serve, proclaim, preach and offer. How? He touched service in His circumcision, proclaimed by His prophecies, preached Himself to humanity, and at last offered Himself as a living sacrifice on the altar of the cross. And He gave Himself as a burnt-offering in chastity; so let those who seek to offer a burnt-offering to Him on the altar imitate His chastity.

They must not only guard chastity in others but preserve it in themselves. How? As a priest should keep himself from contamination with a woman, let him also keep himself from himself; let him take care not to arouse defilement in himself by the touch of his hands, so that the clamor of lust may not make a sinful tumult within him. For the crime of Adam, which brought death to Man, aroused his senses to fornication; so let people restrain their flesh so as not to undergo a shameful death. How? My Son conquered death and gave them life; and since He assumed flesh in the integrity of virginal chastity, those who desire to serve Him ought also to be chaste, as is written in the divine command:

63   Words of Moses on this subject

"Be ready against the third day, and come not near your wives" [Exodus 19:15]. What does this mean? You who wish to serve God alone, be prepared with willing hearts for the day of His serenity, when the holy and ineffable Trinity will truly appear and show Its wonders in a great miracle. And if you wish to be worthy to draw near to Him, take care not to join in carnal unions of physical love, so as not to mingle your blood with blood that is deemed weaker. You, O My priests and other ministers, who fight under a spiritual name, beware of this, for the apostles to whom you have succeeded did not divide themselves between opposites or leave you such an example.

64   A priest should not have two marriages

For I do not want priests to have two unions, one of spiritual and one of carnal desire; the priest should be married to the justice of God, and treat it as his wife, with which to nourish and teach the rest of the people as a father brings up and teaches his children. How is it appropriate for a priest to maintain in the right proportions two different and opposing marriages? How? One carnal and the other spiritual.

65   How the Devil may be the priest of bad priests

The priest is the pastor and father of the people who have physical marriages; so if he has one to the same extent, who will be his priest? No other priest could be his superior, since all priests are ministers of a single office, except the Devil, who is appropriate as his priest because he has imitated the Devil in hiding poison under honey. How? As the Devil hides evil under good, so do such priests, who love their own dishonor better than chastity, try to hide a carnal union under a spiritual marriage, like poison under honey. But, since My Son is wholly chaste, those who touch His body and blood on the altar should also love chastity, as it is written:

66   Words of the Law on this subject

"A priest shall not take to wife a harlot or a base prostitute or a woman repudiated by her husband; for he is sacred to his God and offers the bread of God" [Leviticus 21:7-8]. What does this mean? Let one who is appointed to offer sacrifice to God not love the Devil, the common author of all filth and wickedness, or degrade his senses in such a way that when he tries to bear My yoke he will instead have to follow the will of his flesh, contrary to the justice of God and the examples of the ancient saints; lest he come by bad deeds to the impurity that was spurned by those ancient fathers, who knew it to proceed from the breath of the ancient serpent. Let him therefore leave this filth and become a lover of the righteousness of God; for he is sacred to God in holiness, and thus removed from carnal desire and the deeds that bring children into the world. And so, sober and unpolluted, he may offer that bread which is placed on the table of consecration for human salvation. What does this mean? That sacrifice, which is the life of the living and the refreshment of souls and the mirror of all the virtues, which shine in holy innocence through chastity, is free from every stain; and therefore those who offer the sacrifice should be free of filthy pollution and hold themselves back from feasts and drunkenness, jesting and laughing, and light and undisciplined behavior. Let them be held in the reverence that becomes successors of the ancient fathers who set them up and in the dignity proper to their honorable patrons. So let them not live doubly in two roles, and walk at the same time in the secular and the spiritual way; for it is hard to serve two masters at once, as My Son testifies in the Gospel, saying:

67   Words of the Gospel on this subject

"No one can serve two masters" [Matthew 6:24]. What does this mean? No one who is clothed in mortal flesh can offer two masters similar and equal service, because of the weakness of his senses and his body. What does this mean? He cannot serve at once the Lord of Righteousness and the lord of injustice. Why? Because righteousness casts out injustice, and injustice assails righteousness. And so too a priest cannot at once and with equal devotion have the handmaid and the mistress, carnal marriage and spiritual companionship, for these two cannot exist side by side in perfection; for the carnal assails the spiritual, and the spiritual bears down the carnal. Thus My friend Paul, knowing this to be so, shows My will when he says:

68 Words of the Apostle on this subject

"A bishop therefore should be blameless, the husband of one wife" [1 Timothy 3:2]. What does this mean? One who is superior to others in a spiritual office must regulate his life so that no scandal of offense or reproach will be found in it. How? A priest should not have two roles and be at the same time the husband of a physical wife and of a spiritual spouse; but he should be the husband of one wife, namely the holy Church, which is one in My Son because she arose as one Church in Him. But though the Church is one, she has many husbands, entering into marriage with the priests of My Son who are daily in His service; yet she remains an intact virgin, for in her the faith is uncorrupted. And therefore Paul, My vessel, did not say she was the wife of one husband; for she is joined in marriage to all those priests who will arise in My Only-Begotten till the last day, when the immortal and unfailing nuptials will take place. And those who minister to the altar under the priests are also husbands of the same wife, as Paul said, offering My faithful doctrine to humanity:

69 Again Paul on this subject

"Let deacons be the husbands of one wife, who rule well their children and their houses" [1 Timothy 3:12]. What does this mean? Let those who render service to the priests and assist them be the husbands of one wife by faithful marriage. And who is this wife? The chaste Bride who can be injured by no corruption, as a woman is corrupted when she loses the flower and innocence of virginity, which she had at the beginning of her marriage when not yet corrupted by her husband. So let these bridegrooms live so faithfully with this righteous wife as to offer good examples of virtue to those regenerated by their help in the Spirit and water; let them live to labor in their office, which lies within the rampart of the Church, with faithful care, as a secular man devotes his care to maintaining his children and his house.

For My friend Paul displays that Bride to the priests and the other ministers of My altar so that they will choose her as their wife and not seek a carnal spouse. For neither Paul nor My Son's other disciples nor the rest of the Fathers who were their followers ever served as an example to them that they should take a carnal spouse and desert the spiritual wife, who had been their first choice. For a priest who is so stubborn in sin that he does the will of his flesh and illicitly takes a wife commits adultery; for he deserts his true wife, the Church, who was betrothed to him by his spiritual office, and as his will pleases unchastely marries another. It may be difficult for him to restrain his ardor, but let him restrain himself from these desires for the sake of heavenly love, as My Son shows in the Gospel, saying:

70 The three kinds of eunuchs

"There are eunuchs who were born so from their mothers' wombs; and there are eunuchs who were made so by other people; and there are eunuchs who have made themselves eunuchs for the Kingdom of Heaven's sake. He that can receive this, let him receive it" [Matthew 19:12]. What does this mean? There are some men who have come forth from their mothers' wombs with a bodily coldness or impotence, which makes them unable to have wives; and so they will receive no reward for this continence, except in suffering no penalties for the deeds of sin they did not do. And there are some men who are maimed in body by the will of others, and so cannot give pleasure to their flesh in the deeds of marriage; but they also do not deserve praise for containing themselves, for although they cannot do the burning deed they often burn with wickedness in their wills. And there are other men, those who take the spiritual way, who deprive themselves of what their bodies might easily accomplish, because they scorn and reject carnal bonds for the glory of the celestial inheritance; and these shall have the greatest praise and the blessed reward.

And My priests and all who do service to My altar should imitate these last with all their hearts, that they may receive the crown of continence amid the rapture of celestial joy. So if a person can follow this example in his heart, desiring beatitude enough to conquer the body and cast out carnal desire, let him with ardent devotion repress his flesh and abandon the idea of carnal union; and so he will capture heavenly companionship.

71 He who cannot contain himself must not become a priest or minister

But he who cannot contain himself, and burns with carnal desire, should not become a priest or any other kind of minister for the sake of pride or avarice, lest he then fall into carnal delights and so sustain great damage. For those who approach My altar as ministers shall keep their bodies from contamination with women, and never for any reason enter into marriage, but voluntarily keep themselves chaste in My righteous service. If they are otherwise, they should avoid the holy service of My altar.

72 Why the primitive Church let married men become priests but does not now

It is true that certain people who had previously subjected themselves to the world were at one time allowed to minister. But these were people who had received the carnal yoke before and not after entering My service; and afterward they cast off this yoke, and then the Holy Spirit by His miracles brought about in them praise and celebration. This was granted as an unusual measure at the beginning of the Church's rise, because there were so few priests; but now the Church is adult and strong, and her ministers are many. This is like Church opinion on another prohibition of the same sort: At the beginning of the world it was granted to men to marry women most closely related to them, because there were so few people, whereas now that people are so multiplied it is forbidden. For the shapeless and rough stones are customarily laid in the foundation of a building, and afterward the beautiful and well-formed stones are chosen for the walls. And so in the Church's infancy the priests who were available were installed in office, but now the whole complement can be obtained among the spiritual people who are fitted for the priesthood, not being occupied with the secular burden of earthly bonds. For it is not fitting that the father of a family, following the rules for earthly marriage, should be called as My messenger in the priesthood. Therefore hear this comparison:

73 Analogy of the king

A certain very powerful king gathered a small army and carefully observed its performance. Seeing that it was untrained in an army's business, he chose out of it some men of the common people whom he perceived as suitable for leadership, and set them over the army, for the offspring of the nobles had not yet matured. But later, when the army was larger and there were adult noblemen in it, the king set that army in order and promoted dukes and counts from the nobler classes to command it, as justice required. What does this mean?

The King of Heaven, Whose power is over all, started the Church by gathering a little army of believers. Scrutinizing it most closely, He saw that it was as yet infirm and weak with regard to suffering in body for His name; so He set Peter over it to bind and loose, who had been one of those who had lived an earthly life. And after Peter, He cleansed others who had imbibed the taste of the earthly and been stained by temporal things, and set them up in the office of judgment and mercy; for He knew that, having embraced the Catholic faith, they were wise and faithful both in caring for souls and in sustaining bodies. For the glowing dawn that burns up human contagions in the fire of love for chastity had not yet diffused its flowers of sweetness widely among people. But now the churchly race has been multiplied and widely disseminated through the whole length of the world, and the glory of the Church's honor has been nobly strengthened; and so the supernal King has benignly and fittingly bestowed both secular and spiritual gifts on people, and chosen those who most honorably preserved their sobriety and chastity by Church law and God's justice to be priests and other ministers of the divine offices.

Wherefore, O human, many spiritual people have now arisen who want to fight the world and the Devil, and who hasten to approach My altar in chastity and bodily restraint; and so I will that My priests should appear in My sight uncontaminated by earthly marriage. For in the Old Testament priests were commanded to keep themselves from contamination with women when they approached My altar; and in the New Testament that command was brought to full perfection for My priests, so that whereas the ancient priests observed chastity for an hour, these new ones will fulfil it from the beginning of their boyhood to the end of their old age. And as I refused to receive the sacrifice from the ancients when polluted by connection with women, much more do I want My Son to be handled by the new priests only in a state of chastity.

74 Immature and unconsecrated men must not receive churches

Let no one who is immature and unconsecrated receive a church; and let him not presume to seek several churches. For if one who is young in years and without priestly consecration dares to take a church or, having one, tries to subjugate several, he is a transgressor against justice and a destroyer of strict judgment; he is like one who dares to commit fornication before the lawful time and without lawful marriage, or who has a legitimate wife but hastens to defile himself in adultery with other women.

75 Priests should be elected by Christian people from the good and healthy

Priests of wise thoughts and manly minds are to be chosen from every people that calls itself Christian, such that they will come to My service in right order with proper anointing and willing mind. Those who are crippled in any of their members should not approach the office of My altar, for in the Kingdom of Heaven there will be no trace of disabilities in human souls; and therefore I do not want anyone defective in limb to stand at My altar. But these will not be separated from the Kingdom of Heaven because they are weak in body and defective in members, as long as their souls are healthy and they seek Me in the purity of good works. I do not wish, however, that they should take part in the ministry of My altar, but that they should humbly fulfil their virtue in good works.

76 Women should not approach the office of the altar

So too those of female sex should not approach the office of My altar; for they are an infirm and weak habitation, appointed to bear children and diligently nurture them. A woman conceives a child not by herself but through a man, as the ground is plowed not by itself but by a farmer. Therefore, just as the earth cannot plow itself, a woman must not be a priest and do the work of consecrating the body and blood of My Son; though she can sing the praise of her Creator, as the earth can receive rain to water its fruits. And as the earth brings forth all fruits, so in Woman the fruit of all good works is perfected. How? Because she can receive the High Priest as Bridegroom. How? A virgin betrothed to My Son will receive Him as Bridegroom, for she has shut her body away from a physical husband; and in her Bridegroom she has the priesthood and all the ministry of My altar, and with Him possesses all its riches. And a widow too can be called a bride of My Son when she rejects a physical husband and flees beneath the wings of My Son's protection. And as a bridegroom loves his bride with exceeding love, so does My Son sweetly embrace His brides, who for love of chastity eagerly run to Him.

77 Men and women should not wear each other's clothes except in necessity

A man should never put on feminine dress or a woman use male attire, so that their roles may remain distinct, the man displaying manly strength and the woman womanly weakness; for this was so ordered by Me when the human race began. Unless a man's life or a woman's chastity is in danger; in such an hour a man may change his dress for a woman's or a woman for a man's, if they do it humbly in fear of death. And when they seek My mercy for this deed they shall find it, because they did it not in boldness but in danger of their safety. But as a woman should not wear a man's clothes, she should also not approach the office of My altar, for she should not take on a masculine role either in her hair or in her attire.

78 God will judge all perpetrators of fornication, sodomy and bestiality

Let those who approach My altar appear in My sight in chastity, as also should those who desire to receive the sacrament of the body and blood of

My Son, lest they should fall into ruin. For many are found among both spiritual and secular people who not only pollute themselves in fornication with women but also assume a heavy burden of condemnation by contaminating themselves in perverted forms. How? A man who sins with another man as if with a woman sins bitterly against God and against the union with which God united male and female. Hence both in God's sight are polluted, black and wanton, horrible and harmful to God and humanity, and guilty of death; for they go against their Creator and His creature, which is in them. How?

God united man and woman, thus joining the strong to the weak, that each might sustain the other. But these perverted adulterers change their virile strength into perverse weakness, rejecting the proper male and female roles, and in their wickedness they shamefully follow Satan, who in his pride sought to split and divide Him Who is indivisible. They create in themselves by their wicked deeds a strange and perverse adultery, and so appear polluted and shameful in My sight.

And a man who sins with a woman by this same method of perverted fornication is a voracious wolf of wickedness. How? A person would seem perverted and harmful to other people if he threw away beautiful clean food and ate the ordure that comes out of the body in digestion; and these are in My sight equally unworthy and unclean, since they forsake the proper way of uniting with a woman and seek in her an alien sin. And a woman who takes up devilish ways and plays a male role in coupling with another woman is most vile in My sight, and so is she who subjects herself to such a one in this evil deed. For they should have been ashamed of their passion, and instead they impudently usurped a right that was not theirs. And, having put themselves into alien ways, they are to Me transformed and contemptible.

And men who touch their own genital organ and emit their semen seriously imperil their souls, for they excite themselves to distraction; they appear to Me as impure animals devouring their own whelps, for they wickedly produce their semen only for abusive pollution. And women who imitate them in this unchaste touching, and excite themselves to bodily convulsions by provoking their burning lust, are extremely guilty, for they pollute themselves with uncleanness when they should be keeping themselves in chastity. Hence both women and men who elicit their own seed by touching themselves in the body do a filthy deed and inflict ulcers and wounds on their souls; for they will not keep themselves in a state of chastity for love of Me. What does this mean? When a person feels himself disturbed by bodily stimulation, let him run to the refuge of continence, and seize the shield of chastity, and thus defend himself from uncleanness. How? Let him cast out the tares from the wheat, which is to say, let him separate the clamor of lust from the sweetness of chastity.

And whoever thus casts out of himself the taste for lust is very sweet and lovable to Me. But, O humans, you cast away chastity and love lust when you fornicate not only with other people but even with animals; thus you send your seed not into what lives but into what is dead, and you forsake what is equal to you and desire what is subject to you and serves you. Therefore the elements cry out against you, saying, "Alas, alas! our rulers join with us in the mingling of their seed!" And thus they show their grief at My anger against your deeds. Why then do you, knowing yourselves human, convert your intelligence into bestial stupidity? Did I create you to join with animals? Never. And when you unite with them, the guilt of the most bitter crimes falls upon you, because you scorn the plan I made for the joining of male and female. For whoever transforms himself by his deeds into a depraved follower of his own desires, and pours out his semen with an animal, brings on himself great ruin, as Satan cast himself down by his perversity when he tried to be like God.

Therefore, all you who contaminate yourselves with perverted pollutions, resist your desires; chastise your bodies, and give yourselves over to true and bitter penance with weeping and fasting and torture of your flesh and severe blows, lest you send yourselves impenitent into an excess of cruel guilt.

79   Pollution that occurs in sleep

I want men not only to keep themselves clean of impurity while awake, but also to purify themselves properly from the pollution that happens to them in sleep. For if the semen of a man who sleeps and dreams is stirred up unawares, I do not want him to approach the sacramental office of My altar in that condition of ardent heat; he should first calm that ardor in himself, as it is written:

80   Words of Moses on this subject

"If any man among you is defiled in a dream by night, he shall go forth out of the camp, and not return until he washes himself with water in the evening, and then he shall return into the camp after sunset" [Deuteronomy 13:10–11]. What does this mean? If among the laborers in My service there is anyone who is defiled in a dream while he sleeps at night, he should separate himself from the company of those who serve My altar and not presume to join in the mystery until his injurious heat has passed and he has cleansed himself from the fire of his lust in the bath of penance, with confession and compunction of heart. And after that penance has done its work and illumined his heart, let him return in love of chastity among those who faithfully defend themselves against impurity, and worthily and honorably approach that sacrament, which is wholly in sanctity.

81 One who burns strongly should not add flame to his fire

But one who burns strongly in lust either asleep or awake should take care not to add flame to his fire. How? Let him not inflame himself by those foods that stir up lust. He should humbly abstain from the flesh of animals that come forth from their mothers naked and without covering, that is, beasts; for there is a fire of heat in them that is not as great in the flesh of birds, which are not born uncovered but as an egg covered with a shell, and therefore have less inflammatory power. And he should also abstain from excessive wine, lest by too much drinking his veins become filled with noxious blood and wickedly heated with ardent fire.

82 One who is weighed down by vices should seek God's mercy in confession

But if anyone labors under too great a number of these tendencies and is not able to resist them by himself, let him with devoted purpose seek Me and humbly uncover to Me the wounds of his heart. How? Let him lay bare these wounds to Me by making a humble confession to a priest. And why this? Because true confession is a second resurrection. How? The human race was slain by the fall of the old Adam; the new Adam by His death raised it up. And so the resurrection of souls arose in the death of the new Adam. And so a person should confess his sins, as the old Adam did not; for he concealed his transgression instead of confessing it. How? He did not confess it by repenting, but concealed it by accusing the woman. Hence confession was instituted, to raise people up after they fall. And so anyone who confesses his sins to a priest for love of Me rises again from death to life; as the woman who purged herself from her impurity with tears at the banquet in the presence of My Son was snatched away from uncleanness.

83 The remedy of purgation was long prefigured in the ancient fathers

This remedy of purgation was long prefigured in the ancient fathers. How? Before the Law the patriarchs and prophets were the consolation of humanity; under the Law the high priests and the ordinary priests were its instruction; and then the apostles came and brought true righteousness in My Son, so that many people hastened to them and devoutly implored their help. And thus from the time of Adam to the time of the apostles there were always some who by celestial inspiration consoled and instructed people and helped them in their miseries. And the apostles also showed people, by their preaching and many miracles, that Man had fallen by the Devil's tempting into death and could never rise again by himself, but was snatched from death by My Son. How? By His being in the world and performing many labors in the body, and at last being nailed to the cross for the world's redemption.

So faithful people, to gain salvation, should follow this pattern with their priests. How? They should seek the help of My Son, because when they repeat the ancient crime of Adam after baptism they cannot rise from their fall by themselves. And therefore they should seek counsel as if from the patriarchs and prophets, and derive instruction as if from the high priests and the ordinary priests, and accept help as if from the apostles, laying bare their wounds and displaying their sins truly and purely. How?

They should confess their sins to the priest, who is the minister of My Son, with devoted heart and mouth. And then the priest will give them a remedy of penance and bury their sins in the death of My Only-Begotten. And then they will rise again to life and glorify the Resurrection of My Son.

84   One who refuses to confess his sin deceives himself

But one who refuses to lay bare the wounds of sin, and follows his own wishes by trying to cure them himself in silence without the help of another, is deceiving himself. For he wishes to be his own priest, but without the help of another he cannot rise; as Man did not rise up and stand by himself but was saved by My Son. Hence let one who desires to be saved never despair of confessing his sins, even at the end of his life.

85   A dying man without a priest may confess to another person or to God only

And if someone in the hour of death seeks a remedy for his wounds of sin but does not have a priest near to whom to confess them, let him show them to any other person who is there at the time; or, if he is dying so suddenly that there is no one there, let him lay them open to Me with his heart's utmost affection, while he is still in the body with which he did them, and I will regard the devotion of his heart and not reject his penitence.

86   No one should despair at the weight of his sins

Therefore, let no one despair because of the weight of his iniquity; for if he despairs of My mercy, he shall not rise again to life. One who struggles with despair and at last reduces it to nothing has delivered himself; he has been strong, and manfully conquered. But one whose mind is so inflamed that he does not seek the remedy of salvation is not to be helped; for when he could have found Me, he refused to seek Me. And so, let each person not neglect himself while he has time, but seek the refuge of pure confession, as My Son commanded the leper in the Gospel, saying:

87   Words of the Gospel

"Go, show yourself to the priest, and offer your gift, which Moses commanded for a testimony to them" [Matthew 8:4]. What does this mean? You who are foul with sins and want to cleanse yourself of them, go with good intention and show them to the priest, My minister, by pure confession; and offer with devout heart the gift of true penitence, which by God's will was foreshadowed by the man who was removed by divine power from the many floods of earthly iniquity. And thus those who formerly saw you befouled with evil deeds may now testify that you are purged from them by bitter penitence as in the furnace of trial. But, O human, if a sinner conceals his deeds in his secret heart, who will be a witness to his penitence? No one. Therefore let each person manifest his sins, that he may have a witness to his penitence.

88   Sins should be blotted out by alms and by bodily satisfaction

And let one who desires to practice penitence for his sins turn to alms as a source of help. How? When a person's weak body falters in the work of penitence, his alms will hasten to help him. And because it is hard for a person to practice penitence with just and proper harshness, let him take alms as his mother, so as to accomplish with her what is so laborious for his body. For a mother does not cease to help her child in time of need, even when he has been brought up already; and so too alms give aid to a weak body when a person is penitent, even if he seems to be strong in doing penance and punishing his body. So let a person punish in his body the evil works he has done in his body through the lust of the flesh, so as to wash away from his body by bitter penance the deeds that were dear and sweet to his flesh. For bitter penance, with its helpmeet alms, heals in people the deadly wounds of sin. How? A person represses himself by castigation, but he can refresh himself by alms. How? Because alms represent My mercy. How? When a faithful person helps the poor with his substance for love of Me, he keeps My commandments, because he devotes his mercy to the needy for the honor of My name; just as I do not withdraw My grace from those who seek me in purity of heart. And whoever helps the poor in this way, refreshing them with alms for mercy's sake, is exceedingly lovable to Me, for he has a merciful heart; which fulfils what is written:

89 Words of the Book of Wisdom

"Place your treasure in the commandments of the Most High, and your alms shall bring you more profit than gold" [Ecclesiastes 29:14]. What does this mean?

Think justly and rightly, and take some of your material wealth, which you hold in your bosom and embrace in your heart; as the One Who is above all people commands, divide it, for God has ordered you to turn aside from evil and do good. Let your heart's good will overflow, so that you will not be among the lost sheep; sanctify yourself before God by giving of your substance to refresh those in want, and God will give you His mercy in your misery. And if you do this, the compassion you have on one without treasure will be worth more to you than if you could ascend a high mountain and in your pride possess its gold. How? Because it is better for you to give a little to the little ones in humility than to possess and enjoy the kingdom of the world; if you did the latter, God's reward of mercy could never be yours because of the weight of your pride, for you would not have had pity for the poor in your heart.

90 The elements of the world are the pit of human pleasures

Hence the elements are the pit of human pleasures, as they show by their ways. How? By bringing God's vengeance upon those who are sinning. Therefore, O human, renounce the empty avarice which will wreck you, for your true inheritance is eternal life; leave evil and do good, and so renounce harsh malevolence. And, to follow the way of mercy, give of your substance to the poor, and thereby imitate God Who is merciful.

91 One who gives or receives alms must not do so in vain

Therefore, O human, no liar can deny that you who thus help the poor are fulfilling My will. How?

You should give your alms to the poor as I mete out My grace to you. But let not those who receive alms take them vainly or avariciously. What does this mean? There are many who love laziness and do not want to labor with their bodies to feed themselves, or to do good works with their spirits to help their souls; they are like the beasts, who understand justice neither with their souls nor with their bodies. And if they persevere in this, without correction and without penitence for their apathetic wickedness, they are unworthy in My sight. But there are also many who suffer bodily necessity and receive alms in fear of Me, and pray and work for those who weigh out mercy to them, and avoid filthy and evil deeds. And among these are many from whom I have withdrawn earthly riches in order to give them celestial wealth.

92 Seekers of poverty, riches and honor are rewarded by their intention

Those who gladly suffer poverty for My name's sake are extremely lovable to Me; but those who are greedy and would gladly possess earthly riches but cannot lose the reward of this labor. And one who seeks riches in order to satisfy not his greed but My will has a good intention, and I will reward him with honor. One who desires the power of an office for his own boastful pride and not for the glory of My name is to Me like a putrid corpse; but one who seeks it desiring from it not his pride but My honor will be glorious in My kingdom. And so priests should take on the office of spiritual government not for their own sakes but for Mine, that they may rule more surely and devoutly over My people. How?

93 Priests should admonish the people about confession

They should teach, admonish, exhort and urge My people to keep the law of God worthily and fittingly. And pastors should always be thinking this over; and they should warn and exhort the people not to continue in their sins without confession and without penitence, but to tread evil deeds underfoot and do good ones. And if the people do not obey their priests when they so admonish, the people will incur the guilt and the priests will not be blamed for negligence.

94 Priests who do not use their office's authority are not priests but wolves

But if priests do not show the people the authority of their office, they are not priests but ravenous wolves, for they hold their office by robbery as a wolf cruelly snatches a sheep, doing their own will instead of caring for the sheep. And, because they live perversely, they are afraid to teach true doctrine to the people; they consent to iniquity as to a lord, for they harbor carnal desires, and they close the door of their heart to a helper as if to a stranger; for justice is of God.

95 The elements wail to God at the iniquity of priests and Heaven notes it

Therefore, O ye pastors, wail and lament your crimes, which proclaim your iniquity in dire tones, so that the very elements hear their clamor and join in their wailing before My presence. How do you dare to do your office and touch your Lord with bloody hands, in perverse filth and adulterous wickedness? By your uncleanness you shake the foundations of the earth. How? Because you do not fear to touch your Lord while foul with such crimes, I bring great griefs and oppressions upon the earth; and so I avenge the flesh and blood of My Son, for in this horror you not only cruelly shake the earth but by your filth contaminate Heaven. How?

When you touch your Lord in the stench of uncleanness, as a swine tramples pearls into the mire, the heavens receive your iniquity and shower upon the earth the sentence of My judgment. You should have gone before the people in true justice and with divine law, shining for them with good works, so that when they followed you they would avoid tripping on any stumbling-block; and instead you stain My people with greater iniquity than that with which they stain themselves, giving them a bad and evil example. You should have been a shining jewel, by whose light they could have perceived and entered the path of rectitude; but your example is death to them, and they can find no measure in your iniquity. How can you be their shepherd when you seduce them so? And how will you answer for them, when you cannot give an answer for yourselves? Therefore weep and howl, before Death carries you off. For why do you not consider your own honor, which is given you for the sake of other people? What does this mean?

96 Priests have the power of binding and loosing

That you, rather than others, have received in My Son the keys of Heaven; which are righteous decisions of just judgment made in the knowledge of the Scriptures, as long as you consider rightly what it is you should bind. What does this mean?

When people stubbornly oppose themselves to My Law, you must inspire them with fear of My judgment. And if they do not then correct themselves, extend over them your power of binding. How? You will bind these rebels in My words with a clear voice, and show them the power of the binding; for their stubbornness they are bound in My sight, as My Son showed to the Church's first pastor, saying:

97 Words of the Gospel

"I will give you the keys of the kingdom of Heaven. And whatsoever you shall bind on earth, it will be bound also in Heaven; and whatsoever you shall loose on earth, it will be loosed also in Heaven" [Matthew 16:19]. What does this mean? I, Who have all power in Heaven and earth, by My grace give to you, My devout imitators, those judgments that touch the dignity of the Kingdom of Heaven. As you see people sin on earth, you will bind the wicked deed on earth with just judgment, and it will be entangled in its wickedness and bound in Heaven; it will be separated and driven out from Heaven, for in the heavenly mansions there is no freedom and no place for iniquity. But after I withdraw a person's soul from his body, you will not extend your judgment over him, for that judgment is Mine. Likewise, if a transgressor is penitent, you will loose on earth the chain you fastened on him in his rebellion, and it will be loosed in the secret places of Heaven, for God does not reject the groans of a devout heart. But after the person's death you will pray for his soul, but you cannot then absolve it from being bound.

98 No one is to be bound without a grievous fault

But, O priests, who have received this power thus from My Son, you shall not in anger of heart bind any person in My words unless he has committed a grievous fault; you will consider most carefully before you bind anyone. You will use My words of ecclesiastical censure to separate from My church anyone who cannot be restrained by shame before other people, or by fear of Me, or by your prayers and precepts, but seeks to persevere in his iniquity. But you shall not bind an innocent person; for when you bind such a one you bind yourselves in bonds of dire guilt.

99 One who is bound when innocent must ask to be loosed for God's honor

And if anyone has been bound while innocent, contrary to right, he must ask to be loosed for the honor of My Name; yet humbly and submissively, for if he is stubborn he might incur the guilt of pride. But this is the purpose of that binding: that one who perversely refuses to obey Me or the precepts of his superiors may be separated by My word from celestial things. Thus Adam, when he disobeyed Me, was by My command cast out of Paradise.

And until he repents and obeys, he shall not be received into the company of the faithful; as the human race was recalled to the celestial country by the martyrdom of My obedient Son.

100 Rebels who refuse to return to Christ and ask mercy imitate the Devil

But one who rebels and refuses to return to Christ in humility, and continues in this arrogance, will join the company of those who keep a stone for a heart and remain in infidelity; and such people refuse to know the glory of the Church's beatitude. For one who is so obdurate that in his wickedness he will seek no mercy imitates the ancient serpent, who, when he deceived the first man in Paradise, was saying within himself:

101 Words of the Devil

"I was thrown out of Heaven when I tried to fight with my angels against the army of the Most High; I could not resist Him, and He conquered me. But now I have found Man on earth, and I will avenge myself mightily by working my wrath on him. For I will accomplish in Man on earth that which I tried to do in Heaven, and make myself like the Most High. And if God is just, that power will not be taken from me, for Man will consent to me and disobey God."

Saying these things to himself, the Devil arrayed all his arts against Man, and Man withdrew from God and adhered to the Devil; and the Devil bound him so closely to himself that Man worshipped him instead of God and denied God, his Creator.

102 By the Son of God's Incarnation humanity was led out of the darkness

But when humanity was lying in a great darkness of infidelity and could not raise itself, I sent My Son for its salvation, miraculously incarnate of the Virgin, true God and true man. What does this mean? That His Divinity truly came forth from Me, the Father, and His Humanity truly took flesh from the Virgin Mother. What does this mean? O human, you are soft and delicate of body, but hard and inflexible in your incredulity. For a stone can be smoothed for a building, but you are unwilling to be soothed by the faith. Yet listen. As a person who has a beautiful jewel in a box puts it in a metal setting to show it to people, so I, Who had My Son in My heart, willed him to be incarnate of the Virgin to save the lives of those who believe. But if I had given Him a physical father, who would He be then? Not My Son, but My servant; and that could not be. He, born of the Virgin, ate, drank, lay down to sleep and experienced bodily miseries, but He never felt the taste of sin in His flesh, for He had assumed flesh not through a lie but through truth. What does this mean? Other people, because of Adam and Eve's transgression, are born from the taste of delight, which is to say through a lie and not the truth. But My Son did not originate so, but was born in sanctity from the most chaste Virgin to redeem humanity. For like cannot loose like from a chain; a greater one must come who can save him. What does this mean? That no person born in sin could deliver sinful humanity from the perdition of death. Therefore My Son came, without sin; He conquered death and mercifully delivered humanity therefrom.

But let the one who sees with watchful eyes and hears with attentive ears welcome with a kiss My mystical words, which proceed from Me Who am life.

THE DEVIL BOUND

291

THE TEMPTER

VISION SEVEN
The Devil

*T*hen *I saw a burning light, as large and as high as a mountain, divided at
its summit as if into many tongues. And there stood in the presence of this
light a multitude of white-clad people, before whom what seemed like a
screen of translucent crystal had been placed, reaching from their breasts to their
feet. And before that multitude, as if in a road, there lay on its back a monster
shaped like a worm, wondrously large and long, which aroused an indescribable
sense of horror and rage. On its left stood a kind of market-place, which displayed
human wealth and worldly delights and various sorts of merchandise; and some
people were running through it very fast and not buying anything, while others
were walking slowly and stopping both to sell and to buy. Now that worm was
black and bristly, covered with ulcers and pustules, and it was divided into five
sections from the head down through the belly to its feet, like stripes. One was
green, one white, one red, one yellow and one black; and they were full of deadly
poison. But its head had been so crushed that the left side of its jawbone was
dislocated. Its eyes were bloody on the surface and burning within; its ears were
round and bristly; its nose and mouth were those of a viper, its hands human, its
feet a viper's feet, and its tail short and horrible. And around its neck a chain was
riveted, which also bound its hands and feet; and this chain was firmly fastened
to a rock in the abyss, confining it so that it could not move about as its wicked
will desired. Many flames came forth from its mouth, dividing into four parts:
One part ascended to the clouds, another breathed forth among secular people,
another among spiritual people, and the last descended into the abyss.*

*And the flame that sought the clouds was opposing the people who wanted to
get to Heaven. And I saw three groups of these. One was close to the clouds, one in
the middle space between the clouds and the earth, and one moved along near the
earth; and all were shouting repeatedly, "Let us get to Heaven!" But they were
whirled hither and thither by that flame; some did not waver, some barely kept
their balance, and some fell to the earth but then rose again and started toward
Heaven. The flame that breathed forth among secular people burned some of
them so that they were hideously blackened, and others it transfixed so that it
could move them anywhere it wanted. Some escaped from the flame and moved
toward those who sought Heaven, reiterating shouts of "O you faithful, give us
help!" But others remained transfixed. Meanwhile, the flame that breathed forth
among spiritual people concealed them in obscurity; but I saw them in six*

categories. For some of them were cruelly injured by the flame's fury; but when it could not injure one of them, it burningly breathed on them the deadly poison that flowed from the worm's head to its feet, either green or white or red or yellow or black. But the flame that sought the abyss contained in itself diverse torments for those who had worshipped Satan in place of God, not washed by the font of baptism or knowing the light of truth and faith.

And I saw sharp arrows whistling loudly from its mouth, and black smoke exhaling from its breast, and a burning fluid boiling up from its loins, and a hot whirlwind blowing from its navel, and the uncleanness of frogs issuing from its bowels; all of which affected human beings with grave disquiet. And the hideous and foul-smelling vapor that came out of it infected many people with its own perversity. But behold, a great multitude of people came, shining brightly; they forcefully trod the worm underfoot and severely tormented it, but could not be injured by its flames or its poison. And I heard again the voice from Heaven, saying to me:

1 God strengthens the faithful so that the Devil cannot conquer them

God, Who disposes all things justly and rightly, calls His faithful people to the glory of the celestial inheritance; but the ancient deceiver lurks in ambush and tries to hinder them by using all his wicked arts against them. But he is conquered by them and is confounded as his presumption deserves, for they possess the celestial country, and he suffers the horrors of Hell.

Therefore, *you see a burning light, as large and as high as a mountain, divided at its summit as if into many tongues.* This is the justice of God, which burns in the faith of believers, displaying the greatness of His power, sanctity and glory, and wonderfully declaring in that glory the diverse gifts of the Holy Spirit.

2 The multitude of the faithful and the divine law displayed before them

And there stand in the presence of this light a multitude of white-clad people, a cohort of people in the presence of God's justice, shining with faith and well and honorably constituted in good works. *Before them what seems like a screen of translucent crystal has been placed, reaching from their breasts to their feet;* for, from their decision to do good actions to their completion, they have before their eyes the strong and splendid sight of the divine law. And thus they are so strengthened in these actions that no cunning or deception of false persuasion can conquer them.

3   The deceptions of the Devil lie in the path humans take in this world

And before that multitude, as if in a road, there lies on its back a monster shaped like a worm, wondrously large and long. This means that the ancient serpent is well-known to humanity in the course of the pilgrimage of the good and the bad through the world, not in that visible form but in its inner meaning. Its mouth is gaping upward in order to pull down by deception those who are tending toward the celestial regions; but it is lying down, because the Son of God destroyed so much of its strength that it cannot stand up. *And it arouses an indescribable sense of horror and rage;* for the mental capacity of mortal humans is insufficient to understand the manifold variations of its poisonous fury and malicious exertions.

4   The Devil offers fraudulent riches and delights, and some buy them

On its left stands a kind of marketplace, which displays human wealth and worldly delights and various sorts of merchandise. For the left hand of the destroyer signifies death, and there is seen a marketplace composed of Death's evil works: pride and vainglory in corruptible riches, licentiousness and lust for transitory pleasures, and trafficking in all kinds of earthly desires. Thus those who would be terrified by the horror of the Devil if they met it openly are deceived by these things; they are lightly offered persuasions to vice as a merchant displays his diverse wares to people, and delighted by the display so that they buy what is offered. So the Devil offers humanity his lying arts; and those who desire them buy them. How? They throw away a good conscience as if selling it, and they collect deadly wounds in their souls as if buying them.

5   The strong resist the Devil's offers, the apathetic consent to them

And some people are running through it very fast and not buying anything; they know God, and so they carry the treasure of good will and the sweet spices of virtue and eagerly accumulate more of them, and quickly pass by the pleasures of the world and the filth of the Devil, obeying God's commands and despising the sweetness of their flesh. *But others are walking slowly and stopping both to sell and to buy;* they are slow to do good works and apathetic of heart, and so they smother their own desire for Heaven as if selling it, and nurture the pleasures of their flesh as if buying them.

Therefore, the former will receive the reward of good works, and the latter will suffer the punishment of iniquity, as Ezekiel shows, saying:

BOOK TWO

6 Words of Ezekiel on this subject

"The justice of the just shall be upon him, and the wickedness of the wicked shall be upon him" [Ezekiel 18:20]. What does this mean? The shining works of the pure person bathe him in sanctity and surround him like a thousand eyes that see into the heights and the depths; as the Holy Spirit inspires him, they bear him aloft to great honor and leave his wrong desires behind for dead, as a bird is borne aloft in the air by its wings whenever it pleases. But the person who faithlessly follows the wickedness of the savage viper who hisses at Heaven, covering the pearl with mud and raging at the Most Beautiful among all the beautiful, is degraded by its snakelike poison; he is cut off from the noble work of God's hands, from all honor and from the beatitude of the celestial vision, and exiled from the Living Fruit and the root of the Just Tree.

7 The Devil labors to deceive the five senses of humanity

But you see that *that worm is black and bristly, covered with ulcers and pustules*. This shows that the ancient serpent is full of the darkness of black betrayal, and the bristles of concealed deception, and the ulcers of impure pollution, and the pustules of repressed fury. *And it is divided into five sections from the head down through the belly to its feet, like stripes;* for from the time of his first deception when he tried to put himself forward until the final time when his madness will end, he does not cease to inspire the five human senses with the desire for vices. Simulating a deceitful rectitude, he draws people to the downward slopes of his unclean arts. *One is green, one white, one red, one yellow, and one black; and they are full of deadly poison.* The green indicates worldly melancholy; the white, improper irreverence; the red, deceptive glory; the yellow, biting envy; and the black, shameful deceit, with all other perversities that bring death to the souls of those who consent to them.

8 The Devil's pride was overthrown by the Incarnation

But its head has been so crushed that the left side of its jawbone is dislocated. This means that his pride was so overthrown by the Son of God that even the enmity of Death is already destroyed and cannot exert its full strength of bitterness.

9 What the eyes and ears and nostrils of the serpent signify

Its eyes are bloody on the surface and burning within; because his wicked intent outwardly inflicts harm on human bodies and inwardly drives a fiery dart into their souls. *Its ears are round and bristly;* for the bristles of his arts pierce a person all around, so that if he finds anything that is his in that person, he may quickly throw him down. *Its nose and mouth are those of a viper;* for he shows people unbridled and vile behavior, through which, transfixing them with many vices, he may cruelly slay them.

10 Its hands and feet and tail and what they signify

Its hands are human, for he practices his arts in human deeds; *its feet a viper's feet,* because he ceaselessly ambushes people when they are journeying and inflicts devilish lacerations on them; *and its tail short and horrible,* for it signifies his power in the short but most evil time of the son of perdition, whose desire to run wild exceeds his power to do it.

11 The might of God has broken the Devil's strength to do what he wants

And around its neck a chain is riveted, which also binds its hands and feet; which is to say that the strength of the Devil was so broken and crushed by the power of Almighty God that he cannot freely work his evil and accost humans in the way. *And this chain is firmly fastened to a rock in the abyss, confining it so that it cannot move about as its wicked will desires;* for the power of God abides unfailingly and immovably for eternity, and by saving souls oppresses the Devil so forcibly that he is not able by inner or outer means to take away redemption from the faithful, or keep them from that place of joy from which he perversely exiled himself.

12 The Devil sends his fire to lead astray all kinds of people on earth

Many flames come forth from its mouth, dividing into four parts. This means that in his rapacious voracity he sends forth in cruel flames the terrible and manifold evil of his wicked counsels; he breathes it into all four corners of the world, that the people there may follow him.

One part ascends to the clouds; for the sharpness of the Devil's breath drags down those who with all their mind's longing seek Heaven. *Another breathes forth among secular people;* for its many forms deceive those who live among earthly affairs. *And another among spiritual people;* for its pretence infects those who labor in spiritual disciplines. *And the last descends into the abyss;* for its persuasions put the faithless who consent to it into the torments of Hell. For they have walked the way of falsity and deception and left the way of rectitude, and they have not shown the reverence due to the true God, as David testifies, saying:

13 Words of David

"Destruction and unhappiness in their ways, and the way of peace they have not known; there is no fear of God before their eyes" [Psalm 13:5]. What does this mean?

People who expel God from their hearts by their wicked and damnable deeds are overwhelmed by His innocent and mighty works, which arise in the pure living Fountain, as a great rain submerges an object so that it is no longer visible. And so they are not formidable in the sight of God, for misery is in their ways wherever they go, and most unhappy companionship, and the food of death. How? They taste and eat what is evil. Hence in their deeds they do not know the way that ascends in the sunlight, and do not taste in honor or in love the sweetness of God; they cast away their fear of Him as if it were fear of another person, desiring neither to see Him nor to look Him in the face.

14 The Devil assails spiritual and secular people in many ways

Hence you also see that *the flame that seeks the clouds is opposing the people who want to get to Heaven.* For when that wicked flame feels that the minds of the faithful are tending upward, it rages against them most cruelly with its arts, so that they may not come to the celestial places to which they aspire.

15 The three groups of these people

And you see three groups of these; for they do not cease to worship the true and ineffable Trinity, although greatly fatigued by their struggles. *One is close to the clouds;* these are fighting most strongly against the Devil and raising their thoughts from earthly deeds to heavenly things as a cloud floats above the earth. *And one is in the middle space between the clouds and the earth.* These people control themselves moderately well, but their whole mind is not set on heavenly things nor their whole desire on earthly ones; they take a middle way, seeking inner qualities but not refusing outer ones. *And one moves along near the earth;* for these people have not perfectly renounced the transitory but cling a little to passing things, and so have great labor and suffer much fatigue. But, with the help of Heaven, they are all victors; for *all are shouting repeatedly, "Let us get to Heaven!"* And so the former and the latter people, with sighs of desire, exhort themselves to move toward the secret places of Heaven, even though tired out by the arts of the ancient serpent. *But they are whirled hither and thither by that flame,* being driven to various actions by the wind of the Devil's temptation. *Some do not waver,* for they are exceedingly strong fighters and manfully defend themselves from these illusions. *Some barely keep their balance*, for they keep their feet in the path of rectitude and persevere in God's commandments, but are worn out by their labors and can scarcely conquer the Devil's arts; and *some fall to the earth but then rise again and start toward Heaven*, for they fall into different ways of vice but are then raised up by penitence and place their hope in God and good works.

16   The temptations of secular people

Now *the flame that breathes forth among secular people burns some of them so that they are hideously blackened*. This is to say that the flame of evil deception aims itself at those who pursue worldly affairs and subjects some of them to its perversity; it stains them with dark and iniquitous vices, so that they despise the brightness of the true faith. Thus they slay themselves by a bitter death, and fall to the ground and there do evil deeds. *And others it transfixes so that it can move them anywhere it wants;* for it dominates them by its wickedness and bends them to all the vices of its own depravity, seducing them into the embrace of worldly pleasure, so that according to their desires they have different ways in their speech, hair, clothing, gait and other such things. Therefore they become confused and neglect the justice of God, breaking the law and failing to circumcise their minds; they seek excess in lust and do not observe the times of the Law God constituted for them. And as the sea is stirred into turbulence by the wind, they are stirred into diverse vices by the breath of the ancient dragon. *Some of these escape from the flame and move toward those who seek Heaven, reiterating shouts of "O you faithful, give us help!"* For they withdraw themselves from shameful and harmful companionship and imitate those who fix their mind on celestial things, desiring with heart and voice their solicitude and help. *But others remain transfixed,* continuing to be ensnared in evil actions by their various vices.

17   The six ways of temptation of the spiritual

But the flame that breathes forth among spiritual people conceals them in obscurity. This means that the breath of the Devil's persuasion, when it flames toward those who should be assenting totally to the Spirit, beclouds them with the perversity of its vices, so that they long for the flesh more than for the Spirit.

And you see them in six categories; for the ancient enemy strives to pervert both their five exterior senses and the sixth inner one, the devotion of the heart. *Some of them are cruelly injured by the flame's fury;* for the Devil unlooses his arts on them and inspires them with carnal desires and pleasures, and so enkindles them to lust and unclean pollution. *But when it cannot injure one of them, it burningly breathes on them the deadly poison that flows from the worm's head to its feet, either green or white or red or yellow or black.* How? When they refuse the delights of pollution, he pours into them the sprouting green of mundane sadness, so oppressing them that they have no strength for spiritual or worldly matters; or he sends against them the empty whiteness of vicious irreverence, so that they do not hide their shame before God or Man; or he displays to them the bright red of earthly glory, giving them bitterness and anxiety of heart; or he puts into them the dull yellow of contempt for their neighbor, and thus they become whisperers and hypocrites; or he imposes on them the horrid blackness of feigned justice, through which their hearts are wretchedly darkened.

All these are deadly plagues; they have proceeded from the destroyer from the beginning of his time of deception, and will do so until the end of time, when his madness will end in the world. And through them he injures and burns people up with vices.

18   Concerning the unbaptized

But the flame that seeks the abyss contains in itself diverse torments for those who have worshipped Satan in place of God, not washed by the font of baptism or knowing the light of truth and faith. This is to say that the fire that accompanies perdition inflicts dire and bitter torments on those souls who were not washed clean in the font of salvation and did not see the brightness of the celestial inheritance or the faith instituted by the Church, and who continue to venerate the lurker in ambush who tries to kill human souls, rather than the One Who granted humanity life and salvation.

19   What is meant by his mouth's arrows, breast's smoke and loins' fluid

And you see sharp arrows whistling loudly from its mouth; these are the terrible and evil thrusts of the Devil's rage, which issue forth in madness and iniquity; *and black smoke exhaling from its breast,* which is the outpouring of his malicious impulses of hideous wrath and envy; *and a burning fluid boiling up from its loins,* which is the effusion of his uncleanness in ardent lust.

20   What is meant by his navel's whirlwind and bowels' uncleanness of frogs

And a hot whirlwind is blowing from its navel, which is the suffocating wind of fornication that proceeds from his voracity to dominate; *and the uncleanness of frogs issuing from its bowels,* which is the fetid excrement of his obduracy in desperation and his perverse concentration on it. For the ancient waylayer hopes to subjugate those who follow him completely to his will. *And all of these things affect human beings with grave disquiet;* for such perversities bring those who fix their hope in the earthly and not the heavenly, and so most miserably become involved with them, into extreme ruin.

21 The Devil makes the foolish believe what he falsely shows them

And the hideous and foul-smelling vapor that comes out of it infects many people with its own perversity. This means that the black wrong of a fetid conscience proceeds from the Devil and disturbs the foolish with wicked unbelief. How?

From the time of the beheading of John the Baptist, who declared that the Son of God is the One Who heals the wounds of sin, most evil error arose, whereby the Devil seduces different people by different false images; so that they think that what he shows them, each according to his understanding, is true. And many are deceived thus, because their faith is constantly weak and wavering.

But you, O My children, if you wish to live justly and devoutly, fly from this most wicked error, lest death catch you in your unbelief.

22 Heretics who worship the Devil for God must be avoided and excommunicated

And fly from those who linger in caves and are cloistered supporters of the Devil. Woe to them, woe to them who remain thus! They are the Devil's very viscera, and the advance guard of the son of perdition.

Therefore, O you My beloved children, avoid them with all devotion and with all the strength of your souls and bodies. For the ancient serpent feeds and clothes them by his arts, and they worship him as God and trust in his false deceptions. They are wicked murderers, killing those who join them in simplicity before they can turn back from their error; and they are wicked fornicators upon themselves, destroying their semen in an act of murder and offering it to the Devil. And they also invade My Church with their schisms in the fulness of vice; in their shameful plots they wickedly scoff at baptism, and the sacrament of My Son's body and blood, and the other institutions of the Church. Because they are afraid of My people, they do not openly resist these institutions of Mine, but in their hearts and their deeds they hold them as nothing. By devilish illusion, they pretend to have sanctity; but they are deceived by the Devil, for if he were to show himself to them openly they would understand him and flee him. By his arts he shows them things he pretends are good and holy, and thus deludes them. O woe to those who persevere in this death!

But because the Devil knows he has only a short time for his error, he is now hastening to perfect infidelity in his members: you, you evil deceivers, who labor to subvert the Catholic faith. You are wavering and soft, and thus cannot avoid the poisonous arrows of human corruption, which you employ as you wish against the Law. And after you pour out your lust in the poisonous seed of fornication, you pretend to pray and falsely assume an air of sanctity, which is more unworthy in My eyes than the stinking mire.

And thus for certain the punishment of all the schisms shall fall upon you: The one that arose in Horeb when the Jewish people made a graven image and played before it in devilish mockery, as some wantonly do to this very day; and the one about Baal, in which many perished; and the one about fornications, where the Midianites did shameful deeds; and all the others. For you have part in all of them by your evil actions; but you are worse than the earlier people, because you perceive the true law of God but stubbornly abandon it.

But, O you who desire to be saved and have received baptism and form the holy mountain of God, resist Satan, and do not descend from the height of your salvation.

23 God's grace forsakes His despisers but mercifully helps His seekers

The Devil ceaselessly sets his snares against a person who is so hardhearted as to despise God's help in resisting him; for then he sees a blackness of iniquity rising up in that person, bringing such bitterness into his whole body that its strength dries up. Hence, when a person begins to contemplate his evil and so crushes himself in despair, deeming it impossible for him to avoid evil and do good, the Devil sees this and says, "Behold a person who is like us, denying his God and turning to follow us. Let us hasten and run swiftly to him, urging him by our arts so that he cannot escape us. For to leave God and follow us is what he wants."

But a person who is assailed by these evils through the Devil's agency, and polluted by murder, adultery, voracity, drunkenness and excess of all vices, will fall into death if he continues in them impenitent; while one who resists the Devil and withdraws repenting from these vices will rise again to life. For if a person follows the longing of his flesh and neglects the good desires of his spirit, the Maker of this globe says of him, "He despises Me and sinfully loves his flesh, and rejects the knowledge that he should turn away from perdition. And therefore he must be cast out." But if a person loves the virtuous ardor of his spirit and rejects the pleasure of his flesh, the Creator of the world says of him, "He looks toward Me and does not nourish his body on filth, and desires the knowledge of how to avoid death. And therefore help will be given him." How? As Solomon says, in accordance with My will:

24   Words of Solomon

"Evil pursues sinners; and to the just good shall be repaid" [Proverbs 13:21]. What does this mean? Those who fall into error and slide into ruin are invaded on all sides by deadly sickness; and so they do not wisely regard what is true, but carelessly abandon it. And, because they reject God and choose the Devil, they are not worthy to look at God or take any pleasure in God or other people, and the evil they do brings them much adversity. But in good people, right sense and just thoughts erect a tall building; they receive in their bosom the inheritance of the Father, for they long for the celestial light. For they are not among the deceivers in the derisive marketplace, where this or that is sold without regard for its value, but in God they possess that which is true.

25   True worshippers of God crush the ancient serpent

But you see that *a great multitude of people come, shining brightly; they forcefully tread the worm underfoot and severely torment it.* This is to say that those who are born into human misery, but who constitute the faithful army of believers, hasten to attain their desire for Heaven by the faith of baptism and blessed virtues, which are beautiful adornments; and by their deeds they cast down the ancient seducer. They are virgins, martyrs and all other kinds of worshippers of God, who in full knowledge tread worldly things underfoot and desire the heavenly; and they surround the Devil and crush him with force, weakening him with dire suffering. But *they cannot be injured by its flames or its poison;* for they are protected by God with such strength and constancy that neither the open flame nor the hidden persuasion of the Devil's wickedness can touch them. For they forsake all vain fictions, and with great strength in virtue hold fast to sanctity.

But let the one who sees with watchful eyes and hears with attentive ears welcome with a kiss My mystical words, which proceed from Me Who am life. Amen.

Book Three

THE HISTORY OF SALVATION SYMBOLIZED BY A BUILDING

THE ONE SITTING UPON THE THRONE

THE FALLEN STARS

VISION ONE
God and Man

A nd I, a person taken up from among other people—though unworthy to be called a human, since I have transgressed God's law and have been unjust when I should have been just, except that by God's grace I am His creature and will be saved—I looked toward the East. And there *I saw a single block of stone, immeasurably broad and high and the color of iron, with a white cloud above it; and above the cloud a royal throne, round in shape, on which One was sitting, living and shining and marvellous in His glory, and so bright that I could not behold Him clearly. He held to His breast what looked like black and filthy mire, as big as a human heart, surrounded with precious stones and pearls.*

And from this Shining One seated upon the throne extended a great circle colored gold like the dawn, whose width I could not take in; it circled about from the East to the North and to the West and to the South, and back toward the East to the Shining One, and had no end. And that circle was so high above the earth that I could not apprehend it; and it shone with a terrifying radiance the color of stone, steel and fire, which extended everywhere, from the heights of Heaven to the depth of the abyss, so that I could see no end to it.

And then I saw a great star, splendid and beautiful, come forth from the One seated on the throne. And with that star came a great multitude of shining sparks, which followed the star toward the South, looking on the One seated on the throne like a stranger; they turned away from Him and stared toward the North instead of contemplating Him. But, in the very act of turning away their gaze, they were all extinguished and were changed into black cinders.

And behold, a whirlwind arose from those cinders, which drove them away from the South, behind the One sitting on the throne, and carried them to the North, where they were precipitated into the abyss and vanished from my sight. But when they were extinguished, I saw the light, which was taken from them, immediately return to Him Who sat on the throne.

And I heard the One Who sat on the throne saying to me, "Write what you see and hear." And, from the inner knowledge of that vision, I replied, "I beseech you, my Lord, give me understanding, that by my account I may be able to make known these mystical things; forsake me not, but strengthen me by the daylight of Your justice, in which Your Son was manifested. Grant me to make known the divine counsel, which was ordained of old, as I can and should: how You willed Your Son to become incarnate and become a human being within Time; which You willed before all creation in Your rectitude and the fire of the Dove, the Holy Spirit, so that Your Son might rise from a Virgin in the splendid beauty of the sun and be clothed with true humanity, a man's form assumed for Man's sake."

And I heard Him say to me, "Oh, how beautiful are your eyes, which tell of divinity when the divine counsel dawns in them!" And again I answered from the inner knowledge of the vision, "To my own inner soul I seem as filthy ashes of ashes and transitory dust, trembling like a feather in the dark. But do not blot me out from the land of the living, for I labor at this vision with great toil. When I think of the worthlessness of my foolish bodily senses, I deem myself the least and lowest of creatures; I am not worthy to be called a human being, for I am exceedingly afraid and do not dare to recount Your mysteries. O good and kind Father, teach me what to say according to Your will! O reverend Father, sweet and full of grace, do not forsake me, but keep me in Your mercy!"

And again I heard the same One saying to me, "Now speak, as you have been taught! Though you are ashes, I will that you speak. Speak of the revelation of the bread, which is the Son of God, Who is life in the fire of love; Who raises up everyone dead in soul and body, forgives all repented sins in His serene clarity, and awakens holiness in a person and sets it growing. Thus God, the magnificent, glorious and incomprehensible, gave Him as a great intercessor by sending Him into the purity of the Virgin, who had no corruptible weakness in her virginity. No pollution of the flesh should or could have been in the mind of the Virgin; for when the Son of God came in silence into the dawn, which was the humble maiden, Death, the slayer and destroyer of the human race, was deceived without knowing it as if in a dream. Death went on securely, not realizing what life that sweet Virgin bore, for her virginity had been hidden from it. And that Virgin was poor in worldly goods, for the Divine Majesty willed to have her so. Now write about the true knowledge of the Creator in His goodness."

1   The faithful should venerate the magnitude of the fear of the Lord

God, Who created all things and appointed humanity to that glory from which the lost angel and his followers were cast out, should be worshipped and feared by every creature of His with the greatest honor and awe; for it is just that His creatures should worship the Creator of all things and faithfully adore God above all beings. This is symbolized by that stone that you see. For in this mystery it represents the magnitude of the fear of God, which should always arise and live in the hearts of the faithful with purest purpose.

You see it as *a single block of stone, immeasurably broad and high and the color of iron;* this shows how firmly the fear of God must be held. For God is to be dreaded by every creature with single-heartedness, so that they know He is the one true God, without Whom is no one and like Whom there is no one. *It has immense breadth,* because He is incomprehensible; *and height,* because Divinity is above all else and the highest pitch of any creature's senses cannot understand or attain to it. *Its iron color* means that it is burdensome and hard for human minds to fear God; for this is a heavy burden for soft and fragile dust, and the human creature rebels against it.

2 Every soul that wisely fears God becomes by faith God's throne

The white cloud above that stone is the clear wisdom of the human mind; and *the royal throne above the cloud, round in shape,* is the strong faith of the Christian people. In it, God is faithfully recognized; for wherever the fear of the Lord takes root, human wisdom will also appear, and then God's help will set faith above it, and prepare His rest in it. For when God is feared, He is understood by faith with the help of human wisdom, and these will touch Him as a seat touches its owner. And in them God prepares a seat for Himself, supreme above all else; for neither power nor force can comprehend Him, but He resides in single-minded and pure faith, One above all things.

3 God's mystery is incomprehensible unless He gives faith to do so

And One is sitting on that throne, living and shining and marvellous in His glory, and so bright that you cannot behold Him clearly. He holds to His breast what looks like black and filthy mire, as big as a human heart, surrounded with precious stones and pearls. This is the Living God, Who reigns over all things, shining in goodness and wondrous in His works. The deep mystery of His immense glory can never be perfectly contemplated by anyone, unless faith allows that person to comprehend and bear Him, as a seat contains and surrounds its owner. As the seat is subject to its owner and cannot rise and throw him off, so faith has no proud desire to look upon God, but only touches Him in intimate devotion.

4 In the Father's wisdom the perfection of the elect is revealed

And to His breast, that is in the wisdom of His mystery, for love of His Son He holds that poor, weak, infirm mire that is Man: black in the blackness of sins and filthy in the filthiness of the flesh, but the size of a human heart, which is the breadth of the profound wisdom with which God created Man.

For He has looked upon those who are saving their souls through penitence, and no matter how in their persistent weakness they have sinned against Him, they will come to Him at last. They are surrounded by ornaments, those great ones who rise up among them: martyrs and holy virgins like precious stones, and innocent and penitent children of redemption like pearls; so that by them the mire is surpassingly adorned, and the virtues, which so gloriously shine in God, shine also in the human body. For He Who put breath and life in Man was scrutinizing Himself. How?

Because He foreknew and decided in advance that His Son would be incarnate to bring redemption; therefore, every stain of sin must be washed away from His body. And so too He knows the souls which, after many and great sins while they are still in the body, will end by being justified; which, after their several errors will walk in God's justice, will be steadfast in Him and shake off their forgetfulness, turning from the vices that wounded them in the earthly places where they fell into sin. And He will also take note of the fact that many peoples have arisen from their erring ways and were brought back from the deadly stench of sin, though they were walking covered with wounds and most dreadful sores; but many will arise who have been wounded so severely by the bitter and harsh pains of sin that their crimes are beyond measure and their evil habits are ingrained, and they are too ill even to summon the energy to do their deadly works, murder and adultery and all the other evils.

5   Example from the Gospel

O wretches! Do they not approach like pilgrims from a far-off land? As the Scripture says in the Gospel, the younger son said, "I will arise and go to my father and say to him, 'Father, I have sinned against Heaven and before you, and am no longer worthy to be called your son. Make me as one of your hired servants' " [Luke 15:18]. This is to say: A person who, admonished by the Holy Spirit, comes to himself after a fall into sin says, "I want to rise up from the unendurable sins whose heavy guilt I can no longer bear. I will retrace my steps in memory, lamenting and sorrowing over my sins, until I come to my Father, Who is my Father because He created me. And I will say to him, 'Father, I have sinned against Heaven, wronging the celestial work that is myself; You formed me by Your will, and touched me in creating me, so that I should be only celestial in my deeds, but I have belittled myself by shameful actions. And I have sinned before You, because I have forsaken the humanity of my nature. How? By my many abominations.

" 'Therefore, I am guilty both of losing myself and insulting You, and am not worthy to be called Your son; for in the wickedness of my heart I have led Your creature in me in a path You did not appoint for me. But now, let me be as Your servant, redeemed at the price of Your Son's blood. You gave Him at a price so great that not even death can ever repay it; but that price allows penitence to arise from Your Son's Passion, and so sets sinners free. I have lost my rightful inheritance as a child of Adam, for he, who was created a son in justice, was stripped of that joyful glory; but now the blood of Your Son and penitence have redeemed the sins of humanity.' "

And thus all should speak who have repeated Adam's fall but then return through penitence and attain to salvation. They should remember the many warnings they have heard told from the Scriptures about the suffering and the blood of their Redeemer, and recall with lamentation how they have transgressed the rules of keeping God's word instead of receiving them with longing. For they neglected His law, which was set up for them to keep when the commandments were instituted, and refused to think about what things they should have done and left undone for fear of the Lord. But they come to the truth nonetheless, remembering what they heard and learned from God; even though they previously were blinded, not desiring to know His justice and avoiding whatever would set that justice they despised above their sins; even though they turned their back on God's word and rejected His law.

Many of these will be superabundant in good things; they will not find it sufficient to feast in the house of the Lord, to celebrate His Divine Office and work His justice to the fullest, but will always be weeping and woefully remembering the evils they did when they cherished unlawful works and ignored the deeds God's law allowed.

6   The meaning of the mire on the breast and why the angels may not spurn Man

This is the filthy mire that you see on the breast of the loving Father. How? The Son of God went forth from the Father's heart and entered into the world; He is surrounded by the people who believe, and by their decision to believe in Him hold to Him. And therefore they also appear on the breast of the gentle Father; and thus neither angel nor any other creature may spurn a human being, since the incarnate Son of the Most High God has human form in Himself. For the blessed choir of angels would regard Man as unworthy, for he stinks of vice and sin, while those heavenly angels themselves are invulnerable and free from any deed of injustice; except that they continually see the face of the Father, and love in the Son what is loved by the Father. What is this? That the Son of God was born as a human. For I, the Father, established My Son, born of the Virgin, for the salvation and restoration of humanity, as My servant, the prophet Isaiah, says to you:

7 Words of Isaiah

"He shall feed His flock like a shepherd, He shall gather up the lambs with His arm and raise them to His bosom; and He shall carry those who are with young" [Isaiah 40:11]. Which is to say: As a shepherd feeds his flock, so My Son, the Good Shepherd, feeds the flock of His redeemed. How? He feeds it by His law, which He planted through Me. Because My Son is human, He will extend His power like His arm, and gather together the lambs, who by the innocence of baptism, which strips from them the old man and his works, are innocent of Adam's sin; and by His virtues and His law He will take them up into His bosom. How? By lifting them above the height of the heavens and making them members of Himself.

Therefore the human form is to be seen in the inmost nature of the Deity, where neither angels nor any other creatures appear; because My Only-Begotten, to redeem the human race, assumed human form in the flesh of a Virgin. And He will carry in His heart those who are with young. How? My Son carries human beings in His blood, and saves them by His five wounds, for whatever sins they have committed by means of their five senses are washed away by supreme justice when they repent; and He carries them so because He was incarnate, and suffered wounds on the cross, and died and was buried, and rose again from the dead.

And He has stretched out His hand to them and drawn them back to Himself. How? When He assumed humanity for them, though they thought they were lost when Adam fell. For My Only-Begotten conquered death, and it could no longer triumph over them; and so He knew them in the power of His glory, and knew that they were to come to Him by the purgation of penance.

And you see them appear in the bosom of the Father. This means that the Son of Man is perfected with all His members in the secret heart of His Father. How? Because when the world reaches its end, the elect of Christ, who are His members, are to be perfected. O how beautiful is He! As the Psalmist says:

8 Words of David

"Beautiful of form above the children of men" [Psalm 44:3]. This is to say: In Him shines forth beauty beyond beauty, the noblest form free from any spot of sin, without a splash of human corruption, and lacking all desire for the sinful works demanded by fleshly human weakness. None of these ever touched this Man. And the body of the Son of Man was born more purely than other people, for the stainless Virgin bore her Son in ignorance of sin, and thus ignorant of the sorrow of childbirth. How? She never felt any stubborn urge to sin, and therefore the pains of childbirth were unknown to her; but the wholeness of her body rejoiced within her. Oh, how beautiful then His body!

But let the people know that His bodily beauty was no greater than the profound wisdom that established His human form; for the Father, the Son and the Holy Spirit, one God in Three Persons, does not delight in the beauty of the flesh but in the humility with which the Son of God clothed Himself in humanity. And in His form there were no exterior blemishes. Sometimes an ordinary person is given by God an ugly appearance as bodies go, as when his limbs are distorted and misshapen and he is a cripple. This is not because nature so forms human bodies, but because of God's judgment; a strong nature is expressed in a proper form, and a weak one in various deformities. But the latter was not the case with My Son.

Humans, I say, are widely divergent in bodily form; they can be black, ugly, polluted, leprous, dropsical and full of defects; they can also be persuaded by devilish art into becoming inflamed with sorcery, stupid, blind to the good things of the Lord or forgetful of what they should praise and what they should blame. For they should do the works of justice, but they do the works of evil and omit the good, despising the cross and the martyrdom of their Lord. But God the Father contemplates this work of mire with the purpose of His goodness, as a father looks at his children when he hugs them to his breast. And, because He is God, He has the love of a tender father for his children. For so great is His heart's inmost love for people that He sent His Son to the cross, like a meek lamb that is carried to the slaughter. And so the Son brought back the lost sheep, bearing them on His shoulder by assuming humanity; which caused Him great sufferings, for He deigned to die for His flock.

But among these people there are many surrounded by ornaments and adorned pricelessly with virtue. They are the martyrs, the virgins, the innocents and the penitents, as I said before, and those who have obeyed their masters, and those who accuse themselves of their sins and tirelessly strive to punish themselves for them, denying the self in them. And who or where these elect are must not be stated; for the numbers of them all have been reckoned.

Does anyone think it possible to see into the deep wisdom of the Most High and into the discernment of His knowledge, and count the number of those who are to be saved? His judgments are incomprehensible to all people. Your task is to run; for the kingdom of God is prepared for you. For as great as is the zeal of the faithful, washed in baptism and known in faith, to fulfil God's justice, so great also shall be their reward.

9 The Father does, ordains and perfects all His works through His Son

But you see that *from the One seated upon the throne extends a great circle colored gold like the dawn, whose width you cannot take in.* This means that from the Almighty Father there extends a supremely strong power and action, whose might encircles all things; and He works it through His Son, Who is always with Him in the majesty of Divinity, ordaining and perfecting all His works through Him before all worlds and in the world from its start. His Son glows with the brilliant beauty of the dawn; for He was incarnate in the wisest Virgin, whom the dawn signifies, by the hand of God Which is the Holy Spirit, in Whom also each work of the Father is done. You can never comprehend the full extent of His glory, for no creature has, will have or should have a standard of goodness or power with which to measure His power or His deeds; God's power is inestimable and incomprehensible, and His works are invincible and marvellous.

10 On the revolving circle

And that circle wheels about from the East to the North and to the West and to the South, and back toward the East to the One on the throne, and has no end. This is to say that God's power and His work encircle and include every creature. How? All creatures arose in the will of the Father, Who is One God with the Son and the Holy Spirit, and all feel Him in His power. How? They all feel Him in their creation: He wheels around from the East, the origin of all justice, to the North, where the Devil is confounded, to the West, where the darkness of death tries to extinguish the light of life but the light conquers it and rises again, and to the South, where the ardor of God's justice burns in the hearts of the faithful; and so back to the rising of justice as to the East. What does this mean?

When in God's foreordained time His work shall have been completed in the people of this world, then the circuit of the world will have been made, and the perfection of time and the last day will arrive; and then each work of God, seated in His throne without end, will shine resplendent in His elect. For God is perfect in His power and His work, Who was and is and ever shall be, and His Divinity had no beginning; so that it is not that He will have been, but that He is.

11 God's power is greater than Man can know, and why the angels praise Him

And that circle is so high above the earth that you cannot apprehend it. This is to say that the Supreme Power is so far exalted above the lives of all creatures and above the sense and intellect of Man, and so incomprehensible in and above all, that no creature's senses can grasp it, except to realize that this Power is much higher than it can know. And therefore the angels sing to God in praise; for they see Him in His power and glory, but they also cannot understand or sense Him completely, and they can never have enough of His magnitude or His beauty.

12   God is manifest justice, true and just without alteration

But that *it shines with a terrifying radiance the color of stone, steel and fire;* this means that the divine power radiates formidable and severe virtue against iniquity that is dissimulated, impenitent or unpunished. This strength is like steel, because God's manifest justice yields nothing to weak injustice; whereas dust, as the saying goes, is unjust and does not please God. His justice, like steel, strengthens all other justice, which is weaker than it as iron is weaker than steel. And this strength is like fire; for He Himself is the Fire of Judgment, burning up all sin and injustice, which refused to bow down before Him and seek His mercy.

And God is like the rock in Man; for He is true and just without any alteration, as stone cannot be changed into softness. He is like steel, piercing everything with His all-penetrating gaze, never changing but remaining God of all things. And he is also like fire, because He inflames and enkindles and illuminates all things without changing over time; for He is God.

13   God's strength, justice and judgment have no boundary Man can sense

And you see that *this radiance extends everywhere, from the heights of Heaven to the depth of the abyss, so that you can see no end to it.* This is to say that the strength of God's power and work, His justice and His upright judgment are everywhere, and neither in the heights of Heaven nor in the depths of the abyss is there any boundary to them that human senses can comprehend.

14   Why and how the first angel and his followers fell

Then you see a great star, splendid and beautiful, come forth from the One seated on the throne, and with that star come a great multitude of shining sparks. For, by the command of the Almighty Father, the angel Lucifer, who now is Satan, came forth from his beginnings adorned with great glory and clothed with brightness and beauty; and with him came all the lesser lights that were his followers, who then shone with brightness but now are extinguished in darkness. But he was inclined toward evil and did not look on Me the Perfect One; he trusted in himself and thought he could begin anything he wished and finish anything he began. Thus the great honor he owed to the One on the throne, Who was his creator, he gave to himself, and so descended into sin.

But all the sparks that follow the star toward the South look on the One seated on the throne like a stranger; they turn away from Him and stare toward the North instead of contemplating Him. This is to say that Lucifer and all his company, who were miraculously created by the ardent goodness of God, had a secret sin, which was that their pride disdained the One Who reigns in Heaven. All of them, formed at the beginning of Creation, tasted the impiety that leads to perdition, and contemplated God not in order to know His goodness but in order to exalt themselves above Him as if He were a stranger; in their open elation they turned away from knowledge of Him in His glory and hastened toward their fall. *But, in the very act of turning away their gaze, they are all extinguished and are changed into black cinders.* Which is to say that as soon as they disdained to know God, the splendid brilliance with which the divine power had clothed them was extinguished in Lucifer himself and all the followers of his malice; as he destroyed in himself the inner beauty that was his consciousness of good, and gave himself over to impiety, he was erased from eternal glory and fell into eternal loss. Therefore they were all changed into black cinders; stripped of their bright splendor along with their leader, the Devil, they were smothered in darkness and deprived of the glory of beautitude, like a dead coal without its smoldering spark.

Then a whirlwind arises from those cinders, which drives them away from the South, behind the One sitting on the throne, and carries them to the North, where they are precipitated into the abyss and vanish from your sight. This is to say that when these angels of iniquity tried to prevail over God and oppress Him with their pride, the wind of impiety that arose in them was belched forth in bitter perdition, and blew them backward from the South, which means from goodness, into the North, which means into forgetfulness of God the Ruler of all. Thus when they tried to exalt themselves in pride, they were confounded and met their downfall, and were precipitated by their pride into the abyss of eternal death, which is their doom, never again to be seen in brightness. Even so did I tell the noonday forest, which should ardently have borne the fruit of justice and did not, by My servant Ezekiel:

15 Words of Ezekiel

"Behold, I will kindle a fire in you and will burn in you every green tree and every dry tree. The flame of the fire shall not be quenched; and every face shall be burned in it, from the south to the north. And all flesh shall see that it is I the Lord Who have kindled it; and it shall not be quenched" [Ezekiel 20:47–48]. Which is to say: O fool, who raised yourself up in pride against Me! I Who have neither beginning nor end will bring this to pass: In My zeal I will kindle in you the fire of My wrath, and burn up all your vigor with which you tried to begin a work, trusting in your false energy more than in Me, and choosing to act as your pride dictated on your own foolish wisdom. And I will burn up in you all your dryness, that aridity which belongs to your sin and that of the other lost ones, and in which you tempt humanity, which is ashes, to sin; and this temptation will not bring you back salvation, but will become in you eternal fire. There is no reward of salvation for you or those who follow your example. And that fire of punishment shall not be quenched or abate its tortures, but will burn up that headlong pride in which you looked upon the face of honor and tried to seize it for yourself. And thus were you ejected from all your glory; you rose in the South in clear and ardent light, but you set in the darkness of the North, which is to say in Hell.

And everyone shall see this and know Gehenna, both the elect and the reprobate. The elect will know Gehenna because they have escaped it, and the reprobate because they will remain in it and be punished; knowing that it is the place that I the Lord Almighty have kindled in retribution for your crimes, O Devil, and it will not be extinguished by your evil deeds or those of your followers. So the sin of diabolical pride has cast Satan and his angels into the outer darkness of eternal torment, without any comfort from light; so that there is no place for them in the eternal light, and you, O frail human, cannot see them there any longer. As Ezekiel, imbued with My Spirit, says with mystical significance to the King of Tyre:

"All who see you among the nations will be astonished at you; you are brought to naught, and you shall not be forevermore" [Ezekiel 28:19]. Which is to say: All the upright of heart, O Devil, will be astounded at your filthiness, seeing you drunken with the vices of the nations who embrace you and transgress the laws of God and wither away; for you pollute with temptation God's temple, which is Man. And so, through your pride you are brought to naught and fall from the glory of salvation; for you have no honor and no felicity, and no glory shall be yours in the eternity of Heaven; you are lost from them forever, without end.

16 The glory lost by the Devil and the others was saved by the Father

But when they are extinguished, you see the light that was taken from them immediately return to Him Who sits on the throne. This is to say that when the Devil, because of his pride and obstinacy, lost his exceeding brilliance (for Lucifer was of purer light than all the other angels), and when the seeds of death entered into him and all his followers, that brilliance returned to God the Father to be kept in His secret heart; for the glory of that splendor was not allowed to go for nothing, but God kept it as a light for another of His creations.

For God, Who commanded one variety of His creatures to arise without flesh yet bright in splendor, namely the Devil and all his company, kept this splendor for the mire that He formed into Man, who arose covered with a vile earthly nature, that he might not exalt himself into the likeness of God. For the one created in bright splendor, and not clothed in a miserable form as humans are, could not sustain his self-exaltation; there is only one Eternal God, without beginning or end. And thus comparing oneself to God is the wickedest of all crimes.

And so I, the God of Heaven, kept the illustrious light, which departed from the Devil because of his crime, and hid it within Myself until I gave it to the mire of the earth, which I had formed in My image and likeness; as does a human being when his son dies and his inheritance cannot pass to children of his. When he has no children to inherit, a father holds the inheritance and plans to give it to children yet unborn, and when they are born from him he gives it to them.

17   The Devil fell without leaving an heir, but fallen Man had one

For the Devil fell without leaving an heir, which is to say without the intention of doing good works; he never accomplished or began anything good, and therefore another received his inheritance. This other also fell, but did have an heir, which was the beginning of obedience; and he received this inheritance with devotion, even though he could not complete the work that went with it. But then God's grace completed that work in the Incarnation of the Savior of the nations, and restored the good inheritance. So Man receives his inheritance in Christ, because he did not reject God's commandments when they were first given; whereas the Devil did not want to serve the Creator for good, but to vaunt his own pride, and so was deprived of the glory and perished in perdition.

18   Example of Goliath and David

As Goliath rose up despising David, so the Devil rose up presuming upon himself and wanting to be like the Most High. And as Goliath was unaware of David's strength and despised him as nothing, so the Devil's towering pride despised the humility of the Son of God's humanity, when

He was born into the world and sought not His own glory but in all things the glory of the Father. How? The Devil did not seek to imitate this example and submit himself to his Creator as the Son of God submitted Himself to His Father. But David, with the secret strength given to him by God, cut off Goliath's head, as is written by the inspiration of the Holy Spirit:

"And David, taking the head of the Philistine, carried it into Jerusalem; but his arms he placed in his own tent" [1 Kings 17:54]. This is to say: My Son took the spoils and booty of the Devil with His great power and deprived the ancient serpent of his head. Where? In the womb of the Virgin, who crushed that head. Through whom? Through her Son. What is this crushing? The holy humility, which appears both in the Mother and in the Son, and struck at the origin of pride, which is the head of the Devil. And so, in His humility My Son in the body carried that head into the holy Church, which is the vision of peace, and showed it that the pride of the Devil had been slain. The strong arms are the Devil's stubborn vices, by which he had overcome the human race and made them worship him as God; for he had terrified them by his vices as people are terrified by arms. But My Son broke them and placed them in His tent; that is, in the Passion of His body while He suffered on the cross.

So now He lets the battle continue among the tents, which are the bodies of His chosen members, that they may divide with Him the Devil's arms. How? As He conquered the Devil in His Passion, they too may conquer him by restraining themselves from their desires and not being in harmony with his vices. And, to extend the metaphor, as the glory of Goliath was given to David, so the glory that was taken from the first angel was given by Me to Adam and his race, which confesses Me and keeps My precepts, after the Devil's pride was destroyed.

But let the one who has ears sharp to hear inner meanings ardently love My reflection and pant after My words, and inscribe them in his soul and conscience.

THE BUILDING OF SALVATION

VISION TWO
The Edifice of Salvation

hen I saw, within the circumference of the circle, which extended from the One seated on the throne, a great mountain, joined at its root to that immense block of stone above which were the cloud and the throne with its Occupant; so that the stone was continued on to a great height and the mountain was extended down to a wide base.

And on that mountain stood a four-sided building, formed in the likeness of a four-walled city; it was placed at an angle, so that one of its corners faced the East, one faced the West, one the North and one the South. The building had one wall around it, but made of two materials: One was a shining light like the light of the sky, and the other was stones joined together. These two materials met at the east and north corners, so that the shining part of the wall went uninterruptedly from the east corner to the north corner, and the stone part went from the north corner around the west and south corners and ended in the east corner. But that part of the wall was interrupted in two places, on the west side and on the south side.

This building was a hundred cubits long and fifty cubits wide, so that the two side walls were of equal length and the front and back walls were of equal length. But the four walls were equal in height except for the bulwarks, which were somewhat taller.

And between the building and the light of the circle, which extended from the height to the abyss, at the top of the east corner there was only a palm's breadth; but at the north and west and south corners, the breadth of separation between the building and the light was so great that I could not grasp its extent.

And as I was marvelling, the One seated on the throne again said to me:

1 Faith rose in the circumcision of Abraham and climaxed in the Incarnation

Faith appeared faintly in the saints of the Old Testament, who did that justice which was constructed on high in the goodness of the Father. But at the Incarnation of the Son of God, it burst into burning light by the open manifestation of ardent deeds; for the Son of God did not desire transitory things, and taught by example that they should be trampled underfoot and only celestial things loved. The early patriarchs did not flee or separate themselves from the world, for it had not yet been shown them that they should forsake all things; but they worshipped God with simple faith and humble devotion.

Therefore, *you see within the circumference of the circle, which extends from the One seated on the throne, a great mountain, joined at its root to that immense block of stone above which are the cloud and the throne with its Occupant; so that the stone is continued on to a great height and the mountain is extended down to a wide base.* This is to say that the mountain, which signifies faith, stands within the mighty and strongly built power of the Supreme Father; this faith, great in virtue, first appeared in the circumcision of Abraham and progressed until the coming of the Supreme God's Son. Since the ancient serpent was ruined, this faith has been inspired in people by the Holy Spirit; faithfully working in the Father, they can believe that God is almighty, Who could conquer so great an enemy, and uplifted by this belief, they can attain to that glory from which the Devil was cast out for his pride.

2 Faith and fear of the Lord are joined to one another

And this mountain is rooted in that immense stone, which holds the mystery of the fear of the Lord; for faith is connected to constant fear of the Lord, and fear of the Lord to the strength of faith. This is because the Son was sent from the Father to be born of the Virgin, and from the Son came forth true faith, which was the first foundation of the good works that fear of the Lord brings forth with all the virtues, whose height touches God. And so, in the wise minds of the faithful, God Who reigns over all things is faithfully worshipped. How? Because fear of the Lord, with its sharp contemplative sight, penetrates the secrets of Heaven; for fear is the beginning of a just intention, and when that flowers into sanctity by good works, it joins with blessed faith and reaches God in full perfection.

3 The faithful build good works on faith in all four corners of the earth

And on that mountain stands a four-sided building, formed in the likeness of a four-walled city; which is to say that the goodness of the Father builds good works on faith. Gathering multitudes of the faithful from the four corners of the earth, he draws them to celestial things and fortifies them in constancy of virtue; then the Heavenly Father graciously places them in His bosom, which is to say in His inner power and His mystical counsel, in four categories of faith. How?

VISION TWO

4   On the four categories

I Who am the Most High ordained in My work the first category of people, the race of Adam; which race, after his death, went on weakened by great discord until the second arose. This was at the coming of Noah, when the Flood took place; in which, by the Ark, I foretold the mysteries of My Son. But in the time of Noah, by My commands I showed the shining part of the wall of the building; by drowning sinners in the flood, I implied to people that they should flee death and seek life, and thus opened to them the knowledge of the choice between the two ways. What does this mean?

A person flourishes and thrives in the living life, which is the soul, and in it he contemplates and sees two ways, good and evil; either way is open to him, so that while he is in the body he can do good or evil with soul and body, starting with his mental choice and perfecting his will in his deeds. And so, in Noah, by My command there was shown the knowledge of the choice between the two ways, and a sharp warning to spurn evil and love good. And, with the decree of circumcision, this anticipation of God's will leads to the third category, in which Abraham and Moses were united in circumcision and the Law. Circumcision and the Law continued until the fourth category, the time of the Holy Trinity, when the Old Testament was openly fulfilled in the Son of God. And so, through the Son of God an inner shoot arose in the Church; He was born and suffered for human salvation, rose again and returned to the Father, and so restored that corner of the wall that had been obscured and weakened by Adam's fall, building it up again with saved human souls.

5   People must go forward humbly and wisely flee the Devil's snares

But the fact that *the building is placed at an angle* means that Man, who is the work of God, is too weak to go forward by conquering the Devil by force, without fear of sin or bodily harm; he must humbly avoid the Devil and wisely flee his snares, and faithfully unite himself to good works. Thus he will be established on the Son of God, Who sits in the corner and is the Cornerstone, and thus join himself to the work of human salvation.

6   The four corners of the building and what they mean

But one of its corners faces the East, one faces the West, one the North and one the South. This means the following. The Son of God was born of the Virgin and suffered in the flesh that justice might arise and humanity be restored to life with all justice; and that is the eastern corner. From it arose the salvation of souls when in His Son God fulfilled justice; which was prefigured from the time of Abel till the coming of the Son Himself, and in Him was ended the physical observance of the laws in the Old Testament. Then came the salvation of faithful people by their faith, which in the last times the Son of God Who was sent by the Father brought into the world, which is the western corner. In Abraham and in Moses justice raised itself against the Devil, and they foreshadowed the promised grace through which Man was saved, though the Devil had deceived him and slain him like a robber in Adam's fall, which is the northern corner. And the wretched and fatal fall of the human race was at last through heavenly grace nobly and beautifully restored, and the ardent work of God and man bore full fruit, which is the southern corner.

7 Another meaning for the corners

The southern corner also means that the first man, Adam, was created by God. But the knowledge of the choice of the two roads does not come from this corner; which means that from Adam on the human race was disorderly and did not worship God in wisdom by eager service to the Law, but did its own will in great evil. It did not glow with knowledge of God or true beatitude, but lay in death; but what the Father willed to do with the human race lay hidden only in His heart. The eastern corner designates Noah, in whom justice began to show itself; thus there was openly manifested and foreshadowed the knowledge of sanctity that would later be perfected in the Son of God. And because in the Son of God, Who is the true Orient, every kind of justice began, and for the sake of His sanctity and honor, first truly declared in Noah, the building should always be named starting from the east.

The northern corner also means Abraham and Moses, who, working against Satan, surrounded that knowledge as if with precious stones and roofed it in with the golden roof of God's manifest justice, which was circumcision and the Law. For, before circumcision and the Law, justice was naked and without deeds.

And the fourth, the western corner, also means the true Trinity, which showed Itself when the Savior was baptized; and He returned to Heaven with all his work to save souls, and built there the true holy city Jerusalem.

8 God gives people fortifications and defenses of their good works

The building has one wall around it, but made of two materials: One is a shining light like the light of the sky, and the other is stones joined together.

These two materials meet at the east and north corners. This is to say that the goodness of the Father gives people unbroken security, in the form of a fortification and defense of their good works; and thus, surrounded and strengthened by them, people may forsake the lusts of the flesh and fly to the One God Who is their protection.

The wall is of two materials. The first is the knowledge of the choice of the two roads, which is given to people when they speculate and think clearly with their minds, to make them circumspect in all their affairs; and the second is earthy human flesh, for people were created by God to do active deeds.

9   On the reflective knowledge

And the knowledge shines as brightly as daylight, because through it people know and judge their actions, and the human mind that is carefully considering itself is radiant. For this beautiful knowledge appears in people like a white cloud, and passes through human minds as swiftly as the cloud moves through the air; and it shines like daylight, because when God graciously does His most splendid work in humans and they avoid evil, the good they accomplish is as bright in them as the day.

And every human deed proceeds from this knowledge. How? Each person can have two ways. How? With his sensibilities he knows good and evil; and when he moves away from evil by doing good he imitates God, Who works good in Himself, Who is just and knows no injustice. But when he does evil, the wily Devil entangles him in sins, for the Devil seeks iniquity and flees sanctity, and will not rest until he holds the person bound by evil deeds. But if the person breaks free of evil and does good, the Supreme Goodness will receive him; for he has conquered himself for the love of God, Who handed over his Son for him to the death of the cross.

This knowledge is reflective because it is like a mirror; for as a person sees his face in a mirror and discerns beauty or blemishes, so too in the finished deeds he ponders within himself, he can knowingly discern good and evil. For this discernment is part of the reason with which God inspired Man when He breathed life and soul into his body. The life of animals is deficient, because it is not rational; the human soul is never deficient, but because of its rationality it will live forever. And so a person contemplating good and evil knows whether a deed is wicked or good; he was formed by the grace of God and given reason at the beginning of creation, and in the choice of baptism and the salvation of souls in the New Testament he is restored by that same grace. As My most loving Paul says about this election of grace:

10 Words of Paul

"There is a remnant saved according to the election of grace. And if by grace, it is not by works; otherwise grace is no longer grace" [Romans 11:5–6]. This is to say: The remnant, who are not inside the snare of death, shall not stoop to the Devil's example, for they were openly saved when God sent His Son to become incarnate; and this is the election of grace, manifested for human salvation. How?

The grace of God created Man, but by evil works he fell. Then the election of grace was shown in the chosen vessel; for the Son of God was born from the Virgin, and it was not possible for Him to lapse. For if a person makes something useful for himself and it is taken away from him by someone else, he will get himself something even more useful that no one will take, and be content with it. And this is the way the grace of God acted. It made Adam, the first man, and the Devil drew him away from innocent deeds; but then grace brought the fullness of good works and the salvation of souls through the Son of God. But if the grace of God was the cause of salvation, then it was not caused by the merit of any human deeds. How?

There was no justice in Adam's deeds; therefore, humanity would never have returned to salvation by the merit of its works, except that it was restored by grace through the works of the just Son, Who was obedient to His Father, and cleansed by baptism, which the Son of God gave to humanity along with good works. So in this work the grace of God collaborates with humanity, and humanity with it. And therefore the grace of God goes with this work, and the work has arisen from grace.

But if salvation arose from human merit, and righteous human deeds stemmed from the people themselves and not the grace of God, grace would no longer be grace. How? Because then Man would stem from himself and not from God, and no creature would give thanks to God, and the grace of God would be nothing. But as it is, the grace of God has given people the support of reason, that they may work justice in the knowledge of good and evil; and by this knowledge they can seek the good and cast away evil, and so know life and death and choose which one to stay with. As Solomon says in his knowledge of wisdom:

11 Words of Solomon

"He has set before you water and fire; stretch forth your hand to whichever you will" [Ecclesiasticus 15:17]. This is to say: When the soul awakens God gives it a great and acute power, the knowledge of evil and good, which are water and fire. For as water overflows and conceals in its depths deadly creatures and useless things, so a person overflows with evil deeds and conceals them lest he be discovered. And as fire burns and leaves no impurity unconsumed, or as a craftsman purifies jewelry by fire to remove its rust, so too does good purify a person, melting the rust of wickedness off him. Now water and fire are inimical, extinguishing or evaporating each other. And so too does a person: He kills good by evil, or evil by good, and either way he silently hides his desires within himself and turns them over in his mind.

12 On the working of the two motives

And while he is mulling over these desires, the person's will makes its choice of the way he wants to go, and he stretches out his hand to it and moves along it by his deeds. He does good work by God's help through grace, and he does evil by the Devil's craft and his artful temptations; and the person himself observes his deeds by the exercise of his reason. With this reason he contemplates good and evil, and the desire rises in him to choose between the two ways, good and evil, according to his will. What does this mean?

The person has the choice in that his mind's desires reflect different things to him like a mirror, and he says to himself, "If only I could do this or that!" He has not yet done them in actuality, but he has thought about them. So he stands at the fork of two roads, with knowledge of the motives of good or evil; and as he desires so at last he does, and travels upward or downward.

13 Righteous institutions arose in Abraham and Moses

And the other part of the wall, as you see, is like stones joined together; which symbolizes the human race, but also designates the righteous institutions that came from the minds of people like Abraham, Moses and the others, who were the preliminary offshoots of the Law of God and all its just additions up to the end of time. How? God works in Man and through Man; thus He sent His Son to save humanity at the end of the time of the Law, working in a sinless human body. And He took the foundation of faith on Himself, and carried the whole human race with Him, even the first man who was cast out of Paradise for transgressing justice. And He achieved this wondrous deed for humanity through His Law, in which He embraced all Christians; and they make up this building in the goodness of the Father, because Man will live in the celestial Jerusalem.

14   Reflective knowledge began in Noah but iniquity reigned
     uninterrupted

So the two kinds of wall join each other on the east and on the north. For reflective knowledge and human labor join together to end the injustice in which the human race was entangled when it forgot God. From Adam arose the raging injustice of the world before the flood; and because of that world's iniquity, the injustice was drowned with the people in the flood of waters. And then reflective knowledge first appeared, by My inspiration, in Noah's knowledge of good as in the east corner, as was foretold. But though God's admonition flourished in Noah, bold and greedy evil arose again and marched triumphantly to the North. And the iniquity of division from God was not trodden underfoot until Abraham, in whom, as in the north corner, it was choked off and the penetrating light of God's justice arose.

And truly the shining part of the wall goes uninterruptedly from the east corner to the north corner. This is to say that reflective knowledge to fortify human minds first appeared in the east corner, that is, in the days of Noah. Before Noah, iniquity sought to do all it could to mock God, and so people followed their own lusts instead of loving to worship God; and the first descendants of Adam were completely devoured by the Devil, because the knowledge was hidden from them, until in Noah that knowledge was displayed openly. This had been foreshadowed even when the Devil was confident that the whole human race was in his power. But iniquity went on as far as the north corner, that is, until the coming of Abraham and Moses; for before them, iniquity still reigned almost supreme, not yet interrupted or defeated by the established justice of God's Law, since circumcision and the Law had not yet been given. But by these fathers the Devil began to be confounded, where previously he had reigned confidently in the world; in the words of Paul, My light-giving vessel of election:

15   Words of Paul

"Death reigned from Adam to Moses, even over those who had not sinned in the same way as Adam, who was a type of Him Who was to come" [Romans 5:14]. Which is to say: Death reigned, with no competitors or conquerors, from the time of Adam to the time of Moses. How? Before Moses the severity and dignity of the Law had not yet been given, except the small preview of it in the circumcision Abraham accomplished at God's command; and so deathly vice went from error to error as it pleased. But then, by God's will, there arose the strong soldier Moses, and he prepared stout weapons of justice, which destroyed the worship of death by means of the Law, which contained in itself the complete salvation of souls, because it foreshadowed the Son of God. Death indeed even ruled the innocent, who were simple and moderate and did not repeat in their actions the deeds of Adam. And Adam was a type of Him Who was to come. How? God created Adam just and innocent of all thought or deed of sin; and so too the Son of God was born of the Virgin Mary, with no stains of sin.

16 Righteousness is shown in Abraham and Moses, justice in the Incarnation

But you see that *the stone part goes from the north corner around the west and south corners and ends in the east corner.* This means that the righteous works of humans, with which God fortified them, came forth from the north corner, which is to say from the circumcision of Abraham and the Law of Moses and the justice they inspired in people. They continued to the west corner, where open justice arose in the Incarnation of the Son of God; went on from there to the south corner, where through baptism and the other just works of the new-chosen Bride of the Son of God ardent deeds were enkindled to restore Adam to salvation; and at last returned to the east corner, to end restored to the Supreme Father. How? The Supreme Father in His mystery ordained every work of justice that would bring the first, fallen man back into salvation by a return to God. How? Man had fallen, and so I arose in mercy and sent My Son to restore salvation to souls, as My servant the psalmist David shows, saying:

17 Words of David

"His will is in the law of the Lord, and on that law he shall meditate day and night" [Psalm 1:2]. Which is to say that the will of the Father to save is contained in the law of justice His Only-Begotten showed to the world: Who is One God with the Father and the Holy Spirit and rules the whole globe. And He, the Son of the Father, was incarnate and seen as a visible Man, and in the flesh was uplifted above all creatures. How? The Son of God was begotten of His Father before all worlds and later, in the last times, born into the world of a mother; but while He was not yet incarnate He remained invisible within the Father as the will is invisible in a person before it is shown in a deed, and then later appeared visibly in the flesh for human salvation.

So the Almighty Father meditates with His Son upon an act of justice to counter the original fall of Adam. Where? In the love of His Son, Who was before time began in the Father in the glory of divinity, and then became miraculously incarnate at the appointed epoch of the world, when the Father sent Him from His heart into the world as the High Priest of all justice.

Therefore the Son embodied the law of justice, as He received it from the Father when Christian law was made.

And on that law, which the Father willed to establish and make through His Son, He meditates by day. How? He Himself is the Day; and in that Day, before He made any transitory creature and while no darkness or iniquity existed in any creation of His, He meditated on His Son's law.

And also by night. How? Because when evil arose in His creatures, which is like the darkness of night in angels and people, the Father continued to meditate, and will do so until the last day, as long as His ineffable works shall last; He shows and reveals the law of His Son when in Him He perfects all the good deeds that are to be perfected in Man.

18 Christ's members and the Church still lack the perfection they will have

But you see that *the stone part of the wall is interrupted in two places, on the west side and on the south side.* This is to say that the work of the human race to fortify its defenses is still unfinished in two areas. The members of the Son of God, His chosen, remain imperfect, which is to say that the west side is interrupted, since from there the Son of God was sent in these last times into the world. And the Church is also still imperfect in virtue, not as she will be set up and established in the celestial Jerusalem, so that the south side is interrupted, for the Church will be perfected in Heaven.

19 The number ten, diminished by Adam, is multiplied again by Christ

This building is a hundred cubits long, which means that the mystical number ten was diminished by humanity when it transgressed, but was restored by My Son and multiplied by ten to a hundred, as virtues were multiplied in the salvation of souls. And from the hundred, again multiplied by the ten, there will come the perfect number one thousand, referring to the virtues that will completely destroy the thousand arts of the Devil, which now seduce the whole flock of Almighty God's lovely sheep. What does this mean?

I, the Omnipotent, in the beginning made lights that burned and lived, shining in splendor, some of which stood fast in My love, but some despised Me their Creator and fell. But it did not befit Me, the Creator, to discard what I had made as useless and ruined. How? A part of the angelic creation grew proud of the good the Creator gave it that it might know Him, and decided that it could take on false glory and be like its Creator; and so it fell into death. Then God foresaw that what had fallen in this lost group could be more firmly restored in another. How? He created Man from the mud of the earth, living in soul and body, to attain to that glory from which the apostate Devil and his followers were cast out. Man is thus exceedingly dear to God, Who made him truly in His own image and likeness; he was to exercise all the virtues in the perfection of holiness, as indeed God formed all creatures to do, and to work in humble obedience to do acts of virtue, and so to fulfil the function of praise among the more glorious orders of angels. And thus, in this height of blessedness he was to augment the praise of the heavenly spirits who praise God with assiduous devotion, and so fill up the place left empty by the lost angel who fell in his presumption.

And so Man symbolizes the full number ten, perfecting these things by the power of God. But in this figure ten is multiplied to a hundred. For Man was seduced by the Devil and fell away from God; but at last he was admonished by divine mercy and inspiration, began to acknowledge God in the law and prophecy of the Old Testament, and then attained more insight by the sanctity and the means of constancy in virtue given by the Church.

And so, starting with Abel, Man began to practice all the virtues, and will continue to perfect them until the day of the last just person; and this is why the length of the building is the number one hundred, which God shows to humanity in a mystical figure that it may not despair if it falls back into iniquity, but rise above it and vigorously do the work of God. For anyone who falls into sin but then rises from it again will be stronger than he was before, as God gave greater and stronger virtues to humanity by sending His Son into the world to raise up the prostrate human race than it had had before.

And therefore people work more strongly in soul and body than if they had no difficulty in doing it, since they struggle against themselves in many perils; and, waging these fierce wars together with the Lord God Who fights faithfully for them, they conquer themselves, chastising their bodies, and so know themselves to be in His army. But an angel, lacking the hardships of an earthly body, is a soldier of Heaven only in its harmonious, lucid and pure constancy in seeing God; while a human, handicapped by the filth of his body, is a strong, glorious and holy soldier in the work of restoration, which he does in soul and body for the sake of God. And so by the number one hundred of his present labor he attains to the one thousand of future repayment; on the last day he will receive his full and eternal reward, and rejoice in soul and body without end in the celestial habitations. And so the diminished ten is recovered through My Son, Who was born of the Virgin and suffered on the cross, and brought back humanity to the realms of Heaven. As My Son says in the Gospel:

20 Words of the Gospel

"What woman who has ten coins, if she loses one of them, does not light a candle, and sweep the house until she finds it? And when she has found it, she calls together her friends and neighbors, and says, 'Rejoice with me, for I have found my coin that was lost' " [Luke 15:8–9]. Which is to say: The Holy Divinity had ten coins, namely ten orders of the heavenly hierarchy, including the chosen angels and Man. It lost one coin when Man fell into death by following the Devil's temptations instead of the divine precepts. Hence the Divinity kindled a burning lamp, namely Christ, Who was true God and true Man and the splendid Sun of Justice; and with Him He swept the house, namely the Jewish people, and searched the Law for all the meaning of salvation, and established a new sanctification, and found His coin, Man, whom He had lost. Then He called together His friends, namely earthly deeds of justice, and His neighbors, namely spiritual virtues, and said, "Rejoice with Me in praise and joy, and build the celestial Jerusalem with living stones, for I have found Man, who had perished by the deception of the Devil!"

21 The five wounds of Christ wipe out human sins

And you see that *the building is fifty cubits wide,* which is to say that the whole breadth of the vices of humanity, which should have built on and revered the work of God but instead followed its own lusts, is mercifully wiped out and forgiven by the five wounds that My Son suffered on the cross. So the wounds of His hands obliterated the deed of disobedience done by the hands of Adam and Eve, and the wounds of His feet cleared the path of exile for humanity to return, and the wound of His side, from which sprang the Church, wiped out the sin of Eve and Adam after Eve was made from Adam's side. And therefore My Son was nailed to the tree, to abolish what had been done through the tree that occasioned sin; and therefore He drank vinegar and gall, to take away the taste of the harmful fruit.

22 The Holy Spirit made Man's five senses able to know good and evil

The wall is five cubits high, which refers to the virtue of divine knowledge of the Scriptures, which imbue Man's five senses for the sake of the work of God. The Holy Spirit breathed on them for people's good; for with the five senses people can regard the height of Divinity, and discern both good and evil.

23 Soul and body must work to avoid evil and do good in all circumstances

Thus *the two side walls are of equal length;* for, contained within the edifice of God's goodness, people must work with great constancy with the two side walls of soul and body flanking them. How? To avoid evil and do good. How? The profound and incomprehensible power of God created Man to worship God with all his strength and all his might and with all the devotion of his intelligent reason; and it is right that the Creator of all things should, before and above everything, be worshipped worthily as God.

24 The mind must have the wisdom and discernment to know God

Therefore *the front and back walls are of equal length;* for in the work of God wisdom and discretion are like two walls, with wisdom as the higher part and discretion as the lower. And God imbues the whole of the human mind with these, an equitable and just gift, that the mind may know Him.

25 People should gain devout faith from considering the four elements

But *the four walls are equal in height, except for the bulwarks, which are somewhat taller.* This is to say that Man, living as he does among the four elements, should hold high the Catholic faith with constant devotion and veneration through the goodness of the Father; he should worship the Son with the Father and the Holy Spirit, as the Son does all Their works in Them. How? Every work that the Son of God has done and is doing, He perfects through the goodness of the Father in the Holy Spirit. What does this mean? According to the will of the Father, the Son in His great goodness redeemed humanity through His Incarnation; for the Father ordained that the Son should be born of the Virgin, conceived by the Holy Spirit, and assume humanity for love of Man to bring him back to restored life. Therefore Man has a part in God, and can enter into salvation with Him, if he has the true Catholic faith and knows the Father, the Son and the Holy Spirit as the one true God.

26 The faithful person ascends from virtue to virtue

The bulwarks are much higher. How? Because when a person regards the height of goodness in his mind, he then builds a high wall of faith by virtue of the work of God. Then he ascends above that rational faith, which shows him God in the power of His Divinity, and on it he builds bulwarks of virtue higher than the wall. How? He finds that it is not enough to have faith in God, and so builds virtues that rise higher; and so he grows, like a flourishing palm tree, from virtue to virtue, and by these virtues his righteous faith is exalted and adorned as bulwarks do a city.

27 The Father sent His Son into the world to do His will and redeem Man

And between the building and the light of the circle, which extends from the height to the abyss, at the top of the east corner there is only a palm's breadth. This is the width of the heavenly secrets that lie between the work of the Son of God when He lived in the world and did divine works, here shown as a building, and the power of the Father, which expands in mighty splendor into the places below and the places above. He sent His Son into the world to be the capstone of the corner that faces east, made up of the justice first prefigured in Noah and perfected in the Incarnation of the Son. Thus these secrets were, so to speak, just a hand's breadth wide, the distance from the thumb to the little finger of the flat hand; and that was the time ordained in the heart of the Father when He willed to send His Son. He sent Him with a strong hand, and surrounded Him with all the joints of His fingers, which are His works in the Holy Spirit, that He might accomplish the will of His Father and suffer upon the cross for the wretched and contemptible disobedience with which the Devil inspired the first man. To redeem that man from that sin God's mercy bent down to earth, and the incomprehensible height of divinity was contained in the humanity of the Son of God.

28 The defeat of evil and the goals of justice are secrets of God's will

But at the north and west and south corners the breadth of separation between the building and the light is so great that you cannot grasp its extent. This is to say that no one weighed down by a mortal body can understand the elation of evil in the heart of the Devil in the North; or its consummation in active creatures in the West of fallen Man; or the beginning or end of the supernal justice, which is the ardent South. Nor can such a one see how these things are worked out and differentiated between the deeds of all peoples and the power of My knowledge. Both the elect and the reprobate are subjected to a just scrutiny and examined most diligently and strictly on their [obedience] to My precepts; and all should trust in Me to feed them in all their needs. But all these things are so hidden in My secret counsels that human senses and understanding can never take in or understand the extent of their profundity, except as far as is granted by My permission.

But let the one who has ears sharp to hear inner meanings ardently love My reflection and pant after My words, and inscribe them in his soul and conscience.

TOWER OF GOD'S ANTICIPATING WILL

FIVE VIRTUES

VISION THREE
The Tower of Anticipation of God's Will

fter this I looked, and behold! In the middle of the shining part of the building's outer wall there stood an iron-colored tower, which was built out from the outer side. It was four cubits wide and seven cubits high. In it I saw five figures standing separately, each in its own arch with a conical turret above it. The first of these faced the East, the second the Northeast, the third the North, and the fourth the pillar of the Word of God at whose foot was the patriarch Abraham; and the fifth faced the tower of the Church and the people who were hastening here and there in the building.

And the five figures resembled each other in being dressed in silk garments and white shoes, except the fifth, who was armored at all points. The second and third were bareheaded, with loose white hair, and wore no cloak; the first, third and fourth wore white tunics; and this was all the difference between them.

The first figure wore on her head a bishop's miter, and had loose white hair; and she wore a white pallium, whose two borders were adorned on the inside with embroidered purple. In her right hand she held lilies and other flowers, and in her left hand a palm. And she said, "O sweet life, O sweet embrace of eternal life, O blessed happiness, in which consist the eternal rewards! For You are always in true delight, and so I can never be filled or sated with the inner joy that is in my God."

And the second was clothed in a purple tunic, and stood like a youth who has not yet attained adulthood but is very serious. And she said, "Neither the dreadful foe who is the Devil nor the hostility of humans nor this world shall frighten me, who stand in the discipline of God and am constantly in His sight."

The third covered her face with the white sleeve that clothed her right arm, and said, "O filth and uncleanness of this world! Hide yourselves and flee from my eyes, for my Beloved was born of the Virgin Mary."

The fourth had her head veiled in womanly fashion with a white veil, and was hung about with a yellow cloak. On her breast was a picture of Jesus Christ, and around it was written, "Through the depths of the mercy of our God, in which the Dayspring from on high has visited us" [Luke 1:78]. And she said, "I stretch out my hands always to pilgrims, and the needy, and the poor and weak, and those who groan."

But the fifth was armed and arrayed with a helmet on her head, and a breastplate and greaves, and iron gloves; a shield hung from her left shoulder; she was girded with a sword and she held a spear in her right hand. And under her feet a lion lay, its mouth open and its tongue hanging out, and some people also stood; some were blowing trumpets, some fooling with instruments used in shows, and some playing different games. And that figure trampled the lion under her feet, and at the same time pierced these people with the spear she held in her right hand. And she said, "I conquer the strong Devil, and you also, Hate and Envy and Filth, with your deceptive jesters."

And inside the building I saw two other figures standing opposite this tower. The first stood on the floor of the building, in a niche of fiery splendor whose inside was painted with pictures of various evil spirits and which was across from the tower. The other figure stood next to this niche but was outside it and had no niche of its own. Both figures looked sometimes at the tower and sometimes at the people who were entering and leaving the building. These figures were also dressed in silk garments and veiled in women's fashion in white head-coverings, and wore no cloaks but had on white shoes.

And the first of these had on her head a three-sided crown, of a glowing red like a hyacinth, and was clad in a white tunic, with green embroideries in all the folds. And she said, "I conquer in the East with the mighty Son of God, Who went forth from the Father and came into the world to redeem humanity, and afterward died in great suffering on the cross, rose from the dead, ascended into Heaven and returned to the Father. Therefore I shall not be confounded, but will flee from the miseries and pains of this world."

And the second was clad in a white tunic, which was slightly tinged with color; and on her right arm she carried a cross with the image of the Savior, over which she bent her head. And she said, "This child bore many sorrows in this world, and therefore I will weep and know sorrow always for the sake of eternal joy, into which the good sheep will be led by the Son of God."

And I saw that all these figures were uttering their individual speeches through the mystery of God, to admonish humans. And again the One sitting on the throne, Who was showing me all these things, said to me,

I The divine virtues put forth by the Law bear fruit in the Gospel

By the strength and constancy of God's will, the divine virtues sprang up gradually in the Old Testament; but to those who revered them almost in ignorance, they did not yet taste completely sweet and delightful. For then, the Law was seen only in austerity, sharply correcting the delinquent; but afterward, these virtues by the grace of God brought forth much fruit in the new Law, showing the hungry the sweetest, strongest and most perfect food, the love of celestial things. Previous to this, as was said, certain hidden things were a sign of what was to come; and so this miraculous vision appropriately shows.

For *this tower you see standing in the middle of the shining part of the building's outer wall* is the image of the anticipation of God's will, shown in many different ways and meanings in the circumcision; so that by the sign of circumcision God displayed the Law, and by the Law the grace of the Gospel. For by the faith manifested in Abraham, there arose in him also the circumcision, a true prefiguration of the mystery; beginning in him, the divine power built up strong virtues, as it were in the middle of the road of the knowledge of the two ways, defended by the goodness of the Supreme Father. And these virtues were by God's will destined to appear openly; they foreshadowed His will before He displayed it manifestly in His deeds.

It is iron-colored, and built out from the outer side. This is God's justice, strong and invincible, which first showed itself outwardly in reflective knowledge by means of the circumcision, which was apparent in the outer flesh. And it is established with the blessed virtues among the spiritual things of that spiritual wall that God built within people.

2 Virtues are brought about in people by God's will

The tower is four cubits wide; for these virtues, by God's will, are brought about in people by placing them in the world of the four elements, from which, while they are in the body, they get physical nourishment. *It is seven cubits high;* for there were seven gifts of the Holy Spirit, which are so firm and tall that the tower raised itself on them until, after the Incarnation of My Son, which was prefigured in the circumcision of the Old Testament, the Church came forth from it.

3 On the states of Heavenly Love, Discipline, Modesty, Mercy and Victory

In it you see five figures standing separately, each in its own arch with a conical turret above it. This is to say that in this tower, that is in the strength of the circumcision, there are five strong virtues; not that any virtue is a living form in itself, but a brilliant star given by God that shines forth in human deeds. For humanity is perfected by virtues, which are the deeds of people working in God.

Hence these five virtues stand in this tower in the likeness of a person's five senses. They seized with great zeal upon the circumcision, and cut it off from all iniquity, as the five human senses are circumcised in the Church by baptism. But they do not work in a person by themselves, for the person works with them and they with the person; just as the person's five senses do not work by themselves, but the person with them and they with the person, to bear fruit together. And so each of them works hard, as much as it can, and thus has a turreted apex of authority, the surpassing dignity of virtuous constancy.

The first of these faces the East; for this virtue looked forward with sobs of love to the Son of God whenever He was to come, and spoke openly about the eternal life the circumcision was hiding.

The second looks to the Northeast; for this figure divided her attention between the East and the North, regarding God in the East with great discipline, but also disdaining the behavior of the people in the North, who manifested undisciplined licentiousness and did not regard God or His Law with worthy reverence.

The third faces the North; for she destroys unlawful fornication with great strength, despising it and shielding herself from it by the Law.

The fourth looks toward the pillar of the Word of God at whose foot is the patriarch Abraham; for she cleaves to the Incarnation of the Son of God, touching it through the beginning Abraham made, that miraculous foreshadowing of the ram caught in the thornbush.

And the fifth faces the tower of the Church and the people who are hastening here and there in the building; for this image rises up victorious, and destroys every injustice that originated in Adam. She looks to the strength of the Church to help her conquer the vices of the Devil; she shows herself to the people who are hastening to and fro in the Church and all behaving differently, inspiring them to be the flock of God's justice and worship Him with reverent zeal.

4 Their dress and what it signifies

And *the five figures resemble each other,* which is to say that they worship God in human deeds with equal devotion. *Each of them is dressed in silk garments;* for each of these virtues is sweet and delightful, never weighing people down or constraining them, but softly instilling into their minds the sweetness of the heavenly kingdom as balm distils from a bush, with no crusted filth of injustice. And *they are shod in white shoes,* for they follow My justice in righteousness and celestial purity, trampling down surrender to the Devil and stamping out his traces in human beings.

But *the fifth virtue is armored at all points;* for she looks to the Church, where the fiercest wars are waged against the Devil's vice; she extends her victory everywhere in it, wearing the priceless armor, which is God's invincible strength; and this strength slays all injustice and confounds the deceit of the Devil.

The second and third are bareheaded, with loose white hair. This means that, for love of Me, they avoid assuming burdens of labor or wealth or lust; bareheaded, which is to say with a clear conscience, they open to Me all their secret mind. They cast away all confusion and license of the desires of the flesh; and the first sign of this is their white hair, which symbolizes the purity of the mind that desires good works. *And they wear no cloak;* for they reject the customs of the pagans and the lust and filth of the Devil, and abandon all secular cares, because the wisdom of the world is foolishness with God.

The first, third and fourth wear white tunics. This means they hold fast to innocence, which prefigures with sweet chastity the Incarnation of My Son, Who withdrew humanity from death and clothed it with life in salvation. *And this is all the difference between them;* for each gets her strength from the Holy Spirit, but they use different paths of the soul to attain their one desire in God. And so by them the celestial Jerusalem will be perfectly built, for these virtues are the deeds people do to reach God.

5 On Celestial Love's dress and what it means

Therefore *the first figure* signifies Celestial Love, for this love must exist in people before anything else. She *wears on her head a bishop's miter, and has loose white hair;* for this virtue was crowned in the High Priest Jesus Christ, but also in the high priests of the Old Testament and in those who called to the Son of God, "Would that You would rend the heavens and come down!" [Isaiah 64:1]. She stands without a woman's head-covering, so that her hair flows free and its whiteness is seen; and by this hair she prefigures the freeing of the priesthood from the ties of marriage through the advent of My Son. For His priests should, for the sake of salvation, imitate Him in chastity; they should always hold to the perfect heavenly love and shake off the evil actions of sin-stained humanity, and thus form the clear, white part of God's spiritual gift.

And she wears a white pallium, whose two borders are adorned on the inside with embroidered purple. This is to say that the grace of God surrounds her in gentle purity, its boundaries of protection fortified and adorned with the beautiful ornaments of charity. For divine grace will extend to every good deed, which is made up of two parts, God's love and the doer's.

And in her right hand she holds lilies and other flowers, which means that for her good works she has the reward of the lilies of eternal life and light and holiness. These are her companions, who have joined themselves to her by heavenly love.

And in her left hand she carries a palm, which has grown out of the secret place of blessed virtue in remembrance of death; and with it she can stop death as if by rolling stones in its path. And this she declares in the words, already quoted, that she speaks to the children of God.

6   On Discipline's dress and what it means

And the second represents Discipline; for after the love of the celestial life has arisen, carnal lusts must be restrained by the discipline of contrition. She *is clothed in a purple tunic,* for she is surrounded by My Law and the mortification of human flesh, and the purple garment is the example of My Son, Who was born of the Virgin in charity and gave it every means of working.

She stands like a youth who has not yet attained adulthood but is very serious. For Discipline is always full of childlike fear, the fear of a child under restraint who respects his schoolmaster. I, the Almighty, am the Master of discipline; in Me she appears not as an adult, for she does not try to wield power to do her own will, but faithfully and reverently fears. And she shows this in her words, quoted above.

7   On Modesty's dress and what it means

The third represents Modesty, for modesty appears after discipline to blush and drive away sin. Therefore she *covers her face with the white sleeve that clothes her right arm;* for she protects her inner conscience, which is, as it were, the face of her soul, by flying from fornication and the Devil's pollution. She defends herself with the white garment of innocence and chastity, on the right hand of which is the salvation coming from her deeds. For contempt and utter rejection of the filth of Satan is entwined strongly round her conscience, as she declares in the words of her admonition quoted above.

8   On Mercy

And *the fourth* signifies Mercy; for after modesty appears the virtue of mercy to help the needy. In the heart of the Father is true mercy of His grace, which He ordained in His eternal counsel and mercifully showed to Abraham in the circumcision. For He led him forth from his land and commanded that he and his race be circumcised, and showed him great wonders in the true Trinity; and through this He symbolically foreshadowed His Son, and foreshadowed mercy to Abraham in the sacrifice of Isaac.

And she *has her head veiled in womanly fashion with a white veil,* which is the roof and foundation of salvation, inasmuch as one who has mercy can bring back lost souls to the pure protection of the holy veil from out of the exile of death. It makes souls white and people radiant to be covered with

God's mercy; and so those who disdained God while they were in sin will find Him shining on them like a gentle sunbeam when Mercy is brought to them from Heaven. And so Mercy, in the figure of a woman, is a fruitful mother of souls saved from perdition. For as a woman covers her head, so Mercy averts the death of souls; and as women are sweeter than men, so Mercy is sweeter than the rabid insanity of crime in a sinner before his heart is visited by God. And the virtue of Mercy also appears in feminine form because, when one virginal body was enclosed by womanly chastity, sweetest Mercy arose in the womb of Mary; Mercy had always dwelt in the Father, but now the Father showed her as visible through the Holy Spirit in the Virgin's womb.

She is hung about with a yellow cloak; for she is surrounded by the shining sun, the sign of My Son, Who shines on the world from Heaven as the sun's splendor shines on the earth. For My Son is the true Sun, lighting up the world by the sanctification of the Church.

And on her breast she has a picture of My Only-Begotten, which means that I put My Son on the breast of Mercy when I sent Him into the womb of the Virgin Mary.

And therefore, *around it is written, "Through the depths of the mercy of our God, in which the Dayspring from on high has visited us"* [Luke 1:78]. What does this mean? That everywhere My power extends, the secret of what is on the breast of Mercy shows that My Son is the true Mercy. How? As it was foretold in the words of My servant Zacharias in the Gospel, for it was he who said, "Through the depths of the mercy of our God, in which the Dayspring from on high has visited us." Which is to say that salvation comes from the depths of the Father's mercy; for it was hidden in His heart, as the viscera are hidden in a person, that His Son was to be incarnate and God visit humanity at the end of times. How? In the celestial bread, which is His Son, born in the flesh of the Virgin Mary and come forth from the heart of the Father on high to offer the greatest mercy to those who seek Him, as that virtue tells the children of God in her words quoted above.

9   On Victory's dress and what it means

And *the fifth figure* foreshadows Victory; for after the mercy I showed by the circumcision when I willed to send My Son into the world, the same circumcision gave rise to victory, which then went on with increasing strength till the coming of My Son, and goes on with Him until the last day. For in My Son I defeated the ancient serpent, which had exalted itself over His head and bound the human race by a thousand evil deeds like a chain. My Son triumphed over those evil deeds with all the arms of war that, like flowers of virtue, arose in His Incarnation. What does this mean? That after mercy arises victory in people too, as soon as they conquer themselves and their harmful vices. How? Among the five virtues the first is celestial love, which consists in a person knowing and loving God above all things. Then the person, because of his faith, is bound by the law of discipline; and from there he goes on to repress his tendency to sin through good and righteous modesty. And so by these three powers the person will attain a just heart, and be able to see the next thing, the suffering of his neighbor; and then he will provide all necessities for him as for himself.

And with these three powers the person soon becomes a strong soldier, perfected in mind by imitating My Son, the true Samaritan, in mercy. And then he wins victory over the power of the Devil with the arms of virtue; he conquers himself and governs his neighbor, and by these virtues slays all evil, rejecting the pride that drove Adam from Paradise.

And this fifth virtue *is armed with a helmet on her head;* for Man in the fullness of celestial desire should long for God, Who is the Head of all things, and so attain eternal salvation. *She is arrayed with a breastplate;* this is so that Man may resist the Devil by justly restraining the will of his carnal desires. For he has become subject to God in true fear and trembling, faithfully dreading His stern judgment, as the psalmist David says, instructed by Me:

"Your lightnings lit up the world; the earth shook and trembled" [Psalm 76:19]. This is to say: Your wonders and secrets, O Lord of all, shone forth and miraculously appeared. How? Like lightning, which is partly seen and partly concealed, just as Your mysteries are sometimes understood but sometimes unknown. For throughout the whole world, wondrously created by Your will, there is no race to which the name of Your glory and the power of Your majesty will not come; they will come miraculously by different paths with remarkable signs, even to those whom the light of faith and truth has not yet illumined for their salvation. Therefore, people will turn, shaken by sighs, away from their own will; they will forsake their lusts, trembling at the judgment of Heaven. Formerly Man forgot himself and walked in earthly deeds; but now he will be wise and come to himself.

This virtue *is also arrayed with greaves,* so that when she sees the right path she can leave the paths of death by way of chastisement of the body. And *she has iron gloves,* so that through mental circumcision and right faith she may escape the works of the Devil, believe in God and so evade the snares of the cruel enemy. *A shield hangs from her left shoulder;* for the left is the side of the Devil's combat with Man, and so she is surrounded there with the grace of God's mighty precepts. Man by these is surrounded and defended with such strong faith that the Devil cannot corrupt him by temptations, and he will not succumb to the Devil's vices as long as God's protection circles his shoulders; for God's grace binds the high and strong soul to Himself with the bond of love of God and neighbor.

And *she is girded with a sword,* because people must keep themselves in the austere power of God's words by chastising their bodies and cutting away iniquity both from themselves and from others. *And she holds a spear in her right hand;* which is to say that a person who trusts in God may attack and overcome the Devil's filth with the great peace of the Lord. And this is true justice in the evil combat of Devil against Man, which the latter can hardly win without the help of God.

And under her feet a lion lies, its mouth open; this is the Devil, laid low by Victory at the foot of the righteous path of life and truth as he was gaping with bitter cruelty to swallow the human race. *Its tongue is hanging out,* which represents his plan wickedly to devour the whole race of people descended from Adam.

And some people also stand under her feet. These people, brought to a standstill by her fighting force, are the flutes of the Devil, who are supple that evil may be played upon them. And she, acting righteously in God's zeal, justly strikes them, because their many and various perverse tricks aid and serve the Devil.

Some of them are blowing trumpets. For they are drunk with the sound of evil, and rave in the exaltation of a burning mind; in great pride they hate God's justice, race upon race. *Some are fooling with instruments used in shows;* for they try to deceive with the Devil's fantastic illusions, and stubbornly hold to their twisted pride and envy God's discipline. *And others are playing different games;* they are caught in the perverse filth of vice not by the choice of their own will, as they suppose, but by the snares of the Devil.

And that figure tramples the lion and all these people under her feet; for with great zeal and divine justice she crushes all these vanities of human art and diabolical persuasion. *And at the same time she pierces them with the spear she holds in her right hand;* for, with the confidence and daring she derives from God, she pierces, conquers and wounds all these uncleannesses. For by God they are mocked and judged as naught, as she says in the words of admonition previously seen.

10   On Patience and Longing and what they mean

And inside the building you see two other figures standing opposite this tower. This is to say that in the work the Heavenly Father did through His Son, which showed clearly and visibly the One prefigured in the circumcision, two other virtues sprang up. One of these was to see the example of Christ and how to follow in His steps, and the other was to anticipate with fortitude and reverence the will of God; and they are the fruit that was foreshadowed in the circumcision.

The first of these stands on the floor of the building, in a niche of fiery splendor whose inside is painted with pictures of various evil spirits and which is across from the tower. For this virtue is perfected amid earthly things and treads them underfoot in the goodness of the Father, when it follows the example of the Son of God and passes beyond the desires of the flesh. How? By great endurance it bypasses the worldly misery, depicted in this niche, which is the might of secular power, fierce and terrible in its detaining pride. The Devil's company follows it, and the Devil himself draws to his will the inner desires of the souls of the secular, who love carnal things; and the niche, in its earthly power, often opposes itself to justice and resists the true testament built on God. But Patience is victorious, and in good people conquers everything with the help of God, no matter how they are opposed and exhausted by the snares of the evil spirits.

The other figure stands next to this niche but is outside it and has no niche of its own. For after the first virtue patiently conquers the power of arrogance, even though it inflicts pains on her, the second one surpasses this power, for it arises outside the range of the pains dealt out by arrogance and escapes its rage. Longing stands next to Patience, in remembrance of the griefs from which she took her origin; but she is outside all niches, for she is free from the power of this world and openly carries the cross of Christ.

Both figures are looking sometimes at the tower; which is to say that the work prefigured in God's provident will is completed in them, and so they regard its roots in the circumcision of the Old Testament. They are greater than their start in the circumcision, because the radiant deed excels the beginning of the thought. *And sometimes they are looking at the people who are entering and leaving the building.* This means that they are admonishing in the Holy Spirit both those who are treading the path of justice toward God and those who are entering the orbit of the Devil's crimes and leaving the just path; and they are telling the latter to imitate them in good.

II   Their dress and what it means

These figures *are also dressed in silk garments;* for they possess great sweetness, so that people may not groan under a heavy weight of labor when persecuted. *They are veiled in women's fashion in white head-coverings;* for people should justly be subject to God as their Head, and wrap Him around their minds in pure love, and embrace Him in joy and gladness, as a wife holds her husband according to God's ordinance in fearful and loving honor.

They wear no cloaks; for they lack all care for secular things, but lean only toward the things which are eternal in God and the life to come. *But they have on white shoes;* for they shine in the path of justice by the purity of faith in human minds, so that people may follow their steps and their example.

12 On Patience's dress in particular and what it means

The first figure designates Patience, who arose in the horn of Abraham, which is to say in the time his obedience to God began; and this, with his circumcision, was the first sound of obedience that had occurred after the fall of Adam. It preceded the work of obedience in the true Word, which is in the Son of God, as sound precedes a word; and it came in the North, the side facing the wicked deeds and turbulence of the ancient serpent. And she *has on her head a three-sided crown, of a glowing red like a hyacinth;* for she was first crowned through the faith in the Holy Trinity of the faithful people, who despise their flesh and do not hesitate to shed their blood for the love of God and the true faith. For the Son of God appeared in the flesh to conquer death with the redness of His blood, and it adorned the Church like the glowing red beauty of the noble hyacinth.

She is clad in a white tunic, with green embroideries in all the folds. For she has clothed herself in the garment of God's work in the whiteness of perpetual light, whose folds are embroidered with the sorrows and laments of one who says, "Oh, when shall I come to the sight of the true Light?" And this desire is suffered happily in the present life by thinking of what it foreshadows: The very adversities and calamities of the faithful adorn their souls with greenness, and their suffering them in patience for the sake of God embellishes them. Which, indeed, this virtue declares, in her words already quoted.

13 On Longing's dress in particular and what it means

And *the other figure* represents Longing. For after patience in adversity, there arises among My elect the longing for the remembered life, springing from My admonition that I sent My Son from My heart because of the longing of My people. For My people of both the Old and the New Testaments had and have this remembrance of mind, which ornaments its longing with groans, for it is true compunction of heart.

And so she also stands in the North quarter, to repulse the dissolute uncleanness of the Devil's snares. And she *is clad in a white tunic, which is slightly tinged with color;* for the purity of faith surrounds her with good works, but nonetheless she is pale and troubled, because her faith always sighs and sobs for eternal felicity. *On her right arm she carries a cross with the image of the Savior, over which she bends her head;* which is to say that with her right hand, the hand that strongly does her noble task, she embraces My

Son's Passion. She longs for Him, and bends over Him with her whole desire and intent, imitating Him in suffering and grief; as she shows in the words of her exhortation, already quoted.

And so you see that *all these figures are uttering their individual speeches through the mystery of God, to admonish humans;* for in all the virtues, God's tenderness sweetly instructs the minds of the peoples and exhorts them to put aside evil and raise themselves up to good.

But let the one who has ears sharp to hear inner meanings ardently love My reflection and pant after My words, and inscribe them in his soul and conscience.

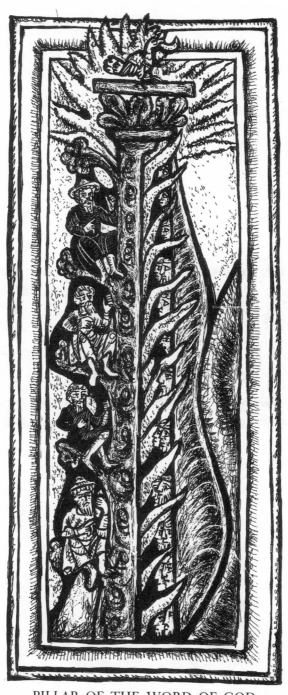

PILLAR OF THE WORD OF GOD

THE VIRTUE OF KNOWLEDGE OF GOD

VISION FOUR
The Pillar of the Word of God

*A*nd then, beyond the tower of anticipation of God's will, one cubit past the corner that faces the North, attached to the outside of the shining part of the main wall of the building, I saw a pillar the color of steel, most dreadful to behold, and so big and tall that I could not form an idea of its measurements. And the pillar was divided from bottom to top into three sides, with edges sharp as a sword; the first edge faced the East, the second the North and the third the South, and the latter was somewhat merged with the outside wall of the building.

From the edge that faced the East, branches grew out from the root to the summit. At the root I saw Abraham sitting on the first branch; then Moses on the second; then Joshua on the third; and then the rest of the patriarchs and prophets, one above the other on each branch, sitting in the order in which they succeeded each other in time. They were all looking toward the edge of the pillar that faced the North, marvelling at the things they could see with spiritual vision going on there in the future.

But between the two edges, the one facing the East and the one facing the North, the side of the pillar to which those patriarchs and prophets turned their faces was from bottom to top as round as if turned in a lathe, and wrinkled like the bark of a tree that puts forth shoots.

And from the second edge, facing the North, there went forth a marvellously bright radiance, which shone and reflected as far as the edge that faced the South. And in the radiance which was so widely diffused, I saw apostles, martyrs, confessors and virgins and many other saints, walking in great joy.

And the third edge, facing the South, was broad and wide in the middle, but thinner and narrower at the bottom and top, like a bow drawn and ready to shoot arrows. And at the top of the pillar I saw a light so bright that human tongue cannot describe it; and in this light appeared a dove, with a gold ray coming out of its mouth, which shed brilliant light on the pillar.

And as I looked at this, I heard from Heaven a terrifying voice, rebuking me and saying, "What you see is divine!" And at this voice I trembled so much that I dared not look there any longer.

Then I saw inside the building a figure standing on the pavement facing this pillar, looking sometimes at it and sometimes at the people who were going to and fro in the building. And that figure was so bright and glorious that I could not *look at her face or her garments for the splendor with which she shone; I saw only that, like the other virtues, she appeared in human form.*

And around her I saw a beautiful multitude, with the appearance and wings of angels, standing in great veneration, for they both feared and loved her. And before her face I saw another multitude, with the appearance of human beings, in dark clothes; and they stood immobile with fear.

And the figure looked upon the people who came in from the world and in the building put on a new garment; and she said to each of them, "Consider the garment you have put on, and do not forget your Creator Who made you." And as I wondered at these things, the One seated on the throne spoke to me again.

1 The austerity of the Law was sweetened by the Incarnation of the Word

The Word of God, by Whom all things were made, was Himself begotten before time in the heart of the Father; but afterward, near the end of time, as the Old Testament saints had predicted, He became incarnate of the Virgin. And, assuming humanity, He did not forsake Deity; but, being one and true God with the Father and the Holy Spirit, he sweetened the world with His sweetness and illumined it with the brilliance of His glory.

Hence, *the pillar you see beyond the tower of anticipation of God's will* designates the ineffable mystery of the Word of God; for in that true Word, the Son of God, all the justice of the New and Old Testaments is fulfilled. This justice was opened to believers for their salvation by divine inspiration, when the Son of the Supreme Father deigned to become incarnate of the sweet Virgin; and the virtues showed themselves to be powerful in the anticipation of God's will, which was the beginning of the circumcision. Then the mystery of the Word of God was also declared in strict justice by the voice of the patriarchs and prophets, who foretold that He would be manifest in justice and godly deeds and great severity, doing the justice of God and leaving no injustice free to evade the commands of the Law.

2 The patriarchs in a mystery showed that the Law was near

And you see that the pillar *is standing one cubit past the corner that faces the North;* which symbolizes in human terms how very near the patriarchs who announced the strict justice of the Word of God were in their meaning to the Law, thus resisting the Devil in the North.

3 No pride can resist the strength of God

The pillar *is the color of steel, and attached to the outside of the shining part of the main wall of the building;* for the power of the Word of God is unconquered and unconquerable, and no one can resist Him by vain rebellion or vile pride. And so the Old Testament fathers were united with the reflective knowledge, as it were, on the outside, by their bulwarks and deeds of justice; but they were not yet imbued with the fiery perfection of the work that arose in the Son of God, and which they but foreshadowed outwardly in their words.

4 God's justice is dreadful and exceeds every creature in height

It is most dreadful to behold; for the justice in the Word of God is fearful to humans, who know only the impious judgment of unjust judges judging according to their own whims. *It is so big and tall that you cannot form an idea of its measurements;* for the Word, Who is the Son of God, exceeds all creatures in paternal majesty by the magnitude of His glory and the height of His divinity, and no human in a corruptible body can fully understand Him.

5 The Word of God has three divisions: Law, Grace and exposition of scripture

And the pillar *is divided from bottom to top into three sides, with edges sharp as a sword;* which is to say that the strength of the Word of God as prefigured in the Old Testament and declared in the New, circling and turning in grace, showed in the Holy Spirit three points of division. These were the old Law, the new Grace, and the exposition of the faithful doctors; and by these the holy person does what is just from the beginning, starting with the good and moving upward to end with the perfect. For all that is just was, is and will be forever in the simple Deity, which is in all things; and no power can stand firm in malice, if He wills to conquer it by the glory of His loving kindness.

6 The knowledge of Law, the work of the Gospel and the wisdom of the doctors

The first edge faces the East, which signifies the start of the knowledge of God through the divine Law, before the perfect day of justice. *The second looks to the North,* for after this good and chosen work was started there came the gospel of My Son and the other precepts of Me, the Father, which rose up against the North where injustice originated. *And the third faces the South, and is somewhat merged with the outside wall of the building.* This is to say that when the works of justice had been confirmed, there came the profound and rich wisdom of the principal doctors, who through the fire of the Holy Spirit made known what was obscure in the Law and the prophets, and showed their fruition in the Gospels. Thus they made these things fruitful to the understanding; they touched on the outward content of the Scriptures in the work of the Father's goodness, and sweetly ruminated on their mystical significance.

7 God worked from the beginning of the Law to the manifestation of His Son

And from the edge which faces the East, branches grow out from the root to the summit. This is to say that when God first became known through the just Law, branches appeared on that eastern edge, which was the time of the patriarchs and prophets. For this sharp-edged pillar of Divinity carries on the work from its root, which is the good beginning in the minds of the elect, to its summit, which is the manifestation of the Son of Man, Who is all justice.

And therefore, *at the root you see Abraham sitting on the first branch;* for the time of inspiration by God began with Abraham, when he obeyed God and with a tranquil mind departed from his country. *Then Moses on the second;* for after this, God inspired Moses to plant the Law, and so foreshadow the Son of the Most High. *Then Joshua on the third;* for he afterward had the spirit of the Lord in him in order to strengthen the custom of the Law as God commanded.

And then you see *the rest of the patriarchs and prophets, one above the other on each branch, sitting in the order in which they succeeded each other in time;* for God inspired each patriarch and prophet in his own time to nurture his particular shoot toward the height of His commands, and all in their day reposed on the disposition and order of the justice He showed them, faithful and obedient to the divine majesty as it showed itself in their times.

8 The patriarchs and prophets marvelled at the Incarnation

They are all looking toward the edge of the pillar that faces the North, marvelling at the things they can see with spiritual vision going on there in the future. For they were all alerted in their souls by the Holy Spirit, and so turned and saw how the Gospel doctrine repulsed the Devil by the strength of the Son of God. They spoke of His Incarnation, and marvelled at how He came from the heart of the Father and the womb of a virgin and showed Himself with great wonders both by Himself and by His followers, who wonderfully imitated Him in new grace and trod the transitory underfoot, greatly thirsting for the joys of the eternal.

9   The Word of God was hidden by prevision in the souls of the
     elect of old

*But between the two edges, the one facing the East and the one facing the
North, the side of the pillar to which those patriarchs and prophets are turning
their faces is from bottom to top as round as if turned in a lathe, and wrinkled
like the bark of a tree that puts forth shoots.* This is to say that between the two
edges, which are the manifest knowledge of Me and the teachings of My
Son, the One Word, which is My Son, was hidden as a foreshadowing image
in the souls of the ancient fathers who abided in My laws, from the first
chosen one until the last holy one. Thus they were decorated all around with
mystical ornaments, for He carefully arranged and polished all His chosen
instruments and showed Himself to them all with swift grace. He was loving
to them all, as is prefigured in the wrinkles of the circumcision, which was
the shadow of things to come; for it contained, hidden in the austerity of the
Law, the apposite meaning of the most righteous offshoot, the high and holy
Incarnation.

10   The words of the Son go from and return to the Father
     through the doctors

*And from the second edge, facing the North, there goes forth a marvellously
bright radiance, which shines and reflects as far as the edge that faces the South.*
This is to say that from the second edge, which is the New Testament and
stands opposed to the Devil, there issue the words of My Son, which come
forth from Me and return to Me. For when the sun, which is My Son, stands
forth in the flesh, the light of the holy Gospel shines in His preaching, and
pours itself out from Him and His disciples as fruits of blessing, and then
returns into the fountain of salvation, where it reaches the guides, those who
profoundly search into the words of the Old and New Testaments. And they
show how wisdom is raised up in that Sun, Who enlightens the world and
burns like noonday in His elect.

11   The apostles, martyrs and other elect were made so by Christ's
     teaching

*And in the radiance, which is so widely diffused, you see apostles, martyrs,
confessors and virgins and many other saints, walking in great joy.* For in the
clear light in which My Son preached and spread the truth there have grown
up apostles who announce that true light, and martyrs who faithfully shed

their blood like strong soldiers, and confessors who officiate after My Son, and virgins who follow the Supernal Branch, and all My other elect, who rejoice in the fountain of happiness and the font of salvation, baptized by the Holy Spirit and ardently going from virtue to virtue.

12 Gospel knowledge was limited, is now broad and will grow weak at the end

And the third edge, facing the South, is broad and wide in the middle, but thinner and narrower at the bottom and top, like a bow drawn and ready to shoot arrows. This is to say that, as the Gospel was spread, the wisdom of the saints broadened; they burned in the Holy Spirit, seeking It in depth so as to find through It the deepening of their understanding of the Word of God, strengthened by the faith of the Christian people. And so the sense of the Scriptures that went forth from the mouth of the holy doctors broadened too; they searched the depths of the Scriptures' astringency and made it known to the many who learned from them, and thus they too enlarged their senses by knowing more of the wisdom and knowledge of the divine writings. At the beginning of the Church's institution—as it were, at the bottom of the edge—this knowledge was narrower and less studied, for the people did not yet embrace it with the love they gave it afterward. And at the end of time—as it were, at the edge's summit—the studies of many will grow cold; divine wisdom will not be lovable to them as deeds are lovable, but they will hide their knowledge and keep it for themselves, as if they had no obligation to do good works. For they will know it only on the outside, as in a dream.

13 People must begin good works timidly, continue strongly and finish humbly

And therefore *the edge is widest and sharpest in the middle.* For the austere works of the worship of God were denuded of their Old Testament darkness and grew from their narrow beginning to their middle, which consists of the strongest virtues and the loftiest zeal. For the people were then swifter against iniquity, wounding the Devil with words from God and casting out and trampling down all his vices with the great austerity of God's justice. But then the people forgot themselves and declined, and as the end of the world drew near lived in a narrower fervor for the Holy Spirit. So, as a bow is stretched tight by the bowstring in time of war, a person must rise up against vice in body and soul, more constricted at each end and broader in the middle; so that the beginning and the end of his work may be circumspect with fear and humility, while its middle is strong and constant, sending forth by the gift of the Holy Spirit the darts of good deeds against the ambushes of the Devil. For when a person begins to do good, his strength is fragile; then when he continues to work good he grows stronger, because the Holy Spirit has poured Itself out in him; but since that power cannot come often, at the end of his good work he will be less in strength again because of the weakness of the flesh. And so the bow should always be bent for defense against the vices of the Devil.

14   God shows people the mysteries of the Son of God by foreshadowing

But at the top of the pillar you see a light so bright that human tongue cannot describe it. This is to say that the Heavenly Father, in His highest and deepest mysteries, made known the mystery of His Son, Who shines in His Father with glorious light, in which there appears all the justice of the giving of the Law and the New Testament. And the latter *is of such clarity and brilliance of wisdom that it is not possible for any earthly person to express it in words,* as long as he is in corruptible flesh.

And in this light appears a dove, with a gold ray coming out of its mouth, which sheds brilliant light on the pillar; for in the heart of the radiant Father, in the brilliance of the light of the Son of God, burns the Holy Spirit, Who comes from on high and declares the mysteries of the Son of the Most High to redeem the people seduced by the ancient serpent. And so the Holy Spirit inspires all the commandments and all the new testimonies, giving before the Incarnation of the Lord the law of His glorious mysteries, and then showing the same glory in the Incarnation itself. And the Spirit's inspiration is a golden splendor and a high and excellent illumination, and by this outpouring It makes known, as was said, the mystical secrets of God's Only-Begotten to the ancient heralds who showed the Son of God through types and marvelled at His coming from the Father and His miraculously arising in the dawn of the perpetual Virgin. And thus the Spirit in Its power fused the Old Testament and the Gospels into one spiritual seed, from which grew all justice.

And so you cannot contemplate the divine glory because of the immense power of Divinity; no mortal can see it except those to whom I will to foreshadow it. Therefore take care not to presume rashly to look at what is divine, as the trembling that seizes you shows.

15   The virtue of the knowledge of God

And you see inside the building a figure standing on the pavement facing this pillar. This is to say that a virtue shows itself within the work of God the Father, which declares the mystery of the Word of God, for it has revealed all the justice in the city of the Omnipotent to the people of the Old and New Testaments. She is standing on the pavement, which is to say above all earthly things in the work of the loving Father, for everything in earth and heaven are foreseen by Him.

And she looks sometimes at the pillar and sometimes at the people who are going to and fro in the building. This is to say that she is contemplating in the Word of God the mystery put forth by His power, and also the people who are working in the Father's goodness, and which of them are succeeding or not succeeding in the work, for she knows the nature of each one at will.

And *this image* signifies the knowledge of God; for she oversees all people and all things in heaven and earth. And she *is so bright and glorious that you cannot look at her face or her garments for the splendor with which she shines.* For she is terrible with the terror of the avenging lightning, and gentle with the goodness of the bright sun; and both her terror and her gentleness are incomprehensible to humans, the terror of divine brilliance in her face and the brightness of her beauty in her garments, as the sun cannot be looked at in its burning face or its beautiful clothing of rays. But she is with everyone and in everyone, and so beautiful is her secret that no person can know the sweetness with which she sustains people, and spares them in inscrutable mercy; spares even the hardest stone, which is a hard and incorrigible person who never wants to turn aside from evil, until it can be penetrated no farther.

But, like the other virtues, she appears in human form. For God in the power of His goodness profoundly imbued Man with reason and knowledge and intellect, that he might dearly love Him and devotedly worship Him and spurn the illusions of demons, and adore Him above all Who gave him such high honor.

16   The angels that surround her and why they are winged

And around her you see a beautiful multitude, with the appearance and wings of angels, standing in great veneration, for they both fear and love her. Which is to say that all the blessed and excellent spirits in the heavenly ministry worship the Knowledge of God with inexpressibly pure praise, as humans cannot worthily do while they are in mortal bodies. These spirits embrace God in their ardor, for they are living light; and they are winged, not in the sense that they have wings like the flying creatures, but in the sense that they circle burningly in their spheres through the power of God, as if they were winged. And so they adore Me the true God, and persevere in proper fear and true subjection, knowing My judgments and burning in My love; for they behold My face forever, and desire and will nothing but those things they see are pleasing to My penetrating vision.

17 On the human beings who are called "compelled sheep"

And before her face you see another multitude, with the appearance of human beings, in dark clothes; and they stand immobile with fear. These are people who live in the Knowledge of God. How? That person whom God foresees will belong to Him stands in great honor in His sight, but one who chooses to stay in perdition rather than in God is lost. Those people you see in this multitude are called "compelled sheep"; they have a human form because of their human deeds, and dark clothes because they have done sinful works in doubt, but they fear the judgment of God with a stringent fear. They are called "compelled sheep" because I compel them by many means to come to life and be snatched from death through My Son's blood. Thus "compelled sheep" are those people who are compelled by Me against their will, by many tribulations and sorrows, to leave their iniquities. These they gladly embraced in the desire of their flesh and the flower of their youth as long as they held to the world, wanting to retain the heat of lust until the fire of the flesh departed from them in cold age; but I forced them all in different ways, according to what I saw in them, to cease from their sins.

18 God constrains some gently, some by a strong lash, some by extreme pain

Some of these, in whom desire for the world does not burn so fiercely, I force with a lighter rather than a heavier scourge; for I do not perceive in them the great bitterness I see in others, since when they feel My correction they renounce the pomps of the world and hastily leave their own will and come to Me. Others I correct with heavier blows, since they so burn and yearn for the sins of their vicious flesh that they would not be fit for the Kingdom unless I forcibly compelled them. And My knowledge sees and knows these, and constrains them in proportion to their bodily excesses.

And others, again, I conquer by the greatest and sharpest misery of mind and body; for they are so rebellious and so extreme in their carnal pleasures that if they were not constrained by the heaviest calamity the wantonness of their flesh would lead them to unceasing crime. These never turn to God while their wills prosper; some fall into desperation through timidity of mind, but others are mocked by prideful ambition, and the former allow despair to trample them underfoot, while the latter cannot contain themselves for the overabundance of their spirits. So, when those who belong to Me resist Me by their deeds, I force them as My knowledge of them directs; and so, through the physical and spiritual calamities they suffer, they are compelled to come to Me and be saved. Thus Pharaoh, having been greatly terrified, finally made the Israelites go forth from his land, as it is written:

19 Example of Pharaoh, Moses and Aaron

"And Pharaoh, calling Moses and Aaron by night, said, 'Rise up, go forth from my people, both you and the children of Israel. Go, sacrifice to the Lord as you say. Take your flocks and your herds as you asked, and as you depart bless me'" [Exodus 12:31–32]. Which is to say: The heavy and burdensome crimes inseparable from this world weigh people down with sorrows and miseries; they say in their hearts, "Alas, alas! Whither shall we flee?" Then these sorrows clash and drive the people away from them, and the people hasten to withdraw; for their bodies are shriveling up from the weight of the scourge in the hand of God, and they cannot live with joy amid the pleasures of the world. For God claims them, calling the just by the many calamities of the dark deeds of the night of sin.

Hence Pharaoh, which is to say the vices of the Devil, amid the clamor of grief and misery calls Moses, which means those people whom God constrains by the keenest spiritual or physical sorrows, and Aaron, that is those people whom He compels by lighter adversities and calls out of the night of evil deeds; and the vices say from amid the oppression of human pleasure, "Arise from your carnal habits, and go forth from the ancient dwelling place you had with us; separate yourselves from the common people whom we possess and who worship us. Separate yourselves from the secular affairs to which we gladly cling, you who were terrified by us when you were our prisoners; and take the children of God with you, who see and acknowledge Him.

"Go therefore by another way; leave us, and offer yourselves to God by means of those invincible fights in which you say you have conquered us by your will. In the newness of mind you now seek, assume the gentleness of the sheep, which prevents you from acting with us because you choose the sorrows of following the Lamb; and assume the victorious arms of the strength of herds, which we cannot resist and which have conquered us. Separate yourselves from us, as you wished when you fiercely fought us; go to the country you long for in your minds, embrace the new life that takes you from us, and bless and praise God for that battle by which you have torn yourselves away from worldly matters and cares."

20 How God, scrutinizing people, chastises and consoles them

And I, Almighty God, in compelling these sheep to come over to Me, strengthen My pillars, which are the strong heirs to Heaven, on a foundation of chastisement. I chastise them according to the degree of wickedness by which they are assailed and implicated in the sin of Adam; for if I do not confirm them by My grace, they cannot stand. Some, who are not weighed down by a very great burden of vice, I punish more lightly; for if I were to correct them with a sharper blow, their spirits would entirely fail and they would fall into desperation. For they are not bound by the force of the great whirlwind of the Devil's temptations.

But others, who in the battle with the Devil are burdened with a greater weight and have savage ways and excessive lusts, I constrain harshly with heavy sufferings, so that they will not withdraw from My covenant; for they belong to it, and wish with all their hearts to lay hold on Me and observe My precepts. But if I chastised these as lightly as the first, they would count My corrections as nothing; for they are assailed by the ancient's serpent's most heavy attack.

And there are also certain people whom I do not know, exiles from the heavenly country, for they completely abandon Me, seducing themselves in the greed of their thoughts with devouring rage. These do not seek Me or desire to know Me, but choke off their good desires; and so they ask no help from Me, but greedily feast on their own goods and please themselves in carnal lusts.

Now some of these latter express their will in excesses and pleasures of the flesh, but do not live in hatred and envy; they are simply engulfed in sweet joys and carnal delights. To these I give the fruits of the earth in prosperity, and do not let them lack and be poor; for they were created by Me, and they do not devour My people with malice. And so what they choose is given to them.

But others are fierce and bitter, full of gall and hatred and envy, rendering evil for evil and suffering no injury to be inflicted on them; and if these obtain worldly honor and riches, they destroy the heavenly virtues in others, and do not let them grow. And so from these I take fruits and riches, and throw them into great miseries, so that they cannot do as much evil as they would want to; for, if they could, they would do the works of the Devil.

And so by a just measure I mark out the ways of good and bad people, and weigh their wills according to what My eye sees of their desires, as Wisdom testifies through Solomon, saying:

21 Words of the Wisdom of Solomon

"All human ways are open to His eyes; the Lord is the weigher of spirits" [Proverbs 16:2]. Which is to say: To the sight of Almighty God all roads are open that the living human mind can choose in the present state of its wisdom; for each person possesses the knowledge of fruitful utility and of vain foolishness. Thus God sees all things, and nothing is hidden from His divine sight; He knows and observes all things, and so He can deal rightly with each and every case. How? He is the weigher of spirits; He treats them tenderly with sweet caresses and peace, or He chastises them with the tribulations of misery and sorrow that they may be conformed to the right measure. They cannot escape Him by running or fleeing, unless He so wills it in accordance with their merits; for they are weighed, both in this world and in the world to come, by the way in which they worshipped God.

And so these spirits are weighed justly, and a person's mind is uplifted to higher things or sunk to lower things exactly as far as God's just judgment requires. No soul has enough power to fight against God, Who resists their attempts; for He judges all things most righteously, and opposes them with His irresistible justice, so that they can do no more than He permits.

And as the leaden counterweight weighs money correctly, so God in His equal scales counterbalances the good and the bad with obstacles, so that they can never escape the equity of His judgment; and the good receive for their merits the glory and joy of life, and the bad the pain and grief of death, according to what God's vision sees in them.

22 How the Knowledge of God scrutinizes those clothed in a new garment

And the figure looks upon the people who come in from the world and in the building put on a new garment. This is to say that the Knowledge of God knows those who leave the wickedness of infidelity and, by the power of God's work, put on the new self in baptism for the sake of eternal life. And she warns them not to turn backward and go toward the Devil, or, if they do thus stray, that they should return to God their Creator, as she says to each of them in the words of her admonition quoted above.

But let the one who has ears sharp to hear inner meanings ardently love My reflection and pant after My words, and inscribe them in his soul and conscience.

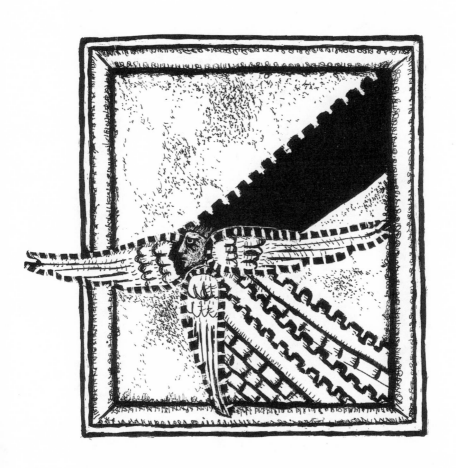

THE ZEAL OF GOD

VISION FIVE
The Jealousy of God

A fter this, I looked, and behold! In the north corner, where the building's two kinds of wall joined, there appeared a head of marvellous form, planted firmly by the neck at the outside of the corner, at the same height from the ground that the wall itself rose to in that corner and no higher, so that the top of the head just equalled the summit of the wall. And this head was fiery in color, sparkling like a fiery flame; and it had a terrible human face, which looked in great anger toward the North.

From the neck down I saw nothing of this figure's body, for the rest of it was hidden by its pressing into the corner. But I saw its head, a bare human head. It was not covered by hair like a man's or by a veil like a woman's; but it was more manly than womanly, and very terrible to see.

It had three wings of wondrous breadth and length, white like a cloud; they were not raised, but extended straight out from each other so that the head was slightly higher than they were. The first rose from the right side of the jaw, and stretched toward the Northeast; the second and middle one pointed from the throat to the North, and the third stretched from the left side of the jaw toward the West. Sometimes these wings moved, very terribly, and struck these regions, but after a while ceased striking. And I did not hear the head uttering any words; it only remained motionless in body and struck with its wings from time to time in the places toward which they extended. And again I heard the One Who sat on the throne, saying to me:

1 The form of the Jealousy of God and what it does

God worked His jealousy very severely on the people of the Old Law; but toward those of the New, for love of His Son, He was mild and sweet. This is not because He overlooked and carelessly dismissed the sins of those who transgressed, but because He was mercifully awaiting the true inner penitence of the pure heart; and at the same time He refused to tolerate the iniquity of the hardened, but punished them with just judgment.

Therefore, *the head that you see in the north corner, where the building's two kinds of wall join,* symbolizes the Jealousy of the Lord, which punishes that inflexible iniquity that desires no curing. This jealousy was prefigured in the symbols of the patriarchs and prophets, and arose openly in the mystery of the Word of God.

So too the Jealousy of God is in the form of a head; for, of all the fear it inspires, it is known best for the severity of its vengeance, as a person is known by his face. And it flames out against the North because it is most swift and sharp in God to slay the Devil and all evil. For in Abraham and in Moses the defense of those who labor, which is to say the knowledge of the two choices, the ways of good and evil, is joined to the human race in the work of God; for in all things, through the goodness of the Father, Man must work strongly against the Devil in the knowledge of good and evil.

But the Jealousy of the Lord avenges sin, the choice expressed in the deeds of people who do not observe God's precepts; for this work is not deserving of remission. Where does this happen? Where there is no acknowledgment of God and therefore no fear of God or Man. And when a heart is thus hardened and deadened by the filth of iniquity, which fears neither the judgment of God nor the countenance of Man, the Jealousy of the Lord confounds it by just judgment and throws it down by vengeance in the Law of God. How?

2   God examines sins to punish or pardon in a person's body and soul

When the commandments were established, it was jealousy that, by righteous judgment, removed the injustice whenever there was transgression of the Law. In the Old Testament injustice was wiped out by a severe reprisal upon the outer person, in whom transgression of the Law caused bodily sores; after the grace of the Gospel, jealousy works through penance; and, after a person's death, it will work in the pains and torments of Hell. For I so examine human iniquities, conceived and brought forth and twisted by the doers of deeds, that I avenge them either physically in the person's body or in the pains of the world to come; or else the person himself will purge them through penance and remission while he is still living with the soul and body that performed them. As My servant Job says, speaking in My Spirit:

3   Words of Job on this subject

"I change my face, and I am twisted with sorrow. I feared all my works, knowing that You do not spare the offender. But if I am wicked, why have I labored in vain?" [Job 9:27–29]. This is to say: I will change my interior aspect. How? I will overthrow the thing I am: changeable, overcome by the blood in my veins, at one time full of delight and at another time anger and at another time unbearable sadness. For I look into myself as one who sees a delightful face, when I gladly pursue these things. But against my will I will change this, and turn myself to good works. And when I do so, I am tortured as by a scourge, for I am forcing myself and tearing myself away from my familiar face, which is my will toward perverse delights; I am joining myself to meditation, and in my good conscience attaining the vision of God, Who cannot be reached by the lusts of the flesh. And, because of these two choices, I fear all my works. How?

When I do a good work, I fear that it is not perfect before God; for I do not see it clearly, but as in a glass darkly. Sometimes I know it in the spirit, but sometimes I do not know it because of being weighed down by the body. But when I do an evil work, my spirit's conscience is in confusion, for I know within me that those who knowingly sin are not spared; that is, when a person understands that his deed is contrary to God, he must be purged either by a penalty in the body, or by penance, or by punishment through tortures in the life to come. And so a transgressor is not spared if he does not repent; he is not given the power to sin in order to use it, and if he does he must be chastised either here or hereafter.

Therefore, if I am so wicked and obstinate that I do not want to give in and turn from my own things, which are my sins; and if I am so weak that I cannot face the great struggle against myself; and if I am always contrary to God in my motives, conceived in sin and desiring to work iniquity and not fearing the Lord's judgment on me; why am I forced to labor in vain, often opposing the evil in myself through my knowledge of God? For I am not so weak that I do not know good from evil. Thus if I drive out my understanding and say, "I do not know God," I am a liar; for the knowledge of my debt to God convicts me when I start to do wickedness. But when I oppose evil with a good conscience I do not labor in vain; for I am the work of God, and so I turn to Him and receive the good reward.

4   Sinners can receive grace by penance or suffer future punishment

Therefore, I Who am the Lord of all things say again that it is needful that each person pay for his sins, either by groaning sorrow or by contrite penitence or by a proper punishment, in this world or the world to come. How? Those who fear their sins and repent in sorrow deserve to rise by God's grace from the sins to their purgation; and when they are not fully purged in this world, they will have purgation unto life in the world to come.

But those who are so hardhearted that they do not wish to acknowledge their sins or repent them in fear and sorrow, but continue to defy God by their wickedness, are not purged of their sins either in this life or in the life to come, but will suffer pains without the consolation of purgation unto life. For they were created by Me with rational minds, yet did not give the proper reply to disobedience. How?

5 Human reason can counter evil with good or good with evil

Human reason can understand two ways to the knowledge of good and evil, and choose two replies, also good and evil. How? Good replies to evil when by God's help it resists it; but evil replies to good when with the Devil's help it attacks it. Those who live in goodness answer evil by refraining from it and taking no pleasure in their own delight. But those who live in evil answer good by not withdrawing from bad deeds; they feast on their own lusts and refuse to answer evil's challenge. How?

6 Man is called two ways, one leading to life and the other to death

Each person has in himself two callings, the desire of fruit and the lust for vice. How? By the desire of fruit he is called toward life, and by the lust for vice he is called toward death. In the desire of fruit a person wishes to do good, and says to himself, "Do good works!" And this is the reply to evil, to avoid it and bring forth useful fruit. But in the lust for vice, a person wants to do evil, and says to himself, "Do the work of your own pleasure!" And this is the reply to good, the refusal to resist iniquity and the delight in attaining to vice, whereby the person despises Me and by not honoring Me treats Me as an impostor. And because he turns away from good, and puts himself into no sorrow or affliction through fear of Me, such a one turns celestial things to scorn, as, enlightened by Me, the psalmist David says:

7 Words of the Psalmist

"They have set their mouth against Heaven, and their tongue has passed over the earth" [Psalm 72:9]. This is to say: Many people are foolish in understanding and unwilling to admit the infinite fear of the Lord. They cast away the good desires they should have for Me and the knowledge of the true God, and refuse assent to the good knowledge that assists people to perform good works in God; and they embrace bitterness and contradict the good, and so despoil themselves and steal from themselves the good treasures, laying up for themselves instead a treasure of multiple iniquities.

And in those iniquities they apply their twisted minds to celestial works, and, opening their mouths in an evil way, destroy those works in rage and mockery, saying in their hearts, "We can do the works of our own will as lawfully as those that are called celestial; for those were established without our knowledge by the people of the Old Testament according to their own pleasure." And thus they mock the words and institutions of the Old Testament fathers, which were established by Me in heavenly works.

And so, tasting wicked deeds as if with their tongues, they excite and surpass themselves in the greatest possible audacity; they boldly fulfil their own wills and have no desire to restrain their bodies from vice. And so, without their minds working, they are, as it were, rolled on the ground by the desires of their flesh, which are the seductions of the Devil.

8 God's wondrous judgments were seen in the Old Testament to make Him feared

So you see this head *of marvellous form*, which is to say that in the Jealousy of the Lord are marvels and wondrous divine judgments, such as no person weighed down by sins can know.

It is planted firmly by the neck at the outside of the corner; this means that, as was shown through Abraham and Moses in the Old Testament, My jealousy against the Devil is plain to the sight of the peoples in reflective knowledge and in human deeds, that they may fear Me and stand face to face with My terror. And My justice faces the North to threaten Satan's cruel iniquity.

9 God's rectitude in judging is not moved by deceitful or adulatory words

It remains immovable, for God cannot be moved, or His righteous judgment of unatoned sins softened, by deceitful or adulatory words. And so it renders to each person who does not observe the precepts of the Law the punishments he deserves for the evil deeds that have sunk him in filth; it is set up by God to establish laws for humans according to their works, and with its excelling strength, like the strength of its neck, it resists the Devil and his followers and opposes itself to their injustice.

10 Supernal vengeance does not exceed the gravity of the deed it punishes

It is at the same height from the ground that the wall itself rises to in that corner; for God, in His supreme avenging justice, towers above all earthly things, and His vengeance exactly matches human deeds, as shown by the Law in the foreshadowing of Abraham and Moses. For divine judgment is as high as any mystical speculation or deed of the people, to throw down their ignorance if they refuse to know God.

But it is no higher, so that the top of the head just equals the summit of the wall. For heavenly vengeance does not surpass human deeds, or punish their evil more than is deserved; it only judges all things equitably and righteously in excelling justice. This the psalmist David knows in the Spirit, when he says:

11 Words of David

"I have known, O Lord, that Your judgments are equity, and in Your truth you have humbled me" [Psalm 118:75]. This is to say: By Your goodness, O Lord, I have experienced in myself that you do not judge the knowing or the ignorant in Your power or Your anger more than they deserve; for you have not slain me for my sins, or taken the power to act from my soul or body.

For I do good to my adversaries, but I do evil in the desires of my flesh; and therefore You reward the good and judge the evil. But You judge only as is equitable and just. How? If You were harshly inflexible about the nature of human deeds, it would not be equity of judgment. But if You carelessly neglected spurring us to penance, and did not try to purge our iniquities, then, O just God, you would be condoning and encouraging injustice. Death, indeed, was a most bitter judgment for the sin of Adam; but now You recall Man to life by the grace restored in penitence, and this would be impossible for anyone but You, Who are God.

And this purgation unto life in grace is Your just and equitable judgment, for Your judgments are meted out in right measure for each case. All that You do is in the truth, and so You never wrongfully exceed the measure; for both excess and deficiency in justice are wrongful. And You use Your power sparingly and in mercy, never slaying anyone just because Your glorious power can do so, but rather choosing to spare by penitence. Therefore I have humbled myself on account of Your mercy, giving glory to Your name; and I am troubled over what my faults deserve in Your judgment.

12 God sees every injustice, and no human can understand His judgment

And you see that this head *is fiery in color, sparkling like a fiery flame;* this is because God's Jealousy is a fierce obstacle to evil, glowing red in the powerful fire of His vengeance. And *it has a terrible human face;* for the eyes of the Lord see all injustices face to face, and no guilt of crime is unsearched by His terrible gaze. He examines all by His just judgment, and turns a human face toward the acting of carnal desires because it is human actions that are thus monstrous and horrifying.

And *it looks in great anger toward the North;* for God in His vengeance scorns all evil that rises from the temptation of the Devil. *And from the neck down you see nothing of this figure's body, for the rest of it is hidden by its pressing into the corner;* which is to say that the righteous judgments with which the Jealousy of God scatters the evil works of the wicked cannot be fully seen by any human sense, for they are hidden and covered by the corner of reflective knowledge and human deeds. Thus they cannot be seen or understood by investigation, except sometimes when something is shown to be a case of God's judgment, which appears as a human face according to His will. And so in such a vengeance there is nothing automatic, except that people always receive just judgment according to their sins; for their crimes, as was said before, are not left unexamined, but are probed by the Jealousy of the Lord.

13 The Jealousy of God, justly judging human acts, is awful to all creatures

And you see its head, *a bare human head;* which is to say that the Jealousy of the Lord is not subject to mortality but is bare of all weakness, justly judging human acts. *It is not covered by hair like a man's or by a veil like a woman's;* for it feels no masculine anxiety about being conquered by one superior in strength, nor has it any feminine weakness as of a timid mind afraid that it cannot conquer its opponents.

But it is more manly than womanly; for the mighty power of God resembles manly virility more than it does soft womanly weakness. *And it is very terrible to see;* for jealousy is terrible and fearsome to all creatures when they feel its vengeance in their case.

14 The Holy Trinity judges all people rightly according to their intentions

It has three wings of wondrous breadth and length, white like a cloud. This symbolizes the expansion of the ineffable power of the Holy Trinity. No one can comprehend the extent of Its glory and the limits of Its power as It shines with the immense sweetness and brightness of Divinity; in Its righteous vengeance it subdues all human minds, as they flit hither and thither diffusely like clouds.

These wings *are not raised, but extend straight out from each other so that the head is slightly higher than they are.* For the vengeance of the Lord is not puffed up by any arrogance, but adapts itself to each case according to its merits; and so it stretches forth within the boundaries of righteousness in the just judgment of its correction, and God's potential strength, like the head of His vengeance, exceeds it in power. And so those human deeds, which the true Trinity does not let go unexamined, are not punished or crushed as severely as that power could if it willed.

15   God's Jealousy beats the Devil by Christ and the elect, and in Antichrist

The first wing rises from the right side of the jaw, and stretches toward the Northeast; for God in His just judgment conquered the Devil and all evil first by His Son, Who is at His right hand for salvation. *The second and middle one points from the throat to the North;* for after salvation was wrought by the Son of God, in the middle times when the faith was already strengthened and its sweetness tasted by the elect, God put the roaring enemy to flight by their means, and snatched them from his jaws. *And the third stretches from the left side of the jaw toward the West;* for Satan, having been put to flight by the elect of God, will be completely crushed and consigned to the perdition on God's left hand, in the person of the son of perdition, when the world approaches the end of its days.

Sometimes these wings move, very terribly, and strike these regions; for the Jealousy of the Lord is moved to vengeance by its terrible and formidable judging of every creature. It exercises its judgments and strikes wherever in their justice it pleases the Divine Majesty. For where fear and love and honor of God are held in faith and reverence, God shows Himself mild and gentle and does not exercise His vengeance; but He chastises terribly those who are hard and rebellious.

16   The hardened who despise God and Man's warnings are lost

And therefore, the first wing of My vengeance strikes and casts into the abyss of perdition those people, hardened more than stones, who ignore their inner faculties and despise My justice; they look to their own intellects, and consent to carnal desire and diabolical temptation rather than seeking true justice. They refuse to turn away from their iniquity by their own decision, or by My admonitions, or by human exhortations; and so they outrage the spirit of their own knowledge, for they seek and perform the injustice of the Devil instead of My justice. They pour, so to speak, melted lead into their hearts, which is to say dissolute desires of evil decadence; and so they make them as hard as iron in forgetfulness of God, and are themselves hardened like iron, and then they spare no one in their wickedness for the sake of God or Man.

17   The elements complain of the hardness of the impenitent, who are punished

And against them the elements and all creation cry out and complain that vile and short-lived human nature is so rebellious against God while they themselves are doing God's will with fear and reverence. And so they are loud and terrible on the subject of Man. How? It is not that the elements cry out with a voice or complain in the words of rational creatures; but that they cry out according to their nature with noisy sounds, and complain by inspiring fear with their terrors. So God's just judgment moves them and the rest of creation to react to humanity, which is ever rebellious; while the elements themselves never go against or swerve from what the Divine Power commands them to do. And so these hardened people cruelly imitate Satan, who in the hardness of his iniquity refused to be subject to God his Creator; and therefore he perished from all beatitude, and those who follow him will perish with him.

18　God brings the punishment of past villains on conscious sinners

And the middle wing of My Jealousy strikes people who rave and the presumptuous and evil deeds that they knowingly and rashly commit. The first such deed cried out in the blood of Abel, whom his brother hated because he was dear to God for offering his substance. Another was Pharaoh's, who was warned by My miraculous deeds and terrified by fear of Me, and so let My people Israel go; but then, in his madness, he tried to bring them back, and therefore My Jealousy swallowed him up. Another arose among that same people of Mine; though they knew Me and saw My miraculous deeds, they adored the idol in Horeb, and therefore the crown fell from their head. And the law of God on the two stone tablets was corrupted by them and others like them, and therefore they fell from their glory and happiness, and My vengeance fell on them. For My servant Moses, in jealousy for Me, meted out punishment to this contrary people who opposed Me so often; he sternly told My chosen that every man should kill his brother and friend and neighbor. And later, he forcefully ordered the judges of that same people to kill their neighbors who were initiated into the rites of Belphegor; and so I avenged Myself, and the iniquity that fought against Me was slain.

19　God's Justice, developing from Abel to Christ, is avenged by His Jealousy

And when God's Justice had first arisen in Abel, in all these evil and perverse generations many other elect were found; they collected and honored My smallest precepts like true children of Israel, and among them rose sorrow and longing for the humanity of My Son. And when My Son appeared, born of the Virgin, all the justice of the Law was baked and salted and became pleasing food for all the people who believed in Me when the apostles showed them the truth. And so, in all those generations, My Jealousy has avenged and will avenge My Justice upon its conscious transgressors; for God was and is and will be, and His Justice, which scours off all the rust of injustice, will not end until all tribes and peoples cease to be.

20 The Jealousy of God will cast down all who harm the Church or its property

Therefore, in My Jealousy, I remove and cast out the iniquity of anyone who, like a dog, despises the Church, which flowers in Me, and of anyone who in insane wickedness destroys a place consecrated to Me or any rights which properly belong to My temple. For these rights were instituted by foreshadowing by My servant Jacob, as the Scripture narrates:

21 Jacob's action prefigured the dedication of churches

"And Jacob, arising in the morning, took the stone he had laid under his head, and set it up as a marker, pouring oil upon the top of it. And he called the name of the city Bethel" [Genesis 28:18–19]. That is to say: Jacob arose in the morning, because he got up as a timely lover of true Justice in the newly constituted Temple. On it he conferred a befitting name, since from it was to arise the most upright of temples, the Virgin Mary, from whom the Sun of Justice would shine forth. And he took the stone, which prefigured an altar, which he had placed under his Head, which is Christ, and sanctified it in the name of Him Who is the true rock, and, having sanctified it, named it. For every sanctification of an altar is under the power of Almighty God, the Head of all the faithful. And he set it up as a marker of the Book of Life, to mark out and prefigure the odor of the heavenly Jerusalem; for as in the heavenly Jerusalem Christ is the Head of His members, so every sanctified altar is the most excelling part of the temple, for oil was poured over it to symbolize the chrism, which is the grace of Almighty God outpoured in holy baptism. And he called that holy place the house and temple of God, which is the name of the city of the heavenly Jerusalem, the living temple of the Living God.

22 A sealed stone legitimizes Communion even without a temple around it

Therefore, by this example and foreshadowing, when a temple is planned in My name, a stone must be erected; for the temple itself is signified by a stone, since I am the firm rock of all justice and Christian law. And wherever the body of My Son is to be sacrificed, there must be a sanctified place where a stone is sealed with My Name, even if by some impossible chance there cannot be a temple there. For I am the strength of truth, and My servant Jacob erected his stone in foreshadowing, as was said, of My Son becoming incarnate of his race.

23 The work of the people should justify the building of a temple

Such a temple, dedicated to Me, should not lack the activity which was the reason for its being put up, but be associated with the work of the people who minister to it; for the celestial Jerusalem, whose Head is Christ, does not lack His justice, but is always mindful of the works of her children whom she will receive in God. How? They are to withdraw from the service of the Devil, restrain themselves from the desires their flesh craves, and for love of the heavenly cut off their own natures and afflict themselves against their own interests. Thus they should not use all they possess, but withhold some and offer it to God in His honor, as My exemplary servant Jacob appointed tithes of all his substance. For, as again it is written, he said:

24 How and why Jacob gave a tenth of all his possessions

"Of all things that You shall give me, I will offer a tenth to You" [Genesis 28:22]. Which is to say: Of all that You give me, I will offer the tenth part to You, because this is Your law; first I will tithe my soul, O my God, and cut away my own will from it, offering You Your own justice against myself, and then I will tithe all the goods I have on earth. What does this mean? That every faithful person who is numbered in the tenth order of the citizens of Heaven should give My temple the tenth of his substance, to reflect the redemption by which he is counted in that tenth order of those numbered in God's knowledge; for they live in and belong to the true temple, that of the celestial Jerusalem.

25 Woe to destroyers, defilers, despisers and cheaters of churches

But those who forget their fear of Me and in insane wickedness destroy temples dedicated in My name, or defile that dedication originated by Jacob by polluting holy places with murderous blood or the impure seed of adultery or fornication, or when offering the supernal sacrifice ignore the Old Testament fathers and neglect to do it in the presence of a sealed stone like Jacob's, or fail to give the tithes or the property to My temples that I justly decreed: O woe to those wretches! O woe to those wretches! O woe to those wretched people who so shamefully misguide themselves and so perversely before My face neglect My institutions, translated out of the old Law! For the new Law was brought forth out of the Old Testament by My Son in the mercy of grace, and all the justice of the Law and the prophets was increased in My Son, since all the signs the ancient fathers uttered secretly in obscurity were in Him shown clearly in total justice.

26 Those who share church property with the wicked are thrown down by God

Those who divide the property of the Church with dogs and swine and other beasts, which is to say with evil people, shall be cast down by the Jealousy of God from the highest to the lowest degree. As for those who despise and disdain the food of life derived from both Testaments, treading it underfoot like mud and using it for their own purposes, I will also despise them and their posterity, casting them down from the highest to the lowest and from riches to poverty in the vengeance of My Jealousy.

27 How God's vengeance strikes both believers and unbelievers

The third wing of My vengeance strikes both believers and unbelievers in their wicked and unjust works. It strikes believers who do not use their will to do good and just works; who clearly see the faith and know God's justice, but nonetheless sit in the gloom of evil deeds, foolishly long for the darkness of iniquity, and perversely will to give themselves to madness. But God does not let them do their will, for He cuts it off from them by His vengeance as long as they forget Him and cover themselves in obscurity and freely avoid Him.

But it strikes unbelievers in their unbelief, so that even their iniquity is taken from them by the retribution of vengeance, and they cannot do the evil they would gladly do. And so the malicious Devil, conquered by the blessedness of the fruitful souls who shine before God's eyes, wants in his wickedness to draw the faithless into the darkness of death; but he has no hold on them greater than their deeds warrant.

28 How fearfully God's vengeance consumes those who gain power by injustice

And there is another kind of people on earth who are rich in a spirit of intelligence; since their minds are illumined they are wise enough to remember God if they would. But because of their intelligence they presumptuously seek to know wisdom for themselves and do whatever they want with it; and so they mingle justice with iniquity. But they are fools in their wisdom, for they think of themselves as completely able to possess and lay hold of and acquire their full wishes, whatever they are.

But as they are seeking to lift their wings in power in the provinces and the cities and the other places and things they are busy governing, and wilfully ignoring the fact that God watches and measures what they do, they are dismissed and cast out from before God's eyes; for they judged with wicked and unjust judgments, and did not make the wise choice of fearing the Lord.

And so, through this My Jealousy, they will become a great lamentation, and speak tearfully before all people, who will see and hear the day when their iniquity is judged. Some of them will go on living in great misery and deprivation, and some will die a terrible death with diverse sufferings. By such a variety of fates, My Jealousy punishes and consumes all injustice, for it is repugnant to Me.

29 God's Jealousy does not loudly warn, but firmly and justly judges

But you do not hear the head uttering any words; it only remains motionless in body and strikes with its wings from time to time in the places toward which they extend, as was mentioned. This is to say that in the Jealousy of the Lord there is no clamorous voice of warning raised in its pride, but a motionless persistence in strength and righteous judgment. It punishes the mad deeds that merit its vengeance, deeds done without fear of the Lord; it confounds and crushes them to the full extent of its justice, as was shown to you, O human, in this most true vision. And because God is just, it is needful to examine all injustice by the standard of His justice; for God Himself knows well the capacity of Man's knowledge to scrutinize all things.

30 Man's knowledge is like a mirror reflecting the desire for good or evil

For knowledge in Man is like a mirror in which lies latent his desire to do good or evil. And each person, standing between these two choices, inclines himself by his will toward the one he desires. The person who turns toward the good and with God's help embraces it in works of faith will be praised and blessedly rewarded, for he has spurned evil and chosen good. But the one who turns toward evil, and absorbs its nature into himself by the perverse conduct suggested by the Devil, will wretchedly undergo a just retribution, for he has neglected good and done evil. Therefore, one who submits himself to God in devotion and humility will faithfully work out his salvation, which comes from the Supreme Good; his soul will be joyfully filled with inner holiness, for he is serving his Creator in well-disposed and ordinate single-heartedness. How?

31 Compunction leads to fear and fear to trembling, and they work justice

Compunction, which is the beginning of anguish, causes fear; fear produces trembling; and by these three a person should do what is just. How? The person feels compunction, and therefore begins to be in anguish, for by the gift of the Holy Spirit his reason tells him to; it means that he cannot refuse to know God, and his knowledge of God causes fear in him so that he respects the things that are of God. And if he knows God and desires these things, the fiery grace of Christ strikes him and tells him to tremble and be terrified in his conscience; and then he may faithfully work God's justice.

32 The first root of human choice and the fiery grace of Christ

Now, therefore, O human, understand and learn. From whence do these things come? What does this mean? It is God Who works in you what is good. How? He has so constituted you that, when you act with wisdom and discretion, you feel Him in your reason. For the irrational animal does all its deeds without intellect or wisdom, without discretion or shame; it does not know God, being irrational, though it feels Him, being His creature. But the rational animal, which is Man, has intellect and wisdom, discretion and shame, and does rational deeds, which is the first root fixed by God's grace in every person given life and soul. These powers flourish where there is reason, for all of them make people know God, so that they may choose what is just. Therefore, the deed that a person embraces in his Savior, the Son of God through Whom the Father does His works in the Holy Spirit, is productive and perfect and prosperous; and the fiery grace of Christ Jesus calls this to the person's mind and kindles his enthusiasm anew.

33 No sinner may murmur against his Creator

Therefore let each person perform works of justice in the joy of the Holy Spirit, and not hesitate and perversely murmur; let him not say that he lacks anything, when he has the first root placed in him by God's gift and the fiery grace of the Holy Spirit, which touches that root by admonition. For if he were thus to fall into perversity, his reprehensible urge would bring him into anguish; his interior root would be diminished, and he would fall farther into compulsion. And then he would truly murmur to himself, "Alas, alas! What have I done, not being able to discern my works in God?" So let him also go forward without the burden of unbelief; let him not distrust God in his works, but avoid evil deeds and thus be safe from tearful lamentation.

But let the one who has ears sharp to hear inner meanings ardently love My reflection and pant after My words, and inscribe them in his soul and conscience.

THE TRIPLE WALL

VISION SIX
The Stone Wall of the Old Law

*A*nd after this I saw the wall of the aforementioned building, which ran between the north and west corners, and its inner side was all arched like a chancel, except that it was not open like chancel arches but unbroken, and each arch had the picture of a human being in it. And on the outer side of this wall I saw two smaller walls, extending from the north to the west corner, and joined to these corners at each end like a vault. The height of these two lesser walls was three cubits. The distance between the inner, arched wall and the middle one was one cubit; between the middle one and the outer one it was one palm, and that a child's.

And inside the building I saw six figures standing on its pavement before the arched wall: three were grouped together before the wall near the north corner, and three were together at the end of the wall that looked to the West. And they were all looking at the pictures in the arches of the wall.

And at that same end of the wall I saw another figure within the building, sitting on a stone resting on the pavement for a seat, and leaning against the wall to her right, but turning her face toward the pillar of the true Trinity. And at the same end I saw another figure, standing on the wall above the first, also turning toward the pillar of the true Trinity.

And in these figures I saw the following resemblances. The last two were clothed in silk garments and white shoes, as were the first six; except that the right-hand figure in the group of three standing at the end of the wall was so pure and bright that I could not discern any detail about her because of her great splendor, and that the one who was standing on the wall was wearing black shoes. And none of these wore a cloak except the middle one of the three who stood at the beginning of the wall; she was wearing a cloak.

And two of these same three, the ones to the right and the left of the middle one, and two of the other three, the middle and the left figures, did not have women's veils on their heads, but stood with bare heads and white hair. But the middle one of the first three and the one who sat on the stone next to the wall had white head-veils in the manner of women. And the middle and the right-hand ones of the second three were clothed in white tunics. And I saw the following differences between them:

The figure who stood in the middle of the three first ones had a yellow circlet like a crown on her head, with this inscription carved on the right side: "*Always burn!" And I saw that a dove was flying at the right side of this figure and breathing out this writing from its beak.* And that figure was saying:

1 Words of Abstinence

"I am poured forth from inner compassion, from which springs the river of mercy, which never tries to hide money or precious stones or pearls from the poor and needy under any pretense, for they do not have the necessities of life and thus are weeping. I will console them and forever refresh their poverty for the love of the sweet and mild Son of God, Who distributes His goods in the souls of the just, and heals the wounds of their sins because of their penitence."

And the second figure, standing at her right, had a lion on her breast that gave off light like a mirror; and hanging from her neck to her breast on a twisted, flexible rod was a pale-colored serpent. And she said:

2 Words of Liberality

"I contemplate the light-giving Lion, and I give for the sake of His love. I flee from the fiery serpent, but I love the serpent hanging from the rod."

And the third figure, on the left, was clad in a tunic of hyacinth red. On her breast was the picture of an angel, a wing out on either side, so that its right wing stretched to the figure's right shoulder and its left wing to her left shoulder. And this figure said:

3 Words of Piety

"My companionship is with angels, and I do not choose to walk with dissembling hypocrites, for I feast with the just."

Now the figure who stood in the middle of the three second ones was dressed in a yellow tunic. Above her right shoulder hovered a dove of exceeding whiteness, breathing into her right ear. On her breast was the picture of a monstrous and shapeless human head; beneath her feet lay the likenesses of people trodden down and crushed by her. In her hands she held a document, fully unrolled; on one side, the side that faced Heaven, there were seven lines of writing. I tried to read it, but could not. And she said:

4 Words of Truth

"I choose to be the rod and scourge of bitter correction against that liar who is the son of the Devil; for the Devil is the persecutor of the ineffable justice of God. Hence I oppose him and trouble him; I am never found in his mouth, and I spit him out of my mouth like a deadly poison, for with all his cunning he has never found me. He is to me the worst and most troublesome of all evils, since all evil originated from him. Therefore, I cast him out and tread him underfoot in the lovable justice of God, which I love unceasingly and without end, and support and lead. For on me the whole edifice of God's virtues, which build on high, is stabilized and will stand. O God, Who art strongest and noblest, hearken!"

The second figure, on her right, had an angelic face and wings capable of flying stretched out to each side. But she was in human form, like the other virtues. And she said:

5   Words of Peace

"I rebuff the attacks of the Devil, which come against me saying, 'I will not suffer tribulation, but I will rid myself of all my adversaries. I am not willing to fear any. Whom should I fear?' But those who utter this evil speech are cast out through me; for I have been appointed always to be glad and rejoice in all good things. For the Lord Jesus abates and consoles all pain, He Who bore pain in His own body.

"And, because He is the restorer of justice, I choose to unite myself to Him and sustain Him always, free of hatred and envy and all evils. And I also choose to present a joyful face to Your justice, O God."

And the third figure, on the left, was clothed in a white tunic, picked out with green; she had in her hands a small vase, pale and shining, which gave off bright light like lightning, and this light shone on the face and neck of the figure. And she said:

6   Words of Beatitude

"I am happy. For the Lord Jesus adorns me and makes me beautiful and white, because I have flown from the deadly counsel of the Devil, which always reverts to misery, seeking by evil deeds what God rejects. I fly from this Satan, I reject him, and I hold him as an enemy forever, for I desire that Lover Whom I may fervently embrace and joyfully possess in and above all things."

Now the figure who sat on the stone at this end of the wall was clothed in a black tunic. On her right shoulder she bore a small cross with the image of Jesus Christ, which turned hither and thither. And as from the clouds there shone on her breast a wondrously bright light, divided into many rays as is the splendor of the sun when it shines through an object's many small openings. In her right hand she held a small branch like a fan, from the top of which three twigs had wonderfully sprouted forth into flower. And in her bosom she carried some minute stones, jewels of all kinds, which she looked at very carefully and diligently as a merchant looks over his goods. And she said:

7   Words of Discretion

"I am the mother of virtues, and I have God's justice in all things. In spiritual war and in secular tumult, within my conscience I always wait upon my God. I do not condemn, I do not trample, I do not spurn kings and dukes and counts and the other secular ruling powers who were ordained by the Ruler of all things. How were it lawful for ashes to spurn ashes? The crucified Son of God turns Himself to all people, admonishing them by His justice and mercy; and I choose to submit to each of His ordinances and institutes according to His will."

And the figure that stood on the wall at the same end was bareheaded, with curly black hair and a swarthy face. She was dressed in a tunic of many different colors. And I saw that she took off the tunic and her shoes, and stood naked; and suddenly her hair and her face gleamed newly white, like a newborn baby, and her whole body shone like light. And then I saw on her breast a splendid cross with the image of Christ Jesus; it was depicted above a little bush with two flowers on it, a lily and a rose, which reached upward toward the cross. And I saw her vigorously beat the tunic and shoes she had taken off, so that a great deal of dust flew out of them. And she said:

8   Words of Salvation

"I take off the Old Testament, and I put on the noble Son of God with His justice in holiness and truth. And thus I am restored to my good deeds and stripped of my vices. Therefore, O my God, I beseech you, 'Do not remember the sins of my youth and my ignorance, and take not revenge on my sins' " [Psalm 24:7, Tobias 3:3].

And as I looked attentively on these things, the One seated on the throne again spoke to me:

9   No Christian should refuse to submit to government, prefigured of old

Let none of the faithful who humbly wish to obey God hesitate to submit to human institutions of government. For through the Holy Spirit the authority of the Church has been ordained for the use of the people while they live; and it was prefigured in the people of the Old Testament that human government is included in churchly authority and should be kept faithfully and firmly.

Hence you see the wall of the aforementioned building, which runs between the north and west corners, and its inner side is all arched like a chancel, except that it is not open like chancel arches but unbroken. This symbolizes the time from Abraham and Moses, who resisted the Devil, as it were, in the northern corner, until the open declaration of the true Trinity in the true and Catholic faith, when the Son of God was sent into the world by God the Father in the last days and set forth His doctrine in abundance, as it were, in the western corner. In that period the wall, which is to say the Israelite people, was set up in the law of God's justice, which built the building of the goodness of the Almighty Father. That is, in the Old Testament the Israelite people were curbed and united, and after the harshness displayed by the Jealousy of God because of the deeds of the early rulers, the reign of the new dignities was foreshadowed.

For the Old Testament extended till the time of the New, and from it sprang the greater precepts of the law of the New Testament. Thus from the lesser the greater was born, the greater and broader new doctrine from the lesser doctrine of the old commands; for the Old Testament was only the foundation, laid down that the profoundest wisdom of all might be built on it, the wisdom manifested in the Incarnation of the Son of God. So the old wisdom lasted from the law of circumcision to the new rule of baptism, which was adorned with greater commands.

10   The Incarnation made clear by the grace of the Spirit what the Law hid

And the wall, which is to say the Jewish people in their inner understanding by which the human soul knows God, was all arched, which is to say surrounded on all sides by their predecessors' wisdom which proclaimed the commands of the Law of God, and walled in and protected by that wisdom, as lesser people are wont to be guided by greater ones. This is the meaning of the structure of the chancel, which is to say the foreshadowing in a type by the Holy Spirit. For, by the Incarnation of the Son of God, Who manifested the archways of His mercy as a refuge to all who ask, the Spirit elucidated the difficult writings.

But the wall was not opened by the Doorkeeper, that is to say the Holy Spirit, Who laid bare the spiritual meaning of the old Law; the archways of mercy were opened in the flesh of the Son of the Most High when He was made manifest, but the old wall remains closed in the harsh precepts of the Law, even though that Law was later made clear through the Holy Spirit in the Fountain of Living Water.

11 A person invested with a government dignity represents God

And each arch has the picture of a human being in it. For as these pictures show human images, so a person in a triumphal arch, which is to say a government dignity, stands in the place of God. How? Because, by the grace of God, profound and excelling wisdom is placed in the mouth of human reason, and so a human being, in the name of God, can exercise an office of instruction as a representative of the justice and mercy of the Most High Himself.

12 A spiritual office is the greater, one which rules the people is lesser

And on the outer side of this wall you see two smaller walls; which is to say that in outward affairs there is an intermittent establishment of greater and lesser people set up by God's authority like two walls. The outer one is people of high birth who by My ordinance have the might of secular power; the middle one is the lesser people who live under the power of both spiritual and secular persons, and thus are between the arches of the inner wall, which is spiritual government, and the outer wall, which, as said, is secular power. And so there are two walls outside the circumference of the inner arched wall; for secular persons in earthly affairs have more outward than inward qualities. And yet they are part of My appointed order. How?

13 The outer authority is an allegory of the inner

Through outward things the inner ones are understood; and so, when people see from the visible and exalted dignity of one in power how he should be feared and honored and loved, they should also understand by the same insight how the invisible and most high God is to be dreaded and worshipped and loved above all things. For by outward and secular dominion people are taught about the inward and spiritual power of the Divine Majesty, which is so concealed and hidden from humanity that no fleshly eye can see it unless faith grasps it. So God is invisible to mortal creatures; but at least through visible authority people can learn to fear and worship the Most High, Who established it. How?

14 Why God lets one kind of person excel and another be subject

God's inspiration gave the human mind, by means of its reason, a sense that great persons should rule the people and be feared and honored by them.

For God has allowed one kind of person to rule and another to be subject so that people would be divided into groups and so would not kill each other off and perish; or because if the example were not given by fearing and honoring human beings, the people would be lazy, and not know how to acknowledge God.

Therefore, the Holy Spirit led the people to the inner spiritual law, which could rule them inwardly and outwardly until the Fountain sprang up and flowed forth in the world in the fullness of justice to rule both body and soul. So secular powers are set up to order earthly things, that the body may seek refreshment and not faint; and spiritual authority is established that the soul might long for celestial things and aspire to the service of God. And so both these things are established by My order, as Isaac said to his son Jacob:

15 Words of Isaac to Jacob

"Be the lord of your brethren, and let your mother's children bow down before you" [Genesis 27:29]. Which is to say, be the lord of your brothers, powerful over them in honors and triumphs, blessed by the benedictions given me by God; and let all the children of your mother's children bow down before you, subject to you because of your exceeding blessing. For out of you shall come forth the great race from which will arise the man most strong and mighty, whom his brothers shall persecute and drive away. But he will escape them like a lion in his strength and rule them with most excellent rule. And he will restrain them in the name of his power, and never dwindle into a mere appendage like a tail; his brothers will become the tail.

And thus too I, the Heavenly Father, said to My incarnate Son, "Be the Lord of all who are born of human seed, who were created by Me through You. For You were born miraculously of a virgin, not conceived by the seed of a man; You went forth from Me as a flaming fire, and appeared on earth as a true man, but the seal of the untouched and chaste Virgin remained closed.

"You, therefore, in the supernal light of divinity, are the Lord of those who by Your Incarnation as a man are Your brothers. And so let the children of the mother of Your Incarnation bow down and be subject to You, and all people born of humanity serve You in loving devotion."

And since the Son of God is thus Lord of all creatures, by the will of the Father and the touch of the Holy Spirit He also established the order of the different powers in the world. How? Thus: There was excess and vaunting because no people honored any other people, and everyone was doing as he pleased; and this would have continued if God, in His infinite wisdom, had not done away with it. Therefore, He made distinctions between one people and another. He made the lesser subject to the greater in the service of obedience, and made the greater help and serve the lesser with intelligence and devotion; just as it was granted to Jacob by his father, inspired by the Holy Spirit, to be lord of his brothers.

16 This means that there are three orders: rulers, free people and servants

And by his being made lord, it was shown that in secular affairs there is a kind of person who is to rule over others' freedom. They honor him for his authority, and thus he spares them and does not oppress them by claiming service from them, but cherishes them with fraternal love. But when it says they are made to bow before him, it symbolizes the services due from those who are released from the bonds of servants, but remain children of the flesh with fleshly cares.

But later, Jacob stole the lordship from his brother through his father's blessing. He then gained heavenly renown by the stone he set up as a sign, and the tithes he vowed to give, as was said; and so he symbolizes each protagonist in the spiritual army. For every faithful person must ascend from the lowest rank to the highest; that is, he must learn from the secular power the higher authority and clearer light of the spiritual life. For in the latter is fulfilled the office of ruler by the way of the immaculate Lamb, Who has lifted Man on high in the plenitude and goodness of justice, raising him up from the snares of the wicked robber who laid him low.

17 How secular and spiritual people are each divided into four categories

And hence the two ways of life, concerned with earthly and with heavenly things, are divided into four parts each. And God gave Man the great power of reason that, inspired by the Holy Spirit, he might know these parts in himself by the pattern of the four elements. And thus he adds variety to the two ways, which I do not spurn or reject; for he who in My name multiplies what is less is worthy of reward and not of rejection. And these four parts pertain as much to the secular as to the spiritual life. For in secular affairs there are lesser and greater nobles, servants and followers; and in spiritual matters there are the excellent and the superior, the obeyers and the enforcers.

18 No one may seize, steal or buy either a spiritual or a secular office

And I do not will that these offices, which I established, should be seized or stolen or put up for sale; I want them given for reasonable cause, that those who receive them may be useful to God and humanity. But there are poisonous scorpions who ignore My justice, and in the deadly venom of their avarice and their pride usurp these positions; and this not just in secular but also in spiritual offices.

The usurping of secular offices, in which the earthly confronts the earthly, will be harshly judged in the wrath of the Jealousy of God; but the usurping of spiritual ones is more serious and more punishable. For secular people are flesh of flesh in outward things, but spiritual people are inwardly joined to the Spirit. Secular people indeed, though occupied with outer things and earthly cares, should seek to be guided by the inner Spirit in their duties; but spiritual people are within the ranks of religion and must scorn earthly things and rest fully in the heart of the Almighty Father, and so they have a much greater obligation to be ardent in imitating the priesthood of the Son. For as the Son went forth from the heart of His Father, so the Father in His Son set up people to be His officials, arrayed in their high rank to serve the Church and be united to God in good works. How?

19 Those worthy of office are intelligent, moral, eloquent and modest

There are those who have compunction and well-searched hearts and mature minds, and all else that is good to Me. They have good consciences, so that they do not seek office wickedly by conflict, or try to obtain it by devilish arts, or buy it with money or with secular power, or seek it for the sake of fleeting words of human praise. Rather, they receive it in humility by My true choice and the election of the people. And these are My most dear and proved guardians, and My surest friends.

20 Those who flee God and seize office devilishly will be punished later

But there are those who go backward and get power in the dark, not caring how; they snatch the celestial mysteries by craft, by secular and earthly means. And such people fly from My face and in bitterness slay their own souls; they deride Me and deny Me, and kick against My will. How?

By despising Me; they do not desire to attain to office through Me, or raise their inner heart's vision to Me and say, "Does this please God or not?" But each of them says within himself, "Even if this is bad in God's sight, I will accept it; I will trust in the Lord, and at some point while I still live I will repent." And thus they get the authority without Me, the Living God, and never ask Me for it or trust to attaining it by My will; in their impatience they flee before My face, snatching at office and running aground from the sea of My mercy.

These people therefore are not inside the heart of the Supreme Father; they are outside, wandering in the region of the North, which rules them in these matters. They choose not to seek Me, the Creator of all, but to seek their own will and hold it in place of God, and follow it and abandon Me. They do not wish to know Me, nor I them; their desires prompt them to do what they wish. And, because they refuse to fear Me, I choose not to stop them at once by the terror of My wrath; and so their deeds will be held against them on that day when they can no longer prevail. If I let them go in this life, they will have to answer in the fearful Last Judgment for what they have done; for they had knowledge of Me in faith, yet chose to ignore Me in the deeds they did.

21 By the ordination of Providence, these human distinctions exist forever

But you see that *the two lesser walls extend from the north to the west corner.* This is to say that when the greater and lesser orders of people were established, from the time of Abraham and Moses as in the North to the manifestation of the Catholic faith of the true Trinity taught by My Son as in the West, the distinction between people and their rulers was set up in My Law. And this was the germ and the prototype of the people of the New Testament, shown in advance and lasting till the time My Son by My Zeal was born in the flesh. So these distinctions were and are and always will be, between people of inner and outer life, spiritual and secular people, and greater and lesser people.

They are joined to these corners at each end like a vault; for the peoples are united in honor and teaching to the Old Testament at the beginning and the New Testament at the end. And it is like a vault because, by the workings of divine Providence, they are well and worthily conformed to the structure of the heavenly Jerusalem.

22 There are three kinds of secular people, greater and lesser

The height of these two lesser walls is three cubits, which indicates that when the two secular conditions are rightfully upheld, there are three divisions between the people: the rulers, those who are free from bonds of servitude, and the common people who are subject to their governors.

23 Spiritual rulers should excel in unity of faith

And so *the distance between the inner, arched wall and the middle one is one cubit;* for that is the distance between the dignity of those high in spiritual authority and those who hold the lesser titles of earthly government, appointed in the unity of faith according to God's will to hold in check those subject to them.

24 The secular rulers and the people must have innocent and loving relations

And between the middle one and the outer one it is one palm, and that a child's; for between the lesser power of the secular government and the servitude of its subjects there must be thoughtful justice, and the two must touch each other with the hands of their joint labor in the single-minded and simple devotion of childlike innocence.

25 In the work of God, six virtues prefigure all the others

And inside the building you see six figures standing on its pavement before the arched wall. This is to say that when God works goodness six virtues appear, which prefigure all the other virtues, as in six days God created His creatures. These virtues stand before the wall as a preview of things to come; they stand before the Israelite people, who were bridled by the divine law and walled about by the authority and defense of their forerunners, and they tread underfoot the pavement of earthly cares, which forms the floor of the Supreme Father's building, to signify that the army of Christians through them can fight the Devil.

26 The positions of these six virtues and the other two

Therefore, *three are grouped together before the wall near the north corner;* for when the Old Testament was begun by Abraham and Moses to oppose the Devil, the holy and inseparable Trinity, in the power of Its majesty, was symbolized by divers secret figures.

And *three are together at the end of the wall that looks to the West;* for when the Son of God was born in the flesh at the end of the time of the Law to redeem the people who looked to the West, the Trinity, which reigns in the Unity of the Divinity, was preached openly by name.

And they are all looking at the pictures in the arches of the wall; for all with equal devotion look to the authority of God's decrees for humanity, designated by His power in the law of the Old and the New Testament, and ponder how those decrees may be perfected in them.

But at that same end of the wall you see another figure within the building, sitting on a stone resting on the pavement for a seat. This is to say that, when the old law of the Old Testament was laid by and the new faith in the true Trinity was begun, and God established all the constant virtues of the Church, this virtue also appeared to do His work and will work through Him in humans until the end of the world.

And therefore she sits on the strongest of rocks, which is to say on God's only Son; for He is the seat and the repose of all the faithful who despise the transitory and with pure faith believe in Him.

And she leans against the wall to her right; for she rightfully reposes on the hope that this people, both the greater and the lesser, who by God's disposition have been placed under authority, may honor her in their works.

But she turns her face toward the pillar of the true Trinity; for she directs her intention toward that Trinity in everything, with sharpest vision and mental powers, as all who worship God must contemplate Him in their deeds, diligently and ceaselessly, as the eternal Trinity inviolably in Three Persons.

But at the same end you see another figure, standing on the wall above the first. This is to say that when the shadows of the old Law were transmuted by the faith of the Holy Trinity into the true light of justice, this virtue was elevated by the authority of rulers and the faithful people to the higher place, the desire for heavenly salvation. She stands there fighting against vice, upright in the Son of God, for she had her origin from Him, and she shall remain with Him in the heavenly Jerusalem when the world has ended.

And she also turns toward the pillar of the true Trinity; for it is in her strength derived from the holy and ineffable Trinity that she brings back souls to their true country.

27   On the virtues' clothing and what it means

And in these figures you see certain resemblances, for the virtues are of one mind though diverse in the gifts of God. *The first six and the last two are clothed in silk garments,* which are the sweet works the worshippers of God offer to Him in divine law and true justice; *and white shoes,* which are their eagerness to follow in purity the example of good human actions.

But *the right-hand figure in the group of three standing at the end of the wall is so pure and bright that you cannot discern any detail about her because of her great splendor.* For this virtue, by the gift of the Holy Trinity, rose up in the true strength of salvation at the end of the ancient severity; so she is completely translucent and pure, devoid of all devilish impurities and shining with the joy of human gladness, and she has in the heavenly places such abundance of glory and honor that no excercise of reason by any mortal can comprehend her incomparable harmony, unless God wills to reveal it.

And the one who is standing on the wall is wearing black shoes; for, before My Son's Incarnation, the sign and footprint of death were in all people both of the higher dignity and of the lesser.

And none of these wears a cloak, which means that they have cast off care for the things of Earth and the outer garments of the Law's commands, and are inwardly contemplating true justice. *But the middle one of the three who stands at the beginning of the wall is wearing a cloak,* for she did her work under God's protection at the beginning of the period of severity. But she is surrounded by the love of God and hides in it her heavenly treasure, rejecting the desire for carnal things.

And two of these same three, the ones to the right and the left of the middle one, and two of the other three, the middle and the left figures, do not have women's veils on their heads, but stand with bare heads and white hair. For Law and Prophecy, which came forth from the power of the Supernal Majesty, displayed in their strength life and death, followed the twofold ways of love and in their inner wisdom were constant against adversity and rejoiced in sweet divinity; and in their Head, Who is Christ My Son, they were faithfully freed from subjection to pain or the noose of death. Their hair is bright with the purity of virginity, for the Divinity greatly loved the virginal nature in the Virgin Mary.

But the middle one of the first three and the one who sits on the stone next to the wall have white head-veils in the manner of women; which is to say that in the height of Heaven and in the constancy of blessed repose they are pleasantly and sweetly bound by the strong bond of subjection. They venerate God, the Head of all the faithful, with a pure and loving devotion, as with sincere love a wife should venerate her husband.

And the middle and the right-hand ones of the second three are clothed in white tunics; for their shining and pure works go forth among people by the power of the Divine Majesty in sweetest beatitude, ordained by the law of the Lord to Whom they are united.

But you also see differences between them; which is to say that, although they worship God in concord, He has given them different powers.

28   Abstinence and her appearance

Therefore, *the figure who stands in the middle of the three first ones* symbolizes Abstinence; for she, in the fight, is like a city and a foundation and an ornament to the virtues near her. By her grave conduct she keeps herself from sin, and having no wantonness in herself she scrutinizes and reproves all childish wrongdoing. She appears like a mother in the midst of those virtues, which showed the glory of the Trinity at the beginning of the time of the Law in the Old Testament.

And *she has a yellow circlet like a crown on her head, with this inscription carved on the right side: "Always burn!"* For she was crowned by the Supreme Head with the yellow ray of the brilliant sun, the Son of God. In His brightness she exists totally, desiring no one but Him; and indeed, He always inflames her from the direction of salvation, which is the right.

And thus, as you see, *a dove is flying at the right side of this figure, and breathing out the writing from its beak.* For the right hand of heavenly bounty gives the gift of true simplicity, which is the Holy Spirit, and It enkindles all good things in Abstinence by divine inspiration, for the purpose of saving souls; and so this virtue shows in the words of her admonition, already quoted.

29 Liberality and her appearance

Now *the second figure, standing at her right,* symbolizes Liberality; she is of childlike simplicity, with no over-subtlety or hardheartedness with respect to human suffering. Together with Abstinence she withdraws herself from all harshness and takes the right path to God; for when Abstinence decides on a work, Liberality begins to carry it out.

She has a lion on her breast, which gives off light like a mirror; which is My Son Christ Jesus, the mighty lion, enclosed in her heart like a tender and wonderful mirror of affection.

And hanging from her neck to her breast on a twisted, flexible rod is a pale-colored serpent. This symbolizes the fact that My wise Son bent His neck, which is to say His patience, to bear the pale agony of the body and the twisting of His pains when He was raised on the cross to heal all wounds. Liberality impresses this upon her heart with heavenly love and causes it to be contemplated in human minds; and so she says in the words of her already quoted declaration.

30 Piety and her appearance

And *the third figure, on the left,* manifests Piety, who never cherishes hatred or envy of human happiness, but always rejoices at and embraces human good fortune. By her freshness and her outpouring of generosity, Abstinence is able to resist the Devil, who whispers to her from the left. For in the struggle for the banner, Piety is the full work of Abstinence, and always is the victor.

VISION SIX

Hence *she is clad in a tunic of hyacinth red;* for her splendid work surrounds her, yet in her beautiful patience she hides bloody injuries beneath it, suffering all of them according to My Son's example in His Passion. *On her breast is the picture of an angel, a wing out on either side.* This means that each person should imitate the angels in his mind by loving each of God's ordinances, and lift himself up into flight on one wing and on two, which is to say by the One God and by twofold virtue; meeting the good and the bad on both sides, not unduly exalted by the good or prostrated by the bad. He should gaze on God in purity of heart, and therefore rise upward and not cast himself down to earth.

And therefore *its right wing stretches to the figure's right shoulder;* for on the right, the side of salvation, human happiness comes to the help of Piety, because My Son brought back Man to his true country. And *its left wing stretches to her left shoulder;* for on the left, the side of the Devil's snares, a faithful person casts off the work of darkness by extending his wing for a flight upward to the refuge of My Son. And thus he is strong against all adversity and imitates the life of the just, as this virtue declares in her already quoted words.

31   Truth and her appearance

The figure who stands in the middle of the three second ones depicts Truth; for in every case, after Abstinence and the virtues that cleave to it have been established, Truth arises. The other figures stand by her because she is their tower and their strong protector; she is at the heart of the virtues that prefigure the Holy Trinity when Jewish custom sets and true faith rises.

Above her right shoulder hovers a dove of exceeding whiteness, breathing into her right ear. This signifies the amazing power of the Holy Spirit, Who appears at the upper right, the direction of the blessed restoration through the Incarnation of the Son of God; Its touch breathes into her right ear, which is to say into the hearts of believers, that they may understand the divine power of God.

On her breast is the picture of a monstrous and shapeless human head; which is to say that God allows the hearts of His elect to be troubled by the miseries and persecutions of rulers, just as His Son chose to suffer at the hands of the chief priests. And, because God is in the hearts of the faithful, they should suffer persecution patiently for the love of God; and, because death arose from the fall of the Devil, they must sustain many struggles and sufferings, often hard and adverse for the body, against the Devil's villainies. For something clings to Man that the ancient serpent always pursues. What is this? The lust of the flesh, which can be ensnared from ambush by that malignant enemy.

And beneath her feet lie the likenesses of people trodden down and crushed by her. This is to say that the lies of the Devil, which reside in human deeds, are reduced to naught under the feet of Truth. She loves the edifice of the Church, where all the virtues shine clearly to be tested by her; before all ages she was hiding invisibly in the heart of the Father, but at the end of time she appeared visibly in the true flesh of the Son of God.

And therefore *in her hands she holds a document fully unrolled, and on the side that faces Heaven there are seven lines of writing.* For in all works of Truth, by God's grace a pattern is unrolled of the law established for the Christian people; and it should be observed with open worship on the side turned toward heavenly desire, and feared on the side of carnal lusts. And it contains the seven gifts of the Holy Spirit, the unassailable bulwark against the Devil's snares of death. *And you try to read it, but cannot.* For though Man yearns to know the mysteries and secrets of God's gifts, it is not possible for him to understand or grasp God's will in His wonders as long as he is burdened with a mortal body. But let Man embrace and truly comprehend those mysteries by faithfully following God's precepts, as this virtue says in her words already quoted.

32   Peace and her appearance

The second figure, on her right, symbolizes Peace, which has the heavenly mark and the company of angels. For she puts forth buds in the full fruitfulness of Truth. Truth is surrounded by marvellous gifts of Heaven, which come from the right, the side of salvation, and so, through the Son of God, she brings Peace. How? As it is written in the angelic song: "Glory be to God on high, and on earth peace to people of good will" [Luke 2:14]. Which is to say: Because the Son of God was miraculously incarnate, humanity shines forth in the Most high God and God in humanity. And therefore God is worthy to be praised and glorified in Heaven by His whole creation. And so will there also be on earth the peace of salvation to those who receive the will of the Father with devotion and faith; for the peace of good will is the will of all the goodness of the Father, His Son, Who is God and Man at once.

And how is He peace? He is the Peace of humans, and defends them from the snares of the ancient serpent. That serpent was the first false one, and lost the light of life and was cast down into darkness; and then the true Peace, which is the true Son of God, brought light to people, so that they became partakers of the Kingdom of God and stood in the blessed place that the Devil had lost.

So, as you see, this virtue *has an angelic face;* for she flies from all evil, and beholds God, as it were, face to face with holy mind and angelic desire. Hence too *she has wings capable of flying stretched out to each side;* for, faced with either tranquillity or trouble, she flies upward to God. She does not deal in terror or bitterness, but remains calm and harmonious; by the joint effort of her two wings she embraces the one God, and persists only in serenity, which is not shaken by changeful tempests either in good or in evil case.

And she is in human form, like the other virtues. For she shines miraculously through the Son of God, and all the other human virtues are made true in her. For she never seeks contention or dispute, but always leniency; and so she opposes the attacks of the Devil, as is manifested in the words of her discourse above.

33   Beatitude and her appearance

And the third figure, on the left, depicts Beatitude, yearning for eternal life. By her faithfulness and quiet gentleness Truth can oppose on her left hand all the craft of the serpent's temptations, which deceive the person who consents to him. For Beatitude is the unconquered serenity of true glory, and fears no miseries in death. Therefore *she is clothed in a white tunic, picked out with green;* for she is surrounded by faithful works, which are bright with celestial desire and fresh with the freshness of the gifts of the Holy Spirit.

She has in her hands a small vase, pale and shining; which is to say that her deeds depict the way Man apprehends God by faith in a small container, the interior of his contrite heart. It is pale with the weakness of human flesh, because faith must be held to even in this mortal life where misery is always with humanity. Therefore *it gives off bright light like lightning, and this light shines on the face and neck of the figure.* For knowledge of eternal light is diffused by both fear and love of God, which reaches from a person's inner heart to his face, which is to say it makes him begin righteous deeds that show his good intent. And then it shines on the neck, which means that the completed work includes strength, and through Beatitude shines before God more brilliantly than the sun, as this virtue declares in her speech quoted above.

34   Discretion and her appearance

But *the figure who sits on the stone at this end of the wall* denotes Discretion. For when the Old Testament observances were fulfilled, she appeared in Christ; she is the wise sifter of all things, holding what should be held and cutting off what should be cut off, as the wheat is separated from the tares.

And *she is clothed in a black tunic;* for she is surrounded by mortification of the flesh, and has cast off all vain levity. And *on her right shoulder she bears a small cross with the image of Jesus Christ;* which is to say that, when Almighty God gave His Son to be miraculously incarnate and humbly suffer, this virtue was firmly rooted in the power of God's strength, which is the right. Discretion united with His love when she was manifested by Him, and through her all justice is decided. And as God determines the stature that best befits Man, Discretion's office is to imitate Him; that is, she fulfils her works in the Giver, His crucified Son, and exists in both His states, divinity and humanity.

It turns hither and thither; for in the sign of the holy cross Discretion moves unceasingly in a round among good and bad people. *And as from the clouds there shines on her breast a wondrously bright light;* which is to say that from God's mercy, the brightest cloud above, divine love is instilled and enkindled in human minds, waking discretion and enlightenment in them.

Therefore, *this light is divided into many rays as is the splendor of the sun when it shines through an object's many small openings.* For the Holy Spirit, with heavenly power, emits diverse rays, which are gifts to humans; and these rays, more brilliant than the sun, diffuse and penetrate the recesses of humility in the clear vision of faithful souls. And thus It enlightens their minds and senses, that they may gain a deep understanding in everything of what they should rightly do in God.

In her right hand she holds a small branch like a fan; which is to say that Discretion, on the right side, which is the side of salvation, contemplates her work in humans through the gifts of the Holy Spirit. These humans are in the flesh, which is fragile like wood; but the flesh has in it her sign, and so by God's help drives away the Devil's temptations, which come like a cloud of flies. Thus Discretion is not dissipated in them by vanities. *And so from the top of this wood three twigs have wonderfully sprouted forth into flower,* that the faithful may believe above all that the Holy Trinity perpetually flowers in wonder and gloriously reigns in the Unity of the Divinity. Thus they must not rashly contemplate the celestial secrets in themselves, but dispose all their actions well and rightly through the power of Discretion, as God disposes His works justly and with discretion in all His creatures.

And in her bosom she carries some minute stones, jewels of all kinds, which she looks at very carefully and diligently as a merchant looks over his goods. This is to say that in the bosom of the human mind she encloses everything that is apt and suitable, that its most minute thoughts and deeds may be jewels of virtue. And with cautious and diligent scrutiny she seeks all God-ordained justice, and influences all human hearts with a sharp awareness of the reward of their work, the recompense from God, which indeed she herself says, as mentioned above.

35 Salvation and her appearance

And *the figure that stands on the wall at the same end* signifies the Salvation of souls, which appeared in the authority of the new grace when the old severity had set. Thus Discretion is the foundation, and Salvation appears above her, who arose in the Son of God when He was born of the Virgin for human salvation. She *is bareheaded, with curly black hair.* For she is bare of subjection or servitude, and remains free in status, because she openly cleaves to the Son of God, Who mercifully raised her up; but her hair is black, because among the Jewish people Salvation was obscured, not shining in true brightness but existing in great diversity of observance, like curls in hair.

She also has a swarthy face; for before the Incarnation of the Son of God, she was in the shadow of death, and seemed not to hope for the happiness of eternal salvation. Therefore, too, *she is dressed in a tunic of many different colors;* for among the people of the Old Testament she was surrounded by many works, including many vices.

But you see that *she takes off the tunic and her shoes, and stands naked.* This is to say that when death was banished by the Passion of My Son, and when the Holy Spirit came and the sound and words of the apostles were heard in the world, Salvation awoke; she spurned evil works and rejected wrong paths and stripped herself bare of the Devil's power. And thus she spoke within herself: "O you most shameful Devil! You would never leave me, except that I am redeemed in the blood of the Lamb. For you wanted to keep me in the pit of Hell, but now by God's grace I am delivered."

And thus *suddenly her hair and her face gleam newly white, like a newborn baby.* For after the Incarnation of My Son, the people represented by her hair increased, well-enlightened in the inner face of their souls. They grasped true and splendid justice and sought eternal happiness, trusting in life's brightness and the liberation of the faithful members who adhere to Christ the Head; and so they are saved in celestial life through regeneration and the innocence of childhood. *And her whole body shines like light;* for she in all her members, the faithful people subject to her through My Son, was made pure in dovelike simplicity and bright in the lucent beauty of the justice of God.

But *you see on her breast a splendid cross with the image of Christ Jesus, which is depicted above a little bush with two flowers on it, a lily and a rose, which reach upward toward the cross.* This is to say that in the Passion of Jesus, this virtue became the strong heart of the believing people. For the Savior Jesus, by His martyrdom and the steps of His righteous example, cast down and broke the tree of Adam's death and perdition, against which the two Testaments had also fought, the Old in white and the New in red. By God's will, then, and in the lofty understanding of the spirit, they turned from the perdition of death to the Passion of that noble and loving Redeemer and all His justice.

So *you see her vigorously beat the tunic and shoes she has taken off, so that a great deal of dust flies out of them.* For Salvation shows, in new and righteous human deeds, that the tunic of early custom and old vice is removed and the evil example of Adam's transgression beaten out of it. She brings these things to naught by vigorous scrutiny, and despises and rejects the dust of vainglory and other sins, as she makes known about herself in the words given above.

But let the one who has ears sharp to hear inner meanings ardently love My reflection and pant after My words, and inscribe them in his soul and conscience.

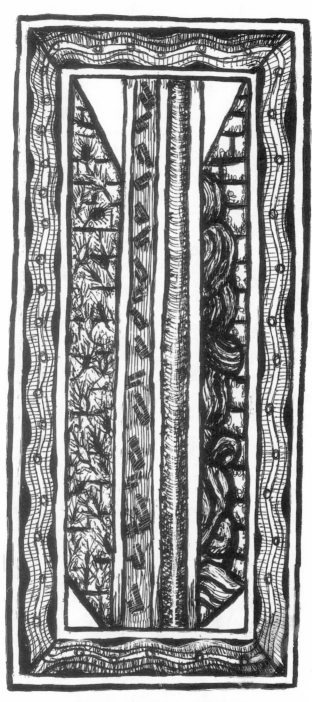

PILLAR OF THE TRINITY

VISION SEVEN
The Pillar of the Trinity

*T*hen I saw in the west corner of the building a wondrous, secret and *supremely strong pillar, purple-black in color. It was so placed in the corner that it protruded both inside and outside the building. And it was so great in extent that neither its size nor its height was clear to my understanding; I only saw that it was miraculously even and without roughnesses.*

The outside part had three steel-colored edges, which stood out like sharp sword-edges from the bottom to the top. One of these faced Southwest, where a great deal of dry straw lay cut and scattered by it; another faced Northwest, where a lot of little wings had been cut off by it and had fallen; and the middle edge faced West, where lay many decaying branches that it had cut away. All of these had been cut off by those edges for their temerity.

And again, the One Who sat on the throne and showed me all these things said to me, "To you I explain these mystical and miraculous unknown gifts in all their fullness, and grant you to speak of them and show them; for, O human, they appear to you clearly in the true light. This I do to enkindle the fiery hearts of the faithful, who are the pure stones that will build the celestial Jerusalem."

1 The Trinity is to be believed humbly and not pried into more than is licit

For the holy and ineffable Trinity of the Supreme Unity, which was hidden from those under the yoke of the Law but manifested in the new Grace to those freed from servitude, must be believed by the faithful with simple and humble heart, One True God in Three Persons; and it must not be rashly scrutinized, nor must anyone be dissatisfied with the gift he has received from the Holy Spirit. If such a one seeks more than is fitting, in the temerity of his self-exaltation he will fall into a worse state, not find what he improperly seeks. And this is shown by the present vision.

For *this pillar you see in the west corner of the building* symbolizes the true Trinity; for the Father, the Word and the Holy Spirit are One God in Trinity, and that Trinity is in Unity. It is the perfect pillar of all good, reaching from the heights to the depths and governing the whole terrestrial globe.

It stands in the west corner because the Son of God was incarnate in the sunset of the world; and He glorified His Father everywhere and promised the Holy Spirit to His disciples. So too, the Son, in undergoing death by the will of the Father, gave a noble example to humans, so that they too could rightfully enter the edifice of the Supreme Father by performing true and just works in the Holy Spirit.

And it *is wondrous, secret and supremely strong.* For God manifests Himself in His creatures so wondrously that they can never exhaust His presence; and so secretly that they cannot scrutinize him by any willful knowledge or sense; and so strongly that all their strength is directed by Him and cannot be compared with His strength.

2 Christ's blood saves the world and shows the Trinity, but incomprehensibly

It is purple-black in color, and is so placed in the corner that it protrudes both inside and outside the building. This is to say that, by the will of the Father, His only Son poured out His purple blood on behalf of humans with their black sins; and thus He saved the world by His Passion and brought the true and right faith to believers. And when the old rituals failed and the new holiness arose, the worship of the Holy Trinity was most plainly proclaimed; for it was openly believed that the Heavenly Father sent His Son, conceived by the Holy Spirit, into the world. And the Son sought the glory of His Father and not His own, and disclosed the profound consolation of the Holy Spirit, as had been foretold; and thus it was hidden on no side, but was proclaimed both to the faithful, who abode in God's work, and to the unbelievers, who stood outside the faith.

But *it is so great in extent that neither its size nor its height is clear to your understanding;* which is to say that the Trinity is of such ineffable glory and power that its greatness of majesty and its altitude of divinity cannot be bounded by any twist or presumption of the human mind. *But it is miraculously even and without roughnesses;* for, wonderful to relate, it is mild and benign in grace, and smooth in its sweet justice to all those who hasten to it, so that no rough place of injustice is in it, but justly and beautifully it confers salvation.

3 The Trinity is manifest in power and pierces even unbelievers' hearts

The outside part has three steel-colored edges, which stand out like sharp sword-edges from the bottom to the top. This is to say that the ineffable Trinity stands against the darkness of the world, appearing openly in the Unity of

Deity. Its sovereignty and power are hidden from none of its creatures except the hearts of unbelievers; from them it is concealed because of their unbelief. Therefore, God's judgment in due recompense deservedly slays them like sharp steel; it yields to no prideful opposition, but extends from one end to the other, which is to say from the creation to the end of the world. And all that exists it has penetrated and does penetrate like a sword of division, in profound Divinity and in all wisdom and power.

4 Unbelief opposes the Catholic faith, and God cuts it down in confusion

And one of these faces Southwest, where a great deal of dry straw lies cut and scattered by it. This is to say that among the Christian people the just and divine Trinity cuts down and burns up all who raise the aridity of heterodoxy and negation and rejection against the righteous Catholic faith. They are utterly confounded, like the grass that is trodden underfoot and burned in the fire, separated from the fruitful grain of the wheat. For faith and works stem from knowledge of Scripture; and all that is contrary to the true faith, though the foolish people follow it like stupid cattle, is scattered and annihilated.

5 God casts down the boasting of the Jewish people

And another faces Northwest, where a lot of little wings have been cut off by it and have fallen. This is to say that the Divinity rejected the high vanity of the Jewish people, which was flying in great pride and mental exaltation, trying to be just in itself and not in God; like the Pharisees, who tried to ascend into the heights of the heavens, trusting with confidence in themselves. But by God's just judgment they fell, rent in pieces for their presumption and their bad conduct.

6 The devilish divisions of the Gentiles are cut down by God and destroyed

And the middle edge faces West, where lie many decaying branches that it has cut away. For by the Trinity the heinous and diabolical schisms of the pagans, who stray from the right faith into the sunset of infidelity, are cut off. And as decaying branches are a nuisance, unfit for human use, so this people, who followed the Devil's lies and not the divine commands, was cut off and rejected from the joy of life.

And therefore all of these have been cut off by those edges for their temerity. For in all these cases, the true and holy Trinity allows the unfaithful people who boldly try to break away from it or stubbornly do not believe in it to cut

themselves off from it and go to perdition; for in their madness and ignorance they attack the Divinity, and choose not to yield to the faith that the
Son of God brought in Himself. This faith He transmitted to humanity
through His disciples, as the following parable shows:

7 Parable on this subject

A certain lord who owned a fire-producing flint decided to command a
numerous people to do a necessary thing, both personally and through messengers. But the messengers did not understand their lord's words, and were
foolish and inexperienced at fulfilling his command, stupidly nattering. So
while they were trying there arose a tumult; there was a great tempest, with
rain and violent thunder, so that the earth quaked and the rocks were rent.
And a vessel that had lain in the earth with its mouth facing away from the
heavens, and which had a lot of small vessels within it, was rooted out of the
earth with great force and its mouth turned to face Heaven.

And then the lord used his flint to produce a violent fire, which ran
through those messengers with such heat that all their veins were inflamed
and all timid indolence was stricken from them, as quickly as something
poured over a dry skin runs off it. And so at last they remembered all the
things they had learned and heard from their lord; and they went forth to the
rootless people, whose cities had been destroyed, and announced to them
their lord's command. For some of these they reconstructed their roots and
rebuilt their cities; but others they did not treat so, but slew them like pigs
and divided them. And therefore that flint is respected by the whole world,
and terrifies and slays all the sins of human flesh.

This means the following. That lord is the Father Almighty, with
Whom is His Only-Begotten, the cornerstone conceived by the ardent Holy
Spirit and born as a man from the intact Virgin, the fairest and most beautiful
flower of all fair and beautiful holiness. For the Son of God in His Divinity
was before all time and all creation with the Father and the fiery Comforter;
and then, when it pleased the Father, He was sent as was foretold, that he
might be conceived by the Holy Spirit, truly incarnate and born of the
Virgin, and bestow on believers the fairness and beauty of life.

When He was incarnate, the Father benignly proclaimed through Him
and His disciples the necessary thing, the deliverance and salvation of those
who believed in Him. But His disciples, while the Son was with them in the
world in His body, were foolish and unknowing and unresponsive, slow to
understand His words in the Spirit and to fulfil them in work. For they heard
them only as in a dream; they were simple, timid and frightened, and had not
yet been strengthened.

And meanwhile there came the time of the raging hearts; the Jews, causing a tumult, sought to stir up many charges against the Son of God and in that great tempest kill Him. And they carried out their malignity even as they wished; in that violent storm a murder was done such as was never seen before and will never be again. And the earth quaked, which is to say that earthly human minds and all of creation were terrified, and because of their criminal deed the laws of the Jews, written on stone, were cracked.

Then the first man, in whom is signified all of creation, and who lay buried in death, bending all his will toward the things of earth and turning his back on Heaven and God, was uprooted from the dust of death, in which he slept with his children, by the great power of the Son of God. And thus he sighed with all his heart and mind and turned to face the celestial country; for he heard Christ, the Son of God, Who was slain for his sake.

But after the Son of God had ascended to the Father, through the Son and according to His promise the Holy Spirit descended. For now the whole earth was full of heavenly dew because the Bread of Heaven had been in it; the faithless had ignored Him like a false rumor, but the faithful had received Him with all their devotion. And so, because the true Word had become incarnate, the Holy Spirit came openly in tongues of fire; for the Son, Who converted the world to the truth by His preaching, was conceived by the Holy Spirit. And, because the apostles had been taught by the Son, the Holy Spirit bathed them in Its fire, so that with their souls and bodies they spoke in many tongues; and, because their souls ruled their bodies, they cried out so that the whole world was shaken by their voices.

And the Holy Spirit took their human fear from them, so that no dread was in them, and they would never fear human savagery when they spoke the word of God; all such timidity was taken from them, so ardently and so quickly that they became firm and not soft, and dead to all adversity that could befall them. And then they remembered with perfect understanding all the things they had heard and received from Christ with sluggish faith and comprehension; they recalled them to memory as if they had learned them from Him in that very hour.

And so, going forth, they made their way among the faithless peoples who did not have roots, which is to say the sign of the knowledge of holy innocence and justice, and whose city, which is to say the instruments of God's law, had been destroyed by faithlessness. And to these they announced the words of salvation and of the true faith in Christ. And thus they brought back many of this throng to the knowledge of God and led them to the center, which is to say the font of baptism, where they received the holiness they had lost by their proud transgressions. And they built the holy city of the commandments of God, thus rebuilding the city which that seducer the Devil had taken from them in Adam, and restored it to them in the faith that leads to salvation.

But there were some who did not believe, and did not choose to receive the faith of baptism and the protection of God's command; and these, reading the signs, the apostles passed by and condemned to death for their hardness and unbelief. For in their crimes and the filth of their carnal pollutions, wallowing in fornication and adultery as a pig wallows in the mud, they were not willing to be converted to the true faith, and therefore they were divided and separated from life.

And thus the Son of God was shown throughout the whole world by many and wondrous signs, ineffably begotten of the Father in His Divinity and then miraculously born of the Virgin in time. And so the hearts of all who hear these things should be alarmed and agitated by fear and trembling, so that the vain and deceitful works they have been pleased to do may be negated in them by contempt of death. For the true Word of God bears testimony to the Holy Trinity and to life-giving salvation through the water of regeneration, as the beloved John shows in the words of his exposition, when he says:

8 Words of John

"And it is the Spirit Which testifies that Christ is the Truth. There are three that give testimony on earth: the spirit, and the water, and the blood; and the three are one. And there are Three Who give testimony in heaven: the Father, the Word and the Spirit. And the Three are One" [1 John 5:6–8; Hildegard has reversed the order of the heaven and earth parts]. This is to say that the human spirit is spiritual; it does not come from the blood, nor is it born out of the flesh, but it emerges from the secret places of God, invisible to the mutable flesh. Therefore it bears testimony to the Son of God, Whose glory is wondrous in mystical breath; no person can perfectly understand that glory, or know how the Only-Begotten of God was conceived by the Holy Spirit and born into the world, just as no person can fully know how the soul permeates the human body and blood to make up one life.

And, as the human spirit is the certain cause of the knowledge granted a person by God, and permeates everything else God gives him, being true and faithful life and not false or deceptive; so too Christ is the perfect Truth, in Whom life has risen and the light of salvation has shone, and from Whom death, which is deceptive, has fallen away.

So three, which signify the Holy Trinity, give testimony on earth, showing and granting in this world the remedy of life-giving salvation; for through that salvation the heavenly things without end must be attained, and in mortal flesh they are only awaited in hope and not possessed in actuality.

Thus the human spirit in itself testifies to Me, for it will not live fully in restored salvation unless it rises again through Me in the water of regeneration. For humanity is deficient in the light that shines in Me, since it was expelled from felicity because it was corrupted into crime and increasingly bloody deeds.

And water testifies to Me, for it purifies all filthy things in it, and clearly purges the fatal pestilence of death; it is joined to the spirit before the blood is, because as the spirit is spiritual, so the water brings spiritual sanctification. It stands in the middle between the spirit and the blood, because its confirming carries both soul and body through spiritual regeneration to life.

And blood too testifies; for it alters its poisoned course toward the house of holiness through the water of salvation, which is the medicine that arises in My Son and remains in His life. For blood by itself carries shameful crimes and turbulent injustice, and runs through uncertain paths, in a twisted sweetness that leads to burning lust and frightful vices, which choke innocence, increasing in appetite by what they feed on; all this by the temptation of that seducer the Devil.

And these three are one. For the spirit without the bloody material of the body is not the living person, and the bloody material of the body without the soul is not the living person; and these two are not strengthened unto life in the grace of the new Law except through the water of regeneration, or perfected in salvation as long as they are separated from this saving water. For then the transcendent honor of life is wanting to the person's reason; the redeemed must always make perfect praise resound in the presence of God, Who gave him that reason.

For God by His own will created Man for that honor, which is consummated in the body of His Son in eternal life; when lost Man lives again in the honor of life, redeemed in God by healing grace. And the spirit, which is invisible to bodily eyes, symbolizes the Father, Who is incomprehensible to every creature; and the water, which purges filth, symbolizes the Word, the Son of God, who by His Passion wiped out human stains; and the blood, which surrounds and warms people, is a symbol of the Holy Spirit, arousing and enkindling the brightest human virtues. So these three, the spirit and the water and the blood, are in one and one in three, and, as was said, one in salvation; and they signify the Trinity in Unity, and the Unity in Trinity. How?

The holy and heavenly Trinity gives heavenly testimony; It is not taken from something else but originates by sure faith in Itself. How? The Father testifies that before the ages He begot His one fruitful Word, through Whom all things were made; and then, at the appointed time, the Word gloriously flowered in the Virgin. The Word testifies that He went forth from the Father and stooped to enter a human nature, becoming incarnate in the purity of virginity. He went forth from the Father a Spirit and returned again to the Father in fruitful flesh; and so He stands in the middle, since He was invisibly begotten by the Father before time began, and conceived in the body within time by the Holy Spirit in the womb of the Virgin. And the Holy Spirit testifies that It quickened the intact Virgin so that she conceived the Word of God, and that It strengthened the doctrine of the same Word in tongues of flame, permeating the apostles so that they proclaimed the true Trinity throughout the world. How?

They cried aloud that God the Father had completed the work whereby He created Man for heavenly happiness, of which he was then robbed. Man was made from the mud of the earth to stand upright, but by his own will had bent down toward the earth again; but now by grace he is able to stand upright a second time through the incarnate Son of God. And, enlightened and confirmed by the Holy Spirit, so as not to perish in perdition but be saved in redemption, he has been restored to eternal glory.

9   On the distinction and unity of the Three Persons

Thus the Father, the Son and the Holy Spirit testify that they are in no way disunited in power, even though they are distinguished in Persons, because they work together in the unity of the simple and immutable substance. How? The Father creates all things through the Word, Who is His Son in the Holy Spirit; the Son is He by Whom all things are perfected in the Father and the Holy Spirit; and the Holy Spirit is He by Whom all things flourish in the Father and the Son. And so these three Persons are in the unity of inseparable substance; but They are not indistinct among themselves. How? He Who begets is the Father; He Who is born is the Son; and He Who in eager freshness proceeds from the Father and the Son, and sanctified the waters by moving over their face in the likeness of an innocent bird, and streamed with ardent heat over the apostles, is the Holy Spirit.

For the Father had the Son before time began, and the Son was with the Father, and the Holy Spirit was co-eternal with the Father and the Son in the Unity of Divinity. Hence it must be seen that if one or two were lacking of these Three Persons, God would not be in fullness. How? They are one Unity of Divinity; and so, if any of Them were lacking, God would not be. For though these Persons are distinct, They are nonetheless one substance, whole and immutable and of indescribable beauty, and remain undivided in unity. How?

10   Three similes for the Trinity

Power, will and fire are the three peaks of a single height of work. How? The will is in the power, and the fire is in the will, and they are inseparable, like expelled human breath. How? The indivisible emission of human breath is the whirling air currents, the moisture and the warmth. So too is the complete human eye. How? The circuit of your eyesight has two transparent parts, but they form one housing for all that is within them. Hear and understand, O human.

Even so there are Three Persons in one immutable essence of Divinity. In the Father is the Son, in both the Holy Spirit, and They are one, and work inseparably with each other; for the Father does not work without the Son, nor the Son without the Holy Spirit, nor the Holy Spirit without Them, nor the Father and the Son without the Holy Spirit, but They are undivided unity. Thus God is Three Persons, eternal before all ages; and the assumption of the flesh by the Son did not occur before the beginning of the world, but at the preordained time near the end of times when God sent His Son. And when the Son became incarnate and the virginal flower blossomed in her intact virginity, God was still in Three Persons and willed to be so invoked; and therefore, no Person was added to the ineffable Trinity, but the Son of God simply assumed flesh.

Hence also these Three Persons are one God in Divinity. And whoever does not believe this will be cast out of the Kingdom of God, for he tears himself away from the wholeness of Divinity in faith, as it is written:

11   Words of the Book of Kings

"And on the third day there appeared a man who came out of Saul's camp with his garments torn, and dust strewed on his head" [2 Kings 1:2]. This is to say: On the day when the Catholic faith arose by the manifestation of the Holy Trinity, humanity, which had now emerged from the camp of the army of death, broke out into many schisms and perversely sought what it was not possible for it to know. Therefore, seduced by the Devil's artful persuasions, some now imagine that they are ascending above the heights, and choose to know more than they should about the incomprehensible Divinity. And therefore the garment of salvation and justice is torn from them, because they oppose God, and they are defiled by the strewing of divisions on the head of their faith. For they lack complete faith, but scatter among many sects the honor due solely to the Deity, and they diminish His high honor by mocking it in schisms. And so God will judge them all, as is clear from the following verses:

"And David said to the young man who told him, 'Where do you come from?' He answered, 'I am the son of a stranger, an Amalekite.' And David said to him, 'Why did you not fear to put out your hand to kill the Lord's anointed?' And David called one of his servants and said to him, 'Go near and fall upon him.' And he struck him so that he died. And David said to him, 'Your blood be upon your own head; for your mouth has spoken against you, saying "I have slain the Lord's anointed." ' " [2 Kings 1:13–16].

This is to say: The Victorious One, incomprehensible to every creature, speaks to the childish and self-exalting ignorance of humanity, which tries to know what it should not know; for in its folly it accosts God and announces to Him with temerity, "Lord, I know You well!" And God answers it thus: "Where do you come from, who, having a beginning, seek to know the Whole, which lacks a beginning?" And the folly that has arisen in the creature with a beginning says, as if it knew: "I am the son of a stranger, who comes from the accursed land; for the first man fell by the taste of the fruit, and journeyed into exile from his country, and I am his descendant."

Then God says to him: "Because you are a person from the accursed land, driven out as an exile from your country, why did you not fear presumptuously to seek out what is not for you to know? This madness chokes your deeds and makes them unable to give hope, and approaches in wickedness to murder. For anyone who rashly searches out what God was before the creation of the world, or what God will do after the last day, is to be cut off from a share in the blessed communion, which is not to be known by a creature with a beginning who is in a state of sin. And so he will be miserable, torn away from the good knowledge that saves, because he obstinately sought out what he should not have sought out.

"And so you, who do these things with presumption and the cruelty of murder, are slaying within yourself the blessed understanding of King David's prophecy; for your soul should seek only pure knowledge, and believe faithfully in God with appropriate simplicity."

And then God commands the Jealousy of His pure justice, which has in it no spot of iniquity, and says to it in the righteous unity of His judgment: "Make haste and fall on him, and take from him the knowledge of good, which he had; let him never repose in any happiness of the senses, since he never prepared his heart for Me to repose in."

And so the blow of the Jealousy of the Lord strikes that creature, so that no spark of eyesight remains to him to see and know God. And so he dies to the justice of life-giving comfort, because he was not able to rule himself. And then God says to him, "Your bloody wickedness, by which you raise yourself to heights you cannot understand, recoil upon your own mind, which you unjustly raised against Me. May evil trample you underfoot in the mud, from which you cannot raise yourself to a right measure of faith, for you did not follow the right paths but sought division in your mind. May words of wisdom forsake your mouth, which spoke against your salvation when you deceitfully sought out the secret and incomprehensible Divinity, and presumed to know what is not to be known. You said rashly within yourself, 'I know well what God is!' and through this temerity you destroyed your inner salvation; you did not choose to believe in God with discretion, but proudly raised yourself against Him."

But let the one who has ears sharp to hear inner meanings ardently love My reflection and pant after My words, and inscribe them in his soul and conscience.

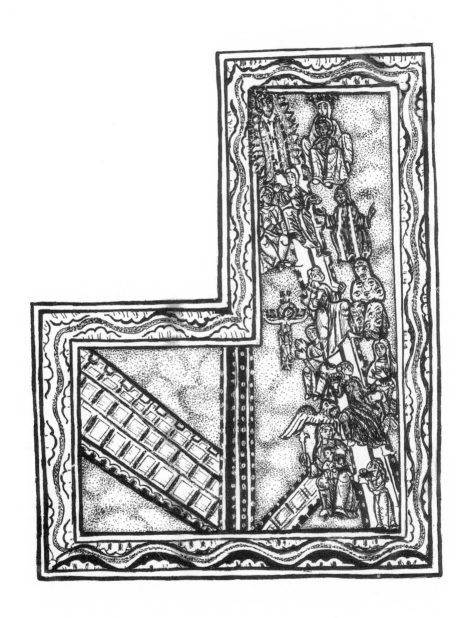

PILLAR OF THE SAVIOR'S HUMANITY

VISION EIGHT
The Pillar of the Humanity of the Savior

*A*nd then I saw, on the south side of the wall of the building beyond the pillar of the true Trinity, a great and shadowed pillar, which protruded both inside and outside the building; and it was so obscure to my sight that I could not tell its size or height. And between this pillar and the pillar of the true Trinity there was a gap three cubits wide in the wall, as mentioned above [p. 325]; only the foundation had been laid.

Thus this shadowed pillar was standing in the same place in the building where I had previously seen, in the celestial mysteries vouchsafed by God from above, a great four-sided radiance of brilliant purity [p. 109]. This radiance, which signifies the secrets of the supernal Creator, was shown to me in the greatest mystery; and in it, another radiance shone forth like dawn, with a deep purple light glowing in it, which was a mystical manifestation of the mystery of the incarnate Son of God. But in the pillar, there was an ascent like a ladder from bottom to top, on which I saw all the virtues of God descending and ascending, laden down with stones and going with keen zeal to their work.

And I heard that Shining One Who was seated on the throne say, "These are God's strongest labourers!" *And among these virtues I saw seven in particular whose form and appearance I especially noted. They resembled each other in this. All of them, like all the other virtues described so far, were clad, as it were, in silk. All of them went with white hair and bare heads, and without a cloak except the first, who wore a woman's head-veil and a mantle like transparent crystal, and the second, who had black hair, and the third, whose form did not seem human. The first, fourth and fifth were wearing white tunics. All had white shoes except the third, who, as mentioned, did not seem to be in human form, and the fourth, who was wondrously shod in shoes of shining crystal.*

And the differences among them were as follows. The first figure wore a gold crown on her head, with three higher prongs; it was radiantly adorned with green and red precious stones and white pearls. On her breast she had a shining mirror, in which appeared with wondrous brightness the image of the incarnate Son of God. And she said:

1 Words of Humility

"I am the pillar of humble minds and the slayer of proud hearts. I began at the lowest point and ascended the steep slope to Heaven; but Lucifer raised himself above himself and fell beneath himself. Whoever wishes to imitate me and be my child and embrace me as a mother and carry out my work, let him start at the foundation and gradually mount upward from virtue to virtue, with a sweet and tranquil mind. For anyone who tries to ascend by taking hold of the highest branch of the tree first will more often than not swiftly fall. But anyone who begins his ascent at the root will not fall so easily, if he proceeds with caution."

And the second figure was a deep sky-blue like a hyacinth, both in person and in tunic. Into her tunic two stripes were marvellously woven and incomparably adorned with gold and gems, so that one stripe descended to the figure's feet over each shoulder in both front and back. And she said:

2 Words of Charity

"When Lucifer in Heaven devoured himself with hatred and pride, I was provoked to indignation. Oh! Oh! Oh! Humility would not tolerate this; and therefore he was cast into great ruin. But when the human race was created, oh! oh! oh! the noble Seed, and oh! oh! oh! the sweetest Offshoot, the Son of God, was born human at the end of times for the sake of humanity. Lucifer wanted and intended to rend my garment and my integrity, but I appeared as a most brilliant splendor in God and in Man. Nowadays the blind and the dead declare that the reality behind my name is brothels and harlots and incest; but just as filth cannot touch Heaven, this filthy accusation cannot touch my will. And so I will make myself wings of the other virtues, and cast out these harmful things Lucifer has scattered throughout the world. Where, O Virtues, is Lucifer? He is in Hell. So let us arise and draw nearer to the true Light, and build high and strong towers throughout all provinces; so that when the Last Day comes we may bear much fruit, both carnal and spiritual. And when the full number of the Gentiles has come in, then we too shall be perfect on earth and in Heaven. O shameful Lucifer, what did your hasty temerity avail you? In the primal splendor in which God created you, you raved and gave yourself over to madness, and tried to tread me underfoot and cast me out of Heaven; but you fell into the abyss and I stayed in Heaven, and later descended to earth in the incarnate Son of God. And through me is perfected the multitude of the faithful, armed with a thousand soldierly arts of justice and goodness; though, had you been able to, you would long since have snatched them away. O Humility, who lifts to the stars the oppressed and the crushed! O Humility, glorious queen of the virtues! What a strong and victorious protector you are to all who are yours! No one falls who loves you with a pure heart. And I too am a valuable and desirable defense to those who are mine; for I am very slender and subtle, and I seek out in those who revere me the smallest openings, and deeply penetrate them."

The third figure I saw in the same form as I had seen her in my previous vision: greater and taller of stature than the other virtues, and non-human in form. She was covered with eyes all over her body, for she lived wholly in wisdom; she wore a shadowy garment through which the eyes could look out. And she trembled in fear before the Shining One seated on the throne. And she said:

3 Words of Fear

"Oh, woe to the miserable sinners who do not fear God but hold Him as an impostor! Who can evade fear of the incomprehensible God, Who allows the wicked who do evil to perish? Therefore I will fear the Lord God much and much. Who will help me in the presence of the true God? And who shall deliver me from His fearsome judgment? No one at all, except God Himself. Therefore I will seek Him, and fly to Him for refuge."

And the fourth was wearing a snow-white chain around her neck, and her hands and feet were chained together with white fetters. And she said:

4 Words of Obedience

"I cannot run in secular paths according to my will, or be infected by human desire; but I choose to return to God the Father of all, Whom the Devil rejected and chose to disobey."

And the fifth had a red chain around her neck. And she said:

5 Words of Faith

"God is One, to be adored in Three Persons of one substance and equal glory. Therefore I will have faith and confidence in the Lord, and never blot out His name from my heart."

And the sixth was clad in a pale-colored tunic. Before her in the air was the cross of the Passion of the crucified Son of God; and toward it she raised her eyes and hands with great devotion. And she said:

6 Words of Hope

"Spare those who sin, O loving Father! You have not forsaken the exiles, but have raised them up upon Your shoulders. And so we do not perish, who have hope in You."

And the seventh was dressed in a tunic more brilliant and pure than crystal, which shone resplendent like water when the sun reflects from it. And a dove was poised over her head, facing her with its wings spread as if to fly. In her womb, as if in a clear mirror, appeared a pure infant, on whose forehead was written "Innocence"; and in her right hand she held a royal scepter, but she had laid her left hand on her breast. And she said:

7 Words of Chastity

"I am free and not fettered, for I have passed through the pure Fountain Who is the sweet and loving Son of God. I have passed through Him, and I have come forth from Him. And I tread underfoot the Devil with his limitless pride, who has not prevailed to fetter me. He is alien from me, because I am always in the Heavenly Father."

Now at the summit of the shadowed pillar I saw another beautiful figure, standing bareheaded; it had curly black hair, and a manly face so ardently bright that I could not look on it clearly like a human one. It was clad in a tunic of purple and black, with a stripe of red over one shoulder and a stripe of yellow over the other, which fell to its feet in front and back. Around its neck it had a bishop's stole, wonderfully adorned with gold and precious gems. But a pure radiance so surrounded it that I could not look at it, except from head to foot in front; its arms and hands and feet were concealed from my sight. And that radiance around it was full of eyes on all sides, and was all alive, changing its form like a cloud and becoming now wider and now narrower. And the figure cried with a loud voice in the world, and said to humanity:

8 Words of the Grace of God, to admonish humans

"I am the Grace of God, my little children; therefore hear and understand me, for my admonition makes radiant the souls of those who do. I keep them in blessedness, so that they will not return to iniquity. And because they have not despised me, I choose to touch them with my admonition so that they will do good works; those, that is, who seek me in simplicity and purity of heart.

"So I admonish and exhort humanity, and grant it pearls of goodness; when a person's mind is touched by me, I am his beginning. That is to say, when a person understands my admonition with his sense of hearing, and his senses consent to my touching his mind, I initiate good in him. And it is needful that he begin thus, with me helping him. Then a struggle follows: Will my gift attain its end or not? How? Understand thus. When I admonish a person, so that he begins to lament and weep for his sins, then if his will consents to my admonition—for he will feel the change in his mind, and according to his mind's desire he will raise his eyes to see and his ears to hear and his mouth to speak and his hands to touch and his feet to walk—his mind will raise itself to conquer his senses, so that they will learn things their habits could not teach them. How?

"They will change themselves, for they must, though unwillingly, follow the will that is set over them. They are subject to it in service, being its inferiors; they will follow it, willing or not. Thus I initiate good, and kindle it in the mind, and give the will work to accomplish; and this I do by admonition, exhortation and the fire of the breath of the Holy Spirit. But if the will resists these gifts, all that I have mentioned comes to naught. And therefore, while a person can still make a start, inflamed by the pre-eminent gifts that come from me, let him hasten to do so; let his will quickly come to good and end its work in splendor.

"For this is why Man has the knowledge of good and evil, that he himself in all his works may know God better by avoiding evil and doing good. For thus he worships God with fear and embraces Him with perfect charity. How? Thus: by opening the inner eyes of the spirit to good, and denying and cutting off the evil that the outer person can do. And so the earthly creation is subject to his power, that he may understand and love God the more, and with that understanding do in Him the work of his knowledge; by which knowledge he fears and loves the Almighty, Who has given him this great honor of having the creatures serve him. Thus Man must wisely distinguish between the creatures, knowing which are to be loved and hated, which are useful and which are useless; and thus all his works will be concluded in faith, through which he understands God, and pleases God and His angels.

"And sometimes I touch a person's mind to warn him to begin to work justice and avoid evil, but he disdains me and thinks he can do what he wants. He postpones the time of repentance until his body is reduced to old age enough to obey him, and he is so old he is tired of sinning. And then I admonish and urge him again to do good and resist in his mind. If he ignores me, he is often brought to the pass of doing good as it were unwillingly and in spite of himself, by monetary and other troubles that come upon him. And, with his mind thus troubled, he has little delight in doing what he planned to do when he was prosperous and unopposed, when he thought he could act as and when he pleased. And such a person receives me in doubt; but yet I choose not to forsake him, for though it was thus he received me, he did not wholly despise me. And so I do not labor vainly in him.

"For I do not find it loathsome to touch ulcerated wounds surrounded by the filthy, gnawing worms that are innumerable vices, stinking with evil report and infamy, and stagnating in habitual wickedness. I do not refuse to close them gently up, drawing forth from them the devouring poison of malice, by touching them with the mild fire of the breath of the Holy Spirit. But often, such a wound grows hardened by old irritation, so that sin grows hot and burning in the person's mind; and in the clotted mass of this filth new wounds of sin appear, swelling and rising from the defilement of worms and the application of dark muck, from which come the deadly poisons of scorpions, serpents, frogs and other poisonous vermin. And such wounds become as hardened as stone, a hardness no one dares try to break open. These things burden such people with insupportable loads; and what happens then? People of little faith cannot believe it is possible for such a one to be converted to God from his iniquity; they see him as already food for the Devil. But I will not forsake this person; I choose, by my help and action, to be on his side in the struggle. I start by gently touching the strong and stony crust of his sin, which is so hard to break, for it stinks so vilely of horrible crimes, which have caused his great filth and wickedness and are like a rotting corpse and the food of the Devil; and he has certainly swallowed them into his stomach. How? The Scripture states that the Son of God said, 'My food is to do the will of My Father' [John 4:34]; and so the opposite is the Devil's food, by which he pulls people down into death, inspiring those who consent to his will and turn aside to follow him. And this is the desire and the continual study of the Devil, for from this filth all evil arises.

"But many of these people recognize me. How? When I begin to touch them, one of them may say to himself, 'What is happening to me? I know nothing of good and am incapable of thinking of it.' And then, in his ignorance, he sighs and says, 'Alas for me, a sinner!' But he feels nothing more, because he is weighed down by his huge weight of sin, and the darkness of iniquity troubles him. Then I touch his wounds again. And, having been admonished by me before, he understands me better this time, and looks at himself, saying, 'Woe is me! What shall I do? I do not know and cannot think what will become of me for my many sins. Oh, where shall I turn, and to whom shall I flee, who can help me cover over my shameful crimes and efface them by repentance?'

"And again he looks at himself, with the same turbulence that formerly propelled him into sin; and then he turns to true repentance, with a desire as great as his former eagerness to sin. And as this person, by my warning, thus wakes from the sleep of death, which he had preferred to life, he no longer desires to sin by thought, word or deed, which before were ardently directed toward crime. And in strong repentance he rises to me; and I wholly receive him, and from henceforward discharge him as free. He will no longer be troubled by the aforesaid things, which I use to warn my dearest children to hold out against the fiery arrows of the Devil's persuasion; for he no longer needs them. For he will always sorrow at the sins he has committed, and in his self-scorn he will do such severe penance that he will deem himself unworthy to be called human. And this victory comes out of the stench of those filthy people, whom I choose not to cast out; for after sinning they have sought me. I am prepared to do anything they ask for those who do not spurn me but receive my admonition and devoutly seek me. But those who despise and reject me are dead, and I do not know them.

"For there are many people who, feeling my presence and understanding that my admonition has touched their minds, fly from me by the evil ways of the sins they conceive, which they have swallowed by their choice, consent and deeds. And therefore they are to God as nothing, with no being at all, since they choose not to know what they can do when I touch them. I do not want to be near the pollution of those sinners, who will not receive my admonition or purify themselves by my exhortation and turn from their sins; they do not desire to eat that food which is the Scripture of the Gospel, with which all the faithful should be satisfied, or to taste the gift of its savor. They flee from the Grace of God; for they do not want to see or hear or think of what they should do when goodness admonishes them. They flee the good admonition like a worm burrowing into the earth. The worm hides itself from all the beauty of the world; and so do the wicked, flying from the commands of God and wrapping themselves in ordure, pollution and death, and hiding in it, afraid to come out of the stench of evil into the light. Such as these do not belong to me, for I do not choose to be apportioned here and there amid the mire. How? I choose to be with those who understand me and repent in purity; and then I join myself to human corruption in order to purge it. But those who refuse to receive me I cast from me, choosing not to be with them; I have no part with them, for their part is that of stupid folly, which will not hear me. And I have no wish to take part in the work that builds up the obdurate perversity that ends in death.

"And those who spurn me thus imitate the lost angel, who saw God but did not want to contemplate and humbly acknowledge Him; and thus suddenly fled from heavenly glory and, trying to gain equal honor with God, fell into death. These people despise me because their deeds are wicked and their pleasures call for illicit carnal desires. And because they despise me, they do what they will. They set little value on God, and so neglect His command. And therefore, I often condemn them in my indignation to do their full will, and so the life of eternal happiness eludes them as if they counted for nothing. And often they fall short in happiness both in this life and in the life to come, because they are hard and unmoved by the happiness that comes from good. For I forsake the obstinate sinner who perseveres in his evil deeds, but I impart life to one who looks at himself and in pure repentance turns to me from his sins.

"For I am the firmly founded pillar, and I never forsake one who seeks me; one who understands me and intimately and faithfully unites with me will never fall into perdition. But one who forgets me in his mind and in his pride raises himself above me is trusting in himself rather than me; he scorns to have faith in me, counting the Grace of God as nothing. I inhabit his mind like a whirlwind, but he regards me with careless mockery, desperately exalting himself in pride. And because of his pride, not because of the gravity of his sins, he mocks me thus: "What is the Grace of God?" And I will cast him down and slay him and never raise him up by my choice; for he is dead to eternal joy.

"And people who do not have confidence that they can rise from a grave state of sin reject Almighty God and His grace; they despair miserably as if they cannot be saved from the enormity of their crimes, and so they fail and are rejected by me. And they run bitterly into death, and live their eternal death in the lowest part of Hell.

"But now I shall speak of my beloved children, who receive me with open senses and willing mind and clear intellect, and touch me with sighs and tears, and follow me with joy to embrace me. O my flowers, who when they feel my presence rejoice in me, and I in them! They are more sweet and pleasant to me than precious stones and pearls to the people who most fervently desire them. They are to me, indeed, the finest cut stones; for in my sight they are always lovable. I will polish and refine them without ceasing, that they may rightly and fitly be placed in the heavenly Jerusalem, for in their minds they are always feasting with me in goodwill, never sated with my justice. When they feel my touch, they hasten to me like the hart to the water-brook. I often withdraw from them, so that it seems to them that they are without help; this I do that their outer person may not be puffed up with pride. Then they weep aloud and lament, thinking I am offended with them; but it is thus I scrutinize their faith.

"And I still hold them with a strong hand, taking away their pride and forcing them to be ignorant of what they are in their secret good deeds; for thus I will to produce in them the fruits of grief and sorrow. And sometimes I let the Devil try to seduce them with the fiery arrows of impurity and burning fornication, which wound their frail bodies; this I permit that they may be imbued with the inspiration of the Holy Spirit, and so become great messengers, glorious in virtue. They are tested like gold in the furnace, tried by mockery and provocation and set at naught; very often they will be stripped of their substance by robbers, and torn like lambs by wolves in the adversities of popular dissensions. But as sheep scattered by the wolf do not die, so these people do not perish in soul but live more fully, purified by their troubles. For a good tree is watered and pruned and dug about that it may bear fruit, and worms are removed from it lest they eat the fruit. What then?

"Let good people, then, not grow hardened or embittered toward God's justice; let them be mild and prepared to receive every good, cutting off evil from themselves and scrutinizing their works so as to repel the hurtful attacks of their enemies. For before a person feels me in his mind and his intellect knows that I am within him, I am his Head, planting fruitfulness and power within him; I establish in him the strength of the city built on the firm rock. Let every faithful person therefore hear me saying to him:

"O human! Is it proper and fitting that a rational person should be mindless like an irrational beast, which does nothing but what it wants? O wretched people, who refuse to know the great glory that God gave them when He made them in His likeness! But they cannot have their wish and freely do all the evil they desire by right, as if their bodily nature gave them permission; they forget that they have that nature so that they can do good. God in His ordinances established all things justly; and who can oppose Him? What then? Can anyone compare himself with God's ordinance, or compete with Him in wisdom or discretion about anything? And why then do they wish to give up the ability that was given them to act rightly or wrongly? How? When I warn those who understand me with my touch, and they feel my presence, by my help they can carry out their good desires; but those who despise me fall into weakness and evil. But the wicked try to excuse themselves, and claim they cannot do good works, so that they can freely work the will of their outer persons.

"So now, my dearest children, sweeter in fragrance to me than spices, hear me admonishing you. While you have time to do good and evil, worship your God with true devotion. Again, O my dearest children, who are rising like the dawn, and who must burn in charity like the sun; run and make haste, dearest ones, in the way of truth, which is the light of the world, Jesus Christ, the Son of God, Who redeemed you in the last days by His blood so that when you die you may joyfully attain to Him."

And again I heard the One Who was seated on the throne saying to me:

"Those who desire heavenly things must faithfully believe, but not wrongfully examine, the Son of God's being sent into the world by the Father and born of the Virgin. For the human mind, weighed down by the frail mortal flesh and the grave burden of sin, cannot know the secrets of God, beyond what the Holy Spirit reveals to those It wills."

9 The humanity of the Savior appears in the works of the faithful people

So, in a mystical mystery, *the pillar you see on the south side of the wall of the building beyond the pillar of the true Trinity* signifies the humanity of the Savior, Who was conceived by the Holy Spirit and born of the sweet Virgin, the Son of the Most High; for He is the strong pillar of sanctity and holds up the whole edifice of the Church. His humanity is manifested in the ardent faith of its stones, which are the faithful people who work hard by the goodness of the Supernal Father when the Trinity has been revealed to them. For when the Trinity in One God was made known to the believing people, the belief also appeared that the incarnate Word of God must be worshipped as true God with the Father and the Holy Spirit in the unity of the divinity of the One True God.

10   The Incarnation, shadowy to the mind, is known to faith and works

It is a great and shadowed pillar, which protrudes both inside and outside the building. For the great and incomprehensible holiness of the true Incarnation is so obscure to human minds that it cannot be contemplated, except insofar as it can be done by faith. It can be understood in faith and works by those who labor in the divine cult, that is, inside the building; and those who stand idle outside can know it by words and sounds.

And it is so obscure to your sight that you cannot tell its size or height. For My Son came among humans in the mortality of the flesh to undergo death for the people, and thus was in shadow because He was mortal; but He came without any spot of sin, so that His true incarnation exceeds all the power of the human intellect, incomprehensible in the mystical greatness of God's mysteries and incalculable in the might of His divine power.

11   God alone knows who and how many will make up the body of Christ

And between this pillar and the pillar of the true Trinity there is a gap three cubits wide in the wall, as mentioned above. This is to say that the incarnate Son of God, Who is true God with the Father and the Holy Spirit, is now inherent in His members; that is, the faithful people who will be born up till the end of the world and made members of their Head through living works, as miraculously and symbolically you were shown above. But who, how many and what kind of people they will be in the long ages to come, who will adore the Trinity in the Unity of Divinity with faithful and devout worship, resides in the mystery of the ineffable Trinity; for the place of those yet to be born is empty, and the wall of their good works has not yet been built.

But the foundation has been laid, which is to say that they are in God's foreknowledge, and the faith that will save them is already strongly established; and so Man must not hope and trust in anyone except God, and never despair of His mercy, since He is the strong foundation of the faithful soul.

12   All the works of the Son and the Church are in the Father's will

But this shadowed pillar is standing in the same place in the building where you had previously seen, in the celestial mysteries vouchsafed by God from above, a great four-sided radiance of brilliant purity. This radiance, which signifies the secrets of the supernal Creator, was shown to you in the greatest mystery. This is to say that the incarnate Son of God did all His works and suffered all His injuries in the body in the world according to the Father's secret will. That great radiance expresses this, in that its four-sidedness is a symbol of God's mysteries; for many who are born in the four corners of the world are to attain to the knowledge of Christ. So does its brilliant purity, for no darkness can obscure the lucent Divinity; and so here the nature of the supernal and glorious Majesty, the Creator, Who made everything in His profound and mysterious knowledge, is revealed to you in symbols. Thus you see that no one helped that Creator, and no one resisted and opposed Him; He created everything through His Word by His will and goodness. *So in it another radiance shines forth like dawn, with a deep purple light glowing in it, which is a mystical manifestation of the mystery of the incarnate Son of God.* For thus God displays in His secret places the purity of the dawn, which is to say the Virgin Mary, who bore in her womb the Son of the Celestial Father. And the Son shed His purple blood, which glowed with the light of salvation, so that by this secret vision, the Incarnation of the Son is shown to you in mystical obscurity.

13   In Christ all virtues work fully and are openly manifested

But in the pillar, there is an ascent like a ladder from bottom to top. This is to say that in the incarnate Son of God all the virtues work fully, and that He left in Himself the way of salvation; so that faithful people both small and great can find in Him the right step on which to place their foot in order to ascend to virtue, so that they can reach the best place to exercise all the virtues. How? In the fine places which are good hearts, the virtues join in the holy work of perfecting the Son of God in His members, the people who are His elect. And so in Him is the example of perfection for all the faithful who concern themselves with the law of God and try to ascend from good to better. They see the manifestation of the true Incarnation, in which the Son of God was truly shown in the flesh; and that is where the certain ascent to the heavenly places is to be found. Therefore, *you see all the virtues of God descending and ascending, laden down with stones;* for in God's Only-Begotten the lucent virtues descend in His Humanity and ascend in His Divinity.

They descend through Him to the hearts of the faithful, who with good heart and eagerness leave their own will and betake themselves to righteous deeds, as a workman bends down to lift a stone that he must carry to a building site. And they ascend through Him when they offer to God the heavenly works that people have done with rejoicing, that the body of Christ may be perfected as quickly as possible in His faithful members. And so they carry stones to the higher places; these are the winged and shining deeds people do, with their help, to win salvation. For each action is given wings by God to rise above the filth of the human mind and gain bright splendor with which to shine before God; for what flows from the fountain of eternal life cannot be obstructed or hidden. And as a fountain should not be concealed, but in plain sight, so that everyone who thirsts may come to it and draw water and drink, so too the Son of God is not obstructed or hidden from the elect, but is in plain sight, preparing to requite all deeds and show by just rewards which ones are done for the sake of His will. Therefore let the faithful person walk to God in his faith and seek His mercy, and it will be given to him. But those who do not seek it will not find it, as a fountain does not flow for people who know of it but do not come to it. They have to approach it if they want to draw its water. Thus let Man do. Let him approach God through the law God established for him, and he shall find Him, and the bread of life and the water of salvation will be given to him, that he may no longer hunger or thirst. Therefore, *these virtues are going with keen zeal to their work;* for they run zealously to their divine labor like torrents of water, that the members of Christ may shine brighter than the sun and be nobly perfected in splendor and united to their Head. And therefore, as you have heard, they are called God's strongest laborers, because they are always active in the good deeds of the faithful.

14 The seven virtues represent the seven gifts of the Holy Spirit

And among these virtues you see seven in particular whose form and appearance you especially note. This is to say that among all virtuous deeds these seven virtues best designate the seven fiery gifts of the Holy Spirit. For it was by the overshadowing of the Holy Spirit that the glorious Virgin conceived the Son of God without sin, sanctified by these holy virtues; they were clearly shown in God's Only-Begotten and illumine the hearts of the faithful as if in His form. And by this appearance they take their place in the unity of faith, as My servant Isaiah testifies, saying:

15 Words of Isaiah

"And there shall come forth a branch out of the root of Jesse; and a flower shall rise up out of his root. And the Spirit of the Lord will rest upon him; the spirit of wisdom and of understanding, the spirit of counsel and of fortitude, the spirit of knowledge and of piety; and the spirit of the fear of the Lord shall fill him" [Isaiah 11:1–3]. This is to say: The Virgin Mary came forth from the troubles of earthly oppression into the sweetness of moral life, as a person might come forth from a house in which he was imprisoned, not by rising above the roof but by walking in the designated path; or as a trickle of wine is pressed from the winepress, not by spurting up above the winepress but by flowing gently down in its proper channel. And why a branch? Because it is not thorny in its manner, or knotted with worldly desires, but straight, unconnected with carnal lusts; arisen, therefore, from the root of Jesse, who was the foundation of the royal race from which the stainless mother had her origin. And so from the root of that branch arose the sweet fragrance of the Virgin's intact fecundity; and when it had so arisen, the Holy Spirit inundated it so that the tender flower was born from her. How? Like a flower born in a field though its seed was not sown there, the Bread of Heaven arose in her without originating in a mingling with a man and without any human burden; it was born in the sweetness of divinity, untouched by unworthy sin, without the knowledge and utterly without the influence of the devious serpent. Hence this Flower deceived the serpent; He ascended on high and lifted up with Him the sinful human race, which the serpent had seduced and drawn down with him into perdition. And because this Flower was the Son of God, the Spirit of the Lord rested upon Him; which is to say, the Spirit of the eternal Divinity. How?

When Humility was exalted by the ascent of the Flower, scorn and disaster overtook Pride; for the first woman had listened to it when she strove to know more than she should have, but the second woman submitted to God's service and confessed Him, acknowledging herself to be small and humble. And so the Holy Spirit ardently rested on Him in Whom was hidden the surpassing charity that saved the lost people and effaced human crime and wickedness. For the fullness of sanctity was in Him, and the living light shone upon Him, and that light withered the fruit of sin and the evils that followed from it; and in that light the dead were healed, and the banner that conquered and destroyed death was raised. Sanctity was completely fulfilled in Him, because He was conceived with no mixture of sin, unlike human children who are born in many different sins. And when that Flower breathed forth a perfume of justice by deed and word, the Holy Spirit brought forth its fruit in fullness; for the Son of God, now clothed in flesh, clearly showed in His deeds what in time past the Holy Spirit had awakened in human minds by Its inspiration mystically and secretly.

The Holy Spirit is said to have rested on the Flower in a sevenfold manner, as God created all things through His Word in the Holy Spirit and on the seventh day rested from His work. But these gifts go in pairs in their meaning; for body and soul are joined together in twofold love by the unction of the Holy Spirit, yet should work as one in fear of the Lord, since fear venerates charity with trembling and adores One above all. And so the Spirit of the Lord is known by the strong virtues that shine forth from It, as branches grow out from a root; so also there is one God from Whom all good things come and through Whom all things are wisely disposed. And, since the Spirit of the Lord rested upon that Flower, the spirit of wisdom was also with Him; for where the Spirit of the Lord was present, wisdom could not be lacking.

And so the spirit of wisdom and understanding was in Him; for when God created all things by His Word, great wisdom appeared, for it was so diffused in the Word that He was Wisdom. That Word was invisible when He was not yet incarnate, but when He was incarnate, He became visible; the Word, Who was in the heart of the Father before all creatures, by Whom all things were made and without Whom nothing was made that was made, shone forth within time as a Flower, visible as a human being and offering good understanding to all humans by His words. What then? Understanding and wisdom should go together; for Man was created by God with wisdom and should worthily have understood his Creator. Thus, before the Virgin Birth, God was to be understood as God without qualification; and after the Virgin Birth, which brought forth the Flower in the flesh, he was to be understood with amazement as both God and Man. And thus what was previously invisible to the intellect became visible and was seen in the Flower; for He was the tangible reason why Man can now understand God in His actions. How? When a person wisely worships his God, his wisdom is the origin of good works. And understanding follows; for when a person does a good work through wisdom, that work shines forth to others, and they apprehend with joy the sweet scent and taste it has because of him.

And in this virginal Flower counsel follows understanding; for Man, who had understanding, had to be freed by divine counsel. Therefore the spirit of counsel and of fortitude rested upon Him; for the Father held the counsel outside of time that His Word would be incarnate within time, perfecting all His works according to the Father's will and showing in Himself obedience, so that when it shone on people through Him they might learn to imitate Him in their actions.

And so, in the great virtue arising from His Divinity, fortitude arose; but by counsel it lay concealed in Him, that it might the more strongly vanquish the Devil. How? Fortitude rightly follows counsel; for God's counsel destroyed the kingdom of the Devil through the fortitude of His Son. The Son of God, the strong Lion, crushed fatal infidelity by the shining light of faith; for it is by great fortitude that people believe through counsel what they cannot see with their bodily sight. What does this mean? Counsel united to fortitude pierces the hardness of stony hearts obdurate in their evil habits; it so overrides that senseless hardness that the work of the flesh is abandoned and the work of God fittingly performed. And so, in the aforesaid Flower, knowledge accompanies fortitude; for, by the fortitude God gives them, people attain to the knowledge of Him. And in His supernal sweetness, the spirit of piety resided in Him along with the spirit of knowledge. For He knowingly has compassion on human miseries, and is the hope by which people enter into salvation; and He knowingly wiped out the sin of the world in great piety by His death. What then?

Piety is rightly linked with knowledge; for the Son of God fulfilled the will of His Father knowingly and in great piety. For He, the only Son, born of the Virgin, scattered among the peoples the seed of heavenly virtue; and so He made it possible for them to follow the company of the angels in the modesty of chastity, since this virtue arose in supernal piety. And so, in the branch that came forth from Jesse, the virtues of this Flower put forth buds. The first woman had fled from these virtues by consenting to the counsel she heard from the serpent, and the whole human race fell in her and was cut off from supernal joy and glory; but the blossoming of this branch uplifted the human race in knowledge through piety to the holiness of salvation. How? The fortitude that conquers the Devil and is joined to knowledge is inspired by the Holy Spirit when faithful people devoutly acknowledge God with ardent desire and embrace Him eagerly in the very depths of their souls.

And in the virginal Flower piety is followed by fear of the Lord; for when the faithful have piety, they fear the Lord in order to fulfil His commands. And so the fear of the Lord filled that Flower. For He Himself was so full of virtues that there was no room in Him for deathly pride or pleasure in honor or transgression of the Law; he was completely full of fear of the Lord, and never sought what was not His like the first of the angels and Adam, but honored his Father in all His works and offered Him fitting obedience. And thus the fear of the Lord is the beginning of all justice, for it is the end and the beginning of the other virtues; as the seventh day of rest was both the end and the origin of all the creatures. How? Fear releases trembling, and trembling stimulates the growth of the buds of fruitful virtues. And therefore this Flower is full of fear of the Lord; for all the buds of good works are attached to Him and draw their material from Him. And the Flower gives fruitfulness in all virtues, filled as He is beyond all others with their fruit and able to perfect all good things, as the Scripture says of Him:

16 Words of Solomon

"As the apple tree among the trees of the woods, so is my beloved among the children. I sat down under the shadow of him whom I desired; and his fruit was sweet to my palate" [Song of Songs 2:3]. Which is to say: The Son of the Virgin is the sweet Lover in chaste affection; and the faithful soul grasps Him to crown her integrity with His sweet embrace, renouncing an earthly husband. She unites herself to Christ, loves Him with binding certainty and regards Him in the mirror of faith. He is the most beautiful fruit of the fruitful tree; which is to say that the Son of the Virgin comes forth from virginal modesty as its fruit, giving refreshing food to those who hunger and sweet drink to those who thirst. And thus He excels all the trees of the woods, which is to say the human children who are conceived and live in sin, not yielding the fruit He yielded; for He came from God bearing the fruit of the sweetness of life, while others have no fruit or fecundity of their own, but only that derived from Him. How? He gave salvation to the world through his Incarnation; he appeared as the beloved Son of God among the sons of men, who through His fervor flourished and bore fruit, but were not fruitful with His great fullness. For He came from God, all-holy, and was born of a virgin. And why is He beloved? Because he treads underfoot whatever obstructs the faithful soul, which is hastening to the heavenly places.

And therefore the faithful soul most rightly calls Him beloved; for she denies herself in faithful love, and strives after Him with devotion, struggling against carnal pleasures and rebuking herself for her desires. And she is close to Him, like a wife to a husband whom she married willingly and joyfully. And so, when she begins to keep herself chaste and sigh for the Son of God, she says to herself, "I want to overthrow carnal desire and unite with this Bridegroom; He has fired me with ardent desire for Him and so kept me from the opposite fire, and under the shadow of His love I sit down." How? "Because my desire is inflamed by His love, my soul consents to my keeping down the fiery love of the flesh. And therefore His sweetest fruit, which I tasted in my soul when I sighed for God, is sweeter to me than all the sweetness of carnal delights I used to feel." And why sweet? Because He was born of the Virgin, and so has the sweetest savor and the strongest unguent, which He distils like balsam; which is the resurrection unto life, by which the dead have been raised. And that unguent has the healing in it that through His incarnation cleanses the wounds of sin; for the Incarnation is full of sanctity and sweetness and all the virtues of virginity.

Therefore, O Virginity, which by the ardent enkindling produced the greatest fruit, which shone in the star of the sea and fights the savage darts of the Devil and despises all shameful filth, rejoice in celestial harmony and hope for the company of angels. How? The Holy Spirit makes music in the tabernacle of Virginity; for she always thinks of how to embrace Christ in full devotion. She burns for love of Him and forgets the human frailties, which burn with carnal desire; she is joined to the One Husband Whom sin never touched, without any lust of the flesh, but flowering perpetually with Him in the joy of the regal marriage.

17 On the appearance and dress of the aforesaid virtues and what it means

So, now, *you see a resemblance in the aforesaid virtues: All of them, like all the other virtues described so far, are clad, as it were, in silk.* This is to say that each of these shining lights in its own rank prepares a devout unanimity in human minds; and, like the rest of the virtues in God, they have soft garments, which is to say gentleness and affection in judging holy souls and an absence of the thorns or hardness of vice. *Some of them go with white hair and bare heads, and without a cloak;* which is to say that the virtues, which are joined in pure innocence in human minds, are without a veil of evil habits, and are not surrounded by worldly leanings, but entirely flee the influence of vice.

But *the first wears a woman's head-veil and a mantle like transparent crystal;* for she wears the chains of humble subjection to God and throws down the pride of the Devil with supernal care. She cleaves to the merciful Head, Who is Christ, and imitates in lucent purity that humble and pure Priest; and so she is without any taint of sins, restrained and humble and pure as befits the priests of that Most High Priest.

And the second has black hair; which clearly shows that through Christ her Head she cleanses the blackness of human sins.

And the third seems to have a non-human form; for her function is to alarm people and make them tremble in terror. And therefore she does not have a human appearance; for humans often disregard God and forget to fear Him, and she never does.

The first, fourth and fifth are wearing white tunics. For they are surrounded by the garment of innocence, which Adam lost when he transgressed the righteous command; it was recovered for salvation in the white Lily, Which flowered from virginity, Who assumed the work of obedience to God. And that work shines before God as the brightest star in the sky to human eyes.

All have white shoes, except the third, who, as mentioned, does not seem to be in human form. For these virtues are the most beautiful deeds of humans, who nullify in themselves the desires of the flesh, following the most splendid example of their Savior. But one does not resemble a human being, because a human is often careless and forgets himself in arrogance, but she is always careful and never takes refuge in audacity; and so she is the dispenser of just warnings, that the faithful may carefully heed God's judgment. *And the fourth is wondrously shod in shoes of shining crystal;* for she constrains herself by her own will to pursue the shining path of Christ, and chokes death within her by the ardent flame of the Holy Spirit.

But there are differences among these virtues; which is to say that, though they are unanimous in their desire, they work diverse works in people.

18   Humility and her appearance

So *the first figure* designates Humility, who first manifested the Son of God when God, Who holds heaven and earth in His power, did not disdain to send His Son into the world. Thus she *wears a gold crown on her head, with three higher prongs,* because she surpasses and sweetly precedes the other virtues, and so is crowned with the gold crown of the precious and resplendent Incarnation of the Savior. For He adorned her head with this mystery when He became incarnate. The crown is triangular, for the Trinity is in the Unity and the Unity in the Trinity; the Son with the Father and the Holy Spirit is One True God, excelling all things in the height of Divinity. *It is radiantly adorned with green and red precious stones and white pearls.* For the Humanity of the Savior manifests the high and profound goodness of His works; the Son of God wrought them in the greenness of the blossoming of the virtues in His teachings, and in the redness of His blood when He suffered death on the cross to save humanity, and in the whiteness of His resurrection and ascension. And with all of these the Church is lighted and adorned, like an object set with precious stones.

And on her breast she has a shining mirror, in which appears with wondrous brightness the image of the incarnate Son of God. This is to say that in Humility, who stands in the heart of the sacred temple in blessed and shining knowledge, gratefully and humbly but splendidly and permanently, there shines forth the Only-Begotten of God, in all the works He performed in the body in which He showed Himself to the world. And so the noblest impulses of the hearts of the faithful elect are sealed by this figure, who sets up her tribunal in them and rules and directs all their actions. For she is the solid foundation of all human good deeds, as she shows in the maternal admonition already quoted.

19   Charity and her appearance

And *the second figure* designates Charity; for, after the Humility with which the Son of God deigned to become incarnate, the true and ardent lamp of Charity was lighted when God so loved humanity that for its love He sent His Only-Begotten to take a human body. She *is a deep sky-blue like a hyacinth, both in person and in tunic;* for through His humanity, the incarnate

Son of God enlightened faithful and heavenly people, as a hyacinth illumines any object on which it is put down. And so He inflamed them with Charity that they might faithfully assist all the needy, and this virtue is clothed with the tunic of God's sweetness that she may shine upon all people with true light for their devotion, use and profit.

Therefore, *into her tunic two stripes are marvellously woven and incomparably adorned with gold and gems.* These are the two commandments of Charity, which issue from the sweetness of God; they are adorned with His good and noble will as if with gold, and by just works as if by bright gems, by the wonderful gift of the Supreme Giver. So that *one stripe descends to the figure's feet over each shoulder in both front and back;* for she carries those commandments very carefully, the one regarding God as on her right shoulder and the one regarding one's neighbor as on her left. As Scripture says, "You shall love the Lord your God with all your heart and with all your soul and with all your strength and with all your mind; and your neighbor as yourself" [Luke 10:27]. This is to say:

You should love the Lord your God, Who is your Lord because He has dominion over every creature, and Who is your God because He has no beginning but only is, the Creator of all things. For the sake of the love of Him in your heart, you should overcome and throw down your material body, which is exceedingly hard to do, because if the flesh has been conquered, the spirit will reign in you, and then you will understand God in your soul. And then you will wisely keep His commandments, and not fulfil them grudgingly. And thus all the powers of your soul and body will be subject to God; for when the first victory is gained in your body, you will understand God securely in your mind in everything you propose to do. For He is a firm bulwark for you against the snares of your enemies, so that no enemy can surpass His strength; and your mind should contain these things, to confirm and consolidate everything you do.

You shall therefore do these things with all your heart, and all your soul, and all your strength, and all your mind, that nothing may be wanting to you in faith, and you may not consent to anything contrary to God; you shall not waste yourself in matters alien to Him, but collect yourself in the sweetness of His love. You shall also love yourself. How? If you love God, you love your salvation. And, loving yourself in all this, you shall also love your neighbor, who is each faithful person who is joined to you by the Christian name and faith; you shall rejoice in his righteous prosperity and heavenly salvation, and his steadfast preservation in faith, in the same way you rejoice in your own salvation.

And this therefore is the double work of Charity in humans, descending to their very feet, which is to say to the appointed end; and it shows before them in loving God, and behind them in helping other people and thus following Charity. And then Death is rejected, and the people may attain the perfection of life, as Charity declares in her words already quoted.

20 Fear of the Lord and her appearance

And *the third figure* signifies Fear of the Lord, who arose in the minds of the faithful after the Charity God showed humanity when He willed His Son to undergo death for its sake. And this Fear arose that people might understand the heavenly commands more fully and perfectly than they previously had when doing them. Now *you see her in the same form as you did in your previous vision;* for the immutable God, as was declared to you before, must be held in equal and similar honor and reverence in every thing and creature of His. And *she is greater and taller of stature than the other virtues, and non-human in form;* for she above all the others brings people anguish and trembling. They look with sharp vision upon the greatness of the Supreme Majesty and the loftiness of His Divinity, and they grow afraid; for God is to be dreaded and venerated by all people, since they were created by Him and not another. For which reason this virtue does not resemble a human being; for, as was mentioned, she rejects the perverseness that opposes God with evil deeds, and fixes her inner eye on God alone and walks the righteous paths of His will. Thus *she is covered with eyes all over her body, for she lives wholly in wisdom.* For, with the eyes of good understanding, she looks all around her and contemplates God in all His wonders, so as to pick out the right path of good works and bypass the Devil's morass of evil works by that knowledge of God. She shines with wisdom, for she despises the deadly things that harm the spirit; she flees death and abandons iniquity, and wisely builds herself a house in life.

She wears a shadowy garment through which the eyes can look out. For she is surrounded by the severe abstinence that destroys carnal desire in humans; and in that abstinence she looks toward the light of life, in which Man is wondrously brilliant in beatitude. *And she trembles in fear before Me.* For into the hearts of ardent people she infuses anguish and trembling, so that they will always hold in dread the turbulence and weakness of their flesh; and thus they will not slide into sin, or place their confidence in themselves or other people, but in Him Who reigns for all time. And so she avows in her speech already quoted.

21 Obedience and her appearance

And the fourth designates Obedience; for when Fear is shown to Me in reverence, it is next fitting that My commands be obeyed. Thus she *is wearing a snow-white chain around her neck;* for when people forsake the strength of the neck of their own wills and join with the innocent Lamb, My Son, she makes their minds pure by the subjection of faithful obedience. *And her hands and feet are chained together with white fetters;* for she is bound by the purity of true faith to the work of Christ and the way of truth. And she does not act or walk as she wishes, but as God the Ruler tells her, as she demonstrates in her words already quoted.

22   Faith and her appearance

And the fifth designates Faith; for when the people have Obedience, and obey My commands upon hearing them, they will become believers in Faith, and faithfully fulfil in deeds what they learn by wisdom and admonition.

She *has a red chain around her neck;* for she perseveres faithfully and steadily, and is adorned with the martyrdom of blood. So she trusts not in deceptive vanities but in God, and this, as already quoted, she declares about herself.

23   Hope and her appearance

And the sixth represents Hope, who rises to life after Faith and belief in God. Her life is not on earth, but hidden in the heavenly places until the time of the eternal reward, for which Hope longs with her whole desire, as does a servant for his pay or a youth for his inheritance. Thus she *is clad in a pale-colored tunic;* for her trust is as yet pallid, because she has not yet been rewarded, but wearily awaits the coming of her longed-for desire.

But *before her in the air is the cross of the Passion of the crucified Son of God; and toward it she raises her eyes and hands with great devotion.* This is to say that she causes in the minds of the faithful a celestial desire, as if it hovered in the air, for the martyrdom of My Only-Begotten, so that they may raise to Him with humble and sincere minds this inner vision of faith and the glorious results of their labor. And so she says in her prayer already quoted.

24   Chastity and her appearance

And the seventh designates Chastity. For after people have placed their hope fully in God, the perfect work increases in them, and then by Chastity they start wanting to restrain themselves from the desires of the flesh. For abstinence in the flower of the flesh feels strongly, as a young girl who does not want to look on a man nonetheless feels the fire of desire. But Chastity renounces all filth and longs with beautiful desire for her sweet Lover, the sweetest and loveliest odor of all good things, for Whom those who love

Him wait in timid beauty of soul. Thus she *is dressed in a tunic more brilliant and pure than crystal, which shines resplendent like water when the sun reflects from it.* It is brilliant because of her simple intent, and pure because not covered with the dust of burning desire; miraculously strengthened by the Holy Spirit, she is enwrapped in the garment of innocence, which shines in the bright light of the Fountain of living water, the splendid Sun of eternal glory.

And a dove is poised over her head, facing her with its wings spread as if to fly. This is to say that Chastity at her beginning, at her head, as it were, is protected by the extended and overshadowing wings of the Holy Spirit; and so she can fly through the Devil's snares, one after another. For the Spirit comes with the ardent love of holy inspiration to wherever Chastity shows her sweet face.

Therefore too, *in her womb as if in a pure mirror appears a pure infant, on whose forehead is written "Innocence."* For in the heart of this purest and brightest of virtues there lives inviolable, beautiful and sure integrity. Its form is immature because it is simple infancy that has integrity; and its forehead, which is to say its knowledge, shows no arrogance and pride but only simple innocence.

And *in her right hand she holds a royal scepter, but she has laid her left hand on her breast.* This is to say that on the right, the side of salvation, life is shown in Chastity through the Son of God who is the King of all people. And through Him as defender, Chastity confounds the left, the side of lust, and reduces it to nought in the hearts of those who love her. How? She allows no liberty to lust; as a fierce bird snatches a rotting corpse and tears it and reduces it to naught, she rejects and crushes stinking lust in God's sight. And, defeated by her, it cannot survive, as she hints in her words, already quoted.

25   The Grace of God and its appearance

But *at the summit of the shadowed pillar you see another beautiful figure.* This is to say that, by the supreme and surpassing loving kindness of the Almighty in the Incarnation of the Savior, another resplendent virtue was manifested, namely the Grace of God. And it is powerful and full of God, admonishing people to repent, so that all their villainies may be forgiven through it.

It stands bareheaded; for its dignity and glory are revealed to all who seek it. *It has curly black hair;* for the Only-Begotten of God clothed Himself in virginal flesh without a stain of sin in the time of the Jewish people, who were tangled and knotted up in their black unfaithfulness.

And *it has a manly face so ardently bright that you cannot look on it clearly like a human one.* For God's Grace, in the powerful might of Divinity, appeared to give life in life, and it burns so ardently in that glorious Divinity that no human being can see it with inner or outer sight while he is still weighed down by the heaviness of the body. So it does not stand with its secrets revealed to human judgment, but is mysterious; for the judgments of divine grace are hidden.

It is clad in a tunic of purple and black, which is to say that the work of Grace, which burns in charity, leans down over the blackness of sins as if it were clothing people. How? It warns people toward salvation, and lifts them from the mire of sin toward the vision of the light by means of penitence. For, as day puts the darkness to flight, it builds up sinners toward life by taking away their misdeeds through repentance.

This tunic has a stripe of red over one shoulder and a stripe of yellow over the other, which fall to its feet in front and back. For the Grace of God, in its strength and piety, bends down to the faithful and lifts them on high to heavenly places. How? By the two ways of the stripes. It grasps the anguish of the frail flesh, worn out by bloody battle, and the strength of the soul, grown tepid in the body, and draws them up to love of heavenly things by the red and yellow splendor of the Humanity and the Divinity of the Son of God, the most serene Sun. And so the faithful person who is touched by the integrity of Grace can resist his own sinful desires; he can put virtue in front of him and mortify vice behind him, and thus courageously consummate his works and be clothed in them as in lovely and delightful clothes.

And *around its neck it has a bishop's stole, wonderfully adorned with gold and precious gems.* This is to say that Christ, the Son of God, Who is the High Priest of the Father, has the high power of the priestly office everywhere in the world; and so that office should be adorned by the Grace of God with the gold of wisdom and the gems of virtues by the faithful who are His imitators and members. But *a pure radiance so surrounds it that you cannot look at it, except from head to foot in front;* for the Grace of the Omnipotent is surrounded by the serene whiteness of His mercy. In the times before the Humanity of the Savior, Grace was hidden, invisible and unknown, in the mystery of the Divinity; only from the time of His Incarnation down to the last of His members, who will live at the end of the world, does Grace show forth as far as possible to human understanding, openly manifested in its works.

But *its arms and hands and feet are concealed from your sight;* for the true power and deeds and goal of the Grace of God working in humans can be fully known to no one who is weighed down by a body.

And *that radiance around it is full of eyes on all sides, and is all alive.* This is to say that the divine pity, which dwells in the Grace of God, manifests His many mercies and His abundant compassion in the form of many eyes, which look upon the sorrows of the people who try to follow God. And that radiance is all alive to console and save their souls, and does not prepare perdition for them, but life.

And that radiance changes its form like a cloud; for Grace goes before the just, that they may watch themselves and not fall, but follows sinners, that they may repent and rise again. And *it becomes now wider and now narrower;* for to the miserable and weeping hearts of the faithful Grace comes in great abundance and fruitfulness, while in the profligate and hard minds of sinners it often contracts itself to a trickle because of their aridity.

And so God's Grace precedes and follows, touches and warms people, as was said; and those who desire to be the children of God can ardently receive and fulfil its words, despising fleeting things and embracing lasting ones. And so this virtue encourages the children of God to do, in its exhortation already quoted.

But let the one who has ears sharp to hear inner meanings ardently love My reflection and pant after My words, and inscribe them in his soul and conscience.

THE TOWER OF THE CHURCH

449

VISION NINE
The Tower of the Church

*A*fter this I saw, in front of the pillar of the humanity of the Savior, a tower of brilliant splendor, set into the stone wall on the south side of the building so that it was visible both inside and outside the building. Its breadth was five cubits across any radius of its interior, but its height was so great that I could not make it out.

And between that tower and the pillar of the humanity of the Savior there was nothing but a foundation laid, on which the wall had not yet been built. Thus there appeared an empty gap, as mentioned [p. 325], which was one cubit long. And this tower was not yet finished, but was being diligently constructed, with great skill and speed, by a great many workers. Around its summit there were seven bulwarks, built with wonderful strength.

And I saw a ladder, which reached from the inside of the building to the summit of this tower, with a multitude of people standing on the rungs from the bottom to the top. They had fiery faces and white garments, but black shoes; and among them were some who were similar in form but taller and more splendid, who looked at the tower with great concentration.

And then, to the north of the building, I saw the world and the people who descended from Adam going to and fro between the building's shining wall of reflective knowledge and the circumference of the circle that surrounded the One seated on the throne. Many of these people went into the building, between the tower of the anticipation of God's will and the pillar of the divinity of His Word, entering and leaving through the wall of reflective knowledge like clouds, which are diffused here and there. And each one who entered the building was clothed in a white garment. Some of them rejoiced with great joy in the smoothness and softness of this garment, and kept it on; but others seemed bothered by its weight and confining nature, and tried to take it off. And that virtue whom I had previously heard called the Knowledge of God often graciously stopped them, and said to each one, "Consider, and keep the garment with which you are clothed."

And I saw that some of them accepted this rebuke, and though the garment seemed to hinder them, they made a great effort and kept it on; but others scoffed at these words, furiously pulled off the garment and threw it away, returning to the world from which they had come. And there they tried out many things and learned a lot about useless worldly vanities. And some of them at last returned into the building, took up the garment they had thrown away and put it on again;

but others did not try to return, but remained ignominiously in the world, stripped of it.

And I saw that some, who were very dirty and black and acted insane, came from the North and burst into the building; they invaded the tower, carrying on and hissing at it like serpents. And some of them left off this madness and were made pure, but the others persevered in their wickedness and filth.

And I also saw, inside the building facing the tower, seven white marble pillars, completely smooth and round, seven cubits high. They supported a round dome of iron, which rose nicely to a fair height. And on top of this dome I saw a very beautiful figure standing and looking out at the people in the world. Her head shone like lightning, with so much brilliance that I could not look directly at it. Her hands were laid reverently on her breast; her feet were hidden from my sight by the dome. She had on her head a circlet like a crown, which shone with great splendor. And she was clad in a gold tunic, with a stripe on it from the breast to the feet, which was ornamented with precious gems; they glittered in green, white, red and brilliant sky-blue. And she cried out to the people in the world, saying:

1 Words of Wisdom

"O slow people, why do you not come? Would not help be given you, if you sought to come? When you begin to go in God's ways, gnats and flies buzz and hinder you; but take up the fan of the inspiration of the Holy Spirit, and drive them away as fast as possible. You should run, and you should hope for God's help. Show that you are unfeignedly in God's service, and you will be strengthened by His hand."

And on the pavement of the building I saw three other images; one of them leaned against the marble pillars, and the other two stood before her on each side. All of them were directing their attention toward the pillar of the humanity of the Savior and the tower that was being built. She who was leaning against the pillars seemed to be as broad as five people standing side by side, and so tall that I could not take in all her height; and thus she could see everything in the building. She had a large head and clear eyes, with which she was looking acutely into the heavens; and she was as white and translucent as an unruffled cloud. But I could see no other human attributes in her. And she cried out in a voice that rang through the whole building, saying to the rest of the virtues:

2 Words of Justice

"Let us swiftly arise; for Lucifer is spreading his darkness through the whole world. Let us build towers, and strengthen them with heavenly bulwarks, for the Devil is the adversary and opponent of the elect of God.

Lucifer began by wanting and trying to get too much in his glory; and now he wants and tries to get too much in his darkness. For he blows and scatters his malice and wickedness all over, and never ceases. And we are the soldiers of Heaven against him, to conquer him in his malice and wickedness; for otherwise, because of his enmity, people will not be able to be saved in the world. And as he, when he first revolted, tried to resist the Divinity, so too will his imitator, the Antichrist, try to resist the Lord's Incarnation in the last days. Lucifer was thrown down at the beginning of time; Antichrist too will fall, at the end of time. Then it will be known Who is the true God; it will be seen Who He is, Who has never fallen. But as Lucifer had demons as supporters, who followed him from the height of Heaven as he fell to damnation, so even now he has people on earth who follow him to the ruin of perdition. So we virtues are appointed to fight his subtleties and mockeries, which he sends into the world to devour souls; and so we will reduce all his arts to naught in the souls of the just, until he is confounded in every respect. And so we acknowledge God, Who is just in all things, and so must not be concealed but made manifest."

And the first of the figures who stood before this one on each side appeared to be armed; she was arrayed in a helmet, breastplate, greaves and iron gloves, and held an unsheathed sword in her right hand and a spear in her left. And she trod a horrible dragon under her feet, sticking the spear into its mouth so that it vomited forth unclean spume. And she held the sword as if to strike with it, brandishing it vigorously. And she said:

3   Words of Fortitude

"O mighty God! Who can resist or oppose You? The ancient serpent, the devilish dragon, cannot. Hence, with Your help, I too choose to resist him so that no one may prevail over me or throw me down, be he strong or weak, prince or outcast, noble or baseborn, rich or poor. I choose to be the strong steel that makes all the arms to be used in God's wars unconquerable; I am the sharp edge of those weapons, and because of You, O mighty God, no one can dash me in pieces. Through You I arise to overthrow the Devil. Hence I am a sure refuge for weak humans, and give their softness a cutting sword for their defense. O merciful and benevolent God, help the broken-hearted!"

The other figure had three heads; one was in the normal place and one was on each of her shoulders, but the middle one was a little higher than the other two. The middle and the right-hand one shone so brightly that their brilliance dazzled my eyes, so that I could not quite see whether their faces were masculine or feminine; the one on the left was a little bit shadowed, and veiled with a woman's white veil. The figure was dressed in a white silk tunic and white shoes. On her breast was the sign of the cross, about which a great radiance shone like the dawn. In her right hand she held a naked sword, which she laid with great devotion against her breast and the cross.

And I saw written on the forehead of the middle head, "Sanctity," and on that of the right-hand one, "The root of goodness," and on that of the left-hand one, "Self-sacrifice." And the middle one looked at the other two, and said:

4   Words of triple-headed Sanctity

"I spring from holy Humility, born of her as an infant is born of its mother. By her I was raised and strengthened, as a child is cherished and strengthened by a nurse. My mother Humility bears down and conquers all opposition, even that which is unbearable to others."

And the right-hand head looked at the middle one, and said:

5   Words of the right-hand head

"I rise from my root in the lofty-headed mountain Which is God. And therefore, O Sanctity, I must be attached to your body to enable you to stand."

And the head at the left also looked at Sanctity's middle head, and said:

6   Words of the left-hand head

"O woe, O woe, O woe! How could I be so rigid and inflexible as not to conquer myself, O Sanctity, and come to your aid? For if I fled, you could not stand without me. Alas, alas, alas for the neglecter of good! I must root out the painful thorn that would prick me toward perdition, and pluck it out before it is completely buried in me and inflames me with foul corruption. O Sanctity, I seek to evade and break, with God's help, the Devil's entangling snare, that you may freely persevere in your work."

And again the One Who, as described above, was seated on the throne, showed these things to me and said:

7   After the Incarnation a new people built a new wall of virtues

When the Son of God became incarnate, a new people was called and arose, supported by His doctrine of salvation in the Holy Spirit. They were fortified against the fearsome enemy, whom no one can resist without the help of God's grace, by the exhortations of the strong toward blessed virtue. And, with God's help, they were so unconquerable that no art of that seducer could tear them or take them away from God. Therefore, *this tower you see in front of the pillar of the humanity of the Savior* represents the Church. It arose when My Son's Incarnation was accomplished, newly built out of all good works and the lofty strength of heavenly deeds; it is a strong and fortified tower, standing against the Devil and resisting his iniquity.

8 The Church, illumined by Christ's humanity, displays all human knowledge

Therefore *this tower is of brilliant splendor, set into the stone wall on the south side of the building so that it is visible both inside and outside the building.* For the Church is illumined by the steady light of the humanity of the Son of God. To construct the divine edifice, she joins together living stones enkindled by the fire of the Holy Spirit; and thus her part in the work the Supreme Father is doing through His Only-Begotten is manifest both to believers and to unbelievers, to the inner understanding that comes from heavenly knowledge of Scripture and to the outer foolishness of secular affairs.

9 The Church gives all her adornments to her Bridegroom

Its breadth is five cubits across any radius of its interior; for the Church honors the Lamb, her Bridegroom, by giving Him all her inner thoughts and meditations, which ornament her by the inspiration of the Holy Spirit, on what she receives through the five senses. And she also gives Him all the virtues the true Lamb shows her.

10 The human heart cannot comprehend what divine wisdom works in the Church

But its height is so great that you cannot make it out; for the height and depth of divine wisdom and knowledge in the work of the Church is too great to be understood by the fragile mortal human heart.

11 The Church is moving toward perfection but only God knows what it will be

And between that tower and the pillar of the humanity of the Savior there is nothing but a foundation laid, on which the wall has not yet been built; thus there appears an empty gap, as mentioned, which is one cubit long. This is to say that the knowledge of God, that firm foundation, conceals from the Church, the betrothed of My Son, that great praise she will have; for she is not yet radiant in complete perfection, and lies in human hearts without fully flowering in them. But the gap is one cubit long, narrow enough to reach across; for the human senses are in the power of the One True Almighty God, and thus people can know good and evil and grasp through their intellect whatever is useful for them. And this was clearly shown you above.

And this tower is not yet finished, but is being diligently constructed, with great skill and speed, by a great many workers. This is to say that the Church has not yet come to the direction and status she will have; but, with great diligence and industry, she incessantly hastens toward her full beauty through swiftly passing time and by means of her children.

12 The Church is surrounded by the seven gifts of the Holy Spirit

And the tower *has around its summit seven bulwarks, built with wonderful strength.* For the Church is surrounded in her high celestial labors by the seven impregnable gifts of the Holy Spirit; and they are so strong that no adversary can destroy them, or even lift his mind so far as to touch them.

13 The Church is fortified by its doctors, flowering in apostolic doctrine

And *you see a ladder, which reaches from the inside of the building to the summit of this tower.* This is to say that the work the Supreme Father worked through His Son in His divine counsel had many stages by which the Church was set up and progressed. These stages, by the simple unity of the plan for the Church, lead to the height of the secret places of Heaven, strengthening and fortifying the Church as they go.

So *a multitude of people are standing on the rungs from the bottom to the top.* For throughout the Church's progress, from her first betrothal to the nuptial day when she will openly rejoice with her Bridegroom in the full number of their children, the shining apostles stand on the rungs of God's commands, giving light and protecting her from the darkness of infidelity.

14 The doctors of the Church have brought back the erring to true faith

And thus *they have fiery faces and white garments, but black shoes.* For in the minds of these apostolic guides the flame of the Holy Spirit kindled wondrous faith in the One God, so that they were resplendent before God and the world in the bright garment of good works. But they have black shoes, because they walked on the roads of infidelity and the filthy crimes of the unbelievers; and they won them over by their example, and finally, with great difficulty, converted them to the way of justice.

15 The apostles and their successors tenderly care for the Church

And *among them are some who are similar in form but taller and more splendid.* This is to say that the apostles stand out among those defenders of the Church as its first founders; after the Son of God, they built her by their preaching. They and their followers who imitate them had the same ideas, which the apostles preached and their successors believed; but the apostles are outstanding, since they had no predecessors from whom to draw the example of the new grace except the Son of God Himself, from Whose mouth they heard the words of life. And they also surpass the others in glory, because it was they and not the others who saw the splendor of the Incarnation. *And they are looking at the tower with great concentration;* for they are always there to help the Bride of God in divine love and solicitous piety, so that she can continue in perfect strength. As it is written:

16 Words of Solomon

"Your neck is like the tower of David, which is built with bulwarks; a thousand bucklers hang upon it, all the armor of the valiant" [Song of Songs 4:4]. This is to say:

The Incarnation of the strong Lion, the Son of the Supreme Ruler, Who arose from the blooming of the Virgin, is the strongest instrument of the new grace; and so too the strength of your incorrupt faith, O Bride, is set as the sure rampart of the faithful people. How? All your children stand and join themselves into walls around your strength, nourished by the new light that trickles from the pure living Fountain. And in this strong joining they hold you as the neck holds the head to the rest of the body; and so you cannot be destroyed or dismembered, anymore than the victorious weapons of true David could be defeated. How?

The strong tower is the strength of Christ Jesus the Son of God, and in it the conquering hosts of the faithful are tested without defeat. No adversary can boast of prevailing over them, for they hold fast to Christ, true God and Man, through Whom in the Second Coming all your children will gloriously attain adulthood in salvation. To this end the pure Incarnation was foretold by the prophets and adorned by precious gems of virtue. And it was manifested through the world for the salvation of believers through those bulwarks of apostolic doctrine who planted the justice of the True Light, as the following parable shows.

17   Parable on the same subject

A certain lord had a marble city; he cried out upon it with a loud voice, and inscribed writings on its inner walls, from which the scrapings of the stone trickled down. And he spoke a single word to the waters of the sea, commanding them to rise above the mountaintops. And, this being done, he told the flames of the fire to burn on the altars of small tabernacles; and when they did, the tabernacles grew so high that they rapidly overtopped the city. Which is to say:

This lord is the One Whom no other ever excelled in dominion. He alone is over all things and in all things, for nothing is before Him or after Him; and so He is Lord of all. He had in His power this noble city, the company of the prophets, who were strong and constant against the raging tempests of the world. And when the Lord cried out upon them, He filled them with the Holy Spirit, and stirred them up to bring forth His mysteries in obscure words, as a distant sound is heard when the words cannot yet be made out. But the true Word, the incarnate Son of God, followed on the sound of their prophecy. And when the Lord infused their understanding richly with the spirit of wisdom, He inscribed many things in their hearts; and thus they prophesied by their sense of the Spirit the mysteries of God in the present and future, and uttered in the Spirit harsh words against wicked human behavior. And so they moved the hard hearts of the Jews to mildness and compassion and good works.

But after the Word of God became incarnate, the Heavenly Father gave a sign to His apostles, who, though human, were set apart from the common people, like pure streams diverted from the other waters that flow in a plain. He told them to flow forth into the world in a flood of true faith, overturning and wearing away the great divisions of pride and idol-worship, that all by their preaching might know the true God and forsake their infidelity. And when this faith was strengthened in the people, the Provider for all gently spoke to His elect, whose minds glowed with the flame kindled by the glowing hearts of those touched by the fiery tongues of the Holy Spirit. And He told them to despise the world and contemplate celestial life, and not to refuse to be humble and poor in spirit, but to dwell in humility so as to prepare for themselves treasure in Heaven. And those martyrs and virgins and other self-rejecters who did despise transitory things and worked in humility, meditating in lofty zeal on God's wise precepts, ascended in that self-denial to the love of heavenly things. And so in the eagerness of their good works they surpassed the vinedressers who worked in the vineyard of the Old Testament, for they counted themselves as nothing and strove with their whole desire toward Heaven.

And so a thousand bucklers, perfect defenses of the perfected faith, hang from the Son of God. And the first shepherds of the Church follow His example and despise themselves for the hope of Heaven; they pour out their blood to protect the Catholic faith from the fiery darts of the Devil, which wound human souls. And the other elect, who follow them, also form a heavenly militia and take arms to establish the love of God in this world. How? The ancient serpent infused into the first man the evil stench of contempt for God, and so the Devil himself is now pierced with the darts of Heaven: the perfume of the spices of charity and continence, and the fetters of God's commandments, and the yoke of Christ's company. And thus, cast out from the city of God, confounded and trodden down into his clear damnation, he is abhorred by all the faithful.

18   Those who live according to the flesh await the knowledge of God's power

But now *to the north of the building you see the world, and the people who descend from Adam going to and fro between the building's shining wall of reflective knowledge and the circumference of the circle that surrounds the One seated on the throne.* This is to say that by the sin of the first parent the world and worldly people are subject to carnal desires, which are centered on earthly weaknesses and worldly longings. But, for one thing, the knowledge of good and evil has been given them, that they may draw near to God by good and fly from evil; and, for another, God has shown them His power, that they may know they are under His rule and all their deeds are judged by Him.

19   The different kinds of people who enter and leave the Church

Many of these people are going into the building, between the tower of the anticipation of God's will and the pillar of the divinity of His Word, entering and leaving through the wall of reflective knowledge like clouds, which are diffused here and there. For some approach the divine work through reflective knowledge, admonished by the Old and New Testaments and renouncing carnal desires. But some follow their pleasure and go out of it in the same way due to their evil desires; their will for good or evil propels them as swiftly as clouds, and they withdraw, carried passively by their thoughts. *And those who enter the building are clothed in a white garment;* which is to say that those who approach God's work with good will are clothed by His mercy in a pure and shining garment of the true faith that knows God. *Some of them rejoice with great joy in the smoothness and softness of this garment, and keep it on.* For they are imbued with sweet and mild Catholic faith and have a contrite and humble spirit, and they are bathed in inner holiness; so they rejoice with their inner vision in heavenly things, and devoutly do and keep what the Holy Spirit inspires in them. *But others seem bothered by its weight and confining nature, and try to take it off.* For they feel weighed down by a heavy burden and impeded by the difficulty of the path; so they tear and torture themselves inwardly by their restless and bitter habits and forbidden desires, and end by trying to reject faith in works and refusing to listen to the divine precepts. *And that virtue whom you heard called the Knowledge of God often graciously stops them, admonishing them in the words already quoted.* For the Most High God, as you saw, knowing how hard human hearts can be softened, in His mercy inclines Himself to them. He reminds them often to pray to Him and inwardly lament and weep, that He may deliver them from their perilous iniquity, to which they came by the Devil's persuasion. And by this penitence He tells them to return to knowing what good will is, and remembering the garment of innocence they received by the regeneration of the Spirit and water.

And you see that some of them accept this rebuke, and though the garment seems to hinder them, they make a great effort and keep it on. This is to say that, when the Holy Spirit admonishes them and they receive the warning in faith, they choose the path that is harsh and difficult for them; and finally, not letting their weariness make them despairing or apathetic, with great labor they complete it.

But others scoff at these words, furiously pull off the garment and throw it away, returning to the world from which they have come; and there they try out many things and learn a lot about useless worldly vanities. These are the people who hold God's law and justice in derision; in their vain error they strip themselves of the Catholic faith and deny it by wicked works, which lead to death, and turn aside to the worldly vanities that they earlier pretended to leave. And there they use perverse arts to probe into lustful deeds, and so learn the strong savor of the world; and the Devil deceives them into perversions and mockeries. *And some of them at last return into the building, take up the garment they threw away and put it on again;* for they return from the way of error to the divine path, and reject the schisms the Devil had imposed on them. And so they resume the dress of true faith, which they received in baptism and threw away in error when they scorned the true God; and they praise Him again with pure and simple heart. *But others do not try to return, but remain ignominiously in the world, stripped of it.* For they disdain to return to God in pure penitence, and remain despoiled of the garment of innocence and stripped of the good that would come from works of faith. And so, full of the Devil's vicious arts in the evil vanities of the world, they live impenitent till death, and so are confounded both in this world and in the life to come.

20   On simoniacs, and the hidden divine judgment on them

And you see that some, who are very dirty and black and act insane, come from the North and burst into the building; they invade the tower, carrying on and hissing at it like serpents. This is to say that there are wicked people, willful and blithely careless, who are blackened by the Devil's point of view, and so despise God. Therefore, they seek what they desire not through the gift of the Holy Spirit, but inspired and incited by devilish arts. So they come from the direction of Hell and craftily get into the divine edifice; and by secret intrigues and open seizure, they insanely ingest the offices ordained by God by means of execrable, horrible, devilishly black money. And by their mad folly they throw the Church into disorder, and so hiss at her with the deceiving hisses of the ancient serpent. How? With diabolical cleverness they mislead the unwary and conquer them with deadly bribes; and their boastful hissing corrupts the Church, for they are stealing the powers God constituted in her. And because they do these things, they are banished from My sight; I do not recognize them as holders of these offices, for they got them by themselves and not through Me. And so My servant Hosea indicates, saying, "They have reigned, but not by Me; they have been princes, and I knew not; of their silver and their gold they have made idols for themselves, that they might perish" [Hosea 8:4]. This is to say:

People who do their own will set up for themselves whatever their own desires dictate. What is that? Their lustful will, which persuades them that they can rule people by offices they have stolen or seized, though they never asked or got them from or were set up in them by Me. Sometimes I allow this to happen, so that their wills may bring them to judgment, punishing them for not seeking Me. What will it profit them? For it will produce nothing in them but aridity; it is not rooted, and will give rise to a useless weed without a trunk. For fruitless plants spring up easily by themselves from the ground; but fruit-bearing ones must be sown and planted with great labor. And so I sometimes allow a person's earthly desires to blossom, if they have no root in evil, though they also seek no root in good and so will lack summer fertility. I also sometimes allow a virtuous desire, well-rooted in good, to bear fruit in misery; for I love to water with sanctity all that lacks winter sterility. And so the vile often surpass the useful common people in power, as weeds are sometimes taller than useful plants; but these people are appointed only by their own desires, not rooted firmly in My planting or touched by My gift of knowledge. And I permit this to happen by just judgment; for they established themselves by themselves and did not ask Me, and they will answer for it in the judgment.

For these people pervert to their vain opposites the felicity of good doctrine, which should be mentally purified from unworthy unbelief as silver is purified from dross, and the utility of deep wisdom, which should make their faith splendid and show them how to worship, venerate and confess God. How? They turn this felicity to profound infelicity, for they give the reason they have from God over to the insatiable lusts of the flesh as if that stinking and putrid flesh were God. They do not seek to raise their eyes to the God Who made them, but they hold their own will as God, living by what they ordain for themselves. And they do this not to possess the field that bears the crop of eternal life, but to flee it and lose themselves forever in impenitence. That which they worship as God is dead, and so they too are dead, these buyers and sellers of spiritual things who wanted to be something without asking Me. For how can one who insanely usurps power and makes the rational gift of the Holy Spirit a thing to be sold get anything out of the sale? For one who sells his substance to others no longer has the use of it. And how can the buyer use the salvation he bought? For he did not try to receive it from God, but hastened to buy it for money. But God in His righteous judgment allowed him to buy it.

For God, in His anger at certain people, allows them to become thieves; but yet He punishes them for it by a secret judgment now and not in the future. He allows them to be confounded by the very thing they loved in place of the Holy Spirit, so that they will be brought by this disaster to penitence, and return to God for forgiveness. And other people He tolerates and does not afflict in the present, but justly delays His judgment till the future; for they hold their wills in place of God, and so God in future will demonstrate to them what their wills are worth amid torments. And still others He punishes both now and in the future; for they willfully make their brilliant minds vile and contemptible, and imitate the evil deeds of the Devil. He allows some to go this far that their evil may be negated by penitence, and that they may punish themselves bitterly and cast away their wrong like a putrid corpse. But He mercifully stops others from reaching this point; for if they did, they would do things that merited the pains of Gehenna, and would not escape them.

Now if someone dishonors and usurps a chair of power by means of his spiritual father, money—for in that transaction money becomes his bishop —he buys himself perdition, and both he who gave and he who received the money must be cast out of their dignities. For if a person's animal is stolen from him and sold to another, the one from whom it was stolen has every right to demand it back if he finds it, while both he who sold it and he who bought it must give it up. And so too an office that should be held according to My rules is governed strictly by those rules; and if by some secret bribe it is stolen and wickedly given to an alien, the one who put it up for sale and the one who bought it shall both justly be deprived of the use of it. For they have made the temple consecrated to My name a den of thieves. How?

The wisdom and counsel I put into their hearts they have put up for sale in the marketplace, and so they are getting the wages of iniquity by the perdition of others. So they must renounce this traffic with bitter penance or they will answer to Me for it in the unquenchable fire. For one who tries to juxtapose a living dignity, vivified by the Spirit, with the stench of corruption by buying it for dead money will be lost, unless he hastens to repent that perverse presumption. As Peter, the son of the Dove, who deserted all error when enkindled by the Spirit, said to the fleeting whirlwind who tried to absorb the light into hideous blackness:

21   Words of Peter the apostle on this subject

"May your money perish with you, because you have thought that the gift of God could be purchased with money. You have no part or lot in this word; for your heart is not right in the sight of God" [Acts 8:20–21]. Which is to say:

This is money with which you falsely believed you could become the master of a thing alien to you, but which regards you as a servant or as nothing at all. May it go with you into the perdition of the fires of Gehenna if you do not repent, and if you keep the gift of the ardent Holy Spirit, which you purchased with money. For in your transitory wisdom you have thought that you could have for money the enkindling of your soul by the great Searcher of Hearts; and you did not trust to get it by God's gift. But if you repent of this wrong, you must give up what you bought, and hold the money you gave for it as lost; for you tried to buy an eternal thing with mud from Him Who created you from the mud. And as long as you keep this purchase, you will never share in the light of the company of the supernal angels; for by your speech you have revealed your heart's rapacity, coveting a thing not desired by the citizens of glorious eternity. And so your heart in this wickedness is unjust in God's sight, for it wants to have by a money purchase what should be given freely by God. And My just judgment likens those who will not seek this divine concord by the free gift of the Holy Spirit to vain idols. For idols are the work of hands, and have no truth in them, but they are worshipped by the infidels instead of God; and so too those who use gifts not illumined by the Holy Spirit are teachers of deceit. For they do not take an office sighing in their souls as being unworthy of it, but receive it with eager pride from other people, and ignore My will about it.

Therefore, I know not whence they come, and hold them as alien to Me; and if they persevere in their injustice, they are cut off from Me. But if they repent with their whole heart, I will receive them; and the angels will rejoice in them.

22 Offices of power are set up by God, and one who resists them resists God

But, though those who strive after these dignities with perverse ardor act unjustly, and, as mentioned, consent must not be given to their usurpation, nonetheless government itself is good for human welfare and well-ordained by God. And so it must not be stubbornly resisted, but obeyed for love of Me. So let no faithful person who wants to obey God oppose himself to the authority that governs him; for, in keeping and feeding God's sheep, it imitates Him in honor, and must not be destroyed by an alien who is a thief and a robber. So, as no one should oppose God, no one should foolishly resist His authorities.

Therefore, everyone who lives in soul and body should obey the offices superior to him and subject himself to them, whether they maintain corporeal or spiritual justice. Human laws should be guided by fear of the authorities, lest people should turn from the right path and follow their undisciplined wills to become laws unto themselves. This would be going astray from the way of the Lord; for powers from God exist to keep people from straying. How?

Human governments are set up by the inspiration of the Holy Spirit, that through them people may learn to fear the Lord. If people pervert them into anarchy by their wills, God does not will it but only permits it, that these people's twisted wants may be satisfied to their ruin.

And thus the powers of office are inspired by God for human advantage, justly ordained by Him of necessity; for otherwise the people of God would live like flocks without a shepherd, and follow every winding path of disorder. Hence he who resists them out of pride and refuses to obey them in just humility opposes not people but Me, the Creator, Who disposes all things justly. He follows Adam's transgression in so opposing Me, and thus increases the darkness of his condemnation; he is driven out of joy into sorrow. This does not mean a person who humbly refuses his consent to perverse wickedness, for if he does so properly he increases God's justice and does not diminish it; it refers to one who tries to overthrow an office improperly because of his exalted pride. For, as mentioned, these offices were constituted by Me for the advantage of the living; and one who proudly defies them resists My inspiration. Nonetheless, some people, in mad ignorance and forgetting to fear Me, obtrude themselves upon these dignities, and transgress the divine commands by their wicked wills. And, by My just judgment, I let it be as they wish; but they will answer for it in a just judgment, either by severe penance or in the fires of Gehenna.

23   On simoniacs who repent and those who do not

But you see that *some of them leave off this madness and are made pure, but the others persevere in their wickedness and filth.* This is to say that some of them, by divine inspiration, come to themselves out of their wickedness and, by pure and true penitence, earn the right to be cleansed and saved. But others are obdurate and impenitent, and remain in their crafty impurity till the end of their life; and therefore they will die miserably by choking, a painful and cruel death.

24   God gave the gifts of the Holy Spirit to defend and adorn the Church

And you see, inside the building facing the tower, seven white marble pillars, completely smooth and round. This is to say that the Omnipotent Father, Who has supreme power without beginning or end in the perfect round of eternity, has worked for the protection and beauty of the new Bride by manifesting the seven modes of the purifying inspiration of the Holy Spirit, which drive away all adverse storms. *And they are seven cubits high,* because these gifts surpass in strength and height all human intellect, and thus show that He Who created all things must be worshipped in pure faith.

They are supporting a round dome of iron, which rises nicely to a fair height. For these pillars, in their excelling glory, manifest the profound and incomprehensible power of the Divinity; and by their perfect straightness, they protect and support in Heaven the people who, by the gifts of the Holy Spirit, separate themselves from carnal pleasures here below.

25   Wisdom and her appearance

And *on top of this dome you see a very beautiful figure standing.* This is to say that this virtue was in the Most High Father before all creatures, giving counsel in the formation of all the creatures made in heaven and earth; so that she is the great ornament of God and the broad stairway of all the other virtues that live in Him, joined to Him in sweet embrace in a dance of ardent love. And *she is looking out at the people in the world;* for she protects and guides the people who want to follow her, and keeps with great love those who are true to her. And this figure represents the Wisdom of God, for through her all things are created and ruled by God. *Her head shines like lightning, with so much brilliance that you cannot look directly at it;* for God,

Who is terrible or mild to every creature, sees and judges all things as a human eye assesses what is before it, but no human can understand fully the profound mystery of the Divinity.

Thus *her hands are laid reverently on her breast;* this represents the power of Wisdom, which she wisely holds to do her work so that no one can oppose her by craft or might. *Her feet are hidden from your sight by the dome;* for her depths are hidden in the heart of the Father and invisible to humans, and her secrets are naked and manifest to God alone. *She has on her head a circlet like a crown, which shines with great splendor.* This is to say that the Majesty of God is without beginning or end and bright with incomparable glory, and the Divinity is so radiant that mortal sight cannot look on it. *And she is clad in a gold tunic;* which is to say that Wisdom is often thought of as pure gold. *It has a stripe on it from the breast to the feet, which is ornamented with precious gems; they glitter in green, white, red and brilliant sky-blue.* For from the beginning of the world, when Wisdom first openly displayed her workings, she extended in a straight line to the end of time. She is adorned with the holy and just commandments, which are green like the first sprouts of the patriarchs and prophets who sighed in their tribulations for the Incarnation of the Son of God, and white like the virginity of Mary, and red like the faith of the martyrs, and brilliant blue like the lucent love of contemplation, which, by the ardor of the Holy Spirit, mandates love for God and one's neighbor. And so she will proceed even to the end of the world, and her admonition will not cease, but will spread as long as the world endures; and so Wisdom declares, in her already-quoted exhortation.

26   The appearance of Justice, Fortitude and Sanctity

And on the pavement of the building you see three other images. This is to say that these virtues, which do the divine work by treading the earthly underfoot and following the heavenly, are the three instruments by which the Church strives toward eternity in her children: nourishment from their teachers, and the fight of the faithful against the Devil, and the rejection of consent to vice. *One of them is leaning against the marble pillars;* for the doctors of the Church, imbued with the gifts of the Holy Spirit, find rest in their strength. *And the other two are standing before her on each side;* for, as the exhortation says, the love of God and of neighbor resides in the united and cooperative action of these virtues.

Therefore *all of them are directing their attention toward the pillar of the humanity of the Savior and the tower that is being built.* For they are showing by their unanimity that the Son of God, true God and true Man, is devoutly worshipped and adored in the Church; and they are raising up justice, demonstrating the way of salvation in the Old Testament saints, the Most High God and the Incarnation of His Son.

27   Justice and her appearance

So *this figure who is leaning against the pillars* represents God's Justice; for she arises after Wisdom, and by the Holy Spirit works in all the justice of human beings. She *seems to be as broad as five people standing side by side;* for she takes in all five human senses and uses them to abide in the law of God, and she contains and keeps all the commandments God instituted for those who love her. *And she is so tall that you cannot take in all her height, and thus she can see everything in the building.* For she is greater than the human mind, and extends up into Heaven, just as she bent down from Heaven in the Incarnation of the Savior when He Who was the Son of God came forth from the Father, Who is true Justice. And so she looks at all the attributes of the Church, for they are made and contained by her, and thus are the higher bulwarks joined to confirm the strong tower. *She has a large head and clear eyes, with which she is looking acutely into the heavens;* for Justice, in her supreme goodness, has shown people a bright vision in the incarnate Son of God, Who showed Himself in a human body to darkened mortal eyes, teaching heavenly things to save their souls. And *she is as white and translucent as an unruffled cloud;* for she dwells in the purity of the minds of the just, who direct all their desire toward obeying the justice of God, and so is as white as a cloud. And thus she prepares for herself a pleasant habitation in just hearts.

But you can see no other human attributes in her; which is to say that she remains heavenly and not terrestrial, as was declared to you. That is, those human deeds that weigh people down do not cling to her, but only those that lead them to justification and life. For God is just; and she, fighting against the Devil, shows it in her exhortation, already quoted, to the other virtues, which work for God.

28   Fortitude and her appearance

And *the first of the figures who stand before this one on each side* represents Fortitude. For Fortitude arises after God's Justice like a prince under the rule of a supreme king, to repel by righteous and holy labor all traps set for humans by their enemies. For she is armed by the power of Almighty God, and, strong in faith, repels the advances of the Devil. Therefore, she *is arrayed in a helmet,* which is to say with supernal power to save believers; *and in a breastplate,* which is to say in Christian law, which can never be destroyed by the Devil's arrows because it is full of justice; *and in greaves,* which is to say in righteous paths walked by the main teachers in their doctrines; *and in iron gloves,* which are the strong and noble works the faithful do in Christ.

She holds an unsheathed sword in her right hand; which is God's admonitions in the divine Scriptures, whose inner meaning the Son of God disclosed when He opened the Law to show the sweetness of its kernel. *And she has a spear in her left hand;* for when carnal desires for the pleasure of the flesh afflict the faithful, they resist by thinking of the eternal.

And she is treading a horrible dragon under her feet; which is to say that, by the path of righteousness, she subjugates to her power the ancient and frightful serpent. *She is sticking the spear into its mouth, so that it is vomiting forth unclean spume;* for, with the mighty daring of chastity, she pierces the gaping jaws of foul and devilish lust, and wrings from it the burning venom with which it polluted humans.

And she holds the sword as if to strike with it, brandishing it vigorously; for God has displayed the vast strength of His pervasive Word to slay all unfaithful idol-worship and other schisms of unbelief. And so this virtue shows, in her admonition already quoted.

29   Sanctity and her appearance

The other figure signifies Sanctity; for when the Devil is repelled by Fortitude, Sanctity arises in the good to adorn them in the heavenly host. *She has three heads;* for three attributes make up her condition. *One is in the normal place and one is on each of her shoulders;* for God, the Head of all dignities, is to be respected and venerated in prosperity and adversity, in human joy and sorrow. *But the middle one is a little higher than the other two;* for He Who is the Judge of the good and the evil rises in His equity above all things. *The middle and the right-hand one shine so brightly that their brilliance dazzles your eyes, so that you cannot quite see whether their faces are masculine or feminine;* which is to say that Sanctity is so honorable and sweet and full of heavenly grace that the depth of her mystery exceeds the human intellect, and, weighed down by mortality, that intellect cannot discern her liberty or her subjection in Christ, except what is seen in Him Himself.

But the head on the left is a little bit shadowed, and veiled with a woman's white veil. For this perfection, sternly constraining itself for love of God, is anxious and careful to defend itself by God's help when attacked by the Devil and people; and so, in the sighs of faithful hearts, it commends itself humbly to the Supreme Redeemer in the purity and beauty of the Christian fight.

The figure *is dressed in a white silk tunic;* which is to say that she is surrounded by works of sweet and lucent zeal, in which perfect Sanctity imitates My Son. *And she is protected by white shoes;* for she shines brightly in human minds, through the death of Christ and the pure regeneration of the Spirit and water, that they too may imitate His death.

On her breast is the sign of the cross, about which a great radiance shines on her breast like the dawn. For Sanctity awakens, in the minds of believers who lovingly embrace her, the repeated remembrance of the Passion of Christ Jesus. She declares with bright faith that He Who obeyed the Father and suffered so much in His holy human state was born without stain of sin from the beautiful dawn, the Virgin Mary.

In her right hand she holds a naked sword, which she lays with great devotion against her breast and the cross. This is to say that her holy works show how much she loves the Scriptures revealed by the Holy Spirit, which the chosen recall to mind as they sweetly remember the Passion of their Redeemer.

And you see written on the forehead of the middle head, "Sanctity"; for Sanctity is known by the inner face of the soul, full of joy in life and without unworthy shame. *And on that of the right-hand one is "The root of goodness";* for that is clearly the beginning and the foundation of Sanctity unto salvation. *And on that of the left-hand one is "Self-sacrifice";* for she sternly restrains herself from sluggishness, softness and vain earthly pleasures, and adorns herself with the other virtues that she may be perfected and persevere.

And the middle one looks at the other two, and they look at it, and they all consult together for their advantage; for they are strongly united in inner vision and in love, and none of them can last without the help of the others. And so they direct their words and adminitions to people, to help them go forward.

But let the one who has ears sharp to hear inner meanings ardently love My reflection and pant after My words, and inscribe them in his soul and conscience.

THE SON OF MAN AND THE FIVE VIRTUES

VISION TEN
The Son of Man

*A*nd after this, I saw on the summit of the eastern corner of the building, where the shining part and the stone part of the wall came together, seven white marble steps, which rose like an arch up to the great stone on which the Shining One sat on the throne.

And on these steps a chair was placed, on which sat a man of youthful appearance. His face was manly and noble, but pale; he had black hair down to his shoulders, and was clad in a purple tunic. He was visible to me from his head to his navel, but from the waist downward he was hidden from my sight. And he looked on the world and cried out loudly to the people in it, saying:

1 Words of the Son of Man

"O foolish people! You languidly and shamefully shrink into yourselves, and do not want to open an eye to see how good your souls could be. You constantly burn to do the evil your flesh desires, and refuse to be of good conscience and think rightly. It is as if you did not know good and evil, or have the glory of knowing how to avoid evil and do good. Hear Me, the Son of Man, saying to you: O human, regard what you were when you were just a lump in your mother's womb! You were mindless and powerless to bring yourself to life; but then you were given spirit and motion and sense, so that you might live and move and come to fruitful deeds.

2 Man has the knowledge of good and evil and so has no excuse

"So you have the knowledge of good and evil, and the ability to work. And so you cannot plead as an excuse that you lack any good thing that would inspire you to love God in truth and justice. You have the power to master yourself and not want and take pleasure in injustice; you can punish yourself and flee from the illicit lusts you delight in, and so honor My martyrdom by fighting against your burning desires and bearing My cross in your body. And why have you this great power? So that you may avoid evil and do good. And you will answer to Me for your knowledge of good and evil, as you know yourself to be human. But you despise good and do evil, and burn with

473

carnal desire; good seems grievous to you, and evil is easily awakened in you. And so you choose not to restrain yourself, but to sin freely.

"What did I not do for you when I, the Son of Man, suffered on the cross in frail flesh, and trembled in great anguish? Because of that, I require of you a self-martyrdom; you must suffer for the lusts of your flesh and your other unruliness, your illicit desires contrary to My will and the bad actions that come from them. And you cannot excuse yourself by saying you do not know your good from your bad actions.

3   Admonition to the married

"But I do not reject the chaste coupling of legitimate marriage, which was set up by divine counsel when the children of Adam were fruitful and multiplied. But it is to be done for the true desire of children and not for the false pleasure of the flesh, and only by those to whom it is allowed and harmless by divine law, those allied to the world and not set apart for the Spirit. You should love the good you have from Me better than yourself. You are heavenly in spirit but earthly in flesh; and so you should love heavenly things and tread the earthly underfoot. When you do heavenly things I show you a supernal reward; but when you seek to do what is unjust by the will of your flesh, I show you My martyrdom and the pains I endured for your sakes, that you may fight your wrong desires for love of My Passion.

"You have been given great intelligence; and so great wisdom is required of you. Much has been given to you, and much will be required of you. But in all these things I am your Head and your helper. For when Heaven has touched you, if you call on Me I will answer you. If you knock at the door, I will open to you. You are given a spirit of profound knowledge, and so have in yourself all that you need. And, this being so, My eyes will search you closely and remember what they find.

"Therefore, I require of your conscience a wounded and sorrowful heart; for thus you can restrain yourself when you feel drawn toward sin and burn in it to the point of suffocation. Behold, I am watching you; what will you do? If you call upon Me in this travail, with a wounded heart and tearful eyes and fear of My judgment, and keep calling on Me to help you against the wickedness of your flesh and the attacks of evil spirits, I will do for you all that you desire, and make My dwelling-place in you.

4   Analogy of the field

"Now therefore, my child, note how much work and sweat goes into a field before it is sown with seed. But after it has been sown, it brings forth the crop. Attend and consider these things. Do I not refuse to let the earth bring forth a crop without the sweat of labor? But when I choose, it bears so abundantly that people have the fullest sufficiency, or even more; and when I choose, it bears so meagerly that people can hardly survive their hunger, or even pine and die. And so too are people sustained by Me. To a person who willingly and with good heart receives the seed of My word, I grant the gifts of the Holy Spirit in superabundance, as to a good field. One who now receives My word and now refuses to accept it is like a field that is sometimes green and sometimes dried-up. But this person does not perish utterly; his soul suffers hunger, but he has some greenness, though not much. But one who never chooses to hear My words, or waken his heart to good by the admonition of the Holy Spirit or by human instruction, will die completely. You wonder at this, O human, and want to know why.

5 Man must not look into what he is not meant to know

"But, just as you cannot look on Divinity with your mortal eyes, you cannot grasp its secrets with your mortal minds, except insofar as God permits you. Your wavering mind turns this way and that; and as water is evaporated by the heat of a furnace, your spirit is dried up by the turbulence of your foolish mind. For you want to know what cannot be known by the sinful seed of Man. Will you raise your finger and touch the clouds? This cannot be done; and neither can this search into what is not for you to know. As plants cannot comprehend the nature of the earth because they lack sense and intellect, and know not what they are or how they bear their fruit, though in their usefulness they encompass the earth; or as gnats or ants or such small creatures do not seek to rule their own kind, or to know or understand the power and nature of lions or greater animals; so you cannot know what is in the knowledge of God.

"Where were you and what were you doing when Heaven and earth were made? He Who created them did not need your help, nor does He now. Why do you search into God's judgment? You are touched by the rain of salvation from above; show Me how you labor in the field of your heart to cultivate it. If that labor pleases Me, I will give you good fruit; the fruit with its reward shall be according to your labor. Do I give the fruits of the earth without labor? Neither, O human, do I give to you without the sweat I ask of you. For through Me you have in yourself all the means to work.

"Exercise yourself therefore diligently in labor, and you shall have the fruit thereof. And when you have the fruit, you shall have its reward. But now what? Many seek me with a devout, pure and simple heart, and having found Me never let Me go.

6 No one may too quickly come into the way of holiness

"But many joke and play and try to approach Me without mental labor or cogitation. They are unwilling to deliberate their course first, calling on Me and examining the habits of their body; they wish only to seize upon Me like one awaking from deep sleep, and take the way of sanctity by their own will with a sudden and deceiving motion. Some therefore take My yoke on their shoulders by rejecting secular affairs, others by fleshly continence, others by modest virginity; and they think it possible to be what they wish without recognizing what they are and what they are capable of. But they remain unaware of Who made them and Who their God may be, wishing only to have Him as their servant and do their will.

"To the person who tries to unite himself to Me thus vainly, while in his ignorance he does not know Me, I will not give My gift; I will not sow an empty field. Therefore his foot will often stumble. And I say to him: 'O human, why have you not examined the field of your mind, and rooted out the weeds and thorns and thistles? Why have you not called on Me and examined yourself? For before you come to Me you are as one drunk and insane and ignorant of self; you can do no shining deed without My help. And, after seeking Me in inconsiderate haste as if in a dream, you grew weary in My service, and remembered your other dream of habitual sins; and so you returned to your former crimes, insane and ignorant of the good, and deprived yourself of the help and consolation of the Spirit, the Paraclete.

" 'But what was your guide and helper in this? Your fallacious and deceitful mind; it led you foolishly into aridity, without the fruitful memory in your intellect that you can do nothing good without Me. And so what do you have? You will be wretched and empty, and will fall down before Me and before the people and be trodden into the vain dust. If you work against Me, what can you do? Nothing. And with Me, what can you do? The most shining works, which are more splendid than the light of the sun and sweeter to taste than honey and milk to the desiring people. For when you seek Me in your inmost soul, as you were taught through faith in baptism, do I not do everything you desire?'

"But some who should have sought Me out before they fell seek Me, sighing and sorrowing, after they fall. And to them I offer My hand, saying, 'Why did you not seek Me before falling? Where was I, and where did you seek for Me? And when you sought Me, did I reject you?' And I say, 'O human! If you stood on a bridge over deep water, and foolishly boasted and forgot yourself the way you have despised Me in these matters, thinking all things were possible to you and you did not need My help; if then you said proudly, "I choose to avoid this bridge and walk on the water!" would you be acting wisely? If you act so presumptuously and foolishly toward this creation, which was made for your profit, you will perish. But this will not happen, because you have a present and visible fear of the water and of drowning, and are on your guard. Or if you saw a large tree that had been sawn through and was falling, would you not flee to avoid being injured by it? Or if you saw lions or bears or wolves coming your way, would you not for fear hide in the ground if you could? But since you flee thus from physical injury, why do you not flee the cruel death of the soul by fearing your Creator? Have you ever seen or heard of one who could rebel against Me? For he who is not with Me will be dissolved, and he upon whom I fall will be broken in pieces. Where were you when Heaven and earth were created, which go on as they were meant to? But you, who were formed by God's counsel and touched by His illumination, transgress His commands. Oh, great mindlessness! For the sake of the creation that serves you, you despise your God, though you tread the earth and watch the heavens, which fear their Creator and fulfil His commands; this you foolishly do not do, for you choose not to know Him in your thoughts or your deeds, or to look toward Him and know Him as you should.

" 'Therefore, if you do not repent, Hell will justly receive you, for you have imitated the one who was thrown in his obduracy down from Heaven. But if you fall, seek Me with a constant outcry, and I will lift you up and receive you. O human, you sometimes try to touch the highest things, when you cannot understand even the lowest.'

7   How virgins and celibates should draw near to sanctity

"Therefore, hear me when I tell you this. If because of My words you wish to bear My yoke, and renounce secular business or abstain from the things of the flesh, before you come to that, cry out and persevere in seeking Me; and I will help you. And if, touched by My admonition, you wish to imitate Me, recognizing that I was born without male seed in modest virginity as a flower is born in an unplowed field, humbly show Me the field of your mind and speak to Me with a flood of inner tears. And say, 'O my God, I, an unworthy human, do not have it in me to carry out my undertaking to keep my virginity unless you, Lord, help me. For I am guilty of upsurges of burning desire and wallow in misery, wondering about the reason for my weakness. By my own strength I cannot vanquish my taste for the sweetness of the flesh, for I am a tree conceived and born in sins. Therefore, O Lord, give me by Your might the fiery gift that will extinguish this perverse kindling and burning in me, that with righteous breath I may drink of the water of the living Fountain that will make me rejoice in life. For now I am dust and ashes, regarding the works of darkness more than the works of light.' And if you are zealous and constant in this supplication, I will prepare for Myself in you the field Isaac saw in his son, when he said, 'See, the smell of my son is as the smell of a plentiful field, which the Lord has blessed' [Genesis 27:27]. And I will bless that field of Mine in My heart. And as Isaac went on to say, 'Be lord of your brethren, and let your mother's children bow down before you' [v. 29], so too you will be a generation raised above the common people. And I will sow in that field roses and lilies and other perfumes of virtue, and I will water it constantly with the inspiration of the Holy Spirit, and I will uproot what is useless and tear out what is evil in it, so that I may survey it with my eyes and feast them on the greenness and the blossoming of this uncorrupt field.

"But this will be My doing and through Me, not yours or through you, O human. For I am the Flower of the field; as a field engenders a flower without being plowed, so I the Son of Man was born of a virgin without her coupling with a man. And therefore this gift is Mine and not yours, for you were conceived in sins and born of corruption. But if you faithfully ask this gift of Me, you may expect it confidently from Me; I will grant that in the sight of My Father you may participate with Me in virginity. But because of the weakness of your body, you will not have it without suffering from your desires; for your weak human nature will often manifest itself in you, and, since you are flesh of flesh, you cannot escape it.

"But in this you should bear My cross and imitate My martyrdom; you should restrain yourself and conquer yourself through Me, which is always pleasing to Me. For I know you are a fragile vessel, and so I choose to share in and pity your pains. But if, because of those pains, you fall, rise up quickly and do penance from the heart; and I will receive you and save you.

8 Inner continence of mind and examples pertaining to it

"But certain people, deceived by the Devil and obdurate in evil, think they are sanctified if they keep their outer selves from marriage; but they remain uncircumcised in mind and spirit, overflowing with impure thoughts and bringing forth evil in their words and works. They ignore the fact that this is disgraceful; they tepidly keep their bodies intact from fornication, but they reject the virginity of the spirit. Hence they are unworthy in My sight, outside both the physical and the spiritual law; for they have lived according to God's justice neither in the flesh nor in the spirit. They have not kept either the law of marriage, which was appointed for them, or what is more than the law's command, the love of virginity. Therefore they are unworthy in My eyes, and I know not what they are. For I have not seen them either walk in the command of the Law or do more than was commanded them; and they are rejected from My sight. I compare them to waste ground, which brings forth thorns and thistles and useless weeds, though their height and color is that of roses and lilies and the other useful flowers and herbs that have healthy sap and sweet fruit and healing fragrance. And I compare them to copper, which pretends to be gold, but is secretly only an imitation and counterfeit of gold. For in the same way these people masquerade as wise virgins, but are inwardly full of craft and unworthiness.

"Therefore they are also in My sight like a tepid breeze, with no briskness of heat or cold. For their mental heat makes them unfit to persevere in the virginity they began in; and in the cold of secular affairs they cannot proceed as they would like. They do not wander outside the confines of the law like the publicans, or sin within it like the unjust, but are inwardly tepid, neither just nor unjust. But, as the young of unclean animals are cast out before they are conscious of living or grown into strength, so these people are cast into death; for they do not know how to live unto life, or know in themselves the strength of the virtues, which are in the house of wisdom. And so I spew them out of My mouth, for if they remain impenitent they are unworthy of My sight. So now, O human, look into yourself.

9   Analogy of the treasure

"If someone who loved you very much gave you a treasure, and said to you, 'Profit from this, and enrich yourself, that it may be known who gave you this treasure,' you would have to consider very carefully. You would have to ponder on how to make the best gain out of it, and say to yourself, 'I should make the best profit possible with my lord's treasure, that he too may be praised for it.' And after it was thus increased to advantage and you had multiplied it, a good report would come to the ears of the one who had given it to you. And he would think of you because of it, and love you more, and confer greater gifts on you.

"This is what your Creator does. He loves you exceedingly, for you are His creature; and He gives you the best of treasures, a vivid intelligence. He commands you in the words of His Law to profit from your intellect in good works, and grow rich in virtue, that He, the Good Giver, may thereby be clearly known. Hence you must think every hour about how to make so great a gift as useful to others as to yourself by works of justice, so that it will reflect the splendor of sanctity from you, and people will be inspired by your good example to praise and honor God. And when you have justly multiplied it to advantage, this praise and thanksgiving will come to the knowledge of God, Who by the Holy Spirit inspired these virtues in you. And He Himself, in the sweetness of His love, will give you grace to overflowing; He will make you burn yet more for love of Him, so that, strengthened by the Holy

Spirit, you may wisely discern the good and do greater deeds, and ardently glorify your Father, Who gave you these things.

"Let My sheep hear these words, and let those who have the inner ears of the spirit lay hold of them; for it pleases Me that people who know and love Me should understand what to do by the gifts of the Holy Spirit."

And in the eastern part of the building, I saw three figures standing on the pavement before that youth; they stood next to each other, and looked at him devotedly. And, opposite the North, between the building and the great circle, which extended from the Shining One Who sat on the throne, I saw a wheel hanging in the air; in it was a human figure who could be seen from the breast up, looking with penetrating gaze on the world.

And in the southern corner of the building, another figure appeared standing on the pavement inside, turning most joyfully toward the youth. And all these figures resembled each other in the following ways. Like the other virtues I had seen, they were all clad in silk garments. All of them were veiled with white head-veils, except the right-hand one of the three mentioned above, who was bareheaded and had white hair. None of them wore a cloak except the middle one of these three, who had a white one. But they were all clothed in white tunics except the one in the wheel, who had a black tunic, and the left-hand one of the three, whose tunic was pale-colored. All were shod in white, except the middle one of the three, whose shoes were black and painted with different colors. But this was the divergence between them:

On the breast of the middle figure of the three who stood together were two little windows. Above them was a hart, facing the right side of the figure, so that its forefeet were above the right window and its hind feet above the left, poised to run. And this figure said:

10   Words of Constancy

"I am the strong pillar, who cannot be moved by light changefulness; a blast of wind cannot shake me like the leaf of a tree, for I abide in the true Rock, which is the true Son of God. Who can prevail to move me? and who can harm me? Neither strong nor weak, prince nor noble, rich nor poor will ever be able to keep me from persevering in the true God, Who will not be moved forever.

"And I will not be moved, for I was founded on the strongest foundation. For I do not choose to be with flatterers, who are blown here and there and all ways by the wind of temptation, and who are never at rest in constancy but always fall to the lower and worse. I do not act so; for I am set on the firm rock."

And the figure on her right contemplated the hart, and said,

11 Words of Celestial Desire

" 'As the hart pants after the water-brook, so my soul pants after You, O God' [Psalm 41:2]. Therefore, I will skip over the mountains and hills, and bypass the sweet weakness of this transitory life, and with pure heart regard only the Fountain of living water. For He is full of immeasurable glory, with whose sweetness no one can ever be sated."

And the figure standing on the left looked at the little windows, and said,

12 Words of Compunction of Heart

"I always gaze on and think of the true and eternal Light; and neither thought nor desire nor contemplation will make me sated with the perpetual sweetness that is in Supernal God."

And the figure who was opposite the North in a wheel had a blossoming twig in her right hand. The wheel revolved without ceasing, but the figure within it remained motionless. And on the perimeter of the wheel was written, "If anyone serves Me, let him follow Me; and where I am, there also shall My servant be" [*John 12:26*]. *And on the breast of the figure was carved,* "I am the sacrifice of praise in all lands." *And that figure said,*

13 Words of Contempt of the World

" 'To him who overcomes, I will give to eat of the tree of life which is in the Paradise of my God' [Revelation 2:7]. For the fountain of salvation has drowned Death, and poured its stream into me to make me blossom in redemption."

And the figure who stood in the southern corner was so bright of face that I could not look fully at her. She had a white wing on either side, each broader than the figure herself. And she said,

14 Words of Concord

"Who is so strong as to try to oppose God? And who is so audacious that he would dare to strip me naked and corrupt me into shameful hatred and envy? God is just, and alone in power and glory. I want to embrace Him always with pure and joyous face, and rejoice in all His judgments. And I do not want to change, but to remain always in one mind and praise God continually. Therefore neither the Devil nor envious Man could ever weaken me or degrade me to the insanity of deceit, or make me stop persevering in peace and concord. And when the world passes away, I will appear more gloriously in the heavenly vision."

BOOK THREE

After this I looked, and behold, all the pavement of the building appeared like white glass, which shone with a calm splendor. But the splendor of the Shining One seated on the throne, Who was showing me all these things, shone brightly through that pavement even into the abyss. And between the building and the circle where it extended from the One on the throne the earth was visible, sloping downward, so that the building suddenly seemed to be placed on a mountain. And the Shining One seated on the throne spoke to me again:

"The Son of the Living God, born of the Virgin, is the Cornerstone, rejected by those who should have built their salvation on the law of God and refused; for they loved darkness more than light and death more than life. But the Son reigns mightily in those who burn with the touch of the Holy Spirit, tread their outer selves under foot and hasten with full consent to the inner things of the Spirit, in fullness of virtue and good works."

15 God's work in humans is consolidated by the gifts of the Holy Spirit

Therefore, *you see on the summit of the eastern corner of the building, where the shining part and the stone part of the wall come together, seven white marble steps.* For the sevenfold ascent of pure fortitude rises in high justice from the true East, which is the Cornerstone of the divine work, where the two parts of the wall of necessity, reflective knowledge and human deeds, hold to each other in secure repose. This ascent is full of the righteous actions God works and perfects in humans, as He worked on six days and rested on the seventh.

16 God unites the deeds of the faithful to Fear of the Lord

These steps *rise like an arch up to the great stone on which the Shining One sits on the throne;* for every act that is done by the faithful in faith and work is fittingly united by God's providence to the Fear of the Lord, upon which He Who rules all things is enthroned in supreme omnipotence.

17 The Son of God guides those who seek to persevere, and destroyed death

And on these steps a chair is placed, which is to say that the firm foundation of protection is set above the works God works in humans, to guide and help them. And whoever chooses to persevere in Him will not sink into error, for He is the mighty support on which all justice is established.

And on the chair sits a man of youthful appearance. This is the constant ruler, the Son of Man, Who reigns as One God in all justice with the Father and the Holy Spirit. His face is manly and noble, for He is the strong Lion Who has destroyed death and the noble Sinless One Who was visibly born of the Virgin. But he is pale; for He did not seek earthly honor by earthly means, but was gentle, poor and humble with a holy humility.

18 The birth and Passion of the Son of God ended the shadow of the Law

He has black hair down to his shoulders; for the Jewish people did not seek the clarity of faith displayed in the Incarnation of My Son, and so they remained in the darkness of the shadow of the mere outward understanding of the Law, and wasted away in obstinacy and faithlessness. They arose from the head of justice, but they only reached as far as the shoulders of fortitude; and when the perfect work blossomed in the humanity of My Son, they ended in unbelief.

And he is clad in a purple tunic; for He poured out His blood in charity to save people who had perished.

19 God's past deeds for the Church can be seen by people but not the future

He is visible to you from his head to his navel; which is to say that from His Incarnation to the present time the works He has done in the Church have been manifest to the faithful. *But from the waist downward he is hidden from your sight;* for the things that will be in the Church from the present time to the end of time are not for people to see or know, except by divine revelation and Catholic faith. For the great splendor of virtues that will be manifested in people before the last day still lie hidden, unknown to humanity.

20 God looks on humanity with mercy and tells them to imitate the saints

And he looks on the world, because the Son of God directs a merciful gaze toward people, *and speaks* faithful words of warning to them about things past and things to come; He tells them to imitate the heavenly army of saints, flee from the dangers of sin, and fight with great strength to attain supernal felicity and escape the punishments of the wicked.

21 Constancy, Celestial Desire, Compunction, Contempt of the World, Concord

And in the eastern part of the building you see three figures standing on the pavement before that youth; they stand next to each other, and look at him devotedly. This is to say that when justice arose and bore down carnal desire, which occurred when by the decision of the Almighty Father the Son of God appeared in the flesh, these three virtues showed themselves unalterably unanimous in their devotion in the power of the Trinity; and they direct their gaze to the Son, because they desire Him and seek Him in all the faithful. Hence also, *opposite the North, between the building and the great circle that extends from the Shining One Who sits on the throne, you see a wheel hanging in the air; and in it is a human figure who can be seen from the breast up, looking with penetrating gaze on the world.* This wheel is the circle of divine mercy, which fights the arts of the Devil by the secret power of God, and builds a spiritual structure in human minds. It rolls in the air, now touching the power of God's justice and now confirming His work in people. And in it appears Contempt of the World, a Christian perfection, seen as far down as the breast of her fortitude. For this virtue, trusting in God in the severest of struggles, reminds people who are living in the secular world with her penetrating warnings to imitate the example of the Son of God, Who went before them, rejecting worldly things and desiring Him with an unalterable mind. *And in the southern corner of the building, another figure appears standing on the pavement inside, turning most joyfully toward the youth.* For when fallen Man was restored to life and fruitful ardor through the goodness of the Supernal Father, this virtue showed itself openly in sweet affection, trod secular things underfoot and turned toward the Son of God in company of the angels and faithful people. For she blossomed by the power of Heaven in the Incarnation of the Savior.

22　Their appearance and dress

And all these figures resemble each other; for with similar devotion they manifest God in those people who magnify Him in their works. So, *like the other virtues you have seen, they are all clad in silk garments.* For they are equal in power to the other virtues you were truly shown before, and they are equally tending upward toward God in the gentle activity of their sweet work in the faithful.

All of them are veiled with white head-veils; which is to say that they all consecrate themselves before God their Head with great devotion to the pure propositions of the Law, as a wife veils herself before her husband. *Except the right-hand one of the three mentioned above, who is bareheaded and has white hair;* for she manifests herself in strength and felicity through the Heavenly Trinity, not weighed down by any earthly care, and in the purity of her heavenly desire seeks only to depart and be with Christ. *None of them wears a cloak,* for they have been divested of all duties of servitude that might hinder them from the duties of freedom: to gaze perpetually into Heaven and long for God, desiring nothing unless it is separate from earthly things. *Except the middle one of these three, who has a white cloak;* this signifies her perseverance in the divine beauty of the conscious keeping of the blessed Law. For this virtue is wrapped and covered in this work as a person is wrapped in his cloak.

But they are all clothed in white tunics; which is to say that they live in the purity of good works, without the blackness of depraved habits darkened by the villainies and vices of blind infidelity. *Except the one in the wheel, who has a black tunic;* for she moves with the swiftness of divine clemency, and lives amid the deeds whose stringency is difficult for the flesh. *And the left-hand one of the three, whose tunic is pale-colored;* for she is surrounded and defended by God's supreme Majesty in adversity, and protected by the sorrow of the work she does, weeping and wailing and sighing to God. *All are shod in white;* for they glow with the death of My Son and prepare the way of peace in human minds so that those minds can desire celestial things. *Except the middle one of the three, whose shoes are black and painted with different colors;* for she, though she remains under God's protection, bears the divisions of the faithless, who turn aside into black mockery from the way of truth. But she is in the path of righteousness, and trusts in the death of My Son; and so she perseveres in strength and beauty through the many attacks of the Devil and the many tribulations of the human spirit, and makes her way toward heavenly things.

But there is a divergence between them; for, though they are of one mind and join to do their work, each one separately shows her powers over the people subject to her in heavenly fervor and clarity.

23   On Constancy

So *the middle figure of the three who stand together* symbolizes Constancy, who is the pillar and rampart of the virtues who join with her. She reveals herself to people in the center of this number, which signifies the Holy Trinity, showing them that they should be constant in good works. For indeed Christ, Who was God and Man, crowned His works in the world with a good end; and so this virtue is the foundation of the other inner virtues in people, and by her discipline leads them to God. And so *on her breast are two little windows;* which is to say that in human hearts the things of Heaven are manifested in two mirrors of faith. For there must be faith in both the divinity and the humanity of the Son of God, through Whom the virtue of Constancy, perfected by the strength of His righteousness, shall not be removed from people. *Above these windows is a hart, facing the right side of the figure.* For the Son of God is elevated by the belief of the Christian people above the faith that He is God and Man, and in His swiftness, which represents Celestial Desire, He faces the right side of Constancy. For eternal life is to be found by perseverance in good works. Therefore *the hart's forefeet are above the right window and its hind feet above the left, poised to run;* for when He hastened with great suffering to the Passion of the Cross, His course brought Him the salvation of souls and true life to those who persevere. And so this virtue points out, in her already quoted words of avowal.

24 On Celestial Desire

And *the figure on her right* prefigures Celestial Desire, who always looks up to Heaven and moves toward salvation, even as Constancy does not seek the joys of the transitory but desires the felicity of the eternal. She *contemplates the hart;* for she continually longs for the Son of God and His shining work, and cannot be sated with His sweet embraces. And so she affirms in her discourse on her desire, already quoted.

25 On Compunction of Heart

But *the figure standing on the left* indicates Compunction of Heart, and that memory in the mind that bemoans and weeps for its exile with intense contrition. By her blessed lamentations Constancy turns away from the left, the side of the soul's perdition, and hastens from death to life. And so she *looks at the little windows;* for, acting in the hearts of the faithful, she directs all her intention to the Son of God, Who reigns in Humanity and Divinity. And she delights in the sweetness of this continuous vision, as she shows openly in her words, already quoted.

26 On Contempt of the World

And *the figure who is opposite the North in a wheel* indicates the perfection of Christ in Contempt of the World; for the Son of God most clearly shows the fullness of virtue in the rejection of secular things. For He, living among humans, did not pant for earthly things; and so He admonished His imitators to strive eagerly after the heavenly. She *has a blossoming twig in her right hand;* for, in the happiness of a saved soul, she holds fast the fresh and beautiful shoot of blessed virtues, bathed in the breath of the Holy Spirit. And so *the wheel revolves without ceasing, but the figure within it remains motionless;* for the mercy of God bends down to humans and has compassion on their miseries, and so is always available to those who seek it, but the perfection of Christ in Contempt of the World has no instability or fickleness, but always turns to what is immutable.

And on the perimeter of the wheel is written, "If anyone serves Me, let him

follow Me; and where I am, there also shall My servant be." This is to say that
the abundant mercy of God has this quality: Whoever does service to the Son
of God by imitating His example will rejoice in heavenly beatitude, and will
attain to the endless company of the angels.

*And so on the breast of the figure is carved, "I am the sacrifice of praise in
all lands."* For Christ wisely taught disdain for secular things, and imparted
to the hearts of His elect that every faithful soul should venerate and adore
Him with deepest devotion as the sacrifice of the Father, offered on the
wood of the cross. For the voices and tongues of all the faithful continually
make His glory and praise resound through the whole world, thanking Him
for their restoration to life, as this virtue clearly manifests in her already
quoted discourse.

27 On Concord

And *the figure who stands in the southern corner* signifies Concord, who
flies from the madness of the evil spirits and embraces the company of the
blessed angels; for love of God she avoids the quarrels of the faithless, and
longs for the vision of eternal peace. Hence *she is so bright of face that you
cannot look fully at her;* for she is devoid of deadly hate and envy, and so
brings greater glory to human souls than the mortal mind, weighed down by
the frail body, can grasp. *She has a white wing on either side, each broader than
the figure herself;* which is to say that this virtue extends the protection of her
shining goodness to those who tire themselves out in righteous work both in
prosperity and in adversity. Her charity to human beings is broader than the
whole expanse of the multitudes of people who are yet to be born. And when
the world has ended, she will fly above the heaven of heavens in greater glory
than she appears in now; for then nothing earthly and transitory will be
sought, but what is celestial and eternal will be sweetly embraced, and all
glorious and beautiful things will endure while all clouds of injustice are
dispersed. And this is truly predicted in this virtue's words.

28 Good deeds are shown in the strong faith and perfect works of believers

And you see that *all the pavement of the building appears like white glass,
which shines with a calm splendor.* This is to say that the strength of true faith
supports and expands the work and the city of God, shining pure and clear in
its candor and mirror-like simplicity. Faith watches and builds the city of
God with all the works done in her. And so when people begin to do good
works with a calm and bright intention, they touch God; and when they
perfect the works, their souls are saved and they know Him profoundly. For

when the work is accomplished, faith herself shows the devotion with which each soul has sought God.

29 God cast down the ancient serpent by the fortitude of faith

And the splendor of the Shining One seated on the throne, Who is showing you all these things, shines brightly through that pavement even into the abyss. For the grace of Almighty God, Who rules all and manifests to you all the things you are learning in this vision, reduced the Devil to nothingness and the perdition of death through the fortitude of faith. How? When the Son of God charged His faithful to publish to the world the teachings received from Him, God in His power pierced the darkness of unbelief with the pure faith that is in the regeneration of the Spirit and water, and cast down the ancient serpent and the eternal death of perdition he brought into the abyss of chaos.

30 Pagans, Jews and false Christians are expelled from the Church on high

But *between the building and the circle where it extends from the One on the throne the earth is visible, sloping downward, so that the building suddenly seems to be placed on a mountain.* This is to say that between the strong power of Almighty God and the chosen works of His goodness there stand people who deny the true faith and follow the temporal instead of the eternal. Such are pagans, Jews and false Christians; they descend from evil to evil, and, ignoring the teaching of the Catholic faith about the transitory, try in their pleasures to draw out wicked deeds into the deepest sins. But the great and beautiful work of God, in the height of His supreme goodness, shines out clearly amid this dark misery to anyone who seeks it, as the beloved Evangelist John testifies by divine revelation, saying:

31 Words of John on this subject

"And he took me up in the spirit to a great and high mountain; and he showed me the holy city Jerusalem, coming down out of Heaven with the glory of God" [Revelation 21:10–11]. This is to say: The Spirit lifts up the spirit. How? The Holy Spirit, by Its power, draws the human mind out of the heavy flesh, that it may share in the vision of the Spirit, Whose eyes are not obscured by the blindness of carnal pleasure, and Who sees the inner things. What does this mean? The Holy Spirit lifts the human spirit upward to the mountain of heavenly desires, that it may clearly see the works to be done in the Spirit, the great works of God. A thousand deeds of the Devil lie prostrate before these works, and they tower over them as a mountain rises above the level surface of the earth; they have an immovable foundation, like a mountain, which does not leave its place; they are so high that mortals cannot encompass them by their reason, for they surpass the most excelling human wisdom, which springs from minds that are of the earth and earthly.

And thus the work of the Spirit is shown to the faithful and holy soul: The heavenly Jerusalem is to be built spiritually, without the work of physical hands, through work given by the Holy Spirit. The greatness and loftiness of these works of the Spirit are manifest, for that city will be adorned by good works performed by people touched by the Holy Spirit. It will be situated upon a hill, with countless buildings assembled from the most noble of stones: the holy souls in the vision of peace, purified from all taint of sin. And so, with these precious stones it will shine like gold; for wisdom displays her brightness in good people. But where did they come from— these works performed in righteous justice, which adorn the celestial Jerusalem? From the height of Heaven; for, as the dew descends from the clouds and sprinkles the earth with its moisture, good works descend on people from God, watered by the rain of the Holy Spirit. And so the person of faith brings forth good sweet fruit, and attains to the company in the supernal city. And the heavenly works, which descend on humans by the gift of the Holy Spirit, have the brightness of Him from Whom they emanated. How? The glory of God shines in the good works of the just, making Him known, adored and worshipped the more ardently on earth. And through the virtues the holy city is adorned with their ornaments, because people who with God's help do good works worship Him in His countless wonders. And so by this revelation the eyes of the spirit see and know that by the inspiration of the Holy Spirit righteous human works appear before God in the regions of Heaven.

32 God will bring the Church to her consummation and confound the Devil

And so, as has been shown, God works from the East to the North to the West to the South, and brings to that consummation which is the last day, for love of the Church in His Son, all that was predestined before the creation of the world. He produces His work through Himself, and draws it back to Himself confirmed and adorned and completed in the highest perfection. And this is mystically symbolized by the aforesaid towers and virtues. How? When Adam fell, the justice of righteous actions was revived in Noah, surrounded with many miracles, and extended throughout time till the last day. And God did not cease to manifest this by His elect in different times: in the preparation of Noah [east corner], the manifestation in Abraham and Moses [north corner], and the consummation in His Son [west corner].

How? Before time began the desire was in the heart of the Celestial Father to send His Son into the world at the end of time, to save and redeem lost humanity. And the Son, born of the Virgin, fulfilled with a perfect work all things foretold by the Old Testament saints, inspired by the Holy Spirit. It was as when, to perform an action, first the human arm bends and then the hand works. What does this mean? When Adam, by God's just judgment, was cast out of the flowering land, justice first began to move in Noah, like the joint of the shoulder. Then it broadened into more definite manifestations in Abraham and Moses, like the more flexible elbow joint. And finally it came to perfection in the Son of God, through Whom all the signs and marvels of the old Law were publicly fulfilled, and through Whom all the virtues, which will adorn the heavenly Jerusalem in her children, are declared in the regeneration of the Spirit and water, as the hand with its fingers accomplishes and puts the final touches on a work. And thus I perfect My work, to My glory and your confusion, O Devil! I have opposed you by the strength of My arm in the North and the West, and resisted you from the East to the South, as far as the sun's course runs. And in the West I have so undermined you that you are utterly confounded. For in My Church, which is the mountain of fortitude, I do the work of justice and sanctity, and destroy you, O shameful impostor. You wanted My people to be destroyed; and you yourself will be conquered and destroyed utterly.

But let the one who has ears sharp to hear inner meanings ardently love My reflection and pant after My words, and inscribe them in his soul and conscience.

THE END OF TIMES

491

VISION ELEVEN
The Last Days and the Fall of the Antichrist

*T*hen I looked to the North, and behold! five beasts stood there. One was like a dog, fiery but not burning; another was like a yellow lion; another was like a pale horse; another like a black pig; and the last like a gray wolf. And they were facing the West. And in the West, before those beasts, a hill with five peaks appeared; and from the mouth of each beast one rope stretched to one of the peaks of the hill. All the ropes were black except the one that came from the mouth of the wolf, which was partly black and partly white. And lo, in the East I saw again that youth whom I had first seen on the corner of the wall of the building where the shining and stone parts came together, clad in a purple tunic. I now saw him on the same corner, but now I could see him from the waist down. And from the waist down to the place that denotes the male he glowed like the dawn, and there a harp was lying with its strings across his body; and from there to the width of two fingers above his heel he was in shadow, but from there down to the bottom of the feet he was whiter than milk. And I saw again the figure of a woman whom I had previously seen in front of the altar that stands before the eyes of God [p. 169]; she stood in the same place, but now I saw her from the waist down. And from her waist to the place that denotes the female, she had various scaly blemishes; and in that latter place was a black and monstrous head. It had fiery eyes, and ears like an ass', and nostrils and mouth like a lion's; it opened wide its jowls and terribly clashed its horrible iron-colored teeth. And from this head down to her knees, the figure was white and red, as if bruised by many beatings; and from her knees to her tendons where they joined her heels, which appeared white, she was covered with blood. And behold! That monstrous head moved from its place with such a great shock that the figure of the woman was shaken through all her limbs. And a great mass of excrement adhered to the head; and it raised itself up upon a mountain and tried to ascend the height of Heaven. And behold, there came suddenly a thunderbolt, which struck that head with such great force that it fell from the mountain and yielded up its spirit in death. And a reeking cloud enveloped the whole mountain, which wrapped the head in such filth that the people who stood by were thrown into the greatest terror. And that cloud remained around the mountain for a while longer. The people who stood there, perceiving this, were shaken with great fear, and said to one another: "Alas, alas! What is this? What do you think this was? Alas, wretches that we are! Who will help us, and who will deliver us? For we know not how we were deceived. O

493

BOOK THREE

Almighty God, have mercy on us! Let us return, let us return; let us hasten to the covenant of Christ's Gospel; for ah, ah, ah! we have been bitterly deceived!" And lo, the feet of the figure of the woman glowed white, shining with a splendor greater than the sun's. And I heard the voice from Heaven saying to me:

1   The five ferocious epochs of temporal rule

All things that are on earth hasten to their end, and the world droops toward its end, oppressed by the weakening of its forces and its many tribulations and calamities. But the Bride of My Son, very troubled for her children both by the forerunners of the son of perdition and by the destroyer himself, will never be crushed, no matter how much they attack her. But at the end of time she will rise up stronger than ever, and become more beautiful and more glorious; and so she will move sweetly and delightfully to the embraces of her Beloved. And this is mystically signified by the vision you are seeing. For *you look to the North, and behold! five beasts stand there.* These are the five ferocious epochs of temporal rule, brought about by the desires of the flesh from which the taint of sin is never absent, and they savagely rage against each other.

2   The fiery dog

One is like a dog, fiery but not burning; for that era will produce people with a biting temperament, who seem fiery in their own estimation, but do not burn with the justice of God.

3   The yellow lion

Another is like a yellow lion; for this era will endure martial people, who instigate many wars but do not think of the righteousness of God in them; for those kingdoms will begin to weaken and tire, as the yellow color shows.

4   The pale horse

Another is like a pale horse; for those times will produce people who drown themselves in sin, and in their licentious and swift-moving pleasures neglect all virtuous activities. And then these kingdoms will lose their ruddy strength and grow pale with the fear of ruin, and their hearts will be broken.

5   The black pig

And another is like a black pig; for this epoch will have leaders who blacken themselves with misery and wallow in the mud of impurity. They will infringe the divine law by fornication and other like evils, and will plot to diverge from the holiness of God's commands.

6 The gray wolf

And the last is like a gray wolf. For those times will have people who plunder each other, robbing the powerful and the fortunate; and in these conflicts they will show themselves to be neither black nor white, but gray in their cunning. And they will divide and conquer the rulers of those realms; and then the time will come when many will be ensnared, and the error of errors will rise from Hell to Heaven. And then the children of light will be pressed in the winepress of martyrdom; and they will not deny the Son of God, but reject the son of perdition who tries to do his will with the Devil's arts.

And these beasts are facing the West; for these fleeting times will vanish with the setting sun. For people rise and set like the sun, and some are born, and some die.

7 The five peaks and the five ropes

And in the West, before those beasts, a hill with five peaks appears; for in these peaks is symbolized the power of carnal desire. *And from the mouth of each beast one rope stretches to one of the peaks of the hill;* for each of those powers will extend throughout the period in question. *All the ropes are black except the one that comes from the mouth of the wolf, which is partly black and partly white.* For the length of the ropes indicates how far people are willing to go in their stubborn pleasures; but though the one that symbolizes greed is partly black and puts forth many evils, yet some will come from that direction who are white with justice. And these latter will hasten to resist the son of perdition by ardent wonders, as My servant Job indicates about the righteous doer of justice, when he says:

8 Words of Job

"The innocent shall be raised up against the hypocrite, and the just shall hold to his path; and to clean hands he shall add strength" [Job 17:8–9]. Which is to say:

One who is innocent of bloody deeds, murder and fornication and the like, will be aroused like a burning coal against one who deceives in his works. How? This latter speaks of honey but deals in poison, and calls a man friend but stifles him like an enemy; he speaks sweet words but has malice within him, and talks blandly to his friend and then slays him from ambush.

But one who has a rod with which to drive away vile brutes from himself walks in the light of the shining sun on the righteous path of his heart; he is raised up in the sight of God as a bright spark and a clear light and a flaming torch. And so, bearing in himself the strongest and purest works, he puts them on like a strong breastplate and a sharp sword, and drives away vice and wins virtue.

9   The Church will shine in her justice until the time of Antichrist

And therefore, *in the East you see again that youth whom you first saw on the corner of the wall of the building where the shining and stone parts come together, clad in a purple tunic, now standing on the same corner.* For here is the Sunrise of Justice, the Son of Man, manifest to you to confirm the truth afresh through His mysteries and miracles; still presiding over the union of reflective knowledge and human deeds, having shed His blood by the will and goodness of the Father for the salvation of the world. So *now you can see him from the waist down;* for now you see Him in the strength of His members who are His elect, and He will flourish as Bridegroom of the Church, with many obscure signs and wonders, until their number is complete. *And from the waist down to the place that denotes the male he glows like the dawn;* for until the time of the son of perdition, who will pretend to be the man of strength, His faithful members will be perfected in fortitude and He will be splendid in the justice of His righteous worshippers. So, *in the same place, a harp is lying with its strings across his body;* which signifies the joyful songs of those who will suffer dire torments in the persecution that the son of iniquity will inflict upon the chosen, torturing their bodies so much that they are released from them and pass over into rest.

10   The Church's faith will be in doubt until the witness of Enoch and Elijah

And from there to the width of two fingers above his heel he is in shadow. For, from the time of the persecution the faithful will suffer from the son of the Devil until the testimony of the two witnesses, Enoch and Elijah, who spurned the earthly and worked toward heavenly desires, faith in the doctrines of the Church will be in doubt. People will say to each other with great sadness, "What is this they say about Jesus? Is it true or not?"

11   Before the end of the world the Devil will perish and the truth be known

But from there down to the bottom of the feet he is whiter than milk. That is to say that, by the testimony of those same witnesses who await the eternal reward when the son of perdition is defeated, before the world ends the Son of Man will be brilliantly and beautifully seen in the Catholic faith. The truth will be plainly shown in Him, and the falsity of the son of iniquity rejected in every way, as My servant David testifies when he says:

12 Words of David

"The king shall rejoice in God; all they that swear by Him shall be praised; for the mouth of them that speak wicked things is stopped" [Psalm 62:12]. Which is to say: The profound knowledge of the beautiful human language that gives voice to the will and disposition of God is a great measure of human stature; and it makes music at the altar of God, for it knows Him. And when the hissing and gaping of the Devil, which taints human minds with shame, is forsaken in the time of desperation, the blessed will be praised in minds that sing, and they will make a flowing path of words to the pure fountain of the mighty Ruler.

13 When justice grows cold the Church will undergo suffering and persecution

And you see again the figure of a woman whom you previously saw in front of the altar that stands before the eyes of God, standing in the same place. For the Bride of the Son of God is shown to you again, to reveal the truth, always present to the pure prayers of the saints and, as was said before, offering them up devotely to the eyes of Heaven. *But now you see her from the waist down;* for you see her in her full dignity as the Church, replete with the full number of her children, in the mysteries and wonders by which she has saved so many. *And from her waist to the place that denotes the female, she has various scaly blemishes.* This is to say that, though she is now flourishing worthily and laudably in her children, before the time in which the son of perdition will try to perfect the trick he played on the first woman, the Church will be harshly reproached for many vices, fornication and murder and rapine. How? Because those who should love her will violently persecute her.

14 Antichrist will horribly rend the faithful and cruelly tear humanity

And thus in the place where the female is recognized is a black and monstrous head. For the son of perdition will come raging with the arts he first used to seduce, in monstrous shamefulness and blackest wickedness. *It has fiery eyes, and ears like an ass', and nostrils and mouth like a lion's;* for he runs wild in acts of vile lust and shameful blasphemy, causing people to deny God and tainting their minds and tearing the Church with the greed of rapine. *It opens wide its jowls and terribly clashes its horrible iron-colored teeth;* for with his voracious and gaping jaws he evilly infuses those who consent to him with his strong vices and mordant madness.

15   The son of perdition, unable to be gentle, will try to persecute

And from this head down to her knees, the figure is white and red, as if bruised by many beatings; for the son of perdition will try to seduce people by evil deceptions, and at first speak to them flatteringly and gently, but then try cruelly to pervert and force them. And then the Church will know purity of faith in her children, but anguished and bloody terror and the tribulations of many sufferings for herself.

16   The Church near the end of the world will be bathed in righteous blood

And from her knees to her tendons where they join her heels, which appear white, she is covered with blood. For at the time near the end of the world when she must endure assault, until the coming of the two witnesses of Truth who will keep the Church together by their strength, she will suffer most terrible persecutions, and the blood of those who despise the Destroyer will be most cruelly shed. What does this mean? When the son of perdition is strengthened through deceit, and derives confidence from his perverse teachings, the Church, as she hastens on, will be bathed in the noblest blood; and then she will be fully constructed as the celestial dwelling. For you, O streets of Jerusalem, will then shine with the purest gold which is the blood of the saints; the Devil will be extinguished for persecuting the members of the Supernal King, and his great terror will be reduced to naught.

17   We are now in the seventh millennium

But, O ye people who desire to dwell in those streets, flee from the Devil and adore God, Who created you! For in six days God completed His works, and on the seventh day He rested. What does this mean? The six days are the six numbered epochs; and in the sixth epoch the latest miracles were brought forth in the world, as God finished His work on the sixth day. But now the world is in the seventh epoch, approaching the end of time, as on the seventh day. How? The prophets have completed their utterances, My Son has accomplished His will in the world, and the Gospel has been preached openly throughout all lands; and throughout the times of this full number and more years after it, despite the diversity of human customs, the world has remained as it was well-established by Me.

18 Why God now utters new mysteries by the mouth of an unlearned person

But now the Catholic faith wavers among the nations and the Gospel limps among the people; and the mighty books in which the excelling doctors had summed up knowledge with great care go unread from shameful apathy, and the food of life, which is the divine Scriptures, cools to tepidity. For this reason, I now speak through a person who is not eloquent in the Scriptures or taught by an earthly teacher; I Who Am speak through her of new secrets and mystical truths, heretofore hidden in books, like one who mixes clay and then shapes it to any form he wishes.

19 God's warning to the learned not to spurn these words but exalt them

O fruitful and rewarding teachers! Redeem your souls and loudly proclaim these words, and do not disbelieve them; for if you spurn them, you contemn not them but Me Who am Truth. For you should nurture My people under My law, and care for them until the time for their supervision is past, and all cares and labors cease. But from now on the predestined epoch is approaching, and you are hastening toward the time when the son of perdition will appear. Grow therefore in vigor and fortitude, My elect! Be on your guard, lest you fall into the snare of death; raise the victorious banner of these words, and rush upon the son of iniquity. For those who forerun and follow the son of perdition whom you call Antichrist are in the way of error; but as for you, follow the footsteps of Him Who taught you the way of truth, when He appeared with humility and not with pride in the world in the body. Hear therefore and understand.

20 The words of the Holy Spirit to the Church about the last days

For the Spirit speaks to the Church about the time of the final error. In the end of times death shall rush upon the Church, when the accursed, the son of the curse, shall come; and he is the curse of curses, as My Son testifies in the Gospel about the worst city of error, saying:

21 The Gospel on this subject

"And you, Capernaum, will you be exalted up to Heaven? You will go down into Hell" [Matthew 11:23]. Which is to say: O you cave of iniquity, you concealing ditch, with your wings of hypocrisy and pretense! How can you stand on the high place of the walls, when your eyes devour the wickedness of vice, hiding the burning light under a bushel of excrement? You say, "Who is as great as the hypocrite and murderer, since the foolish call him Lord?" Will you have the signs and wonders of Heaven, when you dip your finger in Hell? How? Your works probe the bottom of Hell, and in its voracity you will lie swallowed up; and Hell will vomit forth your stench, so that the world may see the bitterness of death for the destroyer who has destroyed.

22 When the world is dissolved in the elements, the Church will be completed

But a head without a body or other members should not be. The Head of the Church is the Son of God; the body and the other members are the Church and her children. The Church is not yet perfect in her members and her children; but on the last day, when the number of the elect is filled up, the Church will also be full. And on that last day the whole world will be confounded; I, God, will take away the four elements and all that is mortal in human flesh, and in the consummation of the world there will be full joy for the offspring of the Church.

23 The world is in its seventh epoch, and Man cannot know what will follow

For, as was said, God completed His work in six days. Five days represent five numbered epochs; and in the sixth, new wonders were manifested on earth, as on the sixth day the first man was created. And now the sixth number is complete and the seventh has come, and the course of the world is fixed in, as it were, the seventh day of rest. For now that work which the mighty doctors kept sealed in the holy Scriptures is revealed; it is openly expounded in gentle words, like the words of this book, as if on a Sabbath of rest. For there are six days of work and a seventh of rest; there is no other number of days. And what lies beyond cannot be known to you, O human, but is in the keeping of the Father. But you, O humans, have a time to traverse from now on, until the coming of that murderer who will try to pervert the Catholic faith. But as to what may happen then, it is not for you to know the time or the moment, even as you cannot know what comes after the seven days of the week; for only the Father knows this, Who has placed these things in His power. And about the days of the week and the times of the ages, it is not for you, O human, to know more.

24 How God willed His Son to be incarnate

But after five numbered epochs I brought forth heavenly miracles for the world, as in five days the other creatures were created before Man and subjected to Man. For up to then there was a large population of pagans and Jews, and various schisms and evils were increasing among both the Gentile and the Jewish peoples. The Law and the prophets had finished their work, and all the peoples had been tested for evil and for good, before my Only-Begotten took flesh from the Virgin. For I did not will to send Him until all these things had first taken place, so that all justice might be tried by Him and all injustice offended by Him. If My Son had come earlier, it would have been premature, like a person who wants to gather his fruits before they ripen; and if His Incarnation had been postponed until the very end of the world, He would have come too abruptly, like a fowler who catches birds by trickery, so that they know not how they fell into his nets. But My Son came, as it were, at the ninth hour, when the day is turning to evening; when the heat of the day is declining, and the cold is setting in. And so after five epochs of the world, My Son showed Himself to the world as it began to move toward its end. What then? He came and laid bare the essence of the Law, changing its water into the wine of the Gospel; and so He caused floods of virtue to stream forth. And He came opportunely to do this, when the churchly virtues the Holy Spirit enkindled could take root and grow in humans, and the virginity He brought in Himself could bud and flower.

25 Antichrist and his mother

But the insane murderer, the son of perdition, will come soon, when the last times descend and the earth forsakes its course; as if at the time when day departs and the sun goes down to its setting. O My faithful ones, hear this testimony, and understand it with devotion that you may be safe, lest the terror of the destroyer should come upon you unawares and cast you into the ruin of infidelity and perdition. Arm yourselves therefore, and prepare yourselves for the most strenuous battle, forewarned with firm defenses. For the time will come in which this vile deceiver will horribly appear. The mother who will bring this deceiver into the world will be nurtured in vice from her infancy to her girlhood by the arts of the Devil, living among the most abominable people in the vilest of waste places. Her parents will not recognize her, and those with whom she stays will not know her; for the

Devil, pretending to be a holy angel, will persuade her to go away from them and guide her deceptively as he wishes. She will separate herself from all people, so as to conceal herself more easily; and then she will secretly engage in vile fornication with men, though only a few, defiling herself with them with a great appetite for wicked doings, as if her holy angel commanded her to do this deed of shame. And in the burning heat of this fornication, she will conceive the son of perdition without knowing which man's semen engendered him.

And Lucifer, the ancient serpent, will take delight in this turpitude, and by My just judgment will breathe on the embryo and possess it with all his power in its mother's womb. And so that destroyer will issue from the womb of that mother full of the Devil's spirit. Then she will stop her habitual fornications and declare to the unwise and foolish people that she has no husband, and knows not the father of her infant. And she will call the fornication she has done holy, and the people will think and call her holy.

And the son of perdition will be nurtured by the Devil's arts until he comes to full adulthood, always withdrawing from people who know him.

26 Antichrist will learn magic from his mother and God will allow it

And throughout this time, his mother by magic arts of hers will show him both to the worshippers and to the non-worshippers of God, and he will be seen and loved by them. And when he reaches maturity, he will teach a doctrine that is clearly perverse, thus fighting against Me and My elect; and he will gain such strength that in his great power he will try to raise himself above the clouds. But it is by My just judgment that I will permit him to do his will on various creatures. For as the Devil said in the beginning, "I will be like the Most High," and fell, I will lead him to fall in the last days, when he will say through this son of his, "I am the savior of the world!" And as every age of the faithful knew that Lucifer was a liar when he tried at the beginning of time to be like God, so now every person of faith will see that the son of iniquity is a liar, making himself like the Son of God before the last day.

27 The power of Antichrist and the miracles he will seem to do

For he is the evil beast, who kills those who deny him; he will join with kings, dukes, princes and the rich, crushing humility and exalting pride, and by the Devil's arts subjecting the whole world to himself. His power will issue forth like the wind; he will seem to set the air in motion and bring forth fire and lightnings from heaven, and raise thunders and hailstorms, to uproot mountains and dry up water, to take the greenness from forests and give it back again. In many parts of Creation he will display his illusions, in moisture and freshness and dryness. And he also will cause unceasing deceptions in people. How? He will seem to make the healthy sick and the sick healthy, to cast out devils, and sometimes to raise the dead. How? When someone departs from this life whose soul is in the power of the Devil, by My permission he will sometimes perform illusions on his corpse, making it move as if alive; but he is allowed to do this only occasionally, for a very short time and no longer, lest his presumption bring God's glory into scorn. Some people who see this will trust in him; and others will wish both to keep their earlier faith and to win his favor. And, choosing not to afflict these latter too severely, he will bring illness upon them. They will seek medicine from doctors, but will not be cured; and so they will return to him to see whether he can cure them. And when he sees them he will take away the weakness he brought upon them; and so they will love him dearly and believe in him. And so many will be deceived, for they will blind their own inner vision with which they should have regarded Me. For they will use their minds to probe this novelty their outer eyes see and their hands touch, and despise the invisible things that abide in Me and must be understood by true faith. For mortal eyes cannot see Me, but I show My miracles in the shadows to those I choose. No one shall see Me while he remains in a mortal body, except in the obscurity of My mysteries; for so I spoke to My servant Moses, as it is written:

28   Words of Moses on the vision of God

"For no one shall see Me and live" [Exodus 33:20]. This is to say that no one who is mortal shall fix his mortal gaze on the glory of My Divinity and continue to live his mortal life in his corruptible ashes; for he changes with passing time, leaving one life and passing to another, while I, Who established all living things, live without change. And as a gnat cannot live if he plunges into a flame, so a mortal could not remain alive if he were to see the glory of My Divinity. And so I show Myself to mortals in obscurity as long as they are weighed down by their mortality; like a painter showing people invisible things by the images in his painting.

But, O human, if you love Me, I embrace you, and I will warm you with the fire of the Holy Spirit. For when you contemplate Me with a good intention and know Me by your faith, I will be with you. But those who despise Me turn to the Devil, and choose not to know Me; and therefore I too reject them.

29 Dupes of the Devil show omens in creatures, but cannot control them

But the Devil makes sport of these people, and deceives them however he likes, so that they think that what he shows them is true. And the Devil imparts this art of deceiving to those who trust in him, so that they can at will show people by this fallacious art various portents in creatures. But they cannot in any way alter the elements or other creations of God; they simply feign monstrosities like nebulous apparitions to deceive those who believe in them. And as Adam, seeking more than was right for him to have, lost the glory of Paradise, so these people let slip their inner vision and hearing, forsaking God and worshipping the Devil.

30 How Antichrist will deceive his followers and why it will be allowed

And in this way the son of perdition will practice his deceitful arts on the elements, and show in them the beauty and sweetness and delight desired by those he deceives. And this power will be permitted to him for one purpose: that the faithful may perceive in their faith that the Devil has no power over the good, but only over the evil, whose lot is eternal death. For whatever this son of iniquity brings to pass, he will do with power, pride and cruelty, for he has no mercy, humility or wisdom; he will incite people to follow him by his domination and the wonders he shows. And he will acquire for himself many peoples, telling them to do their own will and not restrain themselves by vigils or fasting; he will tell them that they need only love their God, Whom he will pretend to be, and then they will be delivered from Hell and attain to life. And they, being so deceived, will say, "Oh, woe to the wretches who lived before these times! For they made their lives miserable with dire pains, not knowing, alas, the loving kindness of our God!" He will show them his treasures and riches, and allow them to feast as they will, confirming his teaching by deceitful signs so that they think they need not restrain or chastise their bodies in any way. He will command them to observe circumcision and the Jewish laws and customs, but will alleviate for them as much as they want the stronger commands of the Law, which the Gospel, by worthy penance, converts into grace. And he will say, "When anyone is converted to me, I will blot out his sins, and he shall live with me forever." He will throw out baptism and the Gospel of My Son, and scorn all the precepts handed down to the Church. And he will say, with devilish mockery: "See what a madman that was, Who through His falsehoods decreed that the simple people should observe these things!

31 The pretended death of Antichrist, and his accursed scripture afterward

"But I will die for you and to your glory, and rise again from death; and so I will deliver my people from Hell, that you may live gloriously with me in my kingdom, as that deceiver pretended He had done before." And he will tell his beloved ones to run him through with a sword and wrap him in a clean shroud, until the day of his resurrection. And he will delude them into thinking they are killing him, and so they will fulfil his commands. Then he will pretend to rise again, and bring out a writing as if for the salvation of souls, which is really a dire curse. And he will give this to people for a sign and command them to adore him. And if any person of faith refuses for love of My name, he will kill that person in great suffering and torture. And thus all who see and hear this will be struck with great wonder and doubtful amazement, as My beloved John shows, saying:

32 Words of John

"And I saw one of his heads as if slain unto death; and his death's wound was healed. And all the earth marvelled at this beast" [Revelation 13:3]. This is to say:

I, the lover of God's mysteries, saw the deceiver and the accursed surrounding the holiness of the saints with great and countless iniquities, and wearying them with many vices. By his lying arts he will pretend he is pouring out his blood in death and perishing; he will be thought to be stricken and dying, but he will not fall in the body but in a deceiving shadow. And, having deceived people with these false wounds and pretended to be dead, he will pretend to come back to life as if from the sleep of death. And everyone in the world will stand in terrible amazement, horrified at this accursed man as the people were amazed at the great size and strength of Goliath when he appeared before them armed for war.

And so, as you see, the pillars of My elect will be troubled by great wonder, both by their torments and by the perverse and marvellous and horrible signs that the son of perdition will produce; and they will lament in mournful anguish.

33 Enoch and Elijah, and why they are reserved to this time

But then I will send forth My two witnesses, whom I will hold back until this time in My secret will: Enoch and Elijah. They will resist him and bring back those who err to the way of truth. They will show the faithful the strongest and solidest virtues; for when the words of their witness in each of their mouths agree with each other, they will augment the faith of their hearers. For these two witnesses of the truth were reserved so long by Me so that now, when they will appear, their discourse may be held and confirmed in the hearts of My elect, and through it the seed of My Church may survive in humility. And to the children of God whose names are written in the book of life, they will say:

34 Their words to the children of God

"O ye who are righteous and elect and gloriously praise the graces of the blessed life, hear and understand what we confidently tell you. This accursed one was sent by the Devil to lead into error the souls who submit to his commands. We have been secluded from this world and reserved in the secret places of God, so that we have had no human care or anguish; and we were reserved and sent to you now so that we may contradict the errors of this destroyer. See therefore if we are like you in bodily stature or age."

35 Their true signs by which the Antichrist will be cast down

And all who choose to know and confess the true God will follow these two aged witnesses of truth, carrying the banner of God's justice and abandoning the iniquitous error. For they will be radiant with praise before God and the people; they will hasten through the villages and roads and cities, wherever the son of perdition has breathed out his perverse doctrine, and perform in them signs by the Holy Spirit, so that all who see them will marvel greatly. These great signs, founded on the firm rock, will be given to them that they may reject the perverse and false signs. For as lightning kindles and burns, so does the son of perdition do his wicked acts in iniquity, burning the people with his magic arts as lightning burns; but Enoch and Elijah will terrify and cast out his whole cohort with the thunderbolt of righteous doctrine, and so fortify the faithful.

36 How they will be killed by God's permission and receive their reward

But by the consent of My will, Enoch and Elijah will at last be killed by Antichrist; and then they will receive in Heaven the reward of their labors. And the flowers of their doctrine will fade because their voices have ceased in the world; but they will bear fruit among the elect, who will despise the words and the ravings of the Devil's arts because they are set on the hope of a heavenly inheritance. Solomon tells this of a good and perfect person, saying,

"The house of the just is in great strength, but in the fruits of the wicked is trouble" [Proverbs 15:6]. Which is to say:

In the righteous person, the reflection of the eye of God is a vivid inner dwelling where weariness and misery are not; and God's eye sees His wonders in this person like a sword eager to strike. But the deeds that come forth like growing fruits from the proud heart, which erects ruins on its pleasures, will bring only sadness; for the proud heart does not trust in that hope which blossoms in the fullness of Heaven.

37 Antichrist, trying to learn the secrets of Heaven, will strike the Church

Now you see that *that monstrous head moves from its place with such a great shock that the figure of the woman is shaken through all her limbs.* This is to say that the son of perdition, the head of iniquity, will raise himself in his great arrogance and pride from the small error of his inherent wickedness, and seize upon a greater one, wanting to be exalted above all people. And when his deceptions are thus about to end, the whole Church and all her children, great and small, will be cast into extreme fear, as they watch his mad presumption. *And a great mass of excrement adheres to the head, which raises itself up upon a mountain and tries to ascend the height of Heaven;* for the mighty arts of the Devil, which bring with them so much filth, will help the son of iniquity, give him the wings of pride, and raise him to such great presumption that he will think he can also penetrate the secrets of Heaven. How? When he has completely fulfilled the Devil's will, and by God's just judgment his great power for iniquity and cruelty is no longer allowed to increase, he will assemble all his cohort and tell those who believe in him that he wants to go to Heaven. But, even as the Devil did not know that the Son of God was born to redeem souls, so also this worst of men, entangling himself in the evil of evils, will be ignorant that the mighty hand of God is about to strike him a blow.

38 God's power will strike the son of perdition and send him to damnation

And behold, there comes suddenly a thunderbolt, which strikes that head with such great force that it falls from the mountain and yields up its spirit in death. For God's power will manifest itself and destroy the son of perdition, striking him with such jealousy that he will fall violently from the height of his presumption, in all the pride with which he stood against God. And, so ending, he will vomit forth his life in the death of eternal perdition. For, as

My Son's temptations ended when He said to His tempter, "Begone, Satan!" and the Devil fled in terror, so now those trials the son of iniquity inflicted on the Church will be ended by My jealousy.

39 The place of pride will become so fetid that the deceived will turn back

And a reeking cloud envelops the whole mountain, which wraps the head in such filth that the people who are standing by are thrown into the greatest terror. For the impure and hellish stench will fill the whole place of his pride, in which that worst of criminals boiled with such uncleanliness. And, by God's just judgment, neither his beginning nor his end will be remembered, and the people, seeing his corpse prostrate on the ground, voiceless and rotting, will know that they were deceived. *And that cloud remains around the mountain for a while longer;* for the smell of that devilish pride will show it to be impure, and thus the people seduced by him will perceive that stench and that impurity, and turn from their error and come back to the truth. *For the people who stand there, perceiving this, are shaken with great fear; when they see these things the greatest horror will assail them, and they will pour out doleful words and tearful plaints, and admit that they have grievously sinned.*

40 When Antichrist is dead the Church will shine to recall the erring

And lo, the feet of the figure of the woman glow white, shining with a splendor greater than the sun's. This is to say that when the son of perdition is laid prostrate, as was said, and many of those who had erred return to the truth, the Bride of My Son, standing on a strong foundation, will manifest purity of faith and the beauty that surpasses all the beauty of the glories of earth.

41 None but God can know the day of judgment

But after the wicked one has fallen, let no mortal ask when the last day and the dissolution of the world will come. For he cannot know it, because the Father has hidden it as a secret. Prepare yourselves therefore, O humans, for the judgment. But, as was said, the son of perdition and his father the Devil with all his arts will be conquered in the last days by My Son, the mighty Warrior. This was prefigured when the enemies of the mighty Samson were cast down, as it is written:

42   Example of Samson

"And when he strongly shook the pillars, the house fell on all the princes and the rest of the multitude that was there. And he killed many more at his death than he had killed before in his life" [Judges 16:30: cf. chaps. 14–16 complete]. This is to say:

The Son of God, symbolized by the mighty Samson, first wed the Synagogue; to her He gave the secrets of His wonderful doctrine, which were hidden in the Old Testament, and benignly disclosed to her the inner sweetness of the Law, which was stronger than a lion. But the Synagogue deceived Him and caused His secrets to be mocked; she refused to respect His doctrine, but despised it in arrogant pride. Troubled by this, He foretold that the kingdom of God would be taken from the Synagogue and given to another nation. Thus, amid many prodigies and amid a great crowd, He went up to Jerusalem; and the unbelief of those who spread their garments in the way came to an end when He paid by miracles what He had promised those to whom His bride had betrayed Him.

And in this turbulence He left His bride, prophesying that her house would be left desolate. But the father of His bride, Seduction of the Devil, married her to another husband, Infidelity. Then the Son of God sent out wise foxes, the apostles, who burned the standing corn of His enemies with the fire of the Holy Spirit; that is, they turned the precepts of the Law to spiritual insight. And so the Synagogue was burned with her father, which is to say that her perverse infidelity was overthrown.

Then, with great signs and wondrous miracles, He struck down the unbelieving, so that all trembled in great amazement. And they said they feared the Romans would come and take away their country and people; and therefore they gathered their cohort to destroy Him. And He hid on a hill, and prayed, if it might be, for this cup to pass from Him.

But Judas Iscariot betrayed Him, delivering Him into the hands of His enemies. And He concealed the might of His strength, which was in His hair, which is to say in His Father; which was unknown to all the people except those who grasped it by faith, as hair can be grasped on a human head. But He showed the might of His strength afterward, when He chose to suffer, wielding as it were the jawbone of an ass; for He told the daughters of Jerusalem to weep not for Him but for themselves, and thus "killed" them by predicting to them the terror of the evils to come.

And in His affliction on the cross, when He thirsted a fountain of faith sprang from the Gentiles; and He did not blush to drink from it, declaring that so it was accomplished. And when He gave up the ghost, He descended into Gehenna, as it were, to the harlot; and His enemies tried to take Him by setting guards at His sepulchre. But He rose again from death, carrying away the two doors, His special elect and the common people whom He freed from Hell. And so He sought the heavenly kingdom. And then His beautiful Bride, the Church, asked Him diligently after their marriage how she might know His strength. And He revealed His powers to her not all at once, but little by little, discreetly.

How? When the faithful first received the Catholic faith, some of them thought to walk in both the old and the new Law until they had reached perfect rectitude; as it were, in sinews still moist and not yet completely dried. And the Church, still inexperienced, said to the crowds, "This is the strength of my Bridegroom!" And the people, hearing these words, wanted to come and worship God all at once by the book and not to live by the promptings of the Holy Spirit. But His strength is not in this. Then virginity was nobly constituted, which had never before been deemed glorious, like new ropes, which had never bound anything. And this binding strongly held the Son of God, but did not capture Him fully. But the Church raised herself and said, "O my friends, these are the greatest powers of my Bridegroom!" And all at once, with great tumult, many people rushed upon Him, saying, "We have seized Him in His greatest strength!" But not thus is His strength manifested. And then the Church was assured of the seven gifts of the Holy Spirit, as it were His seven locks of hair, fastened by a strong nail to the apostolic preachers as a foundation. And when she had thus woven faith, the Church cried out, "Oh, how strong is my Bridegroom in His seven locks of hair!" And all the peoples who heard her seized upon Him, thinking that this was the limit of His strength. But again, His strength is not thus known.

And so the Church shed many tears, because she did not know the strength of the Holy Trinity; she said that she had indeed seen the humanity of the Son of God, but had not yet perfectly understood His Divinity. Moved by this, He manifested by His beloved John such secrets of the Holy Trinity as it was lawful for Man to know, in the honor of the Father and the fire of the Holy Spirit. And He laid His head upon the heart of His Bride; and He will rest there until the great schisms that will come with the son of perdition. And then His strength will be cut off as He is robbed of His hair; for people in that time will choose to follow the son of perdition and not Him, saying, "How is this, O God, that we see such wondrous miracles?" And so His strength will be cajoled, and true faith clouded with the blindness of infidelity. But when Enoch and Elijah appear, His strength will return to Him; and He will shatter by force all pride and presumption. He will hurl down the son of perdition with all the arts and vices of the Devil; and when the Church and the Christian name have passed over from the present temporal age to eternity, He will crush the Devil's evil much more severely than He did when divine worship flourished in the world within time. What does this mean? That when time ends, the temporal persecutions of the Devil and deeds of human virtue will both cease.

But let the one who has ears sharp to hear inner meanings ardently love My reflection and pant after My words, and inscribe them in his soul and conscience.

THE DAY OF JUDGMENT

513

THE NEW HEAVEN AND THE NEW EARTH

VISION TWELVE
The New Heaven and the New Earth

*A*fter this I looked, and behold, all the elements and creatures were shaken by dire convulsions; fire and air and water burst forth, and the earth was made to move, lightning and thunder crashed and mountains and forests fell, and all that was mortal expired. And all the elements were purified, and whatever had been foul in them vanished and was no more seen. And I heard a voice resounding in a great cry throughout the world, saying, "O ye children of men who are lying in the earth, rise up one and all!"

And behold, all the human bones in whatever place in the earth they lay were brought together in one moment and covered with their flesh; and they all rose up with limbs and bodies intact, each in his or her gender, with the good glowing brightly and the bad manifest in blackness so that each one's deeds were openly seen. And some of them had been sealed with the sign of faith, but some had not; and some of those signed had a gold radiance about their faces, but others a shadow, which was their sign.

And suddenly from the East a great brilliance shone forth; and there, in a cloud, I saw the Son of Man, with the same appearance He had had in the world and with His wounds still open, coming with the angelic choirs. He sat upon a throne of flame, glowing but not burning, which floated on the great tempest which was purifying the world. And those who had been signed were taken up into the air to join Him as if by a whirlwind, to where I had previously seen that radiance which signifies the secrets of the Supernal Creator; and thus the good were separated from the bad. And, as the Gospel indicates, He blessed the just in a gentle voice and pointed them to the heavenly kingdom, and with a terrible voice condemned the unjust to the pains of Hell, as is written in the same place. Yet He made no inquiry or statement about their works except the words the Gospel declares would be made there; for each person's work, whether good or bad, showed clearly in him. But those who were not signed stood afar off in the northern region, with the Devil's band; and they did not come to this judgment, but saw all these things in the whirlwind, and awaited the end of the judgment while uttering bitter groans.

And when the judgment was ended, the lightnings and thunders and winds and tempests ceased, and the fleeting components of the elements vanished all at once, and there came an exceedingly great calm. And then the elect became more *splendid than the splendor of the sun; and with great joy they made their way toward Heaven with the Son of God and the blessed armies of the angels. And at the same time the reprobate were forced with great howling toward the infernal regions with the Devil and his angels; and so Heaven received the elect, and Hell swallowed up the reprobate. And at once such great joy and praise arose in Heaven, and such great misery and howling in Hell, as were beyond human power to utter. And all the elements shone calm and resplendent, as if a black skin had been taken from them; so that fire no longer had its raging heat, or air density, or water turbulence, or earth shakiness. And the sun, moon and stars sparkled in the firmament like great ornaments, remaining fixed and not moving in orbit, so that they no longer distinguished day from night. And so there was no night, but day. And it was finished.*

And again I heard the voice from Heaven, saying to me:

1   In the last days the world will be dissolved in disasters like a dying man

These mysteries manifest the last days, in which time will be transmuted into the eternity of perpetual light. For the last days will be troubled by many dangers, and the end of the world will be prefigured by many signs. For, as you see, *on that last day the whole world will be agitated by terrors and shaken by tempests, so that whatever is fleeting and mortal in it will be ended.* For the course of the world is now complete, and it cannot last longer, but will be consummated as God wills. For as a person who is to die is captured and laid low by many infirmities, and in the hour of his death suffers great pain in his dissolution, so too the greatest adversities will precede the end of the world and at last dissolve it in terror. For the elements will then display their terrors, because they will not be able to do so afterward.

2   All creation will be moved and purified of all that is mortal in it

And so, at this consummation, *the elements are unloosed by a sudden and unexpected movement:* all creatures are set into violent motion, fire bursts out, the air dissolves, water runs off, the earth is shaken, lightnings burn, thunders crash, mountains are broken, forests fall, and whatever in air or water or earth is mortal gives up its life. For the fire displaces all the air, and the water engulfs all the earth; and thus all things are purified, and whatever was foul in the world vanishes as if it had never been, as salt disappears when it is put into water.

3 The bodies of the dead will rise again in their wholeness and gender

And when, as you saw, the divine command to rise again resounds, the bones of the dead, wherever they may be, are brought together in one moment and covered with their flesh. They will not be hindered by anything; but if they were consumed by fire or water, or eaten by birds or beasts, they will be speedily restored. And so the earth will yield them up as salt is extracted from water; for My eye knows all things, and nothing can be hidden from Me. And so all people will rise again in the twinkling of an eye, *in soul and body, with no deformity or mutilation but intact in body and in gender; and the elect will shine with the brightness of their good works, but the reprobate will bear the blackness of their deeds of misery.* Thus their works will not there be concealed, but will appear in them openly.

4 The risen who are signed and unsigned

And some of them are sealed with the sign of faith, but some are not; and the consciences of some who have faith shine with the radiance of wisdom, but the consciences of others are murky from their neglect. And thus they are clearly distinguished; for the former have done the works of faith, but the latter have extinguished it in themselves. And those who do not have the sign of faith are those who chose not to know the living and true God either in the old Law or in the new Grace.

5 The Son will come to the judgment in human form

And then the Son of God, in the human form He had at His Passion when He suffered by the will of the Father to save the human race, will come to judge it, surrounded by the celestial army; He will be in the brightness of eternal life, but in the cloud that hides celestial glory from the reprobate. For the Father vouchsafed to Him the judging of the visible things of the world, because He had lived visibly in the world; as He Himself shows in the Gospel, saying:

6 The Gospel on this subject

"And He has given Him power to judge, because He is the Son of Man" [John 5:27]. Which is to say:

The Father has borne witness to His Son. What does this mean? The Father gave power to the Son, because He remained with the Father in divinity but received humanity from a mother; and, because He is human, He received also from the Father that every creature should feel Him as the Son of God, for all creatures were created and formed by God. And therefore all deeds will be judged by the Son, whatever their nobility or baseness, and He will put them in their proper order. For, as He was a man palpable and visible in the world, He can justly distinguish all that is visible in the world. And He will appear in His power of judging terrible to the unjust but gentle to the just, and judge them so that the very elements will feel the purgation.

7 The signed will be taken up easily to meet their Judge

And those who are signed are taken up to meet the Just Judge not with difficulty but with great speed, so that in them, who had faith in God, the works of faith may clearly be seen. And, as was shown you, *the good are separated from the bad,* for their works are dissimilar. For here it is apparent how both the bad and the good have sought God, in infancy and childhood and youth and old age.

8 All God's flowers, the great heroes of the Church, will appear radiant

And here all the flowers of My Son will shine out in radiance; that is to say, the patriarchs and prophets who lived before His Incarnation, the apostles who lived with Him in the world, the martyrs, confessors, virgins and widows who have faithfully imitated Him, the holders of high office, both secular and spiritual, in My Church, and the anchorites and monks who chastised and mortified their flesh and imitated the humility and charity of the angels in their garments, thus belittling themselves for My Son's name. Those who seek Me in the contemplative life because they think that life is more glorious than another are as nothing to Me; but any who seek Me in humility in that life because the Holy Spirit inspired them to do so, I will put in the first ranks in the celestial homeland.

9 Amid the silence of Heaven, the Son will give sentence on all

Then the heavens will subdue their praises and remain awhile in silence, while the Son of God pronounces judicial sentence both on the just and on the unjust. And they will give ear with reverence and honor to how He decides; and *He will gently grant supernal joys to the just, and terribly consign the unjust to the pains of Hell. And there will be no further excuses or questions about human works,* for here the consciences of both the good and the bad are naked and revealed.

10   Why the good and the bad need to be judged

Now the just, who will receive the words of the most equitable Judge, have indeed done many good works, but while they lived in the world they did not act with fullness of perfection, and therefore their deeds must now be judged. And the unjust, who will suffer a severe judgment against them, have indeed done much evil; but they did not act in ignorance of the Divine Majesty, in the wicked unbelief that would damn them without judgment. And so they will not escape the Judge's sentence, for all things must be weighed equitably.

11   Unbelievers are already judged and so will not come to the judgment

But those who are not signed in faith, because they did not believe in God, *will tarry in the North, the region of perdition, with the Devil's band, and not come to this judgment. But they will see it all in obscurity and await its end, groaning deeply* within themselves because they persevered in unbelief and did not know the true God. For they neither worshiped the living God in the Old Testament before the institution of baptism, nor received the remedy of baptism in the Gospel, but continued under the curse of Adam's fall, with its penalty of damnation. And therefore they are already judged, for the crime of infidelity.

12   When the judgment is finished, a great calm will arise

And when the judgment is ended, *the terrors of the elements,* the lightnings and thunders and winds and tempests, *will cease, and all that is fleeting and transitory will* melt away and *no longer be,* like snow melted by the heat of the sun. And so, by God's dispensation, *an exceedingly great calm will arise.*

13   Glory will receive the elect and Hell swallow up the damned

And thus the elect will become splendid with the splendor of eternity, *and with My Son their Head and the glorious celestial army will embrace glory and the heavenly joys; while the reprobate, together with the Devil and his angels, will wretchedly direct their course toward eternal punishment,* where eternal death awaits them for following their lusts instead of My commands. And so *Heaven will receive the elect* into the glory of eternity, because they have loved the Ruler of the heavens; and *Hell will swallow up the reprobate,* because they did not renounce the Devil. And then *such great joy and praise will resound in the glory of Heaven and such great groaning and howling will arise in*

Hell as to exceed the grasp of the human understanding. For the first have eternal life and the second eternal death, as My Son declares in the Gospel, saying:

14 The Gospel on this subject

"And these shall go into everlasting punishment; but the just into life everlasting" [Matthew 25:46]. Which is to say: Those who befoul themselves in the house of evil passions, and do not thirst to drink justice from the Supreme Goodness, will come in the course of their infidelity and wickedness to submersion in the pains of eternal perdition, and according to their deeds will receive the torments of Hell. But the builders of the heavenly Jerusalem, who faithfully stand in the gates of the daughter of Zion, will be radiant in the eternal life, which the fruitfulness of the chaste Virgin miraculously gave to all believers.

15 How the elements and heavenly bodies will be changed, and night ended

And, as you see, *when all these things are over the elements will shine out with the greatest brightness and beauty, and all blackness and filth will be removed from them.* And *fire, without its raging heat,* will blaze like the dawn; *air without density* will be completely limpid; *water without its power to flood or drown* will stand transparent and calm, and *earth without shakiness* or roughness will be firm and level. And so all these will be transformed into great calm and beauty.

And *the sun and moon and stars will sparkle in the firmament* like precious stones set in gold, with great glory and brilliance; and *they will no longer restlessly revolve in orbit* so as to distinguish day from night. For the world will have ended and they will have become immutable; and from that time on *there will be no darkness, and day will be perpetual.* As My beloved John witnesses, when he says:

16 Words of John

"And there shall be no more night, and they will not need the light of the lamp or the light of the sun; for the Lord God will illumine them" [Revelation 22:5]. Which is to say: One who possesses a treasure sometimes hides it and at other times shows it, and even so night conceals the light, and day drives out the darkness and brings light to humanity. But it will not be so when time is transformed; for then the shade of night will be put to flight and its darkness will not appear from that time on. For in this transmutation the light people now light to dispel the darkness will not be needed; and the sun will not move and by its motion bring times of darkness. For then the day will be without end; for the Ruler of all, in the immutable glory of His Divinity, will illumine those who in the world have by His grace escaped the darkness.

But let the one who has ears sharp to hear inner meanings ardently love My reflection and pant after My words, and inscribe them in his soul and conscience.

THE CHOIRS OF THE BLESSED

VISION THIRTEEN
Symphony of the Blessed

*T*hen *I saw the lucent sky, in which I heard different kinds of music, marvellously embodying all the meanings I had heard before. I heard the praises of the joyous citizens of Heaven, steadfastly persevering in the ways of Truth; and laments calling people back to those praises and joys; and the exhortations of the virtues, spurring one another on to secure the salvation of the peoples ensnared by the Devil. And the virtues destroyed his snares, so that the faithful at last through repentance passed out of their sins and into Heaven.*

And their song, like the voice of a multitude, making music in harmony praising the ranks of Heaven, had these words:

1 Songs to holy Mary

O splendid jewel, serenely infused with the Sun!
The Sun is in you as a fount from the heart of the Father;
It is His sole Word, by Whom He created the world,
The primary matter, which Eve threw into disorder.
He formed the Word in you as a human being,
And therefore you are the jewel that shines most brightly,
Through whom the Word breathed out the whole of the virtues,
As once from primary matter He made all creatures.

O sweet green branch that flowers from the stem of Jesse!
O glorious thing, that God on His fairest daughter
Looked as the eagle looks on the face of the sun!
The Most High Father sought for a Virgin's candor,
And willed that His Word should take in her His body.
    For the Virgin's mind was by His mystery illumined,
    And from her virginity sprang the glorious Flower.

And again a song resounded:

2 To the nine orders of heavenly spirits

O glorious living light, which lives in Divinity!
Angels who fix your eyes with ardent desire

Amid the mystical darkness surrounding all creatures
On Him with Whom your desires can never be sated!
O glorious joy, to live in your form and nature!
For you are free from every deed of evil,
Although that evil first appeared in your comrade,
The fallen angel, who tried to soar above God,
And therefore that twisted one was submerged in ruin.
And then for himself a greater fall he prepared
By his suggestions to those whom God's hand made.

O angels with shining faces who guard the people,
O ye archangels, who take just souls into Heaven,
And you, O virtues and powers, O principalities,
Dominions and thrones, who by five are secretly counted,
And you, cherubim and seraphim, seal of God's secrets,
Praise be to you all, who behold the heart of the Father,
And see the Ancient of Days spring forth in the fountain,
And His inner power appear like a face from His heart.

And again they sang:

3   To the patriarchs and prophets

 O eminent men, who traversed the hidden ways,
And looked with the eyes of the spirit, and in lucent shadows
Announced the Living Light that would bud from the stem
Which blossomed alone from the Light that rooted within it!
 O ancient saints, you foretold the souls' salvation
Who were sunk in death; like wheels you turned and circled,
And wondrously spoke of the Mount That touches Heaven.
And then He came, and anointed the many waters,
And so the shining light arose among you,
And, going before Him, displayed the Mount Himself.

 O happy roots, from whom miracles and not vices
Grew in the burning way of lucent shadow!
And you, O fiery voice of meditation
Who went before the abyss-sealing Cornerstone;
Rejoice in your Head, in the One Whom so many among you
Invoked with ardor, yet never on earth beheld.

And another song was sung:

VISION THIRTEEN

4 To the apostles

O warrior cohort of the thornless Flower!
Your sound fills the world, traversing the realm of the senses,
Where madmen feast and defile themselves with swine;
And you, infused with the Comforter, conquered them.
O noble race of the Savior, whose roots are fixed
In the tabernacle of the Word's complete labor,
You take by the Lamb the path of the water's salvation.
He sent you armed with a sword amid dogs most savage,
Who with the work of their fingers destroyed their glory,
Subjecting the Handlessly Made to their hands' own makings.

O lucent crowd of apostles, in truest knowledge
You rose to open the Devil's mighty prisons
And cleanse his slaves in the fount of living waters.
You are the glorious light in the blackest darkness,
The pillars that prop the jewelled Bride of the Lamb,
Whose banner-bearer first was the Virgin Mother,
For joy of the Lamb, Who weds the immaculate Bride.

And another song resounded:

5 To the martyrs

O ye who have poured out your blood in triumph,
And conquered a share in the blood of the Lamb who perished,
Feasting upon the slain calf's sacrifice,
And so built the Church, what a great reward is yours!
Alive, you followed the Lamb, and despised your bodies,
Adorned His pains, and so recaptured your portions.

O rose blossoms, blessed in the joy of your blood's effusion!
Your fragrant blood flowed forth from the inner counsel
Of Him Who has been always, without beginning,
And planned before time began His great redemption.
Your company is honor, whose blood abounded
To build the Church in the stream from your noble wounds.

And another song was sung:

6   To the confessors

O ye who succeed and serve the mighty Lion,
And rule between the temple and the altar,
The angels sing praises and stand to help the peoples,
And so do you, in the Lamb's service careful.

O ye who imitate the Most Exalted,
In His most precious and glorious Sacrament!
How great is your glory, in which the power is given
To loose and bind the indolent and the straying,
To beautify white and black, and lift their burdens.
   Yours too is the office of the angelic order,
And yours is the task of knowing the firm foundations
And where to lay them; and therefore great is your honor.

And another song resounded:

7   To the virgins

O lovely faces who look on the face of God
And build in the dawn; O noble blessed virgins!
The King took thought for you, sealing you to His purpose
And decking you with all ornaments of Heaven,
And so you are a garden adorned in sweetness.

O noble verdure, which grows from the Sun of splendor!
Your clear serenity shines in the Wheel of Godhead,
Your greatness is past all earthly understanding,
And Heaven's wonders surround you in their embrace.
   You glow like dawn, and burn like the Sun in glory.

And another song was heard, like the voice of a multitude breaking out in melodic laments over the people who had to be brought back to that place:

8   The lament over the ones to be recalled

Oh, this is a voice of sorrow and great lamenting!
Ah! ah! what a wonderful victory has arisen:
The desire for God, while carnal pleasure flees!
But oh, alas! how few were the wills that were sinless,
How few the desires that fled from lust to You!

Mourn, mourn then, Innocence, you whose modest goodness
Has never failed, nor craved what the Serpent showed you,
For people respected, though they neglected you.

O Living Fountain, how great is Your sweet compassion!
You never lost sight of the face of the straying people,
But saw in advance the way that You would save them
From the fallen angels, who thought they had reft them from You.
O daughter of Zion, rejoice that God restores you
So many cut off from you by the ancient serpent,
Who now shine brighter than ever they shone before.
The Living Light now says of the ones He rescued,
"The guileful serpent I flouted in his seduction,
His work was not so perfect as once he thought it.
I swore by Myself, and I did more, far more,
For them than he did to them. And so your joy
Is ended, your snares destroyed, and all your greed
Is come to nothing, O wickedest of impostors!"

*And again a song was heard, like the voice of a multitude, exhorting the virtues to
help humanity and oppose the inimical arts of the Devil. And the virtues overcame the vices, and by divine inspiration people turned back to repentance. And
thus the song resounded in harmony:*

9   The exhortation of the virtues and the fight against the Devil

THE VIRTUES: We virtues are in God, and there abide; we wage war
for the King of Kings, and separate evil from good. We appeared in the first
battle, and conquered there, while the one who tried to fly above himself fell.
So let us now wage war and help those who invoke us; let us tread underfoot the Devil's arts, and guide those who would imitate us to the blessed
mansions.

SOULS (in the body, lamenting): Oh, we are strangers, wandering off
toward sin! What have we done? We should have been daughters of the
King, but we fell into the darkness of sin. O living Sun, carry us on Your
shoulders into the just inheritance, which we lost in Adam! O King of Kings,
let us fight in your battle!

A FAITHFUL SOUL: O sweet Divinity and O lovely Life, in Whom I
may put on a robe of glory, and receive what I lost in the beginning! I long
for You, and I call upon the virtues.

VIRTUES (answering): O blessed soul! O sweet creature of God, who
were formed in the depths of God's profound wisdom, you have loved much.

BOOK THREE

THE SOUL: Oh, I come to you gladly; give me the kiss of the heart!

VIRTUES: We must join with you in the battle, O daughter of the King.

THE SOUL (burdened and complaining): Oh, burdensome labor! Oh, heavy load I must endure while garbed in this life! It is most hard for me to fight against the flesh.

VIRTUES: O soul created by God's will, O happy instrument! Why are you so weak against the thing God has crushed by the Virgin? Through us you must conquer the Devil.

THE SOUL: Help, support me, that I may stand firm!

KNOWLEDGE OF GOD: See what it is that you are clothed with, O daughter of salvation, and stand firm! Then you will never fall.

THE SOUL: Oh, I know not what to do or where to flee! Woe is me! I cannot use rightly that which clothes me. I want to tear it off!

VIRTUES: O bad conscience, O wretched soul! Why do you hide your face in the presence of your Creator?

KNOWLEDGE OF GOD: You do not know or see or taste Him Who created you.

THE SOUL: God created the world; I do Him no wrong if I want to enjoy it.

THE DEVIL (whispering to the soul): Fool, fool! What good is your labor? Regard the world, and it will embrace you with honor.

VIRTUES: Alas, alas! Virtues, let us loudly lament and mourn; for a sheep of the Lord is fleeing from life.

HUMILITY: I, Humility, queen of the virtues, say: Come to me, all of you virtues, and I will strengthen you, so that you can seek the lost coin and give it the crown of blessed perseverance!

VIRTUES: O glorious queen, O sweetest mediator! We come gladly.

HUMILITY: Beloved daughters, I keep you in the King's wedding chamber. O daughters of Israel, God raised you under His tree, so now remember your planting. Rejoice, O daughters of Zion!

THE DEVIL (to the virtues): What good is it that there should be no power but God's? I say that I will give everything to the one who follows me and his own will; but you and all your followers have nothing to give, for none of you knows who you are.

HUMILITY: I and my companions know well that you are the ancient dragon, who tried to fly higher than the Most High, and was thrown into the deepest abyss by God Himself.

VIRTUES: But all of us dwell on high.

THE SOUL (in the body, repentant and lamenting): O royal virtues! How beautifully you shine in the Supreme Sun! How sweet is your dwelling! Oh, woe is me, I fled from you!

530

VISION THIRTEEN

VIRTUES: Come, O fugitive, come to us! and God will receive you.

THE SOUL: Alas, alas! Burning sweetness plunged me into sins; I dare not enter with you.

VIRTUES: Do not fear or flee; the Good Shepherd seeks you, His lost sheep.

THE SOUL: Now I need you to take me back, for I fester with wounds the ancient serpent has dealt me.

VIRTUES: Run to us, and follow with us that path in which you will never fall; and God will heal you.

THE SOUL: I am a sinner who fled from Life; I must come to you full of sores, that you may offer me the shield of redemption.

VIRTUES: O fugitive soul, be firm, and put on yourself the armor of light!

THE SOUL: O soldiery of the Queen, O white lilies and crimson roses, look gently upon me! I have lived as a stranger and an exile from you; help me to rise up in the blood of the Son of God! O Humility, who are true healing, help me; for Pride has broken me with many vices, and wounded me with many scars. Now I fly to you; oh, receive me!

HUMILITY (to the virtues): O virtues all, for the sake of Christ's wounds receive this mourning sinner, scarred as she is, and bring her to me.

VIRTUES (to the soul): We will bring you back, and we will not desert you; the whole celestial army rejoices over you! And so we will sing a song of rejoicing.

HUMILITY (to the soul): O unhappy daughter, I will embrace you; for the great Physician for your sake suffered deep and bitter wounds.

THE DEVIL (whispering to the soul): Who are you, and whence do you come? You embraced me, and I led you forth; and now you return and confound me! But I will throw you down in battle.

THE SOUL (to the Devil): I recognized that all your ways are evil, and so I fled from you. And now, O impostor, I fight against you! (To Humility): O Queen Humility, help me with your healing remedy!

HUMILITY (to Victory and the other virtues): O Victory! You conquered the Devil in Heaven; run now with your companions, and all bind this Devil!

VICTORY (to the virtues): O strong and glorious soldiers, come and help me conquer this deceiver!

VIRTUES (to Victory): O sweetest warrior in the flowing fountain that engulfed the ravenous wolf! O you crowned with glory, we gladly fight with you against the deluder of souls.

HUMILITY: Bind him, O splendid virtues!

VIRTUES: O queen, we will obey you, and do your commands in all things.

BOOK THREE

VICTORY: Rejoice, comrades! The ancient serpent is bound!

VIRTUES: Praise be to you, O Christ, King of the angels! O God, Who are You Who had this great counsel in You? It destroyed the hellish drink, which poisoned the publicans and sinners; and they now shine in celestial goodness. Praise therefore be to You, O King! O Father Almighty, from Your ardent heat flows the fountain; guide your children with a favorable wind on the waters, that we may lead them into the celestial Jerusalem.

And these voices were like the voices of a multitude lifting up its sound on high. And their song went through me, so that I understood them perfectly.

And I heard a voice from the shining sky, saying to me:

10 God must be unceasingly praised for His grace with heart and voice

Praises must be offered unceasingly to the Supernal Creator with heart and mouth, for by His grace he sets on heavenly thrones not only those who stand erect but those who bend and fall.

Thus, O human, *you see the lucent sky,* which symbolizes the brilliance of the joy of the citizens of Heaven; *in which you hear different kinds of music, marvellously embodying all the meanings you heard before. You hear the praises of the joyous citizens of Heaven, steadfastly persevering in the ways of Truth, and laments calling people back to those praises and joys.* For, as the air encloses and sustains everything under the heavens, so the wonders of God, which you have already been shown, are enveloped for you in a sweet and delightful song. It sings with joy of the wonders of the elect who dwell in the heavenly city and eternally express their sweet devotion to God; and it laments over the wavering of those the ancient serpent is trying to destroy, but who will be led to blessed joy by the divine power, and know the mysteries no human mind can know that bows down to the earth. *And you hear the exhortations of the virtues, spurring one another on to secure the salvation of the peoples ensnared by the Devil; and the virtues destroy his snares, so that the faithful at last through repentance pass out of their sins and into Heaven.* For the virtues in the minds of the faithful resist the vices by which the Devil wearies them, and redeem them; and when their mighty strength conquers these vices, the people who fell into sin return by God's will to repentance, diligently examining and weeping over their former deeds, and weighing and considering their future ones.

11 The song is sung in unity and concord

And so that song, like the voice of a multitude, makes music in praise among the ranks of Heaven. For the song of rejoicing, sung in consonance and in concord, tells of the glory and honor of the citizens of Heaven, and lifts on high what the Word has shown.

12 The words are the body and the music the spirit

And so the words symbolize the body, and the jubilant music indicates the spirit; and the celestial harmony shows the Divinity, and the words the Humanity of the Son of God.

13 By this song the sluggish soul is aroused to watchfulness

And as the power of God is everywhere and encompasses all things, and no obstacle can stand against it, so too the human intellect has great power to resound in living voices, and arouse sluggish souls to vigilance by the song.

David shows this by his songs of prophecy and rejoicing; and Jeremiah shows it by the sorrowful voice of his lamentation. And you also, O human, with your poor and frail little nature, can hear in the song the ardor of virginal modesty embraced by the blossoming branch; and the acuity of the living lights, which shine in the heavenly city; and the profound utterances of the apostles; and the outpouring of the blood of the faithful who offer themselves; and the secrets of the priestly office; and the procession of virgins, blooming in the verdancy of Heaven. For the faithful creature rejoices to his Creator in a voice of exultation and gladness, and returns Him perpetual gratitude. *And you hear another song, like the voice of a multitude breaking out in melodic laments over the people who have to be brought back to that place.* For the song does not only harmonize and exult over those who persevere in the path of rectitude, but also exults in the concord of those who are resurrected from their fall out of the path of justice, and are at last uplifted to true beatitude. For the Good Shepherd has brought back to the fold with joy the sheep that was lost.

And again you hear a song, like the voice of a multitude, exhorting the virtues to help humanity and oppose the arts of the Devil. And the virtues overcome the vices, and by divine inspiration people turn back to repentance; and so their song resounds in harmony. For the sweet alliance of the virtues draws the faithful to true beatitude, though the vices the Devil uses as snares accumulate direly. But the virtues do not merely conquer the vices, but destroy them; and so they lead people who consent to be helped by God to eternal reward by true penitence. And this is shown by the words of their song.

14 The song of rejoicing softens the hard heart and summons the Holy Spirit

For the song of rejoicing softens hard hearts, and draws forth from them the tears of compunction, and invokes the Holy Spirit. And so *those voices you hear are like the voice of a multitude, which lifts its sound on high;* for jubilant praises, offered in simple harmony and charity, lead the faithful to that consonance in which is no discord, and make those who still live on earth sigh with heart and voice for the heavenly reward.

And their song goes through you so that you understand them perfectly; for where divine grace has worked, it banishes all dark obscurity, and makes pure and lucid those things that are obscure to the bodily senses because of the weakness of the flesh.

15 The faithful should rejoice without ceasing

Therefore, let everyone who understands God by faith faithfully offer Him tireless praises, and with joyful devotion sing to Him without ceasing. As My servant David, filled with the spirit of lofty profundity, exhorts on My behalf, saying:

16 Words of David

"Praise Him with the sound of trumpets; praise Him with psaltery and harp. Praise Him with timbrel and dance; praise Him with stringed instruments and flute. Praise Him on high-sounding cymbals; praise Him on cymbals of joy; let every spirit praise the Lord" [Psalm 150:3–5]. This is to say:

You know, adore and love God with simple mind and pure devotion. Praise Him, then, with the sound of trumpets, which is to say by the use of the reason. For when the lost angel and his consenters fell into perdition, the armies of the blessed spirits stood firm in the truth of reason, and with faithful devotion adhered to God.

And praise Him on the psaltery of deep devotion, and the honey-toned harp. For when the trumpet sounds the psaltery follows, and when the psaltery sounds the harp follows; as first the blessed angels stood fast in the love of truth, and then after the creation of Man the prophets arose with their wonderful voices, and then the apostles followed with their words of sweetness.

And praise Him with the timbrel of mortification and in the dance of exultation. For after the harp sounds, the timbrel exults, and after the timbrel, the dance; as after the apostles preached words of salvation, the martyrs endured many bodily torments for the honor of God, and then arose the truthful doctors of the priestly office.

And praise Him with the stringed instruments of human redemption and the flute of divine protection. For after the dance of joy, the voice of the stringed instruments and the flute emerge; as, after the doctors who served beatitude showed the truth, there appeared the virgins, who loved the Son of God, Who was true Man, like stringed instruments and adored Him, Who was true God, like flutes. For they believed Him to be true Man and true God. What does this mean? When the Son of God assumed flesh for human salvation, He did not lose the glory of Divinity; and so the happy virgins chose Him as their Bridegroom, and knew Him with faithful devotion as true Man in betrothal and true God in chastity.

And praise Him too on high-sounding cymbals, which is to say by loud and joyful declarations, whenever people who lay in the depths of sin are touched by divinely inspired remorse and raise themselves from those depths to the height of Heaven.

And praise Him on cymbals of joy, which is to say by statements of praise, whenever the strong virtues gain the victory and overthrow human vice, and lead people who persevere in good works and holy desires to the beatitude of the true recompense.

And so let every spirit who wills to believe in God and honor Him praise the Lord, Him Who is the Lord of all; for it is fitting that anyone who desires life should glorify Him Who is Life.

And again I heard a voice from the lucent sky, saying: "O King most high, praise be to You, Who bring these things to pass in a simple and untaught person!"

And another voice cried out from Heaven with a great shout, saying:

Hear and attend, all you who desire to have heavenly recompense and bliss. O ye people who have believing hearts and await the heavenly reward, take these words and lay them up in your inmost hearts, and do not reject this admonition that comes to you. For I the Living and True Witness of Truth, the speaking and not silent God, say and say again: Who shall prevail over Me? He who tries it I will overthrow. Let not anyone lay hold of a mountain, which he cannot move, but let him abide in the valley of humility. Who walks a road without water? The one who is swayed by the whirlwind, and divides fruit but does not eat it. And how can My tabernacle be there? My tabernacle is the place where the Holy Spirit pours forth His overflowing waters. What does this mean?

I am in the midst. How? Whoever lays hold of Me worthily shall not fall, either as to height or as to depth or as to breadth. What does this mean?

I am that Charity which emulous pride cannot cast down, a fall into the depths cannot dash to pieces and the wide expanse of evils cannot crush. Can

I not build as high as the footstool of the sun? The strong despise Me, who show their strength in the valleys; the apathetic leave me at the sound of the tempest; and the learned refuse My food; and so do they all who build towers for themselves according to their own will. But I will confound them through the small and the weak, as I overthrew Goliath by a boy, and conquered Holofernes by Judith. And therefore, if anyone rejects the mystical words of this book, I will draw My bow against him and transfix him by the arrows from My quiver; I will knock his crown from his head, and make him like those who fell in Horeb when they murmured against Me. And if anyone utters curses against this prophecy, may the curse that Isaac uttered come upon him. But anyone who embraces it and keeps it in his heart and makes its ways plain, I will fill with the dews of Heaven.

And whoever tastes this prophecy and fixes it in his memory will become the mountain of myrrh, and of frankincense, and of all aromatical spices, and the diffusion of many blessings; he will ascend like Abraham from blessing to blessing. And the new spouse, the Bride of the Lamb, will take him to herself, for he is a pillar in the sight of God. And the shadow of the hand of the Lord will protect him.

But whoever rashly conceals these words written by the finger of God, madly abridging them, or for any human reason taking them to a strange place and scoffing at them, let him be reprobate; and the finger of God shall crush him.

Praise, therefore, praise God, ye blessed hearts, for the miracles God has wrought in the frail earthly reflection of the beauty of the Most High; as He Himself foreshadowed when He first made Woman from the rib of the man He had created.

But let the one who has ears sharp to hear inner meanings ardently love My reflection and pant after My words, and inscribe them in his soul and conscience. Amen.

Bibliography to Introduction

I. Texts

Derolez, Albert, and Peter Dronke, eds. *Liber divinorum operum.* In *Corpus Christianorum: continuatio mediaevalis* (CCCM). Turnhout, Belgium: forthcoming.

Dronke, Peter, ed. "The Text of the *Ordo virtutum.*" In *Poetic Individuality in the Middle Ages.* Oxford: 1970.

Führkötter, Adelgundis, and Angela Carlevaris, eds. *Scivias.* CCCM, vols. 43–43a. Turnhout, Belgium: 1978.

Kaiser, Paul, ed. *Hildegardis Causae et curae.* Leipzig: 1903.

Migne, J.-P., ed. *Sanctae Hildegardis abbatissae Opera omnia.* In *Patrologiae cursus completus: series latina* 197. Paris: 1855. Includes *Vita S. Hildegardis,* 145 *Epistolae, Scivias, Liber divinorum operum, Physica* and several short works.

Newman, Barbara, ed. *Symphonia armonie celestium revelationum:* A critical edition with English translations and commentary. Ithaca, NY: 1988.

Pitra, J.-B., ed. *Analecta S. Hildegardis.* Vol. 8 of *Analecta sacra.* Monte Cassino: 1882. Includes *Liber vitae meritorum, Expositiones evangeliorum,* 145 *Epistolae* not contained in Migne, and fragments of other works.

Schipperges, Heinrich, ed. "Ein unveröffentlichtes Hildegard Fragment." *Sudhoffs Archiv für Geschichte der Medizin* 40 (1956). A collection of medical and theological *sententiae* related to the *Causae et curae.*

Van Acker, Lieven, ed. *Epistolae.* In CCCM. Turnhout, Belgium: forthcoming.

II. German Translations (Otto Müller Verlag)

Barth, Pudentiana, Maria-Immaculata Ritscher, and Joseph Schmidt-Görg, eds. and trans. *Lieder (Symphonia* and *Ordo virtutum).* Salzburg: 1969. Includes texts, translations and music.

BIBLIOGRAPHY

Böckeler, Maura, trans. *Wisse die Wege* (*Scivias*), 8th ed. Salzburg: 1987.

Führkötter, Adelgundis, trans. *Briefwechsel* (*Epistolae*). Salzburg: 1965.

———. *Das Leben der hl. Hildegard von Bingen* (*Vita S. Hildegardis*), by the monks Gottfried of St. Disibod and Dieter of Echternach, 2d ed. Salzburg: 1980.

Riethe, Peter, trans. *Das Buch von den Steinen* (*Physica*), 2d ed. Salzburg: 1986.

———. *Naturkunde: Das Buch von dem inneren Wesen der verschiedenen Naturen in der Schöpfung* (*Physica*), 3d ed. Salzburg: 1980.

Schipperges, Heinrich, trans. *Heilkunde: Das Buch von dem Grund und Wesen der Heilung von Krankheiten* (*Causae et curae*), 4th ed. Salzburg: 1981.

———. *Der Mensch in der Verantwortung: Das Buch der Lebensverdienste* (*Liber vitae meritorum*), 2d ed. Salzburg: 1985.

———. *Welt und Mensch: Das Buch "De operatione Dei"* (*Liber divinorum operum*). Salzburg: 1965.

III. Bibliography

Lauter, Werner. *Hildegard-Bibliographie*. Vol. 1, to 1970; vol. 2, 1970–1982; vol. 3, 1983–(forthcoming). Alzey: 1970 and 1984.

IV. Studies

Brück, Anton, ed. *Hildegard von Bingen, 1179–1979: Festschrift zum 800. Todestag der Heiligen*. Mainz: 1979. Collection of twenty-one essays.

Dronke, Peter. "Hildegard of Bingen as Poetess and Dramatist." In *Poetic Individuality in the Middle Ages*. Oxford: 1970.

———. "Problemata Hildegardiana." *Mittellateinisches Jahrbuch* 16 (1981).

———. *Women Writers of the Middle Ages: A Critical Study of Texts from Perpetua († 203) to Marguerite Porete († 1310)*. Cambridge: 1984. On Hildegard see chap. 6 and appendix.

Flanagan, Sabina. *Hildegard of Bingen 1098–1179: A Visionary Life*. London and New York: 1989.

Führkötter, Adelgundis. *Hildegard von Bingen*. Salzburg: 1972.

———, ed. *Kosmos und Mensch aus der Sicht Hildegards von Bingen*. Mainz: 1987. Essays by Heinrich Schipperges, Irmgard Müller and Monika Klaes.

Gronau, Eduard. *Hildegard von Bingen, 1098–1179*. Stein-am-Rhein, Switzerland: 1985.

Kerby-Fulton, Kathryn. *The Voice of Honest Indignation: Reformist Apocalypticism and Piers Plowman*. Cambridge: 1989.

BIBLIOGRAPHY

Kraft, Kent. "The German Visionary: Hildegard of Bingen." In *Medieval Women Writers*, ed. Katharina Wilson. Athens, GA: 1984.

Liebeschütz, Hans. *Das allegorische Weltbild der hl. Hildegard von Bingen*. Leipzig: 1930.

Meier-Staubach, Christel. *Text und Bild im überlieferten Werk Hildegards von Bingen*. Wiesbaden: 1978.

———. *"Virtus* and *operatio* als Kernbegriffe einer Konzeption der Mystik bei Hildegard von Bingen." In *Theologia Mystica: Grundfragen zur mystischen Theologie*, ed. Margot Schmidt. Stuttgart: 1986.

Newman, Barbara. "Hildegard of Bingen: Visions and Validation." *Church History* 54 (1985).

———. *Sister of Wisdom: St. Hildegard's Theology of the Feminine*. Berkeley: 1987.

Schipperges, Heinrich. *Die Welt der Engel bei Hildegard von Bingen*. 2d ed. Salzburg: 1979.

Schrader, Marianna, and Adelgundis Führkötter. *Die Echtheit des Schrifttums der hl. Hildegard von Bingen*. Cologne: 1956.

Ungrund, Magna. *Die metaphysische Anthropologie der hl. Hildegard von Bingen*. Münster: 1938.

Widmer, Bertha. *Heilsordnung und Zeitgeschehen in der Mystik Hildegards von Bingen*. Basel: 1955.

Indexes

INDEXES

INDEXES

INDEX TO TEXTS

INDEXES

INDEXES

Other Volumes in this Series